I0754536

Schuyler Colfax

HISTORY

OF THE

THIRTY-NINTH CONGRESS

OF THE

UNITED STATES.

By WILLIAM H. BARNES, A.M.,
AUTHOR OF "THE BODY POLITIC."

WITH PORTRAITS.

NEW YORK:
HARPER & BROTHERS, PUBLISHERS,
327 TO 335 PEARL STREET.
1868.

PREFACE.

THE history of the Thirty-Ninth Congress is a sequel to that of the Rebellion. This having been overthrown, it remained for Congress to administer upon its effects. It depended upon the decisions of Congress whether the expected results of our victories should be realized or lost.

Now that the work of the Thirty-Ninth Congress stands forth complete, people naturally desire to know something of the manner in which the rough material was shaped into order, and the workmanship by which the whole was "fitly joined together." It can not be said of this fabric of legislation that it went up without "the sound of the hammer." The rap of the gavel was often heard enforcing order or limiting the length of speeches.

Discussion is the process by which legislation is achieved; hence no history of legislation would be complete without presenting the progress of debate preparatory to the adoption of important measures. The explanation of what our legislators did is found in what they said. Debates, as presented in the following pages, are by necessity much abridged. No attempt has been made to give a summary or synopsis of speeches. That which seemed to be the most striking or characteristic passage in a speech is given, in the words of the orator.

Many things said and done in the Thirty-Ninth Congress, of great importance to the nation, are by necessity omitted. The reader, in forming his opinion of

Congressional character and ability, will bear in mind that those who speak most frequently are not always the most useful legislators. Men from whom no quotation is made, and to whom no measure is attributed in the following pages, may be among the foremost in watchfulness for their constituents, and faithfulness to the country.

If it should seem that one subject — the negro question — occupied too much of the time and attention of Congress, it must be borne in mind that this subject was thrust upon Congress and the country by the issue of the Rebellion, and must be definitely and finally settled before the nation can be at rest. "Unsettled questions have no pity on the repose of mankind."

No attempt has been made to present a journal of Congressional proceedings, giving a detail of what was said and done from day to day in the Senate and the House. There was always some great national question under consideration in one or the other House, forming an uninterrupted series of discussions and transactions. To present these in review is to give a history of the Thirty-Ninth Congress, since they distinguish it from all its predecessors, and make it historical.

CONTENTS.

CHAPTER XXIII.—Other Important Acts.

(Page 552–560.)

CHAPTER XXIV.—The President and Congress.

(Page 561–567.)

CHAPTER XXV.—Personal.

(Page 568–576.)

LIST OF PORTRAITS.

INTRODUCTORY.

BY HON. SCHUYLER COLFAX,
SPEAKER OF THE HOUSE OF REPRESENTATIVES.

THE CONGRESS that has just passed away has written a record that will be long remembered by the poor and friendless, whom it did not forget. Misrepresented or misunderstood by those who denounced it as enemies, harshly and unjustly criticised by some who should have been its friends, it proved itself more faithful to human progress and liberty than any of its predecessors. The outraged and oppressed found in these congressional halls champions and friends. Its key-note of policy was protection to the down-trodden. It quailed not before the mightiest, and neglected not the obscurest. It lifted the slave, whom the nation had freed, to the full stature of manhood. It placed on our statute-book the Civil Rights Bill as our nation's magna charta, grander than all the enactments that honor the American code; and in all the region whose civil governments had been destroyed by a vanquished rebellion, it declared as a guarantee of defense to the weakest that the freeman's hand should wield the freeman's ballot; and that none but loyal men should govern a land which loyal sacrifices had saved. Taught by inspiration that new wine could not be safely put in old bottles, it proclaimed that there could be no safe or loyal reconstruction on a foundation of unrepentant treason and disloyalty.

The first session of the Thirty-ninth Congress proposed, as their plan of Reconstruction, a Constitutional Amendment. It was a bond of public justice and public safety combined, to be embodied in our national Constitution, to show to our posterity that patriotism is a virtue and rebellion is a crime. These terms were more magnanimous than were ever offered in any country under like circumstances. They were kind, they were forbearing, they were less than we had a right to demand; but in our anxiety, in our desire to close up this question, we made the proposition. How was it received? They trampled upon it, they spat upon it, they repudiated it, and said they would have nothing to do with it. They were determined to have more power after the rebellion than they had before.

When this proposition was repudiated, we came together again, at the second session of the same Congress, to devise some other plan of reconstruction in place of the proffer that had been spurned. We put the basis of our reconstruction, first, upon every loyal man in the South, and then we gave the ballot also to every man who had only been a traitor. The persons we excluded, for the present, from suffrage in the South, were not the thousands who struggled in the rebel army, not the millions who had given their adhesion to it, but only those men who had sworn allegiance to the Constitution and then added to treason the crime of perjury.

Though we demand no indemnity for the past, no banishment, no confiscations, no penalties for the offended law, there is one thing we do demand, there is one thing we have the power to demand, and that is security for the future, and that we intend to have, not only in legislation, but imbedded in the imperishable bulwarks of our national Constitution, against which the waves of secession may dash in future but in vain. We intend to have those States reconstructed on such enduring corner-stones that posterity shall realize that our fallen heroes have not died in vain.

THE THIRTY-NINTH CONGRESS.

CHAPTER I.

OPENING SCENES.

MOMENTOUS EVENTS OF THE VACATION—OPENING OF THE SENATE—MR. WADE—MR. SUMNER—MR. WILSON—MR. HARRIS—EDWARD MCPHERSON—AS CLERK OF THE PRECEDING CONGRESS, HE CALLS THE HOUSE TO ORDER—INTERRUPTION OF ROLL-CALL BY MR. MAYNARD—REMARKS BY MR. BROOKS—HIS COLLOQUY WITH MR. STEVENS—MR. COLFAX ELECTED SPEAKER—HIS INAUGURAL ADDRESS—THE TEST OATH.

THE Thirty-ninth Congress of the United States, convened in the Capitol at Washington on the fourth of December, 1865. Since the adjournment of the Thirty-eighth Congress, events of the greatest moment had transpired—events which invested its successor with responsibilities unparalleled in the history of any preceding legislative body.

Abraham Lincoln, sixteenth President of the United States, had been slain by the hand of the assassin. The crime had filled the land with horror. The loss of its illustrious victim had veiled the nation in unaffected grief.

By this great national calamity, Andrew Johnson, who on the fourth of March preceding had taken his seat simply to preside over the deliberations of the Senate, became President of the United States.

Meanwhile the civil war, which had been waged with such terrible violence and bloodshed for four years preceding, came to a sudden termination. The rebel armies, under Generals Lee and Johnston, had surrendered to the victorious soldiers of the United States, who in their generosity had granted to the vanquished terms so mild and easy as to excite universal surprise.

Jefferson Davis, Alexander H. Stephens, and some other leaders in the rebellion, had been captured and held for a time as State prisoners; but, at length, all save the "President of the Confederate States" were released on parole, and finally pardoned by the President.

The President had issued a proclamation granting amnesty and pardon to "all who directly or indirectly participated in the rebellion, with restoration of all rights of property, except as to slaves," on condition of their subscribing to a prescribed oath. By the provisions of this proclamation, fourteen classes of persons were excepted from the benefits of the amnesty offered therein, and yet "any person belonging to the excepted classes" was encouraged to make special application to the President for pardon, to whom clemency, it was declared, would "be liberally extended." In compliance with this invitation, multitudes had obtained certificates of pardon from the President, some of whom were at once elected by the Southern people, to represent them, as Senators and Representatives, in the Thirty-ninth Congress.

The President had further carried on the work of reconstruction by appointing Provisional Governors for many of the States lately in rebellion. He had recognized and entered into communication with the Legislatures of these States, prescribing certain terms on which they might secure representation in Congress, and recognition of "all their rights under the Constitution."

By these and many other events which had transpired since the expiration of the preceding Congress, the legislation pertaining to reconstruction had become a work of vast complexity, involving principles more profound, and questions more difficult, than ever before presented for the consideration and solution of men assembled in a legislative capacity.

At twelve o'clock on the day designated in the Constitution for the meeting of Congress, the Senate assembled, and was called to order by Hon. Lafayette S. Foster, President *pro tempore*. Senators from twenty-five States were in their seats, and answered to their names. Rev. E. H. Gray, Chaplain of the Senate, invoked the blessing of Almighty God upon Congress, and prayed "that all their deliberations and enactments might be such as to secure the Divine approval, and insure the unanimous acquiescence of the people, and command the respect of the nations of the earth."

Soon after the preliminary formalities of opening the Senate had transpired, Benjamin F. Wade, Senator from Ohio, inaugurated the labors of the Thirty-ninth Congress, and significantly foreshadowed one of its most memorable acts by introducing "a bill to regulate the elective franchise in the District of Columbia."

The Senate signified its willingness to enter at once upon active duty by giving unanimous consent to Mr. Sumner, Senator from Massachusetts, to introduce a number of important bills. The measures thus brought before the Senate were clearly indicative of the line of policy which Congress would pursue. The bills introduced were designed "to carry out the principles of a republican form of government in the District of Columbia;" "to present an oath to maintain a republican form of government in the rebel States;" "to enforce the amendment to the Constitution abolishing slavery;" "to enforce the guarantee of a republican form of government in certain States where governments have been usurped or overthrown."

Senator Wilson, of Massachusetts, was not behind his distinguished colleague in his readiness to enter upon the most laborious legislation of the session. He introduced "a bill to maintain the freedom of the inhabitants in the States declared in insurrection by the proclamation of the President on the first of July, 1862."

Senator Harris, of New York, long known as one of the ablest jurists of his State, and recently an eminent member of the Senate's Judiciary Committee, directed attention to his favorite field of legislative labor by introducing "a bill to reörganize the Judiciary of the United States."

While the Senate was thus actively entering upon the labors of the session, a somewhat different scene was transpiring in the other end of the Capitol.

Long before the hour for the assembling of Congress, the halls, the galleries, and corridors of the House of Representatives were thronged with such crowds as had never before been seen at the opening of a session. The absorbing interest felt throughout the entire country in the great questions to be decided by Congress had drawn great numbers to the Capitol from every quarter of the Union. Eligible positions, usually held in reserve for certain privileged or official persons, and rarely occupied by a spectator, were now filled to their utmost capacity. The Diplomatic Gallery was occupied by many unskilled in the mysteries of diplomacy; the Reporters' Gallery held many listeners and lookers on who had no connection with newspapers, save as readers. The "floor" was held not only by the "members," who made the hall vocal with their greetings and congratulations, but by a great crowd of pages, office-seekers, office-holders, and unambitious citizens, who thronged over the new carpet and among the desks.

The hour having arrived for the assembling of Congress, Edward McPherson, Clerk of the last House of Representatives, brought down the gavel on the Speaker's desk, and called the House to order. The members found their seats, and the crowd surged back up the aisles, and stood in a compact mass in the rear of the last row of desks.

Edward McPherson, who at that moment occupied the most prominent and responsible place in the nation, had come to his position through a series of steps, which afforded the country an opportunity of knowing his material and capacity. A graduate of Pennsylvania College in 1848, editor, author, twice a Congressman, and Clerk of the House of Representatives in the Thirty-eighth Congress, he had given evidence that he was reliable. Having shown himself a thoroughly conscientious man in the performance of all his public duties, the great interests of the nation were safe in his hands.

The country had been greatly concerned to know how the Clerk would make up the Roll of the House, and whether the names of members elect from the late rebellious States would be called at the opening of the session. If this should be done, the first step would be gained by the Representatives of those States toward holding seats in Congress to which the majority at the North considered them not entitled. It had even been intimated that the color of constitutionality which they would gain from recognition by the Clerk would be used to justify an assertion of their claims by force. What the Clerk would do, as master of the rolls and presiding officer of the House, was not long in doubt.

The Clerk proceeded to call the roll of Representatives elect, while the subordinates at the desk took note of the responses. He called the names of Congressmen from the States of Maine, New Hampshire, Vermont, Massachusetts, and so forth, in a certain order which had been customary time immemorial in naming the States. In this order Tennessee had place after Kentucky and before Indiana. When the name of the last Representative from Kentucky had been called, the decisive moment arrived. The delegation from Tennessee were on the floor, ready to answer to their names. The Clerk passed over Tennessee and went direct to Indiana. As soon as the first member from Indiana had responded, there arose a tall, black-haired, dark-faced figure, that every body recognized as Horace Maynard, of Tennessee. He shook his certificate of election at the Clerk, and began to speak, but the gavel came down with a sharp rap, and a firm, decided voice was heard from the desk, "The Clerk declines to have any interruption during the call of the roll." The roll-call then proceeded without further interference to the end. When, at last, the Clerk had finished his list of Representatives and Territorial Delegates, Mr. Maynard once more arose. "The Clerk can not be interrupted while ascertaining whether a quorum is present," says the presiding officer. The count of the assistants having been completed, the Clerk announced, "One hundred and seventy-six members having answered to their names, a quorum is present." Mr. Morrill immediately moved that the House proceed to the election of Speaker. "Before that motion is put," said Mr. Maynard, again arising. The Clerk was ready for the emergency, and before Mr. Maynard could complete his sentence, he uttered the imperative and conclusive words, "The Clerk can not recognize as entitled to the floor any gentleman whose name is not on this roll." A buzz of approbation greeted the discreet ruling of the Clerk. The difficult point was passed, and the whole subject of the admission of Southern Representatives was handed over intact, to be deliberately considered after the House should be fully organized for business.

Mr. Morrill, in moving to proceed to the election of a Speaker, had forgotten or neglected to demand the previous question, and thus cut off debate. Mr. James Brooks, most plausible in address, and most ready in talk on the side of the minority, saw the point left unguarded by his opponents, and resolved to enter. Born in

Maine, now a citizen of New York, and editor of the "Express," Mr. Brooks was in Congress for the fourth time a champion of what he deemed the rights of the South, and not in accordance with the prevailing sentiments in his native and adopted States.

Mr. Brooks obtained the floor, and desired to amend the motion. He thought the roll should be completed before proceeding to the election of Speaker. "I trust," said he, "that we shall not proceed to any revolutionary, any step like that, without at least hearing from the honorable gentleman from Tennessee. If Tennessee is not in the Union, by what right does the President of the United States usurp his place in the White House when an alien and a foreigner, and not from a State in the Union?"

At this stage, a man of mark—five times a Representative in Congress, but now twelve years away from the capital and a new member—John Wentworth, of Chicago—elevated his tall and massive form, and with a stentorian voice called Mr. Brooks to order. The Clerk having fairly decided that gentleman entitled to the floor on the question of proceeding to the election of a Speaker, Mr. Wentworth sat down, and Mr. Brooks in resuming his remarks improved his chance to administer rebuke in a manner which provoked some mirth. "When the honorable gentleman from Illinois is better acquainted with me in this House," said Mr. Brooks, "he will learn that I always proceed in order, and never deviate from the rules." Mr. Brooks then returned to his championship of Mr. Maynard: "If he is not a loyal man, and is not from a State in this Union, what man, then, is loyal? In the darkest and most doubtful period of the war, when an exile from his own State, I heard his eloquent voice on the banks of the St. Lawrence arousing the people of my own State to discharge their duties to the country."

Mr. Brooks joined Virginia with Tennessee, and asked the Clerk to give his reasons for excluding the names of Representatives from these States from the roll. The Clerk replied that he had acted in accordance with his views of duty, and was willing to let the record stand; if it was the desire of the House to have his reasons, he would give them.

"It is not necessary," said Thaddeus Stevens; "we know all."

"I know," replied Mr. Brooks, "that it is known to all in one quarter, but that it is not known to many in other quarters in this House, why this exclusion has been made. I should know but little, if I had not the record before me of the resolution adopted by the Republican majority of this House, that Tennessee, Louisiana, and Virginia were to be excluded, and excluded without debate. Why without debate? Are gentlemen afraid to face debate? Are their reasons of such a character that they dare not present them to the country, and have to resort to the extraordinary step of sideway legislation, in a private caucus, to enact a joint resolution to be forced upon this House without debate, confirming that there are no reasons whatever to support this position except their absolute power, and authority, and control over this House? If the gentleman from Pennsylvania would but inform me at what period he intends to press this resolution, I would be happy to be informed."

"I propose to present it at the proper time," was the response of Mr. Stevens, provoking laughter and applause.

Mr. Brooks replied: "Talleyrand said that language was given to man to conceal ideas, and we all know the gentleman's ingenuity in the use of language. The proper time! When will that be?" Mr. Brooks then proceeded at some length to answer this question. He supposed the proper time would be as soon as the House was organized, and before the President's message could be heard and considered, that the action of the House might silence the Executive, and nullify the exposition which he might make, and become a *quasi* condemnation of the action of the President of the United States.

Mr. Brooks was at length ready to close, and sought to yield the floor to a Democratic member. The Republicans, however, were ready to meet the emergency, and objected to the floor being yielded in such a way as would cause delay without furthering the business of organizing the House. Points of order were raised, and efforts made to entangle the Clerk, but in vain. His rulings were prompt, decisive, and effectual. The moment a Republican fairly held the floor, the previous question was moved, the initial contest was over, and the House proceeded to elect a Speaker.

A stoop-shouldered, studious-looking gentleman, now for the sixth successive term a member of Congress—Justin S. Morrill, of Vermont—arose and nominated Schuyler Colfax, of Indiana On the other side of the house, a gentleman from New York portly in his person, now entering on his second Congressional term—Charles H. Winfield—nominated James Brooks, of New York. Four members took their seats behind the Clerk to act as tellers. The responses were at length all given, and the numbers noted. Mr. Morrill, one of the tellers, announced the result—"Mr. Colfax, one hundred and thirty-nine; Mr. Brooks, thirty-six." The Clerk formally announced the result, and stepped aside; his work as presiding officer of the Thirty-ninth Congress was at an end.

In the place thus made vacant appeared the man but a moment before elected to the position by the largest political majority ever given to a Speaker of the House. A well-proportioned figure of medium size, a pleasing countenance often radiant with smiles, a style of movement quick and restless, yet calm and self-possessed, were characteristic of him upon whom all eyes were turned. In the past a printer and editor in Indiana, now in Congress for the sixth term, and elected Speaker the second time, SCHUYLER COLFAX stood to take the oath of office, and enter upon the discharge of most difficult and responsible duties. He said:

"Gentlemen of the House of Representatives: The reässembling of Congress, marking as it does the procession of our national history, is always regarded with interest by the people for whom it is to legislate. But it is not unsafe to say that millions more than ever before, North, South, East, and West, are looking to the Congress which opens its session to-day with an earnestness and solicitude unequaled on similar occasions in the past. The Thirty-eighth Congress closed its constitutional existence with the storm-cloud of war still lowering over us, and after nine months' absence, Congress resumes its legislative authority in these council halls, rejoicing that from shore to shore in our land there is peace.

"Its duties are as obvious as the sun's pathway in the heavens. Representing in its two branches the States and the people, its first and highest obligation is to guarantee to every State a republican form of government. The rebellion having overthrown constitutional State governments in many States, it is yours to mature and enact legislation which, with the concurrence of the Executive, shall establish them anew on such a basis of enduring justice as will guarantee all necessary safeguards to the people, and afford what our Magna Charta, the Declaration of Independence, proclaims is the chief object of government—protection to all men in their inalienable rights. The world should witness, in this great work, the most inflexible fidelity, the most earnest devotion to the principles of liberty and humanity, the truest patriotism and the wisest statesmanship.

"Heroic men, by hundreds of thousands, have died that the Republic might live. The emblems of mourning have darkened White House and cabin alike; but the fires of civil war have melted every fetter in the land, and proved the funeral pyre of slavery. It is for you, Representatives, to do your work as faithfully and as well as did the fearless saviors of the Union in their more dangerous arena of duty. Then we may hope to see the vacant and once abandoned seats around us gradually filling up, until this hall shall contain Representatives from every State and district; their hearts devoted to the Union for which they are to legislate, jealous of its honor, proud of its glory, watchful of its rights, and hostile to its enemies. And the stars on our banner, that paled when the States they represented arrayed themselves in arms against the nation, will shine with a more brilliant light of loyalty than ever before."

Mr. Colfax having finished his address, took the following oath, which stood as the most serious obstacle in the way of many elected to Congress from the Southern States:

"I do solemnly swear that I have never voluntarily borne arms against the United States since I have been a citizen thereof; that I have voluntarily given no aid, countenance, counsel, or encouragement to persons engaged in armed hostility thereto; that I have neither sought nor accepted nor attempted to exercise the functions of any office whatever, under any authority or pretended authority in hostility to the United States; that I have not yielded a voluntary support to any pretended government, authority, power, or constitution within the United States, hostile or inimical thereto. And I do further swear that, to the best of my knowledge and ability, I will support and defend the Constitution of the United States against all enemies, foreign and domestic; that I will bear true faith and allegiance to the same; that I take this obligation freely, without any mental reservation or purpose of evasion; and that I will well and faithfully discharge the duties of the office on which I am about to enter. So help me God!"

The subordinate officers were then elected by resolution, and the House of Representatives being organized, was ready to enter upon its work.

CHAPTER II.

LOCATIONS OF THE MEMBERS AND CAST OF THE COMMITTEES.

Importance of surroundings—Members sometimes referred to by their seats—Senator Andrew Johnson—Seating of the Senators—Drawing in the House—The Senate-chamber as seen from the Gallery—Distinguished Senators—The House of Représentatives—Some prominent characters—Importance of Committees—Difficulty in their appointment—Important Senate Committees—Committees of the House.

THE localities and surroundings of men have an influence on their actions and opinions. A matter which, to the casual observer, seems so unimportant as the selection and arrangement of the seats of Senators and Representatives, has its influence upon the legislation of the country. Ever since parties have had an existence, it has been considered of vital moment that those of one political faith in a deliberative body should occupy, as nearly as possible, the same locality.

It is sometimes of service to a reader, in attempting to understand the reported proceedings of Congress, to know the localities of the members. Each seat has a sort of history of its own, and becomes in some way identified with its occupant. Members are frequently alluded to in connection with the seats they occupy. Sometimes it happens that, years after a man has gone from Congress, it is convenient and suggestive to refer to him by his old place in the chamber. As an illustration, Mr. Trumbull, in his speech on the veto of the Civil Rights Bill, desiring to quote Andrew Johnson, Senator, against Andrew Johnson, President, referred to "a speech delivered in this body by a Senator occupying, I think, the seat now occupied across the chamber by my friend from Oregon (Mr. Williams)."

A necessary and important part of the adjustment of the

machinery, at the opening of each Congress, is the selection of seats. As the Senators serve for six years, and many of them have been reëlected more than once, there are comparatively few changes made at the opening of any Congress. The old members generally choose to retain their accustomed seats, and the small number that come in as new Senators choose among the vacant seats, as convenience or caprice may dictate.

In the House of Representatives the formality of drawing for seats is necessary. That this may be conveniently and fairly done, at the appointed time all the members retire to the antechambers, leaving the seats all unoccupied. The Clerk draws at random from a receptacle containing the names of all the members. As the members are called, one by one, they go in and occupy such seats as they may choose. The unlucky member whose name last turns up has little room for choice, and must be content to spend his Congressional days far from the Speaker, on the remote circumference, or to the right or left extreme.

There are in the Senate-chamber seventy seats, in three tiers of semi-circular arrangement. If all the old Southern States were represented by Senators on the floor, the seats would be more than full. As it was in the Thirty-ninth Congress, there were a number of vacant desks, all of them situated to the right and left of the presiding officer.

In a division of political parties nearly equal, the main aisle from the southern entrance would be the separating line. As it was, the Republican Senators occupied not only the eastern half of the chamber, but many of them were seated on the other side, the comparatively few Democratic Senators sitting still further to the west.

Seated in the gallery, the spectator has a favorable position to survey the grand historic scene which passes below. His eye is naturally first attracted to the chair which is constitutionally the seat of the second dignitary in the land—the Vice-President of the United States. That office, however, has no incumbent, since he who took oath a few months before to perform its duties was called to occupy a higher place, made vacant by a most atrocious crime. The event, however, cost the Senate little loss of dignity, since the chair is filled by a President *pro tempore* of great ability and excellence—Lafayette S. Foster, Senator from Connecticut.

The eye of the spectator naturally seeks out Charles Sumner, who sits away on the outer tier of seats, toward the south-east corner of the chamber; and near him, on the left, are seen the late Governors, now Senators, Morgan and Yates, of New York and Illinois. Immediately in front of them, on the middle tier of seats, is an assemblage of old and distinguished Senators—Trumbull, Wilson, Wade, and Fessenden. To the right of the Vice-President's chair, and in the row of seats neares this desk, sits the venerable and learned lawyer, Reverdy Johnson, of Maryland. Just in his rear sits the youthful Sprague, of Rhode Island, to whose right is seen Sherman, of Ohio. To the rear of these Senators, in the outer segment of seats, sits, or perhaps stands, Garrett Davis, of Kentucky, the most garrulous of old men, continually out of temper with the majority, yet all the time marked by what he calls his "usual courtesy." To the left of Davis, beyond Nesmith, of Oregon, and the other and more silent Senator from Kentucky, sits Saulsbury, of Delaware, unless he should be traversing the carpeted space in the rear of his seat, like a sentinel of the Senate.

Far different is the sight presented to the spectator who looks down from the galleries of the House of Representatives. The immense area below is supplied with two hundred and fifty-three seats, with desks arranged in semi-circular rows, having a point in front of the Speaker's desk as a focus. On the right of the spectator, as he looks from the gallery in front of the Speaker, is the Republican side of the House. But this prosperous organization has grown so rapidly since its birth, ten years ago, that it has overstepped all old and traditional party limitations. One-half of the House is not sufficient to afford its representatives adequate accommodations. Republican members have passed over the main aisle, and occupy half of the Democratic side, having pressed the thin ranks of their opponents to the extreme left.

As the spectator scans the House, his eye will rest on Thaddeus Stevens, whose brown wig and Roman cast of countenance mark the veteran of the House. He sits in the right place for a leader of the Republicans, about half-way back from the Speaker's desk, on the diagonal line which divides the western side of the House, where he can readily catch the Speaker's eye, and be easily heard by all his friends. Immediately in his rear is his successor in the chairmanship of the Committee of Ways and Means—Mr. Morrill, of Vermont. To the right, across the aisle, is Elihu B. Washburn, of Illinois, the oldest member in continuous service in the House; and to his rear is Henry J. Raymond, of the Times. To the right, and partly in the rear of Mr. Stevens, are a number of noteworthy men: among them are General Schenck, General Garfield, and "Long John" Wentworth, of Chicago. Far around to the right, and much nearer the Speaker's desk, is seen a man distinguished in civil and military history, who once occupied the Speaker's chair—General Banks, of Massachusetts. In physical contrast with him, sits—in the adjoining desk, a tall, dark, bearded Californian—General John Bidwell, a new member of the House. On the opposite side of the House, among the Democrats, is the seat of John A. Bingham, who now returns to Congress after an absence of one term, whom his friends describe as the "best-natured and crossest-looking man in the House." James Brooks, most plausible and best-natured of Democrats, notwithstanding the inroads of the Republicans, sturdily keeps his seat near the main aisle. His seat, however, he is destined to lose before many months in favor of a contestant, who will occupy the other side of the chamber.

In looking down upon so large an assemblage, a large part of which is so distant, the eye of the spectator will weary in the attempt to discover and recognize individuals, however familiar, amidst the busy throng.

In preparing for the work of legislation, a matter of more importance than the arrangement of the seats is the cast of the committees. Most of the labor of legislative bodies is done by committees. As it is impossible for any one Congressman to give that minute and particular attention to all the numerous interests demanding legislation, essential to a wise determination as to what bills should be presented, and how they should be drawn in every case, the various subjects are parceled out among those whose opportunities, interests, or inclinations have led them to give particular attention to the matters committed to their charge. The perfection of legislation on particular subjects depends not more on the wisdom of the entire body of legislalators than on the good sense of the committees that deliberate upon them. Much of the efficiency and success of the legislative acts of Congress will depend upon the structure of the committees that do the laborious work of preparing business for the body. Tracing the stream of legislative enactment still nearer to its source, it will be found that the work of a committee takes a decided tinge from the character of its chairman.

It consequently becomes a matter of great interest to the country, at the opening of each Congress, to know who constitute the committees. One of the most arduous and responsible duties of the Speaker of the House of Representatives is the selection of committees and filling their chairmanships. Fitness and special adaptation are supposed to constitute the rule by which choice is made. Many elements, however, enter into the work which are not a part of this philosophy. It is impossible that the presiding officer should know unerringly who is absolutely the fittest man for any position, and if he possessed such superhuman knowledge he would still be trammeled by long-established rules of precedence and promotion. There is often a regular gradation by which men arrive at positions which is not in direct ratio to their fitness for their places.

Notwithstanding all the errors which were unavoidable elements in the work, committees were never better constituted than those of the Thirty-ninth Congress.

The Senate being comparatively small in numbers, and, moreover, by usage, doing most of the details of this business in caucus, the announcement of the committees in this body was made on Wednesday, the third day of the session. On the other hand, the size of the House, the large proportion of new and unknown members appearing every term, the number and magnitude of the committees, and the fact that the duty of appointment devolved upon the Speaker, combined to render the reading out of committeemen in the latter body impossible before the following Monday, one week after the assembling of Congress.

Of the Senate Committee on Foreign Relations, Charles Sumner was appointed chairman. This is a very important committee, being the direct channel of communication between the State Department and the Senate. It being the constitutional duty of the Senate to pass upon all treaties, and to decide upon qualifications of all persons nominated by the Executive to represent the United States in foreign countries, the labors of this committee are arduous and responsible. The chairmanship of this committee was filled by a Senator of most eminent fitness and ability. His literary culture, and attainments as a scholar, his general legal ability and familiarity with the laws of nations, his residence abroad for several years, and his long membership in the Senate, now of fourteen years' duration, all marked him as wisely chosen for his important position.

On account of the immense National debt accumulated in the war, and the complication of the financial affairs of the nation, the Committee on Finance has an important bearing upon the interests of the country, unknown until recent years. William P. Fessenden was the Senator chosen chairman of this committee. His success in his private business, his appointment, in 1864, as the head of the Treasury Department, and his service in the Senate since 1853 as member of the Finance Committee, and since 1859 as its chairman, all indicated the propriety of his continuance in this position. Second on the list of this committee stood Senator Sherman, of Ohio, who has been described as "*au fait* on National Banks, fond of figures, and in love with finances."

The Committee on Commerce was constituted with Senator Chandler, of Michigan, as its chairman. Himself most successful in commercial life, in which he had attained distinction before coming to the Senate, and representing a State having a greater extent of coast and better facilities for commerce than any other inland community in the world, Senator Chandler was eminently suitable as head of the Committee on Commerce. His associates being selected from Maine, New York, Vermont, Wisconsin, Kansas, and Oregon, left unrepresented no important commercial interest in the nation.

The Committee on Manufactures was headed by William Sprague, Senator from Rhode Island, a State having the largest capital invested, and most persons employed in manufactures, in proportion to population, of any in the Union. Senator Sprague himself having been educated in the counting-room of a manufacturing establishment, and having control of one of the largest manufacturing interests in the country, was the appropriate person for such a position.

The agricultural States of Ohio, Kansas, Maryland, Pennsylvania, and Kentucky furnished the members of the Committee on Agriculture, with Senator Sherman at its head.

Of the Committee on the Judiciary, a Senator has given a description. In a speech delivered in the Senate, December 12,

1865, Mr. Doolittle, of Wisconsin, said: "From its very organization the Senate designs to make that committee its constitutional adviser—not that its opinions are to be conclusive or controling on the vote of any member of this body, like the opinion of the bench of Judges in the House of Lords; but its members are chosen in consideration of their high professional ability, their long experience, and well-known standing as jurists, in order that their report upon constitutional questions may be entitled to the highest consideration. And, sir, if you look into the organization of the Judiciary Committee appointed by the Senate at the present session, what is it? There is the Senator from Illinois, [Mr. Trumbull], for years Judge of the Supreme Court of that State before he entered this body, who, for ten years and more, has been a faithful, laborious, distinguished member of that committee, and for the last four years its chairman. And there sits my honorable friend from New York [Mr. Harris], for twenty years before he came here known and distinguished among the able jurists and judges of that great State. And there is the honorable Senator from Vermont [Mr. Poland]. He has, it is true, just entered this body, but his reputation as a jurist preceded his coming, and he comes here to fill the place in this chamber, and is put upon this Judiciary Committee to fill the place of him of whom I will say, without disparagement to any, that he was the ablest jurist of us all—the late distinguished Senator from Vermont [Mr. Collamer]. And there is the Senator from New Hampshire [Mr. Clark], from the far East, and the Senator from Nevada [Mr. Stewart], from the Pacific coast, and the Senator from Indiana [Mr. Hendricks], from the central region, each of whom stands eminent in the profession in the State which he represents, and all of whom are recognized here among the ablest jurists of this body."

Some of the great political questions destined to engage the attention of the Thirty-ninth Congress invested the *Committee on the District of Columbia* with a national interest, although its duties pertained chiefly to the local concerns of the immediate neighborhood of the capital. Its chairman, Mr. Morrill, of Maine, as well as its members, among whom were Wade, Sumner, and Yates, gave it character and ability, and afforded assurance that the great questions involved would be calmly met and honestly answered.

Eng.d by G. E. Perine & Co. N. York

THADDEUS STEVENS,

REPRESENTATIVE FROM PENNSYLVANIA.

In the House of Representatives, the *Committee of Ways and Means* has ever been regarded of first importance, and its chairman has been considered leader of the House. Its duties, though of a somewhat miscellaneous character, relate chiefly to devising the ways and means of raising revenue. The fact that the Constitution provides that "all bills for raising revenue shall originate in the House of Representatives," gives the Committee of Ways and Means a sort of preëminence over all other committees, whether of the Senate or the House.

The work of the Committee of Ways and Means, as it had existed before the Thirty-ninth Congress, was, at the opening of this session, divided among three committees; one retaining the old name and still remaining the leading committee, a second on *Appropriations,* and a third on *Banking and Currency.*

Of the new Committee of Ways and Means, Justin S. Morrill, of Vermont, was appointed chairman—a Representative of ten years' experience in the House, who had seen several years of service on the same committee. While his abilities and habits, as a student and a thinker, well adapted him for the work of conducting his committee by wise deliberation to useful measures, yet they were not characteristics fitting him with readiest tact and most resolute will to "handle the House."

Thaddeus Stevens, the old chairman of the Committee of Ways and Means, was appointed the head of the new Committee on Appropriations. His vigilance and integrity admirably fitted him for this position, while his age made it desirable that he should be relieved of the arduous labors of the Committee of Ways and Means. Of this committee he had been chairman in the two preceding Congresses, and had filled a large space in the public eye as leader of the House. His age—over seventy years—gave him the respect of members the majority of whom were born after he graduated at college—the more especially as these advanced years were not attended with any perceptible abatement of the intellectual vivacity or fire of youth. The evident honesty and patriotism with which he advanced over prostrate theories and policies toward the great ends at which he aimed, secured him multitudes of friends, while these same qualities contributed to make him many enemies. The timid became bold and the resolute were made stronger in seeing the bravery with which he maintained his principles. He had a habit of going straight to the issue, and a rugged manner of presenting his opinions, coupled with a cool assurance, which, one of his unfriendly critics once declared, "sometimes rose almost to the sublime." He alone, of all the members of the Pennsylvania Convention, in 1836, refused to sign the new State Constitution, because it robbed the negro of his vote. It was a fitting reward that he, in 1866, should stand in the United States House of Representatives, at the head of a majority of more than one hundred, declaring that the oppressed race should enjoy rights so long denied.

The Committee on Banking and Currency had as chairman Theodore M. Pomeroy, of New York, who had served four years in Congress. Perhaps its most important member was Samuel Hooper, a Boston merchant and financier, who, from the outset of his Congressional career, now entering upon the third term, had been on the Committee of Ways and Means, of which he still remained a member, the only Representative retaining connection with the old committee and holding a place in one of the new offshoots from it.

Hiram Price, of Iowa, was appointed chairman of the Committee on the Pacific Railroad. The Speaker of the House, in his recent visit to the Pacific coast, had been impressed with the importance of this work, and wisely chose as members of this committee Representatives from Pennsylvania, Minnesota, Massachusetts, New York, Missouri, Kansas, California, and Oregon.

A committee of much importance to Congress and the country—that of Commerce—had for its chairman Elihu B. Washburn, of Illinois, who had been in the previous Congress the oldest member in continuous service, and hence was styled "Father of the House."

The Committee on Elections subsequently lost some of its importance in the public estimation by the creation of a special committee to consider subjects of reconstruction and the admission of Southern members; yet the interests confided to it demanded ability, which it had in its chairman, Henry L. Dawes, of Massachusetts, as well as in the Representatives that constituted its membership.

The legislation relative to our vast unoccupied domain, having to pass through the Committee on Public Lands, renders this committee one of much importance. The honesty and ability of its chairman, George W. Julian, of Indiana, together with his long experience in Congress, gave to the recommendations of this committee great character and weight.

Of the Committee on the Judiciary, James F. Wilson, of Iowa, was appointed for the second time as chairman. George S. Boutwell, of Massachusetts, and other Representatives of ability, were appointed as members of this committee. Since the duty devolved upon it of taking testimony in regard to the impeachment of the President, this committee attracted public attention to a degree never known before.

The interests of manufactures were not likely to suffer in the hands of a committee in which the first place was held by James K. Moorhead, tanner's apprentice, and pioneer of cotton manufactures in Pennsylvania, and the second by Oakes Ames, a leading manufacturer of Massachusetts.

Agriculture—the most gigantic material interest in America—was intrusted to a committee having John Bidwell, of California, as its chairman, and members chosen from Iowa, Indiana, Vermont, Ohio, Kentucky, Michigan, Pennsylvania, and New York.

The chairmanship of the Committee on Military Affairs was bestowed upon a major-general of volunteers from Ohio, Robert C. Schenck; while membership on the committee was given to a Connecticut colonel, Henry C. Deming; a New Hampshire brigadier-general, Gilman Marston; a Kentucky major-general, Lovell H. Rousseau; a New York Colonel, John H. Ketchum, and four civilians.

Nathaniel P. Banks, Henry J. Raymond, and other men of much ability, were appointed on the Committee on Foreign Affairs.

Special committees were appointed on the important subjects of Bankruptcy and the Freedmen. Of the committee on the former, Thomas A. Jenckes was appointed chairman. Thomas D. Eliot, of Massachusetts, was made chairman of the Committee on the Freedmen.

Many other committees were appointed whose labors were arduous and necessary to our legislation, yet, as they had to do with subjects of no great general interest, they need not be named.

There was another committee, however, of great importance

whose members were not yet designated. The resolution by which it should be created, was yet to pass through the ordeal of discussion. The process by which this committee was created will be described in the following chapter.

CHAPTER III.

FORMATION OF THE JOINT COMMITTEE ON RECONSTRUCTION.

Lack of Excitement—Cause—The Resolution—Dilatory Motions—Yeas and Nays—Proposed Amendments in the Senate—Debate in the Senate—Mr. Howard—Mr. Anthony—Mr. Doolittle—Mr. Fessenden—Mr. Saulsbury—Mr. Hendricks—Mr. Trumbull—Mr. Guthrie—Passage of the Resolution in the Senate—Yeas and Nays—Remarks of Mr. Stevens on the Amendments of the Senate—Concurrence of the House—The Committee appointed.

SINCE it was known throughout the country that members-elect from Tennessee and other States recently in rebellion would appear at Washington on the opening of the Thirty-ninth Congress, and demand recognition of their right to represent their constituents, all eyes were turned to observe the action which would be taken on the subject. It was anticipated that the question would be sprung at once, and that a season of storm and excitement would ensue, unparalleled in the political history of the nation. Since the American people are exceedingly fond of excitements and sensations, the expectation of trouble in Congress drew immense numbers to its galleries on the first day of the session. Lovers of sensation were doomed to disappointment. Correspondents and reporters for the press, who were prepared to furnish for the newspapers descriptions of an opening of Congress "dangerously boisterous," were compelled to describe it as "exceptionally quiet."

The cause of this unexpected state of things was the faet that the majority had previously come to the wise conclusion that it would not be well to pass upon the admission of Southern members in open session and amid the confusion of organization. As there was so much difference of opinion concerning the *status* of the communities recently in rebellion, and such a variety of considerations must be regarded in reaching wise conclusions, it was deemed advisable that the whole subject should be calmly and deliberately investigated by a select number of able and patriotic men from both Houses of Congress.

Accordingly, on the first day of the session, soon after the House was organized, Mr. Thaddeus Stevens offered the following important RESOLUTION:

"*Resolved*, by the Senate and House of Representatives in Congress assembled, that a joint committee of fifteen members shall be appointed, nine of whom shall be members of the House, and six members of the Senate, who shall inquire into the condition of the States which formed the so-called Confederate States of America, and report whether they or any of them are entitled to be represented in either House of Congress, with leave to report at any time by bill or otherwise; and until such report shall have been made, and finally acted upon by Congress, no member shall be received into either House from any of the said so-called Confederate States; and all papers relating to the representation of the said States shall be referred to the said committee without debate."

To avoid the delay occasioned by a protracted debate, Mr. Stevens called the previous question. The minority perceived the impossibility of preventing the final passage of the resolution, yet deemed it their duty to put it off as far as possible by their only available means—"dilatory motions." They first objected to the introduction of the resolution, under the rule that unanimous consent must be given to permit a resolution to come before the House without notice given on a previous day. To meet this difficulty, Mr. Stevens moved to suspend the rules to enable him to introduce the resolution. On this motion the yeas and nays were demanded. To suspend the rules under such circumstances required a two-thirds' vote, which was given—one hundred and twenty-nine voting for, and thirty-five against the motion. The rules having been suspended, the resolution was regularly before the House. A motion was then made to lay the resolution on the table, and the yeas and nays demanded. Thirty-seven were in favor of the motion, and one hundred and thirty-three against it. Before a call for the previous question is available to cut off debate, it must, by the rules of the House, be seconded by one-fifth of the members present. This having been done, the vote was taken by yeas and nays on the concurrent resolution submitted by Mr. Stevens. One hundred and thirty-three voted in favor of the resolution, and thirty-six against it, while thirteen were reported as "not voting." As this vote was on an important measure, and is significant as marking with considerable accuracy the political complexion of the House of Representatives, it should be given in detail.

The following are the names of those who voted "Yea:"

Messrs. Alley, Allison, Ames, Anderson, Baker, Baldwin, Banks, Barker, Baxter, Beaman, Benjamin, Bidwell, Bingham, Blow, Boutwell, Brandagee, Bromwell, Broomall, Buckland, Bundy, Reader W. Clark, Sidney Clark, Cobb, Conkling, Cook, Cullom, Culver, Darling, Davis, Dawes, Defrees, Delano, Deming, Dixon, Donnelly, Driggs, Dumont, Eckley, Eggleston, Eliot, Farnsworth, Ferry, Garfield, Grinnell, Griswold, Hale, Abner C. Harding, Hart, Hayes, Henderson, Higby, Hill, Holmes, Hooper, Hotchkiss, Asabel W. Hubbard, John H. Hubbard, Chester D. Hubbard, Demas Hubbard, James R. Hubbell, Hulburd, James Humphrey, Ingersoll, Jenckes, Julian, Kasson, Kelley, Kelso, Ketchum, Kuykendall, Laflin, Latham, George V. Lawrence, William Lawrence, Loan, Longyear, Lynch, Marston, Marvin, McClurg, McIndoe, McKee, McRuer, Mercur, Miller, Moorhead, Morrill, Morris, Moulton, Myers, Newell, O'Neill, Orthe, Paine, Patterson, Perham, Phelps, Pike, Pomeroy, Price, William H. Randall, Raymond, Alexander H. Rice, John H. Rice, Rollins, Sawyer, Schenck, Scofield, Shellabarger, Smith, Spaulding, Starr, Stevens, Stillwell, Thayer, John L. Thomas, Trowbridge, Upson, Van Aernam, Burt Van Horn, Robert Van Horn, Ward, Warner, Elihu B. Washburne, Welker, Wentworth, Whaley, Williams, James F. Wilson, Windom, and Woodbridge.

The following members voted "Nay:"

Messrs. Ancona, Bergen, Boyer, Brooks, Chanler, Dawson, Denison, Eldridge, Finck, Glossbrenner, Goodyear, Grider, Aaron Harding, Hogan, James M. Humphrey, Johnson, Kerr, LeBlond, McCullough, Niblack, Nicholson, Noell, Radford, Samuel J. Randall, Ritter, Rogers, Ross, Shanklin, Sitgreaves, Strouse, Tabor, Taylor, Thornton, Trimble, Winfield, and Wright.

The following are reported as "not voting:"

Messrs. Delos R. Ashley, James M. Ashley, Blaine, Farquhar, Harris, Edwin N. Hubbell, Jones, Marshall, Plants, Rousseau, Sloan, Francis Thomas, Voorhees, and William B. Washburn.

Thus the resolution passed the House. The immense size of this body required that, by stringent rule, debate should have limitation, and even sometimes be cut off altogether by the operation of previous question. This arrangement enabled skillful and resolute leaders to carry through this measure within an hour's time, whereas, in the Senate, a body of less than one-third the size, it passed after a delay of several days, and at the end of a discussion of considerable length.

On the day following the passage of the resolution in the House of Representatives, it was read in the Senate. Mr. Johnson, of Maryland, objecting to its being considered on the day of its reception, under a regulation of the Senate it was postponed.

After the lapse of a week, on Tuesday, December 12, the resolution was taken up for consideration in the Senate. Mr. Anthony moved to amend the enacting clause so as to change it from a joint resolution to a concurrent resolution, since, under its original shape, it would require the President's approval.

This amendment having been made, Mr. Anthony moved to further amend the resolution by striking out all after the word "otherwise." The following are the words proposed to be stricken out:

"And until such report shall have been made and finally acted on by Congress, no member shall be received into either house from any of the said so-called Confederate States; and all papers relating to the representation of said States shall be referred to the said committee without debate."

Mr. Howard, of Michigan, preferred the resolution as it came from the House of Representatives. "It contains within itself a pledge on the part of the two houses, that until the report of this important committee shall have been presented, we will not re-admit any of the rebel States, either by the recognition of their Senators or their Representatives. I think the country expects nothing less than this at our hands. I think that portion of the loyal people of the United States who have sacrificed so much of blood and treasure in the prosecution of the war, and who secured to us the signal victory which we have achieved over the rebellion, have a right to at least this assurance at our hands, that neither house of Congress will recognize as States any one of the rebel States until the event to which I have alluded.

"Sir, what is the present position and *status* of the rebel States? In my judgment they are simply conquered communities, subjugated by the arms of the United States; communities in which the right of self-government does not now exist. Why? Because they have been for the last four years hostile, to the most surprising unanimity hostile, to the authority of the United States, and have, during that period, been waging a bloody war against that authority. They are simply conquered communities, and we hold them, as we know well, as the world knows to-day, not by their own free will and consent as members of the Union, but solely by virtue of our military power, which is executed to that effect throughout the length and breadth of the rebel States. There is in those States no rightful authority, according to my view, at this time, but that of the United States; and every political act, every governmental act exercised within their limits, must necessarily be exercised and performed under the sanction and by the will of the conqueror.

"In short, sir, they are not to-day loyal States; their population are not willing to-day, if we are rightly informed, to perform peaceably, quietly, and efficiently the duties which pertain to the population of a State in the Union and of the Union; and for one I can not consent to recognize them, even indirectly, as entitled to be represented in either house of Congress at this time. The time has not yet come, in my judgment, to do this. I think that, under present circumstances, it is due to the country that we should give them the assurance that we will not thus hastily reädmit to seats in the legislative bodies here the representatives of constituencies who are still hostile to the authority of the United States. I think that such constituencies are not entitled to be represented here."

Mr. Anthony, of Rhode Island, said: "The amendment was proposed from no opposition to what I understand to be the purpose of the words stricken out. That purpose I understand to be that both houses shall act in concert in any measures which they may take for the reconstruction of the States lately in rebellion. I think that that object is eminently desirable, and not only that the two houses shall act in concert, but that Congress shall act in concert with the Executive; that all branches of the Government shall approach this great question in a spirit of comprehensive patriotism, with confidence in each other, with a conciliatory temper toward each other, and that each branch of the Government will be ready, if necessary, to concede something of their own views in order to meet the views of those who are equally charged with the responsibility of public affairs.

"The words proposed to be stricken out refer to the joint committee of the two houses of Congress matters which the Constitution confides to each house separately. Each house is made, by the Constitution, the judge of the elections, returns, and qualifications of its own members.

"There is one other reason why I move this amendment, and that is, that the resolution provides that papers shall be referred to this committee without debate. This is contrary to the practice of the Senate. The House of Representatives has found it necessary, for the orderly transaction of its business, to put limitations upon debate, hence the previous question and the hour rule; but the Senate has always resisted every proposition of this kind, and submitted to any inconvenience rather than check free discussion. Senators around me, who were here in the minority, felt that the right of debate was a very precious one to them at that time, and, as it was not taken from them, they are not disposed to take it from the minority now.

"The purpose of all that is stricken out can be effected by the separate action of the two houses, if they shall so elect. The House of Representatives, having passed this resolution by a great vote, will undoubtedly adopt, in a separate resolution, what is here stricken out; and, except so far as relates to the restriction upon debate, I shall, if this amendment be adopted and the resolution passed, offer a resolution substantially declaring it to be the opinion of the Senate that, until this committee reports—presuming that it will report in a reasonable time—no action should be taken upon the representation of the States lately in rebellion."

Mr. Doolittle, of Wisconsin, said: "All of these great questions, concerning reconstruction, pacification, and restoration of civil government in the Southern States, representation in this body, or any thing which concerns of Federal relations with the several States, ought to be referred to the Committee on the Judiciary. Such has been the practice of this Government from the beginning. Great questions of constitutional law, questions concerning the relations of the Union to the States and the States to the Union, and above all, and without any exception, all questions relating to representation in this body, to its membership, have always been referred to the Judiciary Committee.

"There is nothing in the history of the Senate, there is nothing in the constitution of this committee, which would send these great constitutional questions for advisement and consideration to any other committee than the Committee on the Judiciary.

To place their consideration in the hands of a committee which is beyond the control of the Senate, is to distrust ourselves; and to vote to send their consideration to any other committee, is equivalent to a vote of want of confidence in the Judiciary Committee.

"I object to this resolution, because, upon these great questions which are to go to the joint committee, the Senate does not stand upon an equality with the House. This resolution provides that, of the joint committee of fifteen, nine shall be appointed by the House of Representatives, six only by the Senate, giving to the House portion of the committee a majority of three. We all know that in joint committees the members vote, not as the representatives of the two houses, but *per capita*. The vote of a member of the committee from the House weighs precisely the same as the vote of a member of the committee from the Senate; so that, to all intents and purposes, if we pass this concurrent resolution, which we can not repeal but by the concurrence of the other house, we place the consideration of these grave questions in the hands of a committee which we can not control, and in which we have no equal voice.

"Under the Constitution, upon all subjects of legislation but one, the two houses are equal and coördinate branches of Congress. That one relates to their representation in the bodies, to their membership, that which constitutes their existence, which is essential to their life and their independence. That is confided to each house, and to each house alone, to act for itself. It judges for itself upon the elections, returns, and qualifications of its members. It judges, it admits, it punishes, it expels. It can not share that responsibility with any other department of the Government. It can no more share it with the other house than it can share it with the Supreme Court or with the President. It is a matter over which its jurisdiction is exclusive of every other jurisdiction. It is a matter in which its decisions, right or wrong, are absolute and without appeal. In my opinion the Senate of the United States can not give to a committee beyond its control this question of the representation in this body, without a loss of its self-respect, its dignity, its independence; without an abandonment of its constitutional duty and a surrender of its constitutional powers.

"There is another provision in this resolution, as it stands, that we shall refer every paper to the committee without debate. Yes, sir, the Senate of the United States is to be led like a lamb to the slaughter, bound hand and foot, shorn of its constitutional power, and gagged, dumb; like the sheep brought to the block! Is this the condition to which the Senator from Michigan proposes to reduce the Senate of the United States by insisting upon such a provision as that contained in the resolution as it comes from the House of Representatives?

"There is a still graver objection to this resolution as it stands. The provision that 'until such report shall have been made and finally acted on by Congress, no member shall be received into either house from any of the so-called Confederate States,' is a provision which, by law, excludes those eleven States from their representation in the Union. Sir, pass that resolution as it stands, and let it receive the signature of the President, and you have accomplished what the rebellion could not accomplish, what the sacrifice of half a million men could not accomplish in warring against this Government—you have dissolved the Union by act of Congress. Sir, are we prepared to sanction that? I trust never.

"The Senator from Michigan talks about the *status* of these States. He may very properly raise the question whether they have any Legislatures that are capable of electing Senators to this body. That is a question of fact to be considered; but as to whether they are States, and States still within the Union, notwithstanding their civil form of government has been overturned by the rebellion, and their Legislatures have been disorganized, that they are still States in this Union is the most sacred truth and the dearest truth to every American heart, and it will be maintained by the American people against all opposition, come from what quarter it may. Sir, the flag that now floats on the top of this Capitol bears thirty-six stars. Every star represents a State in this Union. I ask the Senator from Michigan, does that flag, as it floats there, speak the nation's truth to our people and to the world, or is it a hypocritical, flaunting lie? That flag has been borne at the head of our conquering legions through the whole South, planted at Vicksburg, planted at Columbia, Savannah, Charleston, Sumter; the same old flag which came down before the rebellion at Sumter was raised up again, and it still bore the same glorious stars; 'not a star obscured,' not one.

"These people have been disorganized in their civil governments in consequence of the war; the rebels overturned civil government in the first place, and we entered with our armies and captured the rebellion; but did that destroy the States? Not at all. We entered the States to save them, not to destroy them. The guarantee of the Constitution is a guarantee to the States, and to every one of the States, and the obligation that rests upon us is to guarantee to South Carolina a republican form of government as a State in this Union, and not as a Territory. No State nor the people of any State had any power to withdraw from the Union. They could not do it peacefully; they undertook to do it by arms. We crushed the attempt; we trampled their armies under our feet; we captured the rebellion; the States are ours; and we entered them to save, and not to destroy.

"The Constitution of the United States requires the President, from time to time, to give to Congress information of the state of the Union. Who has any right to presume that the President will not furnish the information which his constitutional duty requires? He has at his control all the agencies which are necessary. There is the able Cabinet who surround him, with all the officers appointed under them: the post-masters under the Post-office Department, the treasury agents under the Treasury Department, and almost two hundred thousand men under the control of the War Department, in every part of this 'disaffected' region, who can bring to the President information from every quarter of all the transactions that exist there. That the President of the United States will be sustained, in the views which he takes in his message, by the people of this country, is as certain as the revolutions of the earth; and it is our duty to act harmoniously with him, to sustain him, to hold up his hands, to strengthen his heart, to speak to him words of faith, friendship, and courage.

"I know that in all these Southern States there are a thousand things to give us pain, sometimes alarm, but notwithstanding the bad appearance which from time to time presents itself in the midst of that boiling caldron of passion and excitement which the war has left still raging there, the real progress which we have made has been most wonderful. I am one of those who look forward with hope, for I believe God reigns and rules in the affairs of mankind. I look beyond the excitement of the hour and all the outbreaking passion which sometimes shows itself in the South, which leads them to make enactments in their Legislatures which are disgraceful to themselves, and can never be sanctioned by the people of this country, and also in spite of all the excitement of the North, I behold the future full of confidence and hope. We have only to come up like men, and stand as the real friends of the country and the Administration, and give to the policy of the President a fair and substantial trial, and all will be well."

Mr. Fessenden, of Maine, then remarked: "When this resolution was first promulgated in the newspapers as having been agreed upon, I approved it because I sympathized with its object and purpose. I did not examine it particularly; but, looking simply at what it was designed for, it met my approbation simply for this reason: that this question of the reädmission of these Confederate States, so called, and all the questions connected with that subject, I conceived to be of infinite importance, requiring calm and serious consideration, and I believe that the appointment of a committee, carefully selected by the two houses, to take that subject into consideration, was not only wise in itself, but an imperative duty resting upon the representatives of the people in the two branches of Congress. For myself, I was not prepared to act upon that question at once. I am not one of those who pin their faith upon any body, however eminent in position, or conceive themselves obliged, on a question of great national importance, to follow out any body's opinions simply because he is in a position to make those opinions, perhaps, somewhat more imperative than any other citizen of the republic. Talk about the Administration! Sir, we are a part of the Administration, and a very important part of it. I have no idea of abandoning the prerogatives, the rights, and the duties of my position in favor of any body, however that person or any number of persons may desire it. In saying this, I am not about to express an opinion upon the subject any further than I have expressed it, and that is, that in questions of such infinite importance as this, involving the integrity and welfare of the republic in all future time, we are solemnly bound, and our constituents will demand of us that we examine them with care and fidelity, and act on our own convictions, and not upon the convictions of others.

"I do not agree with the honorable Senator from Wisconsin, that by passing a simple resolution raising a committee of our own body, and referring to it certain papers, if we conclude to do so, we are infringing upon the rights of any body or making an intimation with regard to any policy that the President may have seen fit to adopt and recommend to the country. Sir, I trust there are no such things as exclusive friends of the President among us, or gentlemen who desire to be so considered. I have as much respect for the President of the United States probably as any man. I acted with him long, and I might express the favorable opinions which I entertain of him here, if they would not be out of place and in bad taste in this body. That I am disposed and ready to support him to the best of my ability, as every gentleman around me is, in good faith and with kind feeling in all that he may desire that is consistent with my views of duty to the country, giving him credit for intentions as good as mine, and with ability far greater, I am ready to asseverate.

"But, sir, I do not agree with the doctrine, and I desire to enter my dissent to it now and here, that, because a certain line of policy has been adopted by one branch of the Government, or certain views are entertained by one branch of the Government, therefore, for that reason alone and none other, that is to be tried, even if it is against my judgment; and I do not say that it is or is not. That is a question to be considered. I have a great respect, not for myself, perhaps, but for the position which I hold as a Senator of the United States; and no measure of Government, no policy of the President, or of the head of a department, shall pass me while I am a Senator, if I know it, until I have examined it and given my assent to it; not on account of the source from which it emanates, but on account of its own intrinsic merits, and because I believe it will result in the good of my country. That is my duty as a Senator, and I fear no misconstruction at home on this subject or any other.

"Now, therefore, sir, I hope that, laying aside all these matters, which are entirely foreign, we shall act upon this resolution simply as a matter of business. No one has a right to complain of it that we raise a committee for certain purposes of our own when we judge it to be necessary. It is an imputation upon nobody; it is an insult to nobody; it is not any thing which any sensible man could ever find fault with, or be disposed to do so. It is our judgment, our deliberate judgment, our friendly judgment—a course of action adopted from regard to the good of the community, and that good of the community comprehends the good of every individual in it."

Mr. Saulsbury, of Delaware, said: "This resolution is very objectionable to my mind. It is for the appointment of a committee of the two houses to determine and to report upon what? The right of representation of eleven States in this body. What determines the rights of those States to representation here? Is it the views of the members of the House of Representatives? Do we stand in need of any light, however bright it may be, that may come from that distinguished quarter? Are we going to ask them to illuminate us by wisdom, and report the fact to us whether those States are entitled to representation on this floor?

"Mr. President, on the first day of your assemblage after the battle of Manassas, you and they declared, by joint resolution, that the object for which the war was waged was for no purpose of conquest or subjugation, but it was to preserve the union of the States, and to maintain the rights, dignity, and equality of the several States unimpaired. While that war was being waged there was no action, either of this house or of the House of Representatives, declaring that, when it was over, the existence of those States should be ignored, or their right to representation in Congress denied. Throughout the whole contest the battle-cry was 'the preservation of the Union' and 'the Union of the States.' If there was a voice then raised that those States had ceased to have an existence in this body, it was so feeble as to be passed by and totally disregarded.

"Sir, suppose this committee should report that those States are not entitled to representation in this body, are you bound by their action? Is there not a higher law, the supreme law of the land, which says if they be States that they shall each be entitled to two Senators on this floor? And shall a report of a joint committee of the two houses override and overrule the fundamental law of the land? Sir, it is dangerous as a precedent, and I protest against it as an humble member of this body. If they be not States, then the object avowed for which the war was waged was false."

Mr. Hendricks, of Indiana, said: "I shall vote against this resolution because it refers to a joint committee a subject which, according to my judgment, belongs exclusively to the Senate. I know that the resolution no longer provides in express terms that the Senate, pending the continuance of the investigation of this committee, will not consider the question of credentials from these States, but in effect it amounts to that. The question is to be referred to the committee, and according to usage, and it would seem to be the very purpose of reference that the body shall not consider the subject while the question is before them. I could not vote for a resolution that refers to a joint committee a subject that this body alone can decide. If there are credentials presented here, this body must decide the question whether the person presenting the credentials is entitled to a seat; and how can this body be influenced by any committee other than a committee that it shall raise itself?"

Mr. Trumbull, of Illinois, then followed: "If I understood the resolution as the Senator from Indiana does, I should certainly vote with him; but I do not so understand it. It is simply a resolution that a joint committee be raised to inquire into the condition of the States which formed the so-called Confederate States of America, and to report whether they or any of them are entitled to be represented in either House of Congress, with leave to report at any time by bill or otherwise. It is true, as the Senator says, that after having raised this committee, the Senate will not be likely to take action in regard to the admission of the Senators from any of these States until the committee shall have had a reasonable time at least to act and report; but it is very desirable that we should have joint action upon this subject. It would produce a very awkward and undesirable state of things if the House of Representatives were to admit members from one of the lately rebellious States, and the Senate were to refuse to receive Senators from the same State.

"We all know that the State organizations in certain States of the Union have been usurped and overthrown. This is a fact of which we must officially take notice. There was a time when the Senator from Indiana, as well as myself, would not have thought of receiving a Senator from the Legislature, or what purported to be the Legislature, of South Carolina. When the people of that State, by their Representatives, undertook to withdraw from the Union and set up an independent government in that State, in hostility to the Union, when the body acting as a Legislature there was avowedly acting against this Government, neither he nor I would have received Representatives from it. That was a usurpation which, by force of arms, we have put down. Now the question arises, Has a State government since been inaugurated there entitled to representation? Is not that a fair subject of inquiry? Ought we not to be satisfied upon that point? We do not make such an inquiry in reference to members that come from States which have never undertaken to deny their allegiance to the Government of the United States. Having once been admitted as States, they continue so until by some positive act they throw off their allegiance, and assume an attitude of hostility to the Government, and make war upon it; and while in that condition, I know we should all object that they, of course, could not be represented in the Congress of the United States. Now, is it not a proper subject for inquiry to ascertain whether they have assumed a position in harmony with the Government? and is it not proper that that inquiry should be made the subject of joint action?"

Mr. Guthrie, of Kentucky, wished to ask the friends of this resolution if it was contemplated that this committee should take evidence, and report that evidence to the two houses. "If," said he, "they are only to take what is open to every member of the Senate, the fact that the rebellion has been suppressed; the fact that the President of the United States has appointed officers to collect the taxes, and, in some instances, judges and other officers; that he has sent the post-office into all the States; that there have been found enough individuals loyal to the country to accept the offices; the fact that the President has issued his proclamation to all these States, appointing Provisional Governors; that they have all elected conventions; that the conventions have rescinded the ordinances of secession; that most of them have amended their constitutions and abolished slavery, and the Legislatures of some of them have passed the amendment to the Constitution on the subject of slavery—if they are only to take these facts, which are open and clear to us all, I can see no necessity for such a committee. My principal objection to the resolution is, that this committee can give us no information which we do not now possess, coupled with the fact that the loyal conservative men of the United States, North, South, East, and West, do most earnestly desire that we shall so act that there shall be no longer a doubt that we are the United States of America, in full accord and harmony with each other.

"I know it has been said that the President had no authority to do these things. I read the Constitution and the laws of this country differently. He is to 'take care that the laws be faithfully executed;' he is to suppress insurrection and rebellion. The power is put in his hands, and I do not see why, when he marches into a rebel State, he has not authority to put down a rebel government and put up a government that is friendly to the United States, and in accordance with it. I do not see why he can not do that while the war goes on, and I do not see why he may not do it after the war is over. The people in those States lie at the mercy of the nation. I see no usurpation in what he has done, and if the work is well done, I, for one, am ready to accept it. Are we to send out a commission to see what the men whom he has appointed have done? It is said that they are not to be relied on; that they have been guilty of treason, and we will not trust them. I hope that no such ideas will prevail here. I think this will be a cold shock to the warm feelings of the nation for restoration, for equal privileges and equal rights. They were in insurrection. We have suppressed that insurrection.. They are now States of the Union; and if they come here according to the laws of the States, they are entitled, in my judgment, to representation, and we have no right to refuse it. They are in a minority, and they would be in a minority even if they meant now what they felt when they raised their arms against the Government; but they do not, and of those whom they will send here to represent them, nineteen out of twenty will be just as loyal as any of us—even some of those who took up arms against us.

"I really hope to see some one move a modification of the test oath, so that those who have repented of their disloyalty may not be excluded, for I really believe that a great many of those who took up arms honestly and wished to carry out the doctrines of secession, and who have succumbed under the force of our arms and the great force of public opinion, can be trusted a great deal more than those who did not fight at all.

"To conclude, gentlemen, I see no great harm in this resolution except the procrastination that will result from it, and that will give us nothing but what we have before us."

The question being taken, the resolution, as amended, passed the Senate, thirty-three voting in the affirmative and eleven in the negative. The following are the names of those who voted for the resolution:

Messrs. Anthony, Brown, Chandler, Clark, Conness, Creswell, Fessenden, Foot, Foster, Grimes, Harris, Howard, Howe, Lane of Indiana, Lane of Kansas, Morgan, Morrill, Norton, Nye, Poland, Pomeroy, Ramsey, Sherman, Sprague, Stewart, Sumner, Trumbull, Van Winkle, Wade, Willey, Williams, Wilson, and Yates.

The following Senators voted against the resolution:

Messrs. Buckalew, Cowan, Dixon, Doolittle, Guthrie, Hendricks, Johnson, Riddle, Saulsbury, Stockton, and Wright.

Five Senators were absent: Messrs. Cragin, Davis, Henderson, McDougall, and Nesmith.

On the day succeeding the adoption of the concurrent resolution by the Senate, the amendments of that body came before the House of Representatives. Mr. Thaddeus Stevens moved that the House concur in the amendments of the Senate. He said: "The Senate took what to them appeared to be the proper view of their prerogatives, and, though they did not seem to differ with us as to the main object, the mode of getting at it with them was essential, and they very properly put the resolution in the shape they considered right. They have changed the form of the resolution so as not to require the assent of the President; and they have also considered that each house should determine for itself as to the reference of papers, by its own action at the time. To this I see no objection, and, while moving to concur, I will say now, that when it is in order I shall move, or some other gentleman will move when his State is called, a resolution precisely similar, or very nearly similar, to the provision which the Senate has stricken out, only applicable to the House alone."

The House then concurred in the amendments of the Senate, so the resolution passed in the following form:

"*Resolved*, by the House of Representatives (the Senate concurring), That a joint committee of fifteen members shall be appointed, nine of whom shall be members of the House, and six members of the Senate, who shall inquire into the condition of the States which formed the so-called Confederate States of America, and report whether they, or any of them, are entitled to be represented in either house of Congress, with leave to report at any time, by bill or otherwise."

A resolution subsequently passed the House, "That all papers offered relative to the representation of the late so-called Confederate States of America, shall be referred to the joint committee of fifteen without debate, and no members shall be admitted from either of said so-called States until Congress shall declare such States entitled to representation."

On the fourteenth of December the Speaker announced the names of the committee on the part of the House. They were: Thaddeus Stevens, Elihu B. Washburn, Justin S. Morrill, Henry Grider, John A. Bingham, Roscoe Conkling, George S. Boutwell, Henry T. Blow, and Andrew J. Rogers.

On the twenty-first of December the following gentlemen were announced as members of the committee on the part of the Senate: William Pitt Fessenden, James W. Grimes, Ira Harris, Jacob M. Howard, Reverdy Johnson, and George H. Williams.

Thus, before the adjournment of Congress for the holidays, the Joint Committee of Fifteen on Reconstruction had been appointed and empowered to proceed with investigations of the utmost importance to the country. Hated by the late insurgents of the South, who expected little leniency at its hands; opposed by politicians at the North, who viewed it as an obstacle in the way of their designs, and even misrepresented by the President himself, who stigmatized it as a "Central Directory," this committee went forward in the discharge of its important duties, without fear or favor, having a marked influence upon the doings of Congress and the destinies of the country.

Meanwhile other important measures were enlisting the attention of Congress, and were proceeding, by the slow but steady steps of parliamentary progress, to their final consummation.

CHAPTER IV.

SUFFRAGE IN THE DISTRICT OF COLUMBIA.

Duty of Congress to legislate for the District of Columbia—Suffrage Bill introduced into the House—Speech by Mr. Wilson—Mr. Boyer—Mr. Schofield—Mr. Kelley—Mr. Rogers—Mr. Farnsworth—Mr. Davis—Mr. Chanler—Mr. Bingham—Mr. Grinnell—Mr. Kasson—Mr. Julian—Mr. Thomas—Mr. Darling—Mr. Hale's amendment—Mr. Thayer—Mr. Van Horn—Mr. Clarke—Mr. Johnson—Mr. Boutwell.

WHATEVER differences of opinion may exist as to the authority of Congress to legislate for States loyal or disloyal, or for Territories, there is entire unanimity as to the power and duty of Congress to enact laws for the District of Columbia. Here there is no countercurrent of "reserved rights" or "State sovereignty" opposed to the authority of Congress.

Congress being responsible for the legislation of the District of Columbia, we naturally look in that direction for an exhibition in miniature of the policy of the national legislature on questions relating to the interests of the nation at large. If slavery flourished and the slave-market existed in the capital, it was because a majority of the people of the United States were willing. So soon as the nation became antislavery, the "peculiar institution" could no longer exist in the District of Columbia, although it might still survive in other localities.

The General Government having become completely disenthralled from the dominion of slavery, and a wide-spread opinion prevailing at the North that all loyal men should enjoy the right of suffrage, the members of the Thirty-ninth Congress convened with a sense of duty impelling them to begin the great work of political reform at the capital itself. Hence Mr. Wade, as we have seen, on the first day of the session, introduced "Senate bill Number One," designed, as its title declared, "to regulate the elective franchise in the District of Columbia." In the House of Representatives, on the second day of the session, Mr. Kelley introduced "a bill extending the right of suffrage in the District of Columbia." This bill was referred to the Judiciary Committee.

In the House of Representatives, on the 18th of December, Mr. Wilson, chairman of the Committee on the Judiciary, reported a bill extending the right of suffrage in the District of Columbia. The bill provided that from all laws and parts of laws prescribing the qualification of electors for any office in the District of Columbia, the word "white" should be stricken out; also, that from and after the passage of the bill, no person should be disqualified from voting at any election held in the District of Columbia on account of color; also, that all acts of Congress, and all laws of the State of Maryland in force in the District of Columbia, and all ordinances of the cities of Washington and Georgetown inconsistent with the provisions of the bill, should be repealed and annulled.

This bill was made the special order for Wednesday the 10th of January.

Mr. Wilson, of Iowa, whose duty it was, as chairman of the Judiciary Committee, to report the bill, opened the discussion by speaking as follows in favor of the measure:

"Can we excuse ourselves in continuing a limitation on the right of suffrage in the capital of the republic that has no justification in reason, justice, or in the principles on which we profess to have based our entire political system? Upon this question there seems to have been but little difference of opinion among the men who laid the foundation and built the superstructure of this Government. In those days no limitation was placed upon the enjoyment of the defensive rights of the citizen, including the right of suffrage, on account of the color of the skin, except in the State of South Carolina. All of the other States participating in the formation of the Government of the United States had some limitation, based on sex, or age, or property placed upon the right of suffrage; but none of them so far forgot the spirit of our Constitution, the great words of the Declaration of Independence, or the genius of our institutions, as to inquire into the color of a citizen before allowing him the great defensive right of the ballot. It is true, that as the republic moved off in its grand course among the nations a change occurred in the minds and practices of the people of a majority of the States. The love of liberty, because of its own great self, and not because of its application to men of a particular color, lost its sensitive character and active vitality. The moral sense of the people became dormant through the malign influence of that tolerated enemy to all social and governmental virtue, human slavery. The public conscience slumbered, its eyes closed with dollars and its ears stuffed with cotton. When these things succeeded the active justice, abounding mercy, and love of human rights of the earlier days, State after State fell into the dark line of South Carolinian oppression, and adopted her anti-republican limitation of the right of suffrage. A few States stood firm and kept their faith, and to-day, when compared with the bruised and peeled and oppression-cursed State of South Carolina, stand forth as shining examples of the great rewards that are poured upon the heads of the just. Massachusetts and South Carolina, the one true, the other false to the faith and ideas of the early life of the nation, should teach us how safe it is to do right, and how dangerous it is to do wrong; how much safer it is to do justice than it is to practice oppression.

"But, sir, not the States alone fell into this grievous error. The General Government took its stand upon the side of injustice, and apostatized from the true faith of the nation, by depriving a portion of its citizens of the political right of self-defense, the use of the ballot. What good has come to us from this apostasy? Take the history of the municipal government of this city, and what is there in its pages to make an American feel proud of the results of this departure from the principles of true democracy? Is there a worse governed city in all the republic? Where in all the country was there to be found such evidences of thriftless dependence as in this city before the cold breath of the North swept down here during the rebellion and imparted a little of 'Yankee' vigor to its business and population? Where within the bounds of professed fidelity to the Government was true loyalty at a lower ebb, and sympathy with the rebellion at higher flood; freedom more hated, and emancipation more roundly denounced; white troops harder to raise, and black ones more heartily despised; Union victories more coldly received, and reverses productive of less despondency, than right among that portion of the voting population and its adjuncts which control the local elections in this District? With what complaisance the social elements of this capital fostered the brood of traitors who rushed hence to the service of the rebellion in 1861! Are these fruits of our errors pleasing?

"I would not be vindictive, I would be just. I do not want to legislate against the white citizen for the purpose of advancing the interests of the colored citizen. It is best to guard against all such legislation. Let the laws which we pass here be of such pure republican character, that no person can tell from the reading of them what color is stamped upon the faces of the citizens of the United States. Let us have no class legislation, no class privileges. Let our laws be just and uniform in their operation. This is the smooth sea upon which our ship of state may sail; all others are tempestuous and uncertain.

"And now, Mr. Speaker, who are the persons upon whom this bill will operate, if we shall place it upon the statute-book of the nation? They are citizens of the United States and residents of the District of Columbia. It is true that many of them have black faces, but that is God's work, and he is wiser than we. Some of them have faces marked by colors uncertain; that is not God's fault. Those who hate black men most intensely can tell more than all others about this mixture of colors. But, mixed or black, they are citizens of this republic, and they have been, and are to-day, true and loyal to their Government; and this is vastly more than many of their contemners can claim for themselves. In this District a white skin was not the badge of loyalty, while a black skin was. No traitor breathed the air of this capital wearing a black skin. Through all the gradations of traitors, from Wirz to Jeff. Davis, criminal eyes beamed from white faces. Through all phases of treason, from the bold stroke of Lee upon the battle-field to the unnatural sympathy of those who lived within this District, but hated the sight of their country's flag, runs the blood which courses only under a white surface. While white men were fleeing from this city to join their fortunes with the rebel cause, the returning wave brought black faces in their stead. White enemies went out, black friends came in. As true as truth itself were these poor men to the cause of this imperiled nation. Wherever we have trusted them, they have been true. Why will we not deal justly by them? Why shall we not, in this District, where the first effective legislative blow fell upon slavery, declare that these suffering, patient, devoted friends of the republic shall have the power to protect their own rights by their own ballots? Is it because they are ignorant? Sir, we are estopped from that plea. It comes too late. We did not make this inquiry in regard to the white voter. It is only when we see a man with a dark skin that we think of ignorance. Let us not stand on this now in relation to this District. The fact itself is rapidly passing away, for there is no other part of the population of the District so diligent in the acquisition of knowledge as the colored portion. In spite of the difficulties placed in their pathway to knowledge by the white residents, the colored people, adults and children, are pressing steadily on.

"Taken as a class, they surely show themselves possessed of enough of the leaven of thrift, education, morality, and religion to render it safe for us to make the experiment of impartial suffrage here. Let us make the trial. A failure can work no great harm, for to us belongs the power to make any change which the future may show to be necessary. How can we tell whether success or failure shall be the fruit of a practical application of the principles upon which our institutions rest, unless we put them to a fair test? Give every man a fair chance to show how well he can discharge the duties of fully recognized citizenship. This is the way to solve the problem, and in no other way can it be determined. That success will attend the experiment I do not doubt. Others believe the result will prove quite the reverse. Who is right and who wrong can be ascertained only by putting the two opinions to a practical test. The passage of this bill will furnish this test, and to that end I ask for it the favorable consideration of this house."

Mr. Boyer, of Pennsylvania, said: "The design of this bill is to inaugurate here, upon this most conspicuous stage, the first act of the new political drama which is intended to culminate in the complete political equality of the races and the establishment of negro suffrage throughout the States. Constitutional amendments with this view have been already introduced at both ends of the Capitol. The object of the leaders of this movement is no longer concealed; and if there is any thing in their action to admire, it is the candor, courage, and ability with which they press their cause. The agitation is to go on until the question has been settled by the country, and it may as well be met here upon the threshold. The monstrous proposition is nothing less than the absorption into the body politic of the nation of a colored population equal to one-sixth of all the inhabitants of the country, as the census reports will show. Four millions of the population so to be amalgamated have been just set free from a servitude, the debasing influences of which have many a time been vividly depicted in the antislavery speeches of the very men who are the most prominent champions of this new political gospel.

"The argument in favor of the American negro's right to vote must be measured by his capacity to understand and his ability to use such right for the promotion of the public good. And that is the very matter in dispute. But the point does not turn simply upon the inferiority of the negro race; for differences without inferiority may unfit one race for political or social assimilation with another, and render their fusion in the same government incompatible with the general welfare. It is, as I conceive, upon these principles that we must settle the question whether this is a white man's government.

"The negro has no history of civilization. From the earliest ages of recorded time he has ever been a savage or a slave. He has populated with teeming millions the vast extent of a continent, but in no portion of it has he ever emerged from barbarism, and in no age or country has he ever established any other stable government than a despotism. But he is the most obedient and happy of slaves.

"Of all men, the negroes themselves are best contented with their situation. They are not the prime movers in the agitations which concern them. An examination of the tables of the last census will demonstrate that they do not attach much importance to political rights. It will be found that the free people of color are most numerous in some of those States which accord them the fewest political privileges; and in those States which have granted them the right of suffrage they seem to see but few attractions. In Maryland there were, in 1860, 83,942 free people of color; in Pennsylvania, 56,949; in Ohio, 36,673. In neither of those States were they voters. In the State of New York, where they could not vote except under a property qualification, which excluded the most of them, they numbered 49,005. But in Massachusetts, where they did then and do now vote, there were but

9,602. And in all New England, (except Connecticut, where they are not allowed to vote,) there were at the last census but 16,084. If the American negro, in his desire and capacity for self-government, bore any resemblance to the Caucasian, he would distinguish himself by emigration; and, spurning the soil which had enslaved his race, he would seek equality and independence in a more congenial clime. But the spirit of independence and hardy manhood which brought the Puritans to the shores of a New England wilderness he lacks. He will not even go to Massachusetts now, although, instead of a stormy ocean, his barrier is only an imaginary State line, and instead of a howling wilderness, he is invited to a land resounding with the myriad voices of the industrial arts, and instead of painted savages with uplifted tomahawks, he has reason to expect a crowd of male and female philanthropists, with beaming faces and outstretched hands, to welcome him and call him brother. There will he find lecturers to prove his equality, and statesmen to claim him as an associate ruler in the land. If he cares for these things, or is fit for them, why does he linger outside upon the very borders of his political Eden? Why does he not enter into it—avoiding Connecticut in his route—and take possession? The fact is, that the fine political theories set up in his behalf are not in accordance with the natural instinct of the negro, which, in this particular, is truer than the philosophy of his white advisers.

"They are but superficial thinkers who imagine that the organic differences of races can be obliterated by the education of the schools. The qualities of races are perpetuated by descent, and are the result of historical influences reaching far back into the generations of the past. An educated negro is a negro still. The cunning of the chisel of a Canova could not make an enduring Corinthian column out of a block of anthracite; not because of its color, but on account of the structure of its substance. He might indeed, with infinite pains, give it the form, but he could not impart to it the strength and adhesion of particles required to enable it to brave the elements, and the temple it was made to support would soon crumble into ruin."

Mr. Schofield, of Pennsylvania, said: "The cheapest elevator and best moralizer for an oppressed and degraded class is to inspire them with self-respect, with the belief in the possibility of their elevation. Bestow the elective franchise upon the colored population of this District, and you awaken the hope and ambition of the whole race throughout the country. Hitherto punishment has been the only incentive to sobriety and industry furnished these people by American law. They were kept too low to feel disgrace, and reward was inconsistent with the theory of 'service owed.' Let us try now the persuasive power of wages and protection. If colored suffrage is still considered an experiment, this District is a good place in which to try it. The same objections do not exist here that are urged on behalf of some of the States. No constitutional question intervenes. Here, at least, Congress is supreme. The law can be passed, and if it is found to be bad, a majority can repeal it. The colored race is too small in numbers here to endanger the supremacy of the white people, but large and loyal enough to counteract to some extent disloyal proclivities.

"Both the precept and practice of our fathers refute the allegation that this is exclusively a white man's government. If we can not now consent to so slight a recognition, as proposed by this bill, of the great underlying theory of our Government, as declared and practiced by our fathers, we are thrown back upon that new and monstrous doctrine, that the five millions of our colored population, and their posterity forever, have no rights that a white man is bound to respect.

"Who pronounces this crushing sentence? The political South. And what is this South? The Southern master and his Northern minion. Have these people wronged the South? Have they filled it with violence, outrage, and murder? No, sir; they are remarkably gentle, patient, and respectful. Have they despoiled its wealth or diminished its grandeur? No, sir; their unpaid toil has made the material South. They removed the forests, cleared the fields, built the dwellings, churches, colleges, cities, highways, railroads, and canals. Why, then, does the South hate and persecute these people? Because it has wronged them. Injustice always hates its victim. They are forced to look to the North for justice. And what is the North? Not the latitude of frosts; not New England and the States that border on the lakes, the Mississippi, and the Pacific. The geographical is lost in the political meaning of the word. The North, in a political sense, means justice, liberty, and union, and in the order in which I have named them. Jefferson defined this 'North' when he wrote 'all men are created equal, endowed by their Creator with certain inalienable rights, among which are life, liberty, and the pursuit of happiness.' This North has no geographical boundaries. It embraces the friends of freedom in every quarter of this great republic. Many of its bravest champions hail from the geographical South. The North, that did not fear the slave power in its prime, in the day of its political strength and patronage, when it commanded alike the nation and the mob, and for the same cruel purpose, will not be intimidated by its expiring maledictions around this capital. The North must pass this bill to vindicate its sincerity and its courage. The slave power has already learned that the North is terrible in war, and forgiving and gentle in peace; let its crushed and mangled victims learn from the passage of this bill, that the justice of the North, unlimited by lines of latitude, unlimited by color or race, slumbereth not."

Mr. Kelley, of Pennsylvania, followed: "In preparing to begin the work of reconstructing the grandest of human governments, shattered for a time by treason, and in endeavoring to ascertain what we should do, and how and when it should be done, I have consulted no popular impulse. Groping my way through the murky political atmosphere that has prevailed for more than thirty years, I have seated myself at the feet of the fathers of our country, that I might, as far as my suggestions would go, make them in accordance with the principles of those who constructed our Government. I can make no suggestion for the improvement of the primary principles or general structure of our Government, and I would heal its wounds so carefully that it should descend to posterity unstained and unmarred as it came, under the guidance of Providence, from the hands of those who fashioned it.

"For whom do we ask this legislation? In 1860, according to the census, there were fourteen thousand three hundred and sixteen colored people in this District, and we ask this legislation for the male adults of that number. Are they in rags and filth and degradation? The tax-books of the District will tell you that they pay taxes on $1,250,000 worth of real estate, held within the limits of this District. On one block, on which they pay taxes on fifty odd thousand dollars, there are but two colored freeholders who have not bought themselves out of slavery.

Eng. by Samuel Sartain

HON. WILLIAM D. KELLEY

REPRESENTATIVE FROM PENNSYLVANIA

One of them has bought as many as eight persons beside himself—a wife and seven children. Coming to freedom in manhood, mortgaged for a thousand or fifteen hundred dollars as his own price, he has earned and carried to the Southern robber thousands of dollars, the price extorted for his wife and children, and is now a freeholder in this District. They have twenty-one churches, which they own, and which they maintain at an annual cost of over twenty thousand dollars. Their communing members number over forty-three hundred. In their twenty-two Sunday-schools they gather on each Sabbath over three thousand American children of African descent. They maintain, sir, to the infamous disgrace of the American Congress and people, thirty-three day schools, eight of which are maintained exclusively by contributions from colored citizens of the District; the remainder by their contributions, eked out by contributions from the generous people of the North; and every dollar of their million and a quarter dollars of real estate and personal property is taxed for schools to educate the children of the white people of the District, the fathers of many of those children having been absent during the war fighting for the Confederacy and against our constitutional flag. Who shall reproach them with being poor and ignorant while Congress, which has exclusive jurisdiction over the District, has, till last year, robbed them day by day, and barred the door of the public school against them? Such reproach does not lie in the white man's mouth; at any rate, no member of the Democratic party ought to utter it."

The debate was continued on the day following. Mr. Rogers, of New Jersey, having obtained the floor, addressed the House for two hours. He said: "I hold that there never has been, in the legislation of the United States, a bill which involved so momentous consequences as that now under consideration, because nowhere in the history of this country, from the time that the first reins of party strife were drawn over the land, was any political party ever known to advocate the doctrine now advocated by a portion of the party on the other side of this House, except within the last year, and during the heat and strife of battle in the land. The wisdom of ages for more than five thousand years, and the most enlightened governments that ever existed upon the face of the earth, have handed down to us that grand principle that all governments of a civilized character have been and were intended especially for the benefit of white men and white women, and not for those who belong to the negro, Indian, or mulatto race.

"It is the high prerogative which the political system of this country has given to the masses, rich and poor, to exercise the right of suffrage and declare, according to the honest convictions of their hearts, who shall be the officers to rule over them. There is no privilege so high, there is no right so grand. It lies at the very foundation of this Government; and when you introduce into the social system of this country the right of the African race to compete at the ballot-box with the intelligent white citizens of this country, you are disturbing and embittering the whole social system; you rend the bonds of a common political faith; you break up commercial intercourse and the free interchanges of trade, and you degrade the people of this country before the eyes of the envious monarchs of Europe, and fill our history with a record of degradation and shame.

"Why, then, should we attempt at this time to inflict the system of negro suffrage upon those who happen to be so unfortunate as to reside in the District of Columbia? This city bears the name of George Washington, the father of our country; and as it was founded by him, so I wish to hand it down to those who shall come after us, preserving that principle which declares that the sovereignty is in the white people of the country, for whose benefit this Government was established. I am not ready to believe that those men who have laid down their lives in the battles of the late revolution, who came from their homes like the torrents that sweep over their native hills and mountains, those men who gathered round the sacred precincts of the tomb of Washington to uphold and perpetuate our proud heritage of liberty, intended to inflict upon the people of this District, or of this land, the monstrous doctrine of political equality of the negro race with the white at the ballot-box.

"No such dogma as this was ever announced by the Republican party in their platforms. When that party met at Chicago, in 1860, they took pains to enunciate the great principle of self-government which underlies the institutions of this country, that each State has the right to control its own domestic policy according to its own judgment exclusively. I ask the gentlemen on the other side of the house to allow the people of the District of Columbia to exercise the same great right of self-government, to determine by their votes at the ballot-box whether they desire to inaugurate a system of political equality with the colored people of the District.

"Self-government was the great principle which impelled our fathers to protest against the powers of King George. That was the principle which led the brave army of George Washington across the ice of the river Delaware. It was the principle which struck a successful blow against despotism, and planted liberty upon this continent. It was the principle that our fathers claimed the Parliament of England had no right to invade, and drove the colonies into rebellion, because laws were passed without their consent by a Parliament in which they were unrepresented.

"I am here to-day to plead for the white people of this District, upon the same grounds taken by our fathers to the English Parliament, in favor of self-government and the right of the people of the District to be heard upon this all-important question. Although we may have a legal yet we have no moral right, according to the immutable principles of justice, and according to the declaration of Holy Writ, that we should do unto others as we would they should do unto us, to inflict upon the people of this District this fiendish doctrine of political equality with a race that God Almighty never intended should stand upon an equal footing with the white man and woman in social or civil life."

Mr. Farnsworth, of Illinois, replied: "He [Mr. Rogers] says this is a white man's Government. 'A white man's Government!' Why, sir, did not the Congress of the United States pass a law for enrolling into the service of the United States the black man as well as the white man? Did not we tax the black man as well as the white man? Does he not contribute his money as well as his blood for the protection and defense of the Government? O, yes; and now, when the black man comes hobbling home upon his crutches and his wooden limbs, maimed for life, bleeding, crushed, wounded, is he to be told by the people who called him into the service of the Government, 'This is a white man's Government; you have nothing to do with it?' Shame! I say, eternal shame upon such a doctrine, and upon the men who advocate it!

"What should be the test as to the right to exercise the elective franchise? I contend that the only question to be asked should be, 'Is he a man?' The test should be that of manhood. not that of color, or races, or class. Is he endowed with conscience and reason? Is he an immortal being? If these questions are answered in the affirmative, he has the same right to protection that we all enjoy.

"I am in favor, Mr. Speaker, of making suffrage equal and universal. I believe that greater wisdom is concentrated in the decisions of the ballot-box when all citizens of a certain age vote than when only a part vote. If you apply a test founded on education or intelligence, where will you stop? One man will say that the voter should be able to read the Constitution and to write his name; another, that he should be acquainted with the history of the United States; another will demand a still higher degree of education and intelligence, until you will establish an aristocracy of wisdom, which is one of the worst kinds of aristocracy. Sir, the men who formed this Government, who believed in the rights of human nature, and designed the Government to protect them, believed, I think, as I do, that when suffrage is made universal, you concentrate in the ballot-box a larger amount of wisdom than when you exclude a portion of the citizens from the right of suffrage.

"I grant, sir, that many of the colored men whom I would enfranchise are poor and ignorant, but we have made them so. We have oppressed them by our laws. We have stolen them from their cradles and consigned them to helpless slavery. The shackles are now knocked from their limbs, and they emerge from the house of bondage and stand forth as men. Let us now take the next grand step, a step which must commend itself to our judgment and consciences. Let us clothe these men with the rights of freemen, and give them the power to protect their rights.

"Sir, as I have already remarked, we have passed through a fiery ordeal. There are but few homes within our land that are not made desolate by the loss of a son or a father. The widow and the orphan meet us wherever we turn. The maimed and crippled soldiers of the republic are every-where seen. Many fair fields have become cemeteries, where molder the remains of the noble men who have laid down their lives in defense of our Government. We thought that we had attained the crisis of our troubles during the progress of the war. But it has been said that the ground-swell of the ocean after the storm is often more dangerous to the mariner than the tempest itself; and I am inclined to think that this is true in reference to the present posture of our national affairs. The storm has apparently subsided; but, sir, if we fail to do our duty now as a nation—and that duty is so simple that a child can understand it; no elaborate argument need enforce it, as no sophistry can conceal it; it is simply to give to one man the same rights that we give to another—if we fail now in this our plain duty as a nation, then the ship of state is in more peril from this ground-swell on which we are riding than it was during the fierce tempest of war. I trust that this Congress will have the firmness and wisdom to guide the old ship safely into the haven of peace and security. This we can do by fixing our eyes upon the guiding star of our fathers—the equal rights of all men."

The discussion was resumed on the following day, January 12, by Mr. Davis, of New York: "Republican government can never rest safely, it can never rest peacefully, upon any foundation save that of the intelligence and virtue of its subjects. No government, republican in form, was ever prosperous where its people were ignorant and debased. And in this Government, where our fathers paid so much attention to intelligence, to the cultivation of virtue, and to all considerations which should surround and guard the foundations of the republic, I am sure that we would do dishonor to their memory by conferring the franchise upon men unfitted to receive it and unworthy to exercise it.

"I am perfectly aware that in many States we have given the elective franchise to the white man who is debased and ignorant. I regret it, because I think that intelligence ought always, either as to the black or the white man, to be made a test of suffrage. And I glory in the principles that have been established by Massachusetts, which prescribes, not that a man should have money in his purse, but that he should have in his head a cultivated brain, the ability to read the Constitution of his country, and intelligence to understand his rights as a citizen.

"I have never been one of those who believed that the black man had 'no rights that the white man was bound to respect.' I believe that the black man in this country is entitled to citizenship, and, by virtue of that citizenship, is entitled to protection, to the full power of this Government, wherever he may be found on the face of God's earth; that he has a right to demand that the shield of this Government shall be held over him, and that its powers shall be exerted on his behalf to the same extent as if he were the proudest grandee of the land. But, sir, citizenship is one thing, and the right of suffrage is another and a different thing; and in circumstances such as exist around us, I am unwilling that general, universal, unrestricted suffrage should be granted to the black men of this District, as is proposed by the bill under consideration.

"This whole subject is within the power of Congress, and if we grant restricted privilege to-day, we can extend the exercise of that privilege to-morrow. Public sentiment on this, as on a great many subjects, is a matter of slow growth and development. That is the history of the world. Development upon all great subjects is slow. The development of the globe itself has required countless ages before it was prepared for the introduction of man upon it. And take the progress of the human race through the historic age—kingdoms and empires, systems of social polity, systems of religion, systems of science, have been of no rapid growth, but long centuries intervened between their origin and their overthrow.

"The Creator placed man on earth, not for the perfection of the individual, but the race; and therefore he locked up the mysteries of his power in the bosom of the earth and in the depths of the heavens, rendering them invisible to mankind. He made man study those secrets, those mysteries, in order that his genius might be cultivated, his views enlarged, his intellect matured, so that he might gradually rise in the scale of being, and finally attain the full perfection for which his Creator designed him.

"Thus governments, political systems, and political rights have been the subjects of study and improvement; changes adapted to the advance of society are made; experiments are tried, based upon reason and upon judgment, and those are safest which in their gradual introduction avoid unnecessary violence and convulsion.

"I submit, sir, whether it be wise for us now so suddenly to alter so entirely the political *status* of so great a number of the citizens of this District, in conferring upon them indiscriminately the right of franchise."

Mr. Chanler, of New York, then addressed the House:

"If, sir, it should ever be your good fortune to visit romantic old Spain, and to enter the fortress and palace of Alhambra, the fairest monument of Moorish grandeur and skill, as this Capitol is the pride of American architecture, you may see cut in stone a hand holding a key, surmounting the horse-shoe arch of the main gateway. They are the three types of strength, speed, and secresy, the boast of a now fallen Saracen race, sons of that sea of sand, the desert, who carried the glory of Islam to furthest Gades. In an evil hour of civil strife and bitter hatred of faction, the Alhambra was betrayed to Spain, 'to feed fat an ancient grudge' between political chiefs. The stronghold of the race, with the palace, the sacred courts of justice, and all the rare works of art—the gardens of unrivaled splendor—all that was their own of majesty, strength, and beauty, became the trophies of another.

"The legend of the Saracen exile tells the story of penitence and shame; and to the last moment of his sad life he sighs in the sultry desert for the fair home of his ancestors, the gorgeous Alhambra. We, too, are descended from a race of conquerors, who crossed the ocean to establish the glory of civil and religious liberty, and secure freedom to themselves and their posterity. To-day we are assembled in the Alhambra of America; here is our citadel; here our courts of highest resort; around these halls cluster the proudest associations of the American people; they seem almost sacred in their eyes. No hostile foot of foreign foe or domestic traitor has trodden them in triumph. Above it floats the flag, the emblem of our Union. That Union is the emblem of the triumphs of the white race. That race rules by the ballot. Shall we surrender the ballot, the emblem of our sovereignty; the flag, the emblem of our Union; the Union, the emblem of our national glory, that they may become the badges of our weakness and the trophies of another race? Never, sir! never, never!

"Shall the white laborer bow his free, independent, and honored brow to the level of the negro just set free from slavery, and, by yielding the entrance to this great citadel of our nation, surrender the mastery of his race over the Representatives of the people, the Senate, and Supreme Court of this Union? Then, sir, the white workingman's sovereignty would begin to cease to be.

"Then the most democratic majesty of American liberty would be humbled in the little dust which was lately raised by a brief campaign of two hundred thousand negro troops, and even they led by white officers, while millions of white soldiers held the field in victory by their own strength and valor. Deny it if ye dare! Sir, I know that this is a white man's Government, and I believe the white workingman has the manhood which shall preserve it to his latest posterity, pure and strong, in 'justice tempered with mercy.'

"There may be a legend hereafter telling of the exile of Representatives now on this floor, who, in the hour of party spite, betrayed the dominion of their race here, and the stronghold of their people's liberty, to a servile and foreign race."

Near the close of Mr. Chanler's remarks, his time having been extended by courtesy of the House, a forensic passage at arms occurred between that gentleman and Mr. Bingham, of Ohio. Mr. Chanler had said: "I deny that any obligation rests against this Government to do any thing more for the negro than has already been done. 'On what meats doth this Cæsar feed that he has grown so great?' The white soldier did as much work as he, fought as well, died as bravely, suffered in hospitals and in the field as well as he. More than this, the white soldier fought to liberate the slave, and did do it. The white soldier did more: he fought to preserve institutions and rights endeared to him by every hallowed association; to overthrow the rebellion of his brother against their Commonwealth and glorious Union; to preserve the sovereignty of the people against the conspiracy of a slave aristocracy, if you will; to maintain the fabric of the Government built by their fathers for them and their race in every country of kindred men who, downtrodden and disenfranchised, look to this country as a sure refuge. The white soldier fought as a volunteer, as a responsible, free, and resolute citizen, knowing for what he fought, and generously letting the slave share with him the honor, and bestowing on him more than his share of the profits of the white man's victory over his equal and the negro's master.

"We are willing that the negro should have every protection which the law can throw around him, but there is a majesty which 'hedges in a king.' That he ought not to have until he shows himself 'every inch a king.'

"'Who would be free, themselves must strike the blow.'

"'Some are born great, some achieve greatness, and some have greatness thrust upon them.'

"We are opposed to thrusting honor on the negro. He is to-day, as a race, as dependent on the power and skill of the white race for protection as when he was first brought from Africa. Not one act of theirs has proved the capacity of the black race for self-government. They have neither literature, arts, nor arms, as a race. They have never, during all the changes of dynasties or revolution of States, risen higher than to be the helpers of the contending parties. They have had the same opportunity as the Indian to secure their independence of the white race, but have never systematically even attempted it on this continent, although they have been educated with equal care, and in the same schools as the white man. Their race has been subject to the white man, and has submitted to the yoke."

Mr. Bingham.—"I understood the gentleman to say, that the colored race had failed to strike for their rights during the late rebellion. I wish to remind the gentleman of the fact, which ought to bring a blush to the cheek of every American citizen, that at the beginning of this great struggle, a distinguished general, who, I have no doubt, received the political support of the gentleman himself for the Presidency, and who, then at the head of an American army within the Commonwealth of Virginia, issued his proclamation, as general in command of the army, notifying the insurgents in arms against the Constitution that, if their slaves rose in revolt for their liberty, he, Major-General McClellan, by the whole force of the army at his command, would crush them with an iron hand. Yet the gentleman gets up here to-day, after a record of that sort, to cast censure upon this people because they did not strike for their liberties against the combined armies of the republic and the armies of treason!"

Mr. Chanler.—"My honorable friend from Ohio may have made a good point against General McClellan, but he has made none against me. I admit that they have made successful insurrections, but my argument was not to the effect that the negro race was not capable of the bloodiest deeds. I avoided entering into that question. I asserted that they had made successful insurrection; that they had held the white race under their heel in Hayti and St. Domingo. I would only say, with regard to this question of race, that I assert there is no record of the black race having proved its capacity for self-government as a race; that they have never struck a blow for freedom, and maintained their freedom and independence as individuals when free. I appeal to history, and to the gentleman from Ohio [Mr. Bingham], and I speak as a student of history, and the representative of a race whose proudest boast is that their capacity for self-government is the only charter of their liberty. I assail no race; I assail no man. I have taken the greatest pains to prove that the inalienable rights of the black man are as sacred to me as those inalienable rights I have received from my God. If the gentleman misunderstood me, I hope he will accept this explanation. If I have not met his question, I will now yield the floor to him to continue."

Mr. Bingham.—"And I continue thus far, that the gentleman's speech certainly has relation to the rights of the black man within the Republic of the United States. What he may say of their history outside of the jurisdiction of this country, it is not very important for me to take notice of. But inasmuch as the gentleman has seen fit, in his response to what I said, to refer to the testimony of history, I will bear witness now, by the authority of history, that this very race of which he speaks is the only race now existing upon this planet that ever hewed their way out of the prison-house of chattel slavery to the sunlight of personal liberty by their own unaided arm. So much for that part of the gentleman's argument as relates to history."

Mr. Chanler.—"Does the gentleman allude now to what has been done in other lands than this? I ask the question because he says he does not like me to go outside of the jurisdiction of this country, and I therefore ask him not to go too far into Africa."

Mr. Bingham.—"I am not in Africa. I refer to what the gentleman referred to himself. The insurrection in St. Domingo, I say, stands without a parallel in the history of any race now living on this earth, and I challenge the gentleman to refute that statement from history."

Mr. Chanler.—"That is admitted."

Mr. Bingham.—"That is admitted. Then I want to know, with a fact like that conceded, what sort of logic, what sort of force, what sort of reason, what sort of justice is there in the remark of the gentleman made here in a deliberative assembly touching the question of the personal enfranchisement of the black race, when he says in the statement here, right in the face of that fact, that they only are entitled to their liberty who strike the blow for and maintain their liberty? They did strike the blow in Hayti, and did maintain their liberty there. They struck such a blow for liberty there as no other race of men under like circumstances ever before struck, now represented by any organized community upon this planet; and that the gentleman conceded. And yet this sort of argument is to be adduced here as reason why these people in the District of Columbia should not receive the consideration of this House, and be protected in their rights as men. If the gentleman's remark is not adduced for that purpose, then it is altogether foreign to our inquiry. If the gentleman can assign any other reason for the introduction of any such argument as that, I should like to hear him."

Mr. Chanler.—"I merely wish to say, in reply to the gentleman, that I have read history a little further back. I remember when the British fleet and the British army held out a similar threat to the white race of this country. The proclamation of General McClellan did keep down the negroes; and this fact proves what I assert—that they are a race to be kept under. No race capable of achieving its liberty by its own efforts, would have listened for one moment to the paper threats of all the generals in the world. The negroes listened to McClellan, and they shrank behind the bush. They are bushmen in Africa. They are a dependent race, unwilling—I assert it from the record of history—unwilling to assert their independence at the risk of their lives. By their own efforts they never have attained, and I firmly believe they never will attain, their liberty."

Mr. Bingham replied: "I desire to say to the gentleman from New York, when he talks of being a 'student of history,' that before the tribunal of history the facts are not against me nor against the colored race. I beg leave to say to the gentleman that these people have borne themselves as bravely, as well, and, I may add, as wisely during the great contest just closed, as any people to whom he can point, situated in like circumstances, at any period of the world's history. They were in chains when the rebellion broke out. They constituted but one-sixth of the whole body of the people. By the terms of the Constitution of the United States, if they lifted a hand in the assertion of their right to freedom, they were liable that moment to be crushed by the combined power of the Republic, called out, in pursuance of the very letter of the Constitution, 'to suppress insurrection.'

Yet, notwithstanding the fact that their whole living generation and the generations before them, running back two centuries, had been enslaved and brutalized, reduced to the sad and miserable condition of chattels, which, for want of a better name, we call a 'slave'—an article of merchandise, a thing of trade, with no acknowledged rights in the present, and denied even the hope of a heritage in the great hereafter—yet, sir, the moment that the word 'Liberty' ran along your ranks, the moment that the word 'Emancipation' was emblazoned upon your banners, those men who, with their ancestors, had been enslaved through five generations, rose as one man to stand by this republic, the last hope of oppressed humanity upon the earth, until they numbered one hundred and seventy-five thousand arrayed in arms under your banners, doing firmly, unshrinkingly, and defiantly their full share in securing the final victory of our arms. I have said this much in defense of men who had the manhood, in the hour of the nation's trial, to strike for the flag and the unity of the republic in the tempest of the great conflict, and to stand, where brave men only could stand, on the field of poised battle, where the earthquake and the fire led the charge. Sir, I am not mistaken; and the record of history to which I have referred does not, as the gentleman affirms it does, make against me."

Mr. Grinnell, of Iowa, in reply to Mr. Chanler, said: "He [Mr. Chanler] proceeds to say that they are now, as a class, dependent as when they were brought from their native wilds in Africa. Sir, I believe if the gentleman were master of all languages, if he were to attempt to put into a sentence the quintessence, the high-wines, and sublimation of an untruth, he could not have more concentrated his language into a libel.

"What is the fact, sir? It is perfectly notorious that these four million slaves have not only taken care of themselves amid all the ingenious impediments which tyrants could impose, but they have borne upon their stalwart shoulders their masters, millions of people, for a century. Why, sir, it seemed as impossible for a man to swim the Atlantic with Mount Atlas upon his back, or make harmonious base to the thunders of heaven. But these men have achieved the world's wonder—coming out from the tortures of slavery, from the prison-house, untainted with dishonor or crime, and out of the war free, noble, brave, and more worthy of their friends, always true to the flag.

"Mr. Speaker, it was in fable that a man pointed a lion to the picture which represented the king of the forest prostrate, with a man's foot on his neck, and asked what he thought of that. The reply was, 'Lions have no painters.' For days the unblushing apostles of sham Democracy have in this House drawn pictures of the ignorance and degradation of the people of color in the District of Columbia. Had the subjects of their wanton defamation had a Representative here, there would have been a different coloring to the picture, and I would gladly leave their defense to the Representatives of classes who have by hundreds darkened these galleries with their sable countenances, waiting for days to hear the decisive vote which announces that their freedom is not a mockery.

"Who are they to whom this bill proposes to give suffrage? They are twenty thousand people, owning twenty-one churches, maintaining thirty-three day schools, and paying taxes on more than one and a quarter million dollars' worth of real property. Thirty per cent. of their number were slaves; but the census does not show that there is a Democratic congressional district in the Union where a larger proportion of its population are found attendant at the churches or in the schools.

"They did not follow the example of their pale-faced neighbors, to the number of thousands, crossing the line to join in the rebellion; but three thousand and more of their number went into the Union army, nearly one thousand of whom, as soldiers, fell by disease and battle in the room of those who wept on Northern soil for rebel defeats, and now decry the manhood and withhold just rights from our true national defenders.

"In the South they were our friends. In the language of an official dispatch of Secretary Seward to Minister Adams, 'Everywhere the American general receives his most useful and reliable information from the negro, who hails his coming as the harbinger of freedom.' Not one, but many, of our generals have proclaimed that the negro has gained by the bayonet the ballot. Admiral Du Pont made mention of the negro pilot Small, who brought out the steamer Planter, mounting a rifled and siege gun, from Charleston, as a prize to us, under the very guns of the enemy. He brought us the first trophy from Fort Sumter, and information more valuable than the prize.

"The celebrated charge of the negro brigade at the conflict at

Port Hudson has passed into history. The position of the colored people in the State of Iowa reflects lasting honor on their loyalty, and our brave white soldiers would not have me withhold the facts. In the State there were between nine hundred and a thousand people of their class subject to military duty. Of that number more than seven hundred entered the army. They put to blush the patriotism of the dominant race in all Democratic districts. Seven-tenths of a class, without the inducement of commissions as lieutenants, captains, colonels, commissaries, or quartermasters, braving the hate and vengeance of rebels, rushing into the deadly imminent breach in the darkest hour of our struggle! Where is the parallel to this? They had no flag; it was a mockery. There was no pledge of political franchise. Does history cite us to a country where so large a per cent. of the population went forth for the national defense? It was not under the Cæsars; and Harold, in the defense of Britain, left behind him a larger per cent. of the stalwart and the strong. They were more eager to maintain the national honor than the zealots to rescue Jerusalem from the profanation of infidels. Not Frank or Hun, nor Huguenot or Roundhead, or mountaineer, Hungarian, or Pole, exceeded their sacrifices made when tardily accepted. And this is the race now asking our favor.

"Mr. Speaker, it will be one of the most joyful occasions of my life to give expression to my gratitude by voting a ballot to those who owed us so little, yet have aided us so faithfully and well. My conscience approves it as a humane act to the millions who for centuries have groaned under a terrible realization that on the side of the oppressor there is power.

"My purpose is not to leave that heritage of shame to my children, that I forgot those whose blood fed our rivers and crimsoned the sea, and left them outcasts in the 'land of the free,' preferring white treason to sable loyalty. I rather vote death the penalty for the chief traitor, all honor and reward for our soldiery, and a ballot, safety, and justice for the poor."

On the 15th of January the discussion was continued by Mr. Kasson, of Iowa, who said: "Much has been said in this debate about the gallantry of the negro troops, and about the number of negro troops in the war. Gentlemen have declared here so broadly that we were indebted to them for our victories as to actually convey the impression that they won nearly all the victories accomplished by the armies of the United States, and that to them are we indebted for the salvation of our country and our triumph over the rebellion.

"I do not agree with them in the extent of their praise, nor the grounds upon which it has been placed. One gentleman, I think it was the gentleman from Pennsylvania, speaks of our debt to the negroes, because they have fought *our* battles for us. This is a falsification of the condition of the negroes, and of the history of the country in this particular. *Those negroes fought for their liberty,* which was involved in the preservation of the Union of the States. They fought with us to accomplish the maintenance of the integrity of the country, which carried with it the liberty of their own race; and what would have been said of the negroes if they had not, under such circumstances, come forward and united with us? While I yield to the negro troops the credit of having exhibited bravery and manhood when put to the test, I do not yield to them the exclusive or chief credit of having won the victory for the Government of my country in preserving this Union. Let us not, under false assertions of fact, send out to the country and the world from this floor the declaration that the white race of this country are wanting in the gallantry, the devotion, and the patriotism which ultimately secured for our armies triumph, and for our nation perpetuity.

"Unless intelligence exists in this country, unless schools are supported and education diffused throughout the country, our institutions are not safe, and either anarchy or despotism will be the result; and when you propose substantially to introduce at once three-quarters of a million or a million of voters, the great mass of whom are ignorant and unable to tell when the ballot they vote is right side up, then I protest against such an alarming infusion of ignorance into the ballot-box, into that sacred palladium, as we have always called it, of the liberties of our country. Let us introduce them by fit degrees. Let them come in as fast as they are fit, and their numbers will not shock the character of our institutions.

"I turn for a single moment to call attention to the philanthropy of the proposition. If you introduce all without regard to qualification, without their being able to read or write, and thus to understand the questions on which they are to decide, what would be the effect? You will take away from them the strongest incentive to learn to read or write. As a race, it is not accustomed to position and property; it has no homesteads, it has no stake in the country; and unless they are required to be intelligent, and qualified to understand something about our institutions and our laws, and the questions which are submitted to the people from time to time, you say then to them, 'No matter whether or not you make progress in civilization or education, you shall have all the rights of citizenship,' and in that way you take away from them all special motive to education and improvement. On the contrary, if the ability to read and write and understand the ballot is made the qualification on the part of these people to exercise the right of voting, the remaining portion will see that color is not exclusion. They would all aspire to the qualification itself as preliminary to the act. You can submit no motive to that race so powerful for the purpose of developing in them the education and intelligence required.

"I say, therefore, on whatever grounds you put it, whether you regard the safety of our institutions or the light of philanthropy, you should insist on qualifications substantially the same as those required in the State of Massachusetts. And let me say that, taking the State of Massachusetts as an example of the result of general intelligence and qualified suffrage, and a careful guardianship of the ballot-box, I know of no more illustrious example in this or any other country of its importance.

"With a credit that surpasses that of the United States, with a history that is surpassed by no State in the Union, with wealth that is almost fabulous in proportion to its population, with a prosperity almost unknown in the history of the world, that State stands before us to-day in all her dignity, strength, wealth, intelligence, and virtue. And if we, by adopting similar principles in other States, can secure such results, we certainly have an inducement to consider well how far this condition is to be attributed to her diffused education, and to the provisions of her constitution."

At the close of Mr. Kasson's speech, a colloquy occurred between him and his colleague, Mr. Price, eliciting the fact that the question of negro suffrage in Iowa had been squarely before the people of that State in the late fall election, and their vote had been in favor of the measure by a majority of sixteen thousand.

Mr. Julian, of Indiana, having obtained the floor near the hour of adjournment, made his argument on the following day, when the consideration of the question was resumed. In answer to the objection that negro voting would "lead to the amalgamation of the races or social equality," he said: "On this subject there is nothing left to conjecture, and no ground for alarm. Negro suffrage has been very extensively tried in this country, and we are able to appeal to facts. Negroes had the right to vote in all the Colonies save one, under the Articles of Confederation. They voted, I believe, generally, on the question of adopting the Constitution of the United States. They have voted ever since in New York and the New England States, save Connecticut, in which the practice was discontinued in 1818. They voted in New Jersey till the year 1840; in Virginia and Maryland till 1833; in Pennsylvania till 1838; in Delaware till 1831; and in North Carolina and Tennessee till 1836. I have never understood that in all this experience of negro suffrage the amalgamation of the races was the result. I think these evils are not at all complained of to this day in New England and New York, where negro suffrage is still practiced and recognized by law."

In answer to the argument that a "war of races" might ensue, Mr. Julian said: "Sir, a war of races in this country can only be the result of denying to the negro his rights, just as such wars have been caused elsewhere; and the late troubles in Jamaica should teach us, if any lesson can, the duty of dealing justly with our millions of freedmen. Like causes must produce like results. English law made the slaves of Jamaica free, but England failed to enact other laws making their freedom a blessing. The old spirit of domination never died in the slave-master, but was only maddened by emancipation. For thirty years no measures were adopted tending to protect or educate the freedmen. At length, and quite recently, the colonial authorities passed a whipping act, then a law of eviction for people of color, then a law imposing heavy impost duties, bearing most grievously upon them, and finally a law providing for the importation of coolies, thus taxing the freedmen for the very purpose of taking the bread out of the mouths of their own children! I believe it turns out, after all, that these outraged people even then did not rise up against the local government; but the white ruffians of the island, goaded on by their own unchecked rapacity, and availing themselves of the infernal pretext of a black insurrection, perpetrated deeds of rapine and vengeance that find no parallel anywhere, save in the acts of their natural allies, the late slave-breeding rebels, against our flag. Sir, is there no warning here against the policy of leaving our freedmen to the tender mercies of their old masters? Are the white rebels of this District any better than the Jamaica villains to whom I have referred? The late report of General Schurz gives evidence of some important facts which will doubtless apply here. The mass of the white people in the South, he says, are totally destitute of any national feeling. The same bigoted sectionalism that swayed them prior to the war is almost universal. Nor have they any feeling of the enormity of treason as a crime. To them it is not odious, as very naturally it would not be, under the policy which foregoes the punishment of traitors, and gives so many of them the chief places of power in the South. And their hatred of the negro to-day is as intense and scathing and as universal as before the war. I believe it to be even more so. The proposition to educate him and elevate his condition is everywhere met with contempt and scorn. They acknowledge that slavery, as it once existed, is overthrown; but the continued inferiority and subordination of the colored race, under some form of vassalage or serfdom, is regarded by them as certain. Sir, they have no thought of any thing else; and if the ballot shall be withheld from the freedmen after the withdrawal of military power, the most revolting forms of oppression and outrage will be practiced, resulting, at last, in that very war of races which is foolishly apprehended as the effect of giving the negro his rights."

A serious question confronted Mr. Julian, namely: How could Representatives from States which negroes by constitutional provision are forbidden to enter, be expected to vote for negro suffrage in this District? He said: "In seeking to meet this difficulty, several considerations must be borne in mind. In the first place, the demand for negro suffrage in this District rests not alone upon the general ground of right, of democratic equality, but upon peculiar reasons superinduced by the late war, which make it an immediate practical issue, involving not merely the welfare of the colored man, but the safety of society itself. If civil government is to be revived at all in the South, it is perfectly self-evident that the loyal men there must vote; but the loyal men are the negroes, and the disloyal are the whites. To put back the governing power into the hands of the very men who brought on the war, and exclude those who have proved themselves the true friends of the country, would be utterly suicidal and atrociously unjust. Negro suffrage in the districts lately in revolt is thus a present political necessity, dictated by the selfishness of the white loyalist as well as his sense of justice. But in our Western States, in which the negro population is relatively small, and the prevailing sentiment of their white people is loyal, no such emergency exists. Society will not be endangered by the temporary postponement of the right of negro suffrage till public opinion shall render it practicable, and leaving the question of suffrage in the loyal States to be decided by them on its merits. If Indiana had gone out of her proper place in the Union, and her loyal population had been found too weak to force her back into it without negro bullets and bayonets, and if, after thus coercing her again into her constitutional orbit, her loyalists had been found unable to hold her there without negro ballots, the question of negro suffrage in Indiana would most obviously have been very different from the comparatively abstract one which it now is. It would, it is true, have involved the question of justice to the negroes of Indiana, but the transcendently broader and more vital question of national salvation also. Let me add further, that should Congress pass this bill, and should the ballot be given to the negroes in the sunny South generally, those in our Northern and Western States, many of them at least, may return to their native land and its kindlier skies, and thus quiet the nerves of conservative gentlemen who dread too close a proximity to those whose skins, owing to some providential oversight, were somehow or other not stamped with the true orthodox luster.

"The ballot should be given to the negroes as a matter of justice to them. It should likewise be done as a matter of *retributive* justice to the slaveholders and rebels. According to the best information I can obtain, a very large majority of the white people of this District have been rebels in heart during the war, and are rebels in heart still. That contempt for the negro and scorn of free industry, which constituted the mainspring of the rebellion, cropped out here during the war in every form that was possible, under the immediate shadow of the central Government. Meaner rebels than many in this District could scarcely have been found in the whole land. They have not been punished. The halter has been cheated out of their necks. I am very sorry to say that under what seems to be a false mercy, a misapplied humanity, the guiltiest rebels of the war have thus far been allowed to escape justice. I have no desire to censure the authorities of the Government for this fact. I hope they have some valid excuse for their action. This question of punishment I know is a difficult one. The work of punishment is so vast that it naturally palsies the will to enter upon it. It never can be thoroughly done on this side of the grave. And were it practicable to punish adequately all the most active and guilty rebels, justice would still remain unsatisfied. Far guiltier men than they are the rebel sympathizers of the loyal States, who coolly stood by and encouraged their friends in the South in their work of national rapine and murder, and while they were ever ready to go joyfully into the service of the devil, were too cowardly to wear his uniform and carry his weapons in open day. But Congress in this District has the power to punish by ballot, and there will be a beautiful, poetic justice in the exercise of this power. Sir, let it be applied. The rebels here will recoil from it with horror. Some of the worst of them, sooner than submit to black suffrage, will doubtless leave the District, and thus render it an unspeakable service. To be voted down and governed by Yankee and negro ballots will seem to them an intolerable grievance, and this is among the excellent reasons why I am in favor of it. If neither hanging nor exile can be extemporized for the entertainment of our domestic rebels, let us require them at least to make their bed on negro ballots during the remainder of their unworthy lives. Of course they will not relish it, but that will be their own peculiar concern. Their darling institution must be charged with all the consequences of the war. They sowed the wind, and, if required, must reap the whirlwind. Retribution follows wrong-doing, and this law must work out its results. Rebels and their sympathizers, I am sure, will fare as well under negro suffrage as they deserve, and I desire to leave them, as far as practicable, in the hands of their colored brethren. Nor shall I stop to inquire very critically whether the negroes are *fit* to vote. As between themselves and white rebels, who deserve to be hung, they are eminently fit. I would not have them more so. Will you, Mr. Speaker, will even my conservative and Democratic friends, be particularly nice or fastidious in the choice of a man to vote down a *rebel?* Shall we insist upon a perfectly finished gentleman and scholar to vote down the traitors and white trash of this District, who have recently signalized themselves by mobbing unoffending negroes? Sir, almost any body, it seems to me, will answer the purpose. I do not pretend that the colored men here, should they get the ballot, will not sometimes abuse it. They will undoubtedly make mistakes. In some cases they may even vote on the side of their old masters. But I feel pretty safe in saying that even white men, perfectly free from all *suspicion* of negro blood, have sometimes voted on the wrong side. Sir, I appeal to gentlemen on this floor, and especially to my Democratic friends, to say whether they can not call to mind instances in which white men have voted wrong? Indeed, it rather strikes me that white voting, ignorant, depraved, party-ridden, *Democratic* white voting, had a good deal to do in hatching into life the rebellion itself, and that no results of negro voting are likely to be much worse."

After an hour occupied by Mr. Randall and Mr. Kelley, both of Pennsylvania, in a colloquial discussion of the history and present position of their State upon the subject of negro suffrage, Mr. Thomas, of Maryland, addressed the House. After setting forth the injustice the passage of the bill would work toward the people of his State, he said:

"If I believed that the matter of suffrage was the only mode to help the negro in his elevation, and the only safeguard to his protection, or guarantee to his rights, I would be willing to give it to him now, subject to proper qualifications and restrictions. But I am honest in my conviction that, uneducated and ignorant as he is, a slave from his birth, and subject to the will and caprice of his master, with none of the exalted ideas of what that privilege means, and with but a faint conception of the true position he now occupies, the negro is not the proper subject to have conferred upon him this right. I believe if it is given to him, that in localities where his is the majority vote, parties will spring up, each one bidding higher than the other for his ballot, and that in the end the negro-voting element will be controlled by a few evil and wicked politicians, and as something to be bought and sold as freely as an article of merchandise. I am satisfied of another fact, from my experience of the Southern negro, that if they are ever allowed to vote, the shrewd politician of the South, who has been formerly his master, will exert more influence over his vote than all the exhortations from Beecher or Cheever.

"It is a notorious fact that the Southern planter maintained his political influence over the poor white man of the South, because the poor white man was dependent on him for his living and support. And you will find, when it is too late, that the Southern planter will maintain the same political influence over the poor, uneducated, ignorant, and dependent African, even to a greater extent than he formerly exercised over what used to be called the 'poor white trash.'

"Mr. Speaker, let us not, because we have the majority here to-day, pass upon measures which, if we were evenly divided, we would hesitate to pass. Let us not, because we are called radicals, strike at the roots of society, and of the great social and political systems that have existed for over a century, and attempt to do in a day, without any preparation, what, to do well and safely, will require years of patience on the part of the freedmen, and earnest, honest exertions to elevate, improve, and educate on our part. Let us look at this question as statesmen, not as partisans. Let us not suppose that the parties of to-day will have a perpetual existence, and that because the negro, freed and emancipated by us, would naturally vote on the side of his deliverer to-day, that it is any guarantee, when new parties are formed and a competition arises, that the whole or the major part of his vote will be cast on the right side. White men and black men are liable to the same infirmities.

"Let us rather, sir, rejoice at what has been already done for him, and be content to watch his future. Let us help to elevate and improve him, not only in education, but in morals. Let us see to it that he is not only protected in all his rights of person and of property, but let us insist that the amplest guarantees shall be given. Let us wait until the great problem the African is now working out has been finished, and we find that he thoroughly comprehends and will not abuse what he has got, before we attempt to confer other privileges, which, when once granted, can never be taken from him. Sir, let it not be forgotten that 'revolutions never go backward;' and if you ever confer this right on the negro, and find it will not work well, that you have been too hasty, that you should have waited awhile longer, you will find it is too late, and that, once having possessed it, they will not part with it except with their lives."

On the 17th of January the debate was resumed by Mr. Darling, of New York, who remarked:

"What public necessity exists for the passage of this bill at this time? There are no benefits which the colored people of this District could attain by the exercise of the right of suffrage that Congress could not bestow. Our right and power to legislate for this District are unquestioned, and instead of wasting days and weeks over a question which is exciting bitter feeling among our own people, had we not better give our attention to matters of great national interest which so urgently demand speedy action on our part? Let us pass laws for the education of the people of this District, and fit them ultimately to receive the elective franchise; or, if any thing is required to satisfy the intense desire, manifested by some gentlemen of this House, to bestow the franchise on those not now possessed of it, give it to every soldier who served in the Union Army and was honorably discharged, whether old or young, rich or poor, native or foreign-born, white or black, and show to the world that the American people, recognizing the services and sufferings of their brave defenders, give them, as a recognition, the highest and best gift of American citizenship.

"If I know myself, I know that no unjust or unmanly prejudice warps my judgment or controls my action on any matter of legislation affecting the colored race on this continent. I believe in their equality of rights before the law with the dominant race. I believe in their rights of life, liberty, and the pursuit of happiness. And yet I believe that, before we confer upon them the political right of suffrage, as contemplated by the bill now under consideration, we should seek to elevate their social condition, and lift them up from the depths of degradation and ignorance in which many of them are left by the receding waves of the sea of rebellion. There are many strong objections to conferring upon the colored men of this District the gift of unqualified suffrage without any qualification based on intelligence. The large preponderance which they possess numerically will inevitably lead to mischievous results. Neither would I entirely disregard the views of the people of this District, many of whom I know to be sound, loyal Union men.

"But I do not wish to see the Union party take any step in this direction from which they may desire hereafter to recede.

Let us first rather seek to enlighten this people, and educate them to know the value of the great gift of liberty which has been bestowed upon them; teach them to know that to labor is for their best interests; teach them to learn and lead virtuous and industrious lives, in order to make themselves respected, and encourage them to act as becomes freemen. Then they will vote intelligently, and not be subject to the control of designing men, who would seek to use them for the attainment of their own selfish ends.

"Now, Mr. Speaker, in conclusion I desire to say that, as no election will take place in this District until next June, there can be no reason for special haste in the passage of this bill, and that there is a proposition before this House, which seems to be received with very general favor, to create a commission for the government of this city; and, in order to give an opportunity to mature a bill for that purpose, and have it presented for the consideration of this House, I move the postponement of the pending bill until the first Tuesday in April next."

At a previous stage of the discussion of this measure, Mr. Hale had proposed amendments to the bill. These amendments were now the subject under discussion. They were in the following words:

"Amend the motion to recommit by adding to that motion an instruction to the committee to amend the bill so as to extend the right of suffrage in the District of Columbia to all persons coming within either of the following classes, irrespective of caste or color, but subject only to existing provisions and qualifications other than those founded on caste or color, to wit:

"1. Those who can read the Constitution of the United States.

"2. Those who are assessed for and pay taxes on real or personal property within the District.

"3. Those who have served in and been honorably discharged from the military or naval service of the United States.

"And to restrict such right of suffrage to the classes above named, and to include proper provisions excluding from the right of suffrage those who have borne arms against the United States during the late rebellion, or given aid and comfort to said rebellion."

At the close of Mr. Darling's remarks, in which he had moved to postpone the whole subject, Mr. Hale, of New York, having argued at considerable length in favor of the several clauses of his proposed amendment, remarked: "Of the details of my amendment I am by no means tenacious. I do not expect to bring every member of the House, or even every member on this side of the House, to concur in all my own views. I desire simply to put my measures fairly before the House, and to advocate them as I best can. I am ready and willing to yield my own preferences in matters of detail to their better judgment. More than that, I shall not follow the example that has been set by some on this side of the House who oppose my amendment, and who claim to be the peculiar friends of negro suffrage, by proclaiming that I will adhere to the doctrine of qualified suffrage, and will join our political enemies, the Democrats, in voting down every thing else. No, sir; for one, and I say it with entire frankness, I prefer a restricted and qualified suffrage substantially upon the basis that I have proposed. If the voice of this House be otherwise—if the sentiment of this Congress be that it is more desirable that universal suffrage should be extended to all within this District, then, for one, I say most decidedly I am for it rather than to leave the matter in its present condition, or to disfranchise the black race in this District."

Mr. Thayer, of Pennsylvania, spoke as follows: "The proposition contained in this bill is a new proposition. It contemplates a change which will be a landmark in the history of this country—a landmark which, if it is set up, will be regarded by the present and future generations of men who are to inhabit this continent with pride and satisfaction, or deplored as one of the gravest errors in the history of legislation. The bill, if it shall become a law, will be, like the law to amend the Constitution by abolishing slavery, the deep foot-print of an advancing civilization, or the conspicuous monument of an unwise and pernicious experiment.

"Much has been said, on the part of those who oppose the bill, on the subject of its injustice to the white inhabitants of the District of Columbia. Indeed, the argument on that side of the question is, when divested of all that is immaterial, meretricious, and extravagant, reduced almost entirely to that single position. Abstract this from the excited declamation to which you have listened, and what is left is but the old revolting argument in favor of slavery, and a selfish appeal to prejudice and ignorance. It is insisted that a majority of the white voters of the District are opposed to the contemplated law, that they have recently given a public expression of their opinion against it, and that for that reason it would be unjust and oppressive in Congress to pass this law. In my judgment, this is a question not concerning alone the wishes and prejudices of the seven thousand voters who dwell in this District, but involving, it may be, the honor, the justice, the good faith, and the magnanimity of the great nation which makes this little spot the central seat of its empire and its power.

"If it concerns the honor of the United States that a certain class of its people, in a portion of its territory subject to its exclusive jurisdiction and control, shall, in consideration of the change which has taken place in its condition, and of the fidelity which it has exhibited in the midst of great and severe trials, be elevated somewhat above the political degradation which has hitherto been its lot, shall the United States be prevented from the accomplishment of that great and generous purpose by the handful of voters who temporarily encamp under the shadow of the Capitol? It may be that the determination of a question of so much importance as this belongs rather to the people of the United States, through their Representatives in Congress assembled, than to the present qualified voters of this District. Sir, the field of inquiry is much wider than the District of Columbia, and the problem to be solved one in which not they alone are interested. When Congress determined that the time had come when slavery should be abolished in this District, and the capital of the nation should no longer be disgraced by its presence, did it pause in the great work of justice to which it laid its hand to hear from the mayor of Washington, or to inquire whether the masters would vote for it? It is not difficult to conjecture what the fate of that great measure would have been had its adoption or rejection depended upon the voters of this District.

"Shall we be told, sir, that if the Representatives of the people of twenty-five States are of the opinion that the laws and institutions which exist in the seat of Government of the United States ought to be changed, that they are not to be changed because a majority of the voters who reside here do not desire that change? Will any man say that the voices of these seven thousand voters are to outweigh the voices of all the constituencies of the United States in the capital of their country? I dismiss this objection, therefore, as totally destitute of reason or weight. It is based upon a fallacy so feeble that it is dissipated by the bare touch of the Constitution to it.

"Whatever is the duty of the United States to do, that is for their interest to do. The two great facts written in history by the iron hand of the late war are, first, that the Union is indissoluble, and second, that human slavery is here forever abolished. From these two facts consequences corresponding in importance with the facts themselves must result: from the former, a more vigorous and powerful nationality; from the latter, the elevation and improvement of the race liberated by the war from bondage, as well as a higher and more advanced civilization in the region where the change has taken place. It is impossible to say that the African race occupies to-day the same position in American affairs and counts no more in weight than it did before the rebellion. You can not strike the fetters from the limbs of four million men and leave them such as you found them. As wide as is the interval between a freeman and a slave, so wide is the difference between the African race before the rebellion and after the rebellion. You can not keep to its ancient level a race which has been released from servitude any more than you can keep back the ocean with your hand after you have thrown down the sea-wall which restrained its impatient tides. Freedom is everywhere in history the herald of progress. It is written in the annals of all nations. It is a law of the human race. Ignorance, idleness, brutality—these belong to slavery; they are her natural offspring and allies, and the gentleman from New York, [Mr. Chanler,] who consumed so much time in demonstrating the comparative inferiority of the black race, answered his own argument when he reminded us that the Constitution recognized the negro only as a slave, and gave us the strongest reason why we should now begin to recognize him as a freeman. Sir, I do not doubt that the negro race is inferior to our own. That is not the question. You do not advance an inch in the argument after you have proved that premise of your case. You must show that they are not only inferior, but that they are so ignorant and degraded that they can not be safely intrusted with the smallest conceivable part of political power and responsibility, and that this is the case not on the plantations of Alabama and Mississippi, but here in the District of Columbia. Nay, you must not only prove that this is the general character of this population here, but that this condition is so universal and unexceptional that you can not allow them to take this first step in freedom, although it may be hedged about with qualifications and conditions; for which of you who have opposed this measure on the ground of race has proposed to give the benefit of it to such as may be found worthy? Not one of you. And this shows that your objection is founded really on a prejudice, although it assumes the dignity and proportions of an argument. The real question, sir, is, can we afford to be just—nay, if you please, generous—to a race whose shame has been washed out in the consuming fires of war, and which now stands erect and equal before the law with our own? Shall we give hope and encouragement to that race beginning, as it does now for the first time, its career of freedom, by erecting here in the capital of the republic a banner inscribed with the sacred legend of the elder days, 'All men are born free and equal?' or shall we unfurl in its stead that other banner, with a strange device, around which the dissolving remnants of the Democratic party in this hall are called upon to rally, inscribed with no great sentiment of justice or generosity, but bearing upon its folds the miserable appeal of the demagogue, 'This is a white man's Government?' When you inaugurate your newly-discovered political principle, do not forget to invite the colored troops; beat the assembly; call out the remnants of the one hundred and eighty thousand men who marched with steady step through the flames and carnage of war, and many of whom bear upon their bodies the honorable scars received in that unparalleled struggle and in your defense, and as you send your banner down the line, say to them, 'This is the reward of a generous country for the wounds you have received and the sufferings you have endured.'

"Shall we follow the great law to which I have referred—the law that liberty is progress—and conform our policy to the spirit of that great law? or shall we, governed by unreasonable and selfish prejudices, initiate a policy which will make this race our hereditary enemy, a mine beneath instead of a buttress to the edifice which you are endeavoring to repair? Sir, I do not hesitate to say that, in my opinion, it were better to follow where conscience and justice point, leaving results to a higher Power, than to shrink from an issue which it is the clear intention of Providence we shall face, or to be driven from our true course by the chimeras which the excited imaginations of political partisans have conjured up, or by the misty ghosts of long-buried errors."

Mr. Van Horn, of New York, while willing to accept the bill as originally presented, preferred it as modified by Mr. Hale's amendments. In his speech he charged those who had opposed the bill as laboring in the interest of slavery.

"They seem to have forgotten," he said, "in their advocacy of slavery, that we have passed through a fierce war, begun by slavery, waged against the Government by slavery, and solely in its interest to more thoroughly establish itself upon the Western Continent, and crush out the best interests of freedom and humanity; and that this war, guided on our part by the omnipotent arm of the Invisible, made bare in our behalf, has resulted in a most complete overthrow of this great wrong; and by the almost omnipotent voice of the republic, as now expressed in its fundamental law, it has no right to live, much less entitled to the right of burial, and should have no mourners in the land or going about the streets. Such speeches as those of the gentlemen from New Jersey, [Mr. Rogers,] and from Pennsylvania, [Mr. Boyer,] and my colleague and friend, [Mr. Chanler,] who represents, with myself, in part, the Empire State, carry us back to the days and scenes before the war, when slavery ruled supreme, not only throughout the land, by and through its hold upon power, which the people in an evil hour had given it, but here in these halls of legislation, where liberty and its high and noble ends ought to have been secured by just and equal laws, and the great and paramount object of our system of government carried out and fully developed. They seem to forget that liberty and good government have been on trial during these five years last past of war and blood, and that they have succeeded in the mighty struggle. They forget that Providence, in a thousand ways, during this fierce conflict, has given us evidence of his favor, and led us out of the land of bondage into a purer and higher state of freedom, where slavery, as an institution among us, is no more. Why do they labor so long and so ardently to resurrect again into life this foul and loathsome thing? Why can not they forget their former love and attachments in this direction, and no longer cling with such undying grasp to this dead carcass, which, by its corruptions and rottenness, has well nigh heretofore poisoned them to the death? Why not awake to the new order of things, and accept the results which God has worked out in our recent struggle, and not raise the weak arm of flesh to render null and void what has thus been done, and thus attempt to turn back the flow of life which is overspreading all, and penetrating every part of the body politic with its noble purposes and exalted hopes?"

Thursday, January 18, was the last day of the discussion of this important measure in the House of Representatives. When the subject was in order, Mr. Clarke, of Kansas, "as the only Representative upon the floor of a State whose whole history had been a continual protest against political injustice and wrong," after having advocated the bill by arguments drawn from the history of the country and the record of the negro race, remarked as follows: "This cry of poverty and ignorance is not new. I remember that those who first followed the Son of man, the Savior of the world, were not the learned rabbis, not the enlightened scholar, not the rich man or the pious Pharisee. They were the poor and needy, the peasant and the fisherman. I remember, also, that the more learned the slaveholder, the greater the rebel. I remember that no black skin covered so false a heart or misdirected brain, that when the radiant banner of our nationality was near or before him, he did not understand its meaning, and remained loyal to its demands. The man capable of taking care of himself, of wife and children, and, in addition to his unrequited toil, to hold up his oppressor, must have intelligence enough, in the long run, to wield the highest means of protection we can give.

"But, sir, it is for our benefit, as well as for the benefit of the proscribed class, that I vote for and support impartial manhood suffrage in this District. We can not afford, as a nation, to keep any class ignorant or oppress the weak. We must establish here republican government. That which wrongs one man, in the end recoils on the many. Sir, if we accept, as the Republican party of the Union, our true position and our duty, we shall nobly win. If we are false and recreant, we shall miserably fail. Let us have faith in the people and the grand logic of a mighty revolution, and dare to do right. Class legislation will be the inevitable result of class power; and what would follow, so far as the colored race are concerned, let the recent tragedy of Jamaica answer.

"The principles involved in the arguments put forth on the other side of the House are not alone destructive to the rights of the defenseless, intelligent, and patriotic colored men of this District, but they militate with a double effect and stronger purpose against the poor whites of the North and of the South, against

Eng^d by G.F. Perine & Co. N.York

Sidney Clarke

the German, the Irishman, and the poor and oppressed of every race, who come to our shores to escape the oppression of despotic governments, and to seek the protection of a Government the true theory of which reposes in every citizen a portion of its sovereign power. Against this attempt to deny or abridge in any way the rights of the weak, the poor, and the defenseless, and to transfer the governing power of the nation to the favored classes, to the rich and the powerful, and thus change the very purpose and principles of our republican system, I protest in the name of constitutional freedom, and in behalf of equal rights and equal laws.

"I protest against this stealthy innovation upon popular rights, in the name of the toiling millions of the land; and I warn the House and the country of the untold mischief and disaster which must come to distract and divide the republic in the future, if we follow the pernicious and destructive doctrines founded upon either the prejudices of class, caste, wealth, or power. I protest in the name of a constituency whose early history was a sublime and persistent struggle against the prejudices of pampered and arrogant ruffianism at home, and the worse than ruffian spirit of the Administrations of Pierce and Buchanan, and the Democratic traitors who at that time constituted a majority of this House, and were engaged in preparing the nation for its harvest of blood. We must go back to the spirit and purposes of the founders of our Government. We must accept the grand logic of the mighty revolution from which we are now emerging. We must repudiate, now and forever, these assaults upon the masses of the people and upon the fundamental principles of popular rights. I accept in their full force and effect the principles of the Declaration of Independence, and by constitutional amendment and law of Congress I would stamp them with irrevocable power upon the political escutcheon of the new and regenerated republic. I would avoid the mistakes of the past, and I would spurn that cringing timidity by which, through all history, liberty has been sacrificed and humanity betrayed.

"Sir, I hesitate not to say that if we do not gather up, in the process of national reconstruction, the enduring safeguards of future peace, we shall be false to our history and unmindful of the grand responsibilities now devolving upon us. The establishment of impartial suffrage in this District will be a fitting commencement of the work. It will be hailed by the friends of freedom every-where as a return to a policy of national justice too long delayed. In behalf of the State I have the honor to represent, and upon whose soil this contest for a larger liberty and a nobler nationality was first submitted to the arbitrament of arms, I hail this measure with feelings of satisfaction and pride. It is the legitimate result of the courage and fidelity of the hardy pioneers of Kansas in 1856, who dared to face the blandishment of power and the arrogance and brutality of slavery when compromisers trembled, and Northern sycophants of an oligarchic despotism, then, as now, scowled and fretted at the progress of free principles."

Mr. Johnson, of Pennsylvania, after having adduced a variety of arguments against the bill, finally said: "Sir, we hear a tremendous outcry in this House in favor of popular government and about the guarantee of the Constitution of the United States to the several States that they shall have republican governments. How are the poor people of this District to have a republican form of government if gentlemen who have come to this city, perhaps for the first time in their lives, undertake to control them as absolutely and arbitrarily as Louis Napoleon controls France or Maximilian Mexico? Gentlemen ask, What right have they to hold an election and express their sentiments? What right have they to hold such an election? Surely they ought to have the right to petition, for their rulers are generally arbitrary enough.

"Mr. Speaker, it seems to me ridiculously inconsistent for gentlemen upon this floor to prate so much about a republican form of government, and rise here and offer resolution after resolution about the Monroe doctrine and the downtrodden Mexicans, while they force upon the people of this District a government not of their own choice, because the voter in a popular government is a governor himself. But, sir, this is only part of a grand plan. Gentlemen who dare not go before their white constituents and urge that a negro shall have a vote in their own States, come here and undertake to thrust negro suffrage upon the people here. Gentlemen whose States have repudiated the idea of giving the elective franchise to negroes, come here and are willing to give the suffrage to negroes here, as if they intended to make this little District of Columbia a sort of negro Eden; as if they intended to say to the negroes of Virginia and Maryland and Delaware, 'You have no right to vote in these States, but if you will go to

Washington you can vote there.' I imagine I can see them swarming up from different sections of the country to this city and inquiring where the polls are. Agents, men and women, such as there are at work in this city, will no doubt be at work in these States, telling them to pack their knapsacks and march to Washington, for on such a day there is to be an election, and there they will have the glorious privilege of the white man. Sir, all this doctrine is destructive of the American system of government, which recognizes the right of no man to participate in it unless he is a citizen, which secures to the citizen his voice in the control and management of the Government, and prevents those not citizens from standing in the way of the exercise of his just rights.

"This Government does not belong to any race so that it can be divested or disposed of. The present age have no right to terminate it. It is ours to enjoy and administer, and to transmit to posterity unimpaired as we received it from the fathers."

Mr. Boutwell, of Massachusetts, then addressed the House: "When we emancipated the black people, we not only relieved ourselves from the institution of slavery, we not only conferred upon them freedom, but we did more, we recognized their manhood, which, by the old Constitution and the general policy and usage of the country, had been, from the organization of the Government until the Emancipation Proclamation, denied to all of the enslaved colored people. As a consequence of the recognition of their manhood, certain results follow in accordance with the principles of this Government, and they who believe in this Government are, by necessity, forced to accept those results as a consequence of the policy of emancipation which they have inaugurated and for which they are responsible.

"But to say now, having given freedom to them, that they shall not enjoy the essential rights and privileges of men, is to abandon the principle of the proclamation of emancipation, and tacitly to admit that the whole emancipation policy is erroneous.

"It has been suggested that it is premature to demand immediate action upon the question of negro suffrage in the District of Columbia. I am not personally responsible for the presence of the bill at the present time, but I am responsible for the observation that there never has been a day during a session of Congress since the Emancipation Proclamation, ay, since the negroes of this

District were emancipated, when it was not the duty of the Government, which, by the Constitution, is intrusted with exclusive jurisdiction in this District, to confer upon the men of this District, without distinction of race or color, the rights and privileges of men. And, therefore, there can be nothing premature in this measure, and I can not see how any one who supports the Emancipation Proclamation, which is a recognition of the manhood of the whole colored people of this country, can hesitate as to his duty; and while I make no suggestion as to the duty of other men, I have a clear perception of my own. And, first, we are bound to treat the colored people of this District, in regard to the matter of voting, precisely as we treat white people. And I do not hesitate to express the opinion that if the question here to-day were whether any qualification should be imposed upon white voters in this District, if they alone were concerned, this House would not, ay, not ten men upon this floor would, consider whether any qualifications should be imposed or not.

"Reading and writing, or reading, as a qualification, is demanded, and an appeal is made to the example of Massachusetts. I wish gentlemen who now appeal to Massachusetts would often appeal to her in other matters where I can more conscientiously approve her policy. But it is a different proposition in Massachusetts as a practical measure. When, ten years ago, this qualification was imposed upon the people of Massachusetts, it excluded no person who was then a voter. For two centuries we have had in Massachusetts a system of public instruction open to the children of the whole people without money and without price. Therefore all the people there had had opportunities for education. Now, why should the example of such a state be quoted to justify refusing suffrage to men who have been denied the privilege of education, and whom it has been a crime to teach? Is there no difference?

"We are to answer for our treatment of the colored people of this country, and it will prove in the end impracticable to secure to men of color civil rights unless the persons who claim those rights are fortified by the political right of voting. With the right of voting, every thing that a man ought to have or enjoy of civil rights comes to him. Without the right to vote, he is secure in nothing. I can not consent, after all the guards and safeguards which may be prepared for the defense of the colored men in the enjoyment of their rights—I can not consent that they shall be deprived of the right to protect themselves. One hundred and eighty-six thousand of them have been in the army of the United States. They have stood in the place of our sons and brothers and friends. They have fallen in defense of the country. They have earned the right to share in the Government; and if you deny them the elective franchise, I know not how they are to be protected. Otherwise you furnish the protection which is given to the lamb when he is commended to the wolf.

"There is an ancient history that a sparrow pursued by a hawk took refuge in the chief assembly of Athens, in the bosom of a member of that illustrious body, and that the senator in anger hurled it violently from him. It fell to the ground dead, and such was the horror and indignation of that ancient but not Christianized body—men living in the light of nature, of reason—that they immediately expelled the brutal Areopagite from his seat, and from the association of humane legislators.

"What will be said of us, not by Christian, but by heathen nations even, if, after accepting the blood and sacrifices of these men, we hurl them from us and allow them to be the victims of those who have tyrannized over them for centuries? I know of no crime that exceeds this; I know of none that is its parallel; and if this country is true to itself, it will rise in the majesty of its strength and maintain a policy, here and every-where, by which the rights of the colored people shall be secured through their own power—in peace, the ballot; in war, the bayonet.

"It is a maxim of another language, which we may well apply to ourselves, that where the voting register ends the military roster of rebellion begins; and if you leave these four million people to the care and custody of the men who have inaugurated and carried on this rebellion, then you treasure up for untold years the elements of social and civil war, which must not only desolate and paralyze the South, but shake this Government to its very foundation."

Soon after the close of Mr. Boutwell's speech, Mr. Darling's motion to postpone and Mr. Hale's motion to amend having been rejected, a vote was taken on the bill as reported by the committee. The bill passed by a vote of one hundred and sixteen in the affirmative—fifty-four voting in the negative.

The friends of the measure having received evidence that it

would not meet with Executive approval, and not supposing that a vote of two-thirds could be secured for its passage over the President's veto, determined not to urge it immediately through the Senate.

There was great reluctance on the part of many Senators and members of the House to come to an open rupture with the President. They desired to defer the day of final and irreconcilable difference between Congress and the Executive. If the subject of negro suffrage in the District of Columbia was kept in abeyance for a time, it was hoped that the President's approval might meanwhile be secured to certain great measures for protecting the helpless and maintaining the civil rights of citizens. To accomplish these important ends, the suffrage bill was deferred many months. The will of the majority in Congress relating to this subject did not become a law until after the opening of the second session of the Thirty-ninth Congress.

CHAPTER V.

THE FREEDMEN.

NECESSITIES OF THE FREEDMEN—COMMITTEE IN THE HOUSE—EARLY MOVEMENT BY THE SENATE IN BEHALF OF FREEDMEN—SENATOR WILSON'S BILL—OCCASION FOR IT—MR. COWAN MOVES ITS REFERENCE—MR. REVERDY JOHNSON ADVISES DELIBERATION—A QUESTION OF TIME WITH MR. SHERMAN—MR. TRUMBULL PROMISES A MORE EFFICIENT BILL—MR. SUMNER PRESENTS PROOF OF THE BAD CONDITION OF AFFAIRS IN THE SOUTH—MR. COWAN AND MR. STEWART PRODUCE THE PRESIDENT AS A WITNESS FOR THE DEFENSE—MR. WILSON ON THE TESTIMONY—"CONSERVATISM"—THE BILL ABSORBED IN GREATER MEASURES.

THE necessities of three millions and a half of persons made free as a result of the rebellion demanded early and efficient legislation at the hands of the Thirty-ninth Congress. In vain did the Proclamation of Emancipation break their shackles, and the constitutional amendment declare them free, if Congress should not "enforce" these important acts by "appropriate legislation."

The House of Representatives signified its view of the importance of this subject by constituting an able Committee "on Freedmen," with Thomas D. Eliot, of Massachusetts, as its chairman. The Senate, however, was first to take decided steps toward the protection and relief of freedmen. We have seen that on the first day of the session Senator Wilson, of Massachusetts, introduced a bill "to maintain the freedom of the inhabitants in the States declared in insurrection and rebellion by the proclamation of the President of the 1st of July, 1862," of which the following is a copy:

Be it enacted, etc., That all laws, statutes, acts, ordinances, rules and regulations, of any description whatsoever, heretofore in force or held valid in any of the States which were declared to be in insurrection and rebellion by the proclamation of the President of the 1st of July, 1862, whereby or wherein any inequality of civil rights and immunities among the inhabitants of said States is recognized, authorized, established, or maintained, by reason or in consequence of any distinctions or differences of color, race, or descent, or by reason or in consequence of a previous condition or status of slavery or involuntary servitude of such inhabitants, be, and are hereby, declared null and void; and it shall be unlawful to institute, make, ordain, or establish, in any of the aforesaid States declared to be in insurrection and rebellion, any such law, statute, act, ordinance, rule, or regulation, or to enforce, or to attempt to enforce, the same.

SEC. 2. *And be it further enacted*, That any person who shall violate either of the provisions of this act shall be deemed guilty of a misdemeanor, and shall be punished by a fine of not less than $500 nor exceeding $10,000, and by imprisonment not less than six months nor exceeding five years; and it shall be the duty of the President to enforce the provisions of this act.

On the 13th of December, Mr. Wilson called up his bill, which the Senate proceeded to consider as in Committee of the Whole. The author of the bill presented reasons why it should become a law: "A bill is pending before the Legislature of South Carolina making these freedmen servants, providing that the persons for whom they labor shall be their masters; that the relation between them shall be the relation of master and servant. The bill, as originally reported, provided that the freedmen might be educated, but that provision has already been stricken out, and the bill now lies over waiting for events here. That bill makes the colored people of South Carolina serfs, a degraded class, the slaves of society. It is far better to be the slave of one man than to be the slave of arbitrary law. There is no doubt of the fact that in a great portion of those States the high hopes, the confidence, and the joy expressed last spring by the freedmen, have passed away; that silence and sorrow pervade that section of the country, and that they are becoming distrustful and discontented. God grant that the high-raised expectations of these loyal and deserted people may not be blasted. God forbid that we should violate our plighted faith."

Mr. Cowan moved the reference of the bill to the Committee on the Judiciary, but its author was unwilling that it should be so referred, since it was highly important that action should be had upon it before the holidays.

Mr. Johnson said that the bill gave rise to grave questions on which it was very desirable that the deliberation of the Senate should be very calmly advised. He objected on the ground of its indefiniteness: "There are no particular laws designated in the bill to be repealed. All laws existing before these States got into a condition of insurrection, by which any difference or inequality is created or established, are to be repealed. What is to be the effect of that repeal upon such laws as they exist? In some of those States, by the constitution or by the laws, (and the constitution is equally a law,) persons of the African race are excluded from certain political privileges. Are they to be repealed, and at once, by force of that repeal, are they to be placed exactly upon the same footing in regard to all political privileges with that which belongs to the other class of citizens? Very many of those laws are laws passed under the police-power, which has always been conceded as a power belonging to the States—laws supposed to have been necessary in order to protect the States themselves from insurrection. Are they to be repealed absolutely?

"No man feels more anxious certainly than I do that the rights incident to the condition of freedom, which is now as I personally am glad to believe, the condition of the black race, should not be violated; but I do not know that there is any more pressing need for extraordinary legislation to prevent outrages upon that class, by any thing which is occurring in the Southern States, than there is for preventing outrages in the loyal States. Crimes are being perpetrated every day in the very justly-esteemed State from which the honorable member comes. Hardly a paper fails to give us an account of some most atrocious and horrible crime. Murders shock the sense of that community and the sense of the United States very often; and it is not peculiar to Massachusetts. Moral by her education, and loving freedom and hating injustice as much as the people of any other State, she yet is unable to prevent a violation of every principle of human rights, but we are not for that reason to legislate for her."

Mr. Wilson replied: "The Senator from Maryland says that cruelties and great crimes are committed in all sections of the country. I know it; but we have not cruel and inhuman laws to be enforced. Sir, armed men are traversing portions of the rebel States to-day enforcing these black laws upon men whom we have made free, and to whom we stand pledged before man and God to maintain their freedom. A few months ago these freedmen were joyous, hopeful, confident. To-day they are distrustful, silent, and sad, and this condition has grown out of the wrongs and cruelties and oppressions that have been perpetrated upon them."

Mr. Sherman said: "I believe it is the duty of Congress to give to the freedmen of the Southern States ample protection in all their natural rights. With me it is a question simply of time and manner. I submit to the Senator of Massachusetts whether this is the time for the introduction of this bill. I believe it would be wiser to postpone all action upon this subject until the proclamation of the Secretary of State shall announce that the constitutional amendment is a part of the supreme law of the land. When that is done, there will then be, in my judgment, no doubt of the power of Congress to pass this bill, and to make it definite and general in its terms.

"Then, as I have said, it is a question of manner. When this question comes to be legislated upon by Congress, I do not wish it to be left to the uncertain and ambiguous language of this bill. I think that the rights which we desire to secure to the freedmen of the South should be distinctly specified.

"The language of this bill is not sufficiently definite and distinct to inform the people of the United States of precisely the character of rights intended to be secured by it to the freedmen of the Southern States. The bill in its terms applies only to those States which were declared to be in insurrection; and the same criticism would apply to this part of it that I have already made, that it is not general in its terms."

Mr. Trumbull made some remarks of great significance, as foreshadowing important measures soon to occupy the attention of Congress and the country:

"I hold that under that second section Congress will have the authority, when the constitutional amendment is adopted, not only to pass the bill of the Senator from Massachusetts, but a bill that will be much more efficient to protect the freedman in his rights. We may, if deemed advisable, continue the Freedman's Bureau, clothe it with additional powers, and, if necessary, back it up with a military force, to see that the rights of the men made free by the first clause of the constitutional amendment are protected. And, sir, when the constitutional amendment shall have been adopted, if the information from the South be that the men whose liberties are secured by it are deprived of the privilege to go and come when they please, to buy and sell when they please, to make contracts and enforce contracts, I give notice that, if no one else does, I shall introduce a bill, and urge its passage through Congress, that will secure to those men every one of these rights; they would not be freemen without them. It is idle to say that a man is free who can not go and come at pleasure, who can not buy and sell, who can not enforce his rights. These are rights which the first clause of the constitutional amendment meant to secure to all."

On a subsequent day, December 20, 1865, when this subject was again before the Senate, Mr. Sumner spoke in its favor. Referring to the message of the President on the "Condition of the Southern States," the Senator said:

"When I think of what occurred yesterday in this chamber; when I call to mind the attempt to whitewash the unhappy condition of the rebel States, and to throw the mantle of official oblivion over sickening and heart-rending outrages, where human rights are sacrificed and rebel barbarism receives a new letter of license, I feel that I ought to speak of nothing else. I stood here years ago, in the days of Kansas, when a small community was surrendered to the machinations of slave-masters. I now stand here again, when, alas! an immense region, with millions of people, has been surrendered to the machinations of slave-masters. Sir, it is the duty of Congress to arrest this fatal fury. Congress must dare to be brave; it must dare to be just."

After having quoted copiously from the great Russian act by which the freedom given to the serfs by the Emperor's proclamation "was secured," and having emphasized them as examples for American legislation, Mr. Sumner said:

"My colleague is clearly right in introducing his bill and pressing it to a vote. The argument for it is irresistible. It is essential to complete emancipation. Without it emancipation will be only *half done*. It is our duty to see that it is wholly done. Slavery must be abolished not in form only, but in substance, so that there shall be no black code; but all shall be equal before the law."

He then read extracts from letters and documents, showing the hostile sentiments of the people, and the unhappy condition of the colored population in nearly all of the rebel States, and closed by saying: "I bring this plain story to a close. I regret that I have been constrained to present it. I wish it were otherwise.

But I should have failed in duty had I failed to speak. Not in anger, not in vengeance, not in harshness have I spoken; but solemnly, carefully, and for the sake of my country and humanity, that peace and reconciliation may again prevail. I have spoken especially for the loyal citizens who are now trodden down by rebel power. You have before you the actual condition of the rebel States. You have heard the terrible testimony. The blood curdles at the thought of such enormities, and especially at the thought that the poor freedmen, to whom we owe protection, are left to the unrestrained will of such a people smarting with defeat, and ready to wreak vengeance upon these representatives of a true loyalty. In the name of God let us protect them. Insist upon guarantees. Pass the bill now under consideration; pass any bill; but do not let this crying injustice rage any longer. An avenging God can not sleep while such things find countenance. If you are not ready to be the Moses of an oppressed people, do not become its Pharaoh."

Mr. Cowan rebuked the Senator from Massachusetts for applying the term "whitewash" to the message of the President. He then charged Mr. Sumner with reading from "anonymous letter-writers, from cotton agents, and people of that kind," and placed against them "the testimony of the President of the United States, not a summer soldier, or a sunshine patriot, who was a Union man, and who was in favor of the Union at a time and in a place when there was some merit in it. He then proceeded to read extracts from the President's message and General Grant's report.

On a subsequent day, Mr. Stewart, of Nevada, made a speech in opposition to the positions assumed by Mr. Sumner. He declared his opinion that "if the great mass of the people of the South are capable of the atrocities attributed to them by the anonymous witnesses paraded before this Senate, then a union of these States is impossible; then hundreds and thousands of the bravest and best of our land have fallen to no purpose; then every house, from the gulf to the lakes, is draped in mourning without an object; then three thousand millions of indebtedness hangs like a pall upon the pride and prosperity of the people, only to admonish us that the war was wicked, useless, and cruel."

After making the remark, "In judging of testimony upon

ordinary subjects, we take into consideration not only the facts stated, but the character and standing of the .witness, his means of information, and last, but not least, his appearance upon the stand," Mr. Stewart thus spoke in behalf of the principal witness relied upon in the defense of the South: "In this great cause, the Senate properly called upon the chief Executive of the nation for information. Was he a witness whose character and standing before the country would entitle his testimony to consideration? Let the voice of a great people, who have indorsed his patriotism and administration, answer. Were his means of information such as to entitle him to speak advisedly upon this subject? Let the machinery of the Government, that collects facts from every department, civil and military, upon the table of the Executive, answer. Was not his appearance before the public, in communicating this testimony to the Senate and the country such as to remove all grounds of suspicion? Let the exalted tone, bold and fearless statement, pure and patriotic spirit of both his messages be his best vindication."

The Senator's remarks were principally directed in opposition to the policy of regarding the rebel States as "conquered territories." He finally remarked: "I wish to be distinctly understood as not opposing the passage of the bill. I am in favor of legislation on this subject, and such legislation as shall secure the freedom of those who were formerly slaves, and their equality before the law; and I maintain that it can be fully secured without holding the Southern States in territorial subjugation."

Mr. Wilson replied: "The Senator who has just addressed us questions the testimony adduced here by my colleague yesterday. He might as well question the massacre at Fort Pillow, and the cruelties perpetrated at Andersonville, where eighty-three per cent. of the men who entered the hospitals died—Andersonville, where more American soldiers lie buried than fell throughout the Mexican war; where more American soldiers lie buried than were killed in battle of British soldiers in Wellington's four great battles in Spain, and at Waterloo, Alma, Inkermann, and Sebastopol. The Senator might as well question the atrocities of sacked Lawrence and other atrocities committed during the war. If he will go into the Freedman's Bureau, and examine and study the official records of officers who, for five or six months, have taken testimony and have large volumes of sworn facts; if he will go into the office of General Holt, and read the reports there, his heart and soul will be made sick at the wrongs man does to his fellow-man."

The Senator, in the course of his remarks, took occasion to express his opinion of "conservatism:" "Progress is to be made only by fidelity to the great cause by which we have stood during the past four years of bloody war. For twenty-five years we had a conflict of ideas, of words, of thoughts—words and thoughts stronger than cannon-balls. We have had four years of bloody conflict. Slavery, every thing that belongs or pertains to it, lies prostrate before us to-day, and the foot of a regenerated nation is upon it. There let it lie forever. I hope no words or thoughts of a reactionary character are to be uttered in either house of Congress. I hope nothing is to be uttered here in the name of 'conservatism,' the worst word in the English language. If there is a word in the English language that means treachery, servility, and cowardice, it is that word 'conservative.' It ought never hereafter to be on the lips of an American statesman. For twenty years it has stood in America the synonym of meanness and baseness. I have studied somewhat carefully the political history of the country during the last fifteen or twenty years, and I have always noticed that when I heard a man prate about being a conservative and about conservatism, he was about to do some mean thing. [Laughter.] I never knew it to fail; in fact, it is about the first word a man utters when he begins to retreat."

Mr. Wilson declared his motives in proposing this bill, and yet cheerfully acquiesced in its probable fate: "Having read hundreds of pages of records and of testimony, enough to make the heart and soul sick, I proposed this bill as a measure of humanity. I desired, before we entered on the great questions of public policy, that we should pass a simple bill annulling these cruel laws; that we should do it early, and then proceed calmly with our legislation. That was my motive for bringing this bill into the Senate so early in the session. Many of the difficulties occurring in the rebel States, between white men and black men, between the old masters and the freedmen, grow out of these laws. They are executed in various parts of the States; the military arrest their execution frequently, and the agents of the Freedmen's Bureau set them aside; and this keeps up a continual conflict. If these obnoxious State laws were promptly annulled, it would contribute much to the restoration of good feeling and harmony, relieve public officers from immense labors, and the freedmen from suffering and sorrow; and this is the opinion of the most experienced men engaged in the Freedmen's Bureau. I have had an opportunity to consult with and to communicate with many of the agents of the Bureau, with teachers, officers, and persons who understand the state of affairs in those States.

"But, sir, it is apparent now that the bill is not to pass at present; that it must go over for the holidays at any rate. The constitutional amendment has been adopted, and I have introduced a bill this morning based upon that amendment, which has been referred to the committee of which the Senator from Illinois [Mr. Trumbull] is chairman. This bill will go over; possibly it will not be acted upon at all. We shall probably enter on the discussion of the broader question of annulling all the black laws in the country, and putting these people under the protection of humane, equal, and just laws."

The presentiment of the author of the bill was realized. The bill never saw the light as a law of the land. Nor was it needful that it should. It contributed to swell the volume of other and more sweeping measures.

CHAPTER VI.

THE FREEDMEN'S BUREAU BILL IN THE SENATE.

The bill introduced and referred to Judiciary Committee—Its provisions—Argument of Mr. Hendricks against it—Reply of Mr. Trumbull—Mr. Cowan's amendment—Mr. Guthrie wishes to relieve Kentucky from the operation of the bill—Mr. Creswell desires that Maryland may enjoy the benefits of the bill—Mr. Cowan's gratitude to God and friendship for the negro—Remarks by Mr. Wilson—"The short gentleman's long speech"—Yeas and nays—Insulting title.

ON the 19th of December Mr. Trumbull gave notice that "on some early day" he would "introduce a bill to enlarge the powers of the Freedmen's Bureau so as to secure freedom to all persons within the United States, and protect every individual in the full enjoyment of the rights of person and property, and furnish him with means for their vindication." Of the introduction of this measure, he said it would be done "in view of the adoption of the constitutional amendment abolishing slavery. I have never doubted that, on the adoption of that amendment, it would be competent for Congress to protect every person in the United States in all the rights of person and property belonging to a free citizen; and to secure these rights is the object of the bill which I propose to introduce. I think it important that action should be taken on this subject at an early day, for the purpose of quieting apprehensions in the minds of many friends of freedom, lest by local legislation or a prevailing public sentiment in some of the States, persons of the African race should continue to be oppressed, and, in fact, deprived of their freedom; and for the purpose, also, of showing to those among whom slavery has heretofore existed, that unless by local legislation they provide for the real freedom of their former slaves, the Federal Government will, by virtue of its own authority, see that they are fully protected."

On the 5th of January, 1866, the first day of the session of Congress after the holidays, Mr. Trumbull obtained leave to introduce a bill "to enlarge the powers of the Freedmen's Bureau." The bill was read twice by its title, and as it contained provisions relating to the exercise of judicial functions by the officers and agents of the Freedmen's Bureau, under certain circumstances, in the late insurgent States, it was referred to the Committee on the Judiciary.

On the 11th of January Mr. Trumbull reported the bill from the Judiciary Committee, to whom it had been referred, with some amendments of a verbal character. On the following day these amendments were considered by the Senate, in Committee of the Whole, and adopted. The consideration of the bill as amended was deferred to a subsequent day.

The bill provided that "the act to establish a Bureau for the relief of Freedmen and Refugees, approved March 3, 1865, shall continue until otherwise provided for by law, and shall extend to refugees and freedmen in all parts of the United States. The President is to be authorized to divide the section of country containing such refugees and freedmen into districts, each containing one or more States, not to exceed twelve in number, and by and with the advice and consent of the Senate, to appoint an assistant commissioner for each district, who shall give like bond, receive the same compensation, and perform the same duties prescribed by this act and the act to which it is an amendment. The bureau may, in the discretion of the President, be placed under a commissioner and assistant commissioners, to be detailed from the army, in which event each officer so assigned to duty is to serve without increase of pay or allowances.

"The commissioner, with the approval of the President, is to divide each district into a number of sub-districts, not to exceed the number of counties or parishes in each State, and to assign to each sub-district at least one agent, either a citizen, officer of the army, or enlisted man, who, if an officer, is to serve without additional compensation or allowance, and if a citizen or enlisted man, is to receive a salary not exceeding $1,500 per annum. Each assistant commissioner may employ not exceeding six clerks, one of the third class and five of the first class, and each agent of a sub-district may employ two clerks of the first class.

The President of the United States, through the War Department and the commissioner, is to extend military jurisdiction and protection over all employés, agents, and officers of the bureau, and the Secretary of War may direct such issues of provisions, clothing, fuel, and other supplies, including medical stores and transportation, and afford such aid, medical or otherwise, as he may deem needful for the immediate and temporary shelter and supply of destitute and suffering refugees and freedmen, their wives and children, under such rules and regulations as he may direct.

"It is also provided that the President may, for settlement in the manner prescribed by section four of the act to which this is an amendment, reserve from sale or settlement, under the homestead or preëmption laws, public lands in Florida, Mississippi, and Arkansas, not to exceed three million acres of good land in all, the rental named in that section to be determined in such manner as the commissioner shall by regulation prescribe. It proposes to confirm and make valid the possessory titles granted in pursuance of Major-General Sherman's special field order, dated at Savannah, January 16, 1865. The commissioner, under the direction of the President, is to be empowered to purchase or rent such tracts of land in the several districts as may be necessary to provide for the indigent refugees and freedmen dependent upon the Government for support; also to purchase sites and buildings for schools and asylums, to be held as United States property until the refugees or freedmen shall purchase the same, or they shall be otherwise disposed of by the commissioner.

"Whenever in any State or district in which the ordinary course of judicial proceedings has been interrupted by the rebellion, and wherein, in consequence of any State or local law, ordinance, police or other regulation, custom, or prejudice, any of the civil rights or immunities belonging to white persons (including the right to make and enforce contracts, to sue, be parties, and give evidence, to inherit, purchase, lease, sell, hold, and convey real and personal property, and to have full and equal benefit of all laws and proceedings for the security of person and estate), are refused or denied to negroes, mulattoes, freedmen, refugees, or any other persons, on account of race, color, or any previous condition of slavery or involuntary servitude, except as a punishment for crime whereof the party shall have been duly convicted, or wherein they or any of them are subjected to any other or different punishment, pains, or penalties, for the commission of any act or offense, than are prescribed for white persons committing like acts or offenses, it is to be the duty of the President of the United States, through the commissioner, to extend military protection and jurisdiction over all cases affecting such persons so discriminated against.

"Any person who, under color of any State or local law, ordinance, police, or other regulation or custom, shall, in any State or district in which the ordinary course of judicial proceedings has been interrupted by the rebellion, subject, or cause to be subjected, any negro, mulatto, freedman, refugee, or other person, on account of race or color, or any previous condition of slavery or involuntary servitude, except as a punishment for crime whereof the party shall have been duly convicted, or for any other cause, to the deprivation of any civil right secured to white persons, or to any other or different punishment than white persons are subject to for the commission of like acts or offenses, is to be deemed guilty of a misdemeanor, and be punished by fine not exceeding $1,000 or imprisonment not exceeding one year, or both. It is to be the duty of the officers and agents of this bureau to take jurisdiction of and hear and determine all offenses committed against this provision; and also of all cases affecting negroes, mulattoes, freedmen, refugees, or other persons who are discriminated against in any of the particulars mentioned in this act, under such rules and regulations as the President of the United States, through the War Department, may prescribe. This jurisdiction is to cease and determine whenever the discrimination on account of which it is conferred ceases, and is in no event to be exercised in any State in which the ordinary course of judicial proceedings has not been interrupted by the rebellion, nor in any such State after it shall have been fully restored in all its constitutional relations to the United States, and the courts of the State and of the United States within its limits are not disturbed or stopped in the peaceable course of justice."

Other business occupying the attention of the Senate, the consideration of the Freedman's Bureau Bill was not practically entered upon until the 18th of January. On that day, Mr. Stewart made a speech ostensibly on this bill, but really on the question of reconstruction and negro suffrage, in reply to remarks by Mr. Wade on those subjects.

Mr. Trumbull moved as an amendment to the bill that occupants on land under General Sherman's special field order, dated at Savannah, January 16, 1865, should be confirmed in their possessions for the period of three years from the date of said order, and no person should be disturbed in said possession during the said three years unless a settlement should be made with said occupant by the owner satisfactory to the commissioner of the Freedmen's Bureau.

Mr. Trumbull explained the circumstances under which the freedmen had obtained possessory titles to lands in Georgia, and urged the propriety of their being confirmed by Congress for three years. He said:

"I should be glad to go further. I would be glad, if we could, to secure to these people, upon any just principle, the fee of this land; but I do not see with what propriety we could except this particular tract of country out of all the other lands in the South, and appropriate it in fee to these parties. I think, having gone upon the land in good faith under the protection of the Government, we may protect them there for a reasonable time; and the opinion of the committee was that three years would be a reasonable time."

On the following day, Mr. Hendricks presented his objections to the bill in a speech of considerable length. He was followed by Mr. Trumbull in reply. As both were members of the Judiciary Committee from which the bill was reported, and both had carefully considered the reasons for and against the measure, their arguments are given at length.

Mr. Hendricks said: "At the last session of Congress the original law creating that bureau was passed. We were then in the midst of the war; very considerable territory had been brought within the control of the Union troops and armies, and within the scope of that territory, it was said, there were many freedmen who must be protected by a bill of that sort; and it was mainly upon that argument that the bill was enacted. The Senate was very reluctant to enact the law creating the bureau as it now exists. There was so much hesitancy on the part of the Senate, that by a very large vote it refused to agree to the bill reported by the Senator from Massachusetts, [Mr. Sumner,] from a committee of conference, and I believe the honorable Senator from Illinois, [Mr. Trumbull,] who introduced this bill, himself voted against that bill; and why? That bill simply undertook to define the powers

Eng^d by G.E. Perine & Co. N.York

T. A. Hendricks

HON. T. A. HENDRICKS

SENATOR FROM INDIANA

and duties of the Freedmen's Bureau and its agents, and the Senate would not agree to confer the powers that that bill upon its face seemed to confer, and it was voted down; and then the law as it now stands was enacted in general terms. There was very little gained, indeed, by the Senate refusing to pass the first bill and enacting the latter, for under the law as it passed, the Freedmen's Bureau assumed very nearly all the jurisdiction and to exercise all the powers contemplated in the bill reported by the Senator from Massachusetts.

"Now, sir, it is important to note very carefully the enlargement of the powers of this bureau proposed by this bill; and in the first place, it proposes to make the bureau permanent. The last Congress would not agree to this. The bill that the Senate voted down did not limit the duration of the bureau, and it was voted down, and the bill that the Senate agreed to provided that the bureau should continue during the war and only for one year after its termination. That was the judgment of the Senate at the last session. What has occurred since to change the judgment of the Senate in this important matter? What change in the condition of the country induces the Senate now to say that this shall be a permanent bureau or department of the Government, when at the last session it said it should cease to exist within one year after the conclusion of the war? Why, sir, it seems to me that the country is now, and especially the Southern States are now in better condition than the Senate had reason to expect when the law was enacted. Civil government has been restored in almost all the Southern States; the courts are restored in many of them; in many localities they are exercising their jurisdiction within their particular localities without let or hinderance; and why, I ask Senators, shall we make this bureau a perpetual and permanent institution of the Government when we refused to do it at the last session?

"I ask Senators, in the first place, if they are now, with the most satisfactory information that is before the body, willing to do that which they refused to do at the last session of Congress? We refused to pass the law when it proposed to establish a permanent department. Shall we now, when the war is over, when the States are returning to their places in the Union, when the citizens are returning to their allegiance, when peace and quiet, to a very large extent, prevail over that country, when the courts are reëstablished; is the Senate now, with this information before it, willing to make this a permanent bureau and department of the Government?

"The next proposition of the bill is, that it shall not be confined any longer to the Southern States, but that it shall have a government over the States of the North as well as of the South. The old law allowed the President to appoint a commissioner for each of the States that had been declared to be in rebellion—one for each of the eleven seceding States, not to exceed ten in all. This bill provides that the jurisdiction of the bureau shall extend whereever, within the limits of the United States, refugees or freedmen have gone. Indiana has not been a State in insurrection, and yet there are thousands of refugees and freedmen who have gone into that State within the last three years. This bureau is to become a governing power over the State of Indiana according to the provisions of the bill. Indiana, that provides for her own paupers, Indiana, that provides for the government of her own people, may, under the provisions of this bill, be placed under a government that our fathers never contemplated—a government that must be most distasteful to freemen.

"I know it may be said that the bureau will not probably be extended to the Northern States. If it is not intended to be extended to those States, why amend the old law so as to give this power? When the old law limited the jurisdiction of this bureau to the States that had been declared in insurrection, is it not enough that the bureau should have included one State, the State of Kentucky, over which it had no rightful original jurisdiction? And must we now amend it so as to place all the States of the Union within the power of this irresponsible sub-government? This is one objection that I have to the bill, and the next is the expense that it must necessarily impose upon the people. We are asked by the Freedmen's Bureau in its estimates to appropriate $11,745,050; nearly twelve million dollars for the support of this bureau and to carry on its operations during the coming year. I will read what he says:

"'It is estimated that the amount required for the expenditures of the bureau for the fiscal year commencing January, 1866, will be $11,745,050. The sum is requisite for the following purposes:

Salaries of assistant and sub-assistant commissioners	$147,500
Salaries of clerks	82,800

Stationery and printing	63,000
Quarters and fuel	15,000
Clothing for distribution	1,750,000
Commissary stores	4,106,250
Medical department	500,000
Transportation	1,980,000
School superintendents	21,000
Sites for school-houses and asylums	3,000,000
Telegraphing	18,000

Making in all the sum which I have mentioned. The old system under this law, that was before the commissioner when he made this estimate, requires an expenditure to carry on its operations of nearly twelve million dollars, and that to protect, as it is called, and to govern four millions of the people of the United States—within a few millions of the entire cost of the Government under Mr. Adams's administration, when the population of the States had gone up to many millions. How is it that a department that has but a partial jurisdiction over the people shall cost almost as much for the management of four million people as it cost to manage the whole Government, for its army, its navy, its legislative and judicial departments, in former years? My learned friend from Kentucky suggests that the expenses under John Quincy Adams's administration were about thirteen million dollars. What was the population of the United States at that time I am not prepared to state, but it was far above four millions. Now, to manage four million people is to cost the people of the United States, under the law as it stands, nearly as much as it cost the people to manage the whole affairs of the Government under the administration of Mr. John Quincy Adams.

"I hear Senators speak very frequently of the necessity of economy and retrenchment. Is this a specimen, increasing the number of officers almost without limit, and increasing the expenditures? I think one might be safe in saying that, if this bill passes, we can not expect to get through a year with less than $20,000,000 of an expenditure for this bureau. But that is a mere opinion; for no man can tell until we have the number of officers that are to be appointed under the bill prescribed in the bill itself, and this section leaves the largest discretion to the bureau in the appointment of officers. I appeal to Senators to know whether, at this time, when we ought to adopt a system of retrenchment and reform, they are willing to pass a bill which will so largely increase the public expenditures.

"Then, sir, when this army of officers has been organized, the bill provides: 'And the President of the United States, through the War Department and the commissioner, shall extend military jurisdiction and protection over all employès, agents, and officers of this bureau.'

"Will some Senator be good enough to tell me what that means? If Indiana be declared a State within which are found refugees and freedmen, who have escaped from the Southern States, and if Indiana has a commissioner appointed to her, and if in each county of Indiana there be a sub-commissioner at a salary of $1,500 a year, with two clerks with a salary of $1,200 each, and then the War Department throws over this little army of office-holders in the State of Indiana its protection, what does that mean? The people of Indiana have been ground hard under military authority and power within the last three or four years, but it was borne because it was hoped that when the war would be closed the military power would be withdrawn from the State. Under this bill it may be established permanently upon the people by a body of men protected by the military power of the Government. An officer is appointed to the State of Indiana to regulate the contracts which are made between the white people and the colored people of that State, and because he holds this office, not military in its character, involving no military act whatever, the military throws over him its iron shield of protection. What does that mean? If this officer shall do a great wrong and outrage to one of the people, and the wronged citizen appeals to the court for his redress and brings his suit for damages, does the protecting shield of the War Department prevent the prosecution of that suit and the recovery of a judgment? What is the protection that is thrown over this army of office-holders? Let it be explained.

"It may be said that this is a part of the military department. That will depend not so much upon what we call them in the law as what are the duties imposed upon these sub-agents. It is a little difficult to tell. They are to protect the freedmen; they are to protect refugees; they are to buy asylums and school-houses; they are to establish schools; they are to see to the contracts that are made between white men and colored men. I want to know of the chairman of the committee that reported this bill, in what respect these duties are military in their character? I can understand one thing, that it may be regarded as a war upon the liberties of the people, but I am not able to see in what respect the duties of these officers otherwise are military. But this protection is to be thrown over them. I will not occupy longer time upon that subject.

"The third section of the bill changes the letter of the law in two respects: first, 'That the Secretary of War may direct such issues of provisions, clothing, fuel, and other supplies, including medical stores and transportation,' etc. Those last words, 'medical stores and transportation,' make the change in the law that is proposed in this bill. But, sir, in point of fact it makes no change in the law; for if you will turn to the report of the commissioner of this bureau, it will be found that the bureau, during the past six months, has been furnishing medical supplies and transportation. A very large item in the expenditures estimated for is transportation. But I wish to ask of the Senator who framed this bill why we shall now provide for the transportation of freedmen and refugees. During the war, a very large number of refugees came from the Southern States into the North; but the Commissioner of the Freedmen's Bureau, in his report, says that those refugees have mainly returned, and but few remain now to be carried back from the North to the South, or who desire to be. Then why do we provide in this bill for transportation? Is it simply to give the bureau the power to transport refugees and freedmen from one locality to another at its pleasure? The necessity of carrying them from one section of the country to another has passed away. Is it intended by this bill that the bureau shall expend the people's money in carrying the colored people from one locality in a Southern State to another locality? I ask the Senator from Illinois, when he comes to explain his bill, to tell us just what is the force and purpose of this provision.

"The fourth resolution, as amended, provides for the setting apart of three million acres of the public lands in the States of Florida, Mississippi, and Arkansas for homes for the colored people. I believe that is the only provision of the bill in which I concur. I concur in what was said by some Senator yesterday, that it is desirable, if we ever expect to do any thing substantially for the colored people, to encourage them to obtain homes, and I am willing to vote for a reasonable appropriation of the public lands for that purpose. I shall not, therefore, occupy time in discussing that section.

"The fifth section, as amended by the proposition before the Senate, proposes to confirm the possessory right of the colored people upon these lands for three years from the date of that order, or about two years from this time. I like the amendment better than the original bill; for the original bill left it entirely uncertain what was confirmed, and of course it is better that we should say one year, or three years, or ten years, than to leave it entirely indefinite for what period we do confirm the possession. I have no doubt that General Sherman had the power, as a military commander, at the time, to set apart the abandoned lands along the coast as a place in which to leave the colored people then surrounding his army; but that General Sherman during the war, or that Congress after the war, except by a proceeding for confiscation, can take the land permanently from one person and give it to another, I do not admit; nor did General Sherman undertake to do that. In express terms, he said that they should have the right of possession; for what length of time he did not say, for the reason that he could not say. It was a military possession that he conferred, and that possession would last only during the continuance of the military occupation, and no longer. If General Sherman, by his General Order No. 15, placed the colored people upon the lands along the coast of South Carolina, Georgia, and Florida, for a temporary purpose, what was the extent of the possessory right which he could confer? He did not undertake to give a title for any defined period, but simply the right of possession. It is fair to construe his order as meaning only what he could do, giving the right of possession during military occupancy. Now, sir, the President informs us that the rebellion is suppressed; that the war is over; that military law no longer governs in that country; but that peace is restored, and that civil law shall now govern. What, then, is the law upon the subject? A right of possession is given by the commanding general to certain persons within that region of country; peace follows, and with peace comes back the right of the real owners to the possession. This possession that the General undertook to give, according to law, could not last longer than the military occupancy. When peace comes, the right of the owners return with it. Then how is it that Congress can undertake to say that the property that belongs to A, B, and C, upon the islands and sea-coast of the South, shall, for two years from this date, not belong to them, but shall belong to certain colored people? I want to know upon what principle of law Congress can take the property of one man and give it to another.

"I know very well what may be done in the courts by a proceeding for confiscation. I am not discussing that question. If there has been any property confiscated and disposed of under proceedings of confiscation, I do not question the title here. That is purely a judicial question. But, sir, I deny that Congress can legislate the property of one man into the possession of another. If this section is to pass, I prefer that this confirmation shall be for three years rather than leave it in the uncertain state in which General Sherman's order left it.

"The sixth section provides, 'That the commissioners shall, under the direction of the President, procure in the name of the United States, by grant or purchase, such lands within the districts aforesaid as may be required for refugees and freedmen dependent on the Government for support; and he shall provide, or cause to be erected, suitable buildings for asylums and schools.' Upon what principle can you authorize the Government of the United States to buy lands for the poor people in any State of the Union? They may be very meritorious; their cases may appeal with great force to our sympathies; it may almost appear necessary to prevent suffering that we should buy a home for each poor person in the country; but where is the power of the General Government to do this thing? Is it true that by this revolution the persons and property of the people have been brought within the jurisdiction of Congress, and taken from without the control and jurisdiction of the States? I have understood heretofore that it has never been disputed that the duty to provide for the poor, the insane, the blind, and all who are dependent upon society, rests upon the States, and that the power does not belong to the General Government. What has occurred, then, in this war that has changed the relation of the people to the General Government to so great an extent that Congress may become the purchasers of homes for them? If we can go so far, I know of no limit to the powers of Congress. Here is a proposition to buy a home for each dependent freeman and refugee. The section is not quite as strong as it might have been. It would have been stronger, I think, in the present state of public sentiment, if the word 'refugee' had been left out, and if it had been only for the freedmen, because it does not seem to be so popular now to buy a home for a white man as to buy one for a colored man. But this bill authorizes the officers of the Freedmen's Bureau to buy homes for white people and for black people only upon the ground that they are dependent. If this be the law now, there has come about a startling change in the relation of the States and of the people to the General Government. I shall be very happy to hear from the learned head of the Judiciary Committee upon what principle it is that in any one single case you may buy a home for any man, whether he be rich or poor. The General Government may buy land when it is necessary for the exercise of any of its powers; but outside of that, it seems to me, there is no power within the Constitution allowing it.

"The most remarkable sections of the bill, however, are the seventh and eighth, and to those sections I will ask the very careful attention of Senators; for I think if we can pass those two sections, and make them a law, then indeed this Government can do any thing. It will be useless to speak any longer of limitations upon the powers of the General Government; it will be idle to speak of the reserved power of the States; State rights and State power will have passed away if we can do what is proposed in the seventh and eighth sections of this bill. We propose, first, to legislate against the effects of 'local law, ordinance, police, or other regulation;' then against 'custom,' and lastly, against 'prejudice,' and to provide that 'if any of the civil rights or immunities belonging to white persons' are denied to any person because of color, then that person shall be taken under the military protection of the Government. I do not know whether that will be understood to extend to Indiana or not. That will be a very nice point for the bureau to decide, I presume, after the enactment of the law. The section limits its operation to 'any State or district in which the ordinary course of judicial proceedings has been interrupted by the rebellion.' It will be a little difficult to say whether in the State of Indiana and Ohio the ordinary course of judicial proceeding has or has not been interrupted. We had some war in Indiana; we had a very great raid through that State and some fighting; and I presume that in some cases the proceedings of the courts were interrupted and the courts were unable to go on with their business, so that it might be said that even in some of the Northern States this provision of the bill would be applicable. Suppose that it were applicable to the State of Indiana, then every man in that State, who attempted to execute the constitution and laws of the State, would be liable for a violation of the law. We do not allow to colored people there many civil rights and immunities which are enjoyed by the white people. It became the policy of the State in 1852 to prohibit the immigration of colored people into that State. I am not going to discuss the question whether that was a wise policy or not. At the time it received the approval of my judgment. Under that constitutional provision, and the laws enacted in pursuance of it, a colored man coming into the State since 1852 can not acquire a title to real estate, can not make certain contracts, and no negro man is allowed to intermarry with a white woman. These are civil rights that are denied, and yet this bill proposes, if they are still denied in any State whose courts have been interrupted by the rebellion, the military protection of the Government shall be extended over the person who is thus denied such civil rights or immunities.

"The next section of the bill provides punishments where any of these things are done, where any right is denied to a colored man which under State law is allowed to a white man. The language is very vague, and it is very difficult to say what this section will mean. If it has as broad a construction as is attempted to be given to the second section of the constitutional amendment, I would not undertake to guess what it means. Any man who shall deny to any colored man any civil rights secured to white persons, shall be liable to be taken before the officers of this bureau and to be punished according to the provisions of this section. In the first place, now that peace is restored, now that there is no war, now that men are no longer under military rule, but are under civil rule, I want to know how such a court can be organized; how it is that the citizen may be arrested without indictment, and may be brought before the officers of this bureau and tried without a jury, tried without the forms which the Constitution requires.

"But sir, this section is most objectionable in regard to the offense that it defines. If any portion of the law ought to be certain, it is that which defines crime and prescribes the punishment. What is meant by this general expression, 'the deprivation of any civil right secured to white persons?' The agent in one State may construe it to mean one thing, and the agent in another State another thing. It is broad and comprehensive—'the deprivation of any civil right secured to white persons.' That act of deprivation is the crime that is to be punished. Take the case that I have just referred to. Suppose a minister, when called upon, should refuse to solemnize a marriage between a colored man and a white woman because the law of the State forbade it, would he then, refusing to recognize a civil right which is enjoyed by white persons, be liable to this punisment?

"My judgment is that, under the second section of the constitutional amendment, we may pass such a law as will secure the freedom declared in the first section, but that we can not go beyond that limitation. If a man has been, by this provision of the Constitution, made free from his master, and that master undertakes to make him a slave again, we may pass such laws as are sufficient in our judgment to prevent that act; but if the Legislature of the State denies to the citizen as he is now called, the freedman, equal privileges with the white man, I want to know if that Legislature, and each member of that Legislature, is responsible to the penalties prescribed in this bill? It is not an act of the old master; it is an act of the State government, which defines and regulates the civil rights of the people.

"I regard it as very dangerous legislation. It proposes to establish a government within a government—not a republic within a republic, but a cruel despotism within a republic. In times of peace, in communities that are quiet and orderly, and obedient to law, it is proposed to establish a government not responsible to the people, the officers of which are not selected by the people, the officers of which need not be of the people governed—a government more cruel, more despotic, more dangerous to the liberties of the people than that against which our forefathers fought in the Revolution. There is nothing that these men may not do, under this bill, to oppress the people.

"Sir, if we establish courts in the Southern States, we ought to establish courts that will be on both sides, or on neither side; but the doctrine now is, that if a man is appointed, either to an executive or a judicial office, in any locality where there are colored people, he must be on the side of the negro. I have not heard, since Congress met, that any colored man has done a wrong in this country for many years; and I have scarcely heard that any white man coming in contact with colored people has done right for a number of years. Every body is expected to take sides for the colored man against the white man. If I have to take sides, it will be with the men of my own color and my own race; but I do not wish to do that. Toward these people I hope that the legislation of Congress, within the constitutional powers of Congress, will be just and fair—just to them and just to the white people among whom they live; that it will promote harmony among the people, and not discord; that it will restore labor to its channels, and bring about again in those States a condition of prosperity and happiness. Do we not all desire that? If we do, is it well for us to inflame our passions and the passions of the people of the North, so that their judgments shall not be equal upon the questions between these races? It is all very well for us to have sympathy for the poor and the unfortunate, but both sides call for our sympathy in the South. The master, who, by his wickedness and folly, has involved himself in the troubles that now beset him, has returned, abandoning his rebellion, and has bent down upon his humble knees and asked the forgiveness of the Government, and to be restored again as a citizen. Can a man go further than that? He has been in many cases pardoned by the Executive. He stands again as a citizen of the country.

"What relation do we desire that the people of the North shall sustain toward these people of the South—one of harmony and accord, or of strife and ill will? Do we want to restore commerce and trade with them, that we shall prosper thereby as well as they, or do we wish permanent strife and division? I want this to be a Union in form, under the Constitution of the United States, and, in fact, by the harmony of the people of the North and of the South. I believe, as General Grant says, that this bureau, especially with the enlarged powers that we propose to confer upon it, will not be an instrument of concord and harmony, but will be one of discord and strife in that section of the country. It can not do good, but, in my judgment, will do much harm."

Following immediately upon the close of the above argument, Mr. Trumbull thus addressed the senate: "Mr. President, I feel it incumbent on me to reply to some of the arguments presented by the Senator from Indiana against this bill. Many of the positions he has assumed will be found, upon examination, to have no foundation in fact. He has argued against provisions not contained in the bill, and he has argued also as if he were entirely forgetful of the condition of the country and of the great war through which we have passed.

"Now, sir, what was the object of the Freedmen's Bureau, and why was it established? It was established to look after a large class of people who, as the results of the war, had been thrown upon the hands of the Government, and must have perished but for its fostering care and protection. Does the Senator mean to deny the power of this Government to protect people under such circumstances? The Senator must often have voted for appropriations to protect other classes of people under like circumstances. Whenever, in the history of the Government, there has been thrown upon it a helpless population, which must starve and die but for its care, the Government has never failed to provide for them. At this very session, within the last thirty days, both houses of Congress have voted half a million dollars to feed and clothe people during the present winter. Who were they? Many of them were Indians who had joined the rebellion, and had slain loyal people of the country. Yes, sir, we appropriated money to feed Indians who had been fighting against us. We did not hear the Senator's voice in opposition to that appropriation. What were the facts? It was stated by our Indian agents that the Indian tribes west of Arkansas, a part of whom had joined the rebel armies and some the Union armies, had been driven from their country; that their property had been destroyed; and now, the conflict of arms having ceased, they had nothing to live upon during the winter; that they would encroach upon the white settlements; that unless provision was made for them, they would rob, plunder, and murder the inhabitants nearest them; and Congress was called upon to appropriate money to buy them food and clothing, and we did it. We did it for rebels and traitors. Were we not bound to do it?

Now, sir, we have thrown upon us four million people who have toiled all their lives for others; who, unlike the Indians, had no property at the beginning of the rebellion; who were never permitted to own any thing, never permitted to eat the bread their own hands had earned; many of whom are without support, in the midst of a prejudiced and hostile population who have been struggling to overthrow the Government. These four million people, made free by the acts of war and the constitutional amendment, have been, wherever they could, loyal and true to the Union; and the Senator seriously asks, What authority have we to appropriate money to take care of them? What would he do with them? Would he allow them to starve and die? Would he turn them over to the mercy of the men who, through their whole lives, have had their earnings, to be enslaved again? It is not the first time that money has been appropriated to take care of the destitute and suffering African. For years it has been the law that whenever persons of African descent were brought to our shores with the intention of reducing them to slavery, the Government should, if possible, rescue and restore them to their native land; and we have appropriated hundreds of thousands of dollars for this object. Can any body deny the right to do it? Sir, humanity as well as the constitutional obligation to suppress the slave trade required it. So now the people relieved by our act from the control of masters who supplied their wants that they might have their services, have a right to rely upon us for assistance till they can have time to provide for themselves.

"This Freedmen's Bureau is not intended as a permanent institution; it is only designed to aid these helpless, ignorant, and unprotected people until they can provide for and take care of themselves. The authority to do this, so far as legislative sanction can give it, is to be found in the action of a previous Congress which established the bureau; but, if it were a new question, the authority for establishing such a bureau, in my judgment, is given by the Constitution itself; and as the Senator's whole argument goes upon the idea of peace, and that all the consequences of the war have ceased, I shall be pardoned, I trust, if I refer to those provisions of the Constitution which, in my judgment, authorize the exercise of this military jurisdiction; for this bureau is a part of the military establishment not simply during the conflict of arms, but until peace shall be firmly established and the civil tribunals of the country shall be restored with an assurance that they may peacefully enforce the laws without opposition.

"The Constitution of the United States declares that Congress shall have authority 'to declare war and make rules concerning captures on land and water,' 'to raise and support armies,' 'to provide and maintain a navy,' 'to make rules for the government and regulation of the land and naval forces,' 'to provide for calling forth the militia to execute the laws of the Union, suppress insurrection, and repel invasion,' and 'to make all laws which shall be necessary and proper for carrying into execution the foregoing powers.' It also declares that 'the citizens of each State shall be entitled to all the privileges and immunities of citizens in the several States,' and that 'the United States shall guarantee to every State in the Union a republican form of government.' Under the exercise of these powers, the Government has gone through a four years' conflict. It has succeeded in putting down armed resistance to its authority. But did the military power which was exercised to put down this armed resistance cease the moment the rebel armies were dispersed? Has the Government no authority to bring to punishment the authors of this rebellion after the conflict of arms has ceased? no authority to hold as prisoners, if necessary, all who have been captured with arms in their hands? Can it be that, the moment the rebel armies are dispersed, the military authority ceases, and they are to be turned loose to arm and organize again for another conflict against the Union? Why, sir, it would not be more preposterous on the part of the traveler, after having, at the peril of his life, succeeded in disarming a highwayman by whom he was assailed, to immediately turn round and restore to the robber his weapons with which to make a new assault.

"And yet this is what some gentlemen would have this nation do with the worse than robbers who have assailed its life. They propose, the rebel armies being overcome, that the rebels themselves shall be instantly clothed with all the authority they possessed before the conflict, and that the inhabitants of States who for more than four years have carried on an organized war against the Government shall at once be invested with all the powers they had at its commencement to organize and begin it anew; nay, more, they insist that, without any action of the Government, it is the right of the inhabitants of the rebellious States, on laying down their arms, to resume their former positions in the Union, with all the rights they possessed when they began the war. If such are the consequences of this struggle, it is the first conflict in the history of the world, between either individuals or nations, from which such results have followed. What man, after being despoiled of much of his substance, his children slain, his own life periled, and his body bleeding from many wounds, ever restored the authors of such calamities, when within his power, to the rights they possessed before the conflict without taking some security for the future.

"Sir, the war powers of the Government do not cease with the dispersion of the rebel armies; they are to be continued and exercised until the civil authority of the Government can be established firmly and upon a sure foundation, not again to be disturbed or interfered with. And such, sir, is the understanding of the Government. None of the departments of the Government understand that its military authority has ceased to operate over the rebellious States. It is but a short time since the President of the United States issued a proclamation restoring the privilege of the writ of *habeas corpus* in the loyal States; but did he restore it in the rebellious States? Certainly not. What authority has he to suspend the privilege of that writ anywhere, except in pursuance of the constitutional provision allowing the writ to be suspended 'when in cases of rebellion or invasion the public safety may require it?' Then the President understands that the public safety in the insurrectionary States still requires its suspension.

"The Attorney-General, when asked, a few days ago, why Jefferson Davis was not put upon trial, told you that, 'though active hostilities have ceased, a state of war still exists over the territory in rebellion,' so that it could not be properly done. General Grant, in an order issued within a few days—which I commend to the especial consideration of the Senator from Indiana, for it contains many of the provisions of the bill under consideration—an order issued with the approbation of the Executive, for such an order, I apprehend, could not have been issued without his approbation—directs 'military division and department commanders, whose commands embrace or are composed of any of the late rebellious States, and who have not already done so, will at once issue and enforce orders protecting from prosecution or suits in the State, or municipal courts of such State, all officers and soldiers of the armies of the United States, and all persons thereto attached, or in anywise thereto belonging, subject to military authority, charged with offenses for acts done in their military capacity, or pursuant to orders from proper military authority; and to protect from suit or prosecution all loyal citizens or persons charged with offenses done against the rebel forces, directly or indirectly, during the existence of the rebellion; and all persons, their agents and employés, charged with the occupancy of abandoned lands or plantations, or the possession or custody of any kind of property whatever, who occupied, used, possessed, or controlled the same, pursuant to the order of the President, or any of the civil or military departments of the Government, and to protect them from any penalties or damages that may have been or may be pronounced or adjudged in said courts in any of such cases; and also protecting colored persons from prosecutions, in any of said States, charged with offenses for which white persons are not prosecuted or punished in the same manner and degree.'"

Mr. Saulsbury having asked whether the Senator believed that General Grant or the President had any constitutional authority to make such an order as that, Mr. Trumbull replied: "I am very glad the Senator from Delaware has asked the question. I answer, he had most ample and complete authority. I indorse the order and every word of it. It would be monstrous if the officers and soldiers of the army and loyal citizens were to be subjected to suits and prosecutions for acts done in saving the republic, and that, too, at the hands of the very men who sought its destruction. Why, had not the Lieutenant-General authority to issue the order? Have not the civil tribunals in all the region of country to which order applies been expelled by armed rebels and traitors? Has not the power of the Government been overthrown there? Is it yet reëstablished? Some steps have been taken toward reëstablishing it under the authority of the military, and in no other way. If any of the State governments recently set up in the rebellious States were to undertake to embarrass military operations, I have no doubt they would at once be set aside by order of the Lieutenant-General, in pursuance of directions from the Executive. These governments which have been set up act by permission of the military. They are made use of, to some extent, to preserve peace and order and enforce civil rights between parties; and, so far as they act in harmony with the Constitution and laws of the United States and the orders of the military commanders, they are permitted to exercise authority; but until those States shall be restored in all their constitutional relations to the Union, they ought not to be permitted to exercise authority in any other way.

"I desire the Senator from Indiana to understand that it is under this war power that the authority of the Freedmen's Bureau is to be exercised. I do not claim that its officers can try persons for offenses without juries in States where the civil tribunals have not been interrupted by the rebellion. The Senator from Indiana argues against this bill as if it was applicable to that State. Some of its provisions are, but most of them are not, unless the State of Indiana has been in rebellion against the Government; and I know too many of the brave men who have gone from that State to mantain the integrity of the Union and put down the rebellion to cast any such imputation upon her. She is a loyal and a patriotic State; her civil government has never been usurped or overthrown by trators, and the provisions of the seventh and eighth sections of the bill to which the Senator alludes can not, by their very terms, have any application to the State of Indiana. Let me read the concluding sentence of the eighth section:

"'The jurisdiction conferred by this section on the officers and agents of this bureau to cease and determine whenever the discrimination on account of which it is conferred ceases, and in no event to be exercised in any State in which the ordinary course of judicial proceedings has not been interrupted by the rebellion, nor in any such State after said State shall have been fully restored in all its constitutional relations to the United States, and the courts of the State and of the United States within the same are not disturbed or stopped in the peaceable course of justice.'

"Will the Senator from Indiana admit for a moment that the courts in his State are now disturbed or stopped in the peaceable course of justice? If they were ever so disturbed, they are not now. Will the Senator admit that the State of Indiana does not have and exercise all its constitutional rights as one of the States of this Union? The judicial authority conferred by this bill applies to no State, not even to South Carolina, after it shall have been restored in all its constitutional rights.

"There is no provision in the bill for the exercise of judicial authority except in the eighth section. Rights are declared in the seventh, but the mode of protecting them is provided in the eighth section, and the eighth section then declares explicitly that the jurisdiction that is conferred shall be exercised only in States which do not possess full constitutional rights as parts of the Union. Indiana has at all times had all the constitutional rights pertaining to any State, has them now, and therefore the officers and agents of this bureau can take no jurisdiction of any case in the State of Indiana. It will be another question, which I will answer, and may as well answer now, perhaps, as to what is meant by 'military protection.'

"The second section declares that 'the President of the United States, through the War Department and the commissioner, shall extend military jurisdiction and protection over all employés, agents, and officers of this bureau.' He wants to know the effect of that in Indiana. This bureau is a part of the military establishment. The effect of that in Indiana is precisely the same as in every other State, and under it the officers and agents of the Freedmen's Bureau will occupy the same position as do the officers and soldiers of the United States Army. What is that? While they are subject to the Rules and Articles of War, if they chance to be in Indiana and violate her laws, they are held amenable the same as any other person. The officer or soldier in the State of Indiana who commits a murder or other offense upon a citizen of Indiana, is liable to be indicted, tried, and punished, just as if he were a civilian. When the sheriff goes with the process to arrest the soldier or officer who has committed the offense, the military authorities surrender him up to be tried and punished according to the laws of the State. It has always been done, unless in time of war when the courts were interrupted. The jurisdiction and 'protection' that is extended over these officers and agents is for the purpose of making them subject to the Rules and Articles of War. It is necessary for this reason: in the rebellious States civil authority is not yet fully restored. There would be no other way of punishing them, of holding them to accountability, of governing and controlling them, in many portions of the country; and it is because of the condition of the rebellious States, and their still being under military authority, that it is necessary to put these officers and agents of the Freedmen's Bureau under the control of the military power.

"The Senator says the original law only embraced within its provisions the refugees in the rebellious States; and now this bill is extended to all the States, and he wants to know the reason. I will tell him. When the original bill was passed, slavery existed in Tennessee, Kentucky, Delaware, and in various other States. Since that time, by the constitutional amendment, it has been every-where abolished."

Mr. Saulsbury, aroused by the mention of his own State, interrupted the speaker: "I say, as one of the representatives of Delaware on this floor, that she had the proud and noble character of being the first to enter the Federal Union under a Constitution formed by equals. She has been the very last to obey a mandate, legislative or executive, for abolishing slavery. She has been the last slaveholding State, thank God, in America, and I am one of the last slaveholders in America."

Mr. Trumbull continued: "Well, Mr. President, I do not see particularly what the declaration of the Senator from Delaware has to do with the question I am discussing. His State may have been the last to become free, but I presume that the State of Delaware, old as she is, being the first to adopt the Constitution, and noble as she is, will submit to the Constitution of the United States, which declares that there shall be no slavery within its jurisdiction." [Applause in the galleries.]

"It is necessary, Mr. President, to extend the Freedmen's Bureau beyond the rebel States in order to take in the State of Delaware, [laughter,] the loyal State of Delaware, I am happy to say, which did not engage in this wicked rebellion; and it is necessary to protect the freedmen in that State as well as elsewhere; and that is the reason for extending the Freedmen's Bureau beyond the limits of the rebellious States.

"Now, the Senator from Indiana says it extends all over the United States. Well, by its terms it does, though practically it can have little if any operation outside of the late slaveholding States. If freedmen should congregate in large numbers at Cairo, Illinois, or at Evansville, Indiana, and become a charge upon the people of those States, the Freedmen's Bureau would have a right to extend its jurisdiction over them, provide for their wants, secure for them employment, and place them in situations where they could provide for themselves; and would the State of Illinois or the State of Indiana object to that? The provisions of the bill which would interfere with the laws of Indiana can have no operation there.

"Again, the Senator objects very much to the expense of this bureau. Why, sir, as I have once or twice before said, it is a part of the military establishment. I believe nearly all its officers at the present time are military officers, and by the provisions of the pending bill they are to receive no additional compensation when performing duties in the Freedmen's Bureau. The bill declares that the 'bureau may, in the discretion of the President, be placed under a commissioner and assistant commissioners, to be detailed from the army, in which event each officer so assigned to duty shall serve without increase of pay or allowances.'

"I shall necessarily, Mr. President, in following the Senator from Indiana, speak somewhat in a desultory manner; but I prefer to do so because I would rather meet the objections made directly than by any general speech. I will, therefore, take up his next objection, which is to the fifth section of the bill. That section proposes to confirm for three years the possessory titles granted by General Sherman. The Senator from Indiana admits that General Sherman had authority, when at the head of the army at Savannah, and these people were flocking around him and dependent upon him for support, to put them upon the abandoned lands; but he says that authority to put them there and maintain them there ceased with peace. Well, sir, a sufficient answer to that would be that peace has not yet come; the effects of war are not yet ended; the people of the States of South Carolina, Georgia, and Florida, where these lands are situated, are yet subject to military control. But I deny that if peace had come the authority of the Government to protect these people in their possessions would cease the moment it was declared. What are the facts? The owners of these plantations had abandoned them and entered the rebel army. They were contending against the army which General Sherman then commanded. Numerous colored people had flocked around General Sherman's army. It was necessary that he should supply them to save them from starvation. His commissariat was short. Here was this abandoned country, owned by men arrayed in arms against the Government. He, it is admitted, had authority to put these followers of his army upon these lands, and authorize them to go to work and gain a subsistence if they could. They went on the lands to the number of forty or fifty thousand, commenced work, have made improvements; and now will the Senator from Indiana tell me that upon any principle of justice, humanity, or law, if peace had come when these laborers had a crop half gathered, the Government of the United States, having rightfully placed them in possession, and pledged its faith to protect them there for an uncertain period, could immediately have turned them off and put in possession those traitor owners who had abandoned their homes to fight against the Government?

"The Government having placed these people rightfully upon these lands, and they having expended their labor upon them, they had a right to be protected in their possessions, for some length of time after peace, on the principle of equity. That is all we propose to do by this bill. The committee thought it would not be more than a reasonable protection to allow them to remain for three years, they having been put upon these lands destitute, without any implements of husbandry, without cattle, horses, or any thing else with which to cultivate the land, and having, up to the present time, been able to raise very little at the expense of great labor. Perhaps the Senator thinks they ought not to remain so long. I will not dispute whether they shall go off at the end of one year or two years. The committee propose two years more. The order was dated in January, 1865, and we propose three years from that time, which will expire in January, 1868, or about two years from this time.

"On account of that provision of the bill, the Senator asks me the question whether the Government of the United States has the right, in a time of peace, to take property from one man and give it to another. I say no. Of course the Government of the United States has no authority, in a time of peace, by a legislative act, to say that the farm of the Senator from Indiana shall be given to the Senator from Ohio; I contend for no such principle. But following that up, the Senator wants to know by what authority you buy land or provide school-houses for these refugees. Have we not been providing school-houses for years? Is there a session of Congress when acts are not passed giving away public lands for the benefit of schools? But that does not come out of the Treasury, the Senator from Indiana will probably answer. But how did you get the land to give away? Did you not buy it of the Indians? Are you not appropriating, every session of Congress, money by the million to extinguish the Indian title—money collected off his constituents and mine by taxation? We buy the land and then we give the land away for schools. Will the Senator tell me how that differs from giving the money? Does it make any difference whether we buy the land from the Indians and give it for the benefit of schools, or whether we buy it from some rebel and give—no, sir, use—it for the benefit of schools, with a view ultimately of selling it for at least its cost? I believe I would rather buy from the Indian; but still, if the traitor is to be permitted to have a title, we will buy it from him if we can purchase cheaper.

"Sir, it is a matter of economy to do this. The cheapest way by which you can save this race from starvation and destruction is to educate them. They will then soon become self-sustaining. The report of the Freedmen's Bureau shows that to-day more than seventy thousand black children are being taught in the schools which have been established in the South. We shall not long have to support any of these blacks out of the public Treasury if we educate and furnish them land upon which they can make a living for themselves. This is a very different thing from taking the land of A and giving it to B by an act of Congress.

"But the Senator is most alarmed at those sections of this bill which confer judicial authority upon the officers and agents of the Freedmen's Bureau. He says if this authority can be exercised there is an end to all the reserved rights of the States, and this Government may do any thing. Not at all, sir. The authority, as I have already shown, to be exercised under the seventh and eighth sections, is a military authority, to be exerted only in regions of country where the civil tribunals are overthrown, and not there after they are restored. It is the same authority that we have been exercising all the time in the rebellious States; it is the same authority by virtue of which General Grant issued the order which I have just read. Here is a perfect and complete answer to the objection that is made to the seventh and eighth sections.

"But, says the Senator from Indiana, we have laws in Indiana prohibiting black people from marrying whites, and are you going to disregard these laws? Are our laws enacted for the purpose of preventing amalgamation to be disregarded, and is a man to be punished because he undertakes to enforce them? I beg the Senator from Indiana to read the bill. One of its objects is to secure the same civil rights and subject to the same punishments persons of all races and colors. How does this interfere with the law of Indiana preventing marriages between whites and blacks? Are not both races treated alike by the law of Indiana? Does not the law make it just as much a crime for a white man to marry a black woman as for a black woman to marry a white man, and *vice versa?* I presume there is no discrimination in this respect, and therefore your law forbidding marriages between whites and blacks operates alike on both races. This bill does not interfere with it. If the negro is denied the right to marry a white person, the white person is equally denied the right to marry the negro. I see no discrimination against either in this respect that does not apply to both. Make the penalty the same on all classes of people for the same offense, and then no one can complain.

"My object in bringing forward these bills was to bring to the attention of Congress something that was practical, something upon which I hoped we all could agree. I have said nothing in these bills which are pending, and which have been recommended by the Committee on the Judiciary—and I speak of both of them because they have both been alluded to in this discussion—about the political rights of the negro. On that subject it is known that there are differences of opinion, but I trust there are no differences of opinion among the friends of the constitutional amendment, among those who are for real freedom to the black man, as to his being entitled to equality in civil rights. If that is not going as far as some gentlemen would desire, I say to them it is a step in the right direction. Let us go that far, and, going that far, we have the coöperation of the Executive Department; for the President has told us 'Good faith requires the security of the freedmen in their liberty and their property, their right to labor, and their right to claim the just return of their labor.'

"Such, sir, is the language of the President of the United States in his annual message; and who in this chamber that is in favor of the freedom of the slave is not in favor of giving him equal and exact justice before the law? Sir, we can go along hand in hand together to the consummation of this great object of securing to every human being within the jurisdiction of the republic equal rights before the law, and I preferred to seek for points of agreement between all the departments of Government, rather than to hunt for points of divergence. I have not said any thing in my remarks about reconstruction. I have not attempted to discuss the question whether these States are in the Union or out of the Union, and so much has been said upon that subject that I am almost ready to exclaim with one of old, 'I know not whether they are in the body or out of the body; God knoweth.' It is enough for me to know that the State organizations in several States of the Union have been usurped and overthrown, and that up to the present time no State organization has been inaugurated in either of them which the various departments of Government, or any department of the Government, has recognized as placing the States in full possession of all the constitutional rights pertaining to States in full communion with the Union.

"The Executive has not recognized any one, for he still continues to exercise military jurisdiction and to suspend the privilege of the writ of *habeas corpus* in all of them. Congress has not recognized any of them, as we all know; and until Congress and the Executive do recognize them, let us make use of the Freedmen's Bureau, already established, to protect the colored race in their rights; and when these States shall be admitted, and the authority of the Freedmen's Bureau as a court shall cease and determine, as it must when civil authority is fully restored, let us provide, then, by other laws, for protecting all people in their equal civil rights before the law. If we can pass such measures, they receive executive sanction, and it shall be understood that it is the policy of the Government that the rights of the colored men are to be protected by the States if they will, but by the Federal Government if they will not; that at all hazards, and under all circumstances, there shall be impartiality among all classes in civil rights throughout the land. If we can do this, much of the apprehension and anxiety now existing in the loyal States will be allayed, and a great obstacle to an early restoration of the insurgent States to their constitutional relations in the Union will be removed.

"If the people in the rebellious States can be made to understand that it is the fixed and determined policy of the Government that the colored people shall be protected in their civil rights, they themselves will adopt the necessary measures to protect them; and that will dispense with the Freedmen's Bureau and all other Federal legislation for their protection. The design of these bills is not, as the Senator from Indiana would have us believe, to consolidate all power in the Federal Government, or to interfere with the domestic regulations of any of the States, except so far as to carry out a constitutional provision which is the supreme law of the land. If the States will not do it, then it is incumbent on Congress to do it. But if the States will do it, then the Freedmen's Bureau will be removed, and the authority proposed to be given by the other bill will have no operation.

"Sir, I trust there may be no occasion long to exercise the authority conferred by this bill. I hope that the people of the rebellious States themselves will conform to the existing condition of things. I do not expect them to change all their opinions and prejudices. I do not expect them to rejoice that they have been discomfited. But they acknowledge that the war is over; they agree that they can no longer contend in arms against the Government; they say they are willing to submit to its authority; they say in their State conventions that slavery shall no more exist among them. With the abolition of slavery should go all the badges of servitude which have been enacted for its maintenance and support. Let them all be abolished. Let the people of the rebellious States now be as zealous and as active in the passage of laws and the inauguration of measures to elevate, develop, and improve the negro as they have hitherto been to enslave and degrade him. Let them do justice and deal fairly with loyal Union men in their midst, and henceforth be themselves loyal, and this Congress will not have adjourned till the States whose inhabitants have been engaged in the rebellion will be restored, to their former position in the Union, and we shall all be moving on in harmony together."

On the day following the discussion above given, Mr. Cowan moved to amend the first section of the bill so that its operation would be limited to such States "as have lately been in rebellion." In supporting his amendment, Mr. Cowan remarked: "I have no idea of having this system extended over Pennsylvania. I think that as to the freedmen who make their appearance there, she will be able to take care of them and provide as well for them as any bureau which can be created here. I wish to confine the operation of this institution to the States which have been lately in rebellion."

To this Mr. Trumbull replied: "The Senator from Pennsylvania will see that the effect of that would be to exclude from the operation of the bureau the State of Kentucky and the State of Delaware, where the slaves have been emancipated by the constitutional amendment. The operation of the bureau will undoubtedly be chiefly confined to the States where slavery existed; but it is a fact which may not be known to the Senator from Pennsylvania, that during this war large numbers of slaves have fled to the Northern States bordering on the slaveholding territory.

"It is not supposed that the bill will have any effect in the State of Pennsylvania or in the State of Illinois, unless it might, perhaps, be at Cairo, where there has been a large number of these refugees congregated, without any means of support; they followed the army there at different times.

"The provision of the bill in regard to holding courts, and some other provisions, are confined entirely to the rebellious States, and will have no operation in any State which was not in insurrection against this Government. I make this explanation to the Senator from Pennsylvania, and I think he will see the necessity of the bureau going into Kentucky and some of the other States, as much as into any of the Southern rebellious States."

Mr. Guthrie was opposed to the extension of the bill to his State. He said: "I should like to know the peculiar reasons why this bill is to be extended to the State of Kentucky. She has never been in rebellion. Though she has been overrun by rebel armies, and her fields laid waste, she has always had her full quota in the Union armies, and the blood of her sons has marked the fields whereon they have fought. Kentucky does not want and does not ask this relief. The freedmen in Kentucky are a part of our population; and where the old, and lame, and halt, and blind, and infants require care and attention they obtain it from the counties. Our whole organization for the support of the poor, through the agencies of the magistrates in the several counties, is complete."

On the other hand, Mr. Creswell, of Maryland, saw a necessity for the operation of the bill in his State. He said: "I have re-

Engd by A H Ritchie

H. Wilson

ceived, within the last two or three weeks, letters from gentlemen of the highest respectability in my State, asserting that combinations of returned rebel soldiers have been formed for the express purpose of persecuting, beating most cruelly, and in some cases actually murdering the returned colored soldiers of the republic. In certain sections of my State, the civil law affords no remedy at all. It is impossible there to enforce against these people so violating the law the penalties which the law has prescribed for these offenses. It is, therefore, necessary, in my opinion, that this bill shall extend over the State of Maryland."

Mr. Cowan, in the course of a speech on the bill, said: "Thank God! we are now rid of slavery; that is now gone." He also said: "Let the friends of the negro, and I am one, be satisfied to treat him as he is treated in Pennsylvania; as he is treated in Ohio; as he is treated every-where where people have maintained their sanity upon the question."

Mr. Wilson said: "The Senator from Pennsylvania tells us that he is the friend of the negro. What, sir, he the friend of the negro! Why, sir, there has hardly been a proposition before the Senate of the United States for the last five years, looking to the emancipation of the negro and the protection of his rights, that the Senator from Pennsylvania has not sturdily opposed. He has hardly ever uttered a word upon this floor the tendency of which was not to degrade and to belittle a weak and struggling race. He comes here to-day and thanks God that they are free, when his vote and his voice for five years, with hardly an exception, have been against making them free. He thanks God, sir, that your work and mine, our work which has saved a country and emancipated a race, is secured; while from the word 'go,' to this time, he has made himself the champion of 'how not to do it.' If there be a man on the floor of the American Senate who has tortured the Constitution of the country to find powers to arrest the voice of this nation which was endeavoring to make a race free, the Senator from Pennsylvania is the man; and now he comes here and thanks God that a work which he has done his best to arrest, and which we have carried, is accomplished. I tell him to-day that we shall carry these other measures, whether he thanks God for them or not, whether he opposes them or not." [Laughter and applause in the galleries.]

After an extended discussion, the Senate refused, by a vote of thirty-three against eleven, to adopt the amendment proposed by Mr. Cowan.

The bill was further discussed during three successive days, Messrs. Saulsbury, Hendricks, Johnson, McDougall, and Davis speaking against the measure, and Messrs. Fessenden, Creswell, and Trumbull in favor of it. Mr. Garrett Davis addressed the Senate more than once on the subject, and on the last day of the discussion made a very long speech, which was answered by Mr. Trumbull. The Senator from Illinois, at the conclusion of his speech, remarked:

"What I have now said embraces, I believe, all the points of the long gentleman's speech except the sound and fury, and that I will not undertake to reply to."

"You mean the short gentleman's long speech," interposed some Senator.

"Did I say short?" asked Mr. Trumbull. "If so, it was a great mistake to speak of any thing connected with the Senator from Kentucky as short." [Laughter.]

"It is long enough to reach you," responded Mr. Davis.

The vote was soon after taken on the passage of the bill, with the following result:

YEAS—Messrs. Anthony, Brown, Chandler, Clark, Conness, Cragin, Creswell, Dixon, Doolittle, Fessenden, Foot, Foster, Grimes, Harris, Henderson, Howard, Howe, Kirkwood, Lane of Indiana, Lane of Kansas, Morgan, Morrill, Norton, Nye, Poland, Pomeroy, Ramsey, Sherman, Sprague, Stewart, Sumner, Trumbull, Van Winkle, Wade, Williams, Wilson, and Yates—37.

NAYS—Messrs. Buckalew, Davis, Guthrie, Hendricks, Johnson, McDougall, Riddle, Saulsbury, Stockton, and Wright—10.

ABSENT—Messrs. Cowan, Nesmith, and Willey—3.

The bill having passed, the question came up as to its title, which it was proposed to leave as reported by the committee: "A bill to enlarge the powers of the Freedmen's Bureau."

Mr. Davis moved to amend the title by substituting for it, "A bill to appropriate a portion of the public land in some of the Southern States and to authorize the United States Government to purchase lands to supply farms and build houses upon them for the freed negroes; to promote strife and conflict between the white and black races; and to invest the Freedmen's Bureau with unconstitutional powers to aid and assist the blacks, and to introduce military power to prevent the commissioner and other officers of said bureau from being restrained or held responsible in civil courts for their illegal acts in rendering such aid and assistance to the blacks, and for other purposes."

The President *pro tempore* pronounced the amendment "not in order, inconsistent with the character of the bill, derogatory to the Senate, a reproach to its members."

Mr. McDougall declared the proposed amendment "an insult to the action of the Senate."

The unfortunate proposition was quietly abandoned by its author, and passed over without further notice by the Senate. By unanimous consent, the title of the bill remained as first reported.

CHAPTER VII.

THE FREEDMEN'S BUREAU BILL IN THE HOUSE.

The Bill reported to the House—Mr. Eliot's Speech—History—Mr. Dawson *vs.* the Negro—Mr. Garfield—The Idol Broken—Mr. Taylor counts the Cost—Mr. Donnelly's Amendment—Mr. Kerr—Mr. Marshall on White Slavery—Mr. Hubbard—Mr. Moulton—Opposition from Kentucky—Mr. Ritter—Mr. Rousseau's Threat—Mr. Shanklin's Gloomy Prospect—Mr. Trimble's Appeal—Mr. McKee an exceptional Kentuckian—Mr. Grinnell on Kentucky—The Example of Russia—Mr. Phelps—Mr. Shellabarger's Amendment—Mr. Chanler—Mr. Stevens' Amendments—Mr. Eliot closes the Discussion—Passage of the Bill—Yeas and Nays.

ON the day succeeding the passage of the bill in the Senate, it was sent to the House of Representatives, and by them referred to the Select Committee on the Freedmen.

On the 30th of January, Mr. Eliot, Chairman of this committee, reported the bill to the House with amendments, mainly verbal alterations.

In a speech, advocating the passage of the bill, Mr. Eliot presented something of the history of legislation for the freedmen. He said: "On the 3d day of last March the bill establishing a Freedmen's Bureau became a law. It was novel legislation, without precedent in the history of any nation, rendered necessary by the rebellion of eleven slave States and the consequent liberation from slavery of four million persons whose unpaid labor had enriched the lands and impoverished the hearts of their relentless masters.

"At an early day, when the fortunes of war had shown alternate triumphs and defeats to loyal arms, and the timid feared and the disloyal hoped, it was my grateful office to introduce the first bill creating a bureau of emancipation. It was during the Thirty-seventh Congress. But, although the select committee to which the bill was referred was induced to agree that it should be reported to the House, it so happened that the distinguished Chairman, Judge White, of Indiana, did not succeed in reporting it for our action. At the beginning of the Thirty-eighth Congress it was again presented, and very soon was reported back to the House under the title of 'A bill to establish a Bureau of Freedmen's Affairs.' It was fully debated and passed by the House. The vote was sixty-nine in favor, and sixty-seven against the bill; but of the sixty-seven who opposed it, fifty-six had been counted against it, because of their political affinities. On the 1st of March, 1864, the bill went to the Senate. It came back to the House on the 30th of June, four days before the adjournment of Congress. To my great regret, the Senate had passed an amendment in the nature of a substitute, attaching this bureau to the Treasury Department; but it was too late to take action upon it then, and the bill was postponed until December. At that time the House non-concurred with the Senate, and a committee of conference was chosen. The managers of the two houses could not agree as to whether the War Department or the Treasury should manage the affairs of the bureau. They therefore agreed upon a bill creating an independent department neither attached to the War nor Treasury, but communicating directly with the President, and resting for its support upon the arm of the War Department. That bill was also passed by the House but was defeated in the Senate. Another Conference Committee was chosen, and that committee, whose chairman in the House was the distinguished gentleman from Ohio, then and now at the head of the Military Committee, agreed upon a bill attaching the bureau to the War Department, and embracing refugees as well as freedmen in its terms. That bill is now the law.

"The law was approved on the 3d of March, 1865. Nine months have not yet elapsed since its organization. The order from the War Department under which the bureau was organized bears date on the 12th of May, 1865. General Howard, who was then in command of the Department of Tennessee, was assigned as commissioner of the bureau. The bill became a law so late in the session that it was impossible for Congress to legislate any appropriation for its support. It was necessary, therefore, that the management of it should be placed in the hands of military officers, and fortunately the provisions of the bill permitted that to be done. General Howard was, as I stated, in command of the Department of Tennessee, when he was detailed to this duty. But on the 15th of May, that is to say, within three days after the order appointing him, was issued, he assumed the duties of his office.

"In the course of a few days, the commissioner of the bureau announced more particularly the policy which he designed to pursue. The whole supervision of the care of freedmen and of all lands which the law placed under the charge of the bureau was to be intrusted to assistant commissioners.

"Before a month had expired, head-quarters had been established for assistant commissioners at Richmond, Raleigh, Beaufort, Montgomery, Nashville, St. Louis, Vicksburg, New Orleans, and Jacksonville, and very shortly afterward assistant commissioners were designated for those posts of duty. They were required to possess themselves, as soon as practicable, with the duties incident to their offices, to quicken in every way they could and to direct the industry of the freedmen. Notice was given that the relief establishments which had been created by law under the operations of the War Department should be discontinued as soon as they could be consistently with the comfort and proper protection of the freedmen, and that every effort should be made—and I call the attention of gentlemen to the fact that that policy has been pursued throughout—that every effort should be made to render the freedmen, at an early day, self-supporting. The supplies that had been furnished by the Government were only to be continued so long as the actual wants of the freedmen seemed to require it. At that time there were all over the country refugees who were seeking their homes, and they were notified that, under the care of the bureau, they would be protected from abuse, and directed in their efforts to secure transportation and proper facilities for reaching home.

"Wherever there had been interruption of civil law, it was found impossible that the rights of freedmen could be asserted in the courts; and where there were no courts before which their rights could be brought for adjudication, military tribunals, provost-marshals' courts, were established, for the purpose of determining upon questions arising between freedmen or between freedmen and other parties; and that, also, has been continued to this day.

"The commissioners were instructed to permit the freedmen to select their own employers and to choose their own kind of service. All agreements were ordered to be free and mutual, and not to be compulsory. The old system that had prevailed of overseer labor was ordered to be repudiated by the commissioners who had charge of the laborers, and I believe there has been no time since the organization of the bureau when there have not been reports made to head-quarters at Washington of all labor contracts; and wherever any provisions had been inserted, by inadvertence or otherwise, that seemed unjustly to operate against the freedmen, they have been stricken out by direction of the commissioner here.

"In the course of the next month, action was taken by the commissioner respecting a provision of the law as it was passed in March, authorizing the Secretary of War to make issues of clothing and provisions, and the assistant commissioners were required carefully to ascertain whatever might be needed under that provision of the law, and to make periodical reports as to the demands made upon the Government through the bureau. Directions were given by the commissioner to his assistant commissioners to make repeated reports to him upon all the various subjects which had come under his charge—with regard to the number of freedmen, where they were, whether in camps or in colonies, or whether they were employed upon Government works, and stating, if they obtained supplies, how they were furnished, whether by donations or whether procured by purchase. Reports were also required as to all lands which had been put under the care of the bureau; and statements were called for showing descriptions of the lands, whether, in the language of the law, 'abandoned' or 'confiscated,' so that the bureau here could have full and complete information of all action of its agents throughout these States, and upon examination it could be determined where any specific lands which were under the charge of the bureau came from, and how they were derived.

"In the course of the summer, it became necessary to issue additional instructions. The commissioner found that his way was beset with difficulties; he was walking upon unknown ground; he was testing here and there questions involved in doubt. It was hardly possible at once and by one order to designate all that it would be needful for him to do, and, therefore, different instructions were issued from time to time from his office. The assistant commissioners were called upon thoroughly to examine, either by themselves or their agents, the respective districts allotted to them, to make inquiry as to the character of the freedmen under their charge, their ability to labor, their disposition to labor, and the circumstances under which they were placed, so that the aid, the care, and the protection which the law contemplated might be afforded to them as quickly and as economically as possible.

"The commissioner continually repeated his injunctions to his assistants to be sure that no compulsory or unpaid labor was tolerated, and that both the moral and intellectual condition of the freedmen should be improved as systematically and as quickly as practicable.

"When the bureau was first organized, indeed when it was first urged upon the attention of this House, it was stated and it was believed that the bureau would very shortly be self-sustaining. That was the idea from the beginning. And when it was stated here in debate that the bureau would probably be self-sustaining, it was supposed that from the lands abandoned, confiscated, sold, and the lands of the United States, which by the provisions of the bill had been placed under the care of the commissioner, these freedmen would be given an opportunity to earn substantially enough for the conduct of the bureau. And I have no doubt at all that such would have been the case had the original expectation been carried out.

"There were large tracts of land in Virginia and the other rebel States which were clearly applicable to this purpose. There was the source of supply—the lands and the labor. There were laborers enough, and there was rich land enough. At a very early day the abandoned lands were turned over to the care of the commissioners, and I supposed, and probably we all supposed, that the lands which in the language of the law were known as 'abandoned lands,' and those which were in the possession of the United States, would be appropriated to the uses of these freedmen. Within a week after the commissioner assumed the duties of his office, he found it necessary to issue an order substantially like this: Whereas, large amounts of lands in the State of Virginia and in other States have been abandoned, and are now in the possession of the freedmen, and are now under cultivation by them; and, whereas, the owners of those lands are now calling for their restoration, so as to deprive the freedmen of the results of their industry, it is ordered that the abandoned lands now under cultivation be retained by the freedmen until the growing crops can be secured, unless full and just compensation can be made them for their labor and its products.

"'The above order'—this is the part about which it appeared that some difference of judgment existed between the Executive and the commissioner of the bureau—'the above order will not be construed so as to relieve disloyal persons from the consequences of their disloyalty; and the application for the restoration of their lands by this class of persons will in no case be entertained by any military authority.'

"It was found, not a great while afterward, that the views which the President entertained as to his duty were somewhat in conflict with the provisions of this order; for it was held by the President that persons who had brought themselves within the range of his pardon and had secured it, and who had taken or did afterward take the amnesty oath, would be entitled, as one of the results of the pardon and of their position after the oath had been taken, to a restoration of their lands which had been assigned to freedmen. In consequence of this, an order was subsequently issued, well known as circular No. 15. And under the operation of that circular, on its appearing satisfactorily to any assistant commissioner that any property under his control is not 'abandoned,' as defined in the law, and that the United States have acquired no perfect right to it, it is to be restored and the fact reported to the commissioner. 'Abandoned' lands were to be restored to the owners pardoned by the President, by the assistant commissioners, to whom applications for such restoration were to be forwarded; and each application was to be accompanied by the pardon of the President and by a copy of the oath of amnesty prescribed in the President's proclamation, and also by a proof of title to the land. It must be obvious that the effect of this must have been to transfer from the care of the bureau to the owners very large portions of the land which had been relied upon for the support of the freedmen. Within a few weeks from the date of that order, no less than $800,000 worth of property in New

Orleans was transferred, and about one third of the whole property in North Carolina in possession of the bureau was given up; and the officer having charge of the land department reports that before the end of the year, in all probability, there will be under the charge of the commissioner little, if any, of the lands originally designed for the support of these freedmen.

"It is obvious, if these lands are to be taken, that other lands must be provided, or the freedmen will become a dead weight upon the Treasury, and the bill under consideration assigns other lands, in the place of those thus taken, from the unoccupied public lands of the United States."

On the following day, Mr. Dawson, of Pennsylvania, obtained the floor in opposition to the bill. His speech was not devoted to a discussion of the bill in question, but was occupied entirely with general political and social topics. The following extract indicates the tenor of the speech:

"Negro equality does not exist in nature. The African is without a history. He has never shown himself capable of self-government by the creation of a single independent State possessing the attributes which challenge the respect of others. The past is silent of any negro people who possessed military and civil organization, who cultivated the arts at home, or conducted a regular commerce with their neighbors. No African general has marched south of the desert, from the waters of the Nile to the Niger and Senegal, to unite by conquest the scattered territories of barbarous tribes into one great and homogeneous kingdom. No Moses, Solon, Lycurgus, or Alfred has left them a code of wise and salutary laws. They have had no builder of cities; they have no representatives in the arts, in science, or in literature; they have been without even a monument, an alphabet, or a hieroglyphic."

On the other hand, Mr. Garfield, of Ohio, among the friends of the measure, delivered a speech "on the Freedmen's Bureau Bill," in which the topic discussed was "Restoration of the Rebel States." In the course of his remarks Mr. Garfield said:

"Let the stars of heaven illustrate our constellation of States. When God launched the planets upon their celestial pathway, he bound them all by the resistless power of attraction to the central sun, around which they revolved in their appointed orbits. Each may be swept by storms, may be riven by lightnings, may be rocked by earthquakes, may be devastated by all the terrestrial forces and overwhelmed in ruin, but far away in the everlasting depths, the sovereign sun holds the turbulent planet in its place. This earth may be overwhelmed until the high hills are covered by the sea; it may tremble with earthquakes miles below the soil, but it must still revolve in its appointed orbit. So Alabama may overwhelm all her municipal institutions in ruin, but she can not annul the omnipotent decrees of the sovereign people of the Union. She must be held forever in her orbit of obedience and duty."

After having quoted Gibbon's narrative of the destruction of the collossal statue of Serapis by Theophilus, Mr. Garfield said: "So slavery sat in our national Capitol. Its huge bulk filled the temple of our liberty, touching it from side to side. Mr. Lincoln, on the 1st of January, 1863, struck it on the cheek, and the faithless and unbelieving among us expected to see the fabric of our institutions dissolve into chaos because their idol had fallen. He struck it again; Congress and the States repeated the blow, and its unsightly carcass lies rotting in our streets. The sun shines in the heavens brighter than before. Let us remove the carcass and leave not a vestige of the monster. We shall never have done that until we have dared to come up to the spirit of the Pilgrim covenant of 1620, and declare that all men shall be consulted in regard to the disposition of their lives, liberty, and property. The Pilgrim fathers proceeded on the doctrine that every man was supposed to know best what he wanted, and had the right to a voice in the disposition of himself."

Mr. Taylor, of New York, opposed the bill principally on the ground of the expense involved in its execution. After having presented many columns of figures, Mr. Taylor arrived at this conclusion: "The cost or proximate cost of the bureau for one year, confining its operation to the hitherto slave States, will be $25,251,600. That it is intended to put the bureau in full operation in every county and parish of the hitherto slave States, including Delaware, Maryland, Kentucky, and Missouri, I have not the least doubt, nor have I any doubt but that it is intended to extend it into parts of some of the border States."

Mr. Donnelly moved to amend the bill by inserting the provision that "the commissioner may provide a common-school education for all refugees and freedmen who shall apply therefor."

10

He advocated education as an efficient means of restoration for the South. He presented ample tables of statistics, and summed up the results in their bearing upon his argument as follows:

"The whole United States, with a population of 27,000,000, contains 834,106 illiterate persons, and of these 545,177 are found in the Southern States with a population of 12,000,000. In other words, the entire populous North contains but 288,923, while the sparsely-settled South contains 545,177."

As an argument for the passage of the bill, he answered the question, "What has the South done for the black man since the close of the rebellion?"

"In South Carolina it is provided that all male negroes between two and twenty, and all females between two and eighteen, shall be bound out to some 'master.' The adult negro is compelled to enter into contract with a master, and the district judge, not the laborer, is to fix the value of the labor. If he thinks the compensation too small and will not work, he is a vagrant, and can be hired out for a term of service at a rate again to be fixed by the judge. If a hired negro leaves his employer he forfeits his wages for the whole year.

"The black code of Mississippi provides that no negro shall own or hire lands in the State; that he shall not sue nor testify in court against a white man; that he must be employed by a master before the second Monday in January, or he will be bound out—in other words, sold into slavery; that if he runs away the master may recover him, and deduct the expenses out of his wages; and that if another man employs him he will be liable to an action for damages. It is true, the President has directed General Thomas to disregard this code; but the moment the military force is withdrawn from the State that order will be of no effect.

"The black code of Alabama provides that if a negro who has contracted to labor fails to do so, he shall be punished with damages; and if he runs away he shall be punished as a vagrant, which probably means that he shall be sold to the highest bidder for a term of years; and that any person who entices him to leave his master, as by the offer of better wages, shall be guilty of a misdemeanor, and may be sent to jail for six months; and further, that these regulations include all persons of negro blood to the third generation, though one parent in each generation shall be pure white; that is, down to the man who has but one eighth negro blood in his veins.

After quoting the black codes of other States, the speaker thus epitomized their substance: "All this means simply the reëstablishment of slavery.

"1. He shall work at a rate of wages to be fixed by a county judge or a Legislature made up of white masters, or by combinations of white masters, and not in any case by himself.

"2. He shall not leave that master to enter service with another. If he does he is pursued as a fugitive, charged with the expenses of his recapture, and made to labor for an additional period, while the white man who induced him to leave is sent to jail.

"3. His children are taken from him and sold into virtual slavery.

"4. If he refuses to work, he is sold to the highest bidder for a term of months or years, and becomes, in fact, a slave.

"5. He can not better his condition; there is no future for him; he shall not own property; he shall not superintend the education of his children; neither will the State educate them.

"6. If he is wronged, he has no remedy; for the courts are closed against him."

Mr. Kerr, of Indiana, addressed the House on the subject of reconstruction, maintaining, by extended arguments and quotations from learned authorities, that the rebel States were still in the Union. He concluded his speech by opposing the bill under consideration on the ground of its expense: "It involves the creation of a small army of agents and commissioners, whose jurisdiction and control shall pervade the whole country, shall extend into every State, into every congressional district, into every county, into every township and city of this broad Union; provided, only, that they can find some freedmen or refugees upon whom to exercise their jurisdiction. I submit that, before a measure of this kind should be adopted, we should reflect most carefully upon what we are doing. We should remember that this country is now almost crushed into the very earth with its accumulated burden of public debt, of State debts, of county debts, of city debts, of township debts, of individual debts. We should bear in mind that we may impose upon the people of this country, by this kind of latitudinarian and most dangerous legislation, a burden that is too heavy to be borne, and against which the day may come when the people, as one man, will feel themselves called upon to protest in such a manner as forever to overthrow that kind of legislation, and condemn to merited reproach those who favor it."

On a subsequent day of the discussion, Mr. Marshall, of Illinois, spoke against the bill. He put much stress upon an objection to which nearly all the opponents of the bill had referred, namely, that Congress had no warrant in the Constitution for passing such a measure. He said: "Instead of this being called a bill for the protection of freedmen and refugees, it ought to be called a bill for the purpose of destroying the Constitution of the United States, and subjecting the people thereof to military power and domination. That would be a much more appropriate title."

Mr. Marshall was opposed to bestowing any thing in charity. "I deny," said he, "that this Federal Government has any authority to become the common almoner of the charities of the people. I deny that there is any authority in the Federal Constitution to authorize us to put our hands into their pockets and take therefrom a part of their hard earnings in order to distribute them as charity. I deny that the Federal Government was established for any such purpose, or that there is any authority or warrant in the Constitution for the measures which are proposed in this most extraordinary bill."

He viewed with horror the slavery which the head of the War Department could impose upon the people by virtue of the provisions of this bill. "He is to send his military satraps," said Mr. Marshall, "into every county and district of these States; and they may enslave and put down the entire white people of the country by virtue of this law." He saw in the bill power "to rob the people by unjust taxation; to take the hard earnings from the white people of the West, who, unless wiser counsels prevail, will themselves soon be reduced to worse than Egyptian bondage. I demand to be informed here upon this floor by what power you put your hands into their pockets and drag from them their money to carry out the purposes of this measure."

Mr. Hubbard, of Connecticut, made a short speech in reply to the speaker last quoted. He said: "The gentleman from Illinois, some twenty times in the course of his eloquent speech this morning, called upon some one to tell him where Congress gets the power to enact such a law as this. In the first place, I commend to him to read the second section of the article of the immortal amendment of the Constitution, giving to Congress power to pass all appropriate laws and make all appropriate legislation for the purpose of carrying out its provisions. I commend to his careful study the spirit of the second section of that immortal amendment, and I think, if he will study it with a willingness to be convinced, he will see that it has given to this Congress full power in the premises. Moreover, sir, I read in the Constitution that Congress has been at all times charged with the duty of providing for the public welfare; and if Congress shall deem that the public welfare requires this enactment, it is the sworn duty of every member to give the bill his support.

"Sir, there is an old maxim of law in which I have very considerable faith, that regard must be had to the public welfare; and this maxim is said to be the highest law. It is the law of the Constitution, and in the light of that Constitution as amended I find ample power for the enactment of this law. It is the duty of Congress to exercise its power in such a time as this, in a time of public peril; and I hope that nobody on this side of the House will be so craven as to want courage to come up to the question and give his vote for the bill. It is necessary to provide for the public welfare."

Mr. Moulton, of Illinois, spoke in favor of the bill. Of the oft-repeated objection that "this bill is in violation of the Constitution of the United States," he said: "This is the very argument that we have heard from the other side of this chamber for the last five years with reference to every single measure that has been proposed to this House for the prosecution of the war for the Union. No measure has been passed for the benefit of the country, for the prosecution of this war, for the defense of your rights and mine, but has been assailed by gentlemen on the opposite side of this House with the argument that the whole thing was unconstitutional."

He then proceeded to set forth at length the authority of Congress to pass such a bill.

Very strenuous opposition to the passage of the bill was made by most of the members from Kentucky. Mr. Ritter, of that State, uttered his earnest protest at considerable length against the measure. He presented his views of the "grand purposes and designs of those who introduced this bill." In his opinion they intended "to commence a colony in each one of the five States above named, which is ultimately to drive out the entire white population of those States and fill their places with the negro race. And whether this is the design or not, it is certain, in my judgment, to have this effect. And they could not have devised a more effectual scheme for that purpose.

"Sir, it is not to be expected that the two races will live contentedly where there are large numbers of the colored people living near to neighborhoods settled with white persons. Experience has proved to many of us that wherever large numbers of colored people live, that the white people living within five or ten miles of the place become sufferers to a very large extent. Now, sir, if this should be the case (as I have no doubt it will) in the States in which you propose to establish these people, the whites and blacks will disagree to such an extent that, when people find that the colored people are permanently established, they will be compelled, in self defense, to seek a home somewhere else. No doubt, Mr. Speaker, but that those who prepared this bill saw that the difficulties and disagreements to which I have just alluded would arise, and hence they require that military jurisdiction and protection shall be extended, so as to give safety in their movements; and if the white inhabitants become dissatisfied, the commissioner is prepared with authority by this bill to buy them out and put the negroes upon the land."

He thus presented his calculation of the cost of carrying out the bill as an argument against it: "In 1822 the ordinary expenses of the Government were $9,827,643, and in 1823 the expenses amounted to the sum of $9,784,154. Now, sir, who could have thought at that day that in the comparatively short time of forty-three years it would require the sum of even $12,000,000 to fix up a machinery alone for the benefit of three or four million negroes, and more especially, sir, when it is understood that in 1820 we had a population, including white and colored, of 9,633,545. Mr. Speaker, how long will it be at this rate—when we take into consideration the fact that our Government proper, besides this little bureau machine, is now costing us hundreds of millions of dollars—how long, sir, will it be before we have to call in the services of Mr. Kennedy, of census notoriety, to estimate the amount of the debt we owe?"

Mr. Rousseau, of Kentucky, in defining his position, said: "I am not a Republican; I was a Whig and a Union man, and belong to the Union party, and I am sorry to say that the Union party and the Republican party are not always convertible terms."

Mr. Rousseau urged against the Freedmen's Bureau Bill the wrongs and oppressions which its abuses heaped upon the people of the South. In the course of his speech Mr. Rousseau quoted what he had said on one occasion to an official of the Freedmen's Bureau: "I said to him, 'if you intend to arrest white people on the *ex parte* statements of negroes, and hold them to suit your convenience for trial, and fine and imprison them, then I say that I oppose you; and if you should so arrest and punish me, I would kill you when you set me at liberty; and I think that you would do the same to a man who would treat you in that way, if you are the man I think you are, and the man you ought to be to fill your position here.'"

This extract has considerable importance as being the occasion of an unfortunate personal difficulty between Mr. Rousseau and Mr. Grinnell, of Iowa, narrated in a subsequent chapter. The latter portion of Mr. Rousseau's speech was devoted to the subject of reconstruction. He was followed by Mr. Shanklin, of Kentucky. He characterized the Freedmen's Bureau as a "gigantic monster." He declared that "the effect of this measure upon the negro population will be to paralyze their energy, destroy their industry, and make them paupers and vagabonds." He saw "revolution and ruin" in prospect. "I affirm," said he, "that in legislating for those States, or without allowing them any representation in these halls, you are violating one of the cardinal principles of republican government; you are tearing down the main pillar upon which our whole fabric of Government rests; you are sowing broadcast the seeds of revolution and ruin. Mr. Speaker, if the object of gentlemen here is to restore harmony and peace and prosperity throughout the Union, why do they adopt measures thus insulting, tyrannical, and oppressive in their character? Is this the way to restore harmony and peace and prosperity? How can you expect to gain the respect and affection of those people by heaping upon them insult and injustice? If they have the spirit of their ancestors, you may crush them, you may slay them, but you can never cause them to love you or respect you; and they ought not while you force upon them measures which are only intended to degrade them."

Mr. Trimble, of Kentucky, viewed the question in a similar light to that in which it was regarded by his colleague. "I hold," said he, "this bill is in open and plain violation of that provision of the Constitution. There exists no power in this Government to deprive a citizen of the United States of his property, to take away the hard earnings of his own industry and bestow them upon this class of citizens. The only way you can take property in South Carolina, Georgia, or any other State, is to take that property under the Constitution of the United States and the laws passed in pursuance thereof."

He closed his speech with the following appeal: "I appeal to my friends who love this Union, who love it for all the memories of the past, who love it because it has protected them and theirs; I appeal to them to pause and reflect before they press this measure upon these people; for I tell you that, in my judgment, the effects of the provisions of this bill to us as a nation will not be told in our lifetimes. If legislation of this character is to be pressed here, I awfully fear hope will sink within us. Our love for this Union and desire for its restoration will be greatly weakened and estranged."

Mr. McKee alone, of all the Representatives from Kentucky, was favorable to the bill. The opponents of the measure had spoken of it as a "monstrous usurpation." "We have heard that talk," said Mr. McKee, "for more than four years here. What bill has been introduced into and passed by Congress since this war began that this same party has not been accustomed to denounce as a monstrous usurpation of power? When the President of the United States issued his call for troops they cried out, 'A monstrous usurpation of power.' When he sent a requisition to the Governor of my own State, what was the response? 'Not a man, not a dollar, to prosecute this wicked war against our Southern brethren.' And the Union party, God help them! in Kentucky, indorsed the sentiment at that day. I did not belong to that part of the Union party; I never belonged to that 'neutrality concern.' I never put in my oar to help propel that ship which was in favor of thundering forth with its cannon against the North and the South alike. I never belonged to that party which said, 'We will stand as a wall of fire against either side.'

I thank God I never stood upon but one side, and that was the side of my country, against treason, against oppression, against wrong in all its forms."

In arguing the necessity for some such legislation as that provided in this bill, Mr. McKee asked, "Has any Southern State given the freedmen 'their full rights and full protection?' Is there a solitary State of those that have been in rebellion, (and I include my own State with the rest, because, although she has never been, by proclamation, declared a State in rebellion, I think she has been one of the most rebellious of the whole crew,) is there a single one of these States that has passed laws to give the freedmen full protection? In vain we wait an affirmative response. Until these States have done so, says this high authority, the Freedmen's Bureau is a necessity. This is to my mind a sufficient answer to the arguments of gentlemen on the other side. In none of those States has the black man a law to protect him in his rights, either of person or property. He can sue in a court of justice in my State, but he can command no testimony in his prosecution or defense unless the witness be a white man. We have one code for the white man, another for the black. Is this justice? Where is your court of justice in any Southern State where the black man can secure protection? Again there is no response."

Mr. Grinnell, of Iowa, a member of the committee that had reported this bill, took the floor in its favor. Much having been said by Representatives of Kentucky in reference to that State, Mr. Grinnell remarked: "I can not forget, when I hear these extravagant claims set up here, that her Governor, in the first year of the rebellion, refused to honor the call for troops made by the President of the United States in our darkest hour; nor can I forget that when her soldiers wished to organize regiments they were obliged to cross the Ohio River into the State of Indiana, that they might organize them free from the interference of the power of Kentucky neutrality. That is a fact in history, and I can not overlook it, when gentlemen here arraign the President of the United States because he has seen fit to suspend the privilege of the writ of *habeas corpus* in the State of Kentucky."

"Let us see," said Mr. Grinnell, in a subsequent part of his speech, "what are the laws of Kentucky which are so just and honorable and equitable. The white man in Kentucky can testify in the courts; the black man can testify against himself. The white man can vote; the black man can not. The white man, if he commits an offense, is tried by a jury of his peers; the black man is tried by his enlightened, unprejudiced superiors. The rape of a negro woman by a white man is no offense; the rape of a white woman by a negro man is punishable by death, and the Governor of the State can not commute.

"A white man may come into Kentucky when he pleases; the free negro who comes there is a felon, though a discharged soldier, and wounded in our battles. A white man in Kentucky may keep a gun; if a black man buys a gun he forfeits it, and pays a fine of five dollars if presuming to keep in his possession a musket which he has carried through the war. Arson of public buildings, if committed by a white man, is punished by imprisonment in the penitentiary for a term of from seven to twenty-one years; if committed by a black man, the punishment is death. Arson of a warehouse, etc., when committed by a white man, is punished by imprisonment in the penitentiary from one to six years; when committed by a negro, the penalty is death.

"If a white man is guilty of insurrection or rebellion, he is punished by being called 'chivalrous.' I instance the rebel General Forest, who murdered white men at Fort Pillow, and is reputed the most popular man South. If a negro rebels, or conspires to rebel, he is punished with death. These are specimens."

Referring to the benefits conferred by the Freedmen's Bureau upon Kentucky, Mr. Grinnell remarked: "As it is asserted that this Freedmen's Bureau is a partial, unnecessary, speculating affair, I wish to call attention to the fact that in the State of Kentucky, during the last five months, more white refugees than freedmen, in the proportion of seven and one-fourth to one, have received rations at the hands of the Government; that this bureau has kept in schools in the State of Kentucky fourteen thousand black people.

In further illustration of the work accomplished by this instrumentality, he said: "This bureau is in charge of 800,000 acres of land and 1,500 pieces of town property. It has issued more than 600,000 rations to refugees, and 3,500,000 to freedmen. It has treated 2,500 refugees in hospitals, and decently buried 227 of them. It has treated 45,000 freedmen, and made the graves for 6,000 of the number. Transportation has been furnished to 1,700 refugees and 1,900 freedmen. In the schools there are 80,000 people that have been instructed by this bureau. And now it is proposed to leave all these children of misfortune to the tender mercies of a people of whom it is true by the Spanish maxim, 'Since I have wronged you I have hated you.' I never can. Our authority to take care of them is founded in the Constitution; else it is not worthy to be our great charter. It gives authority to feed Indian tribes, though our enemies, and a just interpretation can not restrain us in clothing and feeding unfortunate friends. In providing schools, we can turn to the same authority which led to the gift of millions of acres of the public domain for the purpose of establishing agricultural colleges in this country."

He referred to Russia for example of what should be done in such an emergency: "We should be worse than barbarians to leave these people where they are, landless, poor, unprotected; and I commend to gentlemen who still cling to the delusion that all is well, to take lessons of the Czar of the Russias, who, when he enfranchised his people, gave them lands and school-houses, and invited school-masters from all the world to come there and instruct them. Let us hush our national songs; rather gird on sack-cloth, if wanting in moral courage to reap the fruits of our war by being just and considerate to those who look up to us for temporary counsel and protection. Care and education are cheaper for the nation than neglect, and nothing is plainer in the counsels of heaven or the world's history."

An allusion made by Mr. Grinnell to the speech of Mr. Rosseau, provoked the personal assault to be described hereafter.

Mr. Raymond having the floor for a personal explanation, took occasion to make the following remarks in reference to the bill: "I have no apprehensions as to the practical workings of this law. So far as I have been able to collect information from all quarters—and I have taken some pains to do so—I find that this law, like most other laws on our statute books, works well where it is well administered. The practical operations of this bureau will depend upon the character of the agents into whose hands its management is intrusted. I certainly have no apprehension in this respect. I do not for one moment fear that the agents who will be appointed to carry this law into execution will not use the powers conferred upon them for the furtherance of the great object which we all have in view—the reconciliation, the protection, the security of all classes of those who are now our fellow-citizens in the Southern States."

Mr. Phelps, of Maryland, made a speech indorsing the principle of the bill, but objecting to some of its details. His objections were removed by the presentation and acceptance of the following amendment by Mr. Shellabarger, of Ohio: "No person shall be deemed destitute, suffering, or dependent upon the Government for support, within the meaning of this act, who, being able to find employment, could, by proper industry and exertion, avoid such destitution, suffering and dependence."

Mr. Chanler made a long speech in opposition to the bill. He gave particular attention to the speech of Mr. Donnelly, of Minnesota, who had advocated education as a necessity for the South. "The malignant party spirit and sectional hate," said Mr. Chanler, "that runs through this whole statement, needs no illustration." After presenting voluminous extracts from speeches, letters, and public documents, Mr. Chanler summed up his objections to the bill in the following words: "Our people are not willing to live under military rule.

"This bureau is under military rule. It proposes to perpetuate and strengthen itself by the present bill.

"It founds an '*imperium in imperio*' to protect black labor against white labor.

"It excludes the foreign immigrant from the lands given to the native-born negro.

"It subjects the white native-born citizen to the ignominy of surrendering his patrimony, his self-respect, and his right to labor into the hands of negroes, idle, ignorant, and misled by fanatic, selfish speculators."

Mr. Stevens desired to amend the bill by striking out the limitation to three years given the possessory titles conferred by General Sherman, and rendering them perpetual. This amendment the House were unwilling to accept. Mr. Stevens further proposed to strike out the proviso "unless as punishment for crime, whereof the party shall have been duly convicted," giving as a reason for this amendment, "I know that men are convicted of assault and battery, and sentenced to slavery down there. I have authentic evidence of that fact in several letters, and, therefore, I propose to strike out those words."

This amendment was adopted. Another important amendment proposed by the committee was the limitation of the operation of the bill to States in which the writ of *habeas corpus* was suspended on the 1st of February, 1866. Mr. Eliot closed the debate by answering some objections to the bill, and presenting some official documents proving the beneficent results of the bureau, especially in the State of Kentucky.

On the 6th of February the question was taken, and the bill passed by the following vote:

Yeas—Messrs. Alley, Allison, Ames, Anderson, Delos R. Ashley, James M. Ashley, Baker, Baldwin, Banks, Barker, Baxter, Beaman, Benjamin, Bidwell, Bingham, Blaine, Blow, Boutwell, Brandegee, Bromwell, Broomall, Bundy, Reader W. Clarke, Sidney Clarke, Cobb, Conkling, Cook, Cullom, Darling, Davis, Dawes, Defrees, Delano, Deming, Dixon, Donnelly, Driggs, Dumont, Eckley, Eggleston, Eliot, Farnsworth, Farquhar, Ferry, Garfield, Grinnell, Griswold, Hale, Abner C. Harding, Hart, Hayes, Henderson, Higby, Hill, Holmes, Hooper, Hotchkiss, Asahel W. Hubbard, Chester D. Hubbard, Demas Hubbard, John H. Hubbard, James R. Hubbell, James Humphrey, Ingersoll, Jenckes, Julian, Kasson, Kelley, Kelso, Ketcham, Kuykendall, Laflin, Latham, George V. Lawrence, William Lawrence, Loan, Longyear, Lynch, Marston, Marvin, McClurg, McIndoe, McKee, McRuer, Mercur, Miller, Moorhead, Morrill, Morris, Moulton, Myers, Newell, O'Neill, Orth, Paine, Patterson, Perham, Phelps, Pike, Plants, Pomeroy, Price, William H. Randall, Raymond, Alexander H. Rice, John H. Rice, Rollins, Sawyer, Schenck, Scofield, Shellabarger, Smith, Spalding, Starr, Stevens, Stilwell, Thayer, Francis Thomas, John L. Thomas, Trowbridge, Upson, Van Aernam, Burt Van Horn, Robert T. Van Horn, Ward, Warner, Elihu B. Washburne, William B. Washburn, Welker, Wentworth, Whaley, Williams, James F. Wilson, Stephen F. Wilson, Windom, and Woodbridge.—136.

Nays—Messrs. Boyer, Brooks, Chanler, Dawson, Eldridge, Finck, Glossbrenner, Grider, Aaron Harding, Harris, Hogan, Edwin N. Hubbell, James M. Humphrey, Kerr, Le Blond, Marshall, McCullough, Niblack, Nicholson, Noell, Samuel J. Randall, Ritter, Rogers, Ross, Rosseau, Shanklin, Sitgreaves, Strouse, Taber, Taylor, Thornton, Trimble, and Wright—33.

Not Voting—Messrs. Ancona, Bergen, Buckland, Culver, Denison, Goodyear, Hulburd, Johnson, Jones, Radford, Sloan, Voorhees, and Winfield—13.

CHAPTER VIII.

THE SENATE AND THE VETO MESSAGE.

MR. TRUMBULL ON THE AMENDMENTS OF THE HOUSE—MR. GUTHRIE EXHIBITS FEELING—MR. SHERMAN'S DELIBERATE CONCLUSION—MR. HENDERSON'S SOVEREIGN REMEDY—MR. TRUMBULL ON PATENT MEDICINES—MR. MCDOUGALL A WHITE MAN—MR. REVERDY JOHNSON ON THE POWER TO PASS THE BILL—CONCURRENCE OF THE HOUSE—THE VETO MESSAGE—MR. LANE, OF KANSAS—HIS EFFORTS FOR DELAY—MR. GARRETT DAVIS—MR. TRUMBULL'S REPLY TO THE PRESIDENT—THE QUESTION TAKEN—YEAS AND NAYS—FAILURE OF PASSAGE.

ON the 7th of February the amendments of the House to the Freedmen's Bureau Bill were presented to the Senate, and referred to the Committee on the Judiciary.

On the following day Mr. Trumbull, chairman of this committee, reported certain amendments to the amendments made by the House of Representatives. Mr. Trumbull said: "The House of Representatives have adopted a substitute for the whole bill, but it is the Senate bill *verbatim*, with a few exceptions, which I will endeavor to point out. The title of the bill has been changed, to begin with. It was called as it passed the Senate 'A bill to enlarge the powers of the Freedmen's Bureau.' The House has amended the title so as to make it read, 'A bill to amend an act entitled "An act to establish a Bureau for the Relief of Freedmen and Refugees," and for other purposes.' Of course, there is no importance in that.

"The first amendment which the House has made, and the most important one, will be found to commence in the eighth line of the first section. The House has inserted words limiting the operation of the Freedmen's Bureau to those sections of country within which the writ of *habeas corpus* was suspended on the 1st day of February, 1866. As the bill passed the Senate, it will be remembered that it extended to refugees and freedmen in all parts of the United States, and the President was authorized to divide the section of country containing such refugees and freedmen into districts. The House amend that so as to authorize the President to divide the section of country within which the privilege of the writ of *habeas corpus* was suspended on the 1st day of February, 1866, containing such refugees and freedmen, into districts. The writ of *habeas corpus* on the 1st day of February last was suspended in the late rebellious States, including Kentucky, and in none other. The writ of *habeas corpus* was restored by the President's proclamation in Maryland, in Delaware, and in Missouri, all of which have been slaveholding States.

"As the bill passed the Senate, it will be observed it only extended to refugees and freedmen in the United States, wherever they might be, and the President was authorized to divide the region of country containing such refugees and freedmen, and it had no operation except in States where there were refugees and freedmen. The House has limited it so that it will not have operation in Maryland, or Delaware, or Missouri, or any of the Northern States."

After Mr. Trumbull had stated the other and less important amendments made by the House, the Senate proceeded to consider the amendments proposed by the Judiciary Committee, the first of which was to strike out the words "within which the privileges of the writ of *habeas corpus* was suspended on the 1st day of February, 1866."

Mr. Trumbull said: "I wish to say upon that point that the bill as it passed the Senate can have no operation except in regions of country where there are refugees and freedmen. It is confined to those districts of country, and it could not have operation in most of the loyal States. But it is desirable, as I am informed, and it was so stated by one of the Senators from Maryland, that the operations of this bill should be extended to Maryland. It may be necessary that it should be extended to Missouri, and possibly to Delaware. I trust not; but the authority to extend it there ought to exist, if there should be occasion for it. The only objection I have to limiting the operation of the bill to the late slaveholding States is, that I think it bad legislation, when we are endeavoring to break down discrimination and distinction, to pass a law which is to operate in one State of the Union and not in another. I would rather that the law should be general, although I am fully aware that there is nothing for the law to operate upon in most of the States of the Union. I do not feel quite willing to vote upon Kentucky, for instance, a law that I am not willing to have applicable to the State of Illinois, if such a state of facts exists as that the law can operate in Illinois. I prefer, therefore, to have the bill in the shape in which it passed the Senate, and such was the opinion of the Committee on the Judiciary."

Mr. Guthrie, of Kentucky, spoke with much feeling upon the bearings of the bureau upon his State: "You will have to acknowledge these States or you will have to do worse. The passage of this system of bills is a dissolution of the Union, and you can not help it. It will be impossible for you to carry on this Government under any such system. When the Union is not to be restored, when there is nothing of that feeling to make the people endure, do you suppose they will endure forever? Do you suppose this bill will attach the people in these eleven States more thoroughly to the Union than they felt when they reörganized their State governments, passed laws manumitting their slaves, electing their Legislatures, and doing all that was indicated as necessary to be done? Do you suppose that there will ever come a time, under this bill, that they will desire to become members of this Union once more? I see in this bill exactly how Kentucky is tolerated here; for as to having part in this legislation, when she is charged openly with being ruled at home by rebels, our counsels can be of no good here; but still we are not to be driven from the Union, and from raising our voice in favor of it, and raising it in favor of conciliation and confidence from one section to the other. Gentlemen do not get these doctrines of hatred and vengeance from the Gospel. These are not the doctrines taught by the Savior of the world. While you cry for justice to the African, you are not slow to commit wrong and outrage on the white race.

"Sir, there were rebels in all the States, and will be again if you drive these people to desperation. The Senator from Massachusetts, if I understood his language aright, threatened us with war or worse if we did not yield to his suggestions, and the Senator from Indiana intimated very strongly the same thing. You have strength enough to carry these measures, if it is the sentiment of the nation; but we are not a people to be alarmed by words or threats."

Mr. Sherman had been, as he said, "during this whole debate, rather a spectator than a participant." Not desiring to commit himself too hastily, he had reserved his opinion that he might act and vote understandingly, without feeling, or prejudice, or passion. It was after full reflection that he voted for the bill so harshly characterized by the Senator from Kentucky, who had evinced a degree of feeling entirely uncalled for. Mr. Sherman said further: "I look upon the Freedman's Bureau Bill as simply a temporary protection to the freedmen in the Southern States. We are bound by every consideration of honor, by every obligation that can rest on any people, to protect the freedmen from the rebels of the Southern States; ay, sir, and to protect them from the loyal men of the Southern States. We know that, on account of the prejudices instilled by the system of slavery pervading all parts of the Southern States, the Southern people will not do justice to the freedmen of those States. We know that in the course of the war the freedmen have been emancipated; that they have aided us in this conflict; and, therefore, we are bound, by every consideration of honor, faith, and of public morals, to protect and maintain all the essential incidents of freedom to them. I have no doubt that in doing this we shall encounter the prejudices not only of rebels, but of loyal men; but still the obligation and guarantee is none the less binding on us. We must maintain their freedom, and with it all the incidents and all the rights of freedom."

Mr. Henderson, of Missouri, like the Senator from Ohio, had hitherto taken no part in the discussion. He was opposed to the limitations placed upon the bill by the House of Representatives. "I would not have voted for it if it had not been carried to my own State; and if this amendment of the House of Representatives is to be adopted, I will not vote for the bill. I want the bill to be made general.. If it is to be made special, if it is to be applied to Kentucky only, I appreciate the feeling that drove my friend from Kentucky to make the most unfortunate remark that has been made upon the floor of the Senate since 1861. I sincerely hope, for the good of the country, that the distinguished Senator may see fit to take back what he said a few moments ago.

"Sir, we have had enough of disunion. I hope that no Senator in the future will rise upon this floor and talk, under any circumstances whatever, of another war of rebellion against the constituted authorities of this country. My God! are we again to pass through the scenes of blood through which we have passed for the last four years? Are we to have this war repeated? No Freedmen's Bureau Bill, no bill for the protection of the rights of any body, shall ever drive me to dream of such a thing."

Mr. Henderson thought a better protection for the negro than the Freedmen's Bureau would be the ballot. He said: "I live in a State that was a slaveholding State until last January a year ago. I have been a slaveholder all my life until the day when the ordinance of emancipation was passed in my State. I advocated it, and have advocated emancipation for the last four years, at least since this war commenced. Do you want to know how to protect the freedmen of the Southern States? This bill is useless for that purpose. It is not the intention of the honorable Senators on this floor from Northern States, who favor this bill, to send military men to plunder the good people of Kentucky. It is an attempt to enforce this moral and religious sentiment of the people of the Northern States. Sir, these freedmen will be protected. The decree of Almighty God has gone forth, as it went forth in favor of their freedom originally, that they shall be endowed with all the rights that belong to other men. Will you protect them? Give them the ballot, Mr. President, and then they are protected."

In reference to the remarks by Mr. Henderson, Mr. Trumbull said: "The zeal of my friend from Missouri seems to have run away with him. Having come from being a slaveholder to the position of advocating universal negro suffrage as the sovereign remedy for every thing, he manifests a degree of zeal which I have only seen equaled, I confess, by some of the dicoverers of patent medicines who have found a grand specific to cure all diseases! Why, he says this bureau is of no account; give the negro the ballot, and that will stop him from starving; that will feed him; that will educate him! You have got on your hands to-day one hundred thousand feeble, indigent, infirm colored population that would starve and die if relief were not afforded; and the Senator from Missouri tells you, 'This is all nonsense; give them the right of suffrage, and that is all they want.' This to feed the hungry and clothe the naked! He has voted for these bills; but if you will only just give the right of suffrage, you do not want to take care of any starving man, any orphan child, any destitute and feeble person that can not take care of himself! It is the most sovereign remedy that I have heard of since the days of Townsend's Sarsaparilla."

Referring to the feeling manifested by Mr. Guthrie, Mr. Trumbull said: "God forbid that I should put a degradation on the people of Kentucky. I never thought of such a thing. I would sooner cut off my right hand than do such a thing. What is it that so excites and inflames the mind of the Senator from Kentucky that he talks about the degradation that is to be put upon her, the plunder of her people, the injustice that is to be done her inhabitants? Why, sir, a bill to help the people of Kentucky to take care of the destitute negroes, made free without any property whatever, without the means of support, left to starve and to die unless somebody cares for them; and we propose in the Congress of the United States to help to do it. Is that a degradation? Is that an injustice? Is that the way to rob a people?"

Mr. McDougall having subsequently obtained the floor, made the remark: "I, being a white man, say for the white men and white women that they will take care of themselves. This bill was not made for white women or white men, or white men and women's children."

This brought out the following statistical statement from Mr. Trumbull: "I have before me the official report, which shows the consolidated number of rations issued in the different districts and States during the month of June, July, August, September, and October, 1865. In June there were issued to refugees three hundred and thirteen thousand six hundred and twenty-seven rations, and thirty six thousand one hundred and eighty-one to freedmen. In August, in Kentucky and Tennessee, there were issued to refugees eighty-seven thousand one hundred and eighty rations, and to freedmen eighty-seven thousand one hundred and ninety-five—almost an equality."

Mr. Johnson, of Maryland remarked: "The object of the bill is a very correct one; these people should be taken care of; and as it is equally applicable to the whites and to the blacks, and the whites in many of the States requiring as much protection as the blacks, I would very willingly vote for the bill if I thought we had the power to pass it; but on the question of power I have no disposition now or perhaps at any time in the present stage of the bill to trouble the Senate."

The bill soon after passed the Senate as amended in the House, and reämended in the Senate, by a vote of twenty-nine to seven.

On the following day, the amendments of the Senate were concurred in by the House without debate, and the Freedmen's Bureau Bill was ready to be submitted to the Executive.

Ten day's after the final passage of the bill, the President sent to the Senate a message, "with his objection thereto in writing."

The Senate immediately suspended other business to hear the VETO MESSAGE, which was read by the Secretary, as follows:

"*To the Senate of the United States:*

"I have examined with care the bill which originated in the Senate, and has been passed by the two houses of Congress, to amend an act entitled 'An act to establish a Bureau for the relief of Freedmen and Refugees,' and for other purposes. Having, with much regret, come to the conclusion that it would not be consistent with the public welfare to give my approval to the measure, I return the bill to the Senate with my objections to its becoming a law.

"I might call to mind, in advance of these objections, that there is no immediate necessity for the proposed measure. The act to establish a Bureau for the relief of Freedmen and Refugees, which was approved in the month of March last, has not yet expired. It was thought stringent and extensive enough for the purpose in view in time of war. Before it ceases to have effect, further experience may assist to guide us to a wise conclusion as to the policy to be adopted in time of peace.

"I share with Congress the strongest desire to secure to the freedmen the full enjoyment of their freedom and property, and their entire independence and equality in making contracts for their labor; but the bill before me contains provisions which, in my opinion, are not warranted by the Constitution, and are not well suited to accomplish the end in view.

"The bill proposes to establish by authority of Congress, military jurisdiction over all parts of the United States containing refugees and freedmen. It would, by its very nature, apply with most force to those parts of the United States in which the freedmen most abound; and it expressly extends the existing temporary jurisdiction of the Freedmen's Bureau, with greatly enlarged powers, over those States 'in which the ordinary course of judicial proceeding, has been interrupted by the rebellion.' The source from which this military jurisdiction is to emanate is none other than the President of the United States, acting through the War Department and the commissioner of the Freedmen's Bureau. The agents to carry out this military jurisdiction are to be selected either from the army or from civil life; the country is to be divided into districts and sub-districts; and the number of salaried agents to be employed may be equal to the number of counties or parishes in all the United States where freedmen and refugees are to be found.

"The subjects over which this military jurisdiction is to extend in every part of the United States include protection to 'all employés, agents, and officers of this bureau in the exercise of the duties imposed' upon them by the bill. In eleven States it is further to extend over all cases affecting freedmen and refugees discriminated against 'by local law, custom, or prejudice.' In those eleven States the bill subjects any white person who may be charged with depriving a freedman of 'any civil rights or immunities belonging to white persons' to imprisonment or fine, or both, without, however, defining the 'civil rights and immunities' which are thus to be secured to the freedmen by military law. This military jurisdiction also extends to all questions that may arise respecting contracts. The agent who is thus to exercise the office of a military judge may be a stranger, entirely ignorant of the laws of the place, and exposed to the errors of judgment to which all men are liable. The exercise of power, over which there is no legal supervision, by so vast a number of agents as is contemplated by the bill, must, by the very nature of man, be attended by acts of caprice, injustice, and passion.

"The trials, having their origin under this bill, are to take place without the intervention of a jury, and without any fixed rules of law or evidence. The rules on which offenses are to be 'heard and determined' by the numerous agents, are such rules and regulations as the President, through the War Department, shall prescribe. No previous presentment is required, nor any indictment charging the commission of a crime against the laws; but the trial must proceed on charges and specifications. The punishment will be, not what the law declares, but such as a court-martial may think proper; and from these arbitrary tribunals there lies no appeal, no writ of error to any of the courts in which the Constitution of the United States vests exclusively the judicial power of the country.

"While the territory and the classes of actions and offenses that are made subject to this measure are so extensive, the bill itself, should it become a law, will have no limitation in point of time, but will form a part of the permanent legislation of the country. I can not reconcile a system of military jurisdiction of this kind with the words of the Constitution, which declare that 'no person shall be held to answer for a capital or otherwise infamous crime unless upon a presentment or indictment of a grand jury, except in cases arising in the land and naval forces, or in the militia when in actual service in time of war or public danger;' and that 'in all criminal prosecutions the accused shall enjoy the right to a speedy and public trial, by an impartial jury of the State or district wherein the crime shall have been committed.' The safeguards which the experience and wisdom of ages taught our fathers to establish as securities for the protection of the innocent, the punishment of the guilty, and the equal administration of justice, are to be set aside, and for the sake of a more vigorous interposition in behalf of justice, we are to take the risk of the many acts of injustice that would necessarily follow from an almost countless number of agents established in every parish or county in nearly a third of the States of the

Union, over whose decisions there is to be no supervision or control by the Federal courts. The power that would be thus placed in the hands of the President is such as in time of peace certainly ought never to be intrusted to any one man.

"If it be asked whether the creation of such a tribunal within a State is warranted as a measure of war, the question immediately presents itself whether we are still engaged in war. Let us not unnecessarily disturb the commerce and credit and industry of the country by declaring to the American people and to the world, that the United States are still in a condition of civil war. At present there is no part of our country in which the authority of the United States is disputed. Offenses that may be committed by individuals should not work a forfeiture of the rights of whole communities. The country has returned, or is returning, to a state of peace and industry, and the rebellion is in fact at an end. The measure, therefore, seems to be as inconsistent with the actual condition of the country as it is at variance with the Constitution of the United States.

"If, passing from general considerations, we examine the bill in detail, it is open to weighty objections.

"In time of war it was eminently proper that we should provide for those who were passing suddenly from a condition of bondage to a state of freedom. But this bill proposes to make the Freedmen's Bureau, established by the act of 1865 as one of many great and extraordinary military measures to suppress a formidable rebellion, a permanent branch of the public administration, with its powers greatly enlarged. I have no reason to suppose, and I do not understand it to be alleged, that the act of March, 1865, has proved deficient for the purpose for which it was passed, although at that time, and for a considerable period thereafter, the Government of the United States remained unacknowledged in most of the States whose inhabitants had been involved in the rebellion. The institution of slavery, for the military destruction of which the Freedmen's Bureau was called into existence as an auxiliary, has been already effectually and finally abrogated throughout the whole country by an amendment of the Constitution of the United States, and practically its eradication has received the assent and concurrence of most of those States in which it at any time had an existence. I am not, therefore, able to discern, in the condition of the country, any thing to justify an apprehension that the powers and agencies of the Freedmen's Bureau, which were effective for the protection of freedmen and refugees during the actual continuance of hostilities and of African servitude, will now, in a time of peace and after the abolition of slavery, prove inadequate to the same proper ends. If I am correct in these views, there can be no necessity for the enlargement of the powers of the bureau, for which provision is made in the bill.

"The third section of the bill authorizes a general and unlimited grant of support to the destitute and suffering refugees and freedmen, their wives and children. Succeeding sections make provision for the rent or purchase of landed estates for freedmen, and for the erection for their benefit of suitable buildings for asylums and schools, the expenses to be defrayed from the Treasury of the whole people. The Congress of the United States has never heretofore thought itself empowered to establish asylums beyond the limits of the District of Columbia, except for the benefit of our disabled soldiers and sailors. It has never founded schools for any class of our own people, not even for the orphans of those who have fallen in the defense of the Union; but has left the care of education to the much more competent and efficient control of the States, of communities, of private associations, and of individuals. It has never deemed itself authorized to expend the public money for the rent or purchase of homes for the thousands, not to say millions, of the white race, who are honestly toiling from day to day for their subsistence. A system for the support of indigent persons in the United States was never contemplated by the authors of the Constitution, nor can any good reason be advanced why, as a permanent establishment, it should be founded for one class or color of our people more than another. Pending the war, many refugees and freedmen received support from the Government, but it was never intended that they should thenceforth be fed, clothed, educated, and sheltered by the United States. The idea on which the slaves were assisted to freedom was that, on becoming free, they would be a self-sustaining population. Any legislation that shall imply that they are not expected to attain a self-sustaining condition must have a tendency injurious alike to their character and their prospects.

"The appointment of an agent for every county and parish will create an immense patronage; and the expense of the numerous officers and their clerks, to be appointed by the President, will be great in the beginning, with a tendency steadily to increase. The appropriations asked by the Freedmen's Bureau, as now established, for the year 1866, amount to $11,745,000. It may be safely estimated that the cost to be incurred under the pending bill will require double that amount—more than the entire sum expended in any one year under the administration of the second Adams. If the presence of agents in every parish and county is to be considered as a war measure, opposition, or even resistance, might be provoked, so that, to give effect to their jurisdiction, troops would have to be stationed within reach of every one of them, and thus a large standing force be rendered necessary. Large appropriations would therefore be re-required to sustain and enforce military jurisdiction in every county or parish from the Potomac to the Rio Grande. The condition of our fiscal affairs is encouraging, but, in order to sustain the present measure of public confidence, it is necessary that we practice not merely customary economy, but, as far as possible, severe retrenchment.

"In addition to the objections already stated, the fifth section of the bill proposes to take away land from its former owners without any legal proceedings being first had, contrary to that provision of the Constitution which declares that no person shall 'be deprived of life, liberty, or property, without due process of law.' It does not appear that a part of the lands to which this section refers may not be owned by minors or persons of unsound mind, or by those who have been faithful to all their obligations as citizens of the United States. If any portion of the land is held by such persons, it is not competent for any authority to deprive them of it. If, on the other hand, it be found that the property is liable to confiscation, even then it can not be appropriated to public purposes until, by due process of law, it shall have been declared forfeited to the Government.

"There is still further objection to the bill on grounds seriously affecting the class of persons to whom it is designed to bring relief; it will tend to keep the mind of the freedman in a state of uncertain expectation and restlessness, while to those among whom he lives it will be a source of constant and vague apprehension.

"Undoubtedly the freedman should be protected, but he should be protected by the civil authorities, especially by the exercise of all the constitutional powers of the courts of the United States and of the States. His condition is not so exposed as may at first be imagined. He is in a portion of the country where his labor can not well be spared. Competition for his services from planters, from those who are constructing or repairing railroads, and from capitalists in his vicinage or from other States, will enable him to command almost his own terms. He also possesses a perfect right to change his place of abode; and if, therefore, he does not find in one community or State a mode of life suited to his desires, or proper remuneration for his labor, he can move to another, where that labor is more esteemed and better rewarded. In truth, however, each State, induced by its own wants and interests, will do what is necessary and proper to retain within its borders all the labor that is needed for the development of its resources. The laws that regulate supply and demand will maintain their force, and the wages of the laborer will be regulated thereby. There is no danger that the exceedingly great demand for labor will not operate in favor of the laborer.

"Neither is sufficient consideration given to the ability of the freedmen to protect and take care of themselves. It is no more than justice to them to believe that, as they have received their freedom with moderation and forbearance, so they will distinguish themselves by their industry and thrift, and soon show the world that, in a condition of freedom, they are self-sustaining, capable of selecting their own employment and their own places of abode, of insisting for themselves on a proper remuneration, and of establishing and maintaining their own asylums and schools. It is earnestly hoped that, instead of wasting away, they will, by their own efforts, establish for themselves a condition of respect, ability, and prosperity. It is certain that they can attain to that condition only through their own merits and exertions.

"In this connection the query presents itself, whether the system proposed by the bill will not, when put into complete operation, practically transfer the entire care, support, and control of four million emancipated slaves to agents, overseers, or task-masters, who, appointed at Washington, are to be located in every county and parish throughout the United States containing freedmen and refugees? Such a system would inevitably tend to a concentration of power in the Executive which would enable him, if so disposed, to control the action of this numerous class and use them for the attainment of his own political ends.

"I can not but add another very grave objection to this bill: The Constitution imperatively declares, in connection with taxation, that each State shall have at least one Representative, and fixes the rule for the number to which, in future times, each State shall be entitled. It also provides that the Senate of the United States shall be composed of two Senators from each State, and adds, with peculiar force, 'that no State, without its consent, shall be deprived of its equal suffrage in the Senate.' The original act was necessarily passed in the absence of the States chiefly to be affected, because their people were then contumaciously engaged in the rebellion. Now the case is changed, and some, at least, of those States are attending Congress by loyal Representatives, soliciting the allowance of the constitutional right of representation. At the time, however, of the consideration and the passing of this bill, there was no Senator or Representative in Congress from the eleven States which are to be mainly affected by its provisions. The very fact that reports were and are made against the good disposition of the people of that portion of the country is an additional reason why they need, and should have, Representatives of their own in Congress to explain their condition, reply to accusations, and assist, by their local knowledge, in the perfecting of measures immediately affecting themselves. While the liberty of deliberation would then be free, and Congress would have full power to decide according to its judgment, there could be no objection urged that the States most interested had not been permitted to be heard. The principle is firmly fixed in the minds of the American people that there should be no taxation without representation.

"Great burdens have now to be borne by all the country, and we may best demand that they shall be borne without murmur when they are voted by a majority of the Represetatives of all the people. I would not interfere with the unquestionable right of Congress to judge, each house for itself, 'of the elections, returns, and qualifications of its own members,' but that authority can not be construed as including the right to shut out, in time of peace, any State from the representation to which it is entitled by the Constitution. At present, all the people of eleven States are excluded—those who were most faithful during the war not less than others. The State of Tennessee, for instance, whose authorities engaged in rebellion, was restored to all her constitutional relations to the Union by the patriotism and energy of her injured and betrayed people. Before the war was brought to a termination, they had placed themselves in relation with the General Government, had established a State government of their own; as they were not included in the Emancipation Proclamation, they, by their own act, had amended their Constitution so as to abolish slavery within the limits of their State. I know no reason why the State of Tennessee, for example, should not fully enjoy 'all her constitutional relations to the United States.'

"The President of the United States stands toward the country in a somewhat different attitude from that of any member of Congress. Each member of Congress is chosen from a single district or State; the President is chosen by the people of all the States. As eleven are not at this time represented in either branch of Congress, it would seem to be his duty, on all proper occasions, to present their just claims to Congress. There always will be differences of opinion in the community, and individuals may be be guilty of transgressions of the law; but these do not constitute valid objections against the right of a State to representation. I would in nowise interfere with the discretion of Congress with regard to the qualifications of members; but I hold it my duty to recommend to you, in the interests of peace and in the interests of union, the admission of every State to its share in public legislation when, however insubordinate, insurgent, or rebellious its people may have been, it presents itself, not only in an attitude of loyalty and harmony, but in the persons of Representatives whose loyalty can not be questioned under any existing constitutional or legal test.

"It is plain that an indefinite or permanent exclusion of any part of the country from representation must be attended by a spirit of disquiet and complaint. It is unwise and dangerous to pursue a course of measures which will unite a very large section of the country against another section of the country, however much the latter may preponderate. The course of emigration, the development of industry and business, and natural causes will raise up at the South men as devoted to the Union as those of any other part of the land. But if they are all excluded from Congress—if, in a permanent statute, they are declared not to be in full constitutional relations to the country—they may think they have cause to become a unit in feeling and sentiment against the Government. Under the political education of the American people, the idea is inherent and ineradicable that the consent of the majority of the whole people is necessary to secure a willing acquiescence in legislation.

"The bill under consideration refers to certain of the States as though they had not 'been fully restored in all their constitutional relations to the United States.' If they have not, let us at once act together to secure that desirable end at the earliest possible moment. It is hardly necessary for me to inform Congress that, in my own judgment, most of these States, so far, at least, as depends upon their own action, have already been fully restored, and are to be deemed as entitled to enjoy their constitutional rights as members of the Union. Reasoning from the Constitution itself, and from the actual situation of the country, I feel not only entitled but bound to assume that, with the Federal courts restored, and those of the several States in the full exercise of their functions, the rights and interests of all classes of the people will, with the aid of the military in cases of resistance to the laws, be essentially protected against unconstitutional infringement or violation. Should this expectation unhappily fail—which I do not anticipate—then the Executive is already fully armed with the powers conferred by the act of March, 1865, establishing the Freedmen's Bureau, and hereafter, as heretofore, he can employ the land and naval forces of the country to suppress insurrection or to overcome obstructions to the laws.

"In accordance with the Constitution, I return the bill to the Senate, in the earnest hope that a measure involving questions and interests so important to the country will not become a law unless, upon deliberate consideration by the people, it shall receive the sanction of an enlightened public judgment.

"ANDREW JOHNSON."

Engd. by G. E. Perine & Co. N.Y.

S. C. Pomeroy

HON. S. C. POMEROY.

The majority of the Senate was in favor of proceeding immediately to the consideration of the message, and to have a vote as to whether the bill should be passed, "the objections of the President to the contrary notwithstanding." To this Mr. Lane, of Kansas, was opposed. He said: "There are several Senators absent, and I think it but just to them that they should have an opportunity to be present when the vote is taken on this bill. I can not consent, so long as I can postpone this question by the rules of the Senate, to have a vote upon it to-night." Mr. Lane accordingly made four successive motions to adjourn, in each of which he called for the yeas and nays. Finally, the motion for adjournment having been made for the fifth time, it was carried, with the understanding that the bill should be the pending question at one o'clock on the following day.

On that day, February 20th, the bill and the message came duly before the Senate. Mr. Davis obtained the floor, and made a long speech in opposition to the bill and in favor of the Veto Message. He expressed his aversion to the bill, and the objects sought to be attained under it in very emphatic terms, but added nothing to the arguments which had already been adduced.

Mr. Trumbull replied to the objections urged against the bill in the President's Message. The President said, "The bill, should it become a law will have no limitation in point of time, but will form a part of the permanent legislation of the country."

"The object of the bill," replied Mr. Trumbull, "was to continue in existence the Freedmen's Bureau—not as a permanent institution. Any such intent was disavowed during the discussion of the bill. It is true, no time is expressly limited in the bill itself when it shall cease to operate, nor is it customary to insert such a clause in a law; but it is declared that the bill shall operate until otherwise provided by law. It is known that the Congress of the United States assembles every year, and no one supposed that this bill was to establish a bureau to be ingrafted upon the country as a permanent institution; far from it. Nor is it a bill that is intended to go into the States and take control of the domestic affairs of the States."

"There is no immediate necessity for the proposed measure," said the President; "the act to establish a Bureau for the Relief of Freedmen and Refugees, which was approved in the month of

March last, has not yet expired. It was thought stringent and extensive enough for the purpose in view in time of war."

Mr. Trumbull replied: "By the terms of the act, it was to continue 'during the present war of rebellion and for one year thereafter.' Now, when did the war of rebellion cease? So far as the conflict of arms is concerned, we all admit that the war of rebellion ceased when the last rebel army laid down its arms, and that was some time in the month of May, when the rebel army in Texas surrendered to the Union forces. I do not hold that the consequences of the war are over. I do not understand that peace is restored with all its consequences. We have not yet escaped from the evils inflicted by the war. Peace and harmony are not yet restored, but the war of rebellion is over, and this bureau must expire in May next, according to the terms of the act that was passed on the 3d of March, 1865, and according to the views of the President as expressed in his Veto Message."

"The bill," said the President, "proposes to establish by authority of Congress, military jurisdiction over all parts of the United States containing refugees and freedmen."

"I would like to know," said Mr. Trumbull, "where in that bill is any provision extending military jurisdiction over all parts of the United States containing refugees and freedmen? The bill contains no such clause. It is a misapprehension of the bill. The clause of the bill upon that subject is this:

"'And the President of the United States, through the War Department and the commissioner, shall extend military jurisdiction and protection over all employés, agents, and officers of this bureau in the exercise of the duties imposed or authorized by this act or the act to which this is additional.'

"Is not the difference manifest to every body between a bill that extends military jurisdiction over the officers and employés of the bureau and a bill which should extend military jurisdiction over all parts of the United States containing refugees and freedmen? This bill makes the Freedmen's Bureau a part of the War Department. It makes its officers and agents amenable to the Rules and Articles of War. But does that extend jurisdiction over the whole country where they are? How do they differ from any other portion of the army of the United States? The army of the United States, as every one knows, is governed by the Rules and Articles of War, wherever it may be, whether in Indiana or in Florida, and all persons in the army and a part of the military establishment are subject to these Rules and Articles of War; but did any body ever suppose that the whole country where they were was under military jurisdiction? If a company of soldiers are stationed at one of the forts in New York harbor, the officers and soldiers of that company are subject to military jurisdiction; but was it ever supposed that the people of the State of New York were thereby placed under military jurisdiction? It is an entire misapprehension of the provisions of the bill. It extends military jurisdiction nowhere; it merely places under jurisdiction the persons belonging to the Freedmen's Bureau who, nearly all of them, are now under military jurisdiction."

"The country," objected the President, "is to be divided into districts and sub-districts, and the number of salaried agents to be employed may be equal to the number of counties or parishes in all the States where freedmen and refugees are to be found."

Mr. Trumbull replied: "A single officer need not be employed other than those we now have. I have already stated that it is in the power and discretion of the President to detail from the army officers to perform all the duties of the Freedmen's Bureau, and, in case they are detailed, the bill provides that they shall serve without any additional compensation or allowance. But, sir, is it necessary, or was it ever contemplated, that there should be an officer or agent of the Freedmen's Bureau in every county and every parish where refugees and freedmen are to be found? By no means. What is the bill upon that subject? Does it make it imperative upon the President to appoint an agent in each county and parish? It authorizes him 'when the same shall be necessary for the operations of the bureau;' not otherwise. He has no authority, under the bill, to apppoint a single agent unless it is necessary for the operations of the bureau, and then he can only appoint so many as may be needed. Sir, it never entered the mind, I venture to say, of a single advocate of this bill, that the President of the United States would so abuse the authority intrusted to him as to station an agent in every county in these States; but it was apprehended that there might be localities in some of these States where the prejudice and hostility of the white population and the former masters were such toward the negroes that it would be necessary to have an agent in every county in that locality for their protection; and, in order to give the President the necessary discretion where this should be requisite, the bill authorized, when it was necessary for the operations of the bureau, the appointment of an agent in each county or parish. In order to vest the President with sufficient power in some localities, it was necessary, legislating by general law, to give him much larger power than would be necessary in other localities.

"Sir, the country is not to be divided, I undertake to say, into districts and sub-districts unless the President of the United States finds it necessary to do so for the protection of these people; and if the law should be abused in that respect, it would be because he abused the discretion vested in him by Congress, and not because the law required it. It makes no such requirement."

"This military jurisdiction," said the President, "also extends to all questions that may arise respecting contracts."

"So far," replied Mr. Trumbull, "from extending this military jurisdiction over all questions arising concerning contracts, and so far from extending military jurisdiction anywhere, it is expressly provided, by the very terms of the bill, that no such jurisdiction shall be exercised except where the President himself has established and is maintaining military jurisdiction, which he is now doing in eleven States; and the very moment that he ceases to maintain military jurisdiction, that very moment the military jurisdiction conferred over freedmen by this act ceases and terminates.

"Sir, the whole jurisdiction to try and dispose of cases by the officers and agents of the Freedmen's Bureau is expressly limited to the time when these States shall be restored to their constitutional relations, and when the courts of the United States and of the States are not interrupted nor interfered with in the peaceable course of justice. So far, then, from the bill establishing a military jurisdiction, upon which the Senator from Kentucky and other Senators have so much harped, it confers no jurisdiction to try cases one moment after the courts are restored, and are no longer interrupted in the peaceable administration of justice. Let me ask by what authority is it that military tribunals are sitting to-day at Alexandria, Virginia? By what authority is it that the writ of *habeas corpus* is suspended to-day in eleven States, when the Constitution of the United States says that the writ shall not be suspended except when, in cases of rebellion and invasion, the public safety may require it. By what authority dose the President of the United States object to the exercise of military jurisdiction by that part of the army charged with the execution of the provisions of the Freedmen's Bureau when he exercises that military jurisdiction himself by other portions of the army? But a few days since a military commission was sitting in Alexandria, trying persons charged with crimes—and they are held all over the South—and yet that part of the army connected with the Freedmen's Bureau can not exercise any such authority because it is unconstitutional—unconstitutional to do by virtue of a law of Congress what is done without any law!

"Where does the Executive get the power? The Executive is but the Commander-in-chief of the armies, made so by the Constitution; but he can not raise an army or a single soldier, he can not appoint a single officer, without the consent of Congress. He can not make any rules and regulations for the government of the army without our permission. The Constitution of the United States declares, in so many words, that Congress shall have power 'to make rules for the government and regulation of the land and naval forces' of the United States. Can it be that that department of the Government, vested in express terms by the Constitution itself with authority to make rules for the government and regulation of the land and naval forces, has no authority to direct that portion of the land and naval forces employed in the Freedmen's Bureau to exercise this jurisdiction instead of department commanders? Sir, it is competent for Congress to declare that no department commanders shall exercise any such authority; it is competent for Congress to declare that a court-martial shall never sit, that a military commission shall never be held, and the President is as much bound to obey it as the humblest citizen in the land."

The President said: "The trials having their origin under this bill are to take place without the intervention of a jury, and without any fixed rules of law or evidence."

"Do not all military trials take place in that way," asked Mr. Trumbull. "Did any body ever hear of the presentment of a grand jury in a case where a court-martial set for the trial of a military offense, or the trial of a person charged with any offense cognizable before it? This Freedmen's Bureau Bill confers no authority to do this except in those regions of country where military authority prevails, where martial law is established, where persons exercising civil authority act in subordination to the military power, and where the moment they transcend the proper limits as fixed by military orders, they are liable to be arrested and punished without the intervention of a grand jury, or without the right of appeal to any of the judicial tribunals of the country. I would as soon think of an appeal from the decision of the military tribunal that sat in the city of Washington, and condemned to death the murderers of our late President, to the judicial tribunals of the country! Where military authority bears sway, where the courts are overborne, is it not an absurdity to say that you must have a presentment of a grand jury, and a trial in a court."

"I can not reconcile a system of military jurisdiction of this kind with the words of the Constitution," said the President.

"If you can not reconcile a system of military jurisdiction of this kind with the words of the Constitution, why have you been exercising it," asked Mr. Trumbull. "Why have you been organizing courts-martial and military commissions all over the South, trying offenders, and punishing some of them with death? Why have you authorized the present Freedmen's Bureau to hold bureau courts all through the South? This has all been done by your permission, and is being done to-day. Then, sir, if you are still in the exercise of this power now, if you have been exercising it from the day you became President of the United States, how is it that you can not reconcile a system of jurisdiction of this kind with the words of the Constitution?

"Sir, does it detract from the President's authority to have the sanction of law? I want to give that sanction. I do not object to the exercise of this military authority of the President in the rebellious States. I believe it is constitutional and legitimate and necessary; but I believe Congress has authority to regulate it. I believe Congress has authority to direct that this military jurisdiction shall be exercised by that branch of the army known as the Freedmen's Bureau, as well as by any other branch of the army."

"The rebellion is at an end," said the President. "The measure, therefore, seems to be as inconsistent with the actual condition of the country as it is at variance with the Constitution of the United States."

Mr. Trumbull replied: "If the rebellion is at an end, will any body tell me by what authority the President of the United States suspends the writ of *habeas corpus* in those States where it existed. The act of Congress of March, 1863, authorized the President of the United States to suspend the writ of *habeas corpus* during the present rebellion. He says it is at an end. By what authority, then, does he suspend the writ? By his own declaration, let him stand or fall. If it is competent to suspend the writ, if it is competent for military tribunals to sit all through the South, and entertain military jurisdiction, this bill, which does not continue military jurisdiction, does not establish military jurisdiction, but only authorizes the officers of this bureau, while military jurisdiction prevails, to take charge of that particular class of cases affecting the refugee or freedman where he is discriminated against, can not be obnoxious to any constitutional objection."

"This bill," said the President, "proposes to make the Freedmen's Bureau, established by the act of 1865, as one of many great and extraordinary military measures to suppress a formidable rebellion, a permanent branch of the public administration, with its powers greatly enlarged."

"This is a mistake," replied Mr. Trumbull; "it is not intended, I apprehend, by any body, certainly not by me, to make it a permanent branch of the public administration; and I am quite sure that the powers of the bureau are not, by the amendatory bill, greatly enlarged. A careful examination of the amendment will show that it is in some respects a restriction on the powers already exercised."

"The third section of the bill," the President objected, "authorizes a general and unlimited grant of support to the destitute and suffering refugees and freedmen, their wives and children."

"What is the third section of the bill," asked Mr. Trumbull, "which the President says contains such an unlimited grant of support to the destitute and suffering refugees, their wives and children? I will read that third section:

"'That the Secretary of War may direct such issues of provisions, clothing, fuel, including medical stores and transportation, and afford such aid, medical or otherwise, as he may deem needful for the immediate and temporary shelter and supply of destitute and suffering refugees and freedmen, their wives and children, under such rules and regulations as he may direct: *Provided*, That no person shall be deemed "destitute," "suffering," or "dependent upon the Government for support," within the meaning of this act, who, being able to find employment, could, by proper industry and exertion, avoid such destitution, suffering, or dependence.'

"Does the President object to this bill on the ground that it authorizes medical aid to be furnished the sick? Or does he object to it because of the proviso which limits its operation, and declares that nobody shall be deemed destitute and suffering under the provisions of the act who is able, by proper industry and exertion, to avoid such destitution? Why, sir, it is a limitation on the present existing law. Does that look much like taking care of four million of people—a provision that expressly limits the operations of this act to those only who can not find employment? A statement of the fact is all that is necessary to meet this statement in the Veto Message."

"The Congress of the United States," said the President, "has never heretofore thought itself empowered to establish asylums beyond the limits of the District of Columbia, except for the benefit of our disabled soldiers and sailors. It has never founded schools for any class of our own people. It has never deemed itself authorized to expend the public money for the rent or purchase of homes for the thousands, not to say millions of the white race who are honestly toiling from day to day for their subsistence."

"The answer to that is this," said Mr. Trumbull: "We never before were in such a state as now; never before in the history of this Government did eleven States of the Union combine together to overthrow and destroy the Union; never before in the history of this Government have we had a four years' civil war; never before in the history of this Government have nearly four million people been emancipated from the most abject and degrading slavery ever imposed upon human beings; never before has the occasion arisen when it was necessary to provide for such large numbers of people thrown upon the bounty of the Government unprotected and unprovided for. But, sir, wherever the necessity did exist the Government has acted. We have voted hundreds of thousands and millions of dollars, and are doing it from year to year, to take care of and provide for the destitute and suffering Indians. We appropriated, years ago, hundreds of thousands of dollars to take care of and feed the savage African who was landed upon our coast by slavers. We provided by law that whenever savages from Africa should be brought to our shores, or whenever they should be captured on board of slavers, the President of the United States should make provision for their maintenance and support, for five years, on the coast of Africa. He was authorized by law to appoint agents to go to Africa to provide means to feed them, and we paid the money to do it. And yet, sir, can we not provide for these Africans who have been held in bondage all their lives, who have never been permitted to earn one dollar for themselves, who, by the great Constitutional Amendment declaring freedom throughout the land, have been discharged from bondage to their masters, who had hitherto provided for their necessities in consideration of their services? Can we not provide for these destitute persons of our own land on the same principle that we provide for the Indians, that we provide for the savage African?"

"But," continued Mr. Trumbull, "the President says we have never rented lands for the white race, we have never purchased lands for them. What do we propose to do by this bill? This authorizes, if the President thinks proper to do it—it is in his discretion—the purchase or renting of lands on which to place these indigent people; but before any land can be purchased or rented, before any contract can be made on the subject, there must be an appropriation made by Congress. This bill contains no appropriation. If the President is opposed to the rent or purchase of land, and Congress passes a bill appropriating money for that purpose, let him veto it if he thinks it unconstitutional; but there is nothing unconstitutional in this bill. This bill does not purchase any land; but it prevents even a contract on the subject until another law shall be passed appropriating the money for that purpose.

"But, sir, what is the objection to it if it did appropriate the money? I have already undertaken to show, and I think I have shown, that it was the duty of the United States, as an independent nation, as one of the powers of the earth, whenever there came into its possession an unprotected class of people, who must suffer and perish but for its care, to provide for and take care of them. When an army is marching through an enemy's country, and poor and destitute persons are found within its lines who must die by starvation if they are not fed from the supplies of the army, will any body show me the constitutional provision or the act of Congress that authorizes the general commanding to open his commissariat and feed the starving multitude? And has it not been done by every one of your commanders all through the South? Whenever a starving human being, man, woman, or child, no matter whether black or white, rebel or loyal, came within the lines of the army, to perish and die unless fed from our supplies, there has never been an officer in our service, and, thank God! there has not been, who did not relieve the sufferer. If you want to know where the constitutional power to do this is, and where the law is, I answer, it is in that common humanity that belongs to every man fit to bear the name, and it is in that power that belongs to us as a Christian nation, carrying on war upon civilized principles.

"If we had the right then to feed those people as we did, have we not the right to take care of them in the cheapest way we can? If, when General Sherman was passing through Georgia, he found the lands abandoned; if their able-bodied owners had entered the rebel army to fight against us; if the women and children had fled and left the land a waste, and he had, as is the fact, thousands of persons hanging upon his army dependent upon him for supplies; if it was believed that it would be cheaper to support these people upon these lands than to buy provisions to feed them, might we not do so? May we not resort to whatever means is most judicious to protect from starvation that multitude which common humanity requires us to feed?

"Nor, sir, is it true that no provision has been made by Congress for the education of white people. We have given all through the new States one section of land in every township for the benefit of common schools. We have donated hundreds of thousands of acres of land to all the States for the establishment of colleges and seminaries of learning. How did we get this land? It was purchased by our money, and then we gave it away for purposes of education. The same right exists now to provide for these people, and it is not simply for the black people, but for the white refugees as well as the black, that this bill provides."

Said the President: "The appropriations asked by the Freedmen's Bureau, as now established, for the year 1866, amounts to $11,745,000. It may be safely estimated that the cost to be incurred under the pending bill will require double that amount."

Mr. Trumbull replied: "A far larger sum, in proportion to the number that were thrown upon our hands, was expended before the creation of the Freedmen's Bureau, in feeding and taking care of refugees and freedmen, than since the establishment of the Freedmen's Bureau. Since that time, the authority of the Government has been extended over all the rebellious States, and we have had a larger number of refugees and freedmen to provide for, but in proportion to the number I have no doubt that the expense is less now than it was before the establishment of the bureau."

"The query again presents itself," said the President, "whether the system proposed by the bill will not, when put into complete operation, practically transfer the entire care, support, and control of four million emancipated slaves to agents, overseers, or task-masters, who, appointed at Washington, are to be located in every county and parish throughout the United States containing freedmen and refugees."

"I scarcely know how to reply to that most extravagant statement," said Mr. Trumbull. "I have already shown that it would be a great abuse of the power conferred by this bill to station an agent in every county. I have already stated that but a small proportion of the freedmen are aided by the Freedmen's Bureau. In this official document the President has sent to Congress the exaggerated statement that it is a question whether this bureau would not bring under its control the four million emancipated slaves. The census of 1860 shows that there never were four million slaves in all the United States, if you counted every man, woman, and child, and we know that the number has not increased during the war. But, sir, what will be thought when I show, as I shall directly show by official figures, that, so far from providing for four million emancipated slaves, the Freedmen's Bureau never yet provided for a hundred thousand, and, as restricted by the proviso to the third section of the present bill, it could never be extended, under it, to a larger number. Is it not most extraordinary that a bill should be returned with the veto from the President on the ground that it provides for four million people, when, restricted in its operations as it is, and having been in operation since March last, it has never had under its control a hundred thousand? I have here an official statement from the Freedmen's Bureau, which I beg leave to read in this connection:

"'The greatest number of persons to whom rations were issued, including the Commissary Department, the bureau issues to persons without the army, is one hundred and forty-eight thousand one hundred and twenty.'

"Who are they? I said there were not a hundred thousand freedmen provided for by the bureau.

"'Whites, 57,369; colored, 90,607; Indians, 133. The greatest number by the bureau was 49,932, in September. The total number for December was 17,025.'

"That sounds a little different from four millions. Seventeen thousand and twenty-five were all that were provided for by the Freedmen's Bureau in the month of December last, the number getting less and less every month. Why? Because, by the kind and judicious management of that bureau, places of employment were found for these refugees and freedmen. When the freedmen were discharged from their masters' plantations they were assisted to find places of work elsewhere.

"The President says," continued Mr. Trumbull, "that Congress never thought of making these provisions for the white people. Let us see what provisions have been made for the white people. Major-General Fisk, Commissioner of the Freedmen's Bureau for the State of Tennessee, in his testimony given before the Reconstruction Committee, said:

"'During the last year, the rations issued to white people in Tennessee have been much in excess of those issued to freedmen. When I took charge of my district the Government was feeding twenty-five thousand people; in round numbers, about seventeen thousand five hundred white persons and seven thousand blacks. The month preceding the establishment of the Freedmen's Bureau, for rations alone for that class of people the sum of $97,000 was paid. My first efforts were to reduce the number of those beneficiaries of the Government, to withhold the rations, and make the people self-supporting as far as possible; and in the course of four months I reduced the monthly expenses from $97,000 to $5,000.'

"In addition to the objections already stated," said the President, "the fifth section of this bill proposes to take away land from its former owners, without any legal proceedings first had."

"I regret," said Mr. Trumbull, "that a statement like that should inadvertently (for it must have been inadvertent) have found a place in this Veto Message. The fifth section of the bill does not propose to take away lands from any body. I will read it, and we shall see what it is:

"'That the occupants of land under Major-General Sherman's special field order, dated at Savannah, January 16, 1865, are hereby confirmed in their possession.'

"Is not this a different thing from taking away land from any body? Do you take a thing away from another person when you have it in your possession already? This fifth section, so far from taking land from any body, provides simply for protecting the occupants of the land for three years from the 16th of January, 1865, a little less than two years from this time. If the section does any thing, it simply prevents the restoration of this property to its former owners within that period, except upon terms to be entered into, satisfactory to the commissioner, between the occupant and the former owner. This is all there is of it. It is a very different thing from taking away land from its former owners."

"Undoubtedly," said the President, "the freedmen should be protected by the civil authorities, especially by the exercise of all the constitutional powers of the courts of the United States and of the States."

"Let us see," replied Mr. Trumbull, "how they are protected by the civil authority." After having read from documents setting forth laws in reference to freedmen in force in Texas and Mississippi, Mr. Trumbull continued: "I have here a number of communications of a similar character, showing that, by the laws in some of the Southern States, a pass system still exists, and that the negro really has no protection afforded him either by the civil authorities or judicial tribunals of the State. I have letters showing the same thing in the State of Maryland, from persons whose character is vouched for as reliable. Under this state of things, the President tells us that the freedman should be protected 'by the exercise of all the constitutional powers of the courts of the United States and of the States!'"

"He also possesses," said the President, referring to the freedman, "a perfect right to change his place of abode; and if, therefore, he does not find in one community or State a mode of life suited to his desires, or proper remuneration for his labor, he can move to another where that labor is more esteemed and better rewarded."

"Then, sir," said Mr. Trumbull, "is there no necessity for some supervising care of these people? Are they to be coldly told that they have a perfect right to change their place of abode, when, if they are caught in a strange neighborhood without a pass, they are liable to be whipped? when combinations exist against them that they shall not be permitted to hire unless to their former master? Are these people, knowing nothing of geography, knowing not where to go, having never in their lives been ten miles from the place where they were born, these old women and young children, these feeble persons who are turned off because they can no longer work, to be told to go and seek employment elsewhere? and is the Government of the United States, which has made them free, to stand by and do nothing to save and protect them? Are they to be left to the mercy of such legislation as that of Mississippi, to such laws as exist in Texas, to such practices as are tolerated in Maryland and in Kentucky? Sir, I think some protection is necessary for them, and that was the object of this bureau. It was not intended, and such is not its effect, to interfere with the ordinary administration of justice in any State, not even during the rebellion. The moment that any State does justice and abolishes all discrimination between whites and blacks in civil rights, the judicial functions of the Freedmen's Bureau cease.

"But," continued Mr. Trumbull, "the President, most strangely of all, dwells upon the unconstitutionality of this act, without ever having alluded to that provision of the Constitution which its advocates claim gives the authority to pass it. Is it not most extraordinary that the President of the United States returns a bill which has passed Congress, with his objections to it, alleging it to be unconstitutional, and makes no allusion whatever in his whole message to that provision of the Constitution which, in the opinion of its supporters, clearly gives the authority to pass it? And what is that? The second clause of the constitutional amendment, which declares that Congress shall have authority by appropriate legislation to enforce the article which declares that there shall be neither slavery nor involuntary servitude throughout the United States. If legislation be necessary to protect the former slaves against State laws, which allow them to be whipped if found away from home without a pass, has not Congress, under the second clause of the amendment, authority to provide it? What kind of freedom is that which the Constitution of the United States guarantees to a man that does not protect him from the lash if he is caught away from home without a pass? And how can we sit here and discharge the constitutional obligation that is upon us to pass the appropriate legislation to protect every man in the land in his freedom, when we know such laws are being passed in the South, if we do nothing to prevent their enforcement? Sir, so far from the bill being unconstitutional, I should feel that I had failed in my constitutional duty if I did not propose some measure that would protect these people in their freedom. And yet this clause of the Constitution seems to have escaped entirely the observation of the President.

"The President objects to this bill because it was passed in the absence of representation from the rebellious States. If that objection be valid, all our legislation affecting those States is wrong, and has been wrong from the beginning. When the rebellion broke out, in the first year of the war, we passed a law for collecting a direct tax, and we assessed that tax upon all the rebellious States. According to the theory of the President, that was all wrong, because taxation and representation did not go together. Those States were not represented. Then, according to this argument, (I will not read all of it,) we were bound to have received their Representatives, or else not legislate for and tax them. He insists they were States in the Union all the time, and according to the Constitution, each State is entitled to at least one Representative.

"If the argument that Congress can not legislate for States unrepresented is good now, it was good during the conflict of arms, for none of the States whose governments were usurped are yet relieved from military control. If we have no right to legislate for those States now, we had no right to impose the direct tax upon them. We had no right to pass any of our laws that affected them. We had no right to raise an army to march into the rebellious States while they were not represented in the Congress of the United States. We had no right to pass a law declaring these States in rebellion. Why? The rebels were not here to be represented in the American Senate. We had no right to pass a law authorizing the President to issue a proclamation discontinuing all intercourse with the people of those rebellious States; and why? Because they were not represented here. We had no right to blockade their coast. Why? They were not represented here. They are States, says the President, and each State is entitled to two Senators, and to at least one Representative. Suppose the State of South Carolina had sent to Congress, during the war, a Representative; had Congress nothing to do but to admit him, if found qualified? Must he be received because he comes from a State, and a State can not go out of the Union? Why, sir, is any thing more necessary than to state this proposition to show its absolute absurdity?"

The President said: "The President of the United States stands toward the country in a somewhat different attitude from that of any member of Congress. Each member of Congress is chosen from a single district or State; the President is chosen by the people of all the States. As eleven States are not at this time represented in either branch of Congress, it would seem to be his duty, on all proper occasions, to present their just claims to Congress."

"If it would not be disrespectful," said Mr. Trumbull, "I should like to inquire how many votes the President got in those eleven States. Sir, he is no more the representative of those eleven States than I am, except as he holds a higher position. I came here as a Representative chosen by the State of Illinois; but I came here to legislate, not simply for the State of Illinois, but for the United States of America, and for South Carolina as well as Illinois. I deny that we are simply the Representatives of the districts and States which send us here, or that we are governed by such narrow views that we can not legislate for the whole country; and we are as much the Representatives, and, in this particular instance, receive as much of the support of those eleven States as did the President himself."

Mr. Trumbull finally remarked: "The President believes this bill unconstitutional; I believe it constitutional. He believes that it will involve great expense; I believe it will save expense. He believes that the freedmen will be protected without it; I believe he will be tyrannized over, abused, and virtually reënslaved, without some legislation by the nation for his protection. He believes it unwise; I believe it to be politic."

Without further debate, the vote was taken on the question, "Shall the bill pass, the objections of the President of the United States notwithstanding?" The Senators voted as follows:

YEAS—Messrs. Anthony, Brown, Chandler, Clark, Conness, Cragin, Creswell, Fessenden, Foster, Grimes, Harris, Henderson, Howard, Howe, Kirkwood, Lane of Indiana, Lane of Kansas, Morrill, Nye, Poland, Pomeroy, Ramsey, Sherman, Sprague, Sumner, Trumbull, Wade, Williams, Wilson, and Yates—30.

NAYS—Messrs. Buckalew, Cowan, Davis, Dixon, Doolittle, Guthrie, Hendricks, Johnson, McDougall, Morgan, Nesmith, Norton, Riddle, Saulsbury, Stewart, Stockton, Van Winkle, and Willey—18.

ABSENT—Messrs. Foot and Wright—2.

The President *pro tempore* then announced, "On this question the yeas are thirty and the nays are eighteen. Two-thirds of the members present not having voted for the bill, it is not a law."

CHAPTER IX.

THE CIVIL RIGHTS BILL IN THE SENATE.

DUTY OF CONGRESS CONSEQUENT UPON THE ABOLITION OF SLAVERY—CIVIL RIGHTS BILL INTRODUCED—REFERENCE TO JUDICIARY COMMITTEE—BEFORE THE SENATE—SPEECH BY MR. TRUMBULL—MR. SAULSBURY—MR. VAN WINKLE—MR. COWAN—MR. HOWARD—MR. JOHNSON—MR. DAVIS—CONVERSATIONS WITH MR. TRUMBULL AND MR. CLARK—REPLY OF MR. JOHNSON—REMARKS BY MR. MORRILL—MR. DAVIS "WOUND UP"—MR. GUTHRIE'S SPEECH—MR. HENDRICKS—REPLY OF MR. LANE—MR. WILSON—MR. TRUMBULL'S CLOSING REMARKS—YEAS AND NAYS ON THE PASSAGE OF THE BILL.

THE preceding Congress having proposed an amendment to the Constitution by which slavery should be abolished, and this amendment having been "ratified by three-fourths of the several States," four millions of the inhabitants of the United States were transformed from slaves into freemen. To leave them with their shackles broken off, unprotected, in a new and undefined position, would have been a sin against them only surpassed in enormity by the original crime of their enslavement.

As provided in the amendment itself, it devolved upon Congress "to enforce this article by appropriate legislation." The Thirty-ninth Congress assembled, realizing that it devolved upon them to define the extent of the rights, privileges, and duties of the freedmen. That body was not slow in meeting the full measure of its responsibility.

Immediately on the reässembling of Congress after the holidays, January 5, 1866, Mr. Trumbull, in pursuance of previous notice, introduced a bill "to protect all persons in the United States in their civil rights, and furnish the means of their vindication." This bill, having been read twice, was referred to the Committee on the Judiciary.

It was highly appropriate that this bill, involving the relations of millions of the inhabitants of the United States to the Government, should be referred to this able committee, selected from among the men of most distinguished legal ability in the Senate. Its members were chosen in consideration of their high professional ability, their long experience, and exalted standing as jurists. They are the legal advisers of the Senate, whose report upon constitutional questions is entitled to the highest consideration.

To such a committee the Senate appropriately referred the Civil Rights Bill, and the nation could safely trust in their hands the great interests therein involved.

The bill declares that "there shall be no discrimination in civil rights or immunities among the inhabitants of any State or Territory of the United States on account of race, color, or previous condition of slavery; but the inhabitants, of every race and color, without regard to any previous condition of slavery or involuntary servitude, except as a punishment for crime whereof the party shall have been duly convicted, shall have the same right to make and enforce contracts, to sue, be parties, and give evidence, to inherit, purchase, lease, sell, hold, and convey real and personal property, and to full and equal benefit of all laws and proceedings for the security of person and property, and shall be subject to like punishment, pains, and penalties, and to none other, any law, statute, ordinance, regulation, or custom to the contrary notwithstanding. Any person who, under cover of any law, statute, ordinance, regulation, or custom, shall subject, or cause to be subjected, any inhabitant of any State or Territory to the deprivation of any right secured or protected by the act, or to different punishment, pains, or penalties, on account of such person having at any time been held in a condition of slavery or involuntary servitude, except as a punishment for crime whereof the party shall have been duly convicted, or by reason of his color or race, than is prescribed for the punishment of white persons, is to be deemed guilty of a misdemeanor, and, on conviction, to be punished by a fine not exceeding $1,000, or imprisonment not exceeding one year, or both, in the discretion of the court."

Other provisions of the bill relate to the courts which shall have jurisdiction of cases which arise under the act, and the means to be employed in its enforcement.

That no question might arise as to the constitutionality of the law, all the provisions which relate to the enforcement of the act were borrowed from the celebrated Fugitive Slave Law, enacted in 1850. It was a happy thought to compel the enemies of the negro themselves, as judges, to pronounce in favor of the constitutionality of this ordinance. It is an admirable illustration of the progress of the age, that the very instruments which were used a few years before to rivet tighter the chains of the slave, should be employed to break those very chains to fragments. It shall forever stand forth to the honor of American legislation that it attained to more than poetic justice in using the very means once employed to repress and crush the negro for his defense and elevation.

Within less than a week after the reference of this bill to the Judiciary Committee, it was reported back, with no alteration save a few verbal amendments. On account of pressure of other business, it did not come up for formal consideration and discussion in the Senate until the 29th of January. On that day Mr. Trumbull, having called up the bill for the consideration of the Senate, said:

"I regard the bill to which the attention of the Senate is now called, as the most important measure that has been under its consideration since the adoption of the constitutional amendment abolishing slavery. That amendment declared that all persons in the United States should be free. This measure is intended to give effect to that declaration, and secure to all persons within the United States practical freedom. There is very little importance in the general declaration of abstract truths and principles unless they can be carried into effect, unless the persons who are to be affected by them have some means of availing themselves of their benefits. Of what avail was the immortal declaration 'that all men are created equal; that they are endowed by their Creator with certain inalienable rights; that among these are life, liberty, and the pursuit of happiness,' and 'that to secure these rights governments are instituted among men,' to the millions of the African race in this country who were ground down and degraded, and subjected to a slavery more intolerable and cruel than the world ever before knew? Of what avail was it to the citizen of Massachusetts, who, a few years ago, went to South Carolina to enforce a constitutional right in court, that the Constitution of the United States declared that the citizens of each State shall be entitled to all the privileges and immunities of citizens in the several States? And of what avail will it now be that the Constitution of the United States has declared that slavery shall not exist, if in the late slaveholding States laws are to be enacted and enforced depriving persons of African descent of privileges which are essential to freemen?

"It is the intention of this bill to secure those rights. The laws in the slaveholding States have made a distinction against persons of African descent on account of their color, whether free or slave. I have before me the statutes of Mississippi. They provide that if any colored person, any free negro or mulatto, shall come into that State for the purpose of residing there, he shall be sold into slavery for life. If any person of African descent residing in that State travels from one county to another without having a pass or a certificate of his freedom, he is liable to be committed to jail, and to be dealt with as a person who is in the State without authority. Other provisions of the statute prohibit any negro or mulatto from having fire-arms; and one provision of the statute declares that for 'exercising the functions of a minister of the Gospel, free negroes and mulattoes, on conviction, may be punished by any number of lashes not exceeding thirty-nine, on the bare back, and shall pay the costs." Other provisions of the statute of Mississippi prohibit a free negro or mulatto from keeping a house of entertainment, and subject him to trial before two justices of the peace and five slaveholders for violating the provisions of this law. The statutes of South Carolina make it a highly penal offense for any person, white or colored, to teach slaves; and similar provisions are to be found running through all the statutes of the late slaveholding States.

"When the constitutional amendment was adopted and slavery abolished, all these statutes became null and void, because they were all passed in aid of slavery, for the purpose of maintaining and supporting it. Since the abolition of slavery, the Legislatures which have assembled in the insurrectionary States have passed laws relating to the freedmen, and in nearly all the States they have discriminated against them. They deny them certain rights, subject them to severe penalties, and still impose upon them the very restrictions which were imposed upon them in consequence of the existence of slavery, and before it was abolished.

The purpose of the bill under consideration is to destroy all these discriminations, and to carry into effect the constitutional amendment."

After having stated somewhat at length the grounds upon which he placed this bill, Mr. Trumbull closed by saying: "Most of the provisions of this bill are copied from the late Fugitive Slave Act, adopted in 1850 for the purpose of returning fugitives from slavery into slavery again. The act that was passed at that time for the purpose of punishing persons who should aid negroes to escape to freedom is now to be applied by the provisions of this bill to the punishment of those who shall undertake to keep them in slavery. Surely we have the authority to enact a law as efficient in the interests of freedom, now that freedom prevails throughout the country, as we had in the interest of slavery when it prevailed in a portion of the country."

Mr. Saulsbury took an entirely different view of the subject under consideration: "I regard this bill," he said, "as one of the most dangerous that was ever introduced into the Senate of the United States, or to which the attention of the American people was ever invited. During the last four or five years, I have sat in this chamber and witnessed the introduction of bills into this body which I thought obnoxious to many very grave and serious constitutional objections; but I have never, since I have been a member of the body, seen a bill so fraught with danger, so full of mischief, as the bill now under consideration.

"I shall not follow the honorable Senator into a consideration of the manner in which slaves were treated in the Southern States, nor the privileges that have been denied to them by the laws of the States. I think the time for shedding tears over the poor slave has well nigh passed in this country. The tears which the honest white people of this couutry have been made to shed from the oppressive acts of this Government, in its various departments, during the last four years, call more loudly for my sympathies than those tears which have been shedding and dropping and dropping for the last twenty years in reference to the poor, oppressed slave—dropping from the eyes of strong-minded women and weak-minded men, until, becoming a mighty flood, they have swept away, in their resistless force, every trace of constitutional liberty in this country.

"I suppose it is a foregone conclusion that this measure, as one of a series of measures, is to be passed through this Congress regardless of all consequences. But the day that the President of the United States places his approval and signature to that Freedmen's Bureau Bill, and to this bill, he will have signed two acts more dangerous to the liberty of his countrymen, more disastrous to the citizens of this country, than all the acts which have been passed from the foundation of the Government to the present hour; and if we on this side of the chamber manifest anxiety and interest in reference to these bills, and the questions involved in them, it is because, having known this population all our lives, knowing them in one hour of our infancy better than you gentlemen have known them all your lives, we feel compelled, by a sense of duty, earnestly and importunately, it may be, to appeal to the judgment of the American Senate, and to reach, if possible, the judgment of the great mass of the American people, and invoke their attention to the awful consequences involved in measures of this character. Sir, stop, stop! the mangled, bleeding body of the Constitution of your country lies in your path; you are treading upon its bleeding body when you pass these laws."

After having argued at considerable length that this bill would be a most unconstitutional interference on the part of the Federal Government with "the powers of the States under the Federal Constitution," the Senator from Delaware thus concluded:

"Sir, from early boyhood I was taught to love and revere the Federal Union and those who made it. In early childhood I read the words of the Father of his country, in which he exhorted the people to cling to the union of these States as the palladium of liberty, and my young heart bounded with joy in reading the burning words of lofty patriotism. I was taught in infancy to admire, as far as the infant mind could admire, our free system of government, Federal and State; and I heard the old men say that the wit of man never devised a better or more lovely system of government. When I arrived at that age when I could study and reflect for myself, the teachings of childhood were approved by the judgment of the man.

"I have seen how under this Union we had become great in the eyes of all nations; and I see now, notwithstanding the horrible afflictions of war, if we can have wisdom in council and sincere purpose to subserve the good of the whole people of the

13

United States, though much that was dear to us has been blasted as by the pestilence that walketh in darkness and the destruction that wasteth at noonday, how we might, in the providence of God, resume our former position among the nations of the earth, and command the respect of the whole civilized world. But, sir, to-day, in viewing and in considering this bill, the thought has occurred to me, how happy were the founders of our Federal system of government, that they had been taken from the council chambers of this nation and from among their fellow-men before bills of this character were seriously presented for legislative consideration. Happily for them, they sleep their last sleep, and—

"'How sleep the brave who sink to rest,
By all their country's wishes blest!
When Spring, with dewy fingers cold,
Returns to deck their hallowed mold,
She there shall dress a sweeter sod
Than Fancy's feet have ever trod.

"'By fairy hands their knell is rung;
By forms unseen their dirge is sung;
There Honor comes, a pilgrim gray,
To bless the turf that wraps their clay;
And Freedom shall henceforth repair
And dwell a weeping hermit there.'"

On the following day, Mr. Van Winkle, of West Virginia, addressed the Senate on the merits of the bill. He thought that the objects sought could only be attained through an amendment to the Constitution. He moreover said:

"We hear a great deal about the sentence from the Declaration of Independence, that 'all men are created equal.' I am willing to admit that all men are created equal; but how are they equal? Can a citizen of France, for instance, by going into England, be entitled to all the rights of a citizen of that country, or by coming into this country acquire all the rights of an American, unless he is naturalized? Can a citizen of our country, by going into any other, become entitled to the rights of a citizen there? If not, it may be said that they are not equal. I believe that the division of men into separate communities, and their living in society and association with their fellows, as they do, are both divine institutions, and that, consequently, the authors of the Declaration of Independence could have meant nothing more than that the rights of citizens of any community are equal to the rights of all other citizens of that community. Whenever all communities are conducted in accordance with these principles, these very conditions of their prosperous existence, then all mankind will be equal, each enjoying his equality in his own community, and not till then. Therefore, I assert that there is no right that can be exercised by any community of society more perfect than that of excluding from citizenship or membership those who are objectionable. If a little society is formed for a benevolent, literary, or any other purpose, the members immediately exercise, and claim the right to exercise, that right; they determine who shall come into their community. We have the right to determine who shall be members of our community; and much as has been said here about what God has done, and about our obligations to the Almighty in reference to this matter, I do not see where it comes in that we are bound to receive into our community those whose minglings with us might be detrimental to our interests. I do not believe that a superior race is bound to receive among it those of an inferior race, if the mingling of them can only tend to the detriment of the mass. I do not mean strict miscegenation, but I mean the mingling of two races in society, associating from time to time with each other."

Mr. Cowan, of Pennsylvania, spoke against the bill. He said: "The identical question came up in my State—the question whether the negro was a citizen, and whether he possessed political power in that State—and it was there decided that he was not one of the original corporators, that he was not one of the freemen who originally possessed political power, and that they had never, by any enactment or by any act of theirs, admitted him into a participation of that power, except so far as to tax him for the support of Government. And, Mr. President, I think it a most important question, and particularly a most important question for the Pacific coast, and those States which lie upon it, as to whether this door shall now be thrown open to the Asiatic population. If it be, there is an end to republican government there, because it is very well ascertained that those people have no appreciation of that form of government; it seems to be obnoxious to their very nature; they seem to be incapable either of understanding it or of carrying it out; and I can not consent to say that California, or Oregon, or Colorado, or Nevada, or any of those States, shall be given over to an irruption of Chinese. I, for my part, protest against it.

"There is a great deal more in this bill that is exceedingly objectionable. It is the first time, I think, in the history of civilized legislation, that a judicial officer has been held up and subjected to a criminal punishment for that which may have been a conscientious discharge of his duty. It is, I say, the first case that I know of, in the legislation of modern and civilized nations, where a bill of indictment is to take the place of a writ of error, and where a mistake is to be tortured into a crime.

"I may state that I have another objection to this bill at the present time; and that is, that the people of several States in the Union are not represented here, and yet this law is mainly to operate upon those people. I think it would be at least decent, respectful, if we desire to maintain and support this Government on the broad foundation upon which it was laid—namely, the consent of the governed—that we should wait, at any rate, until the people upon whom it is to operate have a voice in these halls."

Mr. Cowan then proceeded in a somewhat "devious course," as it was characterized by another Senator, to make remarks upon the subject of reconstruction. Many questions and remarks were interposed by other Senators, giving the discussion an exceedingly colloquial style.

At length, Mr. Howard, of Michigan, having obtained the floor, spoke in favor of the bill. He said: "If I understand correctly the interpretation given by several Senators to the constitutional amendment abolishing slavery, it is this: that the sole effect of it is to cut and sever the mere legal ligament by which the person and the service of the slave was attached to his master, and that beyond this particular office the amendment does not go; that it can have no effect whatever upon the condition of the emancipated black in any other respect. In other words, they hold that it relieves him from his so-called legal obligation to render his personal service to his master without compensation, and there leaves him, totally, irretrievably, and without any power on the part of Congress to look after his well-being from the moment of this mockery of emancipation. Sir, such was not the intention of the friends of this amendment at the time of its initiation here, and at the time of its adoption; and I undertake to say that it is not the construction which is given to it by the bar throughout the country, and much less by the liberty-loving people.

"But let us look more closely at this narrow construction. Where does it leave us? We are told that the amendment simply relieves the slave from the obligation to render service to his master. What is a slave in contemplation of American law, in contemplation of the laws of all the slave States? We know full well; the history of two hundred years teaches us that he had no rights, nor nothing which he could call his own. He had not the right to become a husband or a father in the eye of the law; he had no child; he was not at liberty to indulge the natural affections of the human heart for children, for wife, or even for friend. He owned no property, because the law prohibited him. He could not take real or personal estate either by sale, by grant, or by descent or inheritance. He did not own the bread he earned and ate. He stood upon the face of the earth completely isolated from the society in which he happened to be. He was nothing but a chattel, subject to the will of his owner, and unprotected in his rights by the law of the State where he happened to live. His rights, did I say? No, sir, I use inappropriate language. He had no rights; he was an animal; he was property, a chattel. The Almighty, according to the ideas of the times, had made him to be property, a chattel, and not a man.

"Now, sir, it is not denied that this relation of servitude between the former negro slave and his master was actually severed by this amendment. But the absurd construction now forced upon it leaves him without family, without property, without the implements of husbandry, and even without the right to acquire or use any instrumentalities of carrying on the industry of which he may be capable; it leaves him without friend or support, and even without the clothes to cover his nakedness. He is a waif upon the current of time; he has nothing that belongs to him on the face of the earth, except solely his naked person. And here, in this State, we are called upon to abandon the poor creature whom we have emancipated. We are coolly told that he has no right beyond this, and we are told that under this amendment the power of the State within whose limits he happens to be is not at all restrained in respect to him, and that the State, through its Legislature, may at any time declare him to be a vagrant, and as such commit him to jail, or assign him to uncompensated service."

Mr. Johnson, of Maryland, made a speech, in which he expressed himself as in favor of conferring citizenship upon the negro, and yet unable to vote for this bill from the opinion he entertained on "the question of power." He referred to the Dred Scott and other decisions, and showed their bearing upon the legislation now proposed. He said: "I have been exceedingly anxious individually that there should be some definition which will rid this class of our people from that objection. If the Supreme Court decision is a binding one, and will be followed in the future, this law which we are now about to pass will be held, of course, to be of no avail, as far as it professes to define what citizenship is, because it gives the rights of citizenship to all persons without distinction of color, and, of course, embraces Africans or descendants of Africans."

He referred to a precedent when Congress had conferred the rights of citizenship: "The citizens of Texas, who, of course, were aliens, it has never been doubted became citizens of the United States by the annexation of Texas; and that was not done by treaty, it was done by legislation. If the power was in Congress by legislation to make citizens of all the inhabitants of the State of Texas, why is it not in the power of Congress to make citizens by legislation of all who are inhabitants of the United States, and who are not citizens? That is what this bill does, or what it proposes to do. There are within the United States millions of people who are not citizens, according to the view of the Supreme Court of the United States. Ought they to be citizens? I think they ought. I think it is an anomaly that says there shall not be the rights of citizenship to any of the inhabitants of any State of the United States.

"While they were slaves, it was a very different question; but now, when slavery is terminated, and by terminating it you have got rid of the only obstacle in the way of citizenship, two questions arise: First, whether that fact itself does not make them citizens? Before they were not citizens, because of slavery, and only because of slavery. Slavery abolished, why are they not just as much citizens as they would have been if slavery had never existed? My opinion is that they become citizens, and I hold that opinion so strongly that I should consider it unnecessary to legislate on the subject at all, as far as that class is concerned, but for the ruling of the Supreme Court to which I have adverted."

Mr. Davis, of Kentucky, spoke against the propriety and constitutionality of making all negroes citizens of the United States. He said: "There never was a colony before the Declaration of Independence, and there never was a State after the Declaration of Independence, up to the time of the adoption of the Constitution, so far as I have been able to learn by the slight historical examination which I have given to the subject, that ever made or attempted to make any other person than a person who belonged to one of the nationalities of Europe a citizen. I invoke the chairman of the committee to give me an instance, to point to any history or any memento, where a negro, although that negro was born in America, was ever made a citizen of either of the States of the United States before the adoption of this Constitution. The whole material out of which citizens were made previous to the adoption of the present Constitution was from the European nationalities, from the Caucasian race, if I may use the term. I deny that a single citizen was ever made by one of the States out of the negro race. I deny that a single citizen was ever made by one of the States out of the Mongolian race. I controvert that a single citizen was ever made by one of the States out of the Chinese race, out of the Hindoos, or out of any other race of people but the Caucasian race of Europe.

"I come, then, to this position: that whenever the States, after the Declaration of Independence and before the present Constitution was adopted, legislated in relation to citizenship, or acted in their governments in relation to citizenship, the subject of that legislation or that action was the Caucasian race of Europe; that none of the inferior races of any kind were intended to be embraced or were embraced by this work of Government in manufacturing citizens."

Mr. Trumbull inquired, "Will the Senator from Kentucky allow me to ask him if he means to assert that negroes were not citizens of any of these colonies before the adoption of the Constitution?"

"I say they were not," said Mr. Davis.

"Does the Senator wish any authority to show that they were?" asked Mr. Trumbull.

"When I get through," said Mr. Davis, "you can answer me."

Mr. Trumbull replied: "I understood the Senator to challenge me to produce any proof on that point, and I thought he would like to have it in his speech. I can assert to him that by a solemn decision of the Supreme Court of North Carolina, they were citizens before the adoption of the Constitution."

"If the honorable Senator will allow me," said Mr. Davis, "I will get along with my remarks."

"I think you will get along better," replied Mr. Trumbull, "by not being exposed in your statements."

"The honorable Senator is full of conceit, but I have seen less conceit with a great deal more brains," said Mr. Davis, who then proceeded "to throw up" what he termed "the main buttress for the defense of the positions" that he took.

"My main position," said he, "is, that no native-born person of the United States, of any race or color, can be admitted a citizen of the United States by Congress under the power conferred in relation to naturalization by the Constitution upon Congress."

After reading some authorities, the Senator proceeded to say: "A grave hallucination in this day is to claim all power; and a minor error is that every thing which passion, or interest, or party power, or any selfish claims may represent to the judgment or imagination of gentlemen who belong to strong parties, to be necessary or useful for the good and the domination of such parties, is seized upon in defiance of a fair construction of language, in outrage of the plain meaning of the Constitution. That is not the rule by which our Constitution is to be interpreted. It is not the rule by which it is to be administered. On the contrary, if the able, honorable, and clear-headed Senator from Illinois would do himself and his country the justice to place himself in the position of the framers of the Constitution; if he would look all around on the circumstances and connections of that day, on the purposes of those men not only in relation to forming a more perfect Union, but also in relation to securing the blessings of life, liberty, and property to themselves and their posterity forever; if the honorable Senator would construe the Constitution according to the light, the sacred and bright light which such surrounding circumstances would throw upon his intellect, it seems to me that he would at once abandon this abominable bill, and would also ask to withdraw its twin sister from the other House that both might be smothered here together upon the altar of the Constitution and of patriotism."

At the close of Mr. Davis' speech, much debate and conversation ensued among various Senators upon a proposed amendment by Mr. Lane, of Kansas, by which Indians "under tribal authority" should be excluded from the benefits conferred by this bill. After this question was disposed of, Mr. Davis was drawn out in another speech by what seemed to him to be the necessity of defending some positions which he had assumed. He said:

"I still reiterate the position that the negro is not a citizen here according to the essential fundamental principles of our system; but whether he be a citizen or not, he is not a foreigner, and no man, white or black, or red or mixed, can be made a citizen by naturalization unless he is a foreigner."

Mr. Clark, of New Hampshire, interposed: "I wish the Senator from Kentucky would tell us what constitutes a citizen under the Constitution."

"A foreigner is not a citizen in the fullest sense of the word at all," said Mr. Davis.

"The Senator is now telling us," said Mr. Clark, "who is not a citizen, but my question is, What constitutes a citizen?"

"I leave that to the exercise of your own ingenuity," replied Mr. Davis.

"That is it," said Mr. Clark. "Washington is dead; Marshall is dead; Story is dead; I hoped the Senator from Kentucky would have enlightened us. He says a negro is not a citizen, and a negro is not a foreigner and can not be made a citizen. He says that a person who might be and was a citizen before the Constitution, is not a citizen since the Constitution was adopted. What right was taken away from him by the Constitution that disqualifies him from being a citizen? The free negroes in my State, before the Constitution was adopted, were citizens."

Mr. Davis, having admitted that free negroes were citizens before the Constitution in New Hampshire, Mr. Clark said:

"I desired that the Senator should tell me what, in his opinion, constituted a citizen under the Constitution."

Mr. Davis replied: "I will answer the honorable Senator. We sometimes answer a positive question by declaring what a thing is not. Now, the honorable Senator asks me what a citizen is. It is easier to answer what it is not than what it is, and I say that a negro is not a citizen."

"Well, that is a lucid definition," said Mr. Clark.

"Sufficient for the subject," said Mr. Davis.

"That is begging the question," Mr. Clark replied. "I wanted to find why a negro was not a citizen, if the gentleman would tell me. If he would lay down his definition, I wanted to see whether the negro did not comply with it and conform to it, so as to be a citizen; but he insists that he is not a citizen."

"I will answer that question, if the honorable Senator will permit me," said Mr. Davis. "Government is a political partnership. No persons but the partners who formed the partnership are parties to the government. Here is a government formed by the white man alone. The negro was excluded from the formation of our political partnership; he had nothing to do with it; he had nothing to do in its formation."

"Is it a close corporation, so that new partners can not be added?" asked Mr. Stewart, of Nevada.

"Yes, sir," said Mr. Davis; "it is a close white corporation. You may bring all of Europe, but none of Asia and none of Africa into our partnership."

"Let us see," said Mr. Clark, "how that may be. Take the gentleman's own ground that government is a partnership, and those who did not enter into it and take an active part in it can not be citizens. Is a woman a citizen under our Constitution?"

"Not to vote," said Mr. Davis.

"I did not ask about voting," said Mr. Clark. "The gentleman said awhile ago that voting did not constitute citizenship. I want to know if she is a citizen. Can she not sue and be sued, contract, and exercise the rights of a citizen?"

"So can a free negro," said Mr. Davis.

"Then, if a free negro can do all that," said Mr. Clark; "why is he not a citizen?"

"Because he is no part of the governing power; that is the reason," Mr. Davis replied.

"I deny that," said Mr. Clark, "because in some of the States he is a part of the governing power. The Senator only begs the question; it only comes back to this, that a nigger is a nigger." [Laughter.]

"That is the whole of it," said Mr. Davis.

BEVERLY JOHNSON

SENATOR FROM MARYLAND

"That is the whole of the gentleman's logic," said Mr. Clark.

In answer to the statement insisted on by Mr. Davis, "You can not make a citizen of any body that is not a foreigner," Mr. Johnson said:

"That would be an extraordinary condition for the country to be in. Here are four million negroes. They are not foreigners, because they were born in the United States. They have no foreign allegiance to renounce, because they owed no foreign allegiance. Their allegiance, whatever it was, was an allegiance to the Government of the United States alone. They can not come, therefore, under the naturalizing clause; they can not come, of course, under the statutes passed in pursuance of the power conferred upon Congress by that clause; but does it follow from that that you can not make them citizens; that the Congress of the United States, vested with the whole legislative power belonging to the Government, having within the limits of the United States four million people anxious to become citizens, and when you are anxious to make them citizens, have no power to make them citizens? It seems to me that to state the question is to answer it.

"The honorable member reads the Constitution as if it said that none but white men should become citizens of the United States; but it says no such thing, and never intended, in my judgment, to say any such thing. If it had designed to exclude from all participation in the rights of citizenship certain men on account of color, and to have confined, at all times thereafter, citizenship to the white race, it is but fair to presume, looking to the character of the men who framed the Constitution, that they would have put that object beyond all possible doubt; they would have said that no man should be a citizen of the United States except a white man, or rather would have negatived the right of the negro to become a citizen by saying that Congress might pass uniform rules upon the subject of the naturalization of white immigrants and nobody else; but that they did not do. They left it to Congress. Congress, in the exercise of their discretion, have thought proper to insert the term 'white' in the naturalization act; but they may strike it out, and if it should be stricken out, I do not think any lawyer, except my friend from Kentucky, would deny that a black man could be naturalized, and by naturalization become a citizen of the United States.

"But to go back to the point from which the questions of my

honorable friend from Kentucky caused me to digress, we have now within the United States four million colored people, the descendants of Africans, whose ancestors were brought into the United States as chattels. It was because of that condition that they were considered as not entitled to the rights of citizenship. We have put an end to that condition. We have said that at all times hereafter men of any color that nature may think proper to impress upon the human frame, shall, if within the United States, be free, and not property. Then, we have four million colored people who are now as free as we are; and the only question is, whether, being free, they can not be clothed with the rights of citizenship. The honorable member from Kentucky says no, because the naturalization clause does not include them. I have attempted to answer that. He says no, because the act passed in pursuance of that clause does not include them. I have answered that by saying that that act in that particular may be changed."

On the following day, February 1st, the discussion of the bill was resumed by Mr. Morrill, of Maine. He said of the bill: "It marks an epoch in the history of this country, and from this time forward the legislation takes a fresh and a new departure. Sir, to-day is the only hour since this Government began when it was possible to have enacted it. Such has been the situation of politics in this country, nay, sir, such have been the provisions of the fundamental law of this country, that such legislation hitherto has never been possible. There has been no time since the foundation of the Government when an American Congress could by possibility have enacted such a law, or with propriety have made such a declaration. What is this declaration? All persons born in this country are citizens. That never was so before. Although I have said that by the fundamental principles of American law all persons were entitled to be citizens by birth, we all know that there was an exceptional condition in the Government of the country which provided for an exception to this general rule. Here were four million slaves in this country that were not citizens, not citizens by the general policy of the country, not citizens on account of their condition of servitude; up to this hour they could not have been treated by us as citizens; so long as that provision in the Constitution which recognized this exceptional condition remained the fundamental law of the country, such a declaration as this would not have been legal, could not have been enacted by Congress. I hail it, therefore, as a declaration which typifies a grand fundamental change in the politics of the country, and which change justifies the declaration now.

"The honorable Senator from Kentucky has vexed himself somewhat, I think, with the problem of the naturalization of American citizens. As he reads it, only foreigners can be naturalized, or, in other words, can become citizens; and upon his assumption, four million men and women in this country are outside not only of naturalization, not only of citizenship, but outside of the possibility of citizenship. Sir, he has forgotten the grand principle both of nature and nations, both of law and politics, that birth gives citizenship of itself. This is the fundamental principle running through all modern politics both in this country and in Europe. Every-where, where the principles of law have been recognized at all, birth by its inherent energy and force gives citizenship. Therefore the founders of this Government made no provision—of course they made none—for the naturalization of natural-born citizens. The Constitution speaks of 'natural-born,' and speaks of them as citizens in contradistinction from those who are alien to us. Therefore, sir, this amendment, although it is a grand enunciation, although it is a lofty and sublime declaration, has no force or efficiency as an enactment. I hail it and accept it simply as a declaration.

"The honorable Senator from Kentucky, when he criticises the methods of naturalization, and rules out, for want of power, four million people, forgets this general process of nations and of nature by which every man, by his birth, is entitled to citizenship, and that upon the general principle that he owes allegiance to the country of his birth, and that country owes him protection. That is the foundation, as I understand it, of all citizenship, and these are the essential elements of citizenship: allegiance on the one side, and protection on the other."

In reply to statements made by Mr. Davis, Mr. Morrill remarked: "The Senator from Kentucky denounces as a usurpation this measure, and particularly this amendment, this declaration. He says it is not within the principles of the Constitution. That it is extraordinary I admit. That the measure is not ordinary is most clear. There is no parallel, I have already said, for it in the history of this country; there is no parallel for it in the history of any country. No nation, from the foundation of government, has ever undertaken to make a legislative declaration so broad. Why? Because no nation hitherto has ever cherished a liberty so universal. The ancient republics were all exceptional in their liberty; they all had excepted classes, subjected classes, which were not the subject of government, and, therefore, they could not so legislate. That it is extraordinary and without a parallel in the history of this Government, or of any other, does not affect the character of the declaration itself.

"The Senator from Kentucky tells us that the proposition is revolutionary, and he thinks that is an objection. I freely concede that it is revolutionary. I admit that this species of legislation is absolutely revolutionary. But are we not in the midst of revolution? Is the Senator from Kentucky utterly oblivious to the grand results of four years of war? Are we not in the midst of a civil and political revolution which has changed the fundamental principles of our Government in some respects? Sir, is it no revolution that you have changed the entire system of servitude in this country? Is it no revolution that now you can no longer talk of two systems of civilization in this country? Four short years back, I remember to have listened to eloquent speeches in this chamber, in which we were told that there was a grand antagonism in our institutions; that there were two civilizations; that there was a civilization based on servitude, and that it was antagonistic to the free institutions of the country. Where is that? Gone forever. That result is a revolution grander and sublimer in its consequences than the world has witnessed hitherto.

"I accept, then, what the Senator from Kentucky thinks so obnoxious. We are in the midst of revolution. We have revolutionized this Constitution of ours to that extent; and every substantial change in the fundamental constitution of a country is a revolution. Why, sir, the Constitution even provides for revolutionizing itself. Nay, more, it contemplates it; contemplates that in the changing phases of life, civil and political, changes in the fundamental law will become necessary; and is it needful for me to advert to the facts and events of the last four or five years to justify the declaration that revolution here is not only radical and thorough, but the result of the events of the last four years? Of course, I mean to contend in all I say that the revolution of which I speak should be peaceful, as on the part of the Government here it has been peaceful. It grows out, to be sure, of an assault upon our institutions by those whose purpose it was to overthrow the Government; but, on the part of the Government, it has been peaceful, it has been within the forms of the Constitution; but it is a revolution nevertheless.

"But the honorable Senator from Kentucky insists that it is a usurpation. Not so, sir. Although it is a revolution radical, as I contend, it was not a usurpation. It was not a usurpation, because it took place within the provisions contemplated in the Constitution. More than that, it was a change precisely in harmony with the general principles of the Government. This great change which has been wrought in our institutions was in harmony with the fundamental principles of the Government. The change which has been made has destroyed that which was exceptional in our institutions; and the action of the Government in regard to it was provoked by the enemies of the Government. The opportunity was afforded, and the change which has been wrought was in harmony with the fundamental principles of the Government."

The Senator from Maine opposed the theory that this is a Government exclusively for white men. He remarked: "It is said that this amendment raises the general question of the antagonism of the races, which, we are told, is a well-established fact. It is said that no rational man, no intelligent legislator or statesman, should ever act without reference to that grand historical fact; and the Senator from Pennsylvania, [Mr. Cowan,] on a former occasion, asserted that this Government, that American society, had been established here upon the principle of the exclusion, as he termed it, of the inferior and the barbarian races. Mr. President, I deny that proposition as a historical fact. There is nothing more inaccurate. No proposition could possibly be made here or anywhere else more inaccurate than to say that American society, either civil or political, was formed in the interest of any race or class. Sir, the history of the country does not bear out the statement of the honorable Senator from Pennsylvania. Was not America said to be the land of refuge? Has it not been, since the earliest period, held up as an asylum for the oppressed of all nations? Hither, allow me to ask, have not all the peoples of the nations of the earth come for an asylum and for refuge? All the nations of the earth, and all the varieties of the races of the nations of the earth, have gathered here. In the early settlements of the country, the Irish, the French, the Swede, the Turk, the Italian, the Moor, and so I might enumerate all the races, and all the variety of races, came here; and it is a fundamental mistake to suppose that settlement was begun here in the interests of any class, or condition, or race, or interest. This Western Continent was looked to as an asylum for the oppressed of all nations and of all races. Hither all nations and all races have come. Here, sir, upon the grand plane of republican democratic liberty, they have undertaken to work out the great problem of man's capacity for self-government without stint or limit."

Mr. Davis then made another speech in opposition to the bill. When the hour for adjournment had arrived, and Mr. Johnson interrupted him with a proposition that "the bill be passed over for to-day," Mr. Davis said, "I am wound up, and am obliged to run down." The Senate, however, adjourned at a late hour, and resumed the hearing of Mr. Davis on the following day.

In alluding to Mr. Johnson's strictures on his assertion that Congress had no power to confer the right of citizenship on "the native born negro," Mr. Davis said: "The honorable Senator, [Mr. Johnson,] as I said the other day, is one of the ablest lawyers, and, I believe, the ablest living lawyer in the land. I have seen gentlemen sometimes so much the lawyer that they had to abate some of the statesman [laughter]; and I am not certain, I would not say it was so—I will not arrogate to myself to say so—but sometimes a suspicion flashes across my mind that that is precisely the predicament of my honorable friend.

"I maintain that a negro can not be made a citizen by Congress; he can not be made a citizen by any naturalization laws, because the naturalization laws apply to foreigners alone. No man can shake the legal truth of that position. They apply to foreigners alone; and a negro, an Indian, or any other person born within the United States, not being a foreigner, can not be naturalized; therefore they can not be made citizens by the uniform rule established by Congress under the Constitution, and there is no other rule. Congress has no power, as I said before, to naturalize a citizen. They could not be made citizens by treaty. If they are made so at all, it is by their birth, and the locality of their birth, and the general operation and effect of our Constitution. If they are so made citizens, that question is a judicial question, not a legislative question. Congress has no power to enlarge or extend any of the provisions of the Constitution which bear upon the birth or citizenship of negroes or Indians born in the United States.

"If there was any despot in Europe or in the world that wanted a master architect in framing and putting together a despotic and oppressive law, I would, if my slight voice could reach him, by all means say to him, Seek the laboratory of the Senator from Illinois. If he has not proved himself an adept in this kind of legislation, unconstitutional, unjust, oppressive, iniquitous, unwise, impolitic, calculated to keep forever a severance of the Union, to exclude from all their constitutional rights, privileges, and powers under the Government eleven States of the Union—if he has not devised such a measure as that, I have not reason enough to comprehend it.

Mr. Davis closed his speech by saying: "Was it for these fruits and these laws that we went into this war? Was it for these fruits and these laws and these oppressions that two million and a quarter of men were ordered into the field? Was it that the American people might enjoy these as the fruits of the triumphant close of this war, that hundreds of thousands of them have been mutilated on the battle-field and by the diseases of the camp, and that a debt of four or five thousand million dollars has been left upon the country? If these are to be the results of the war, better that not a single man had been marshaled in the field nor a single star worn by one of our officers. These military gentlemen think they have a right to command and control every-where. They do it. They think they have a right to do it here, and we are sheep in the hands of our shearers. We are dumb."

Mr. Trumbull said: "I will occupy a few moments of the attention of the Senate, after this long harangue of the Senator from Kentucky, which he closed by declaring that we are dumb in the presence of military power. If he has satisfied the Senate that he is dumb, I presume he has satisfied the Senate of all the other positions he has taken; and the others are about as absurd as that declaration. He denounces this bill as 'outrageous,' 'most

14

monstrous,' 'abominable,' 'oppressive,' 'iniquitous,' 'unconstitutional,' 'void.'

"Now, what is this bill that is obnoxious to such terrible epithets? It is a bill providing that all people shall have equal rights. Is not that abominable? Is not that iniquitous? Is not that monstrous? Is not that terrible on white men? [Laughter.] When was such legislation as this ever thought of for white men?

"Sir, this bill applies to white men as well as black men. It declares that all men in the United States shall be entitled to the same civil rights, the right to the fruit of their own labor, the right to make contracts, the right to buy and sell, and enjoy liberty and happiness; and that is abominable and iniquitous and unconstitutional! Could any thing be more monstrous or more abominable than for a member of the Senate to rise in his place and denounce with such epithets as these a bill, the only object of which is to secure equal rights to all the citizens of the country—a bill that protects a white man just as much as a black man? With what consistency and with what face can a Senator in his place here say to the Senate and the country, that this is a bill for the benefit of the black men exclusively, when there is no such distinction in it, and when the very object of the bill is to break down all discrimination between black men and white men?"

Mr. Guthrie, of Kentucky, said: "My doctrine is that slavery exists no longer in this country; that it is impossible to exist in the face of that provision; and with slavery fell the laws of all the States providing for slavery, every one of them. I do not see what benefit can arise from repealing them by this bill, because, if they are not repealed by the Constitution as amended, this bill could not repeal them. I hope that all the States in which slavery formerly existed will accept that constitutional provision in good faith. I myself accept it in good faith. Believing that all the laws authorizing slavery have fallen, I have advised the people of Kentucky, and I would advise all the States, to put these Africans upon the same footing that the whites are in relation to civil rights. They have all the rights that were formerly accorded to the free colored population in all the States just as fully this day as they will have after this bill has passed, and they will continue to have them.

"Now, to the States belong the government of their own population, and those within their borders, upon all subjects. We, in Kentucky, prescribe punishment for those who violate the laws; we prescribe it for the white population; we prescribe it for the free African population, and we prescribe it for the slave population. All the laws prescribing punishment for slaves fell with slavery, and they were subject afterward only to the penalties which were inflicted upon the free colored population, they then being free. Slaves, for many offenses, were punished far less than the free colored people. No slave was sent to the penitentiary and punished for stealing, or any thing of that kind, whereas a free person was. But all these States will now, of course, remodel their laws upon the subject of offenses. I would advise that there should be but one code for all persons, black as well as white; that there shall be one general rule for the punishment of crime in the different States. But, sir, the States must have time to act on the subject; and yet we are here preparing laws and penalties, and proposing to carry them into execution by military authority, before the States have had time to legislate, and even before some of their Legislatures have had time to convene.

"Kentucky has had her share of talking here, and, sir, she has had her share of suffering during the war. At one time she was invaded by three armies of the rebellion; all but seven or eight counties of the State, at one time, were occupied by its armies, and her whole territory devastated by guerrillas. We have suffered in this war. We have borne it as best we could. We feel it intensely that now, at the end of the war, we should be subjected to a military despotism, our houses liable to be entered at any time when our families are at rest, by military men who can arrest and send to prison without warrant, and we are obliged to go, and we are obliged to pay any fines they may impose. I do not believe that you will lose any thing if you pause before passing such legislation as this, and establishing these military despotisms, for we do not know where they are to end."

Mr. Hendricks, of Indiana, had proposed to strike out the last clause of the bill, which provided that "such part of the land and naval forces of the United States, or of the militia," as should be necessary, might be employed to prevent the violation, and enforce the due execution of this act. The Senator from Indiana opposed the bill on the ground that it employed the machinery of the Fugitive Slave Law, and that it was to be enforced by the military authority of the United States. He said:

"This bill is a wasp; its sting is in its tail. Sir, what is this bill? It provides, in the first place, that the civil rights of all men, without regard to color, shall be equal; and, in the second place, that if any man shall violate that principle by his conduct, he shall be responsible to the court; that he may be prosecuted criminally and punished for the crime, or he may be sued in a civil action and damages recovered by the party wronged. Is not that broad enough? Do Senators want to go further than this? To recognize the civil rights of the colored people as equal to the civil rights of the white people, I understand to be as far as Senators desire to go; in the language of the Senator from Massachusetts [Mr. Sumner], to place all men upon an equality before the law; and that is proposed in regard to their civil rights."

In reference to the reënactment of the odious features of the Fugitive Slave Law in this bill, Mr. Hendricks said: "I recollect how the blood of the people was made to run cold within them when it was said that the white man was required to run after the fugitive slave; that the law of 1850 made you and me, my brother Senators, slave-catchers; that the *posse comitatus* could be called to execute a writ of the law, for the recovery of a runaway slave, under the provisions of the Constitution of the United States; and the whole country was agitated because of it. Now slavery is gone; the negro is to be established upon a platform of civil equality with the white man. That is the proposition. But we do not stop there; we are to reënact a law that nearly all of you said was wicked and wrong; and for what purpose? Not to pursue the negro any longer; not for the purpose of catching him; not for the purpose of catching the great criminals of the land; but for the purpose of placing it in the power of any deputy marshal in any county of the country to call upon you and me, and all the body of the people, to pursue some white man who is running for his liberty, because some negro has charged him with denying to him equal civil rights with the white man. I thought, sir, that that frame-work was enough; I thought, when you placed under the command of the marshal, in every county of the land, all the body of the people, and put every one upon the track of the fleeing white man, that that was enough; but it is not. For the purpose of the enforcement of this law, the President is authorized to appoint somebody who is to have the command of the military and naval forces of the United States—for what purpose? To prevent a violation of this law, and to execute it.

"You clothe the marshals under this bill with all the powers that were given to the marshals under the Fugitive Slave Law. That was regarded as too arbitrary in its provisions, and you repealed it. You said it should not stand upon the statute-book any longer; that no man, white or black, should be pursued under the provisions of that law. Now, you reënact it, and you claim it as a merit and an ornament to the legislation of the country; and you add an army of officers and clothe them with the power to call upon any body and every body to pursue the running white man. That is not enough, but you must have the military to be called in, at the pleasure of whom? Such a person as the President may authorize to call out the military forces. Where it shall be, and to whom this power shall be given, we do not know."

Mr. Lane, of Indiana, replied to the argument of his colleague. He said: "It is true that many of the provisions of this bill, changed in their purpose and object, are almost identical with the provisions of the Fugitive Slave Law, and they are denounced by my colleague in their present application; but I have not heard any denunciation from my colleague, or from any of those associated with him, of the provisions of that Fugitive Slave Law which was enacted in the interest of slavery, and for purposes of oppression, and which was an unworthy, cowardly, disgraceful concession to Southern opinion by Northern politicians. I have suffered no suitable opportunity to escape me to denounce the monstrous character of that Fugitive Slave Act of 1850. All these provisions were odious and disgraceful in my opinion, when applied in the interest of slavery, when the object was to strike down the rights of man. But here the purpose is changed. These provisions are in the interest of freemen and of freedom, and what was odious in the one case becomes highly meritorious in the other. It is an instance of poetic justice and of apt retribution that God has caused the wrath of man to praise Him. I stand by every provision of this bill, drawn as it is from that most iniquitous fountain, the Fugitive Slave Law of 1850.

"Then my colleague asks, Why do you invoke the power of the

military to enforce these laws? And he says that constables, and sheriffs, and marshals, when they have process to serve, have a right to call upon the *posse comitatus*, the body of the whole people, to enforce their writs. Here is a justice of the peace in South Carolina or Georgia, or a county court, or a circuit court, that is called upon to execute this law. They appoint their own marshal, their deputy marshal, or their constable, and he calls upon the *posse comitatus*. Neither the judge, nor the jury, nor the officer, as we believe, is willing to execute the law. He may call upon the people, the body of the whole people, a body of rebels steeped in treason and rebellion to their lips, and they are to execute it; and the gentleman seems wonderfully astonished that we should call upon the military power. We should not legislate at all if we believed the State courts could or would honestly carry out the provisions of the constitutional amendment; but because we believe they will not do that, we give the Federal officers jurisdiction.

"But what harm is to result from it? Who is to be oppressed? What white man fleeing, in the language of my colleague, pursued by these harpies of the law, is in danger of having his rights stricken down? What does the bill provide? It places all men upon an equality, and unless the white man violates the law, he is in no danger. It takes no rights from any white man. It simply places others on the same platform upon which he stands; and if he would invoke the power of local prejudice to override the laws of the country, this is no Government unless the military may be called in to enforce the order of the civil courts and obedience to the laws of the country."

Mr. Wilson, of Massachusetts, said, in answer to some objections to the bill urged by Mr. Guthrie: "The Senator tells us that the emancipated men ought to have their civil rights, that the black codes fell with slavery; but the Senator forgets that at least six of the reörganized States in their new Legislatures have passed laws wholly incompatible with the freedom of these freedmen; and so atrocious are the provisions of these laws, and so persistently are they carried into effect by the local authorities, that General Thomas, in Mississippi, General Swayne, in Alabama, General Sickles, in South Carolina, and General Terry, in Virginia, have issued positive orders, forbidding the execution of the black laws that have just been passed.

"So unjust, so wicked, so incompatible are these new black laws of the rebel States, made in defiance of the expressed will of the nation, that Lieutenant-general Grant has been forced to issue that order, which sets aside the black laws of all these rebellious States against the freedmen, and allows no law to be enforced against them that is not enforced equally against white men. This order, issued by General Grant, will be respected, obeyed, and enforced in the rebel States with the military power of the nation. Southern legislators and people must learn, if they are compelled to learn by the bayonets of the Army of the United States, that the civil rights of the freedmen must be and shall be respected; that these freedmen are as free as their late masters; that they shall live under the same laws, be tried for their violation in the same manner, and if found guilty, punished in the same manner and degree.

"This measure is called for, because these reconstructed Legislatures, in defiance of the rights of the freedmen, and the will of the nation, embodied in the amendment to the Constitution, have enacted laws nearly as iniquitous as the old slave codes that darkened the legislation of other days. The needs of more than four million colored men imperatively call for its enactment. The Constitution authorizes and the national will demands it. By a series of legislative acts, by executive proclamations, by military orders, and by the adoption of the amendment to the Constitution by the people of the United States, the gigantic system of human slavery that darkened the land, controlled the policy, and swayed the destinies of the republic has forever perished. Step by step we have marched right on from one victory to another, with the music of broken fetters ringing in our ears. None of the series of acts in this beneficent legislation of Congress, none of the proclamations of the Executive, none of these military orders, protecting rights secured by law, will ever be revoked or amended by the voice of the American people. There is now

> "'No slave beneath that starry flag,
> The emblem of the free.'

"By the will of the nation freedom and free institutions for all, chains and fetters for none, are forever incorporated in the fundamental law of regenerated and united America. Slave codes and auction blocks, chains and fetters and blood-hounds, are things of the past, and the chattel stands forth a man, with the rights and the powers of the freemen. For the better security of these new-born civil rights we are now about to pass the greatest and the grandest act in this series of acts that have emancipated a race and disinthralled a nation. It will pass, it will go upon the statute-book of the republic by the voice of the American people, and there it will remain. From the verdict of Congress in favor of this great measure, no appeal will ever be entertained by the people of the United States."

Mr. Cowan spoke again, and denounced the section of the bill which provided for its enforcement by the military. He said: "There it is; words can not make it plainer; reason can not elucidate it; no language can strengthen it or weaken it, one way or the other. There is the question whether a military man, educated in a military school, accustomed to supreme command, unaccustomed to the administration of civil law among a free people, is to be intrusted with these appellate jurisdiction over the courts of the country; whether he can in any way, whether he ought in any way, to be intrusted with such a power. I, for my part, will never agree to it; and I should feel myself recreant to every duty that I owed to myself, to my country, to my country's history, and I may say to the race which has been for hundreds and thousands of years endeavoring to attain to something like constitutional liberty, if I did not resist this and all similar projects."

Mr. Trumbull answered some objections to the bill. "The Senator from Indiana [Mr. Hendricks] objects to the bill because he says that the same provisions which were enacted in the old Fugitive Slave Law are incorporated into this, and that it has been heralded to the country that it was a great achievement to do this; and he insists that if those provisions of law were odious and wicked and wrong which provided for punishing men for aiding the slave to escape, therefore they must be wicked and wrong now when they are employed for the punishing a man who undertakes to put a person into slavery. Sir, that does not follow at all. A law may be iniquitous and unjust and wrong which undertakes to punish another for doing an innocent act, which would be righteous and just and proper to punish a man for doing a wicked act. We have upon our statute-books a law punishing a man who commits murder, because the commission of murder is a high crime, and the party who does it forfeits his right to live; but would it be just to apply the law which punishes a person for committing murder to an innocent person who had killed another accidentally, without malice? That is the difference. It is the difference between right and wrong, between good and evil. True, the features of the Fugitive Slave Law were abominable when they were used for the purpose of punishing, not negroes, as the Senator from Indiana says, but white men. The Fugitive Slave Law was enacted for the purpose of punishing white men who aided to give the natural gift of liberty to those who were enslaved. Now, sir, we propose to use the provisions of the Fugitive Slave Law for the purpose of punishing those who deny freedom, not those who seek to aid persons to escape to freedom. The difference was too clearly pointed out by the colleague of the Senator [Mr. Lane] to justify me in taking further time in alluding to it.

"But the Senator objects to this bill because it authorizes the calling in of the military; and he asserts that it is the only law in which the military is brought in to enforce it. The Senator from Pennsylvania [Mr. Cowan] follows this up with a half hour's speech, denouncing this law as obnoxious to the objection that it is a military law, that it is taking the trial of persons for offenses out of the hands of the courts and placing them under the military—a monstrous proposition, he says. Is that so? What is the law?

"It is a court bill; it is to be executed through the courts, and in no other way. But does the Senator mean to say it is a military bill because the military may be called in, in aid of the execution of the law through the courts? Does the Senator from Pennsylvania—I should like his attention, and that of the Senator from Indiana, too—deny the authority to call in the military in aid of the execution of the law through the courts?

"Let me read a clause from the Constitution, which seems to have been forgotten by the Senator from Pennsylvania and the Senator from Indiana. The Senator from Pennsylvania, who has denounced this law, has been living under just such a law for thirty years, and it seems never found it out. What says the Constitution? 'Congress shall have power to provide for calling forth the militia to execute the laws of the Union.'

"Then, can not the militia prevent persons from violating the law? They are authorized by the Constitution to be called out for the purpose of executing the law, and here we have a law that is to be carried into execution, and when you find persons combined together to prevent its execution, you can not do any thing with them! Suppose that the county authorities in Muscogee County, Georgia, combine together to deny civil rights to to every colored man in that county. For the purpose of preventing it, before they have done any act, I say the militia may be called out to prevent them from committing an act. We are not required to wait until the act is committed before any thing can be done. That was the doctrine which led to this rebellion, that we had no authority to do any thing till the conflict of arms came. I believed then, in 1860, that we had authority; and if it had been properly exercised, if the men who were threatening rebellion, who were in this chamber defying the authority of the Government, had been arrested for treason—of which, in my judgment, by setting on foot armed expeditions against the country, they were guilty—and if they had been tried and punished and executed for the crime, I doubt whether this great rebellion would ever have taken place.

"There is another statute to which I beg leave to call the attention of the Senator from Pennsylvania, and under which he has lived for thirty years without ever having known it; and his rights have been fully protected. I wish to call attention to a section from which the tenth section of the bill under consideration, at which the Senator from Indiana is so horrified, is copied word for word, and letter for letter. The act of March 10, 1836, 'supplementary to an act entitled "An act in addition to the act for the punishment of certain crimes against the United States, and to repeal the acts therein mentioned," approved 20th of April, 1818,' contains the very section that is in this bill, word for word. It did not horrify the country; it did not destroy all the liberties of the people; it did not consolidate all the powers of the Constitution in the Federal Government; it did not overthrow the courts, and it has existed now for thirty years!"

The question was first taken on the amendment offered by Mr. Hendricks, to strike out the tenth section of the bill. The vote resulted yeas, twelve; nays, thirty-four.

At this stage of the proceedings, Mr. Saulsbury moved to

amend the bill by adding in the first section of the bill after the words "civil rights," the words, "except the right to vote in the States." He desired that if the Senate did not wish to confer the right of suffrage by this bill, they should say so. The question being taken on Mr. Saulsbury's amendment, the vote resulted seven in the affirmative and thirty-nine in the negative.

The vote was finally taken on the passage of the bill, which resulted thirty-three in the affirmative and twelve in the negative. The following Senators voted in favor of the bill:

Messrs. Anthony, Brown, Chandler, Clark, Connor, Cragin, Dixon, Fessenden, Foot, Foster, Harris, Henderson, Howard, Howe, Kirkwood, Henry S. Lane, James H. Lane, Morgan, Morrill, Nye, Poland, Pomeroy, Ramsey, Sherman, Sprague, Stewart, Sumner, Trumbull, Wade, Willey, Williams, Wilson, and Yates—33.

The following voted against the bill, namely:

Messrs. Buckalew, Cowan, Davis, Guthrie, Hendricks, McDougall, Nesmith, Norton, Riddle, Saulsbury, Stockton, and Van Winkle—12.

Five Senators were absent, to wit:

Messrs. Creswell, Doolittle, Grimes, Johnson, and Wright—5.

CHAPTER X.

THE CIVIL RIGHTS BILL IN THE HOUSE OF REPRESENTATIVES.

THE BILL REFERRED TO THE JUDICIARY COMMITTEE AND REPORTED BACK—SPEECH BY THE CHAIRMAN OF THE COMMITTEE—MR. ROGERS—MR. COOK—MR. THAYER—MR. ELDRIDGE—MR. THORNTON—MR. WINDOM—MR. SHELLABARGER—MR. BROOMALL—MR. RAYMOND—MR. DELANO—MR. KERR—AMENDMENT BY MR. BINGHAM—HIS SPEECH—REPLY BY HIS COLLEAGUE—DISCUSSION CLOSED BY MR. WILSON—YEAS AND NAYS ON THE PASSAGE OF THE BILL—MR. LE BLOND'S PROPOSED TITLE—AMENDMENTS OF THE HOUSE ACCEPTED BY THE SENATE.

ON the 5th of February, four days after the passage of the Civil Rights Bill in the Senate, it came before the House of Representatives, and having been read a first and second time, was referred to the Committee on the Judiciary. On the 1st of March, the Chairman of the Judiciary Committee, Mr. Wilson, brought the bill again before the House, proposing some verbal amendments which were adopted. He then made a motion to recommit the bill, pending which, he made a speech on the merits of the measure. He referred to many definitions, judicial decisions, opinions, and precedents, under which negroes were entitled to the rights of American citizenship. In reference to the results of his researches, he said:

"Precedents, both judicial and legislative, are found in sharp conflict concerning them. The line which divides these precedents is generally found to be the same which separates the early from the later days of the republic. The further the Government drifted from the old moorings of equality and human rights, the more numerous became judicial and legislative utterances in conflict with some of the leading features of this bill."

He argued that the section of the bill providing for its enforcement by the military arm was necessary, in order "to fortify the declaratory portions of this bill with such sanctions as will render it effective." In conclusion he said:

"Can not protection be rendered to the citizen in the mode prescribed by the measure we now have under consideration? If not, a perpetual state of constructive war would be a great blessing to very many American citizens. If a suspension of martial law and a restoration of the ordinary forms of civil law are to result in a subjection of our people to the outrages under the operation of State laws and municipal ordinances which these orders now prevent, then it were better to continue the present state of affairs forever. But such is not the case; we may provide by law for the same ample protection through the civil courts that now depends on the orders of our military commanders; and I will never consent to any other construction of our Constitution, for that would be the elevation of the military above the civil power.

"Before our Constitution was formed, the great fundamental rights which I have mentioned belonged to every person who became a member of our great national family. No one surrendered a jot or tittle of these rights by consenting to the formation of the Government. The entire machinery of Government, as organized by the Constitution, was designed, among other things, to secure a more perfect enjoyment of these rights. A legislative department was created, that laws necessary and proper to this end might be enacted; a judicial department was erected to expound and administer the laws; an executive department was formed for the purpose of enforcing and seeing to the execution of these laws; and these several departments of Government possess the power to enact, administer, and enforce the laws 'necessary and proper' to secure those rights which existed anterior to the ordination of the Constitution. Any other view of the powers of this Government dwarfs it, and renders it a failure in its most important office.

"Upon this broad principle I rest my justification of this bill. I assert that we possess the power to do those things which governments are organized to do; that we may protect a citizen of the United States against a violation of his rights by the law of a single State; that by our laws and our courts we may intervene to maintain the proud character of American citizenship; that this power permeates our whole system, is a part of it, without which the States can run riot over every fundamental right belonging to citizens of the United States; that the right to exercise this power depends upon no express delegation, but runs with the rights it is designed to protect; that we possess the same latitude in respect to the selection of means through which to exercise this power that belongs to us when a power rests upon express delegation; and that the decisions which support the latter maintain the former. And here, sir, I leave the bill to the consideration of the House."

Mr. Rogers, of New Jersey, followed with an argument against the bill, because it interfered with "States' Rights." Under its provisions, Congress would "enter the domain of a State and interfere with its internal police, statutes, and domestic regulations." He said:

"This act of legislation would destroy the foundations of the Government as they were laid and established by our fathers, who reserved to the States certain privileges and immunities which ought sacredly to be preserved to them.

"If you had attempted to do it in the days of those who were living at the time the Constitution was made, after the birth of that noble instrument, the spirit of the heroes of the Revolution and the ghosts of the departed who laid down their lives in defense of the liberty of this country and of the rights of the States, would have come forth as witnesses against the deadly infliction, and the destruction of the fundamental principle of the sovereignty of the States in violation of the Constitution, and the breaking down of the ties that bind the States, and the violation of the rights and liberties of the white men and white women of America.

"If you pass this bill, you will allow the negroes of this country to compete for the high office of President of the United States. Because if they are citizens at all, they come within the meaning and letter of the Constitution of the United States, which allows all natural-born citizens to become candidates for the Presidency, and to exercise the duties of that office if elected.

"I am afraid of degrading this Government; I am afraid of danger to constitutional liberty; I am alarmed at the stupendous strides which this Congress is trying to initiate; and I appeal in behalf of my country, in behalf of those that are to come after us, of generations yet unborn, as well as those now living, that conservative men on the other side should rally to the standard of sovereign and independent States, and blot out this idea which is inculcating itself here, that all the powers of the States must be taken away, and the power of the Czar of Russia or the Emperor of France must be lodged in the Federal Government.

"I ask you to stand by the law of the country, and to regulate these Federal and State systems upon the grand principles upon which they were intended to be regulated, that we may hand down to those who are to come after us this bright jewel of civil liberty unimpaired; and I say that the Congress or the men who will strip the people of these rights will be handed down to perdition for allowing this bright and beautiful heritage of civil liberty embodied in the powers and sovereign jurisdiction of the States to pass away from us.

"I am willing to trust brave men—men who have shown as much bravery as those who were engaged on battle-fields against the armed legions of the North; because I believe that even when they were fighting against the flag of their country, the great mass of those people were moved by high and conscientious convictions of duty. And in the spirit of Christianity, in the spirit which Jesus Christ exercised when he gave up his own life as a propitiation for a fallen world, I would say to those Southern men, Come here in the Halls of Congress, and participate with us in passing laws which, if constitutionally carried into effect, will control the interests and destinies of four millions people, mostly living within the limits of your States."

Mr. Cook, of Illinois, replied: "Mr. Speaker, in listening to the very eloquent remarks of the gentleman from New Jersey [Mr. Rogers], I have been astonished to find that in his apprehension this bill is designed to deprive somebody, in some State of this Union, of some right which he has heretofore enjoyed. I am only sorry that he was not specific enough; that he did not inform us what rights are to be taken away. He has denounced this bill as dangerous to liberty, as calculated in its tendency at least to destroy the liberties of this country. I have examined this bill with some care, and, so far as I have been able to understand it, I have found nothing in any provision of it which tends in any way to take from any man, white or black, a single right he enjoys under the Constitution and laws of the United States.

"I would have been glad if he would have told us in what manner the white men of this country would have been placed in a worse condition than they are now, if this becomes the law.

This general denunciation and general assault of the bill, without pointing out one single thing which is to deprive one single man of any right he enjoys under the Government, seems to me not entitled to much weight.

"When those rights which are enumerated in this bill are denied to any class of men, on account of race or color, when they are subject to a system of vagrant laws which sells them into slavery or involuntary servitude, which operates upon them as upon no other part of the community, they are not secured in the rights of freedom. If a man can be sold, the man is a slave. If he is nominally freed by the amendment to the Constitution, he has nothing in the world he can call his own; he has simply the labor of his hands on which he can depend. Any combination of men in his neighborhood can prevent him from having any chance to support himself by his labor. They can pass a law that a man not supporting himself by labor shall be deemed a vagrant, and that a vagrant shall be sold. If this is the freedom we gave the men who have been fighting for us and in defense of the Government, if this is all we have secured them, the President had far better never have issued the Proclamation of Emancipation, and the country had far better never have adopted the great ordinance of freedom.

"Does any man in this House believe that these people can be safely left in these States without the aid of Federal legislation or military power? Does any one believe that their freedom can be preserved without this aid? If any man does so believe, he is strangely blind to the history of the past year; strangely blind to the enactments passed by Legislatures touching these freedmen. And I shuddered as I heard the honorable gentleman from New Jersey [Mr. Rogers] claiming that he was speaking and thinking in the spirit which animated the Savior of mankind when he made atonement for our race; that it was in that spirit he was acting when he was striving to have these people left utterly defenseless in the hands of men who were proving, day by day, month by month, that they desire to oppress them, for they had been made free against their consent. Every act of legislation, every expression of opinion on their part, proves that these people would be again enslaved if they were not protected by the military arm of the Federal Government; without that they would be slaves to-day. And I submit, with all deference, that it is any thing but the spirit which the gentleman claims to have exercised, which prompted the argument he has made.

"For myself, I trust that this bill will be passed, because I consider it the most appropriate means to secure the end desired, and that these people will be protected. I trust that we will say to them, Because upon our call you aided us to suppress this rebellion, because the honor and faith of the nation were pledged for your protection, we will maintain your freedom, and redeem that pledge."

On the following day, the House of Representatives resumed the consideration of this bill. A speech was made by Mr. Thayer, of Pennsylvania. He said:

"This bill is the just sequel to, and the proper completion of, that great measure of national redress which opened the dungeon-doors of four million human beings. Without this, in my judgment, that great act of justice will be paralyzed and made useless. With this, it will have practical effect, life, vigor, and enforcement. It has been the fashion of gentlemen, holding a certain set of opinions, in this House to characterize that great measure to which I have referred as a revolutionary measure.

"Sir, it was a revolutionary measure. It was one of the greatest, one of the most humane, one of the most beneficial revolutions which ever characterized the history of a free State; but it was a revolution which, though initiated by the conflict of arms and rendered necessary as a measure of war against the public enemy, was accomplished within and under the provisions of the Constitution of the United States. It was a revolution for the relief of human nature, a revolution which gave life, liberty, and hope to millions whose condition, until then, appeared to be one of hopeless despair. It was a revolution of which no freeman need be ashamed, of which every man who assisted in it will, I am sure, in the future be proud, and which will illumine with a great glory the history of this country.

"There is nothing in this bill in respect to the employment of military force that is not already in the Constitution of the United States. The power here conferred is expressly given by that instrument, and has been exercised upon the most stupendous scale in the suppression of the rebellion. What is this bill? I hope gentlemen, even on the opposite side of the House, will not suffer their minds to be influenced by any such vague, loose, and groundless denunciations as these which have proceeded from the gentleman from New Jersey. The bill, after extending these fundamental immunities of citizenship to all classes of people in the United States, simply provides means for the enforcement of these rights and immunities. How? Not by military force, not through the instrumentality of military commanders, not through any military machinery whatever, but through the quiet, dignified, firm, and constitutional forms of judicial procedure. The bill seeks to enforce these rights in the same manner and with the same sanctions under and by which other laws of the United States are enforced. It imposes duties upon the judicial tribunals of the country which require the enforcement of these rights. It provides for the administration of laws to protect these rights. It provides for the execution of laws to enforce them. Is there any thing appalling in that? Is that a military despotism? Sir, it is a strange abuse of language to say that a military despotism is established by wholesome and equal laws. Yet the gentleman declaimed by the hour, in vague and idle terms, against this bill, which has not a single offensive, oppressive, unjust, unusual, or tyrannical feature in it. These civil rights and immunities which are to be secured, and which no man can conscientiously say ought to be denied, are to be enforced through the ordinary instrumentalities of courts of justice.

"While engaged in this great work of restoration, it concerns our honor that we forget not those who are unable to help themselves; who, whatever may have been the misery and wretchedness of their former condition, were on our side in the great struggle which has closed, and whose rights we can not disregard or neglect without violating the most sacred obligations of duty and of honor. To us they look for protection against the wrongs with which they are threatened. To us alone can they appeal in their helplessness for succor and defense. To us they hold out to-day their supplicating hands, asking for protection for themselves and their posterity. We can not disregard this appeal, and stand acquitted before the country and the world of basely abandoning to a miserable fate those who have a right to demand the protection of your flag and the immunities guaranteed to every freeman by your Constitution."

Mr. Eldridge, of Wisconsin, opposed the bill, in a speech of which the following are the concluding remarks:

"I had hoped that this subject would be allowed to rest. Gentlemen refer us to individual cases of wrong perpetrated upon the freedmen of the South as an argument why we should extend the Federal authority into the different States to control the action of the citizens thereof. But, I ask, has not the South submitted to the altered state of things there, to the late amendment of the Constitution, to the loss of their slave property, with a cheerfulness and grace that we did not expect? Have they not acquiesced more willingly than we dared to hope? Then why not trust them? Why not meet them with frankness and kindness? Why not encourage them with trust and confidence?

"I deprecate all these measures because of the implication they carry upon their face, that the people who have heretofore owned slaves intend to do them wrong. I do not believe it. So far as my knowledge goes, and so far as my information extends, I believe that the people who have held the freedmen slaves will treat them with more kindness, with more leniency, than those of the North who make such loud professions of love and affection for them, and are so anxious to pass these bills. They know their nature; they know their wants; they know their habits; they have been brought up together, and have none of the prejudices and unkind feelings which many in the North would have toward them.

"I do not credit all these stories about the general feeling of hostility in the South toward the negro. So far as I have heard opinions expressed upon that subject, and I have conversed with many persons from that section of the country, they do not blame the negro for any thing that has happened. As a general thing, he was faithful to them and their interests until the army reached the place and took him from them. He has supported their wives and children in the absence of the husbands and fathers in the armies of the South. He has done for them what no one else could have done. They recognize his general good feeling toward them, and are inclined to reciprocate that feeling toward him.

"I believe that is the general feeling of the Southern people to-day. The cases of ill-treatment are exceptional cases. They are like the cases which have occurred in the Northern States where the unfortunate have been thrown upon our charity. Take for instance the stories of the cruel treatment of the insane in the State of Massachusetts. They may have been barbarously confined in the loathsome dens, as stated in particular instances, but is that any evidence of the general ill-will of the people of the State of Massachusetts toward the insane? Is that any reason why the Federal arm should be extended to Massachusetts to control and protect the insane there?

"It has also been said that certain paupers in certain States have been badly used—paupers, too, who were whites. Is that any reason why we should extend the arm of the Federal Government to those States to protect the poor who are thrown upon the charities of the people there?

"Sir, we must yield to the altered state of things in this country. We must trust the people; it is our duty to do so; we can not do otherwise. And the sooner we place ourselves in a position where we can win the confidence of our late enemies, where our counsels will be heeded, where our advice may be regarded, the sooner will the people of the whole country be fully reconciled to each other and their changed relationship; the sooner will all the inhabitants of our country be in the possession of all the rights and immunities essential to their prosperity and happiness."

Mr. Thornton, of Illinois, feared there was "something hidden, something more than appears in the language" of the bill. He feared "a design to confer the right of suffrage upon the negro," and urged that a proviso should be accepted "restricting the meaning of the words 'civil rights and immunities.'" He remarked further: "The most serious objection that I have to this bill is, that it is an interference with the rights of the South. It was remarked by my friend from Wisconsin that it has often been intimated on this floor, and throughout the country, that whenever a man talks about either the Constitution or the rights of the States, he is either a traitor or a sympathizer with treason. I do not assume that the States are sovereign. They are subordinate to the Federal Government. Sovereignty in this country is in the people, but the States have certain rights, and those rights are absolutely necessary to the maintenance of our system of government. What are those rights? The right to determine and fix the legal *status* of the inhabitants of the respective States; the local powers of self-government; the power to regulate all the relations that exist between husband and wife, parent and child, guardian and ward; all the fireside and home rights, which are nearer and dearer to us than all others.

"Sir, this is but a stepping-stone to a centralization of the Government and the overthrow of the local powers of the States. Whenever that is consummated, then farewell to the beauty, strength, and power of this Government. There is nothing left but absolute, despotic, central power. It lives no longer but as a naked despotism. There is nothing left to admire and to cherish."

Mr. Windom, of Minnesota, next obtained the floor. Referring to the speech of Mr. Rogers, he said: "I wish to make another extract from the speech of the gentleman from New Jersey. He said, 'If you pass this bill, you will allow negroes to compete for the high office of the President of the United States.' You will actually allow them to compete for the Presidency of the United States! As for this fear which haunts the gentleman from New Jersey, if there is a negro in the country who is so far above all the white men of the country that only four millions of his own race can elect him President of the United States over twenty-six millions of white people, I think we ought to encourage such talent in the country.

"Sir, the gentleman has far less confidence in the white race than I have, if he is so timid in regard to negro competition. Does he really suppose that black men are so far superior to white men that four millions of them can elect a President of their own race against the wishes of thirty millions of ours? Ever since I knew any thing of the party to which the gentleman belongs, it has entertained this same morbid fear of negro competition; and sometimes I have thought that if we were to contemplate the subject from their stand-point we would have more charity than we do for this timidity and nervous dread which haunts them. I beg leave, however, to assure the gentleman that there is not the slightest danger of electing a black President, and that he need never vote for one, unless he thinks him better fitted for the office than a white man."

With more direct reference to the merits of the question, Mr. Windom said: "Our warrant for the passage of this bill is found in the genius and spirit of our institutions; but not in these alone. Fortunately, the great amendment which broke the shackles from every slave in the land contains an express provision that 'Congress shall have power to enforce this article by appropriate legislation.'

"When this amendment was acted upon, it was well understood, as it is now, that although the body of slavery might be destroyed, its spirit would still live in the hearts of those who have sacrificed so much for its preservation, and that if the freedmen were left to the tender mercy of their former masters, to whose heartless selfishness has been superadded a malignant desire for vengeance upon the negro for having aided us in crushing the rebellion, his condition would be more intolerable than it was before the war. And hence the broad grant of power was made to enable Congress to enforce the spirit as well as the letter of the amendment. Now, sir, in what way is it proposed to enforce it? By denying to any one man a single right or privilege which he could otherwise constitutionally or properly enjoy? No. By conferring on any one person or class of persons a single right or immunity which every other person may not possess? By no means. Does it give to the loyal negro any preference over the recent would-be assassins of the nation? Not at all. It merely declares that hereafter there shall be no discrimination in civil rights or immunities among the citizens of any State or territory of the United States on account of race, color, or previous condition of slavery, and that every person, except such as are excluded by reason of crime, shall have the same right to enforce contracts, to sue, be parties, and give evidence, to inherit, purchase, sell, hold, and convey real and personal property, and to full and equal benefit of all laws and proceedings for the security of person and property, and shall be subject to like punishment, pains, and penalties, and to none other.

"We know, and the whole world knows, that when in the hour of our extremity we called upon the black race to aid us, we promised them not liberty only, but all that that word liberty implies. All remember how unwilling we were to do any thing which would inure to the benefit of the negro. I recall with shame the fact that when, five years ago, the so-called Democracy—now Egyptians—were here in this capital, in the White House, in the Senate, and on this floor, plotting the destruction of the Government, and we were asked to appease them by sacrificing the negro, two-thirds of both houses voted to rivet his chains upon him so long as the republic should endure. A widening chasm yawned between the free and slave States, and we looked wildly around for that wherewith it might be closed. In our extremity we seized upon the negro, bound and helpless, and tried to cast him in. But an overruling Providence heard the cries of the oppressed, and hurled his oppressors into that chasm by hundreds of thousands, until the whole land was filled with mourning, yet still the chasm yawned. In our anguish and terror, we felt that the whole nation would be speedily ingulfed in one common ruin. It was then that the great emancipator and savior of his country, Abraham Lincoln, saw the danger and the remedy, and seizing four million bloody shackles, he wrenched them from their victims, and standing with these broken manacles in his hands upraised toward heaven, he invoked the blessing of the God of the oppressed, and cast them into the fiery chasm. That offering was accepted, and the chasm closed.

"When the reports from Port Hudson and Fort Wagner thrilled all loyal hearts by the recital of the heroic deeds of the black soldier, we were not reminded that if the negro were permitted to enjoy the same rights under the Government his valor helped to save that are possessed by the perjured traitors who sought its destruction, it would 'lead to a war of races.' O no! Then we were in peril, and felt grateful even to the negro, who stood between us and our enemies. Then our only hope of safety was in the brave hearts and strong arms of the soldier at the front. Now, since by the combined efforts of our brave soldiers, white and black, the military power of the South has been overthrown, and her Representatives are as eager to resume their places on this floor as five years ago they were to quit them for a place in the rebel army, we are told that, having been victorious, it becomes a great nation like ours to be magnanimous. I answer, it is far more becoming to be just. I am willing to carry my magnanimity to the verge of justice, but not one step beyond. I will go with him who goes furthest in acts of generosity toward our former enemies, unless those acts will be prejudicial to our friends. But when you advise me to sacrifice those who have stood by us during the war, in order to conciliate unrepentant rebels, whose hearts still burn with ill-suppressed hatred to the Government, I scorn your counsel."

Mr. Shellabarger, of Ohio, said: "I agree with the gentleman on the other side of the House, that this bill can not be passed under that clause of the Constitution which provides that Congress may pass uniform rules of naturalization. Under that clause it is my opinion that the act of naturalization must not only be the act of the Government, but also the act of the individual alien, by which he renounces his former allegiance and accepts the new one. And that proposition and distinction will be found, I think, in all judicious arguments upon the subject.

"There is another class of persons well recognized, not only in our constitutional history, but also by the laws of nations, who are not foreigners, who occupy an intermediate position, and that intermediate position is defined by the laws of nations by the word 'subjects.' Subjects are all persons who, being born in a given country, and under a given government, do not owe an allegiance to any other government.

"To that class in this country, according to the decisions of our courts hitherto, belong American Indians and slaves, and, according to the Dred Scott decision, persons of African descent whose ancestors were slaves. All these were subjects by every principle of international as well as of settled constitutional law in this country.

"Now, then, to that class belong the persons who are naturalized by this bill. If they were not, indeed, citizens hitherto, they were at least subjects of this Government, by reason of their birth, and by reason of the fact that they owed no foreign allegiance.

"That brings me to the next remark, and it is this: that these subjects, not owing any foreign allegiance, no individual act of theirs is required in order to their naturalization, because they owe no foreign allegiance to be renounced by their individual acts, and because, moreover, being domiciled in our own country, and continuing here to reside, it is the individual election of each member of the tribe, or race, or class, to accept our nationality; therefore, no additional individual act is required in order to his citizenship.

"That being proved, it is competent for the nationality, or for the government, wherever that subject may reside, to naturalize that class of persons by treaty or by general law, as is proposed by the amendment of the gentleman from New York [Mr. Raymond]. It is the act of the sovereign alone that is requisite to the naturalization of that class of persons, and it may be done either by a single act naturalizing entire races of men, or by adopting the heads of families out of those races, or it may be done to any extent, greater or less, that may please the sovereign.

For this proposition, I refer gentlemen who desire to examine this subject to the authorities that may be found collected in any judicious work on public law, and they will find them very fully collected, certainly, in the notes to Wheaton.

"Now, then, what power may do that act of naturalization, and how may it be exercised? That is also answered by these same authorities. It may be done in this country either by an act of Congress, or it may be done by treaty. It has been done again and again and again in both ways in this country. It was done once in the case of the Choctaw Indians, as you will find in the Statutes-at-Large, where, in case the heads of families desired to remain and not to remove to the West, it was provided by the treaty of September 27, 1830, that those families should be naturalized as a class.

"Then, again, it was done in the other way, by an act of Congress, in the case cited by my learned friend from Iowa [Mr. Wilson], in the case of the Stockbridge Indians.

"It was done again, as you may remember, in the case of the Cherokees, in December, 1835. There again a class was naturalized by treaty."

Some amendments having been proposed, the bill was recommitted to the Committee on the Judiciary, with the understanding that it should be returned for consideration on Thursday of the following week.

Accordingly, on that day, March 8, the consideration of the bill being resumed, Mr. Broomall, of Pennsylvania, addressed the House. He viewed the bill as beneficent in its provisions, since it made no discriminations against the Southern rebels, but granted them, as well as the negro, the rights of citizenship.

"A question might naturally arise whether we ought again to trust those who have once betrayed us; whether we ought to give them the benefits of a compact they have once repudiated. Yet the spirit of forgiveness is so inherent in the American bosom, that no party in the country proposes to withhold from these people the advantages of citizenship; and this is saying much. With a debt that may require centuries to pay; with so many living and mutilated witnesses of the horrors of war; with so many saddened homes, so many of the widowed and fatherless pleading for justice, for retribution, if not revenge, it speaks well for the cause of Christian civilization in America that no party in the country proposes to deprive the authors of such immeasurable calamity of the advantages of citizenship.

"But the election must be made. Some public legislative act is necessary to show the world that those who have forfeited all claims upon the Government are not to be held to the strict rigor of the law of their own invoking, the decision of the tribunal of their own choosing; that they are to be welcomed back as the prodigal son, whenever they are ready to return as the prodigal son.

"The act under consideration makes that election. Its terms embrace the late rebels, and it gives them the rights, privileges, and immunities of citizens of the Uuited States, though it does not propose to exempt them from punishment for their past crimes.

"I might consent that the glorious deeds of the last five years should be blotted from the country's history; that the trophies won on a hundred battle-fields, the sublime visible evidences of the heroic devotion of America's citizen soldiery, should be burned on the altar of reconstruction. I might consent that the cemetery at Gettysburg should be razed to the ground; that its soil should be submitted to the plow, and that the lamentation of the bereaved should give place to the lowing of cattle. But there is a point beyond which I will neither be forced nor persuaded. I will never consent that the Government shall desert its allies in the South, and surrender their rights and interests to the enemy, and in this I will make no distinction of caste or color, either among friends or foes."

Mr. Raymond, of New York, was impressed with the importance of the measure. "Whether we consider it by itself, simply as a proposed statute, or in its bearings upon the general question of the restoration of peace and harmony to the Union, I regard it as one of the most important bills ever presented to this House for its action, worthy, in every respect, to enlist the coolest and the calmest judgment of every member whose vote must be recorded upon it."

He was in favor of the first part of the bill, which declares "who shall be citizens of the United States, and declares that all shall be citizens without distinction of race, color, or previous condition of servitude, who are, have been, or shall be born within the limits and jurisdiction of the United States.

"Now, sir, assuming, as I do, without any further argument, that Congress has the power of admitting to citizenship this great class of persons just set free by the amendment to the Constitution of the United States abolishing slavery, I suppose I need not dwell here on the great importance to that class of persons of having this boon conferred upon them.

"We have already conferred upon them the great, inestimable, priceless boon of personal liberty. I can not for one moment yield to what seems to be a general disposition to disparage the freedom we have given them. I think the fact that we have conferred upon four million people that personal liberty and freedom from servitude from this time forward for evermore, is one of the highest and most beneficent acts ever performed by any Government toward so large a class of its people.

"Having gone thus far, I desire to go on by successive steps still further, and to elevate them in all respects, so far as their faculties will allow and our power will permit us to do, to an equality with the other persons and races in this country. I desire, as the next step in the process of elevating that race, to give them the rights of citizenship, or to declare by solemn statute that they are citizens of the United States, and thus secure to them whatever rights, immunities, privileges, and powers belong as of right to all citizens of the United States. I hope no one will be prepared or inclined to say this is a trifling boon. If we do so estimate this great privilege, I fear we are scarcely in the frame of mind to act upon the great questions coming before us from day to day here. I, for one, am not prepared or inclined to disparage American citizenship as a personal qualification belonging to myself, or as conferred upon any of our fellow-citizens."

Mr. Raymond expressed doubts as to the constitutionality of that part of the bill "that provides for that class of persons thus made citizens protection against anticipated inequality of legislation in the several States."

In this direction he was desirous of avoiding a veto. He said: "Moreover, on grounds of expediency, upon which I will not dwell, I desire myself, and I should feel much relieved if I thought the House fully and heartily shared my anxiety, not to pass here any bill which shall be intercepted on its way to the statute-book by well-grounded complaints of unconstitutionality on the part of any other department of the Government."

Mr. Delano, of Ohio, followed, expressing doubts as to the constitutionality of the measure. He considered it a serious infringement of the rights of the States. He said: "Now, sir, should this bill be passed, that law of the State might be overthrown by the power of Congress. In my opinion, if we adopt the principle of this bill, we declare, in effect, that Congress has authority to go into the States and manage and legislate with regard to all the personal rights of the citizen—rights of life, liberty, and property. You render this Government no longer a Government of limited powers; you concentrate and consolidate here an extent of authority which will swallow up all or nearly all of the rights of the States with respect to the property, the liberties, and the lives of its citizens."

He added, near the close of his address: "I am not to be understood as denying the power of this Government, especially that great war power which, when evoked, has no limit except as it is limited by necessity and the laws of civilized warfare. But, sir, in time of peace I would not and I can not stand here and attempt the exercise of powers by this General Government, which, if carried out with all the logical consequences that follow their assumption, will, in my opinion, endanger the liberties of the country."

Mr. Kerr, of Indiana, maintained the theory that the States should settle questions of citizenship as relating to those within their borders; that "the privileges and immunities of citizenship in the States are required to be attained, if at all, *according to the laws or Constitutions of the States*, and never in *defiance* of them." To sustain this theory, he read from a number of authorities, and finally remarked:

"This bill rests upon a theory utterly inconsistent with, and in direct hostility to, every one of these authorities. It asserts the right of Congress to regulate the laws which shall govern in the acquisition and ownership of property in the States, and to determine who may go there and purchase and hold property, and to protect such persons in the enjoyment of it. The right of the State to regulate its own internal and domestic affairs, to select its own local policy, and make and administer its own laws, for the protection and welfare of its own citizens, is denied. If Congress can declare what rights and privileges shall be enjoyed in the States by the people of one class, it can, by the same kind of reasoning, determine what shall be enjoyed by every class. If it can say who may go into and settle in and acquire property in a State, it can also say who shall not. If it can determine who may testify and sue in the courts of a State, it may equally determine who shall not. If it can order the transfer of suits from the State to the Federal courts, where citizens of the same State alone are parties, in such cases as may arise under this bill, it can, by parity of logic, dispense with State courts entirely. Congress, in short, may erect a great centralized, consolidated despotism in this capital. And such is the rapid tendency of such legislation as this bill proposes."

On the succeeding day, March 9th, Mr. Wilson having demanded the previous question, on the motion to recommit, was entitled to the floor, but yielded portions of his time to Mr. Bingham and Mr. Shellabarger.

The former had moved to amend the motion to recommit, by adding instructions "to strike out of the first section the words, 'and there shall be no discrimination in civil rights or immunities among citizens of the United States, in any State or Territory of the United States, on account of race, color, or previous condition of slavery,' and insert in the thirteenth line of the first section, after the word 'right,' the words, 'in every State and Territory of the United States.' Also, to strike out all parts of said bill which are penal, and which authorize criminal proceedings, and in lieu thereof to give to all citizens injured by denial or violation of any of the other rights secured or protected by said act, an action in the United States courts with double costs in all cases of recovery, without regard to the amount of damages; and also to secure to such persons the privilege of the writ of *habeas corpus*."

Mr. Bingham said: "And, first, I beg gentlemen to consider that I do not oppose any legislation which is authorized by the Constitution of my country to enforce in its letter and its spirit the bill of rights as embodied in that Constitution. I know that the enforcement of the bill of rights is the want of the republic. I know if it had been enforced in good faith in every State of the Union, the calamities, and conflicts, and crimes, and sacrifices of the past five years would have been impossible.

"But I feel that I am justified in saying, in view of the text of the Constitution of my country, in view of all its past interpretations, in view of the manifest and declared intent of the men who framed it, the enforcement of the Bill of Rights, touching the life, liberty, and property of every citizen of the republic, within every organized State of the Union, is of the reserved powers of the States, to be enforced by State tribunals and by State officials, acting under the solemn obligations of an oath imposed upon them by the Constitution of the United States. Who can doubt this conclusion who considers the words of the Constitution, 'the powers not delegated to the United States by the Constitution, nor prohibited by it to the States, are reserved to the States respectively, or to the people?' The Constitution does not delegate to the United States the power to punish offenses against the life, liberty, or property of the citizen in the States, nor does it prohibit that power to the States, but leaves it as the reserved power of the States, to be by them exercised. The prohibitions of power by the Constitution to the States are express prohibitions, as that no State shall enter into any treaty, etc., or emit bills of credit, or pass any bill of attainder, etc. The Constitution does not prohibit States from the enactment of laws for the general government of the people within their respective limits.

"The law in every State should be just; it should be no respecter of persons. It is otherwise now, and it has been otherwise for many years in many of the States of the Union. I should remedy that, not by arbitrary assumption of power, but by amending the Constitution of the United States, expressly prohibiting the States from any such abuse of power in the future. You propose to make it a penal offense for the judges of the States to obey the Constitution and laws of their States, and for their obedience thereto to punish them by fine and imprisonment as felons. I deny your power to do this. You can not make an official act, done under color of law, and without criminal intent, and from a sense of public duty, a crime."

Mr. Shellabarger of Ohio said: "I do not understand that there is now any serious doubt anywhere as to our power to admit by law to the rights of American citizenship entire classes or races who were born and continue to reside in our territory or in territory we acquire. I stated, the other day, some of the cases in which we naturalized races, tribes, and communities in mass, and by single exercises of national sovereignty. This we did by the treaty of April 30, 1800, by which we acquired Louisiana; also in the treaty of 1819, by which we acquired Florida; also in the treaty of 1848, by which we acquired part of Mexico; also by

Eng.d by G. E. Perine & Co. N. York.

James F. Wilson

JAMES F. WILSON

the resolution of March 1, 1845, annexing Texas, and the act of December 29, same year, admitting Texas into the Union, we made all the people not slaves citizens; also by the treaty of September 27, 1830, we admitted to citizens certain heads of families of Choctaws; also by the treaty of December 29, 1855, we did the same as to the Cherokees; also by the act of March 3, 1843, we admitted to full citizenship the Stockbridge tribe of Indians." Referring to the first section which his colleague had proposed to amend, he said: "Self-evidently this is the whole effect of this first section. It secures, not to all citizens, but to all races as races who are citizens, equality of protection in those enumerated civil rights which the States may deem proper to confer upon any races. Now, sir, can this Government do this? Can it prevent one race of free citizens from being by State laws deprived as a race of all the civil rights for the securement of which his Government was created, and which are the only considerations the Government renders to him for the Federal allegiance which he renders? It does seem to me that that Government which has the exclusive right to confer citizenship, and which is entitled to demand service and allegiance, which is supreme over that due to any State, may—nay, must—protect those citizens in those rights which are fairly conducive and appropriate and necessary to the attainment of his 'protection' as a citizen. And I think those rights to contract, sue, testify, inherit, etc., which this bill says the races shall hold as races in equality, are of that class which are fairly conducive and necessary as means to the constitutional end; to-wit, the protection of the rights of person and property of a citizen. It has been found impossible to settle or define what are all the indispensable rights of American citizenship. But it is perfectly well settled what are some of these, and without which there is no citizenship, either in this or any other Government. Two of these are the right of petition and the right of protection in such property as it is lawful for that particular citizen to own."

The debate was closed by Mr. Wilson, Chairman of the Judiciary Committee. He said: "This bill, sir, has met with opposition in both houses on the same ground that, in times gone by, before this land was drenched in blood by the slaveholders' rebellion, was urged by those who controlled the destinies of the southern portion of the country, and those who adhered to their fortunes in the North, for the purpose of riveting the chains of slavery and converting this republic into a great slave nation. The arguments which have been urged against this bill in both houses are but counterparts of the arguments used in opposition to the authority the Government sought to exercise in controlling and preventing the spread of slavery.

"Citizens of the United States, as such, are entitled to certain rights, and, being entitled to those rights, it is the duty of the Government to protect citizens in the perfect enjoyment of them. The citizen is entitled to life, liberty, and the right to property. The gentleman from Ohio tells us, in the protection of these rights, the citizen must depend upon the 'honest purpose of the several States,' and that the General Government can not interpose its strong right arm to defend the citizen in the enjoyment of life, liberty, and in possession of property. In other words, if the States of this Union, in their 'honest purpose,' like the honesty of purpose manifested by the Southern States in times past, should deprive the citizen, without due process of law, of life, liberty, and property, the General Government, which can draw the citizen by the strong bond of allegiance to the battle-field, has no power to intervene and set aside a State law, and give the citizen protection under the laws of Congress in the courts of the United States; that at the mercy of the States lie all the rights of the citizens of the United States; that while it was deemed necessary to constitute a great Government to render secure the rights of the people, the framers of the Government turned over to the States the power to deprive the citizen of those things for the security of which the Government was framed. In other words, the little State of Delaware has a hand stronger than the United States; that revolted South Carolina may put under lock and key the great fundamental rights belonging to the citizen, and we must be dumb; that our legislative power can not be exercised; that our courts must be closed to the appeal of our citizens. That is the doctrine this House of Representatives, representing a great free people, just emerged from a terrible war for the maintenance of American liberty, is asked to adopt.

"The gentleman from Ohio tells the House that civil rights involve all the rights that citizens have under the Government; that in the term are embraced those rights which belong to the citizen of the United States as such, and those which belong to a citizen of a State as such; and that this bill is not intended merely to enforce equality of rights, so far as they relate to citizens of the United States, but invades the States to enforce equality of rights in respect to those things which properly and rightfully depend on State regulations and laws. My friend is too sound a lawyer, is too well versed in the Constitution of his country, to indorse that proposition on calm and deliberate consideration. He knows, as every man knows, that this bill refers to those rights which belong to men as citizens of the United States and none other; and when he talks of setting aside the school laws, and jury laws, and franchise laws of the States, by the bill now under consideration, he steps beyond what he must know to be the rule of construction which must apply here, and, as the result of which this bill can only relate to matters within the control of Congress."

Comparing Mr. Bingham's proposed amendment with the original bill, Mr. Wilson said: "What difference in principle is there between saying that the citizen shall be protected by the legislative power of the United States in his rights by civil remedy and declaring that he shall be protected by penal enactments against those who interfere with his rights? There is no difference in the principle involved. If we may adopt the gentleman's mode, we may also select the mode provided in this bill. There is a difference in regard to the expense of protection; there is also a difference as to the effectiveness of the two modes. Beyond this, nothing. This bill proposes that the humblest citizen shall have full and ample protection at the cost of the Government, whose duty it is to protect him. The amendment of the gentleman recognizes the principle involved, but it says that the citizen despoiled of his rights, instead of being properly protected by the Government, must press his own way through the courts and pay the bills attendant thereon. This may do for the rich, but to the poor, who need protection, it is mockery. The highest obligation which the Government owes to the citizen, in return for the allegiance exacted of him, is to secure him in the protection of his rights. Under the amendment of the gentleman, the citizen can only receive that protection in the form of a few dollars in the way of damages, if he shall be so fortunate as to recover a verdict against a solvent wrong-doer. This is called protection. This is what we are asked to do in the way of enforcing the bill of rights. Dollars are weighed against the right of life, liberty,

16

and property. The verdict of a jury is to cover all wrongs and discharge the obligations of the Government to its citizens.

"Sir, I can not see the justice of that doctrine. I assert that it is the duty of the Government of the United States to provide proper protection and to pay the costs attendant on it. We have gone out with the strong arm of the Government and drawn from their homes, all over this land, in obedience to the bond of allegiance which the Government holds on the citizen, hundreds of thousands of men to the battle-field; and yet, while we may exercise this extraordinary power, the gentleman claims that we can not extend the protecting hand of the Government to these men who have been battling for the life of the nation, but can only send them, at their own cost, to juries for verdicts of a few dollars in compensation for the most flagrant wrong to their most sacred rights. Let those support that doctrine who will, I can not."

At the conclusion of Mr. Wilson's speech, Mr. Eldridge, of Wisconsin, moved to lay the whole subject on the table. This motion was rejected—yeas, 32; nays, 118.

The House then rejected Mr. Bingham's proposed amendment, and recommitted the bill to the Committee on the Judiciary.

On the 13th of March the bill was reported back from the committee with some amendments, one of which was to strike out in section one the following words:

"Without distinction of color, and there shall be no discrimination in civil rights, or immunities among citizens of the United States in any State or Territory of the United States on account of race, color, or previous condition of slavery."

The words were omitted to satisfy some who feared that it might be held by the courts that the right of suffrage was conferred thereby.

Another amendment proposed was the addition of a section to the bill, to-wit:

"*And be it further enacted*, That upon all questions of law arising in any case under the provisions of this act, a final appeal may be taken to the Supreme Court of the United States."

Other amendments proposed and adopted were chiefly of a verbal character.

The main question was finally taken, and the bill passed by the following vote:

Yeas—Messrs. Alley, Allison, Ames, Anderson, James M. Ashley, Baker, Baldwin, Banks, Baxter, Beaman, Bidwell, Blaine, Blow, Boutwell, Bromwell, Broomall, Buckland, Bundy, Sidney Clarke, Cobb, Conkling, Cook, Cullom, Darling, Davis, Dawes, Delano, Deming, Dixon, Donnelly, Driggs, Dumont, Eliot, Farnsworth, Farquhar, Ferry, Garfield, Grinnell, Abner C. Harding, Hart, Hayes, Higby, Hill, Holmes, Hooper, Asahel W. Hubbard, Chester D. Hubbard, Demas Hubbard, John H. Hubbard, Hulburd, James Humphrey, Ingersoll, Jenckes, Julian, Kelley, Kelso, Ketcham, Kuykendall, Laflin, George V. Lawrence, William Lawrence, Loan, Longyear, Lynch, Marston, Marvin, McClurg, McRuer, Mercur, Miller, Moorhead, Morrill, Morris, Moulton, Myers, Newell, O'Neill, Orth, Paine, Perham, Pike, Plants, Price, Alexander H. Rice, Sawyer, Schenck, Scofield, Shellabarger, Sloan, Spalding, Starr, Stevens, Thayer, Francis Thomas, John L. Thomas, Trowbridge, Upson, Van Aernam, Burt Van Horn, Ward, Warner, Elihu B. Washburne, William B. Washburn, Welker, Wentworth, Whaley, Williams, James F. Wilson, Stephen F. Wilson, Windom, and Woodbridge—111.

Nays—Messrs. Ancona, Bergen, Bingham, Boyer, Brooks, Coffroth, Dawson, Denison, Glosbrenner, Goodyear, Grider, Aaron Harding, Harris, Hogan, Edwin N. Hubbell, Jones, Kerr, Latham, Le Blond, Marshall, McCullough, Nicholson, Phelps, Radford, Samuel J. Randall, Willam H. Randall, Ritter, Rogers, Ross, Rosseau, Shanklin, Sitgreaves, Smith, Taber, Taylor, Thornton, Trimble, and Winfield—38.

Not Voting—Messrs. Delos R. Ashley, Barker, Benjamin, Brandegee, Chanler, Reader W. Clarke, Culver, Defrees, Eckley, Eggeston, Eldridge, Finck, Griswold, Hale, Henderson, Hotchkiss, James R. Hubbell, James M. Humphrey, Johnson, Kasson, McIndoe, McKee, Niblack, Noell, Patterson, Pomeroy, Raymond, John H. Rice, Rollins, Stilwell, Strouse, Robert T. Van Horn, Henry D. Washburn, and Wright—34.

It is an illustration of the opinion which the minority entertained of the bill to the last, that after it had finally passed, and the previous question had been moved on the adoption of the title, Mr. Le Blond moved to amend the title of the bill by making it read, "A bill to abrogate the rights and break down the judicial system of the States."

On the 15th of March the amendments made by the House came before the Senate for adoption in that body. While these were under consideration by the Senate, Mr. Davis, of Kentucky, made two motions to amend, which were rejected. He then moved to lay the bill on the table, and was proceeding to make a speech, when he was informed that his motion was not debatable. He then withdrew his motion to lay on the table, and moved to postpone the bill until the first Monday of December following. Finding that the last amendment proposed by the House of Representatives was before the Senate, and that his motion could not be entertained, he proceeded to make a speech on the question before the Senate. He asserted that "Congress has no authority or jurisdiction whatever" over the subject of legislation which the bill contains. He closed his remarks with the following words: "I therefore, on the grounds that I have stated, oppose this bill. I know that they weigh nothing with the dominant power here. What care I for that? What care I for the manner in which my suggestions may be received by the majority? Nothing—less than nothing, if possible. I am performing my duty according to my sense of that duty; and in despite of all opposition, of frowns or scoffs, or of any other opposition, come in what form it may, I will stand up to the last hour of my service in this chamber, and will, endeavor, as best I can, to perform my duty whatever may betide me."

The amendments of the House were agreed to, and the CIVIL RIGHTS BILL wanted only Executive approval to become a law of the land.

CHAPTER XI.

THE CIVIL RIGHTS BILL AND THE VETO.

DOUBTS AS TO THE PRESIDENT'S DECISION—SUSPENSE ENDED—THE VETO MESSAGE—MR. TRUMBULL'S ANSWER—MR. REVERDY JOHNSON DEFENDS THE MESSAGE—REJOINDER—REMARKS OF MR. YATES—MR. COWAN APPEALS TO THE COUNTRY—MR. STEWART SHOWS HOW STATES MAY MAKE THE LAW A NULLITY—MR. WADE—MR. MCDOUGALL ON PERSIAN MYTHOLOGY—MR. J. H. LANE DEFENDS THE PRESIDENT—MR. WADE—THE PRESIDENT'S COLLAR—MR. BROWN—MR. DOOLITTLE—MR. GARRETT DAVIS—MR. SAULSBURY—YEAS AND NAYS IN THE SENATE—VOTE IN THE HOUSE—THE CIVIL RIGHTS BILL BECOMES A LAW.

THE Civil Rights Bill having finally passed through Congress, on the 15th of March, by the concurrence of the Senate in the amendments of the House, was submitted to the President for his approval. Much anxiety was felt throughout the country to know what would be the fate of the bill at the hands of the Executive. Some thought it incredible that a President of the United States would veto so plain a declaration of rights, essential to the very existence of a large class of inhabitants. Others were confident that Mr. Johnson's approval would not be given to a bill interfering, as they thought, so flagrantly with the rights of the States under the Constitution.

All doubts were dispelled, on the 27th of March, by the appearance of the President's Secretary on the floor of the Senate, who said, in formal phrase: "Mr. President, I am directed by the President of the United States to return to the Senate, in which house it originated, the bill entitled 'An act to protect all persons in the United States in their civil rights, and to furnish the means of their vindication,' with his objections thereto in writing."

The Secretary of the Senate then read the message, which was heard with profound attention by the Senators, and a large assembly which thronged the galleries, drawn thither in anticipation of the President's veto message.

"*To the Senate of the United States:*

"I regret that the bill which has passed both houses of Congress, entitled 'An act to protect all persons in the United States in their civil rights, and furnish the means for their vindication,' contains provisions which I can not approve, consistently with my sense of duty to the whole people and my obligations to the Constitution of the United States. I am therefore constrained to return it to the Senate, the house in which it originated, with my objections to its becoming a law.

"By the first section of the bill, all persons born in the United States, and not subject to any foreign power, excluding Indians not taxed, are declared to be citizens of the United States. This provision comprehends the Chinese of the Pacific States, Indians subject to taxation, the people called Gypsies, as well as the entire race designated as blacks, people of color, negroes, mulattoes, and persons of African blood. Every individual of those races, born in the United States, is by the bill made a citizen of the United States. It does not purport to declare or confer any other right of citizenship than Federal citizenship. It does not purport to give these classes of persons any *status* as citizens of States, except that which may result from their *status* as citizens of the United States. The power to confer the right of State citizenship is just as exclusively with the several States as the power to confer the right of Federal citizenship is with Congress.

"The right of Federal citizenship thus to be conferred on the several excepted races before mentioned is now, for the first time, proposed to be given by law. If, as is claimed by many, all persons who are native-born, already are, by virtue of the Constitution, citizens of the United States, the passage of the pending bill can not be necessary to make them such. If, on the other hand, such persons are not citizens, as may be assumed from the proposed legislation to make them such, the grave question presents itself, whether, when eleven of the thirty-six States are unrepresented in Congress, at this time it is sound policy to make our entire colored population and all other excepted classes citizens of the United States? Four millions of them have just emerged from slavery into freedom. Can it be reasonably supposed that they possess the requisite qualifications to entitle them to all the privileges and immunities of citizens of the United States? Have the people of the several States expressed such a conviction? It may also be asked whether it is necessary that they should be declared citizens in order that they may be secured in the enjoyment of civil rights? Those rights proposed to be conferred by the bill are, by Federal as well as by State laws, secured to all domiciled aliens and foreigners even before the completion of the process of naturalization, and it may safely be assumed that the same enactments are sufficient to give like protection and benefits to those for whom this bill provides special legislation. Besides, the policy of the Government, from its origin to the present time, seems to have been that persons who are strangers to and unfamiliar with our institutions and our laws should pass through a certain probation, at the end of which, before attaining the coveted prize, they must give evidence of their fitness to receive and to exercise the rights of citizens as contemplated by the Constitution of the United States.

"The bill, in effect, proposes a discrimination against large numbers of intelligent, worthy, and patriotic foreigners, and in favor of the negro, to whom, after long years of bondage, the avenues to freedom and intelligence have now been suddenly opened. He must, of necessity, from his previous unfortunate condition of servitude, be less informed as to the nature and character of our institutions than he who, coming from abroad, has to some extent at least, familiarized himself with the principles of a Government to which he voluntarily intrusts 'life, liberty, and the pursuit of happiness.' Yet it is now proposed by a single legislative enactment to confer the rights of citizens upon all persons of African descent, born within the extended limits of the United States, while persons of foreign birth, who make our land their home, must undergo a probation of five years, and can only then become citizens upon proof that they are of 'good moral character, attached to the principles of the Constitution of the United States, and well disposed to the good order and happiness of the same.'

"The first section of the bill also contains an enumeration of the rights to be enjoyed by these classes, so made citizens, 'in every State and Territory in the United States.' These rights are, 'To make and enforce contracts, to sue, be parties, and give evidence, to inherit, purchase, lease, sell, hold, and convey real and personal property,' and to have 'full and equal benefit of all laws and proceedings for the security of persons and property as is enjoyed by white citizens.' So, too, they are made subject to the same punishment, pains, and penalties in common with white citizens, and to none others. Thus a perfect equality of the white and black races is attempted to be fixed by Federal law, in every State of the Union, over the vast field of State jurisdiction covered by these enumerated rights. In no one of these can any State ever exercise any power of discrimination between the different races.

"In the exercise of State policy over matters exclusively affecting the people of each State, it has frequently been thought expedient to discriminate between the two races. By the statutes of some of the States, Northern as well as Southern, it is enacted, for instance, that no white person shall intermarry with a negro or mulatto. Chancellor Kent says, speaking of the blacks, that 'marriages between them and whites are forbidden in some of the States where slavery does not exist, and they are prohibited in all the slaveholding States, and when not absolutely contrary to law, they are revolting, and regarded as an offense against public decorum.'

"I do not say this bill repeals State laws on the subject of marriage between the two races, for as the whites are forbidden to intermarry with the blacks, the blacks can only make such contracts as the whites themselves are allowed to make, and therefore can not, under this bill, enter into the marriage contract with the whites. I cite this discrimination, however, as an instance of the State policy as to discrimination, and to inquire whether, if Congress can abrogate all State laws of discrimination between the two races in the matter of real estate, of suits, and of contracts generally, Congress may not also repeal the State laws as to the contract of marriage between the two races? Hitherto every subject embraced in the enumeration of rights contained in this bill has been considered as exclusively belonging to the States. They all relate to the internal policy and economy of the respective States. They are matters which in each State concern the domestic condition of its people, varying in each according to its own peculiar circumstances, and the safety and well-being of its own citizens. I do not mean to say that upon all these subjects there are not Federal restraints, as, for instance, in the State power of legislation over contracts, there is a Federal limitation that no State shall pass a law impairing the obligations of contracts; and as to crimes, that no State shall pass an *ex post facto* law; and as to money, that no State shall make any thing but gold and silver a legal tender. But where can we find a Federal prohibition against the power of any State to discriminate, as do most of them, between aliens and citizens, between artificial persons called corporations and natural persons, in the right to hold real estate?

"If it be granted that Congress can repeal all State laws discriminating between whites and blacks, in the subjects covered by this bill, why, it may be asked, may not Congress repeal in the same way all State laws discriminating between the two races on the subject of suffrage and office? If Congress can declare by law who shall hold lands, who shall testify, who shall have capacity to make a contract in a State, then Congress can by law also declare who, without regard to color or race, shall have the right to sit as a juror or as a judge, to hold any office, and, finally, to vote, 'in every State and Territory of the United States.' As respects the Territories, they come within the power of Congress, for, as to them, the law-making power is the Federal power; but as to the States, no similar provisions exist, vesting in Congress the power 'to make rules and regulations' for them.

"The object of the second section of the bill is to afford discriminating protection to colored persons in the full enjoyment of all the rights secured to them by the preceding section. It declares 'that any person who, under color of any law, statute, ordinance, regulation, or custom, shall subject, or cause to be subjected, any inhabitant of any State or Territory to the deprivation of any right secured or protected by this act, or to different punishment, pains, or penalties on account of such person having at one time been held in a condition of slavery or involuntary servitude, except as a punishment for crime whereof the party shall have been duly convicted, or by reason of his color or race, than is prescribed for the punishment of white persons, shall be deemed guilty of a misdemeanor, and, on conviction, shall be punished by fine not exceeding $1,000, or by imprisonment not exceeding one year, or both, in the discretion of the court.' This section seems to be designed to apply to some existing or future law of a State or Territory which may conflict with the provisions of the bill now under consideration. It provides for counteracting such forbidden legislation by imposing fine and imprisonment upon the legislators who may pass such conflicting laws, or upon the officers or agents who shall put, or attempt to put, them into execution. It means an official offense, not a common crime committed against law upon the persons or property of the black race. Such an act may deprive the black man of his property, but not of the right to hold property. It means a deprivation of the right itself, either by the State Judiciary or the State Legislature. It is therefore assumed that, under this section, members of State Legislatures who should vote for laws conflicting with the provisions of the bill; that judges of the State courts who should render judgments in antagonism with its terms; and that marshals and sheriffs, who should, as ministerial officers, execute processes, sanctioned by State laws and issued by State judges, in execution of their judgments, could be brought before other tribunals, and there subjected to fine and imprisonment for the performance of the duties which such State laws might impose.

"The legislation thus proposed invades the judicial power of the State. It says to every State court or judge, If you decide that this act is unconstitutional; if you refuse, under the prohibition of a State law, to allow a negro to testify; if you hold that over such a subject-matter the State law is paramount, and 'under color' of a State law refuse the exercise of the right to the negro, your error of judgment, however conscientious, shall subject you to fine and imprisonment. I do not apprehend that the conflicting legislation which the bill seems to contemplate is so likely to occur as to render it necessary at this time to adopt a measure of such doubtful constitutionality.

"In the next place, this provision of the bill seems to be unnecessary, as adequate judicial remedies could be adopted to secure the desired end without invading the immunities of legislators, always important to be preserved in the interest of public liberty; without assailing the independence of the judiciary, always essential to the preservation of individual rights; and without impairing the efficiency of ministerial officers, always necessary for the maintenance of public peace and order. The remedy proposed by this section seems to be, in this respect, not only anomalous, but unconstitutional; for the Constitution guarantees nothing with certainty, if it does not insure to the several States the right of making and executing laws in regard to all matters arising within their jurisdiction, subject only to the restriction that, in cases of conflict with the Constitution and constitutional laws of the United States, the latter should be held to be the supreme law of the land.

"The third section gives the district courts of the United States exclusive 'cognizance of all crimes and offenses committed against the provisions of this act,' and concurrent jurisdiction with the circuit courts of the United States of all civil and criminal cases 'affecting persons who are denied or can not enforce in the courts or judicial tribunals of the State or locality where they may be any of the rights secured to them by the first section.' The construction which I have given to the second section is strengthened by this third section, for it makes clear what kind of denial or deprivation of the rights secured by the first section was in contemplation. It is a denial or deprivation of such rights 'in the courts or judicial tribunals of the State.' It stands, therefore, clear of doubt, that the offense and the penalties provided in the second section are intended for the State judge, who, in the clear exercise of his function as a judge, not acting ministerially, but judicially, shall decide contrary to this Federal law. In other words, when a State judge, acting upon a question involving a conflict between a State law and a Federal law, and bound, according to his own judgment and responsibility, to give an impartial decision between the two, comes to the conclusion that the State law is valid and the Federal law is invalid, he must not follow the dictates of his own judgment, at the peril of fine and imprisonment. The legislative department of the Government of the United States thus takes from the judicial department of the States the sacred and exclusive duty of judicial decision, and converts the State judge into a mere ministerial officer, bound to decree according to the will of Congress.

"It is clear that, in States which deny to persons whose rights are secured by the first section of the bill any one of those rights, all criminal and civil cases affecting them will, by the provisions of the third section, come under the exclusive cognizance of the Federal tribunals. It follows that if, in any State which denies to a colored person any one of all those rights, that person should commit a crime against the laws of the State—murder, arson, rape, or any other crime—all protection and punishment through the courts of the State are taken away, and he can only be tried and punished in the Federal courts. How is the criminal to be tried? If the offense is provided for and punished by Federal law, that law, and not the State law, is to govern.

"It is only when the offense does not happen to be within the purview of the Federal law that the Federal courts are to try and punish him under any other law; then resort is to be had to 'the common law, as modified and changed' by State legislation, 'so far as the same is not inconsistent with the Constitution and laws of the United States.' So that over this vast domain of criminal jurisprudence, provided by each State for the protection of its own citizens, and for the punishment of all persons who violate its criminal laws, Federal law, wherever it can be made to apply, displaces State law.

"The question here naturally arises, from what source Congress derives the power to transfer to Federal tribunals certain classes of cases embraced in this section. The Constitution expressly declares that the judicial power of the United States 'shall extend to all cases in law and equity arising under this Constitution, the laws of the United States, and treaties made, or which shall be made, under their authority; to all cases affecting embassadors, other public ministers, and consuls; to all cases of admiralty and maritime jurisdiction; to controversies to which the United States shall be a party; to controversies between two or more States, between a State and citizens of another State, between citizens of different States, between citizens of the same State claiming land under grants of different States, and between a State, or the citizens thereof, and foreign States, citizens, or subjects.'

"Here the judicial power of the United States is expressly set forth and defined; and the act of September 24, 1789, establishing the judicial courts of the United States, in conferring upon the Federal courts jurisdiction over cases originating in State tribunals, is careful to confine them to the classes enumerated in the above recited clause of the Constitution. This section of the bill undoubtedly comprehends case, and authorizes the exercise of powers that are not, by the Constitution, within the jurisdiction of the courts of the United States. To transfer them to those courts would be an exercise of authority well calculated to excite distrust and alarm on the part of all the States; for the bill applies alike to all of them—as well to those that have as to those that have not been engaged in rebellion.

"It may be assumed that this authority is incident to the power granted to Congress by the Constitution, as recently amended, to enforce, by appropriate legislation, the article declaring that 'neither slavery nor involuntary servitude, except as a punishment for crime whereof the party shall have been duly convicted, shall exist within the United States, or any place subject to their jurisdiction.' It can not, however, be justly claimed that, with a view to the enforcement of this article of the Constitution, there is, at present, any necessity for the exercise of all the powers which this bill confers.

Slavery has been abolished, and, at present, nowhere exists within the jurisdiction of the United States; nor has there been, nor is it likely there will be, any attempt to revive it by the people of the States. If, however, any such attempt shall be made, it will then become the duty of the General Government to exercise any and all incidental powers necessary and proper to maintain inviolate this great constitutional law of freedom.

"The fourth section of the bill provides that officers and agents of the Freedmen's Bureau shall be empowered to make arrests, and also that other officers may be specially commissioned for that purpose by the President of the United States. It also authorizes circuit courts of the United States and the superior courts of the Territories to appoint, without limitation, commissioners, who are to be charged with the performance of *quasi* judicial duties. The fifth section empowers the commissioners so to be selected by the courts to appoint, in writing, under their hands, one or more suitable persons, from time to time, to execute warrants and other processes described by the bill. These numerous official agents are made to constitute a sort of police, in addition to the military, and are authorized to summon a *posse comitatus* and even to call to their aid such portion of the land and naval forces of the United States, or of the militia, 'as may be necessary to the performance of the duty with which they are charged.'

"This extraordinary power is to be conferred upon agents irresponsible to the Government and to the people, to whose number the discretion of the commissioners is the only limit, and in whose hands such authority might be made a terrible engine of wrong, oppression, and fraud. The general statutes regulating the land and naval forces of the United States, the militia, and the execution of the laws, are believed to be adequate for every emergency which can occur in time of peace. If it should prove otherwise, Congress can, at any time, amend those laws in such manner as, while subserving the public welfare, not to jeopard the rights, interests, and liberties of the people.

"The seventh section provides that a fee of ten dollars shall be paid to each commissioner in every case brought before him, and a fee of five dollars to his deputy, or deputies, 'for each person he or they may arrest and take before any such commissioner,' 'with such other fees as may be deemed reasonable by such commissioner,' 'in general for performing such other duties as may be required in the premises.' All these fees are to be 'paid out of the Treasury of the United States,' whether there is a conviction or not;

but, in case of conviction, they are to be recoverable from the defendant. It seems to me that, under the influence of such temptations, bad men might convert any law, however beneficent, into an instrument of persecution and fraud.

"By the eighth section of the bill, the United States courts, which sit only in one place for white citizens, must migrate, with the marshal and district attorney (and necessarily with the clerk, although he is not mentioned), to any part of the district, upon the order of the President, and there hold a court 'for the purpose of the more speedy arrest and trial of persons charged with a violation of this act;' and there the judge and the officers of the court must remain, upon the order of the President, 'for the time therein designated.'

"The ninth section authorizes the President, or such person as he may empower for that purpose, to employ such part of the land and naval forces of the United States, or of the militia, as shall be necessary to prevent the violation and enforce the due execution of this act.' This language seems to imply a permanent military force, that is to be always at hand, and whose only business is to be the enforcement of this measure over the vast region where it is intended to operate.

"I do not propose to consider the policy of this bill. To me the details of the bill seem fraught with evil. The white race and the black race of the South have hitherto lived together under the relation of master and slave—capital owning labor. Now, suddenly, that relation is changed, and, as to the ownership, capital and labor are divorced. They stand, now, each master of itself. In this new relation, one being necessary to the other, there will be a new adjustment, which both are deeply interested in making harmonious. Each has equal power in settling the terms, and, if left to the laws that regulate capital and labor, it is confidently believed that they will satisfactorily work out the problem. Capital, it is true, has more intelligence; but labor is never so ignorant as not to understand its own interests, not to know its own value, and not to see that capital must pay that value. This bill frustrates this adjustment. It intervenes between capital and labor, and attempts to settle questions of political economy through the agency of numerous officials, whose interest it will be to foment discord between the two races; for, as the breach widens, their employment will continue, and when it is closed, their occupation will terminate.

"In all our history, in all our experience as a people living under Federal and State law, no such system as that contemplated by the details of this bill has ever before been proposed or adopted. They establish, for the security of the colored race, safeguards which go infinitely beyond any that the General Government has ever provided for the white race. In fact, the distinction of race and color is, by the bill, made to operate in favor of the colored and against the white race. They interfere with the municipal legislation of the States, with the relations existing exclusively between a State and its citizens, or between inhabitants of the same State—an absorption and assumption of power by the General Government which, if acquiesced in, must sap and destroy our federative system of limited powers, and break down the barriers which preserve the rights of the States. It is another step, or rather stride, to centralization and the concentration of all legislative power in the National Government. The tendency of the bill must be to resuscitate the spirit of rebellion, and to arrest the progress of those influences which are more closely drawing around the States the bonds of union and peace.

"My lamented predecessor, in his proclamation of the 1st of January, 1863, ordered and declared that all persons held as slaves within certain States and parts of States therein designated, were and thenceforward should be free; and, further, that the Executive Government of the United States, including the military and naval authorities thereof, would recognize and maintain the freedom of such persons. This guarantee has been rendered especially obligatory and sacred by the amendment of the Constitution abolishing slavery throughout the United States. I, therefore, fully recognize the obligation to protect and defend that class of our people whenever and wherever it shall become necessary, and to the full extent compatible with the Constitution of the United States.

"Entertaining these sentiments, it only remains for me to say that I will cheerfully coöperate with Congress in any measure that may be necessary for the protection of the civil rights of the freedmen, as well as those of all other classes of persons throughout the United States, by judicial process under equal and impartial laws, in conformity with the provisions of the Federal Constitution.

"I now return the bill to the Senate, and regret that, in considering the bills and joint resolutions—forty-two in number—which have been thus far submitted for my approval, I am compelled to withhold my assent from a second measure that has received the sanction of both houses of Congress.

"ANDREW JOHNSON.

"WASHINGTON, D. C., *March* 27, 1866."

The death and funeral obsequies of Senator Foot prevented the Senate from proceeding to the consideration of the President's veto message for more than a week after it was read. On the 4th of April the Civil Rights Bill came up to be reconsidered, the question being, "Shall the bill pass, the objections of the President notwithstanding."

It devolved upon Mr. Trumbull, the author of the bill, to answer the objections of the President. In answer to the President's position that the bill conferred only Federal citizenship, and did not give any *status* as citizens of States, Mr. Trumbull said: "Is it true that when a person becomes a citizen of the United States he is not also a citizen of every State where he may happen to be? On this point I will refer to a decision pronounced by the Supreme Court of the United States, delivered by Chief-Justice Marshall, the most eminent jurist who ever sat upon an American bench. In the case of Gassies *vs.*

Ballon, reported in 6 Peters, the Chief-Justice, in delivering the opinion of the court, says:

"'The defendant in error is alleged in the proceedings to be a citizen of the United Stated States, naturalized in Louisiana, and residing there. This is equivalent to an averment that he is a citizen of that State. *A citizen of the United States residing in any State of the Union is a citizen of that State.*'"

The message declared "that the right of Federal citizenship is now for the first time proposed to be given by law." "This," said Mr. Trumbull, "is not a misapprehension of the law, but a mistake in fact, as will appear by references to which I shall call the attention of the Senate." Mr. Trumbull then referred to the "collective naturalization" of citizens of Louisiana, Texas, and Cherokees, Choctaw, and Stockbridge Indians.

To the remark in the message that "if, as many claim, native-born persons are already citizens of the United States, this bill can not be necessary to make them such," Mr. Trumbull replied: "An act declaring what the law is, is one of the most common of acts known by legislative bodies. When there is any question as to what the law is, and for greater certainty, it is the most common thing in the world to pass a statute declaring it."

To the objection that eleven States were unrepresented, the Senator replied: "This is a standing objection in all the veto messages, yet the President has signed some forty bills. If there is any thing in this objection, no bill can pass Congress till the States are represented here. Sir, whose fault is it that eleven States are not represented? By what fault of theirs is it that twenty-five loyal States which have stood by this Union and by the Constitution are to be deprived of their right to legislate? If the reason assigned is a good one now, it has been a good one all the time for the last five years. If the fact that some States have rebelled against the Government is to take from the Government the right to legislate, then the criminal is to take advantage of his crime; the innocent are to be punished for the guilty.

"But the President tells us that 'the bill, in effect, proposes a discrimination against large numbers of intelligent, worthy, and patriotic foreigners, and in favor of the negro.' Is that true? What is the bill? It declares that there shall be no distinction in civil rights between any other race or color and the white race.

It declares that there shall be no different punishment inflicted on a colored man in consequence of his color than that which is inflicted on a white man for the same offense. Is that a discrimination in favor of the negro and against the foreigner—a bill the only effect of which is to preserve equality of rights?

"But perhaps it may be replied to this that the bill proposes to make a citizen of every person born in the United States, and, therefore, it discriminates in that respect against the foreigner. Not so; foreigners are all upon the same footing, whether black or white. The white child who is born in the United States a citizen is not to be presumed at its birth to be the equal intellectually with the worthy, intelligent, and patriotic foreigner who emigrates to this country. And, as is suggested by a Senator behind me, even the infant child of a foreigner born in this land is a citizen of the United States long before his father. Is this, therefore, a discrimination against foreigners?

"The President also has an objection to the making citizens of Chinese and Gypsies. I am told that but few Chinese are born in this country, and where the Gypsies are born, I never knew. [Laughter.] Like Topsy, it is questionable, whether they were born at all, but 'just come.' [Laughter.]

"But, sir, perhaps the best answer to this objection that the bill proposes to make citizens of Chinese and Gypsies, and this reference to the foreigners, is to be found in a speech delivered in this body by a Senator occupying, I think, the seat now occupied across the chamber by my friend from Oregon, [Mr. Williams,] less than six years ago, in reply to a message sent to this body by Mr. Buchanan, the then President of the United States, returning, with his objections, what was known as the Homestead Bill. On that occasion the Senator to whom I allude said:

"'But this idea about "poor foreigners," somehow or other, bewilders and haunts the imagination of a great many. * * * * *

"'I am constrained to say that I look upon this objection to the bill as a mere quibble on the part of the President, and as being hard-pressed for some excuse in withholding his approval of the measure; and his allusion to foreigners in this connection looks to me more like the *ad captandum* of the mere politician or demagogue, than a grave and sound reason to be offered by the President of the United States in a veto message upon so important a measure as the Homstead Bill.'

"That was the language of Senator Andrew Johnson, now

President of the United States. [Laughter.] That is probably the best answer to this objection, though I should hardly have ventured to use such harsh language in reference to the President as to accuse him of quibbling and of demagoguery, and of playing the mere politician in sending a veto message to the Congress of the United States."

The President had urged an objection that if Congress could confer civil rights upon persons without regard to color or race, it might also confer upon them political rights, and among them that of suffrage. In reply to this, Mr. Trumbull referred to the policy of the President himself in undertaking to "reörganize State governments in the disloyal States." He "claimed and exercised the power to protect colored persons in their civil rights," and yet, when "urged to allow loyal blacks to vote," he held that "he had no power; it was unconstitutional."

"But, sir," continued Mr. Trumbull, "the granting of civil rights does not and never did, in this country, carry with it rights, or, more properly speaking, political privileges. A man may be a citizen in this country without a right to vote or without a right to hold office. The right to vote and hold office in the States depends upon the legislation of the various States; the right to hold certain offices under the Federal Government depends upon the Constitution of the United States. The President must be a natural-born citizen, and a Senator or Representative must be a citizen of the United States for a certain number of years before he is eligible to a seat either in this or the other House of Congress; so that the fact of being a citizen does not necessarily qualify a person for an office, nor does it necessarily authorize him to vote. Women are citizens; children are citizens; but they do not exercise the elective franchise by virtue of their citizenship. Foreigners, as is stated by the President in this message, before they are naturalized are protected in the rights enumerated in this bill, but because they possess those rights in most, if not all, the States, that carries with it no right to vote.

"But, sir, what rights do citizens of the United States have? To be a citizen of the United States carries with it some rights, and what are they? They are those inherent, fundamental rights which belong to free citizens or free men in all countries, such as the rights enumerated in this bill, and they belong to them in all the States of the Union. The right of American citizenship means something. It does not mean, in the case of a foreigner, that when he is naturalized he is to be left entirely to the mercy of State legislation. He has a right, when duly naturalized, to go into any State of the Union, and to reside there, and the United States Government will protect him in that right. It will protect a citizen of the United States, not only in one of the States of the Union, but it will protect him in foreign lands.

"Every person residing in the United States is entitled to the protection of that law by the Federal Government, because the Federal Government has jurisdiction of such questions. American citizenship would be little worth if it did not carry protection with it.

"How is it that every person born in these United States owes allegiance to the Government? Every thing that he is or has, his property and his life, may be taken by the Government of the United States in its defense, or to maintain the honor of the nation. And can it be that our ancestors struggled through a long war and set up this Government, and that the people of our day have struggled through another war, with all its sacrifices and all its desolation, to maintain it, and at last that we have got a Government which is all-powerful to command the obedience of the citizen, but has no power to afford him protection? Is that all that this boasted American citizenship amounts to? Go tell it, sir, to the father whose son was starved at Andersonville; or the widow whose husband was slain at Mission Ridge; or the little boy who leads his sightless father through the streets of your city, made blind by the winds and the sand of the Southern coast; or the thousand other mangled heroes to be seen on every side, that this Government, in defense of which the son and the husband fell, the father lost his eyes, and the others were crippled, had the right to call these persons to its defense, but has no right to protect the survivors or their friends in any right whatever in any of the States. Sir, it can not be. Such is not the meaning of our Constitution. Such is not the meaning of American citizenship. This Government, which would go to war to protect its meanest—I will not say citizen—inhabitant, if you please, in any foreign land, whose rights were unjustly encroached upon, has certainly some power to protect its own citizens in their own country. Allegiance and protection are reciprocal rights."

To the President's objection to the second section of the bill, that it discriminated in favor of colored persons, Mr. Trumbull replied: "It says, in effect, that no one shall subject a colored person to a different punishment than that inflicted on a white person for the same offense. Does that discriminate in favor of the colored person? Why, sir, the very object and effect of the section is to prevent discrimination, and language, it seems to me, could not more plainly express that object and effect. It may be said that it is for the benefit of the black man, because he is now, in some instances, discriminated against by State laws; but that is the case with all remedial statutes. They are for the relief of the persons who need the relief, not for the relief of those who have the right already; and when those needing the relief obtain it, they stand upon the precise footing of those who do not need the benefit of the law."

The President had further objected to this section, that "it provides for counteracting such forbidden legislation by imposing fine and imprisonment upon the legislators who may pass such conflicting laws."

"Let us see," said Mr. Trumbull, "if that is the language or the proper construction of the section. I will read again the first lines of it. It declares 'that any person who, under color of any law, ordinance, regulation, or custom, shall subject, or cause to be subjected, etc., * * * shall be punished,' etc.

"Who is to be punished? Is the law to be punished? Are the men who make the law to be punished? Is that the language of the bill? Not at all. If any person, 'under color of any law,' shall subject another to the deprivation of a right to which he is entitled, he is to be punished. Who? The person who, under the color of the law, does the act, not the men who made the law. In some communities in the South a custom prevails by which different punishment is inflicted upon the blacks from that meted out to whites for the same offense. Does this section propose to punish the community where the custom prevails? or is it to punish the person who, under color of the custom, deprives the party of his right? It is a manifest perversion of the meaning of the section to assert any thing else.

"But it is said that under this provision judges of the courts and ministerial officers who are engaged in execution of any such statutes may be punished, and that is made an objection to this bill. I admit that a ministerial officer or a judge, if he acts corruptly or viciously in the execution or under color of an illegal act, may be and ought to be punished; but if he acted innocently, the judge would not be punished. Sir, what is a crime? It is a violation of some public law, to constitute which there must be an act, and a vicious will in doing the act; or, according to the definition in some of the law-books, to constitute a crime there must be a violation of a public law, in the commission of which there must be a union or joint operation of act and intent, or criminal negligence; and a judge who acted innocently, and not viciously or oppressively, would never be convicted under this act. But, sir, if he acted knowingly, viciously, or oppressively, in disregard of a law of the United States, I repeat, he ought to be punished, and it is no anomaly to prescribe a punishment in such a case. Very soon after the organization of this Government, in the first years of its existence, the Congress of the United States provided for punishing officers who, under color of State law, violated the laws of the United States."

Mr. Trumbull then read from an act of Congress passed in 1790, providing for the punishment of certain offenses against foreign ministers, and said: "By this provision all officers executing any process in violation of the laws of the United States are to be subject to a much longer imprisonment than is provided by this bill.

"But, sir, there is another answer, in my judgment, more conclusive, to all these objections to this second section, which is the vital part of the bill. Without it, it would scarcely be worth the paper on which the bill is written. A law without a penalty, without a sanction, is of little value to any body. What good does it do for the Legislature to say, 'Do this, and forbear to do that,' if no consequence is to follow the act of disobedience? This is the vitality of the bill. What is the objection that is made to it, and which seems even to have staggered some friends of the measure? It is because it reads in the first section that any person who, 'under color of law,' shall commit these offenses, shall be subject to the penalties of the law. Suppose those words had been left out, and the bill read, 'any person who shall subject any inhabitant of a State to different punishment by reason of his color shall be punished,' would there have been any objection to the bill then? That is the way most criminal laws read. That is the way the law punishing conspiracies against the Government reads. If two or more persons conspire together to overthrow the Government, or by force to resist its authority, they are liable to indictment, and, upon conviction, to imprisonment in the penitentiary and to heavy fine. Would the fact that the persons engaged in the conspiracy were judges or governors or ministerial officers, acting under color of any statute or custom, screen them from punishment? Surely not.

"The words 'under color of law' were inserted as words of limitation, and not for the purpose of punishing persons who would not have been subject to punishment under the act if they had been omitted. If an offense is committed against a colored person simply because he is colored, in a State where the law affords him the same protection as if he were white, this act neither has nor was intended to have any thing to do with his case, because he has adequate remedies in the State courts; but if he is discriminated against, under color of State laws, because he is colored, then it becomes necessary to interfere for his protection.

"The assumption that State judges and other officials are not to be held responsible for violations of United States laws when done under color of State statutes or customs is akin to the maxim of the English law that the king can do no wrong. It places officials above the law; it is the very doctrine out of which the rebellion was hatched.

"Every thing that was done by that wicked effort to overturn our Government was done under color of law. The rebels insisted that they had a right to secede; they passed ordinances of secession, they set up State governments, and all that they did was under color of law. And if parties committing these high crimes are to go free because they acted under color of law, why is not Jeff. Davis and every other rebel chief discharged at once? Why did this country put forth all its resources of men and money to put down the rebellion against the authority of the Government except it had a right to do so, even as against those who were acting under color of law? Lee, with his rebel hordes, thundering upon the outskirts of this very city, was acting under color of law; every judge who has held a court in the Southern States for the last four years, and has tried and convicted of treason men guilty of no other offense than loyalty to the Union, acted under color of law.

"Sir, if we had authority by the use of the army and the war power to put down rebels acting under color of law, I put the question to every lawyer, if we had not authority to do that through the courts and the judicial tribunals if it had been practicable? Suppose it had been practicable, through the marshals, to arrest the Legislature which convened at Montgomery, and undertook to take the State of Alabama out of the Union and set up a government in hostility thereto, ought it not to have been done? Was not that a conspiracy against this Government? When the Legislature assembled at Montgomery in 1861, and resolved that the connection between Alabama and the United States was dissolved, and when its members took steps to maintain that declaration; when the same thing was done in South Carolina, and courts were organized to carry out the scheme, will any body tell me it would not have been competent, had it been practicable, for the United States courts in those States to have issued process for the arrest of every one of those legislators, governors, judges, and all. And, sir, had this been done, and it had turned out upon trial that any of the parties arrested had been engaged in armed hostility against the United States, as some of them had been when, with arms in their hands, they seized the arsenals and other public property of the United States, would they not have been found guilty of treason and hung for treason? and would the fact that they had acted under color of law have afforded them any protection?"

The President, in his Veto Message, had said, "I do not apprehend that the conflicting legislation which the bill seems to contemplate is so likely to occur as to render it necessary, at this time, to adopt a measure of such doubtful constitutionality."

"That statement," replied Mr. Trumbull, "makes it necessary that I should advert to the facts and show whether there is any likelihood of such conflicting legislation; and my testimony comes from the President himself, or those acting under his authority."

After having referred to legislative enactments of several of the Southern States very oppressive to the colored people, Mr. Trumbull remarked: "Now, sir, what becomes of this declaration that there is no necessity for any measure of this kind? Here are the laws of Texas, of Mississippi, of Virginia, to which I have referred; and laws equally oppressive exist in some of the other States. Is there no necessity to protect a freedman when he is liable to be whipped if caught away from home? no necessity to protect a freedman in his rights when he is not permitted to hold or lease a piece of ground in a State? no necessity to protect a freedman in his rights, who will be reduced to a slavery worse than that from which he has been emancipated if a law is permitted to be carried into effect? Sir, these orders emanate and this information comes from officers acting by presidential authority, and yet the President tells us there is no danger of conflicting legislation."

After having answered other objections of the President, Mr. Trumbull said: "I have now gone through this Veto Message, replying with what patience I could command to its various objections to the bill. Would that I could stop here, that there was no occasion to go further; but justice to myself, justice to the State whose representative I am, justice to the people of the whole country, in legislation for whose behalf I am called to participate, justice to the Constitution I am sworn to support, justice to the rights of American citizenship it secures, and to human liberty, now imperiled, require me to go further. Gladly would I refrain speaking of the spirit of this message, of the dangerous doctrines it promulgates, of the inconsistencies and contradictions of its author, of his encroachments upon the constitutional rights of Congress, of his assumption of unwarranted powers, which, if persevered in and not checked by the people, must eventually lead to a subversion of the Government and the destruction of liberty.

"Congress, in the passage of the bill under consideration, sought no controversy with the President. So far from it, the bill was proposed with a view to carry out what were supposed to be the views of the President, and was submitted to him before its introduction in the Senate. I am not about to relate private declarations of the President, but it is right that the American people should know that the controversy which exists between him and Congress in reference to this measure is of his own seeking. Soon after Congress met, it became apparent that there was a difference of opinion between the President and some members of Congress in regard to the condition of the rebellious States and the rights to be secured to freedmen.

"The President, in his annual message, had denied the constitutional power of the General Government to extend the elective franchise to negroes, but he was equally decided in the assertion of the right of every man to life, liberty, and the pursuit of happiness. This was his language:

"'But while I have no doubt that now, after the close of the war, it is not competent for the General Government to extend the elective franchise in the several States, it is equally clear that good faith requires the security of the freedmen in their liberty and their property.'

"There were some members of Congress who expressed the opinion that in the reörganization of the rebellious States the right of suffrage should be extended to the colored man, though this was not the prevailing sentiment of Congress. All were anxious for a reörganization of the rebellious States, and their admission to full participation in the Federal Government as soon as these relations could be restored with safety to all concerned. Feeling the importance of harmonious action between the different departments of the Government, and an anxious desire to sustain the President, for whom I had always entertained the highest respect, I had frequent interviews with him during the early part of the session. Without mentioning any thing said by him, I may with propriety state that, acting from the considerations I have stated, and believing that the passage of a law by Congress, securing equality in civil rights to freedmen and all other inhabitants of the United States, when denied by State authorities, would do much to relieve anxiety in the North, to induce the Southern States to secure these rights by their own action, and thereby remove many of the obstacles to an early reconstruction, I prepared the bill substantially as it is now returned with the President's objections. After the bill was introduced and printed, a copy was furnished him, and at a subsequent period, when it was reported that he was hesitating about signing the Freedmen's Bureau Bill, he was informed of the condition of the Civil Rights Bill then pending in the House, and a hope expressed that if he had objections to any of its provisions he would make them known to its friends, that they might be remedied, if not destructive of the measure; that there was believed to be no disposition on the part of Congress, and certainly none on my part, to have bills presented to him which he could not approve. He never indicated to me, nor, so far as I know, to any of its friends, the least objection to any of the provisions of the bill till after its passage. And how could he, consistently with himself? The bill was framed, as was supposed, in entire harmony with his views, and certainly in harmony with what he was then and has since been doing in protecting freedmen in their civil rights all through the rebellious States. It was strictly limited to the protection of the civil rights belonging to every freeman, the birthright of every American citizen, and carefully avoided conferring or interfering with political rights or privileges of any kind.

* * * * "If the bill now before us, and which goes no further than to secure civil rights to the freedman, can not be passed, then the constitutional amendment proclaiming freedom to all the inhabitants of the land is a cheat and a delusion.

"I can not better conclude what I have to say than in the language of Mr. Johnson on the occasion of the veto of the Homestead Bill, when, after stating that the fact that the President was inconsistent and changed his opinion with reference to a great measure and a great principle, is no reason why a Senator or Representative, who has acted understandingly, should change his opinion. He said:

"'I hope the Senate and House of Representatives, who have sanctioned this bill by more than a two-thirds majority, will, according to the Constitution, exercise their privilege and power, and let the bill become a law of the land, according to the high behest of the American people.'"

On the next day, April 5th, Mr. Johnson, of Maryland, made a speech sustaining the Veto Message. He argued that negroes were not citizens of the United States by reason of their birth in the United States, and that Congress had no authority by law to declare them such. To sustain his position, he made quotations from the opinion of the minority in the Dred Scott case, as rendered by Mr. Justice Curtis. He then proceeded to reply to some of Mr. Trumbull's arguments against the Veto Message: "The honorable member from Illinois disposes of the President's objection to the first section of this bill by saying that it is merely declaratory. I know it is competent for any legislative body, on a question where difference of opinions exist in relation to any legal proposition, to remove them by declaratory legislation; but that is not the purpose of this bill. It professes to be passed in the exercise of a positive and absolute power to change the law—not to declare what the law was in order to remove doubts, but to make the law. It assumes, or otherwise there would be no occasion for it, that birth alone does not confer citizenship; and assuming that no citizenship would exist in consequence of birth alone, it declares that birth alone, in spite of State constitution and State laws, shall confer citizenship. Now, with all deference to the opinion of the honorable Chairman of the Committee on the Judiciary, that seems to me to be a proposition as clearly erroneous as any proposition can be in relation to constitutional law. The States were sovereign before the Constitution was adopted; and the Constitution not only, according to its very terms, does not profess to confer upon the Government of the United States all governmental power, but as far as Congress is concerned, professes to confer upon that department of the Government only the particular delegated powers there enumerated; but so anxious were the framers of that instrument and the great men of that day, to whom the subsequent organization of this Government was left, that although they had no doubt as to the principle that only the delegated powers were granted, (and the debates in the Convention itself as well as the debates in the conventions of the several States, when the Constitution was before them for adoption or rejection, all went upon the theory that no powers were conferred except such as were expressly granted, or as were reasonably implied to be as necessary to carry out the powers expressly granted,) by the tenth amendment adopted recently after the Constitution went into operation, and recommended by the men, many of whom were the framers of the Constitution itself, that the powers not delegated by the Constitution, and not denied to the States by the same instrument, were to be considered reserved to the States respectively, or to the people.

"Standing, therefore, as well upon the nature of the Government itself, as a Government of enumerated powers specially delegated, as upon the express provision that every thing not granted was to be considered as remaining with the States unless the Constitution contained some particular prohibition of any power before belonging to the States, what doubt can there be that if a State possessed the power to declare who should be her citizens before the Constitution was adopted that power remains now as absolute and as conclusive as it was when the Constitution was adopted? The bill, therefore, changes the whole theory of the Government.

"The President, then, I think, is right. I go further than he does. He expresses a doubt whether Congress has the power; I affirm, with all deference to the better judgment of the majority of the Senate who voted for the bill, and to that of the honorable Chairman of the Committee on the Judiciary, that it is perfectly clear that no such power exists in Congress as the one attempted to be exercised by the first section. I hold, with Mr. Justice Curtis—and his opinion to this day has never been questioned—that citizenship of the United States consequent upon birth in a State is to depend upon the fact whether the constitution and laws of the State make the party so born a citizen of the State.

"But that is not all. This first section has another provision. Not satisfied with making the parties citizens and clothing them with all the rights belonging to white citizens by the laws of the States, it says that they 'shall be subject to like punishment, pains, and penalties, and to none other.' That invades the jurisdiction of the States over their criminal code. Congress assumes to define a crime, and defining a crime gives to its own courts exclusive jurisdiction over the crime and the party charged with its perpetration. It strikes at the criminal code of the States. The result, therefore, of the three provisions in this section is, that contrary to State constitutions and State laws, it converts a man that is not a citizen of a State into a citizen of the State; it gives him all the rights that belong to a citizen of the State; and it provides that his punishment shall only be such as the State laws impose upon white citizens. Where is the authority to do that? If it exists, it is still more obvious that the result is an entire annihilation of the power of the States. It seems to be the fashion of the hour—I do not know that my honorable friend from Illinois goes to that extent—to hold to the doctrine that the sooner every thing is vested in the Government of the United States the better for the country. It is a perilous delusion. If such a proposition had been supposed to be found any where in the Constitution of the United States, it never would have been adopted by the people; and if it is assumed, or if it is considered as constitutionally existing by virtue of some power not before known, the Government will not last half a century. I have not time to read from the writings of Mr. Madison and Mr. Hamilton and the decisions of the Supreme Court on the question.

"But you, Mr. President, know very well that consolidation

of power in the Government of the United States was looked upon as certain ruin to republican institutions. In the first place, it would be sure to result in anarchy; and in the second place, in order to be saved from the horrors of anarchy, we should be compelled to take refuge in despotic power, and the days of constitutional liberty would soon be numbered. The doubt then was, and the doubt now should be more firmly settled in the public mind, that a country as extensive as that of the United States can not exist except by means of divided sovereignties; one sovereignty having charge of all external matters, or matters between the States to which the powers of the States are inadequate; the other sovereignties having power over all internal matters to the management of which they are adequate. Despotism would soon be our fate, preceded by anarchy; the military chieftain instead of being looked upon, as he should be by every republican, with alarm and concern, would be hailed as a savior in order to save us from the horrors of disorganization.

"The honorable member referred to the act of 1790, but it relates entirely to different subjects, and all the statutes to which he adverted are statutes of the same description. What is the twenty-sixth section of the act of 1790 to which he referred? The preceding section provided that no one should sue a foreign minister, and the section to which my friend referred particularly, said that if a party did sue a foreign minister he should be liable to be punished. Certainly; but why? Because the Government of the United States was vested with the exclusive authority in all cases depending upon the law of nations; and the law of nations saving from responsibility embassadors accredited to the United States, for civil debts, he who attempted to interfere offended against the Government, and he offended in relation to a subject exclusively committed to the General Government. The power, therefore, which Congress exerted in the particular legislation to which the honorable member reverted is just the power which they exert when they provide for the punishment of any man who counterfeits the currency of the United States, or forges its paper, or forges its bonds, or interferes with the administration of the Post-office Department. These are all powers incidental to the possession of the express power, and in the case to which he adverted the express power was one necessarily belonging to the Government, because it was a power belonging to and regulated by the law of nations, and not by any municipal regulation.

"The honorable member from Illinois tells us that the President's objection, that there are eleven States not now represented, is entitled to no consideration whatever. The honorable member seems to suppose that the President adverted to the fact that there were eleven States not represented as showing that Congress possessed no constitutional authority to legislate upon the subject, supposing that they would have had the authority if those States were represented. That is not the view taken by the President; it is an entire misapprehension of the doctrine of the President. He says no such thing, and he intimates no such thing. But assuming, what in another part of the message he denies, that the authority might be considered as existing, he submits as a question of policy whether it is right to change the whole domestic economy of those eleven States, in the absence of any representation upon this floor from them. My honorable friend asks whose fault it is that they are not represented. Why are they not here? He says their hands are reeking with the blood of loyal men; that they are unable to take the oath which a statute that he assumes to be constitutional has provided; and he would have the country and the Senate to believe that that is the reason why they are not here. Is that the fact, Mr. President? These States are organized, and how organized? What have they done? They have abolished slavery by an astonishing unanimity; they have abolished nearly all the distinctions which antecedently existed between the two races. They have permitted the negroes to sue. they have permitted them to testify; they have not yet permitted them to vote.

"Why are they not received? Because, in the judgment of the Senate, before the States can be considered as restored, Congressional legislation on the subject is necessary. Whose fault is it that there has not been Congressional legislation? Is it the fault of the eleven States? Certainly not; it is our own fault. And why is it that we are in point of fact delaying their admission, whether it is to be considered as a fault or not? Because we want to inquire into the condition of these States. Why, in the name of Heaven! how long have we been here? We came here early in December, and this is the month of April; and here we may remain until July, or, as rumor has it, until next December;

and shall we be satisfied within that time that Congressional legislation may be safely adopted?

"I have a word or two more to say. My honorable friend from Illinois, as it seemed to me—his nature is impulsive, and perhaps he was carried further than he intended—seemed to intimate that the President of the United States had not acted sincerely in this matter; that his usurpation was a clear one, and that he was to be censured for that usurpation. What has he done? He has vetoed this bill. He had a constitutional right to do so. Not only that; if he believed that the effect of the bill would be that which he states in his Veto Message, he was not only authorized but bound to veto it. His oath is to 'preserve' as well as to 'protect and defend' the Constitution of the United States; and believing, as he does, and in that opinion I concur, that this bill assails the Constitution of the United States, he would have been false to his plighted faith if he had not returned it with his objections.

"He desires—and who does not?—that the Union shall be restored as it originally existed. He has a policy which he thinks is best calculated to effect it. He may be mistaken, but he is honest. Congress may differ with him. I hope they will agree sooner or later, because I believe, as I believe in my existence, that the condition in which the country now is can not remain without producing troubles that may shake our reputation, not only in our own eyes, but in the eyes of the civilized world. Let the day come when we shall be again together, and then, forgetting the past, hailing the present, and looking forward to the future, we shall remember, if we remember the past at all, for the exhibition of valor and gallantry displayed on both sides, and find in it, when we become one, a guarantee that in the future no foreign hostilities are to be dreaded, and that no civil discord need be apprehended."

Mr. Trumbull said: "The opinion of Judge Curtis, from which the Senator read, was the opinion of a dissenting judge, entitled to very great credit on account of the learning and ability of that judge, but it was not the opinion of the court, and an examination of the entire opinion, which is very lengthy, would perhaps not sustain the precise principles the Senator from Maryland laid down. But, sir, I have another authority which I think of equal weight with that of Judge Curtis—not pronounced in a judicial tribunal it is true, but by one of the most eminent members of the bar in this nation; I may say by a gentleman who stands at the head of the bar in America at this time—an opinion pronounced, too, in the exercise of official duties; and I propose to read a few sentences from that opinion, for it is to be found reported in the Congressional Globe containing the proceedings of this body less than ninety days ago. This is the language:

"'While they [negroes] were slaves, it was a very different question; but now, when slavery is terminated, and by terminating it you have got rid of the only obstacle in the way of citizenship, two questions arise: first, Whether that fact itself does not make them citizens? Before they were not citizens, because of slavery, and only because of slavery. Slavery abolished, why are they not just as much citizens as they would have been had slavery never existed? My opinion is that they become citizens, and I hold that opinion so strongly that I should consider it unnecessary to legislate on the subject at all, as far as that class is concerned, but for the ruling of the Supreme Court, to which I have adverted.'

"Sir, that opinion was held by the honorable Senator from Maryland who made this speech to-day. He holds the opinion so strongly now that slavery is abolished, which was the only obstacle in the way of their being citizens, that he would want no legislation on the subject but for the Dred Scott decision! What further did the Senator from Maryland say less than ninety days ago? It is possible, doubtless—it is not only possible but it is certainly true—that the Senator from Maryland, by reading the conclusive arguments of the Veto Message in regard to Chinese and Gypsies, has discovered that he was in error ninety days ago. I by no means mean to impute any wrong motive to the Senator from Maryland, but simply to ask that he will pardon me if I have not been able to see the conclusive reasoning of the Veto Message."

After quoting still further from Mr. Johnson's speech, made on a previous occasion, Mr. Trumbull said: "But as I am up, I will refer to one other point to which the Senator alluded, and that is in regard to the quotation which I made yesterday from the statute of 1790. I quoted that statute for the purpose of showing that the provisions in the bill under consideration, which it was insisted allowed the punishment of ministerial officers and judges who should act in obedience to State laws and under color of State laws, were not anomalous. I read a statute of 1790 to show that the Congress of the United States, at that day, provided for punishing both judges and officers who acted under color of State law in defiance of a law of the United States. How does the Senator answer that? He says that was on a different subject; the law of 1790 provided for punishing judges and officers who did an act in violation of the international law, jurisdiction over which is conferred upon the nation. Let me ask the Senator from Maryland, if the bill under discussion does not provide for the punishment of persons who violate a right secured by the Constitution of the United States? Is a right which a citizen holds by virtue of the Constitution of his country less sacred than a right which he holds by virtue of international law?"

Mr. Johnson replied as follows: "It is singular, in my estimation, how a gentleman with a mind as clear as Mr. Trumbull's, with a perspicacity that is a little surprising, could have fallen into the error of supposing that there is any inconsistency between the doctrine contained in the speech to which he has adverted and the one which I have mantained to-day. What I said then I say now, that as far as the United States are concerned, all persons born within the limits of the United States are to be considered as citizens, and that without reference to the color or the race; and after the abolition of slavery the negro would stand precisely in the condition of the white man. But the honorable member can hardly fail, I think—certainly he can not when I call his attention to it—to perceive that that has nothing to do with the question now before the Senate. His bill makes them citizens of the United States because of birth, and gives them certain rights within the States."

Mr. Fessenden asked: "Were not your remarks made on this very question in this bill?"

"No," replied Mr. Johnson; "on another bill." He continued: "What I maintain is this—and I have never doubted it, because I entertained the same opinion when I made those remarks that I entertain now—that citizenship of the United States, in consequence of birth, does not make a party a citizen of the State in which he is born unless the Constitution and laws of the State recognize him as a citizen. Now, what does this bill propose? All born within the United States are to be considered citizens of the United States, and as such shall have in every State all the rights that belong to any body else in the State as far as the particular subjects stated in the bill are concerned. Now, I did suppose, and I shall continue to suppose, it to be clear, unless I am met with the almost paramount authority of the Chairman of the Judiciary Committee, that citizenship, by way of birth, conferred on the party as far as he and the United States were concerned, is not a citizenship which entitles him to the privilege of citizenship within the State where he is born; if it be true, and I submit that it is true beyond all doubt, that over the question of State citizenship the authority of the State Government is supreme.

"Now, the honorable member is counfounding the *status* of a citizen of the United States and the *status* of a citizen of the United States who as such is a citizen of the State of his residence. Maintaining, as I do, that there is no authority to make any body a citizen of the United States so as to convert him thereby into a citizen of a State, there is no authority in the Constitution for this particular bill, which says that because he is a citizen of the United States he is to be considered a citizen of any State in which he may be at any time with reference to the rights conferred by this bill.

Mr. Trumbull replied: "I desire simply to remark that the speech from which I quoted, made by the Senator from Maryland, was made upon this very bill. It was in reference to this bill that he was speaking when he laid down the proposition that every person born in the United States since the abolition of slavery was a citizen of the United States, and if there was any doubt about it, it was proper for us to declare them so, and not only proper, but our duty to do so; and to make the matter specific, the honorable Senator voted for this proposition, which I will now read, on the yeas and nays:

"'All persons born in the United States, and not subject to any foreign Power, excluding Indians not taxed, are hereby declared to be citizens of the United States, without distinction of color.'

"Upon the adoption of that proposition as an amendment, it not being in the bill as originally introduced, the Senator from Maryland, with thirty others, voted in the affirmative. So we have his high authority for saying that all persons born in the United States, and not subject to any foreign Power, are citizens of the United States, exactly as it appears in this bill."

"Mr. Yates, of Illinois, remarked: "I remember very well

that the Senator from Maryland offered an amendment to the Freedmen's Bureau Bill to this effect: to strike out the words 'without distinction of color.' The Freedmen's Bureau Bill applied legislation by Congress to the freedmen in the States and to the condition of the freedmen in the States. It was legislation that affected the freedmen in the rebellious States. If I remember aright the Senator from Maryland moved to strike out the words 'without distinction of color' in one section of that bill, and for that motion he gave this reason: because, under the Constitution of the United States, as amended, abolishing slavery in all the States and Territories of the United States, the freedmen occupied precisely the same position with any other citizen of the United States in any State or Territory. I understood him as taking the broad position, which I have maintained, and which Republican Senators have maintained, and which I think the country maintains, that under the Constitution, as amended, the freedman occupies precisely the same position as any man born in any State or Territory of the United States; and that was the object, if I understood the Senator from Maryland, of his moving to amend the Freedmen's Bureau Bill by striking out the words 'without distinction of color.'

"I recognize the authority of the decisions quoted by the Senator from Maryland before the adoption of the amendment to the Constitution. The States had the power over the question of slavery in the States before the amendment to the Constitution; but by the amendment to the Constitution, in which the States have concurred, the freedman becomes a free man, entitled to the same rights and privileges as any other citizen of the United States."

Mr. Cowan, of Pennsylvania, spoke in favor of the veto, premising that his words, "if they are not to convince any body in the Senate, may go to the country and be reflected on there." Mr. Cowan said he was quite willing that all the people of this country should enjoy the rights conferred upon them by this bill. But, supposing the bill had all the merit in the world, it would not be effective to attain the ends hoped for by its friends; and apart from that, its provisions were exceedingly dangerous. It gave married women and minors the right to make and enforce contracts. The grammatical structure of a portion of the bill was such as to enable a corrupt, passionate, or prejudiced judge to take advantage of it in order to widen the jurisdiction of the United States courts, and drag into them all the business which had heretofore occupied the State courts. This would be enough in this nineteenth century to make a man tremble for the fate of constitutional government. "If," said Mr. Cowan, "we had undoubted authority to pass this bill, under the circumstances I would not vote for it, on account of its objectionable phraseology, its dubious language, and the mischief which might attend upon a large and liberal construction of it in the District and Circuit Courts of the United States." The trouble and expense of obtaining justice in the United States courts, but one, or at most two existing in any of the Southern States, would debar the African from applying to them for redress. "Your remedy," said the Senator, "is delusive; your remedy is no remedy at all; and to hold it up to the world as a remedy is a gross fraud, however pious it may be. It is no remedy to the poor debtor that you prosecute his judge, and threaten him with fine and imprisonment. It is no remedy to the poor man with a small claim that you locate a court one or two hundred miles away from him which is so expensive in its administration of justice that he can not enter there.

"There is another provision of the bill, which, notwithstanding the act of Congress relied upon by the honorable Senator from Illinois, I think is unquestionably anomalous, and to me not only anomalous, but atrocious; and that is, the substitution of an indictment for the writ of error. What has been the law of these United States heretofore? When an act of Congress came in contact with a State law, and the judge of a State court decided that the law of Congress was unconstitutional, there was an appeal given to the defeated party to the Supreme Court of the United States in order to determine the constitutionality of the law. But, sir, who, until the last few months, ever heard of making the judge a criminal because he decided against the constitutionality of a law of the United States? One would think we were being transported back to the dark ages of the world when a man is to be accused and perhaps convicted of a crime who has done nothing more than honestly and conscientiously discharged his duty. I know that the persons of embassadors are sacred, and I know that it is a very high offense against the law of nations, which no civil judge of any court could justify, to in-

Eng.d by G.E. Perine & Co. N.York.

Wm M. Stewart

W.M M. STEWART

SENATOR FROM NEVADA

vade this sacred right of the embassador, but every body knows that that is an exceptional case. Every body knows that in all times and at all ages the judge was punishable who did not respect the person of an embassador. But that is not this case. That analogy will not help the third section of this bill. It is openly avowed upon the floor of the Senate of the United States, in the year of our Lord 1866, in the full blaze and light of the nineteenth century, that the indictment is to be a substitute for the writ of error, and it is justified because a judge ought to be indicted who violates the sacred person of an embassador! What potency there must be in the recent amendment of the Constitution which has foisted the negro and set him upon the same platform as the envoy extraordinary and minister plenipotentiary of Great Britain or of all the Russias to the United States of America, and made him as sacred as an embassador, and the judge who decides against him is to be punished as a criminal!"

Mr. Stewart showed that States might easily avoid all the annoying operations of this bill which were feared by its opponents: "When I reflect how very easy it is for the States to avoid the operation of this bill, how very little they have to do to avoid the operation of the bill entirely, I think that it is robbed of its coercive features, and I think no one has any reason to complain because Congress has exercised a power, which it must be conceded it has, when it has exercised it in a manner which leaves it so easy for the States to avoid the operation of this bill. If passed to-day, it has no operation in the State of Georgia; it is impossible to commit a crime under this bill in the State of Georgia; and the other States can place themselves in the same position so easily that I do not believe they ought to complain."

He then read the second section of an act passed in Georgia, precisely similar to the first section of the Civil Rights Bill. Nothing could be done in Georgia under "color of law," which would subject officers to the penalties provided by the Civil Rights Bill. "It being so easily avoided by being complied with, by doing a simple act of justice, by carrying out the spirit of the constitutional amendment, I can not give my consent to defeat a bill the purpose of which is good, the operation of which is so innocent, and may be so easily avoided."

The Republican Senators were desirous of bringing the bill to a final vote on this evening, but on account of the illness of

Senator Wright, of New Jersey, it was proposed by Democratic members to appoint some hour on the following day when the vote should be taken in order that they might have a full vote.

Mr. Wade, of Ohio, said: "If this was a question in the ordinary course of legislation, I certainly would not object to the proposition which the gentlemen on the other side make; but I view it as one of the greatest and most fundamental questions that has ever come before this body for settlement, and I look upon it as having bearings altogether beyond the question on this bill. The bill is, undoubtedly, a very good one. There is no constitutional objection to it; there has been no objection to it raised that creates a doubt in the mind of any mortal man; but, nevertheless, we are at issue with the President of the United States upon a question peculiarly our own. The President of the United States has no more power under the Constitution to interpose his authority here, to prescribe the principle upon which these States should be admitted to this Union, than any man of this body has out of it. The Constitution makes him the executive of the laws that we make, and there it leaves him; and what is our condition? We who are to judge of the forms of government under which States shall exist; we, who are the only power that is charged with this great question, are to be somehow or other wheedled out of it by the President by reason of the authority that he sets up.

"Sir, we can not abandon it unless we yield to a principle that will unhinge and unsettle the balances of the Constitution itself. If the President of the United States can interpose his authority upon a question of this character, and can compel Congress to succumb to his dictation, he is an emperor, a despot, and not a President of the United States. Because I believe the great question of congressional power and authority is at stake here, I yield to no importunities of the other side. I feel myself justified in taking every advantage which the Almighty has put into my hands to defend the power and authority of this body, of which I claim to be a part. I will not yield to these appeals of comity on a question like this; but I will tell the President and every body else that, if God Almighty has striken one member so that he can not be here to uphold the dictation of a despot, I thank him for his interposition, and I will take advantage of it if I can."

Mr. McDougall, of California, replied to Mr. Wade. This wayward Senator from California has wide notoriety from his unhappy habits of intemperance. He has been described by a writer unfriendly to his politics as "the most brilliant man in the Senate; a man so wonderfully rich, that though he seeks to beggar himself in talents and opportunities, he has left a patrimony large enough to outdazzle most of his colleagues." He frequently would enter the Senate-chamber in a condition of apparent stupor, unable to walk straight; and after listening a few moments to what was going on, has arisen and spoken upon the pending question in words of great beauty and force.

On this occasion Mr. McDougall is described as having been in a worse condition than usual. His words were muttered rather than spoken, so that only those immediately about him could hear; and yet his remarks were termed by one of his auditors as "one of the neatest little speeches ever heard in the Senate." His remarks were as follows: "The Senator from Ohio is in the habit of appealing to his God in vindication of his judgment and conduct; it is a common thing for him to do so; but in view of the present demonstration, it may well be asked who and what is his God. In the old Persian mythology there was an Ormudz and an Ahriman—a god of light and beauty, and a god of darkness and death. The god of light sent the sun to shine, and gentle showers to fructify the fields; the god of darkness sent the tornado, and the tempest, and the thunder, scathing with pestilence the nations. And in old Chaldean times men came to worship Ahriman, the god of darkness, the god of pestilence and famine; and his priests became multitudinous; they swarmed the land; and when men prayed then their offerings were, 'We will not sow a field of grain, we will not dig a well, we will not plant a tree.' These were the offerings to the dark spirit of evil, until a prophet came who redeemed that ancient land; but he did it after crucifixion, like our great Master.

"The followers of Ahriman always appealed to the same spirit manifested by the Senator from Ohio. Death is to be one of his angels now to redeem the Constitution and the laws, and to establish liberty. Sickness, suffering, evil, are to be his angels; and he thanks the Almighty, his Almighty, that sickness, danger, and evil are about! It may be a good god for him in this world; but if there is any truth in what we learn about the orders of religion in this Christian world, his faith will not help him when he shall ascend up and ask entrance at the crystal doors. If there can be evil expressed in high places that communicates evil thoughts, that communicates evil teachings, that demoralizes the youth, who receive impressions as does the wax, it is by such lessons as the Senator from Ohio now teaches by word of mouth as Senator in this Senate hall.

"Sir, the President of the United States is a constitutional officer, clothed with high power, and clothed with the very power which he has exercised in this instance; and those who conferred upon him these powers were men such as Madison, and Jay, and Hamilton, and Morris, and Washington, and a host of worthies; men who, I think, knew as much about the laws of government, and how they should be rightly balanced, as any of the wisest who now sit here in council. It is the duty of the President of the United States to stand as defender of the Constitution in his place as the conservator of the rights of the people, as tribune of the people, as it was in old Rome when the people did choose their tribunes to go into the senate-chamber among the aristocracy of Rome, and when they passed laws injurious to the Roman people, to stand and say, 'I forbid it.'

"That is the veto power, incorporated wisely by our fathers in the Constitution, conferred upon the President of the United States, and to be treated with consideration; and no appeal of the Senator to his God can change the Constitution or the rights of the President of the United States, or can prevent a just consideration of the dignity of this Senate body by persons who have just consideration, who feel that they are Senators.

"It is a strange thing, an exceedingly strange thing, that when a few Senators in the city of Washington, ill at their houses, give assurance that they can be here to act upon a great public question on the day following this, we should hear a piece of declamation, the Senator appealing to his God, and saying, with an *Io triumphe* air, 'Well or ill, God has made them ill.' Sir, the god of desolation, the god of darkness, the god of evil is his god. I never expected to hear such objections raised among honorable men; and men to be Senators should be honorable men. I never expected to hear such things in this hall; and I rose simply to say that such sentiments were to be condemned, and must receive my condemnation, now and here; and if it amounts to a rebuke, I trust it may be a rebuke."

The Senate adjourned, with the understanding that the vote should be taken on the following day. In the morning hour on that day, as the States were called for the purpose of giving Senators an opportunity of introducing petitions or resolutions, Mr. Lane, of Kansas, presented a joint resolution providing for admitting Senators and Representatives from the States lately in insurrection. This bill, emanating from a Republican Senator, who professed to have framed it as an embodiment of the President's policy, was evidently designed to have an influence upon the action of the Senate upon the Civil Rights Bill. It proposed that Senators and Representatives from the late rebellious States should be admitted into Congress whenever it should appear that they had annulled their ordinances of secession, ratified the constitutional amendment abolishing slavery, repudiated all rebel debts, recognized the debts of the United States, and extended the elective franchise to all male persons of color residing in the State, over twenty-one years of age, who can read and write, and who own real estate valued at not less than two hundred and fifty dollars.

As a reason for introducing this measure, Mr. Lane, of Kansas, remarked: "I have been laboring for months to harmonize the President of the United States with the majority on the floor of Congress. I thought yesterday that there was a hope of securing such a result. It did seem that some of the members of this body were disposed to harmonize with the President. I proposed to go very far yesterday to secure that harmony. But while pursuing this course, we were awakened by one of the most vindictive assaults ever made upon any official, by either friend or opponent, from the Senator from Ohio [Mr. Wade]—an assault upon my personal friend, a man who for two years sat side by side with me here, whom I learned to respect and admire for his pluck, his ability, and integrity, and to love for his manly virtues; a man whom I originally selected as the candidate of the Republican party for the second office within the gift of that party; a man whom I urged on the Republican convention at Baltimore as their candidate; a man whose election I did my utmost to secure against the efforts of the Senator from Ohio. In the most critical moment of that political campaign, an assault was made on our presidential candidate in the same spirit evinced by him yesterday in his attack upon the President. I defended the candidate of the Republican party against that assault, and I defend the President of the Republican party against the assault of yesterday.

"'A despot!' 'A dictator!' In what? In seeking to reconstruct the rebellious States in violation of the wishes of the Congress of the United States? When Mr. Johnson took his seat in the presidential chair, I ask you, sir, what had Congress done? The people of the United States had done this: Mr. Lincoln had marked out the policy of reconstruction, since adopted by Mr. Johnson, and the people of the United States, the party to which the Senator from Ohio and myself belong, indorsed by triumphant majorities that very reconstruction policy. A despot for proposing, in violation of the wishes of the Congress of the United States, to reconstruct the insurrectionary States upon the theory expressed in that joint resolution annulling the ordinances of secession, ratifying the amendment to the Constitution abolishing slavery, repudiating the Confederate debt, indorsing the national debt, and extending suffrage to all colored men who can read the Constitution of the United States and sign their names, and to all colored men owning and paying taxes upon $250 worth of property!

"Mr. President, I am not as conversant with the constituency of the Senator from Ohio as he is, but I venture the assertion that outside of New England there is not a single Northern State in this Union but will by a majority vote to indorse the policy of reconstruction advised by President Johnson and expressed in that joint resolution. You can not carry before the people of this country suffrage to the unqualified black man. You can not find a State in this Union outside of New England, in my judgment, that will indorse that policy. Restrict it to a qualification clause, as the President of the United States recommends, and you can carry the Republican Union party every-where, and with unanimity.

"The President of the United States 'a despot' for exercising a constitutional right in vetoing a bill passed by Congress! Mr. President, had the Senator from Ohio occupied the position which is occupied by President Johnson, in my judgment, he would have vetoed the Civil Rights Bill. 'A despot!' What is the exercise of the veto power? It amounts merely to a vote to reconsider, with the lights given in his reasons for the veto. When before has the exercise of a constitutional right justified a political friend of the President of the United States in denouncing that President as a despot and a dictator? He has been and is now, in my judgment, as anxious to harmonize the difficulties in the Union party as any Senator upon this floor. If he was met in the same spirit, that party would be reunited and this Union would be restored. His advances are met by insult; his advances are met by denunciation from the leader of the Republican party upon this floor in language without a parallel. Mr. President, so far as I am concerned, I propose to-day and hereafter to take my position alongside the President of the Republican party, and stand there unflinchingly so long as he remains faithful to the principles of that party, defending him against the Senator from Ohio as I defended his predecessor against the same Senator."

Mr. Lane then expressed his desire that his proposition should lie upon the table and be printed. An order having been entered to that effect, Mr. Wade addressed the Senate. He remarked: "It is said I made an attack on the President of the United States. As a Senator upon this floor, I care no more about the opinions of the President of the United States than I do about those of any respectable Senator upon this floor, or any Senator on this floor. Who is your President, that every man must bow to his opinion? Why, sir, we all know him; he is no stranger to this body. We have measured him; we know his height, his depth, his length, his breadth, his capacity, and all about him. Do you set him up as a paragon and declare here on the floor of this Senate that you are going to make us all bow down before him? Is that the idea? You [to Mr. Lane, of Kansas,] are going to be his apologist and defender in whatever he may propose to do! Is that the understanding of the Senator from Kansas?

"I do not believe that his constituents will be quite satisfied with so broad a declaration, that he is to wear any man's collar, and follow him wherever he may go. Did I use harsh language toward the President yesterday? All that I said I stand by today and forever. What was the question upon which I made those observations, and what has been the opinion of the President heretofore? what has been his action since? Here are three million people, our friends, friends to the Government, who generously came forward in its difficulty, and helped us throughout the war, sacrificed their blood and their lives to maintain the issue on our side, and who were faithful beyond all men that were ever faithful before, to us during the whole of the difficulty, every-where assisting our brave soldiers in the field, laying down their lives to maintain our principles, and ministering in every way to the misfortunes of our brave men whenever they fell into the hands of those worse than savages with whom we were warring; and now these men are laboring, are under one of the most frightful despotisms that ever settled down upon the heads of mankind. Three million people are exposed to the outrages, the insolence, the murder of those worse than savages, their former masters, murdered as we hear every day, oppressed every-where, their rights taken away, their manhood trampled under foot; and Congress, under the Constitution of the United States, endeavors to extend to them some little protection, and how are we met here? Every attempt of your Moses has been to trample them down worse, and to throw every obstruction in the way of any relief that could be proposed by Congress. He has from all appearances become their inveterate and relentless foe, making violent war upon any member of Congress who dares raise his voice or give his vote in favor of any measure having for its object the amelioration of the condition of these poor people. Talk to me about the President being their friend! When did it ever happen before that a great measure of relief to suffering humanity on as broad a scale as this was met by the stern veto of the President of the United States, and without being able when he undertakes to make his obstruction to our measures to designate a single clause of the Constitution that he pretends has been violated.

"Yesterday what was the issue? I was charged with great cruelty on this floor, because I was unwilling to wait for recruits to be brought in here for the purpose of overthrowing the ground we had taken upon this important question whether these poor people shall have relief or not. Now, I wish to say that I am willing to extend courtesy to our old associates on this floor under other circumstances; but when you extend this kind of courtesy to them, the result is death and destruction to three million people, trampled under the feet of their former masters. My courtesy is extended to those poor men, and I would not wait a moment that their enemies may be brought in here in order to prevent our doing any thing for their relief, joining with the

President, who is determined, if we may judge by his acts, that no measure having for its object any relief shall be extended to them.

"Did you hear the fact stated here the other day, that bills were drawn with a view to escape the anathemas of your President, and were exhibited to him, and he asked 'if he had any objection to them to look them over well, because if we can, consistent with the object aimed at, make them clear of any objection you may have, we will do it?'

"I said, sir, that he seemed to have meditated a controversy with Congress from the beginning, and he has. He has treated our majorities as hostile to the people; two thirds of both branches of Congress have been treated by him as mere factionists, disunionists, enemies to the country, bent upon its destruction, bargaining with the enemy to destroy the Government. This is the way the President has treated Congress, and every bill they have passed, which promised any relief to the men whom we are bound to protect, has been trampled under the Executive heel; and even when members of this body did what I say they ought not to have done—for I do not approve of my brother Trumbull's going up to the President, when he has a measure pending here as a Senator, to ask the President, in the first place, whether he will approve of it or not; even when he was asked if he objected to this measure, and made no objection, he still undertakes to veto it.

"If Congress should recede from the position they have taken to claim jurisdiction over this great question of reädmitting these States, from that hour they surrender all the power that the Constitution places in their hands and that they were sworn to support, and they are the mere slaves of an accidental Executive; of a man who formerly associated with us upon this floor; who was no more infallible than the rest of us poor mortals; and yet the moment, by death or accident, he is placed in the executive chair, it would seem as if some Senators believed him to be endowed with superhuman wisdom, and ought to be invested with all the powers of this Government; that Congress ought to get on their knees before him, and take his insults and his dictation without resentment and without even an attempt to resist. Some States may send such instrumentalities here, but God knows some will not; and I pity those that do, for they would hold their freedom on a very uncertaim tenure.

"Some gentlemen may be patient under the charge of treason, perhaps the more so because treason is becoming popular in this day; but, sir, I am a little too old-fashioned to be charged by the executive branch of this Government as a traitor on the floor of Congress, and not resent it. I do not care whether he be King or President that insinuates that I am a disunionist or traitor, standing upon the same infamous platform with the traitors of the South; I will not take it from any mortal man, high or low, without repelling the charge. If any man here is tame enough to do it, he is too tame to be the Senator of a proud-spirited people, conscious of their own freedom. I claim to be their representative, and they will censure me if they do not like my doctrine.

"And now, Mr. President, I wish to make an appeal to those great, patriotic statesmen on this floor, who, by their love of principle, by their unswerving honesty, unseduced by the blandishments of executive power, unawed by threats of violence, stand here to defend the rights of the people upon this floor, and will stand here forever. I say to you Senators, we, the majority who are stigmatized as traitors, are the only barrier to-day between this nation and anarchy and despotism. If we give way, the hope of this nation is lost by the recreancy—yea, sir, I will say the treachery—of a man who betrayed our confidence, got into power, and has gone into the camp of the enemy, and joined those who never breathed a breath of principle in common with us."

Mr. Lane replied: "I stated that the party to which I belong nominated the present President of the United States and elected him, and that as long as he fought within our lines and remained in our party, I would endeavor to defend him upon this floor against all unjust assaults. After making that statement, the Senator from Ohio, forgetting the position he occupies, has suggested that I have taken upon myself the collar of the President of the United States. I hurl the suggestion in the teeth of the Senator from Ohio as unworthy a Senator. I wear a collar! The pro-slavery party of the United States, backed by a Democratic Administration, sustained and supported by the army of the United States, could not fasten a collar upon the handful of Kansas squatters of whom I had the honor to be the leader. The gallant fight made in this Senate-chamber by the Senator from Ohio, aided by the Senators from Massachusetts and other Senators, would have been of but little avail had it not been for that other fight that was made upon the prairies of Kansas under the lead of your humble speaker. I wear a collar! Indicted for treason by a pro-slavery grand jury, hunted from State to State by a writ founded upon that indictment for treason, and $100,000 offered for my head! Jim Lane wear a collar! Wherever he is known, that charge will be denounced as false by both friends and enemies."

Mr. Brown, of Missouri, made a short speech, in which he set forth the position of Mr. Lane, of Kansas, on questions previously before the Senate, showing their inconsistency with some of his recent remarks.

Mr. Doolittle next delivered a speech, in the course of which he called attention to a bill which he had drawn "to provide appropriate legislation to enforce article thirteen of the Amendments to the Constitution, abolishing slavery in the United States." His object in presenting this bill was to "avoid the objections raised by men not only in this body, but in the other house, and the objections raised by the President of the United States, to the bill now pending.

He endeavored to explain his position and changes of opinion upon the Civil Rights: "While this measure was upon its passage, I took no part in its discussion except upon a single point in relation to the Indian tribes. The bill passed, and the final vote was taken when I was not present in the Senate; but it was not under such circumstances that, had I been here, I should not have voted for the bill. I have no doubt that if I had been present I should have voted for it. My attention was not drawn very earnestly to the consideration of all the provisions of this bill until the bill had passed from Senate and had gone to the House of Representatives, when the speeches of Mr. Bingham, of Ohio, and of Mr. Delano, of Ohio, both able and distinguished lawyers of that State, arrested my attention and called me very carefully to the consideration of the great questions which are involved in the bill. The bill was passed by the House of Representatives; it went to the President. From the fact that it was not signed and returned to this body at once, and from all I heard, I became satisfied that, at least, if the bill was not to be returned with objections, it was being withheld for most earnest and serious consideration by the Executive.

"Then, Mr. President, it was, in view of all that had occurred, what had been said by gentlemen in whom I had the utmost—I may say unbounded—confidence, that I began to look into this measure and to study it for myself. It is not my purpose now to go into a discussion of the provisions of this bill any further than to say that there are provisions in it upon which the judgments of the best patriots, the best jurists, the most earnest men disagree. There are men, in whom I have entire confidence, who maintain that all its provisions are within the purview of the Constitution; there are others in whom I have confidence, and equal confidence, who maintain directly the contrary; and this has brought me seriously to consider whether there be no common ground upon which friends can stand and stand together. Sir, I may have failed to find it; but if I have, it is not because I have not most earnestly sought for it with some days of study and most earnest reflection. I have endeavored to put upon paper what I believe would carry this constitutional provision into effect and yet would be a common ground on which we could unite without violating the conscientious convictions of any."

In concluding his remarks, Mr. Doolittle referred to instructions received by him from the Legislature of Wisconsin: "Mr. President, I have received, in connection with my colleague, a telegraphic dispatch from the Governor of the State of Wisconsin, which I have no doubt is correct, although I have not seen the resolution which is said to have been passed by the Legislature, in which it is stated that the Legislature has passed a resolution instructing the Senators in Congress from Wisconsin to vote for the passage of the Senate bill commonly known as the Civil Rights Bill, the veto of the President to the contrary notwithstanding. I have already stated, from my stand-point, the reasons why, in my judgment, I can not do it; I have stated them freely and frankly, and, as a matter of course, I expect to abide the consequences. I know that it has sometimes been said to me, by those, too, in whom I would have confidence, that for me, under circumstances like these, not to follow the instructions of the Legislature of my State, would be to terminate my political life. Sir, be it so. I never held or aspired to any other office politically than the one I now hold; and God knows, if I know my own heart, if I can see this Union restored after this gigantic war which has put down the rebellion, and to which I have lent my support, I shall be satisfied. I do not desire to remain in political life beyond that hour. There is nothing in that which will have the slightest influence whatever upon me. The duty which I owe to myself, the duty which I owe to the country, the duty which I owe to the union of these States, and the preservation of the rights of the States, and the duty which I owe to the great Republican party, which I would still desire to save, prompts me to pursue the course which I now do."

Mr. Garrett Davis, of Kentucky, addressed the Senate in a long speech, of which the following is the closing paragraph: "Public justice is often slow, but generally sure. Think you that the people will look on with folded arms and stolid indifference and see you subvert their Constitution and liberties, and on their ruins erect a grinding despotism. No; erelong they will rise up with earthquake force and fling you from power and place. I commend to your serious meditation these words: 'Go tell Sylla that you saw Caius Marius sitting upon the ruins of Carthage!'"

Mr. Saulsbury thought a revolution would result from the passage of this bill: "In my judgment the passage of this bill is the inauguration of revolution—bloodless, as yet, but the attempt to execute it by the machinery and in the mode provided in the bill will lead to revolution in blood. It is well that the American people should take warning in time and set their house in order, but it is utterly impossible that the people of this country will patiently entertain and submit to this great wrong. I do not say this because I want a revolution; Heaven knows we have had enough of bloodshed; we have had enough of strife; there has been enough of mourning in every household; there are too many new-made graves on which the grass has not yet grown for any one to wish to see the renewal of strife; but, sir, attempt to execute this act within the limits of the States of this Union, and, in my judgment, this country will again be plunged into all the horrors of civil war."

Mr. McDougall said: "I agree with the Senator from Delaware that this measure is revolutionary in its character. The majority glory in their giant power, but they ought to understand that it is tyrannous to exercise that power like a giant. A revolution now is moving onward; it has its center in the North-east. A spirit has been radiating out from there for years past as revolutionary as the spirit that went out from Charleston, South Carolina, and perhaps its consequences will be equally fatal, for when that revolutionary struggle comes it will not be a war between the North and its power and the slaveholding population of the South; it will be among the North men themselves, they who have lived under the shadows of great oaks, and seen the tall pine-trees bend."

At the conclusion of the remarks by the Senator from California, the vote was taken, with the following result:

YEAS—Messrs. Anthony, Brown, Chandler, Clark, Conness, Cragin, Creswell, Edmunds, Fessenden, Foster, Grimes, Harris, Henderson, Howard, Howe, Kirkwood, Lane of Indiana, Morgan, Morrill, Nye, Poland, Pomeroy, Ramsey, Sherman, Sprague, Stewart, Sumner, Trumbull, Wade, Willey, Williams, Wilson, and Yates—33.

NAYS—Messrs. Buckalew, Cowan, Davis, Doolittle, Guthrie, Hendricks, Johnson, Lane of Kansas, McDougall, Nesmith, Norton, Riddle, Saulsbury, Van Winkle, and Wright—15.

ABSENT—Mr. Dixon.

The President *pro tempore* then made formal announcement of the result: "The yeas being 33 and the nays 15, the bill has passed the Senate by the requisite constiutional majority, notwithstanding the objection of the President to the contrary."

On the 9th of April, 1866, three days after the passage of the bill in the Senate, the House of Representatives proceeded to its consideration. The bill and the President's Veto Message having been read, Mr. Wilson, of Iowa, demanded the previous question on the passage of the bill, the objections of the President to the contrary notwithstanding, and gave his reasons for so doing: "Mr. Speaker, the debate which occurred on this bill occupied two weeks of the time of this House. Some forty speeches were made, and the debate was not brought to a close until all had been heard who expressed a desire to speak upon the bill. At the close of that debate, the bill was passed by more than two-thirds of this House. It has been returned to us with the objections of the President to its becoming a law. I do not propose to reöpen the discussion of this measure; I am disposed to leave the close of this debate to the President by the message which has just been read. I ask the friends of this great measure to answer the argument and statements of that message by their votes."

The vote was finally taken on the question, 'Shall this bill pass, notwithstanding the objections of the President?" The following is the record of the vote:

YEAS—Messrs. Alley, Allison, Delos R. Ashley, James M. Ashley, Baker, Baldwin, Banks, Barker, Baxter, Beaman, Benjamin, Bidwell, Boutwell, Brandegee, Bromwell, Broomall, Buckland, Bundy, Reader W. Clarke, Sidney Clarke, Cobb, Colfax, Conkling, Cook, Cullom, Darling, Davis, Dawes, Defrees, Delano, Deming, Dixon, Dodge, Donnelly, Eckley, Eggleston, Eliot, Farnsworth, Farquhar, Ferry, Garfield, Grinnell, Griswold, Hale, Abner C. Harding, Hart, Hayes, Henderson, Higby, Hill, Holmes, Hooper, Hotchkiss, Asahel W. Hubbard, Chester D. Hubbard, John H. Hubbard, James R. Hubbell, Hulburd, James Humphrey, Ingersoll, Jenckes, Kasson, Kelley, Kelso, Ketcham, Laflin, George V. Lawrence, William Lawrence, Loan, Longyear, Lynch, Marston, Marvin, McClurg, McIndoe, McKee, McRuer, Mercur, Miller, Moorhead, Morrill, Morris, Moulton, Myers, Newell, O'Neill, Orth, Paine, Patterson, Perham, Pike, Plants, Pomeroy, Price, Alexander H. Rice, John H. Rice, Rollins, Sawyer, Schenck, Scofield, Shellabarger, Spalding, Starr, Stevens, Thayer, Francis Thomas, John L. Thomas, Trowbridge, Upson, Van Aernam, Burt Van Horn, Robert T. Van Horn, Ward, Elihu B. Washburne, Henry D. Washburn, William B. Washburn, Welker, Wentworth, James F. Wilson, Stephen F. Wilson, Windom, and Woodbridge—122.

NAYS—Messrs. Ancona, Bergen, Boyer, Coffroth, Dawson, Dennison, Eldridge, Finck, Glossbrenner, Aaron Harding, Harris, Hogan, Edwin N. Hubbell, James M. Humphrey, Latham, Le Blond, Marshall, McCullough, Niblack, Nicholson, Noell, Phelps, Radford, Samuel J. Randall, William H. Randall, Raymond, Ritter, Rogers, Ross, Rosseau, Shanklin, Sitgreaves, Smith, Strouse, Taber, Taylor, Thornton, Trimble, Whaley, Winfield, and Wright—41.

NOT VOTING—Messrs. Ames, Anderson, Bingham, Blaine, Blow, Chanler, Culver, Driggs, Dumont, Goodyear, Grider, Demas Hubbard, Johnson, Jones, Julian, Kerr, Kuykendall, Sloan, Stilwell, Warner, and Williams—21.

The Speaker then made the following announcement: "The yeas are 122, and the nays 41. Two-thirds of the House having, upon this reconsideration, agreed to the passage of the bill, and it being certified officially that a similar majority of the Senate, in which the bill originated, also agreed to its passage, I do, therefore, by the authority of the Constitution of the United States, declare that this bill, entitled 'An act to protect all persons in the United States in their civil rights, and furnish the means of their vindication,' has become a law."

This announcement was followed by prolonged applause on the floor of the House and among the throng of spectators in the galleries.

The following is the form in which the great measure so long pending became a law of the land:

"*Be it enacted by the Senate and House of Representatives of the United States of America in Congress assembled*, That all persons born in the United States and not subject to any foreign Power, excluding Indians not taxed, are hereby declared to be citizens of the United States; and such citizens of every race and color, without regard to any previous condition of slavery or involuntary servitude, except as a punishment for crime whereof the party shall have been duly convicted, shall have the same right in every State and Territory in the United States to make and enforce contracts, to sue, be parties, and give evidence, to inherit, purchase, lease, sell, hold, and convey real and personal property, and to full and equal benefit of all laws and proceedings for the security of person and property as is enjoyed by white citizens, and shall be subject to like punishment, pains, and penalties, and to none other, any law, statute, ordinance, regulation, or custom to the contrary notwithstanding.

"SEC. 2. *And be it further enacted*, That any person who, under color of any law, statute, ordinance, regulation, or custom, shall subject, or cause to be subjected, any inhabitant of any State or Territory to the deprivation of any right secured or protected by this act, or to different punishment, pains, or penalties on account of such person having at any time been held in a condition of slavery or involuntary servitude, except as a punishment for crime whereof the party shall have been duly convicted, or by reason of his color or race, than is prescribed for the punishment of white persons, shall be deemed guilty of a misdemeanor, and, on conviction, shall be punished by a fine not exceeding $1,000, or imprisonment not exceeding one year, or both, in the discretion of the court.

"SEC. 3. *And be it further enacted*, That the district courts of the United States, within their respective districts, shall have, exclusively of the courts of the several States, cognizance of all crimes and offenses committed against the provisions of this act, and also, concurrently with the circuit courts of the United States, of all causes, civil and criminal, affecting persons who are denied or can not enforce in the courts or judicial tribunals of the State or locality where they may be, any of the rights secured to them by the first section of this act; and if any suit or prosecution, civil or criminal, has been or shall be commenced in any State court against any such person, for any cause whatsoever, or against any officer, civil or military, or other person, for any arrest or imprisonment, trespasses or wrongs, done or committed by virtue or under color of authority derived from this act or the act establishing a Bureau for the Relief of Freedmen and Refugees, and all acts amendatory thereof, or for refusing to do any act upon the ground that it would be inconsistent with this act, such defendant shall have the right to remove such cause for trial to the proper district or circuit court in the manner prescribed by the 'Act relating to *habeas corpus* and regulating judicial proceedings in certain cases,' approved March 3, 1863, and all acts amendatory thereof. The jurisdiction in civil and criminal matters hereby conferred on the district and circuit courts of the United States shall be exercised and enforced in conformity with the laws of the United States, so far as such laws are suitable to carry the same into effect; but in all cases where such laws are not adapted to the object, or are deficient in the provisions necessary to furnish suitable remedies and punish offenses against law, the common law, as modified and changed by the constitution and statutes of the States wherein the court having jurisdiction of the cause, civil or criminal, is held, so far as the same is not inconsistent with the Constitution and laws of the United States, shall be extended to and govern said courts in the trial and disposition of such cause, and, if of a criminal nature, in the infliction of punishment on the party found guilty.

"SEC. 4. *And be it further enacted*, That the district attorneys, marshals, and deputy-marshals of the United States, the commissioners appointed by the circuit and territorial courts of the United States, with powers of arresting, imprisoning, or bailing offenders against the laws of the United States, the officers and agents of the Freedmen's Bureau, and every other officer who may be specially empowered by the President of the United States, shall be, and they are hereby, specially authorized and required, at the expense of the United States, to institute proceedings against all and every person who shall violate the provisions of this act, and cause him or them to be arrested and imprisoned, or bailed, as the case may be, for trial before such court of the United States, or territorial court, as by this act has cognizance of the offense. And with a view to affording reasonable protection to all persons in their constitutional rights of equality before the law, without distinction of race or color, or previous condition of slavery or involuntary servitude, except as a punishment for crime whereof the party shall have been duly convicted, and to the prompt discharge of the duties of this act, it shall be the duty of the circuit courts of the United States and the superior courts of the Territories of the United States, from time to time, to increase the number of commissioners, so as to afford a speedy and convenient means for the arrest and examination of persons charged with a violation of this act. And such commissioners are hereby authorized and required to exercise and discharge all the powers and duties conferred on them by this act, and the same duties with regard to offenses created by this act, as they are authorized by law to exercise with regard to other offenses against the laws of the United States.

"SEC. 5. *And be it further enacted*, That it shall be the duty of all marshals and deputy-marshals to obey and execute all warrants and precepts issued under the provisions of this act, when to them directed; and should any marshal or deputy-marshal refuse to receive such warrant or other process when tendered, or to use all proper means diligently to execute the same, he shall, on conviction thereof, be fined in the sum of $1,000, to the use of the person upon whom the accused is alleged to have commmitted the offense. And the better to enable the said commissioners to execute their duties faithfully and efficiently, in conformity with the Constitution of the

United States and the requirements of this act, they are hereby authorized and empowered, within their counties respectively, to appoint, in writing, under their hands, any one or more suitable persons, from time to time, to execute all such warrants and other process as may be issued by them in the lawful performance of their respective duties; and the persons so appointed to execute any warrant or process as aforesaid, shall have authority to summon and call to their aid the bystanders or the *posse comitatus* of the proper county, or such portion of the land and naval forces of the United States, or the militia, as may be necessary to the performance of the duty with which they are charged, and to insure a faithful observance of the clause of the Constitution which prohibits slavery, in conformity with the provisions of this act; and said warrants shall run and be executed by said officers anywhere in the State or Territory within which they are issued.

"SEC. 6. *And be it further enacted*, That any person who shall knowingly and willfully obstruct, hinder, or prevent any officer, or other person, charged with the execution of any warrant or process issued under the provisions of this act, or any person or persons lawfully assisting him or them, from arresting any person for whose apprehension such warrant or process may have been issued, or shall rescue or attempt to rescue such person from the custody of the officer, other person or persons, or those lawfully assisting as aforesaid, when so arrested pursuant to the authority herein given and declared, or who shall aid, abet, or assist any person so arrested as aforesaid, directly or indirectly, to escape from the custody of the officer or other person legally authorized as aforesaid, or shall harbor or conceal any person for whose arrest a warrant or process shall have been issued as aforesaid, so as to prevent his discovery and arrest after notice or knowledge of the fact that a warrant has been issued for the apprehension of such person, shall, for either of said offenses, be subject to a fine not exceeding $1,000, and imprisonment not exceeding six months, by indictment and conviction before the district court of the United States for the district in which said offense may have been committed, or before the proper court of criminal jurisdiction, if committed within any one of the organized Territories of the United States.

"SEC. 7. *And be it further enacted*, That the district attorneys, the marshals, the deputies, and the clerks of the said district and territorial courts shall be paid for their services the like fees as may be allowed to them for similar services in other cases; and in all cases where the proceedings are before a commissioner, he shall be entitled to a fee of ten dollars in full for his services in each case, inclusive of all services incident to such arrest and examination. The person or persons authorized to execute the process to be issued by such commissioners for the arrest of offenders against the provisions of this act, shall be entitled to a fee of five dollars for each person he or they may arrest and take before any such commissioner as aforesaid, with such other fees as may be deemed reasonable by such commissioner for such other additional services as may be necessarily performed by him or them, such as attending at the examination, keeping the prisoner in custody, and providing him with food and lodging during his detention, and until the final determination of such commissioner, and in general for performing such other duties as may be required in the premises; such fees to be made up in conformity with the fees usually charged by the officers of the courts of justice within the proper district or county, as near as may be practicable, and paid out of the Treasury of the United States on the certificate of the judge of the district within which the arrest is made, and to be recoverable from the defendant as part of the judgment in case of conviction.

"SEC. 8. *And be it further enacted*, That whenever the President of the United States shall have reason to believe that offenses have been or are likely to be committed against the provisions of this act within any judicial district, it shall be lawful for him, in his discretion, to direct the judge, marshal, and district attorney of such district to attend at such place within the district, and for such time as he may designate, for the purpose of the more speedy arrest and trial of persons charged with a violation of this act; and it shall be the duty of every judge or other officer, when any such requisition shall be received by him, to attend at the place, and for the time therein designated.

"SEC. 9. *And be it further enacted*, That it shall be lawful for the President of the United States, or such person as he may empower for that purpose, to employ such part of the land or naval forces of the United States, or of the militia, as shall be necessary to prevent the violation and enforce the due execution of this act.

"SEC. 10. *And be it further enacted*, That upon all questions of law arising in any cause under the provisions of this act a final appeal may be taken to the Supreme Court of the United States."

CHAPTER XII.

THE SECOND FREEDMEN'S BUREAU BILL BECOMES A LAW.

THE DISCOVERY OF THE MAJORITY—THE SENATE BILL—THE HOUSE BILL—ITS PROVISIONS—PASSAGE OF THE BILL—AMENDMENT AND PASSAGE IN THE SENATE—COMMITTEE OF CONFERENCE—THE AMENDMENTS AS ACCEPTED—THE BILL AS PASSED—THE VETO—THE PROPOSITION OF A DEMOCRAT ACCEPTED—CONFUSION IN LEADERSHIP—PASSAGE OF THE BILL OVER THE VETO—IT BECOMES A LAW.

CONGRESS having succeeded in placing the Civil Rights Bill in the statute-book in spite of Executive opposition, was not disposed to allow other legislation which was regarded as important to go by default. The disposition of the President, now plainly apparent, to oppose all legislation which the party that had elevated him to office might consider appropriate to the condition of the rebel States, the majority in Congress discovered that, if they would make progress in the work before them, they must be content to do without Executive approval. The defection of the President from the principles of the party which had elected him, so far from dividing and destroying that party, had rather given it consolidation and strength. After the veto of the Civil Rights Bill, a very few members of the Senate and House of Representatives who had been elected as Republicans adhered to the President, but the most of those who had wavered stepped forward into the ranks of the "Radicals," as they were called, and a firm and invincible "two-thirds" moved forward to consummate legislation which they deemed essential to the interests of the nation.

So fully convinced were the majority that some effective legislation for the freedmen should be consummated, that two days after the final vote in which the former bill failed to pass over the veto, Senator Wilson introduced a bill "to continue in force the Bu reau for the relief of Freedmen and Refugees," which was read twice and referred to the Committee on Military Affairs.

The bill, however, which subsequently became a law, originated in the House of Representatives. In that branch of Congress was a Special Committee on the Freedmen, who were able to give more immediate and continuous attention to that class of people than could committees such as those of the Judiciary and Military Affairs, having many other subjects to consider.

The Committee on the Freedmen, having given much time and attention to the perfection of a measure to meet the necessities of the case, on the 22d of May reported through their chairman, Mr. Eliot, "A bill to continue in force and amend an act entitled 'an act to establish a Bureau for the relief of Freedmen and Refugees, and for other purposes.'"

This bill provided for keeping in force the Freedmen's Bureau then in existence for two years longer. Some of the features to which the President had objected in his veto of the former bill had been modified and in part removed. In providing for the education of freedmen, the commissioner was restricted to cooperating so far with the charitable people of the country as to furnish rooms for school-houses and protection to teachers. The freedmen's courts were to be kept in existence till State legislation should conform itself to the Civil Rights Bill, and the disturbed relations of the States to the Union were restored. The President was required to reserve from sale public lands, not exceeding in all one million of acres, in Arkansas, Mississippi, Florida, Alabama, and Louisiana, to be assigned in parcels of forty acres and less to loyal refugees and freedmen.

One week after the introduction of the bill, its consideration was resumed. The question was taken without debate, and the bill passed by a vote of ninety-six in favor and thirty-two against the measure. Fifty-five members failed to vote.

On the day following, May 30th, the clerk of the House conveyed the bill to the Senate. It was there referred to the Committee on Military Affairs, as that committee already had before them seven bills relating to the same subject. Nearly a fortnight subsequently, the committee reported back to the Senate the House bill with certain amendments. The report of the committee, and the amendments proposed therein, could not be considered in the Senate until the lapse of another fortnight. On the 26th of June, the amendments devised by the committee were read in the Senate and adopted. Mr. Davis made a number of attempts to have the bill laid on the table or deferred to a subsequent day, but without success. Mr. Hendricks and Mr. Buckalew made ineffectual attempts to amend the bill by proposing to strike out important sections.

The Senate indulged in but little discussion of the bill or the amendments. The bill as amended finally passed the Senate by a vote of twenty-six for and six against the measure. The bill then went to the House for the concurrence of that body in the amendments passed by the Senate.

The Committee on the Freedmen made a report, which was adopted by the House, to non-concur in the amendments of the Senate. A Committee of Conference was appointed on the part of the Senate and the House. They, after consultation, made a report by which the Senate amendments, with some modifications, were adopted.

Mr. Eliot, Chairman of the Committee on the Freedmen, and of the Committee of Conference on the part of the House, at the request of a member, thus explained the amendments proposed by the Senate: "The first amendment which the Senate made to the bill, as it was passed by the House, was simply an enlargement of one of the sections of the House bill, which provided that the volunteer medical officers engaged in the medical department of the bureau might be continued, inasmuch as it was expected that the medical force of the regular army would be speedily reduced to the minimum, and in that case all the regular officers would be wanted in the service. It was therefore thought right that there should be some force connected with the Bureau of Refugees and Freedmen. The Senate enlarged the provisions of the House bill by providing that officers of the volunteer service now on duty might be continued as assistant commissioners and other officers, and that the Secretary of War might fill vacancies until other officers could be detailed from the regular army. That is the substance of the first material amendment.

"The next amendment strikes out a portion of one of the sections of the House bill, which related to the officers who serve as medical officers of the bureau, because it was provided for in the amendment to which I have just referred.

"The next amendment strikes out from the House bill the

section which set apart, reserved from sale, a million acres of land in the Gulf States. It may perhaps be recollected that when the bill was reported from the committee, I stated that, in case the bill which the House had then passed, and which was known as the Homestead Bill, and which was then before the Senate, should become a law, this section of the bill would not be wanted. The bill referred to has become a law, and this section five, providing for that reservation, has, therefore, been stricken from the bill.

"The next amendment made by the Senate was to strike out a section of the House bill which simply provided that upon application for restoration by the former owners of the land assigned under General Sherman's field order, the application should not be complied with. That section is stricken out and another substituted for it, which provides that certain lands which are now owned by the United States, having been purchased by the United States under tax commissioners' sales, shall be assigned in lots of twenty acres to freedmen who have had allotments under General Sherman's field order, at the price for which the lands were purchased by the United States; and not only that those freedmen should have such allotments, but that other freedmen who had had lots assigned to them under General Sherman's field order, and who may have become dispossessed of their land, should have assignments made to them of these lands belonging to the United States. I think the justice of that provision will strike every one. And it will be perhaps a merit in the eyes of many that it does not call upon the Treasury for the expenditure of any money. In the bill which was passed by the House, it will be recollected that there was a provision under which there should be purchased by the commissioner of the bureau enough public lands to be substituted for the lands at first assigned to freedmen. Instead of that, provision is made by which they can have property belonging to the United States which has come into its possession under tax sales, and where the titles have been made perfect by lapse of time.

"The next amendment of the Senate provides that certain lands which were purchased by the United States at tax sales, and which are now held by the United States, should be sold at prices not less than ten dollars an acre, and that the proceeds should be invested for the support of schools, without distinction of color or race, on the islands in the parishes of St. Helena and St. Luke. That is all the provision which was made for education.

"The only other material amendment made by the Senate gives to the commissioner of the bureau power to take property of the late Confederate States, held by them or in trust for them, and which is now in charge of the commissioner of the bureau, to take that property and devote it to educational purposes. The amendment further provides that when the bureau shall cease to exist, such of the late so-called Confederate States as shall have made provision for education, without regard to color, should have the balance of money remaining on hand, to be divided among them in proportion to their population."

The vote followed soon after the remarks of Mr. Eliot, and the bill, as amended, passed the House of Representatives.

The following is the bill as it went to the President for his approval:

"AN ACT to continue in force and to amend 'An Act to establish a Bureau for the relief of Freedmen and Refugees,' and for other purposes.

"*Be it enacted by the Senate and House of Representatives of the United States of America in Congress assembled*, That the act to establish a bureau for the relief of freedmen and refugees, approved March third, eighteen hundred and sixty-five, shall continue in force for the term of two years from and after the passage of this act.

"SEC. 2. *And be it further enacted*, That the supervision and care of said bureau shall extend to all loyal refugees and freedmen, so far as the same shall be necessary, to enable them, as speedily as practicable, to become self-supporting citizens of the United States, and to aid them in making the freedom conferred by proclamation of the commander-in-chief, by emancipation under the laws of States, and by constitutional amendment, available to them and beneficial to the republic.

"SEC. 3. *And be it further enacted*, That the President shall, by and with the advice and consent of the Senate, appoint two assistant commissioners, in addition to those authorized by the act to which this is an amendment, who shall give like bonds and receive the same annual salaries provided in said act; and each of the assistant commissioners of the bureau shall have charge of one district containing such refugees or freedmen, to be assigned him by the commissioner, with the approval of the President. And the commissioner shall, under the direction of the President, and so far as the same shall be, in his judgment, necessary for the efficient and economical administration of the affairs of the bureau, appoint such agents, clerks, and assistants as may be required for the proper conduct of the bureau. Military officers or enlisted men may be detailed for service and assigned to duty under this act; and the President may, if, in his judgment, safe and judicious so to do, detail from the army all the officers and agents of this bureau; but no officer so assigned shall have increase of pay or allowances. Each agent or clerk, not heretofore authorized by law, not being a military officer, shall have an annual salary of not less than five hundred dollars, nor more than twelve hundred dollars, according to the service required of him. And it shall be the duty of the commissioner, when it can be done consistently with public interest, to appoint, as assistant commissioners, agents, and clerks, such men as have proved their loyalty by faithful service in the armies of the Union during the rebellion. And all persons appointed to service under this act, and the act to which this is an amendment, shall be so far deemed in the military service of the United States as to be under the military jurisdiction and entitled to the military protection of the Government while in discharge of the duties of their office.

"SEC. 4. *And be it further enacted*, That officers of the Veteran Reserve Corps or of the volunteer service, now on duty in the Freedmen's Bureau as assistant commissioners, agents, medical officers, or in other capacities, whose regiments or corps have been or may hereafter be mustered out of service, may be retained upon such duty as officers of said bureau, with the same compensation as is now provided by law for their respective grades; and the Secretary of War shall have power to fill vacancies until other officers can be detailed in their places without detriment to the public service.

"SEC. 5. *And be it further enacted*, That the second section of the act to which this is an amendment shall be deemed to authorize the Secretary of War to issue such medical stores or other supplies, and transportation, and afford such medical or other aid as may be needful for the purposes named in said section: *Provided*, That no person shall be deemed 'destitute,' 'suffering,' or 'dependent upon the Government for support,' within the meaning of this act, who is able to find employment, and could, by proper industry or exertion, avoid such destitution, suffering, or dependence.

"SEC. 6. Whereas, by the provisions of an act approved February sixth, eighteen hundred and sixty-three, entitled 'An act to amend an act entitled "An act for the collection of direct taxes in insurrectionary districts within the United States, and for other purposes," approved June seventh, eighteen hundred and sixty-two,' certain lands in the parishes of Saint Helena and Saint Luke, South Carolina, were bid in by the United States at public tax sales, and, by the limitation of said act, the time of redemption of said lands has expired; and whereas, in accordance with instructions issued by President Lincoln on the sixteenth day of September, eighteen hundred and sixty-three, to the United States direct tax commissioners for South Carolina, certain lands bid in by the United States in the parish of Saint Helena, in said State, were in part sold by the said tax commissioners to 'heads of families of the African race,' in parcels of not more than twenty acres to each purchaser; and whereas, under the said instructions, the said tax commissioners did also set apart as 'school-farms' certain parcels of land in said parish, numbered in their plats from one to sixty-three inclusive, making an aggregate of six thousand acres, more or less: *Therefore, be it further enacted*, That the sales made to 'heads of families of the African race,' under the instructions of President Lincoln to the United States direct tax commissioners for South Carolina, of date of September sixteenth, eighteen hundred and sixty-three, are hereby confirmed and established; and all leases which have been made to such 'heads of families' by said direct tax commissioners shall be changed into certificates of sale in all cases wherein the lease provides for such substitution; and all the lands now remaining unsold, which come within the same designation, being eight thousand acres, more or less, shall be disposed of according to said instructions.

"SEC. 7. *And be it further enacted*, That all other lands bid in by the United States at tax sales, being thirty-eight thousand acres, more or less, and now in the hands of the said tax commissioners as the property of the United States, in the parishes of Saint Helena and Saint Luke, excepting the 'school-farms,' as specified in the preceding section, and so much as may be necessary for military and naval purposes at Hilton Head, Bay Point, and Land's End, and excepting also the city of Port Royal, on Saint Helena island, and the town of Beaufort, shall be disposed of in parcels of twenty acres, at one dollar and fifty cents per acre, to such persons, and to such only, as have acquired and are now occupying lands under and agreeably to the provisions of General Sherman's special field order, dated at Savannah, Georgia, January sixteenth, eighteen hundred and sixty-five; and the remaining lands, if any, shall be disposed of, in like manner, to such persons as had acquired lands agreeably to the said order of General Sherman, but who have been dispossessed by the restoration of the same to former owners: *Provided*, That the lands sold in compliance with the provisions of this and the preceding section shall not be alienated by their purchasers within six years from and after the passage of this act.

"SEC. 8. *And be it further enacted*, That the 'school-farms' in the parish of Saint Helena, South Carolina, shall be sold, subject to any leases of the same, by the said tax commissioners, at public auction, on or before the first day of January, eighteen hundred and sixty-seven, at not less than ten dollars per acre; and the lots in the city of Port Royal, as laid down by the said tax commissioners, and the lots and houses in the town of Beaufort, which are still held in like manner, shall be sold at public auction; and the proceeds of said sales, after paying expenses of the surveys and sales, shall be invested in United States bonds, the interest of which shall be appropriated, under the direction of the commissioner, to the support of schools, without distinction of color or race, on the islands in the parishes of Saint Helena and Saint Luke.

"SEC. 9. *And be it further enacted*, That the assistant commissioners for South Carolina and Georgia are hereby authorized to examine the claims to lands in their respective States which are claimed under the provisions of General Sherman's special field order, and to give each person having a valid claim a warrant upon the direct tax commissioners for South Carolina for twenty acres of land; and the said direct tax commissioners shall issue to every person, or to his or her heirs, but in no case to any assigns, presenting such warrant, a lease of twenty acres of land, as provided for in section seven, for the term of six years; but, at any time thereafter, upon the payment of a sum not exceeding one dollar and fifty cents per acre, the person holding such lease shall be entitled to a certificate of sale of said tract of twenty acres from the direct tax commissioner or such officer as may be authorized to issue the same; but no warrant shall be held valid longer than two years after the issue of the same.

"SEC. 10. *And be it further enacted,* That the direct tax commissioners for South Carolina are hereby authorized and required, at the earliest day practicable, to survey the lands designated in section seven into lots of twenty acres each, with proper metes and bounds distinctly marked, so that the several tracts shall be convenient in form, and, as near as practicable, have an average of fertility and woodland; and the expense of such surveys shall be paid from the proceeds of sales of said lands, or, if sooner required, out of any moneys received for other lands on these islands, sold by the United States for taxes, and now in the hands of the direct tax commissioners.

"SEC. 11. *And be it further enacted,* That restoration of the lands now occupied by persons under General Sherman's special field order, dated at Savannah, Georgia, January sixteenth, eighteen hundred and sixty-five, shall not be made until after the crops of the present year shall have been gathered by the occupants of said lands, nor until a fair compensation shall have been made to them by the former owners of said lands, or their legal representatives, for all improvements or betterments erected or constructed thereon, and after due notice of the same being done shall have been given by the assistant commissioner.

"SEC. 12. *And be it further enacted,* That the commissioner shall have power to seize, hold, use, lease, or sell, all buildings and tenements, and any lands appertaining to the same, or otherwise, held under claim or title by the late so-called Confederate States, and any buildings or lands held in trust for the same by any person or persons, and to use the same or appropriate the proceeds derived therefrom to the education of the freed people; and whenever the bureau shall cease to exist, such of the late so-called Confederate States as shall have made provision for the education of their citizens, without distinction of color, shall receive the sum remaining unexpended of such sales or rentals, which shall be distributed among said States for educational purposes in proportion to their population.

"SEC. 13. *And be it further enacted,* That the commissioner of this bureau shall at all times coöperate with private benevolent associations of citizens in aid of freedmen, and with agents and teachers, duly accredited and appointed by them, and shall hire or provide by lease buildings for purposes of education whenever such associations shall, without cost to the Government, provide suitable teachers and means of instruction; and he shall furnish protection as may be required for the safe conduct of such schools.

"SEC. 14. *And be it further enacted,* That in every State or district where the ordinary course of judicial proceedings has been interrupted by the rebellion, and until the same shall be fully restored, and in every State or district whose constitutional relations to the Government have been practically discontinued by the rebellion, and until such State shall have been restored in such relations, and shall be duly represented in the Congress of the United States, the right to make and enforce contracts, to sue, be parties, and give evidence, to inherit, purchase, lease, sell, hold, and convey real and personal property, and to have full and equal benefit of all laws and proceedings concerning personal liberty, personal security, and the acquisition, enjoyment, and disposition of estate, real and personal, including the constitutional right to bear arms, shall be secured to and enjoyed by all the citizens of such State or district, without respect to race or color, or previous condition of slavery. And whenever in either of said States or districts the ordinary course of judicial proceedings has been interrupted by the rebellion, and until the same shall be fully restored, and until such State shall have been restored in its constitutional relations to the Government, and shall be duly represented in the Congress of the United States, the President, shall, through the commissioner and the officers of the bureau, and under such rules and regulations as the President, through the Secretary of War, shall prescribe, extend military protection and have military jurisdiction over all cases and questions concerning the free enjoyment of such immunities and rights; and no penalty or punishment for any violation of law shall be imposed or permitted because of race or color, or previous condition of slavery, other or greater than the penalty or punishment to which white persons may be liable by law for the like offense. But the jurisdiction conferred by this section upon the officers of the bureau shall not exist in any State where the ordinary course of judicial proceedings has not been interrupted by the rebellion, and shall cease in every State when the courts of the State and the United States are not disturbed in the peaceable course of justice, and after such State shall be fully restored in its constitutional relations to the Government, and shall be duly represented in the Congress of the United States.

"SEC. 15. *And be it further enacted*, That the officers, agents, and employees of this bureau, before entering upon the duties of their office, shall take the oath prescribed in the first section of the act to which this is an amendment; and all acts or parts of acts inconsistent with the provisions of this act are hereby repealed.

On the 16th of July the President returned the bill to the House of Representatives, in which it originated, with his "objections thereto" in writing. The following is

THE VETO MESSAGE.

"*To the House of Representatives:*

"A careful examination of the bill passed by the two houses of Congress, entitled 'An act to continue in force and to amend "An act to establish a bureau for the relief of freedmen and refugees," and for other purposes,' has convinced me that the legislation which it proposes would not be consistent with the welfare of the country, and that it falls clearly within the reasons assigned in my message of the 19th of February last, returning without my signature a similar measure which originated in the Senate. It is not my purpose to repeat the objections which I then urged. They are yet fresh in your recollection, and can be readily examined as a part of the records of one branch of the National Legislature. Adhering to the principles set forth in that message, I now reäffirm them, and the line of policy therein indicated.

"The only ground upon which this kind of legislation can be justified is that of the war-making power. The act of which this bill was intended as amendatory was passed during the existence of the war. By its own provisions, it is to terminate within one year from the cessation of hostilities and the declaration of peace. It is therefore yet in existence, and it is likely that it will continue in force as long as the freedmen may require the benefit of its provisions. It will certainly remain in operation as a law until some months subsequent to the meeting of the next session of Congress, when, if experience shall make evident the necessity of additional legislation, the two houses will have ample time to mature and pass the requisite measures. In the mean time the questions arise, Why should this war measure be continued beyond the period designated in the original act? and why, in time of peace, should military tribunals be created to continue until each 'State shall be fully restored in its constitutional relations to the Government, and shall be duly represented in the Congress of the United States?' It was manifest with respect to the act approved March 3, 1865, that prudence and wisdom alike required that jurisdiction over all cases concerning the free enjoyment of the immunities and rights of citizenship, as well as the protection of person and property, should be conferred upon some tribunal in every State or district where the ordinary course of judicial proceeding was interrupted by the rebellion, and until the same should be fully restored. At that time, therefore, an urgent necessity existed for the passage of some such law. Now, however, war has substantially ceased; the ordinary course of judicial proceedings is no longer interrupted; the courts, both State and Federal, are in full, complete, and successful operation, and through them every person, regardless of race or color, is entitled to and can be heard. The protection granted to the white citizen is already conferred by law upon the freedman; strong and stringent guards, by way of penalties and punishments, are thrown around his person and property, and it is believed that ample protection will be afforded him by due process of law, without resort to the dangerous expedient of 'military tribunals,' now that the war has been brought to a close. The necessity no longer existing for such tribunals, which had their origin in the war, grave objections to their continuance must present themselves to the minds of all reflecting and dispassionate men. Independently of the danger in representative republics of conferring upon the military, in time of peace, extraordinary powers—so carefully guarded against by the patriots and statesmen of the earlier days of the republic, so frequently the ruin of governments founded upon the same free principle, and subversive of the rights and liberties of the citizen—the question of practical economy earnestly commends itself to the consideration of the law-making power. With an immense debt already burdening the incomes of the industrial and laboring classes, a due regard for their interests, so inseparably connected with the welfare of the country, should prompt us to rigid economy and retrenchment, and influence us to abstain from all legislation that would unnecessarily increase the public indebtedness. Tested by this rule of sound political wisdom, I can see no reason for the establishment of the 'military jurisdiction' conferred upon the officials of the bureau by the fourteenth section of the bill.

"By the laws of the United States, and of the different States, competent courts, Federal and State, have been established, and are now in full practical operation. By means of these civil tribunals ample redress is afforded for all private wrongs, whether to the person or to the property of the citizen, without denial or unnecessary delay. They are open to all, without regard to color or race. I feel well assured that it will be better to trust the rights, privileges, and immunities of the citizens to tribunals thus established, and presided over by competent and impartial judges, bound by fixed rules of law and evidence, and where the rights of trial by jury is guaranteed and secured, than to the caprice and judgment of an officer of the bureau, who, it is possible, may be entirely ignorant of the principles that underlie the just administration of the law. There is danger, too, that conflict of jurisdiction will frequently arise between the civil courts and these military tribunals, each having concurrent jurisdiction over the person and the cause of action—the one judicature administered and controlled by civil law, the other by the military. How is the conflict to be settled, and who is to determine between the two tribunals when it arises? In my opinion it is wise to guard against such conflict by leaving to the courts and juries the protection of all civil rights and the redress of all civil grievances.

"The fact can not be denied that since the actual cessation of hostilities many acts of violence—such, perhaps, as had never been witnessed in their previous history—have occurred in the States involved in the recent rebellion. I believe, however, that public sentiment will sustain me in the assertion that such deeds of wrong are not confined to any particular State or section, but are manifested over the entire country—demonstrating that the cause that produced them does not depend upon any particular locality, but is the result of the agitation and derangement incident to a long and bloody civil war. While the prevalence of such disorders must be greatly deplored, their occasional and temporary occurrence would seem to furnish no necessity for the extension of the bureau beyond the period fixed in the original act. Besides the objections which I have thus briefly stated, I may urge upon your consideration the additional reason that recent developments in regard to the practical operations of the bureau, in many of the States, show that in numerous instances it is used by its agents as a means of promoting their individual advantage, and that the freedmen are employed for the advancement of the personal ends of the officers, instead of their own improvement and welfare—thus confirming the fears originally entertained by many that the continuation of such a bureau for any unnecessary length of time would inevitably result in fraud, corruption, and oppression.

"It is proper to state that in cases of this character investigations have been promptly ordered, and the offender punished, whenever his guilt has been satisfactorily established. As another reason against the necessity of the legislation contemplated by this measure, reference may be had to the 'Civil Rights Bill,' now a law of the land, and which will be faithfully executed as long as it shall remain unrepealed, and may not be declared unconstitutional by courts of competent jurisdiction. By that act, it is enacted 'that all persons born in the United States, and not subject to any foreign power, excluding Indians not taxed, are hereby declared to be citizens of the United States; and such citizens, of every race and color, without regard to any previous condition of slavery or involuntary servitude, except as a punishment for crime, whereof the party shall have been duly convicted, shall have the same right in every State and Territory of the United States, to make and enforce contracts, to sue, to be parties, and give evidence, to inherit, purchase, lease, sell, hold, and convey real and personal property, and to full and equal benefit of all laws and proceedings for the security of person and property, as is enjoyed by white citizens, and shall be subject to like punishment, pains, and penalties, and to none other, any law, statute, ordinance, regulation, or custom to the contrary notwithstanding.'

"By the provisions of the act full protection is afforded, through the district courts of the United States, to all persons injured, and whose privileges, as they are declared, are in any way impaired, and heavy penalties are denounced against the person who wilfully violates the law. I need not state that that law did not receive my approval, yet its remedies are far preferable to those proposed in the present bill—the one being civil and the other military.

"By the sixth section of the bill herewith returned, certain proceedings by which the lands in the 'parishes of St. Helena and St. Luke, South Carolina,' were sold and bid in, and afterward disposed of by the tax commissioners, are ratified and confirmed. By the seventh, eighth, ninth, tenth, and eleventh sections, provisions by law are made for the disposal of the lands thus acquired to a particular class of citizens. While the quieting of titles is deemed very important and desirable, the discrimination made in the bill seems objectionable, as does also the attempt to confer upon the commissioners judicial powers, by which citizens of the United States are to be deprived of their property in a mode contrary to that provision of the Constitution which declares that no person 'shall be deprived of life, liberty, or property, without due process of law.' As a general principle, such legislation is unsafe, unwise, partial, and unconstitutional. It may deprive persons of their property who are equally deserving objects of the nation's bounty, as those whom, by this legislation, Congress seeks to benefit. The title to the land thus to be proportioned out to a favored class of citizens must depend upon the regularity of the tax sale under the law as it existed at the time of the sale, and no subsequent legislation can give validity to the rights thus acquired against the original claimants. The attention of Congress is therefore invited to a more mature consideration of the measures proposed in these sections of the bill.

"In conclusion, I again urge upon Congress the danger of class legislation, so well calculated to keep the public mind in a state of uncertain expectation, disquiet, and restlessness, and to encourage interested hopes and fears that the National Government will continue to furnish to classes of citizens, in the several States, means for support and maintenance, regardless of whether they pursue a life of indolence or labor, and regardless, also, of the constitutional limitations of the national authority in times of peace and tranquillity.

"The bill is herewith returned to the House of Representatives, in which it originated, for its final action.

"ANDREW JOHNSON.

"WASHINGTON, D. C., *July* 16, 1866."

As soon as the reading of this document had been completed, a motion was passed that it should be laid on the table and printed. Notice was given that it would be called up for the action of the House on the following day. Mr. Le Blond, a Democrat, suggested that it would be too long to wait until to-morrow to pass it over the veto, and without debate. The sooner action was taken, the more apparent would be the bad *animus*.

"I have no objection," said Mr. Eliot, taking him at his word. Others said, "There is no objection," whereupon the vote was reconsidered by which the matter was postponed.

The motion to reconsider the postponement was carried, and the previous question called, "Shall this bill become a law, the objections of the President to the contrary notwithstanding?"

"I do not see why we need be in such a hurry," said Mr. Rogers.

"One of your own side suggested that the vote better be taken now," replied Mr. Ashley.

"Well, he was not in earnest, of course," said Mr. Rogers, creating some mirth by the remark.

"I hope the gentleman will make no objection," said Mr. Le Blond, addressing his remark to Mr. Rogers.

Mr. Ward suggested that "the Democrats should choose their leader, and not confuse us in this way."

Without further parley, the vote was one hundred and four in the affirmative, thirty-three in the negative, and forty-five "not voting." The Speaker then announced, "Two-thirds having voted in the affirmative, the bill has, notwithstanding the objections of the President, again passed."

The Clerk of the House of Representatives immediately announced the action of that body to the Senate. Other business was at once laid aside, and the Veto Message was read in the Senate.

Mr. Hendricks and Mr. Saulsbury then addressed the Senate in support of the position of the President. The question being taken, thirty-three voted for and twelve against the bill. Thereupon the President *pro tempore* announced, "Two-thirds of this body have passed the bill, and it having been certified that two-thirds of the House of Representatives have voted for this bill, I now pronounce that this bill has become a law."

Eng'd by G.E. Perine & Co. N.Y.

HON. EBEN C. INGERSOLL.

REPRESENTATIVE FROM ILLINOIS.

CHAPTER XIII.

FIRST WORDS ON RECONSTRUCTION.

Responsibility of the Republican Party—Its Power and Position—Initiatory Step—Mr. Stevens steaks for Himself—Condition of the Rebel States—Constitutional Authority under which Congress should act—Estoppel—What constitutes Congress—The First Duty—Basis of Representation—Duty on Exports—Two important Principles—Mr. Raymond's Theory—Rebel States still in the Union—Consequences of the Radical Theory—Conditions to be required—State Sovereignty—Rebel Debt—Prohibition of Slavery—Two Policies contrasted—Reply of Mr. Jenckes—Difference in Terms, not in Substance—Logic of the Conservatives leads to the Results of the Radicals.

HAVING traced the progress through Congress of the great measures relating to civil rights and protection of the freedmen, it is now proper to go back to an earlier period in this legislative history, and trace what was said and done upon a subject which, more than any other, awakened the interest and solicitude of the American people—the subject of *Reconstruction.*

The Republican party had a majority of more than one hundred in the House, and after all its losses, retained more than two thirds of the Senate. As a consequence of this great preponderance of power, the party possessing it was justly held responsible for the manner in which the country should pass the important political crisis consequent upon the termination of the war in the overthrow of the rebellion.

It became an important question for members of the Republican party in Congress to determine among themselves what line of policy they should pursue.

The appointment of the Joint Committee of Fifteen on Reconstruction, was every-where regarded by the constituents of the majority as a most happy initiatory step. The whole country listened with eagerness to hear what words would be spoken in

Congress to give some clue to the course the committee would recommend. Words of no uncertain significance and weight were uttered at an early period in the session.

On the 18th of December, a fortnight after the opening of the session, Mr. Stevens announced his opinions on reconstruction with great boldness and distinctness. At the same time, seeing himself much in advance of many of his party, and fearing lest his opinions might alarm the less resolute, he declared: "I do not profess to speak their sentiments, nor must they be held responsible for them."

Mr. Stevens opened his speech with remarks on the condition of the rebel States. He said: "The President assumes, what no one doubts, that the late rebel States have lost their constitutional relations to the Union, and are incapable of representation in Congress, except by permission of the Government. It matters but little, with this admission, whether you call them States out of the Union, and now conquered territories, or assert that because the Constitution forbids them to do what they did do, that they are, therefore, only dead as to all national and political action, and will remain so until the Government shall breathe into them the breath of life anew and permit them to occupy their former position. In other words, that they are not out of the Union, but are only dead carcasses lying within the Union. In either case, it is very plain that it requires the action of Congress to enable them to form a State government and send Representatives to Congress. Nobody, I believe, pretends that with their old constitutions and frames of government they can be permitted to claim their old rights under the Constitution. They have torn their constitutional States into atoms, and built on their foundations fabrics of a totally different character. Dead men can not raise themselves. Dead States can not restore their own existence 'as it was.' Whose especial duty is it to do it? In whom does the Constitution place the power? Not in the judicial branch of Government, for it only adjudicates and does not prescribe laws. Not in the Executive, for he only executes and can not make laws. Not in the commander-in-chief of the armies, for he can only hold them under military rule until the sovereign legislative power of the conqueror shall give them law.

"There is fortunately no difficulty in solving the question. There are two provisions in the Constitution, under one of which the case must fall. The fourth article says: 'New States may be admitted by the Congress into this Union.' In my judgment, this is the controlling provision in this case. Unless the law of nations is a dead letter, the late war between two acknowledged belligerents severed their original compacts, and broke all the ties that bound them together. The future condition of the conquered power depends on the will of the conqueror. They must come in as new States or remain as conquered provinces. Congress—the Senate and House of Representatives, with the concurrence of the President—is the only power that can act in the matter. But suppose, as some dreaming theorists imagine, that these States have never been out of the Union, but have only destroyed their State governments so as to be incapable of political action, then the fourth section of the fourth article applies, which says, 'The United States shall guarantee to every State in this Union a republican form of government.' Who is the United States? Not the judiciary; not the President; but the sovereign power of the people, exercised through their Representatives in Congress, with the concurrence of the Executive. It means the political Government—the concurrent action of both branches of Congress and the Executive. The separate action of each amounts to nothing either in admitting new States or guaranteeing republican governments to lapsed or outlawed States. Whence springs the preposterous idea that either the President, or the Senate, or the House of Representatives, acting separately, can determine the right of States to send members or Senators to the Congress of the Union?"

Mr. Stevens then cited authorities to prove that "if the so-called Confederate States of America were an independent belligerent, and were so acknowledged by the United States and by Europe, or had assumed and maintained an attitude which entitled them to be considered and treated as a belligerent, then, during such time, they were precisely in the condition of a foreign nation with whom we were at war; nor need their independence as a nation be acknowledged by us to produce that effect."

Having read from a number of authorities to support his position, Mr. Stevens continued: "After such clear and repeated decisions, it is something worse than ridiculous to hear men of respectable standing attempting to nullify the law of nations, and declare the Supreme Court of the United States in error, because, as the Constitution forbids it, the States could not go out of the Union in fact. A respectable gentleman was lately reciting this argument, when he suddenly stopped and said: 'Did you hear of that atrocious murder committed in our town? A rebel deliberately murdered a Government official.' The person addressed said, 'I think you are mistaken.' 'How so? I saw it myself.' 'You are wrong; no murder was or could be committed, for the law forbids it.'

"The theory that the rebel States, for four years a separate power and without representation in Congress, were all the time here in the Union, is a good deal less ingenious and respectable than the metaphysics of Berkeley, which proved that neither the world nor any human being was in existence. If this theory were simply ridiculous it could be forgiven; but its effect is deeply injurious to the stability of the nation. I can not doubt that the late Confederate States are out of the Union to all intents and purposes for which the conqueror may choose so to consider them.

Mr. Stevens further maintained that the rebel States should be adjudged out of the Union on the ground of estoppel. "They are estopped," said he, "both by matter of record and matter *in pais*. One of the first resolutions passed by seceded South Carolina in January, 1861, is as follows:

"*Resolved, unanimously*, That the separation of South Carolina from the Federal Union is final, and she has no further interest in the Constitution of the United States; and that the only appropriate negotiations between her and the Federal Government are as to their mutual relations as foreign States."

"Similar resolutions appear upon all their State and Confederate Government records. The speeches of their members of Congress, their generals and executive officers, and the answers of their Government to our shameful suings for peace, went upon the defiant ground that no terms would be offered or received except upon the prior acknowledgment of the entire and permanent independence of the Confederate States. After this, to deny that we have a right to treat them as a conquered belligerent, severed from the Union in fact, is not argument but mockery. Whether it be our interest to do so is the only question hereafter and more deliberately to be considered.

"But suppose these powerful but now subdued belligerents, instead of being out of the Union, are merely destroyed, and are now lying about, a dead corpse, or with animation so suspended as to be incapable of action, and wholly unable to heal themselves by any unaided movements of their own. Then they may fall under the provision of the Constitution which says, "the United States shall guarantee to every State in the Union a republican form of government." Under that power, can the judiciary, or the President, or the commander-in-chief of the army, or the Senate or House of Representatives, acting separately, restore them to life and reädmit them into the Union? I insist that if each acted separately, though the action of each was identical with all the others, it would amount to nothing. Nothing but the joint action of the two houses of Congress and the concurrence of the President could do it. If the Senate admitted their Senators, and the House their members, it would have no effect on the future action of Congress. The Fortieth Congress might reject both. Such is the ragged record of Congress for the last four years."

He cited a decision of the Supreme Court to show that "it rests with Congress to decide what government is the established one in a State," and then remarked: "But Congress does not mean the Senate, or the House of Representatives, and President, all acting severally. Their joint action constitutes Congress. Hence a law of Congress must be passed before any new State can be admitted or any dead ones revived. Until then, no member can be lawfully admitted into either house. Hence, it appears with how little knowledge of constitutional law each branch is urged to admit members separately from these destroyed States. The provision that "each house shall be the judge of the elections, returns, and qualifications of its own members," has not the most distant bearing on this question. Congress must create States and declare when they are entitled to be represented. Then each house must judge whether the members presenting themselves from a recognized State possesses the requisite qualifications of age, residence, and citizenship, and whether the election and returns are according to law. The houses separately can judge of nothing else.

"It is obvious from all this, that the first duty of Congress is to pass a law declaring the condition of these outside or defunct States, and providing proper civil government for them. Since the conquest, they have been governed by martial law. Military rule is necessarily despotic, and ought not to exist longer than is absolutely necessary. As there are no symptoms that the people of these provinces will be prepared to participate in constitutional government for some years, I know of no arrangement so proper for them as territorial government. There they can learn the principles of freedom and eat the fruit of foul rebellion. Under such governments, while electing members to the territorial legislatures, they will necessarily mingle with those to whom Congress shall extend the right of suffrage. In territories Congress fixes the qualifications of electors, and I know of no better place nor better occasion for the conquered rebels and the conqueror to practice justice to all men and accustom themselves to make and obey equal laws."

Mr. Stevens proceeded to specify amendments to the Constitution which should be made before the late rebel States "would be capable of acting in the Union." The first of those amendments would be to change the basis of representation among the States from federal numbers to actual voters. After explaining the operation of this amendment, he depicted the consequences of reädmitting the Southern States without this guarantee. "With the basis unchanged," said he, "the eighty-three Southern members, with the Democrats that will in the best of times be elected from the North, will always give them the majority in Congress and in the Electoral College. They will, at the very first election, take possession of the White House and the halls of Congress. I need not depict the ruin that would follow. Assumption of the rebel debt or repudiation of the Federal debt would be sure to follow; the oppression of the freedmen, the reämendment of their State constitutions, and the reëstablishment of slavery would be the inevitable result."

Mr. Stevens thus set forth the importance of a proposed amendment to allow Congress to lay a duty on exports: "Its importance can not well be overstated. It is very obvious that for many years the South will not pay much under our internal revenue laws. The only article on which we can raise any considerable amount is cotton. It will be grown largely at once. With ten cents a pound export duty, it would be furnished cheaper to foreign markets than they could obtain it from any other part of the world. The late war has shown that. Two million bales exported, at five hundred pounds to the bale, would yield $100,000,000. This seems to be the chief revenue we shall ever derive from the South. Besides, it would be a protection to that amount to our domestic manufactures. Other proposed amendments—to make all laws uniform, to prohibit the assumption of the rebel debt—are of vital importance, and the only thing that can prevent the combined forces of copperheads and secessionists from legislating against the interests of the Union whenever they may obtain an accidental majority.

"But this is not all that we ought to do before these inveterate rebels are invited to participate in our legislation. We have turned, or are about to turn, loose four million slaves, without a hut to shelter them or a cent in their pockets. The infernal laws of slavery have prevented them from acquiring an education, understanding the commonest laws of contract, or of managing the ordinary business of life. This Congress is bound to provide for them until they can take care of themselves. If we do not furnish them with homesteads, and hedge them around with protective laws; if we leave them to the legislation of their late masters, we had better have left them in bondage. Their condition would be worse than that of our prisoners at Andersonville. If we fail in this great duty now, when we have the power, we shall deserve and receive the execration of history and of all future ages.

"Two things are of vital importance: 1. So to establish a principle that none of the rebel States shall be counted in any of the amendments of the Constitution until they are duly admitted into the family of States by the law-making power of their conqueror. For more than six months the amendment of the Constitution abolishing slavery has been ratified by the Legislatures of three-fourths of the States that acted on its passage by Congress, and which had Legislatures, or which were States capable of acting, or required to act, on the question.

"I take no account of the aggregation of whitewashed rebels, who, without any legal authority, have assembled in the capitals of the late rebel States and simulated legislative bodies. Nor do I regard with any respect the cunning by-play into which they deluded the Secretary of State by frequent telegraphic announcements that 'South Carolina had adopted the amendment,' 'Alabama has adopted the amendment, being the twenty-seventh State,' etc. This was intended to delude the people and accustom Congress to hear repeated the names of these extinct States as if they were alive, when, in truth, they have now no more existence than the revolted cities of Latium, two-thirds of whose people were colonized, and their property confiscated, and their rights of citizenship withdrawn by conquering and avenging Rome."

A second thing of vital importance to the stability of this republic, Mr. Stevens asserted to be "that it should now be solemnly decided what power can revive, recreate, and reïnstate these provinces into the family of States, and invest them with the rights of American citizens. It is time that Congress should assert its sovereignty, and assume something of the dignity of a Roman senate. It is fortunate that the President invites Congress to take this manly attitude. After stating, with great frankness, in his able message, his theory—which, however, is found to be impracticable, and which, I believe, very few now consider tenable—he refers the whole matter to the judgment of Congress. If Congress should fail firmly and wisely to discharge that high duty, it is not the fault of the President."

Mr. Stevens closed his speech by setting the seal of reprobation upon a doctrine which is becoming too fashionable, that "this is a white man's Government." He uttered a severe rebuke to those who thus "mislead and miseducate the public mind."

There were some Republicans in Congress who disagreed with Mr. Stevens in his theory of the condition of the late rebel States, yet no one ventured immediately, to use a contemporary expression, "to take the Radical bull by the horns."

At length, three days afterward, Mr. Raymond, as a representative of the "Conservatives," ventured a reply. He thus set forth his theory as in opposition to that of Mr. Stevens: "I can not believe that these States have ever been out of the Union, or that they are now out of the Union. I can not believe that they ever have been, or are now, in any sense a separate power. If they were, sir, how and when did they become so? They were once States of this Union—that every one concedes; bound to the Union and made members of the Union by the Constitution of the United States. If they ever went out of the Union, it was at some specific time and by some specific act. Was it by the ordinance of secession? I think we all agree that an ordinance of secession passed by any State of this Union is simply a nullity, because it encounters in its practical operation the Constitution of the United States, which is the supreme law of the land. It could have no legal, actual force or validity. It could not operate to effect any actual change in the relations of the States adopting it to the National Government, still less to accomplish the removal of that State from the sovereign jurisdiction of the Constitution of the United States.

"Well, sir, did the resolutions of these States, the declarations of their officials, the speeches of members of their Legislatures, or the utterances of their press accomplish the result? Certainly not. They could not possibly work any change whatever in the relations of these States to the General Government. All their ordinances and all their resolutions were simply declarations of a purpose to secede. Their secession, if it ever took place, certainly could not date from the time when their intention to secede was first announced. After declaring that intention, they proceeded to carry it into effect. How? By war. By sustaining their purpose by arms against the force which the United States brought to bear against it. Did they sustain it? Were their arms victorious? If they were, then their secession was an accomplished fact; if not, it was nothing more than an abortive attempt, a purpose unfulfilled. This, then, is simply a question of fact, and we all know what the fact is. They did not succeed. They failed to maintain their ground by force of arms; in other words, they failed to secede.

"But the gentleman from Pennsylvania [Mr. Stevens] insists that they did secede, and that this fact is not in the least affected by the other fact that the Constitution forbids secession. He says that the law forbids murder, but that murders are, nevertheless, committed. But there is no analogy between the two cases. If secession had been accomplished; if these States had gone out, and overcome the armies that tried to prevent their going out, then the prohibition of the Constitution could not have altered the fact. In the case of murder the man is killed, and murder is thus committed in spite of the law. The fact of killing is essential to the committal of the crime, and the fact of going out is essential to secession. But in this case there was no such fact. I think I need not argue any further the position that the rebel States have never for one moment, by any ordinances of secession, or by any successful war, carried themselves beyond the rightful jurisdiction of the Constitution of the United States. They have interrupted for a time the practical enforcement and exercise of that jurisdiction; they rendered it impossible for a time for this Government to enforce obedience to its laws; but there has never been an hour when this Government, or this Congress, or this House, or the gentleman from Pennsylvania himself, ever conceded that those States were beyond the jurisdiction of the Constitution and laws of the United States."

Referring to the citation of authorities made by Mr. Stevens, Mr. Raymond maintained that they did not lend the "slightest countenance to the inference which was drawn from them."

In reply to the theory maintained by Mr. Stevens, that States forfeited their State existence by the fact of rebellion, Mr. Raymond said: "I do not see how there can be any such forfeiture involved or implied. The individual citizens of those States went into the rebellion. They thereby incurred certain penalties under the laws and Constitution of the United States. What the States did was to endeavor to interpose their State authority between the individuals in rebellion and the Government of the United States, which assumed, and which would carry out the assumption, to declare those individuals traitors for their acts. The individuals in the States who were in rebellion, it seems to me, were the only parties who, under the Constitution and laws of the United States, could incur the penalties of treason. I know of no law, I know of nothing in the Constitution of the United States, I know of nothing in any recognized or established code of international law, which can punish a State as a State for any act it may perform. It is certain that our Constitution assumes nothing of the kind. It does not deal with States, except in one or two instances, such as elections of members of Congress and the election of electors of President and Vice-President.

"Indeed, the main feature which distinguishes the Union under the Constitution from the old Confederation is this: that whereas the old Confederation did deal with States directly, making requisitions upon them for supplies and relying upon them for the execution of its laws, the Constitution of the United States, in order to form a more perfect Union, made its laws binding on the individual citizens of the several States, whether living in one State or in another. Congress, as the legislative branch of this Government, enacts a law which shall be operative upon every individual within its jurisdiction. It is binding upon each individual citizen, and if he resists it by force, he is guilty of a crime, and is punished accordingly, any thing in the constitution or laws of his State to the contrary notwithstanding. But the States themselves are not touched by the laws of the United States or by the Constitution of the United States. A State can not be indicted; a State can not be tried; a State can not be hung for treason. The individuals in a State may be so tried and hung, but the State as an organization, as an organic member of the Union, still exists, whether its individual citizens commit treason or not."

Mr. Raymond subsequently cited some of the consequences which he thought must follow the acceptance of the position assumed by Mr. Stevens. "If," said Mr. Raymond, "as he asserts, we have been waging war with an independent Power, with a separate nation, I can not see how we can talk of treason in connection with our recent conflict, or demand the execution of Davis or any body else as a traitor. Certainly if we were at war with any other foreign Power, we should not talk of the treason of those who were opposed to us in the field. If we were engaged in a war with France, and should take as prisoner the Emperor Napoleon, certainly we could not talk of him as a traitor or as liable to execution. I think that by adopting any such assumption as that of the honorable gentleman, we surrender the whole idea of treason and the punishment of traitors. I think, moreover, that we accept, virtually and practically, the doctrine of State sovereignty, the right of a State to withdraw from the Union, and to break up the Union at its own will and pleasure.

"Another of the consequences of this doctrine, as it seems to me, would be our inability to talk of loyal men in the South. Loyal to what? Loyal to a foreign, independent Power, as the United States would become under those circumstances? Certainly not. Simply disloyal to their own Government, and deserters, or whatever you may choose to call them, from that to which they would owe allegiance, to a foreign and independent State.

"Now, there is another consequence of the doctrine which I shall not dwell upon, but simply suggest. If that confederacy was an independent Power, a separate nation, it had the right to contract debts; and we, having overthrown and conquered that independent Power, according to the theory of the gentleman from Pennsylvania, would become the successors, the inheritors, of its debts and assets, and we must pay them."

Mr. Raymond set forth his theory of the conditions and relations of the late rebel States in the following language: "I certainly do not think these States are to be dealt with by us as provinces—as simply so much territory—held to us by no other ties than those of conquest. I think we are to deal with them as States having State governments, still subject to the jurisdiction of the Constitution and laws of the United States, still under the constitutional control of the National Government; and that in our dealings with them we are to be guided and governed, not simply by our sovereign will and pleasure as conquerors, but by the restrictions and limitations of the Constitution of the United States, precisely as we are restrained and limited in our dealings with all other States of the American Union."

In answer to the question how we are to deal with the late rebel States, Mr. Raymond remarked: "I think we have a full and perfect right to require certain conditions in the nature of guarantees for the future, and that right rests, primarily and technically, on the surrender we may and must require at their hands. The rebellion has been defeated. A defeat always implies a surrender, and, in a political sense, a surrender implies more than the transfer of the arms used on the field of battle. It implies, in the case of civil war, a surrender of the principles and doctrines, of all the weapons and agencies, by which the war has been carried on. The military surrender was made on the field of battle, to our generals, as the agents and representatives of the Commander-in-chief of the armies of the United States.

"Now, there must be at the end of the war, a similar surrender on the political field of controversy. That surrender is due as an act of justice from the defeated party to the victorious party. It is due, also, and we have a right to exact it, as a guarantee for the future. Why do we demand the surrender of their arms by the vanquished in every battle? We do it that they may not renew the contest. Why do we seek, in this and all similar cases, a surrender of the principles for which they fought? It is that they may never again be made the basis of controversy and rebellion against the Government of the United States.

"Now, what are those principles which should be thus surrendered? The principle of State sovereignty is one of them. It was the corner-stone of the rebellion—at once its animating spirit and its fundamental basis. Deeply ingrained as it was in the Southern heart, it must be surrendered. The ordinances in which it was embodied must not only be repealed, the principle itself must be abandoned, and the ordinances, so far as this war is concerned, be declared null and void, and that declaration must be embodied in their fundamental constitutions."

The speech was here interrupted by Mr. Bingham, who insisted that the adoption of the principle in the State constitutions would not be sufficient guarantee. Adoption in the Constitution of the United States was essential to its permanent effective force.

Mr. Raymond thought the Constitution of the United States as plain as possible in its declaration against the doctrine of State sovereignty. If any more explicit denial could be got into the Constitution, he would favor it.

"Another thing," said Mr. Raymond, "to be surrendered by the defeated rebellion is the obligation to pay the rebel war debt. We have the right to require this repudiation of their debt, because the money represented by that debt was one of the weapons with which they carried on the war against the Government of the United States.

"There is another thing which we have the right to require, and that is the prohibition of slavery. We have the right to require them to do this, not only in their State constitutions, but in the Constitution of the United States. And we have required it, and it has been conceded. They have also conceded that Congress may make such laws as may be requisite to carry that prohibition into effect, which includes such legislation as may be required to secure for them protection of their civil and personal rights—their 'right to life, liberty, and the pursuit of happiness.'"

Mr. Spalding having inquired whether there was any limit to the right to make these requisitions, except the good judgment of Congress, Mr. Raymond answered:

"My impression is that these requisitions are made as a part of the terms of surrender which we have a right to demand at the hands of the defeated insurgents, and that it belongs, therefore, to the President, as Commander-in-chief of the army and navy of the United States, to make them, and to fix the limit as to what they shall embrace."

By way of setting forth the opinions of the "Radicals" in as strong a light as possible, Mr. Raymond said: "It may be for the welfare of this nation that we shall cherish toward the millions of our people lately in rebellion feelings of hatred and distrust; that we shall nurse the bitterness their infamous treason has naturally and justly engendered, and make that the basis of our future dealings with them. Possibly we may best teach them the lessons of liberty, by visiting upon them the worst excesses of despotism. Possibly they may best learn to practice justice toward others, to admire and emulate our republican institutions, by suffering at our hands the absolute rule we denounce in others. It may be best for us and for them that we discard, in all our dealings with them, all the obligations and requirements of the Constitution, and assert as the only law for them the unrestrained will of conquerors and masters."

In contrast with this, he placed what he supposed to be a different policy: "I would exact from them, or impose upon them through the constitutional legislation of Congress, and by enlarging and extending, if necessary, the scope and powers of the Freedmen's Bureau, proper care and protection for the helpless and friendless freedmen, so lately their slaves. I would exercise a rigid scrutiny into the character and loyalty of the men whom they may send to Congress, before I allowed them to participate in the high prerogative of legislating for the nation. But I would seek to allay rather than stimulate the animosities and hatred, however just they may be, to which the war has given rise. But for our own sake as well as for theirs, I would not visit upon them a policy of confiscation which has been discarded in the policy and practical conduct of every civilized nation on the face of the globe."

Mr. Raymond having closed his speech, it was moved that the Committee of the Whole should rise, but the motion was withdrawn to allow Mr. Jenckes, of Rhode Island, five minutes for reply. He said: "The gentleman states, and properly, that every act or ordinance of secession was a nullity. Undoubtedly it was. Upon that question of law we do not disagree. But he seems to me to overlook entirely what was the state of facts from the time of the passage of the ordinances of secession until the time of the surrender of Lee's army. During that period what were the relations which all that territory—I will not use the term States, but all that territory—between the Potomac and the Rio Grande sustained to the Government of the United States? Who could see States there for any purpose for which legislation was required by the Constitution of the United States?

"At the time of the passage of the ordinance of secession, States were organized there, in existence, in action, known to the Constitution and the constitutional authorities under it. But were they loyal? Did they obey the Constitution of the United States? This is a question that needs no answer other than that which is conveyed to every mind by the recollection of the last four years of war, with their expenditure of treasure and blood. Those States were not destroyed, in the technical language of the law—they simply died out. As their Governors passed out of office, as the terms of their legislatures expired, who knew those facts? None but themselves. And yet, behind this grand cordon of armies, stretching from here to the Rio Grande, there were States in existence, organized as States, but States in rebellion, occupying the territory belonging to the people of the United States. They were not acting in concert with this Government, but against it. That, Mr. Chairman, is a matter of fact. My eyes are not dimmed or blinded by the parchment upon which constitutions or laws are written. I, like the men who carried the bayonets and planted the cannon, recognize the fact that was before us during all this time. There was a state of rebellion. There were in that part of our territory no States known to our Constitution or the laws that we enact, or the officers whose duty it is to enforce those laws.

"I recognize, too, the next fact. Bear in mind, I am simply stating now what I conceive to be the facts. The question as to what may be the law can be reserved for discussion on another occasion. I recognize fully the duties of the Executive. And it was the duty of the President of the United States, as the head of the civil and military power of this great republic—not 'empire;' God forbid that this country should ever be so designated with applause or even with toleration—to beat down armed opposition to it, whether it came from a foreign power or from domestic insurrection. That was the duty of the President, and he recognized it; and it was not the duty of any one in this Congress to gainsay it. It was written on the face of the Constitution that the President was to see that the laws should be faithfully executed, and the power of this republic maintained, and he did so.

"The next fact—the fact which seems to me to be the one most pertinent for consideration now—is that the military power which was opposed to this Government has been destroyed. It was the duty of the Executive to see that this was done, and to report to the Congress of the United States that it has been done. But what then? Then there comes the third question of fact, intimately connected with the last, and hardly separable from it, because it requires the immediate action of the Executive and of Congress. All the power that existed in the shape of Confederated States behind rebel bayonets and fortifications has fallen to the earth. The territory which these States in rebellion occupied was the property of the people of the United States, and never could be taken from us. I hold it to be a question of public law, worthy of consideration by the representatives of the American people, by the President and the Administration generally, to ascertain what existed in the shape of civil constitutions and laws behind the military government that has been overthrown. I hesitate not to say, here or elsewhere, that the Executive of this Government has done his duty in this matter. All conquering nations, when they overcome a rebellious people by overthrowing their military power, look, as did the Government of Great Britain when it had overcome the mutiny in India, to see what government of a civil kind has existed or may exist from custom among the people who are conquered. I see no reason in this view to discriminate between the argument of the gentleman from Pennsylvania and the argument of the gentleman from New York. It seems to me, that if they will look at the particular questions which are now before us, and which require our action, the differences would be in terms and not in substance."

The people of the predominant party generally acquiesced in the opinion of Mr. Jenckes, as expressed in the conclusion of his remarks as above presented. They conceived that the difference between the various views of the whole question was "one of details and not of essence." The question of reconstruction was purely practical. All shades of opinion in the Republican party blended in this: that the States in question were not to be restored until satisfactory pledges were given to the United States. All speculation or attempt at argument in reference to their abstract condition was consequently superfluous—"a pernicious abstraction," in the language of Mr. Lincoln.

If some were not prepared to accept the deductions of Mr. Stevens, yet accepting the logic of Mr. Raymond, they would be carried almost as far. The latter held that the citizens of those States were defeated insurgents who must submit to any conditions of surrender imposed by the victorious commander. Certain concessions could be rightfully demanded as parts of their surrender and conditions of their restoration. Their acquiescence had been required in a constitutional amendment affecting the great social and industrial interests of Southern society. After this none could deny the right, whatever might be the expediency, of requiring their assent to other amendments bearing upon the political structure of the Southern States.

Some of the predominant party were willing to stop short in their demands upon the rebel States with requiring acceptance of the emancipation amendment, repudiation of the rebel debt, legal protection of freedmen, and revocation of the ordinances of secession. The majority, however, were disposed to go still further, and demand other conditions and guarantees which should become a part of the fundamental law of the land. This was the practical work of reconstruction for which the Joint Committee of Fifteen was preparing the way, and upon which Congress was soon to enter.

CHAPTER XIV.

THE BASIS OF REPRESENTATION—IN THE HOUSE.

First work of the Joint Committee—The joint resolution proposing a constitutional amendment—Mr. Stevens' reasons for speedy action—Protracted discussion commenced—Objections to the bill by Mr. Rogers—Defense by Mr. Conkling—Two other modes—How States might evade the Law—Not a finality—Wisconsin and South Carolina—Amendment for Female Suffrage proposed—Orth on Indiana and Massachusetts—Obscuration of the sun—More Radical remedy desired—A Kentuckian gratified—Citations from the Census—Premium for Treason—White Slaves—Power to amend well-nigh exhausted—Objections to the Suffrage Basis—"Race" and "Color" ambiguous—Condition of the Question—Recommitted—Final passage.

ALTHOUGH the Joint Committee of Fifteen were assiduous in their attention to the work assigned them, it was not until the 22d of January, 1866, that they were ready to make a partial report and recommend a practical measure for the consideration of Congress.

On that day Mr. Fessenden, of the Senate, and Mr. Stevens, of the House of Representatives, brought before those bodies respectively a partial report from the committee, recommending the passage of the following joint resolution:

Resolved by the Senate and House of Representatives of the United States of America in Congress assembled, (two-thirds of both houses concurring,) That the following article be proposed to the Legislatures of the several States as an amendment to the Constitution of the United States, which, when ratified by three-fourths of the said Legislatures, shall be valid as part of said Constitution, namely:

Article —. Representatives and direct taxes shall be apportioned among the several States which may be included within this Union according to their respective numbers, counting the whole number of persons in each State, excluding Indians not taxed: *Provided*, That whenever the elective franchise shall be denied or abridged in any State on account of race or color, all persons of such race or color shall be excluded from the basis of representation.

In the Senate this subject was laid over, and was not reached for several days, as the Freedmen's Bureau Bill was then under discussion.

The subject was pressed upon the attention of the House for immediate action. Mr. Stevens had no intention to make a speech, since the question had been under consideration by every member for the last six weeks. He remarked, however: "There are twenty-two States whose Legislatures are now in session, some of which will adjourn within two or three weeks. It is very desirable, if this amendment is to be adopted, that it should go forth to be acted upon by the Legislatures now in session. It proposes to change the present basis of representation to a representation upon all persons, with the proviso that wherever any State excludes a particular class of persons from the elective franchise, that State to that extent shall not be entitled to be represented in Congress. It does not deny to the States the right to regulate the elective franchise as they please; but it does say to a State, 'If you exclude from the right of suffrage Frenchmen, Irishmen, or any particular class of people, none of that class of persons shall be counted in fixing your representation in this House. You may allow them to vote or not, as you please; but if you do allow them to vote, they will be counted and represented here; while if you do not allow them to vote, no one shall be authorized to represent them here; they shall be excluded from the basis of representation.'"

As indicative of the apparent harmony of sentiments prevailing on the question, Mr. Wilson said that the Committee on the Judiciary had determined to report a proposition substantially identical with that offered by Mr. Stevens.

It was deemed important to have the joint resolution passed as soon as possible, that it might go before the State Legislatures then in session for their ratification before their adjournment. The member who had the measure in charge desired, after one or two speeches on either side, to have the question put to vote, and have the resolution passed before the sun went down. Such action, however, seemed to the House too hasty, and a discussion of the measure was entered upon, which ran through many days.

Mr. Rogers, a member of the committee, offered a minority report, and addressed the House in opposition to the proposed amendment of the Constitution. He thus presented his view of the object of the measure proposed: "It appears to have in its body, in its soul, and in its life only one great object and aim; that is, to debase and degrade the white race, and to place upon a higher footing than the white men are placed, under the Constitution, this African race. It is a proposition to change the organic law of the land with regard to one of the fundamental principles which was laid down by our fathers at the formation of the Constitution as an axiom of civil and political liberty, that taxation and representation should always go together. If gentlemen will examine this proposed amendment of the Constitution, they will see that it is in violation of that great doctrine which was proclaimed by the fathers of the republic when they enunciated the Declaration of Independence, and protested against the tyranny and despotism of England, because she attempted to tax the people of the colonies without allowing them representation in the councils of the kingdom. The amendment now under consideration proposes the very same identical thing that the Parliament of England proposed when it attempted to inflict upon the American colonies taxation without allowing the people of the colonies to have representatives in the Parliament of England to represent them upon the question whether they should be taxed by the mother country or not.

"The first objection I have to the passage of this joint resolution is, that it is violative of the main principle upon which the Revolutionary War was conducted, and which induced our fathers to enter the harbors of Boston and New York and throw the tea into the water. Because the British people attempted to inflict taxation upon them with regard to that tea, and refused to allow them representation in the Parliament of England, our fathers rebelled against their mother country. What has come over the fortunes and happiness of the people of this country that the great principle of the Constitution should now be violated, that principle for which our fathers spilt their blood to sustain, the great axiom of American liberty, that taxation never should be imposed upon a people unless that people have a corresponding representation? If this amendment to the Constitution should be carried into effect, it will prevent any State, North or South, from allowing qualified suffrage to its colored population, except upon forfeiture of representation; and if qualified suffrage should be allowed to the colored population of any State in this Union, on account of race of color, and but one single negro should be deprived of his vote by failure to meet the requirements of the qualification imposed, that State would be denied representation for the whole of that colored population—men, women, and children.

"More than that: this bill attempts, in an indirect manner, to have passed upon, by the Legislatures of the different States, a question which the party in power dare not boldly and openly meet before the people of this country, because there can be but one object lying at the foundation of this bill—an object which has been explained and expatiated upon in this House—and that object, as I have said, is, through the Federal power, to force the States to adopt unqualified negro suffrage, by holding over them the penalty of being deprived of representation according to population.

"But I object to this joint resolution upon another ground—upon the same ground that I objected to the passage of the Negro Suffrage Bill for the District of Columbia—without consulting the people. It has been said in this country that all power emanates from the people. And I say that to submit this grave question to the consideration and decision of partisan Legislatures in the different States—Legislatures which were elected without any regard to this question—is violative of the great principles which lie at the foundations of the liberties of this country; that no organic law, affecting the whole people, should be passed before submitting it to the people for their ratification or rejection. Now this joint resolution proposes simply to submit this amendment for ratification to the Legislatures of the different States. The Legislatures are not the States; the Legislatures are not the people in their sovereign capacity; Legislatures are not the source from which all power emanates. But the people, the *sacred people*, in the exercise of their sovereign power, either at the ballot-box or in conventions, are the only true and proper forum to which such grave and serious questions should be submitted.

"I maintain that the Constitution of the United States, as it now exists, is not as liberal toward the Southern States, now that slavery has been abolished, as it was before the abolition of slavery. Why, sir, in the days of the past, under our Constitution, the Southern States have been allowed a representation for a population that was not classed as citizens or people; they were allowed a representation for people who had no political *status* in the State; persons who were not entitled even to exercise the right of coming into a court of civil justice as a plaintiff or defendant in the prosecution or defense of a suit.

"Now, after the raging fires of war have swept from the domain of every State in the South the pernicious institution of slavery; after the result has been that every slave has received his freedom; after the slaves have gained more by the success of this war than any other class of people in the United States, white men, men who are the representatives of the white race, come here proposing to compel the States, on pain of being deprived of a portion of their representation, to allow all the negroes within their limits to vote, without regard to qualification or any thing else, while under the same provision the State may, by its organic law, impose qualifications and conditions upon the exercise of the right of suffrage by the white population. The proposed amendment to the Constitution undertakes to consolidate the power in the Federal Government. It throws out a menace to the States, and the inevitable result of the passage would be to induce every State in the Union to adopt unqualified negro suffrage, so as not to deprive them of the great and inestimable right of representation for that class of population in the halls of the legislation of the United States."

Mr. Conkling, also a member of the Reconstruction Committee, made an argument in favor of the proposed amendment: "Emancipation vitalizes only natural rights, not political rights. Enfranchisement alone carries with it political rights, and these emancipated millions are no more enfranchised now than when they were slaves. They never had political power. Their masters had a fraction of power as masters. But there are no masters now. There are no slaves now. The whole relationship in which the power originated and existed is gone. Does this fraction of power still survive? If it does, what shall become of it? Where is it to go?

"We are told the blacks are unfit to wield even a fraction of power, and must not have it. That answers the whole question. If the answer be true, it is the end of controversy. There is no place, logically, for this power to go, save to the blacks; if they are unfit to have it, the power would not exist. It is a power astray, without a rightful owner. It should be resumed by the whole nation at once. It should not exist; it does not exist. This fractional power is extinct.

"A moral earthquake has turned fractions into units, and units into ciphers. If a black man counts at all now, he counts five-fifths of a man, not three-fifths. Revolutions have no such fractions in their arithmetic; war and humanity join hands to blot them out. Four millions, therefore, and not three-fifths of four millions, are to be reckoned in here now, and all these four millions are, and are to be, we are told, unfit for political existence.

"Did the framers of the Constitution ever dream of this? Never, very clearly. Our fathers trusted to gradual and voluntary emancipation, which would go hand in hand with education and enfranchisement. They never peered into the bloody epoch when four million fetters would be at once melted off in the fires of war. They never saw such a vision as we see. Four millions, each a Caspar Hauser, long shut up in darkness, and suddenly led out into the full flash of noon, and each, we are told, too blind to walk, politically. No one foresaw such an event, and so no provision was made for it. The three-fifths rule gave the slaveholding States, over and above all their just representation, eighteen Representatives beside, by the enumeration of 1860.

"The new situation will enable those States, when relationships are resumed, to claim twenty-eight Representatives beside their just proportion. Twenty-eight votes to be cast here and in the Electoral College for those held not fit to sit as jurors, not fit to testify in court, not fit to be plaintiff in a suit, not fit to approach the ballot-box! Twenty-eight votes to be more or less controlled by those who once betrayed the Government, and for those so destitute, we are assured, of intelligent instinct as not to be fit for free agency!

"Shall all this be? Shall four million beings count four millions, in managing the affairs of the nation, who are pronounced by their fellow-beings unfit to participate in administering government in the States where they live, or in their counties, towns, or precincts; who are pronounced unworthy of the least and most paltry part in local political affairs? Shall one hundred and twenty-seven thousand white people in New York cast but one vote in this House, and have none but one voice here, while the same number of white people in Mississippi have three votes and three voices? Shall the death of slavery add two-fifths to the entire power which slavery had when slavery was living? Shall one white man have as much share in the Government as three other white men merely because he lives where blacks outnumber whites two to one? Shall this inequality exist, and exist only in favor of those who without cause drenched the land with blood and covered it with mourning? Shall such be the reward of those who did the foulest and guiltiest act which crimsons the annals of recorded time? No, sir; not if I can help it."

Two other modes of meeting the case had been considered by the committee, namely: *First,* To make the basis of representation in Congress and the Electoral College consist of sufficiently qualified voters alone; *Second,* To deprive the States of the power to disqualify or discriminate politically on account of race or color.

After presenting some reasons why the committee saw proper to recommend neither of these plans, Mr. Conkling further argued in favor of the proposed amendment: "It contains but one condition, and that rests upon a principle already imbedded in the Constitution, and as old as free government itself. That principle I affirmed in the beginning; namely, that representation does not belong to those who have not political existence, but to those who have. The object of the amendment is to enforce this truth. It therefore provides that whenever any State finds within its borders a race of beings unfit for political existence, that race shall not be represented in the Federal Government. Every State will be left free to extend or withhold the elective franchise on such terms as it pleases, and this without losing any thing in representation if the terms are impartial as to all. Qualifications of voters may be required of any kind—qualifications of intelligence, of property, or of any sort whatever, and yet no loss of representation shall thereby be suffered. But whenever in any State, and so long as a race can be found which is so low, so bad, so ignorant, so stupid, that it is deemed necessary to exclude men from the right to vote merely because they belong to that race, in that case the race shall likewise be excluded from the sum of Federal power to which the State is entitled. If a race is so vile or worthless that to belong to it is alone cause of exclusion from political action, the race is not to be counted here in Congress."

Mr. Conkling maintained that the pending proposition commended itself for many reasons. "*First.* It provides for representation coëxtensive with taxation. I say it provides for this; it does not certainly secure it, but it enables every State to secure it. It does not, therefore, as the gentleman from New Jersey [Mr. Rogers] insists, violate the rule that representation should go with taxation. If a race in any State is kept unfit to vote, and fit only to drudge, the wealth created by its work ought to be taxed. Those who profit by such a system, or such a condition of things, ought to be taxed for it. Let them build churches and school-houses, and found newspapers, as New York and other States have done, and educate their people till they are fit to vote. 'Fair play,' 'A fair day's wages for a fair day's work,' 'Live and let live'—these mottoes, if blazoned over the institutions of a State, will insure it against being cursed for any length of time with inhabitants so worthless that they are fit only for beasts of burden. I have said that the amendment provides for representation going hand in hand with taxation. That is its first feature.

"*Second.* It brings into the basis both sexes and all ages, and so it counteracts and avoids, as far as possible, the casual and geographical inequalities of population.

"*Third.* It puts every State on an equal footing in the requirement prescribed.

"*Fourth.* It leaves every State unfettered to enumerate all its people for representation or not, just as it pleases.

Thus every State has the sole control, free from all interference, of its own interests and concerns. No other State, nor the General Government, can molest the people of any State on the subject, or even inquire into their acts or their reasons, but all the States have equal rights. If New York chooses to count her black population as political persons, she can do so. If she does not choose to do so, the matter is her own, and her rights can not be challenged. So of South Carolina. But South Carolina shall not say, 'True, we have less than three hundred thousand "persons" in this State, politically speaking, yet we will have, in governing the country, the power of seven hundred thousand persons.'

"The amendment is common to all States and equal for all; its operation will, of course, be practically only in the South. No Northern State will lose by it, whether the Southern States extend suffrage to blacks or not. Even New York, in her great population, has so few blacks that she could exclude them all from enumeration and it would make no difference in her representation. If the amendment is adopted, and suffrage remains confined as it is now, taking the census of 1860 as the foundation of the calculation, and the number of Representatives as it then stood, the gains and losses would be these: Wisconsin, Indiana, Illinois, Michigan, Ohio, Pennsylvania, Massachusetts, New Jersey, and Maine would gain one Representative each, and New York would gain three; Alabama, Kentucky, North Carolina, South Carolina, and Tennessee would each lose one; Georgia, Louisiana, and Virginia would each lose two, and Mississippi would lose three."

On the following day, January 23d, the proposed joint resolution came up in the regular order of business.

Mr. Jenckes, of Rhode Island, feared that a construction might be put upon the bill which would be fatal to its efficiency for the purposes had in view by its friends. He said: "It says nothing about the qualification of property. Suppose this amendment is adopted by three-fourths of the States, and becomes a part of the fundamental law of the land, and after its adoption the State of South Carolina should reinstate the constitution of 1790, striking out the word 'white' and reëstablishing the property qualification of fifty acres of land, or town lots, or the payment of a tax, there would then be no discrimination of color in the State of South Carolina, yet the number of electors would not be enlarged five hundred, and the basis of representation would be exactly as it is, with the addition of two-fifths of the enfranchised freedmen. A Representative to this House would be reëlected by the same voting constituency as now, perhaps with the addition of five hundred black men in the State. If it bears this construction, and I believe it does, I shall vote against it.

"If any of the States should establish property qualification based upon lands, then the same oligarchy would be enthroned on the whole basis of representation, entitled to a larger number of Representatives than now in this House, and elected by a slightly enlarged number of qualified electors, giving power more firmly to that very aristocracy we have sought to overthrow."

A number of queries were propounded, several amendments proposed, and a considerable desire for discussion expressed, until

Mr. Stevens, much disappointed at the reception the measure met in the House, withdrew the demand for the previous question, and left the subject open for unlimited debate.

Mr. Blaine, of Maine, addressed the House, detailing some objections to the measure. He said: "While I shall vote for the proposition, I shall do so with some reluctance unless it is amended, and I do not regret, therefore, that the previous question was not sustained. I am egotistic enough to believe that the phraseology of the original resolution, as introduced by me, was better than that employed in the pending amendment. The phrase 'civil or political rights or privileges,' which I employed, is broader and more comprehensive than the term 'elective franchise,' for I fear, with the gentleman from Illinois, [Mr. Farnsworth,] that under the latter phrase the most vicious evasions might be practiced. As that gentleman has well said, they might make suffrage depend on ownership of fifty acres of land, and then prohibit any negro holding real estate; but no such mockery as this could be perpetrated under the provisions of the amendment as I originally submitted it."

In relation to taxation, Mr. Blaine remarked: "Now, I contend that ordinary fair play—and certainly we can afford fair play where it does not cost any thing—calls for this, namely, that if we exclude them from the basis of representation they should be excluded from the basis of taxation. Ever since this Government was founded, taxation and representation have always gone hand in hand. If we shall exclude the principle in this amendment, we will be accused of a narrow, illiberal, mean-spirited, and money-grasping policy. More than that, we do not gain any thing by it. What kind of taxation is distributed according to representation? Direct taxation. Now, we do not have any direct taxation. There has been but twenty millions of direct taxation levied for the last fifty years. That tax was levied in 1861, and was not collected, but distributed among the States and held in the Treasury Department as an offset to the war claims of the States; so that, as a matter of fact, we are putting an offensive discrimination in this proposition and gaining nothing by it except obloquy."

Mr. Donnelly, of Minnesota, said: "It follows, as a logical conclusion, that if men have no voice in the National Government, other men should not sit in this hall pretending to represent them. And it is equally clear that an oppressed race should not lend power to their oppressors, to be used in their name and for their destruction. It is a mockery to say that a man's agent shall be his enemy, and shall be appointed without his consent and against his desire, and by other enemies.

"In fact, I can not see how any Northern man can vote against this measure, unless he wishes to perpetuate an injustice to his section, because the effect of it will clearly be to increase the representation of the North and decrease that of the South; and this, too, upon a basis of undoubted justice. It means simply that those who do not take part in the Government shall not be represented in the Government."

Mr. Donnelly did not, however, regard the proposed amendment as "a grand panacea for all the ills that affect the nation." He would vote for the law, "not as a finality, but as a partial step as one of a series of necessary laws." Said he, "When we vote for this measure, it must be because we think it right and necessary, not that it may furnish us with an excuse for failing to do all other right and necessary things expected of us by the people. We must take direct, not sidelong measures. We must make laws, not arguments. We must enforce, not induce.

"To pass this law and then hope that South Carolina, moved by the hope of future power, would do justice to the negro, is absurd. She has 291,300 whites and 412,406 negroes. To pass such a law would be for the governing power to divest itself of the government and hand it over to a subject and despised caste, and that, too, for a faint hope of some future advantage that might never be realized under the most favorable circumstances, and certainly could never be realized by the aspiring class abdicating and relinquishing power. The same is true, more or less, of all the South. In Mississippi there are 353,901 whites, and 436,631 negroes; and in all the States the negro vote would be large enough to turn the scale against the disloyal party."

Mr. Sloan, of Wisconsin, thus presented the practical workings of the "Constitution as it is:" "Look at the practical operation of the question we are discussing to-day. In the State I represent there are eight hundred thousand free white people loyal to the Constitution, who have done their whole duty in sustaining their Government during this terrible war. The bones of our soldiers are moldering in the soil of every rebel State. They have stood around our flag in the deadly hail of every battle of the war. The State of Wisconsin has six Representatives on this floor. South Carolina has three hundred thousand white inhabitants, disloyal, who have done all in their power to overthrow and destroy the Government, and yet, sir, under the Constitution as it now stands, the three hundred thousand disloyal white inhabitants of South Carolina will exercise as much political power in the Government as the eight hundred thousand loyal people of the State of Wisconsin."

Mr. Sloan called attention to a proposition which he had submitted to the preceding Congress, providing that the right of representation should be based upon the right of suffrage—upon the numbers allowed the right to vote in the respective States.

In answer to a supposed objection to this plan, that "there might be some inequality in the representation of the respective States," he said: "We all know that the young men of the old States go out in large numbers to settle in the new States and Territories, while the women and children do not emigrate to so great an extent, and hence there would be a larger number of voters in the new States in proportion to population than in the old. And yet this is a consideration which, in my judgment, ought not to weigh a hair with any member on this floor. It would be only a temporary inequality. In the rapidly increasing settlement and in the natural increase of population of our new States, that inequality would very soon be entirely swept away. I believe the difference to-day between Massachusetts and Wisconsin would be very slight, if any, so rapid has been the increase of our population and the settlement of our State. We are now proposing to adopt an amendment to the Constitution which we expect to stand for all time, and any temporary inequality which could continue but for a few years ought not to have any weight."

Mr. Brooks, of New York, thought that Mr. Stevens would better "at the start have named what are States of this Union. The opinion of the honorable gentleman himself, that there are no States in this Union but those that are now represented upon this floor, I know full well; but he knows as well that the President of the United States recognizes thirty-six States of this Union, and that it is necessary to obtain the consent of three-fourths of those thirty-six States, which number it is not possible to obtain. He knows very well that if his amendment should be adopted by the Legislatures of States enough, in his judgment, to carry it, before it could pass the tribunal of the Executive chamber it would be obliged to receive the assent of twenty-seven States in order to become an amendment to the Constitution."

Mr. Brooks, in the course of his speech, presented a petition from certain ladies of New York, asking an amendment of the Constitution, prohibiting the several States from disfranchising any of their citizens on the ground of sex. He then proposed to amend the joint resolution by inserting the words "or sex" after the word "color," so that it would read, "*Provided,* That whenever the elective franchise shall be denied or abridged in any State on account of race or color or sex, all persons of such race or color or sex shall be excluded from the basis of representation."

"Is the gentleman in favor of that amendment?" asked Mr. Stevens.

"I am," replied Mr. Brooks, "if negroes are allowed to vote."

"That does not answer my question," said Mr. Stevens.

"I suggested that I would move it at a convenient time," said Mr. Brooks.

"Is the gentleman in favor of his own amendment?" Mr. Stevens again asked.

"I am in favor of my own color in preference to any other color, and I prefer the white women of my country to the negro," was the response of Mr. Brooks, which was followed by applause in the galleries.

Mr. Orth, of Indiana, obtained the floor for the purpose of offering an amendment, which he prefaced with the following remarks: "My position is that the true principle of representation in Congress is that voters alone should form the basis, and that each voter should have equal political weight in our Government; that the voter in Massachusetts should have the same but no greater power than the voter in Indiana; and that the voter in Indiana should have the same power, but no greater, than the voter in the State of South Carolina. The gentleman from Maine, however, states that the census tables will show that by the amendment which I desire to offer at this time you will curtail the representative power of the State of Massachusetts. And why? Because he has shown by his figures that although Massachusetts has a male population of 529,244, her voting population is only 175,487, being a percentage of twenty-nine, while Indiana, with a white male population of 693,469, has a voting population of 280,655, being about forty per cent. Why is this difference? Is it because our voting population is so much greater in proportion than the voting population of Massachusetts? Not at all. The difference arises from the fact that the State of Massachusetts has seen fit to exclude a portion of her citizens from the ballot-box. Indiana has done the same thing. Indiana has excluded one class of citizens; Massachusetts has excluded another class. Indiana has seen fit, for reasons best known to herself, to exclude the colored population from the right of suffrage; Massachusetts, on the contrary, has seen fit to exclude from the ballot-box those of her citizens who can not read or write. While we in Indiana are governed by a prejudice of color, the people of Massachusetts, I might say, are governed by a prejudice as regards ignorance. But here is the difference: under the amendment that I propose, while Indiana excludes the black man from the right to participate in the decisions of the ballot-box, she does not ask that the black man shall be represented on this floor. On the contrary, while Massachusetts excludes black and white persons who can not read and write, she yet asks that that population excluded from the ballot shall have representation on this floor. I regard this as wrong in theory, wrong in principle, and injurious to the State which I have the honor to represent, giving to Massachusetts a power upon this floor of which my State is deprived. Why? Because the exclusion which drives from the ballot-box in Massachusetts a large portion of her citizens, yet admits them to representative power on this floor."

Mr. Orth's amendment proposed that Representatives should "be apportioned among the several States according to the number of male citizens over twenty-one years of age, having the qualifications requisite for electors of the most numerous branch of the State Legislature." There being objection to the reception of this amendment under the rules of the House, it could not be considered.

Mr. Chanler, of New York, alluding to Mr. Stevens' desire to have the joint resolution passed on the day of its introduction, before the sun went down, said: "Sir, this measure, if passed, will tend to obscure the sun from which the liberties of this country derive their nourishment and life, the brilliant orb, the Constitution, whose light has spread itself to the farthest ends of the earth. The vital principle of that Constitution, the soul of its being, is that balance of power between the States which insures individual liberty to every citizen of each State, and harmony among all the States of the Union.

"I affirm, sir, that the discussion of this subject in the Constitutional Convention of 1787 was conducted in a spirit worthy of a great people, and resulted in the noble instrument under whose authority we now live. That era furnishes us a sad comparison with the present epoch, when it may well be said that our Rome has 'lost the breed of noble bloods,' and when, so far as the agitation of these fanatical and partisan questions is concerned, reason seems to have 'fled to brutish beasts.' How differently and with what wise moderation did the framers of the Constitution act! No narrow and fanatical partisanship marks their opinions or their acts."

After reading an extract from Curtis' History of the Constitution, Mr. Chanler, contrasting former legislation with the present on the subject of suffrage, said: "From the above historical statement, it will be found that the framers of the Constitution considered the question of suffrage of so vital importance in fixing the balance of power between the States, that it was, after full discussion in Congress by the whole body, referred to a select committee of one from each State, again reported and fully discussed, and then referred to a committee of five, whose thorough examination of the subject gave rise to new difficulties, and caused the matter to be referred to another committee of one member from each State. All differences were compromised in a spirit of patriotism and justice. How different is all this from the hasty partisan legislation on this very suffrage question by the present Congress!

"A caucus met before Congress organized, and chalked out a line of policy and action for the Republican party on the floor of Congress. The whole matter of reconstruction was referred to a grinding committee, whose dictation should govern Congress in every measure brought before it for consideration. Is this wise, just, or reasonable? I hold that this resolution is too narrow to be of use and too weak to last. It will totter to an untimely grave, and hobble, a feeble and contemptible instrument, from this Congress to every State Legislature to which it may be submitted, to be rejected for its feebleness in a time like this, amid the overwhelming issues which agitate this country."

Mr. Farnsworth, of Illinois, remarked: "It is necessary, it seems to me, that whatever constitutional provision we may make should be made clear, manifest, certain. If possible, we should make it enforce itself, so that by no cunningly-devised scheme or shift can they nullify it. It seems to me that the resolution reported by the joint Committee on Reconstruction is not so clear as it ought to be; I am afraid that it will be worthless. A State may enact that a man shall not exercise the elective franchise except he can read and write, making that law apply equally to the whites and blacks, and then may also enact that a black man shall not learn to read and write, exclude him from their schools, and make it a penal offense to instruct or to teach him, and thus prevent his qualifying to exercise the elective franchise according to the State law. And they may do in regard to the elective franchise just what they are doing now in regard to slavery. They may provide that no man shall exercise the elective franchise who has been guilty of a crime, and then they may denounce these men as guilty of a crime for every little, imaginary, petty offense. They may declare that no man shall exercise the right of voting who has not a regular business or occupation by which he may obtain a livelihood, and then they may declare that the black man has no settled occupation and no business. It seems to me, therefore, necessary that we should, by some provision in this amendment, settle this beyond a peradventure, so that none of these shifts or devices may defeat the purpose of the enactment."

Mr. Farnsworth was in favor of more radical remedies: "I protest here that I will not accept any such constitutional amendment as this as a substitute for that full measure of justice which it is our duty to mete out. I will not promise that hereafter I will not propose, and vote for, and advocate with whatever power I possess, a measure which will give to all the people of the States that which is their due. By no vote of mine shall there be incorporated in the Constitution a provision which shall, even by implication, declare that a State may disfranchise any portion of its citizens on account of race or color. We have no right to give our countenance to any such injustice. All provisions in reference to representation which are based upon any other principle than that of the people of this country, who are the subjects of government, have the right to vote and to be represented, are false in principle. Such a measure may, perhaps, answer for a temporary expedient, but it will not do as a fundamental rule to be embodied in the Constitution for the people of this country to live by. I deny that a State has the right to disfranchise a majority or even a minority of its citizens because of class or race. And I say that that provision of the Constitution which makes it the duty of the General Government to 'guarantee to every State in this Union a republican form of government' ought to be taken into consideration by this Congress and enforced. Does a State that denies the elective franchise to one-half of its citizens possess a republican form of government? Where a large portion of the citizens of a State—the men who are required to pay taxes and perform military duty, to contribute their money and their strength in support of the Government—are denied the elective franchise, is that a republican form of government? I say that it is a libel upon republicanism; it is not a republican form of government; it is neither republican in form nor in substance."

Mr. Baker, of Illinois, although anxious to have an amendment of the Constitution "achieving the general purpose of supplying a more just basis of representation," saw points of objection to the proposition before the House, some of which had been raised by previous speakers. He said: "I am reluctant to indorse an amendment to the Constitution framed in this day of growing liberty, framed by the party of progress, intended to make representative power in this Government correspond with the quantum of political justice on which it is based, and yet which leaves any State in the Union perfectly free to narrow her suffrage to any extent she pleases, imposing proprietary and other disqualifying tests, and still strengthening her aristocratic power in the Government by the full count of her disfranchised people, provided only she steers clear of a test based on race or color."

Mr. Jenckes was desirous of having a more just and comprehensive enactment than the one proposed: "In my judgment," said he, "justice requires that the qualification of electors for members of this House and for electors of President and Vice-President of the United States—in other words, for the two popular branches of this great Government—should be defined in the fundamental law. Upon this point let me quote the words of Madison, written in his mature years to a distinguished son of the republic seeking advice from him. He says: 'The right of suffrage, the rule of apportioning representation, and the mode of appointing to and removing from office, are fundamentals in a free government, and ought to be fixed by the Constitution.'

"Certainly, sir, it is less difficult, in a Congress composed of less than three hundred men, to agree to a proposition which will meet the views of the whole country on this question of suffrage than to adopt a proposition which, when submitted to and adopted by the requisite number of States, must be carried into effect by as many Legislatures as there are States, and in a different manner by each, and which, in being carried into effect, must be acted upon by as many thousands of men in State conventions and Legislatures as there are hundreds in this Congress.

"There is no equality, and there can be no equality, in the proposed amendment. It seems to me, therefore, if we undertake to amend the fundamental law at all in this respect, we ought to agree upon what should be the qualification of voters for members of this House, embodying them in the proposed amendments to submit to the Legislatures of the States. Then there would be a definite proposition; and that, I believe, if it emanated from this House, would have substantial equality and justice—would have the elements of equality and uniformity, and be enforced without difficulty in every State of the Union."

Referring to a mode which might be adopted for evading the legitimate results of the proposed amendment, Mr. Jenckes remarked: "I was alluding to another one. Some of the Southern States, up to the breaking out of the war, had constitutions which prescribed a property qualification. Suppose this amendment were adopted, and the State of South Carolina chose to annul the Constitution recently proclaimed and to go back to that of 1790, and that the word 'white' should be stricken out of it, I desire to ask how many freedmen, how many persons of African descent, can be found who own in fee fifty acres of land or a town lot, or who have paid a tax of three shillings sterling. As far as I can ascertain from the statistics, there would not be, if that constitution were restored and the word 'white' omitted, over five hundred additional qualified voters in that State.

"Ever since the adoption of the Constitution of 1790 down to the time of firing on Fort Sumter, South Carolina was in practical relation to this Government as a State of this Union. She had been considered as having a republican form of government, and that which we had guaranteed as such for many years we would be bound to guarantee to her hereafter. Stronger than ever this oligarchy would be enthroned upon their old seat of power, not upheld merely by slaves beneath it, but by the power of the General Government above and around it. She might make any of the discriminations which I have suggested, of age, of residence, of previous servitude, and of ignorance or poverty."

Mr. Trimble, of Kentucky, was "exceedingly gratified at the disposition manifested among the party in opposition here, by reason of their own differences of opinion, to allow an opportunity to us to present our objections to the measure now under consideration. This subject of amending the Constitution under which we have lived so long, so happily, and so prosperously, is one of great moment; and while I have some confidence in the ability and capacity of some of the friends on the opposite side to make a constitution, yet I prefer the Constitution as made by our fathers eighty years ago.

"In my opinion, the amendment proposed is in violation of the reserved rights of the people of the States under that instrument. The object and purpose of this resolution is to enfranchise a million men in this country whom no political party in this country ever had the boldness to propose the enfranchisment of prior to the present session of Congress. I remember that, in 1860 and 1861, the party known in this country as the Union party took the ground, from one end of the country to the other, that neither Congress nor the people of the States had the power, under the Constitution of the United States, to interfere with slavery in the States where it existed; much less, sir, did they claim the power not only to destroy it, but to strike down the provisions of the Constitution that protected me and my constituents in our right to our property. Sir, there was an amendment submitted then for the purpose of peace, for the purpose of restoring peace and quiet throughout the country. It met, at the time, my hearty support, and I regret, from the bottom of my heart, that the people, North, South, East, and West, did not agree to that proposition, and make it part and parcel of the Constitution. I refer to the amendment proposed in 1861, declaring that Congress should never thereafter interfere with the question of slavery in the States.

"Sir, it is a well-established principle that no one should be permitted to take advantage of his own wrong. If the party in power have succeeded in freeing the slaves of the South, ought they not, at least, to allow the Southern States to enjoy the increased representation to which, according to the rule established by the Constitution, they are now entitled? Or, if the Northern States sincerely desire that the negroes of the South shall vote and shall be represented in Congress, let them transport those negroes to the North and take them under their guardianship; they are welcome to them.

"I believe that the people of Kentucky, whom I in part represent, and I have no doubt the people of the whole South, will submit in good faith to the constitutional amendment abolishing slavery. While they may believe that the amendment is revolutionary and unjust, in violation of the rights of Kentucky and the South, still the Southern States, having in a way yielded up this question, for representation and peace, they will stand by the Constitution as amended."

Finally, Mr. Trimble presented the following argument against the measure: "This proposition is a direct attack upon the President of the United States; it is a direct attack upon the doctrines and principles taught by that distinguished man now holding the presidential chair. This amendment is in violation, in my judgment, of every principle that that man has held from his boyhood up to the present hour. Sir, the President of the United States does not believe that the Congress of the United States has the right, or that the people have the right, to strike down the inalienable right of the States to settle for themselves who shall be clothed with that high privilege—suffrage."

The subject being resumed on the following day, January 24th, Mr. Lawrence, of Ohio, addressed the House, premising his remarks by a motion that the resolution and amendments be recommitted to the Committee on Reconstruction, "with instructions to report an amendment to the Constitution which shall, first, apportion direct taxes among the States according to property in each; and which shall, second, apportion Representatives among the States on the basis of adult male voters who may be citizens of the United States."

He argued that "the rule which gave representation to three-fifths of the slave population was wrong in principle, and unjust in practical results. It was purely arbitrary, the result of compromise, and not of fixed political principles, or of any standard of abstract justice. If slavery was a just element of political strength, I know of no rule which could properly divide it into 'fractional quantities;' if it was not a just element of political strength, I know of no rule which could properly give it 'fractional power.'

"The basis of representation was unjust in practical results, because it gave to chattel slavery political power—a power accorded to no other species of property—thus making what the slave States regarded as wealth an element of political strength."

After having given a statistical table showing how representation was apportioned among the several States having free and slave population, Mr. Lawrence deduced the following facts: "New Hampshire, with a white population of 325,579, has but three Representatives, while Louisiana, with a white population of 357,629, had five. California, with a white population of 323,177, has but three Representatives, while Mississippi, with a similar population of 353,901, had five. In South Carolina 72,847 white persons had one Representative, while the ratio of representation is one for 127,000 persons.

"Under this mode of apportionment, the late slave States had eighteen Representatives, by the census of 1860, more than their just share, if based on free population. The whole political power of Ohio was counterbalanced by slave representation. It was equal to two-thirds of all the representation from New England. In South Carolina 14,569 votes carried as much political power as 25,400 in the free States."

Freedom having been given to the slaves, "the effect will be, so soon as lawful State Governments are created in the rebel States, to largely increase their representation in Congress and the Electoral College. The slave population, by the census of 1860, was 3,950,531. Three-fifths of this, or 2,370,318, has heretofore entered into the basis of representation. Now, the additional 1,580,213 is to be added to that basis. This will give ten additional Representatives to the late slave States—in all twenty-eight more than their just proportion upon a basis excluding the late slaves. If this injustice can be tolerated and perpetuated, and the late rebel States shall soon be admitted to representation, they will enjoy as the reward of their perfidy and treason an increased political power. This will reward traitors with a liberal premium for treason."

As to the proper time for amending the Constitution, Mr. Lawrence said: "But if ever there could be a time for making fundamental changes in our organic law, and ingrafting on it irreversible guarantees, that time is now. The events of the past four years demonstrate their necessity, and our security for the future imperatively demands them at our hands. The great events which have transpired, and the altered circumstances that surround us, admonish us that we will be recreant to our trusts if we fail to inscribe justice on the Constitution, and fortify it against the encroachments of treason, so that it shall be eternal. One of the elements of our past misfortunes, and which gave power for evil to the enemies who assailed us in this temple, was unequal and unjust representation—political power wielded by a dominant class, augmented by concessions on behalf of a disfranchised and servile race, insultingly declared almost in the very citadel of national justice as having no rights which a white man was bound to respect. By this amendment we strike down the iniquity of one class wielding political power for another, and arrogant because in the exercise of unjust power."

Maintaining that representation should be based upon suffrage, Mr. Lawrence said: "The reason which conclusively justifies it is, that a people declared by law, if in fact unprepared for suffrage, should not be represented as an element of power by those interested in forever keeping them unprepared. But children never can be qualified and competent depositaries of political power, and, therefore, should not enter into the basis of representation. It never has been deemed necessary for the protection of females that they should be regarded as an element of political power, and hence they should not be an element of representation. If the necessity shall come, or if our sense of justice should so change as to enfranchise adult females, it will be time enough then to make them a basis of representation."

Mr. Shellabarger, of Ohio, though having "fifteen times as much respect for the opinions of the Committee on Reconstruction" as for his own, yet suggested the following as objections to their report:

"1. It contemplates and provides for, and in that way, taken by itself, authorizes the States to wholly disfranchise entire races of its people, and that, too, whether that race be white or black, Saxon, Celtic, or Caucasian, and without regard to their numbers or proportion to the entire population of the State.

"2. It is a declaration made in the Constitution of the only great and free republic in the world, that it is permissible and right to deny to the races of men all their political rights, and that it is permissible to make them the hewers of wood and drawers of water, the mud-sills of society, provided only you do not ask to have these disfranchised races represented in that Government, provided you wholly ignore them in the State. The moral teaching of the clause offends the free and just spirit of the age, violates the foundation principles of our own Government, and is intrinsically wrong.

"3. The clause, by being inserted into the Constitution, and being made the companion of its other clauses, thereby construes and gives new meanings to those other clauses; and it thus lets down and spoils the free spirit and sense of the Constitution. Associated with that clause relating to the States being 'republican,' it makes it read thus: 'The United States shall guarantee to every State in this Union a republican form of government;' provided, however, that a government shall be deemed to be republican when whole races of its people are wholly disfranchised, unrepresented, and ignored.

"4. The report of the committee imposes no adequate restraint upon this disfranchisement of races and creation of oligarchies in the States, because after a race is disfranchised in a State it gives to one vote cast in such State by the ruling race just the same power as a vote has in a State where no one is disfranchised.

"5. These words of the amendment, to-wit, 'denied or abridged on account of color,' admit of dangerous construction, and also of an evasion of the avowed intent of the committee. Thus, for example, the African race may, in fact, be disfranchised in the States, and yet enumerated as part of the basis of representation, by means of a provision disfranchising all who were slaves, or all whose ancestors were slaves.

"6. The pending proposition of the committee is a radical departure from the principles of representative republican government, in this, that it does not provide for nor secure the absolute political equality of the people, or, relatively, of the States. It does not secure to each vote throughout the Government absolute equality in its governing force. It, for example, permits twenty-five thousand votes in New York city to elect two members of Congress, provided one-half of its population should happen to be foreigners unnaturalized, and not electors of the State, whom the law deems unfit to vote; whereas, twenty-five thousand votes in Ohio would elect but one member of Congress, provided her citizens were all Americans instead of foreigners."

Mr. Eliot submitted an amendment to the effect that population should be the basis of representation, and that "the elective franchise shall not be denied or abridged in any State on account of race or color." He stated the following grounds of objection to the resolution offered by the committee: "First, the amendment as it is now reported from the committee is objectionable, to my mind, because it admits by implication that a State has the right to disfranchise large masses of its citizens. No man can show that in that Constitution which the fathers made, and under which we have lived, the right is recognized in any State to disfranchise large masses of its citizens because of race. And I do not want now, at this day, that the Congress of the United States, for the purpose of effecting a practical good, shall put into the Constitution of the land any language which would seem to recognize that right.

"The next objection I have to the amendment is this: that it enables a State, consistently with its provisions, by making the right to vote depend upon a property qualification, to exclude large classes of men of both races. A State may legislate in such a way as to be, in fact, an oligarchy, and not a republican State. South Carolina may legislate so as to provide that no man shall have the right to vote unless he possesses an annual income of $1,000, and holds real estate to the amount of five hundred acres. Every one sees that that would exclude multitudes of all classes of citizens, making the State no longer republican, but oligarchical. Yet gentlemen say that under the Constitution Congress is bound to see to it that each State shall have a republican form of government.

"The third objection I have to this amendment is, that it controls by implication that power; because, while the Constitution now says that Congress shall guarantee to every State a republican form of government, this amendment, as reported by the committee, admits by implication that, although a State may so legislate as to exclude these multitudes of men, not on account of race or color, but on account of property, yet, nevertheless, she would have a republican form of government, and that Congress will not and ought not to interfere."

Mr. Pike, of Maine, had, on the assembling of Congress after the holidays, offered a resolution expressing the idea contained in the report of the committee, but on reflection had come to the conclusion that the resolution would not accomplish the purpose desired. He stated his reasons for changing his opinion. He thought that the provisions of the proposed amendment might be evaded. "Suppose," said he, "this constitutional amendment in full force, and a State should provide that the right of suffrage should not be exercised by any person who had been a slave, or who was the descendant of a slave, whatever his race or color. I submit that it is a serious matter of doubt whether or not that simple provision would not be sufficient to defeat this constitutional amendment which we here so laboriously enact and submit to the States."

Mr. Conkling thought that this criticism could have no practical importance, from the fact that the proposed amendment was to operate in this country, where one race, and only one, has been held in servitude.

Mr. Pike replied: "In no State in the South has slavery been confined to any one race. So far as I am acquainted with their statutes, in no State has slavery been confined to the African race. I know of no slave statute, and I have examined the matter with some care, which says that Africans alone shall be slaves. So much for race. As to color, it was a common thing throughout the whole South to advertise runaway slaves as having light hair and blue eyes, and all the indications of the Caucasian race, and 'passing themselves off for white men.' I say further to the honorable gentleman from New York, that well-authenticated instances exist in every slave State where men of Caucasian descent, of Anglo-Saxon blood, have been confined in slavery, and they and their posterity held as slaves; so that not only free blacks were found every-where, but white slaves also abounded."

Mr. Kelley, who next addressed the House, also brought proof to controvert the "hasty assertion" that but one race had been enslaved: "The assertion that white persons have been sold into slavery does not depend on common report, but is proven by the reports of the superior courts of almost every Southern State. One poor German woman, who had arrived in our country at thirteen years of age, was released from slavery by the Supreme Court of Louisiana, but not until she had become the mother of three mulatto children, her owner having mated her with one of his darker slaves. Toward the close of the last century, the Supreme Court of New Jersey decided that American Indians could be reduced to and legally held in slavery. And so long ago as 1741 white slave women were so common in North Carolina, that the Legislature passed a law dooming to slavery the child of every 'white servant woman' born of an Indian father."

Mr. Kelley thought that the enforcement of this long-dormant power of the Constitution would be for the benefit not merely of the poor, the ignorant, and the weak, but also of the wise, "the strong, and the wealthy of our country." "There is now pending," said he, "before the Legislature of regenerated and, as gentlemen would have us believe, reconstructed Virginia, a bill to require five years' residence on the part of citizens of other States who may invest their capital and settle within the sacred limits of the Old Dominion before they can acquire citizenship. If they may pass a limitation of five years, why may they not pass a limitation of fifty? Why will not any limitation that comes within the ordinary duration of human life be admissible?"

Mr. Bromwell, obtaining the floor, inquired whether the question was in such condition that any amendment or substitute could be offered. The Speaker replied: "Six amendments are pending now. The only one that could be offered would be to amend the amendment of the gentleman from Pennsylvania, [Mr. Stevens,] which was, to add the word 'therein' in the fifteenth line. No other amendment would be in order now, the whole legislative power to amend being exhausted."

Mr. Bromwell had desired to offer an amendment which, in his opinion, would obviate many of the objections to pending joint resolution, and the amendments thereto; but the way not being open for this, he addressed the House in a brief speech. He said: "When this amendment was introduced, on last Monday morning, the differences of opinion which have been developed in reference to the principles of the amendment were not anticipated. But to-day we see that it has, so far, not an advocate upon this floor. Such may be the result with every amendment which may be presented. It is difficult to see, among all the amendments which are now pending, any one of them, or any combination of them, that will meet the desire of the majority, not to say two-thirds of this House. I apprehend that the members of this House desire to act so as to secure the support of a proper majority here. I apprehend, also, that they desire to make this amendment such that it will meet with the sanction of a sufficient number of the States of the Union to make it effectual. Now, sir, it is in vain for this Congress to launch an amendment which shall die on the road through the Legislatures."

Notwithstanding the difficulties in the way of all the plans proposed, Mr. Bromwell was heartily in favor of modifying the basis of representation. "I think," said he, "seventy years is long enough for fifteen, twenty, or thirty Representatives to sit here and make laws to apply to Northern people, with no constituencies behind them. I think it has been seen long enough that a large number of persons called property, made property by the laws of the States, shall give to the oligarchs of those particular districts of country the right to outvote the independent men of the North, of the free States, where some approximation has been made to securing God-given rights to all inhabitants. I think that it is wrong that the further a State recedes from common right and common justice the more power the oligarchy which controls it shall grasp in their hands; and I desire that this amendment shall be made so that it shall bear down upon that abuse with the crushing power of three-fourths of the legislatures of the Union."

After the House had heard so many objectors to the basis of representation, as proposed by the committee, Mr. Cook, of Illinois, took the floor in favor of the measure. He said: "We have now, as I believe, the golden opportunity to remedy this evil which will never come again to the men of this generation. The system of slavery has fallen. The States whose representation was increased by it have, with two or three exceptions, destroyed their loyal and legal State governments, and now seek reconstruction. The adoption of this amendment by the States lately in rebellion should be one of the guarantees to be insisted upon as a condition precedent to their taking equal authority and rank in the Union with the loyal States."

To the proposition that the basis of representation should be voters only, Mr. Cook presented the following objections:

"1. It is difficult to enumerate voters accurately; their qualifications are fixed by State laws. We can not send Federal officers into every State to adjudicate, in disputed cases, the rights of those claiming to be voters under the State laws, as we should have to do.

"2. It would not be just; the voters of the country are unequally distributed. The old States have fewer, the new States more, voters according to the white population. In other words, there is a greater proportion of women and children in the old States. These should be and are represented. They are represented, in the true sense of that word, by their fathers and brothers. The man who represents them does so really and practically, and not by legal fiction, like the man who represents 'three-fifths of all other persons.'

"3. It takes from the basis of representation all unnaturalized foreigners. I do not wish to discuss the question whether this would be judicious or not, but I do not want a measure of this almost supreme importance loaded down with these questions, and its passage jeopardized by the incorporation of provisions which would render it so liable to attack and misrepresentation."

Mr. Cook referred as follows to some objections urged against the basis of representation proposed by the Reconstruction Committee: "It is said that the Southern States may impose a property qualification, and so exclude the negroes, not on account of race or color, but for want of a property qualification, or that they might provide for a qualification of intelligence, and so disfranchise the negroes because they could not read or write, and still enumerate them. To do this they must first repeal all the laws now denying suffrage to negroes; and, second, provide qualifications which will disfranchise half their white voters; two things neither of which will, in any human probability, occur. And in the event that it was possible that both these measures should be adopted, and all the blacks and half the whites disqualified, it would become a grave question whether the provision of the Constitution which requires the United States to guarantee to each State a republican form of government would not authorize the Government to rectify so gross a wrong. There is no measure to which fanciful objections may not be urged; but I believe this to be the least objectionable of any measure which has been suggested to meet this evil. But above all, I am well persuaded that it is the only measure that can meet the approval of three-fourths of the States; consequently, that this is the only practical measure before the House."

Mr. Marshall, of Illinois, declared the proposition, as reported by the committee, to be "wholly untenable, is monstrous, absurd, damnable in its provisions, a greater wrong and outrage on the black race than any thing that has ever been advocated by others."

He thus set forth the measure in the light of injustice to the negro: "The gentlemen who report it profess to be, and doubtless are, the peculiar advocates of the African race. I wish to ask them upon what principle of justice, upon what principle of free government, they have provided that if, after this amendment is adopted, South Carolina, Mississippi, or any other State shall adopt a provision that all white men over twenty-one years of age shall be voters, and all black men who have two hundred dollars' worth of property, and if there shall be ten thousand legal black voters in such State, upon what principle will you place in the Constitution of the United States a provision which would deprive these ten thousand legal black voters of any representation upon the floor of Congress, or of being considered in the basis of representation? And I wish to ask the honorable gentleman who reported this amendment if that is not the effect and result of the amendment reported from the committee."

In reference to the time and place of inaugurating constitutional amendments, Mr. Marshall used the following language: "If any amendments are necessary to the Constitution of our country, this is not the time, and more especially is this not the place, to inaugurate such amendments. I believe, notwithstanding the conceded wisdom, ability, and virtue of this House, that the fathers who framed our glorious Constitution were wiser, better, and nobler than we are; yet every day we have offered here some dozen or twenty proposed amendments to the Constitution, offered as if we were discussing resolutions in a town meeting."

Among the propositions before the House relating to this subject, was an amendment proposed by Mr. Schenck, of Ohio, pro-

Eng^d by G.E. Perine & Co N York

Robt. C. Schenck

ROBERT C. SCHENCK

[illegible]ESENTATIVE FROM OHIO

viding that representation should be based upon "the number of male citizens of the United States over twenty-one years of age, having the qualifications requisite for electors of the most numerous branch of the State legislature."

Mr. Schenck addressed the House, and thus gave a history of his own connection with the measure: "At a very early day in this session, I was one of those disposed to ask the attention of Congress to the subject, to propose in proper form the submission of the question to the Legislatures of the several States. On the first day of the session, on the 4th of December last, as soon as the House was organized, I gave notice that I would on the next, or some succeeding day, introduce a proposition to amend the Constitution. On the ensuing day I did accordingly present a joint resolution. It stands as House Resolution No. 1 of the session.

"In that I propose representation hereafter shall be based upon suffrage. I propose that representation shall be apportioned among the several States of the Union according to the number of voters having qualifications requisite for electors of the most numerous branch of the Legislature of the State where they reside, following in this the language of the Constitution; these voters, however, to be further limited in their descriptions and definitions as being male citizens of the United States over twenty-one years of age. Now, whether the proposition be a good one or not; whether the limitation be such as should commend itself to the masses of our people, I will not for the present inquire. I will only remark they have seemed to me to embrace as many qualifications as we ought to include when we are going to lay down a new organic law on this subject."

An objection urged by Mr. Schenck against the plan proposed by the committee was, that it failed to offer inducements for a gradual enfranchisement of the negro. He said: "Now, sir, I am not one of those who entertain Utopian ideas in relation, not merely to the progress, but to the immediate change of sentiment, opinions, and practice among the people of those States that have so lately been slave States, and so recently in rebellion. I believe that, like all other people, their growth toward good and right and free institutions must necessarily be gradual; and if we pass the amendment which I have proposed, or any thing similar to it, and say to them, 'You shall have representation proportioned to the portion of your population to which you extend this inestimable franchise,' my belief is that they will not, on the next day after it becomes a part of the organic law of the United States, at once enfranchise all the negroes in their midst. I am not sure that they ought to do it; but we are dealing with the matter now as it presents itself as a practical question. What will they probably do? My belief is, that if you persuade them to do right, if you hold out to them an inducement for letting their negroes vote, and striking out these disqualifications and putting all upon the basis of manhood, they will probably begin, after the amendment becomes part of the organic law, by extending this right to those who have acquired certain property; perhaps they will also extend it, after awhile, to those who have certain qualifications of education. However they may proceed, whether rapidly or slowly, it will be a work of progress and a work of time. But by this amendment you would say to them, 'We do not want you to enter upon any such gradual bringing up of these people to the level plain of right to be enjoyed by them equally with others of other races in your midst.' We say to them, 'You may enfranchise one-third or one-fourth of your people who are black and deprived of the privilege of voting by introducing the qualification of property, up to which one-third or one-fourth may come; you may introduce a qualification of education, up to which a number of them may come; but that will all be of no value; so long as there is any denial or any abridgement of the right to vote of a single man on account of his race or color, you shall have no part of the population of that race or color counted to measure to you your share of representation.'

"Now, I will not go into the abstract question whether they ought to enfranchise the negroes at once or not; I will not go into the question of how soon they ought to do it as a matter of expediency; I say that, in all human probability, when they come to enfranchise, if they do it at all, this portion of their population, they will do it gradually; yet, by this amendment, as it comes from the committee, you say that they shall not be represented for any part of it at all till they completely enfranchise them and put them on the same footing with the white population."

In conclusion, Mr. Schenck remarked: "New England, if she should even lose a vote, or two votes, or a fraction of a vote, can not afford, any more than Ohio or Indiana, or any other of those States can, having these particular objections to the scheme, to let the opportunity go by now and not introduce a general amendment which will remedy the one great evil under which we are all laboring together. I hold that Ohio must give up her objections on account of her negro population; that the North-western States must give up their objections on account of the fact that they are permitting persons to vote who are not yet citizens of the United States. Those persons would have to wait, 'to tarry at Jericho until their beards are grown.' I hold that New England must give up her objections; and, if we are to amend the organic law at all, we must do it by uniting upon a common principle, a common sympathy, a common feeling, at least on this side of the House, upon which the entire responsibility is thrown, acting harmoniously, and adopting such an amendment to the organic law as shall be entirely democratic and fair in all its scope and action upon all the people of the States of this Union."

The discussion was continued on the day following, Mr. Eldridge, of Wisconsin, having the floor for the first speech. After having expressed his satisfaction that the sun was allowed to go down on the deliberations upon this resolution, he confessed himself opposed to the amendment of the Constitution. He said: "I believe that this is not the time for its amendment, and I believe, further, that there are other States than those represented upon this floor which are entitled to deliberate with us on that question, and to that point I shall mainly address the remarks which I have to make at this time."

He made a protracted speech on the general subject of reconstruction. At the close of his remarks, he said: "It would much more comport with the dignity and sense of justice of the American Congress to let the legally elected members from the Southern States be admitted, and participate in the proceedings and debates, especially in matters of so great importance as a change in our organic law. Let us have a representation for our whole country. Wherever the American flag floats, from the St. Lawrence to the Gulf of Mexico—wherever the Star-spangled Banner waves—that is our country. And let us legislate as Americans, as Representatives of our whole country, in a spirit of justice, liberality, and patriotism, and we will again have one country."

Mr. Higby, of California, was opposed to the joint resolution from the fact that the proviso in the proposed amendment is in conflict with that portion of the Constitution which requires that "the United States shall guarantee to every State in this Union a republican form of government." "I say it," said he, "without fear or favor, that that amendment will allow any State government in its organization to exclude one-half of its population from the right of suffrage; and I say such State governments will not be republican in form."

In a conversation which ensued with some members, Mr. Higby maintained that no State excluding any class of citizens on account of race or color was republican in form. "I do not believe," said he, "there is a single State in the Union, except it may be one of the New England States, which is an exception to that general rule."

Mr. Hill, of Indiana, asked whether the gentleman would favor the House with his opinion as to what would be a republican form of government.

Mr. Higby was sorry that the gentleman had lived to his time of life, and obtained a position as the Representative of a large constituency, without finding out what a republican form of government is. "I will ask the gentleman," said he, "if he thinks that those States that have excluded and disfranchised more than half of their native population have a republican form of government?"

"In my opinion," said Mr. Hill, "when the framers of the Constitution placed in that instrument the declaration or the provision that the Government of the United States would guarantee to each State a republican form of government, they spoke with reference to such governments as then existed, and such as those same framers recognized for a long time afterward as republican governments."

"Well, that is a very good answer," said Mr. Higby. "It is an answer from a stand-point seventy-five years ago. I speak from the stand-point of the present time."

Mr. Higby desired that the joint resolution should go back to the committee. He said: "I do not wish it disposed of here, to be voted down. I want, if it is possible, that it shall be so framed that it shall receive the full constitutional majority required, and be a proposition that shall operate with full force in all those

States that now have a great population excluded from the rights of citizenship."

"If the gentleman proposes," said Mr. Stevens, "to send it back to the committee without instructions, I would ask him what we are to do. There are not quite as many views upon this floor as there are members; but the number lacks very little of it. And how are we to gather up all those views spread through all this discussion, and accommodate all, when each view would now probably receive from one to three votes in its favor?"

"I have only this to say," replied Mr. Higby: "with my views of the Constitution, I never can vote for this proposition with this proviso in its present language. I say that it gives a power to the States to make governments that are not republican in form."

"I say to my friend," said Mr. Stevens, "that if I thought, that by any fair construction of language, such an interpretation could be given as he gives, I would vote against it myself; but I do not believe there is any thing in that objection."

Mr. Bingham took the floor in favor of the proposed joint resolution. In "giving this and other amendments to the Constitution my support," said he, "I do not subject myself to the gratuitous imputation of a want of reverence either for the Constitution or its illustrious founders. I beg leave, at all events, to say, with all possible respect for that gentleman, that I do not recognize the right of any man upon this floor, who was a representative of that party which denied the right to defend the Constitution of his country by arms against armed rebellion, to become my accuser.

"In seeking to amend, not to mar, the Constitution of the United States, we ought to have regard to every express or implied limitation upon our power imposed by that great instrument. When gentlemen object to amending the Constitution, when they talk sneeringly about tinkering with the Constitution, they do not remember that it is one of the express provisions of that instrument that Congress shall have power to propose amendments to the Legislatures of the several States. Do gentlemen mean, by the logic to which we have listened for the past five days on this subject of our right to amend, that we are not to add any thing to the Constitution, and that we are to take nothing from it? I prefer to follow, in this supreme hour of the nation's trial, the lead of a wiser and nobler spirit, who, by common consent, was called, while he lived, 'the Father of his Country,' and, now that he is dead, is still reverenced as 'the Father of his Country,' and to be hailed, I trust, by the millions of the future who are to people this land of ours as 'the Father of his Country.' In his Farewell Address, his last official utterance, Washington used these significant words, which I repeat to-day for the consideration of gentlemen: "The basis of our political systems is the right of the people to make and to alter their constitutions of government.' We propose, sir, simply to act in accordance with this suggestion of Washington. We propose, in presenting these amendments, to alter, in so far as the changed condition of the country requires, the fundamental law, in order to secure the safety of the republic and furnish better guarantees in the future for the rights of each and all.

"The question that underlies this controversy is this: whether we will stand by the Constitution in its original intent and spirit, or, like cravens, abandon it. I assert it here to-day, without fear of contradiction, that the amendment pending before this House is an amendment conforming exactly to the spirit of the Constitution, and according to the declared intent of its framers.

"My friend from California [Mr. Higby] has informed us that there are one hundred thousand more free colored citizens of the United States in the State of Mississippi to-day than there are of white citizens; that there are one hundred thousand more free colored citizens of the United States in South Carolina than there are of white citizens; and then we are gravely told that we must not press this amendment, because we are abandoning the Constitution and the intent of our fathers. That is a new discovery, one for which the Democracy ought to take out letters patent, that it was ever intended that a minority of free citizens should disfranchise the majority of free male citizens, of full age, in any State of the Union! For myself, I will never consent to it."

In answer to the objection that the proviso in the proposed amendment seemed to acknowledge the right to deny or abridge the elective franchise on account of race or color, Mr. Bingham said: "I beg the gentleman to consider that a grant of power by implication can not be raised by a law which only imposes a penalty, and nothing but a penalty, for a non-performance of a duty or the violation of a right. Within the last hundred years, in no country where the common law obtains, I venture to say, has any implication of a grant of power ever been held to be raised by such a law, and especially an implied power, to do an act expressly prohibited by the same law. The guarantee of your Constitution, that the people shall elect their Representatives in the several States, can not be set aside or impaired by inserting in your Constitution, as a penalty for disregarding it, the provision that the majority of a State that denies the equal rights of the minority shall suffer a loss of political power.

"I have endeavored to show that the words of the Constitution, the people of 'the States shall choose their Representatives,' is an express guarantee that a majority of the free male citizens of the United States in every State of this Union, being of full age, shall have the political power subject to the equal right of suffrage in the minority of free male citizens of full age. There is a further guarantee in the Constitution of a republican form of government to every State, which I take to mean that the majority of the free male citizens in every State shall have the political power. I submit to my friend that this proviso is nothing but a penalty for a violation on the part of the people of any State of the political right or franchise guaranteed by the Constitution to their free male fellow-citizens of full age.

"The guarantee in the first article of the second section of the Constitution, rightly interpreted, is, as I claim, this: that the majority of the male citizens of the United States, of full age, in each State, shall forever exercise the political power of the State with this limitation: that they shall never by caste legislation impose disabilities upon one class of free male citizens to the denial or abridgement of equal rights. The further provision is, that the United States shall guarantee to each State a republican form of government, which means that the majority of male citizens, of full age, in each State, shall govern, not, however, in violation of the Constitution of the United States or of the rights of the minority."

In closing his address, Mr. Bingham said: "I pray gentlemen to consider long before they reject this proviso. It may not be the best that the wisest head in this House can conceive of, but I ask gentlemen to consider that the rule of statesmanship is to take the best attainable essential good which is at our command. The reason why I support the proposed amendment is, that I believe it essential and attainable. I do not dare to say that it could not be improved. I do dare to say that it is in aid of the existing grants and guarantees of the Constitution of my country, that it is simply a penalty to be inflicted upon the States for a specific disregard in the future of those wise and just and humane grants 'to the people' to elect their Representatives and maintain a republican government in each State.

"Mr. Speaker, the republic is great; it is great in its domain, equal in extent to continental Europe, abounding in productions of every zone, broad enough and fertile enough to furnish bread and homes to three hundred million freemen. The republic is great in the intelligence, thrift, industry, energy, virtue, and valor of its unconquered and unconquerable children, and great in its matchless, wise, and beneficent Constitution. I pray the Congress of the United States to propose to the people all needful amendments to the Constitution, that by their sovereign act they may crown the republic for all time with the greatness of justice."

Mr. Broomall, of Pennsylvania, presented an objection to the resolution which had not been alluded to by any gentleman on the floor. He said: "The resolution provides that whenever the elective franchise shall be denied or abridged in any State, on account of race or color, all persons of such race or color shall be excluded from the basis of representation. Now, there is a great deal of indefiniteness in both those terms, 'race' and 'color.'

"What is a race of men? Writers upon the subject of races differ very materially on this point. Some of them would make four or five races; others fifteen; and one, whom I might name, seems inclined not to limit the number short of a thousand. I myself am inclined to think that the Celtic race is a distinct one from ours. I think that any gentleman who has studied this subject attentively will at least have doubts whether or not the race that appears to have inhabited Europe in the early historic period, and has been partly dispossessed there by ours, is not a distinct race from ours.

"Again: the word 'color' is exceedingly indefinite. If we had a constitutional standard of color, that of sole-leather, for example, by which to test the State laws upon this subject, there might be less danger in incorporating this provision in the Constitution. But the term 'color' is nowhere defined in the Constitution or the law. We apply the term to persons who are of African descent, whether their color is whiter or darker than ours.

Every one who is familiar with the ethnological condition of things here in the United States, and who sees the general mixing up of colors, particularly in the Democratic portion of the country—I allude to that portion south of Mason and Dixon's line—must say with me that the word 'color' has no very distinct meaning when applied to the different peoples of the United States of America."

Two Representatives from New York—Mr. Davis and Mr. Ward—expressed opinions favorable to a modification of the basis of representation, and yet were opposed to the details of the proposition before the House.

Mr. Nicholson, of Delaware, in emphatic terms, denounced the acts of a majority of the House in attempting to amend the Constitution. "If they shall finally triumph," said he, "in the mad schemes in which they are engaged, they will succeed in converting that heretofore sacred instrument, reverenced and obeyed till the present dominant party came into power, from a bond of union to a galling yoke of oppression—a thing to be loathed and despised."

The discussion was still much protracted. Many members had an opportunity of presenting their views and opinions without adding much to the arguments for or against the measure. The power of debate, as well as "the power of amendment," seemed to have exhausted itself, and yet gentlemen continued to swell the volume of both through several days.

On Friday, January 26th, Mr. Harding, of Kentucky, made a violent political speech, ostensibly in opposition to the measure before the House. The following is an extract from his remarks:

"The Republican party have manufactured a large amount of capital out of the negro question. First they began with caution, now they draw on it as if they thought it as inexhaustible as were the widow's barrel of meal and cruse of oil. The fact that the negro question has continued so long has been owing to the great care with which the Republican party has managed it."

Mr. McKee, of Kentucky, followed. Referring to his colleague who had preceded him, he said: "I regret extremely that he has pursued the same line of policy that gentlemen belonging to the same political party have pursued ever since the idea took possession of the Government that the negro was to be a freeman. His whole speech has been made up of the negro and nothing else.

"I would like it if the amendment could go a little beyond what it does. I would like so to amend the Constitution that no man who had raised his hand against the flag should ever be allowed to participate in any of the affairs of this Government. But it is not probable that we can go that far. Let us go just as far as we can.

"Gentlemen say that they are not willing to vote for an amendment that strikes off a part of the representation of the States; they are not willing to vote for an amendment that lessens Kentucky's representation upon this floor. The whole course of my colleague's remarks on this point is as the course of his party—and I may say of the loyal party in Kentucky—has been through a great part of the war, that Kentucky is the nation, and the United States a secondary appendage to her."

Mr. Kerr, of Indiana, did not desire to be heard at length upon the main question before the House, but upon some questions incidentally connected with it. He then proceeded to discuss the question whether Congress has "the power so to regulate the suffrage as to give the right of suffrage to every male citizen of the country of twenty-one years of age." "I propose now," said he, "for a few moments, to examine this question with a somewhat extensive reference to the history of the Constitution in this connection, and if possible to arrive at a conclusion whether the honorable gentleman from Pennsylvania has given greater attention to the history of this question than the President, and whether the conclusion which he has reached is a safer one for the country, or more in harmony with the history and true intent of the Constitution, than that of the President."

Near the close of his remarks, referring to the measure before the House, Mr. Kerr remarked: "I can see but one single clear result that will follow from this amendment if it is adopted by the people of this country, and that is an effect that will inure not to the advantage of the nation, nor of any State in the Union, nor of any class or race of men in any State; but it will inure solely to the benefit and advantage of the Republican party. In my judgment, the only persons who will gain by this provision will be the now dominant party in this country. They will thereby increase their power; they will thereby degrade the South; they will reduce her representation here, and relatively increase their own representation; they will confirm the sectional supremacy of the North in the legislation and administration of the Government. They may thus compel the South to become suppliants at their feet for justice, and it may be for mercy."

Mr. Kasson, of Iowa, and Mr. Wright, of New Jersey, made extended remarks, avowedly in opposition to the measure, but dwelling, for the greater portion of their time, upon subjects remotely connected with the resolution before the House.

Discussion was resumed in the House on Monday, January 29th. The question having become much complicated by the numerous propositions to amend, the Speaker, by request of Mr. Conkling, stated the exact position of the subject before the House, and the various questions pending. The Speaker said: "The committee having reported this joint resolution, the gentleman from Pennsylvania [Mr. Stevens] moved to amend by inserting the word 'therein' after the words 'all persons,' in the last clause of the proposed amendment to the Constitution.

"Pending that motion, the gentleman from Pennsylvania [Mr. Kelley] moved an entirely new proposition in the nature of a substitute for the joint resolution reported from the joint committee, proposing an amendment to the Constitution differing from the one reported from the committee. The gentleman from Illinois [Mr. Baker] also submitted for his colleague [Mr. Ingersoll] a proposition in the nature of a substitute for the one reported from the committee, as an amendment to the amendment.

"Pending those two propositions, the gentleman from Ohio [Mr. Lawrence] moved to recommit the joint resolution to the joint committee with certain instructions. The gentleman from Massachusetts [Mr. Eliot] moved to amend the instructions, and the gentleman from Ohio [Mr. Schenck] moved to amend the amendment.

"The gentleman from Ohio [Mr. Le Blond] also moved to commit the whole subject to the Committee of the Whole on the State of the Union. The first question will, therefore, be upon the motion to commit to the Committee of the Whole, as that committee is higher in rank than the joint Committee on Reconstruction.

"Next after that will be the various motions to recommit with instructions. If all those propositions should fail, then the motion of the gentleman from Pennsylvania, [Mr. Stevens,] being for the purpose of perfecting the original proposition, will come up for consideration. Then propositions in the nature of substitutes will come up for consideration; first the amendment to the amendment, proposed by the gentleman from Illinois, [Mr. Baker,] and next the substitute amendment of the gentleman from Pennsylvania [Mr. Kelley]."

Mr. Raymond, of New York, made a speech three hours in length, in opposition to the proposed amendment to the Constitution. He discussed the general questions of reconstruction, affirming that the Southern States had resumed their functions of self-government in the Union, that they did not change their constitutional relations by making war, and that Congress should admit their Representatives by districts, receiving only loyal men as members.

The closing words of Mr. Raymond's speech excited great sensation and surprise. They were as follows: "The gigantic contest is at an end. The courage and devotion on either side which made it so terrible and so long, no longer owe a divided duty, but have become the common property of the American name, the priceless possession of the American Republic through all time to come. The dead of the contending hosts sleep beneath the soil of a common country, and under one common flag. Their hostilities are hushed, and they are the dead of the nation forever more. The victor may well exult in the victory he has achieved. Let it be our task, as it will be our highest glory, to make the vanquished, and their posterity to the latest generation, rejoice in their defeat."

Mr. Julian could not accept heartily the proposition reported by the joint committee. He thus presented what he considered a preferable plan: "Under the constitutional injunction upon the United States to guarantee a republican form of government to every State, I believe the power already exists in the nation to regulate the right of suffrage. It can only exercise this power through Congress; and Congress, of course, must decide what is a republican form of government, and when the national authority shall interpose against State action for the purpose of executing the constitutional guarantee. No one will deny the authority of Congress to decide that if a State should disfranchise one-third, one-half, or two-thirds of her citizens, such State would cease to be republican, and might be required to accept a different rule of suffrage. If Congress could intervene in such a case, it could obviously intervene in any other case in which it might deem it necessary or proper. It certainly might decide that the disfranchisement by a State of a whole race of people within her borders is inconsistent with a republican form of government, and in their behalf, and in the execution of its own authority and duty, restore them to their equal right with others to the franchise. It might decide, for example, that in North Carolina, where 631,000 citizens disfranchise 331,000, the government is not republican, and should be made so by extending the franchise. It might do the same in Virginia, where 719,000 citizens disfranchise 533,000; in Alabama, where 596,000 citizens disfranchise 437,000; in Georgia, where 591,000 citizens disfranchise 465,000; in Louisiana, where 357,000 citizens disfranchise 350,000; in Mississippi, where 353,000 citizens disfranchise 436,000; and in South Carolina, where only 291,000 citizens disfranchise 411,000. Can any man who reverences the Constitution deny either the authority or the duty of Congress to do all this in the execution of the guarantee named? Or if the 411,000 negroes in South Carolina were to organize a government, and disfranchise her 291,000 white citizens, would any body doubt the authority of Congress to pronounce such government antirepublican, and secure the ballot equally to white and black citizens, as the remedy? Or if a State should prescribe as a qualification for the ballot such an ownership of property, real or personal, as would disfranchise the great body of her people, could not Congress most undoubtedly interfere? So of an educational test, which might fix the standard of knowledge so high as to place the governing power in the hands of a select few. The power in all such cases is a reserved one in Congress, to be exercised according to its own judgment, with no accountability to any tribunal save the people; and without such power the nation would be at the mercy of as many oligarchies as there are States. It is true that the power of Congress to guarantee republican governments in the States through its intervention with the question of suffrage has not hitherto been exercised, but this certainly does not disprove the existence of such power, nor the expediency of its exercise now, under an additional and independent constitutional grant, and when a fit occasion for it has come through the madness of treason. Why temporize by adopting half-way measures and a policy of indirection? The shortest distance between two given points is a straight line. Let us follow it in so important a work as amending the Constitution.

"How do you know that the broad proposition I advocate will fail in Congress or before the people? These are revolutionary days. Whole generations of common time are now crowded into the span of a few years. Life was never before so grand and blessed an opportunity. The man mistakes his reckoning who judges either the present or the future by any political almanac of bygone years. Growth, development, progress are the expressive watchwords of the hour. Who can remember the marvelous events of the past four years, necessitated by the late war, and then predict the failure of further measures, woven into the same fabric, and born of the same inevitable logic?"

On Monday, January 30th, the proposed constitutional amendment was recommitted to the joint Committee on Reconstruction. On the following day Mr. Stevens reported back the joint resolution, with an amendment striking out the words "and direct taxes," so as to fix simply the basis of representation in Congress upon population, excluding those races or colors to which the franchise is denied or abridged.

Mr. Schenck offered a substitute making "male citizens of the United States over twenty-one years" the basis of representation. Mr. Schenck occupied a few minutes in advocating his proposition.

On the other hand, Mr. Benjamin, of Missouri, objected to the substitute as greatly to the detriment of Missouri, since it would reduce her representation in Congress from nine to four, because she has endeavored to place the Government in loyal hands by disfranchising the rebel element of that State. In doing this, she had disfranchised one-half her voters.

The previous question having been called, Mr. Stevens made the closing speech of the protracted discussion. In the opening of his speech, Mr. Stevens said: "It is true we have been informed by high authority, at the other end of the avenue, introduced through an unusual conduit, that no amendment is necessary to the Constitution as our fathers made it, and that it is better to let it stand as it is. Now, sir, I think very differently, myself, for one individual. I believe there is intrusted to this Congress a high duty, no less important and no less fraught with the weal or woe of future ages than was intrusted to the august body that made the Declaration of Independence. I believe now, if we omit to exercise that high duty, or abuse it, we shall be held to account by future generations of America, and by the whole civilized world that is in favor of freedom, and that our names will go down to posterity with some applause or with black condemnation if we do not treat the subject thoroughly, honestly, and justly in reference to every human being on this continent."

That the above paragraph may be understood, it will be necessary to state that the President of the United States himself had taken part in the discussion of the measure pending before Congress. The "unusual conduit" was the telegraph and the press—the means by which his opinions were given to Congress and the public. The President's opinions were expressed in the following paper, as read by the Clerk of the House, at the request of several members:

"The following is the substance of a conversation which took place yesterday between the President and a distinguished Senator, as telegraphed North by the agent of the Associated Press:

"The President said that he doubted the propriety at this time of making further amendments to the Constitution. One great amendment had already been made, by which slavery had forever been abolished within the limits of the United States, and a national guarantee thus given that the institution should never exist in the land. Propositions to amend the Constitution were becoming as numerous as preambles and resolutions at town meetings called to consider the most ordinary questions connected with the administration of local affairs. All this, in his opinion, had a tendency to diminish the dignity and prestige attached to the Constitution of the country, and to lessen the respect and confidence of the people in their great charter of freedom. If, however, amendments are to be made to the Constitution, changing the basis of representation and taxation, (and he did not deem them at all necessary at the present time,) he knew of none better than a simple proposition, embraced in a few lines, making in each State the number of qualified voters the basis of representation, and the value of property the basis of direct taxation. Such a proposition could be embraced in the folling terms:

"'Representatives shall be apportioned among the several States which may be included within this Union according to the number of qualified voters in each State.

"'Direct taxes shall be apportioned among the several States which may be included within this Union according to the value of all taxable property in each State.'

"An amendment of this kind would, in his opinion, place the basis of representation and direct taxation upon correct principles. The qualified voters were, for the most part, men who were subject to draft and enlistment when it was necessary to repel invasion, suppress rebellion, and quell domestic violence and insurrection. They risk their lives, shed their blood, and peril their all to uphold the Government, and give protection, security, and value to property. It seemed but just that property should compensate for the benefits thus conferred by defraying the expenses incident to its protection and enjoyment.

"Such an amendment, the President also suggested, would remove from Congress all issues in reference to the political equality of the races. It would leave the States to determine absolutely the qualifications of their own voters with regard to color; and thus the number of Representatives to which they would be entitled in Congress would depend upon the number upon whom they conferred the right of suffrage.

"The President, in this connection, expressed the opinion that the agitation of the negro-franchise question in the District of Columbia, at this time was the mere entering-wedge to the agitation of the question throughout the States, and was ill-timed, uncalled for, and calculated to do great harm. He believed that it would engender enmity, contention, and strife between the two races, and lead to a war between them which would result in great injury to both, and the certain extermination of the negro population. Precedence, he thought, should be given to more important and urgent matters, legislation upon which was essential for the restoration of the Union, the peace of the country, and the prosperity of the people."

"This," said Mr. Stevens, I take to be an authorized utterance of one at the other end of the avenue. I have no doubt that this is the proclamation, the command of the President of the United States, made and put forth by authority in advance, and at a time when this Congress was legislating on this very question; made, in my judgment, in violation of the privileges of this House; made in such a way that centuries ago, had it been made to Parliament by a British king, it would have cost him his head. But, sir, we pass that by; we are tolerant of usurpation in this tolerant Government of ours."

In answer to those who contended that Congress should regulate the right of suffrage in the States, Mr. Stevens said: "If you should take away the right which now is and always has been exercised by the States, by fixing the qualifications of their electors, instead of getting nineteen States, which is necessary to ratify this amendment, you might possibly get five. I venture to say you could not get five in this Union. And that is an answer, in the opinion of the committee, to all that has been said on this subject. But it grants no right. It says, however, to the State of South Carolina and other slave States, True, we leave where it has been left for eighty years the right to fix the elective franchise, but you must not abuse it; if you do, the Constitution will impose upon you a penalty, and will continue to inflict it until you shall have corrected your actions.

"Now, any man who knows any thing about the condition of aspiration and ambition for power which exists in the slave States, knows that one of their chief objects is to rule this country. It was to ruin it if they could not rule it. They have not been able to ruin it, and now their great ambition will be to rule it. If a State abuses the elective franchise, and takes it from those who are the only loyal people there, the Constitution says to such a State, You shall lose power in the halls of the nation, and you shall remain where you are, a shriveled and dried-up nonentity instead of being the lords of creation, as you have been, so far as America is concerned, for years past.

"Now, sir, I say no more strong inducement could ever be held out to them; no more severe punishment could ever be inflicted upon them as States. If they exclude the colored population, they will lose at least thirty-five Representatives in this hall; if they adopt it, they will have eighty-three votes."

Mr. Stevens urged several objections to the proposition of Mr. Schenck. He said: "If I have been rightly informed as to the number, there are from fifteen to twenty Representatives in the Northern States founded upon those who are not citizens of the United States. In New York I think there are three or four Representatives founded upon the foreign population—three certainly. And so it is in Wisconsin, Iowa, and other Northern States. There are fifteen or twenty Northern Representatives that would be lost by that amendment and given to the South whenever they grant the elective franchise to the negro.

"Now, sir, while I have not any particular regard for any foreigner who goes against me, yet I do not think it would be wise to put into the Constitution or send to the people a proposition to amend the Constitution which would take such Representatives from those States, and which, therefore, they will never adopt.

"But I have another objection to the amendment of my friend from Ohio. His proposition is to apportion representation according to the male citizens of the States. Why has he put in

24

the word 'male?' It was never in the Constitution of the United States before. Why make a crusade against women in the Constitution of the nation? [Laughter.] Is my friend as much afraid of their rivalry as the gentlemen on the other side of the House are afraid of the rivalry of the negro? [Laughter.] I do not think we ought to disfigure the Constitution with such a provision. I find that every unmarried man is opposed to the proposition. Whether married men have particular reason for dreading interference from that quarter I know not. [Laughter.] I certainly shall never vote to insert the word 'male' or the word 'white' in the national Constitution. Let these things be attended to by the States."

In answer to the objection that the amendment proposed by the committee "might be evaded by saying that no man who had ever been a slave should vote, and that would not be disfranchisement on account of race or color," Mr. Stevens said: "Sir, no man in America ever was or ever could be a slave if he was a white man. I know white men have been held in bondage contrary to law. But there never was a court in the United States, in a slave State or a free State, that has not admitted that if one held as a slave could prove himself to be white, he was that instant free. And, therefore, such an exclusion, on account of previous condition of slavery, must be an exclusion on account of race or color. Therefore that objection falls to the ground."

In reply to the closing paragraph of Mr. Raymond's speech, Mr. Stevens said: "I could not but admire (an admiration mingled with wonder) the amiability of temper, the tenderness of heart, the generosity of feeling which must have prompted some of the closing sentences of the excellent and able speech delivered by the gentleman on last Monday. His words were these:

"'The gigantic contest is at an end. The courage and devotion on either side, which made it so terrible and so long, no longer owe a divided duty, but have become the common property of the American name, the priceless possession of the American Republic, through all time to come. The dead of the contending hosts sleep beneath the soil of a common country, under their common flag. Their hostilities are hushed, and they are the dead of the nation for evermore.'

"Sir, much more than amiable, much more than religious, must be the sentiment that would prompt any man to say that 'the courage and devotion' which so long withstood our arms, prolonging the terrible conflict of war, and sacrificing the lives of thousands of loyal men, are hereafter to be the common boast of the nation, 'the priceless possession of the American Republic through all time to come;' that it is the pride of our country so many infamous rebels were so ferocious in their murders.

"Sir, we are to consider these dead on both sides as the dead of the nation, the common dead! And so, I suppose, we are to raise monuments beside the monuments to Reynolds and others, to be erected in the cemetery on the battle-field of Gettysburg. We must there build high the monumental marble for men like Barksdale, whom I have seen in this hall draw their bowie-knives on the Representatives of the people; men who died upon the battle-field of Gettysburg in arms against the Government, and where they now lie buried in ditches, 'unwept, unhonored, and unsung!' They are, I suppose, to be raised and put into the fore-front ranks of the nation, and we are to call them through all time as the dead of the nation! Sir, was there ever blasphemy before like this? Who was it burnt the temple of Ephesus? Who was it imitated the thunder of Jove? All that was poor compared with this blasphemy. I say, if the loyal dead, who are thus associated with the traitors who murdered them, put by the gentleman on the same footing with them, are to be treated as the 'common dead of the nation'—I say, sir, if they could have heard the gentleman, they would have broken the cerements of the tomb, and stalked forth and haunted him until his eye-balls were seared."

The question was first taken on the substitute offered by Mr. Schenck, which was rejected by a vote of one hundred and thirty-one to twenty-nine.

The question was then taken on agreeing to the joint resolution as modified by the committee, and it was decided in the affirmative by the following vote:

YEAS—Messrs. Alley, Allison, Ames, Anderson, James M. Ashley, Baker, Banks, Barker, Baxter, Beaman, Benjamin, Bidwell, Bingham, Blaine, Blow, Boutwell, Brandegee, Bromwell, Broomall, Buckland, Bundy, Reader W. Clarke, Sidney Clarke, Cobb, Conkling, Cook, Cullom, Darling, Davis, Dawes, Defrees, Delano, Deming, Dixon, Donnelly, Eckley, Eggleston, Farnsworth, Farquhar, Ferry, Garfield, Grinnell, Griswold, Abner C. Harding, Hart, Hayes, Hill, Holmes, Hooper, Hotchkiss, Asahel W. Hubbard, Chester D.

Hubbard, Demas Hubbard, John H. Hubbard, James R. Hubbell, Hulburd, James Humphrey, Ingersoll, Julian, Kasson, Kelley, Kelso, Ketcham, Kuykendall, Laflin, George V. Lawrence, William Lawrence, Longyear, Lynch, Marston, Marvin, McClurg, McIndoe, McKee, Mercur, Miller, Moorhead, Morrill, Morris, Moulton, Myers, O'Neill, Orth, Paine, Patterson, Perham, Pike, Plants, Pomeroy, Price, Alexander H. Rice, John H. Rice, Rollins, Sawyer, Schenck, Scofield, Shellabarger, Sloan, Spalding, Starr, Stevens, Stilwell, Thayer, Francis Thomas, John L. Thomas, Upson, Van Aernam, Burt Van Horn, Robert T. Van Horn, Ward, Warner, Elihu B. Washburne, William B. Washburn, Welker, Wentworth, Williams, James F. Wilson, Stephen F. Wilson, Windom, and Woodbridge—120.

NAYS—Messrs. Baldwin, Bergen, Boyer, Brooks, Chanler, Dawson, Dennison, Eldridge, Eliot, Finck, Grider, Hale, Aaron Harding, Harris, Hogan, Edwin N. Hubbell, James M. Humphrey, Jenckes, Johnson, Kerr, Latham, Le Blond, Marshall, McCullough, Niblack, Nicholson, Noell, Phelps, Samuel J. Randall, William H. Randall, Raymond, Ritter, Rogers, Ross, Rosseau, Shanklin, Sitgreaves, Smith, Strouse, Taber, Taylor, Thornton, Trimble, Voorhees, Whaley, and Wright—46.

NOT VOTING—Messrs. Ancona, Delos R. Ashley, Culver, Driggs, Dumont, Glossbrenner, Goodyear, Henderson, Higby, Jones, Loan, McRuer, Newell, Radford, Trowbridge, and Winfield—16.

Two-thirds having voted in the affirmative, the Speaker declared the joint resolution adopted.

The strong vote by which this measure was passed, after so general an expression of dissent from it, excited some surprise. Many gentlemen evidently surrendered their individual preferences for the sake of unanimity. They believed that this was the best measure calculated to secure just representation, which would pass the ordeal of Congress and three-fourths of the States. They accepted the "rule of statesmanship," to "take the best attainable, essential good which is at our command."

A disposition to rebuke supposed Executive dictation had some effect to produce an unexpected unanimity in favor of the measure. One Rhode Island and two Massachusetts members insisted on national negro suffrage, and voted against the amendments. Mr. Raymond and Mr. Hale, of New York, were the only Republicans who voted against the measure in accordance with the President's opinions. Of the border slave State members, ten voted for the amendment and sixteen against it.

CHAPTER XV.

THE BASIS OF REPRESENTATION—IN THE SENATE.

The Joint Resolution goes to the Senate—Counter-proposition by Mr. Sumner—He Speaks Five Hours—Mr. Henderson's Amendment—Mr. Fessenden—Mr. Henry S. Lane—Mr. Johnson—Mr. Henderson—Mr. Clark's Historical Statements—Fred. Douglass' Memorial—Mr. Williams—Mr. Hendricks—Mr. Chandler's "Blood-letting Letter"—Proposition of Mr. Yates—His Speech—Mr. Buckalew against New England—Mr. Pomeroy—Mr. Sumner's Second Speech—Mr. Doolittle—Mr. Morrill—Mr. Fessenden meets Objections—Final Vote—The Amendment Defeated.

THE joint resolution, providing for amending the basis of representation, having passed the House of Representatives on the last day of January, 1866, the action of that body was communicated to the Senate. The Civil Rights Bill at that time occupying the attention of the Senate, Mr. Fessenden gave notice that unless something should occur to render that course unwise, he would ask that the consideration of the proposed constitutional amendment should be taken up on the following Monday, February 5th.

On the second of February, Mr. Sumner gave notice of his intention to move a joint resolution as a counter-proposition to the proposed constitutional amendment. Mr. Sumner's resolution was as follows:

Whereas, it is provided in the Constitution that the United States shall guarantee to every State in the Union a republican form of government; and whereas, by reason of the failure of certain States to maintain Governments which Congress can recognize, it has become the duty of the United States, standing in the place of guarantor, where the principal has made a lapse, to secure to such States, according to the requirement of the guarantee, governments republican in form; and whereas, further, it is provided in a recent constitutional amendment, that Congress may 'enforce' the prohibition of slavery by 'appropriate legislation,' and it is important to this end that all relics of slavery should be removed, including all distinction of rights on account of color; now, therefore, to carry out the guarantee of a republican form of government, and to enforce the prohibition of slavery,

"*Be it resolved by the Senate and House of Representatives of the United States of America in Congress assembled*, That in all States lately declared to be in rebellion there shall be no oligarchy, aristocracy, caste, or monopoly invested with peculiar privileges or powers, and there shall be no denial of rights, civil or political, on account of color or race; but all persons shall be equal before the law, whether in the court-room or at the ballot-box; and this statute, made in pursuance of the Constitution, shall be the supreme law of the land, any thing in the constitution or laws of any such State to the contrary notwithstanding."

According to notice given by the Chairman of the joint Committee on Reconstruction on the part of the Senate, the proposed constitutional amendment came up for consideration on the fifth of February.

Mr. Sumner addressed the Senate in opposition to the measure. His speech was five hours in length, and occupied parts of the sessions of two days in its delivery. Mr. Sumner argued that the proposed amendment would introduce "discord and defilement into the Constitution," by admitting that rights could be "denied or abridged on account of race or color," and that by its adoption Congress would prove derelict to its constitutional duty to guarantee a republican form of government to each State, and that having already legislated to protect the colored race in civil rights, it is bound to secure to them political rights also.

Concerning the Committee on Reconstruction and their proposition, Mr. Sumner said: "Knowing, as I do, the eminent character of the committee, its intelligence, its patriotism, and the moral instincts by which it is moved, I am at a loss to understand the origin of a proposition which seems to me nothing else than another compromise of human rights, as if the country had not already paid enough in costly treasure and more costly blood for such compromises in the past. I had hoped that the day of compromise with wrong had passed forever. Ample experience shows that it is the least practical mode of settling questions involving moral principles. A moral principle can not be compromised."

He thought the proposed change in the Constitution could not properly be called an amendment. "For some time we have been carefully expunging from the statute-book the word 'white,' and now it is proposed to insert in the Constitution itself a distinction of color. An amendment, according to the dictionaries, is 'an improvement'—'a change for the better.' Surely the present proposition is an amendment which, like the crab, goes backward."

This measure would not accomplish the results desired by its authors. "If by this," said he, "you expect to induce the recent slave-master to confer the right of suffrage without distinction of color, you will find the proposition a delusion and a snare. He will do no such thing. Even the bribe you offer will not tempt him. If, on the other hand, you expect to accomplish a reduction of his political power, it is more than doubtful if you will succeed, while the means you employ are unworthy of our country. There are tricks and evasions possible, and the cunning slave-master will drive his coach and six through your amendment, stuffed with all his Representatives."

Drawing toward the close of his speech, Mr. Sumner gave the following review of his remarks that had preceded: "We have seen the origin of the controversy which led to the revolution, when Otis, with such wise hardihood, insisted upon equal rights, and then giving practical effect to the lofty demand, sounded the battle-cry that 'Taxation without Representation is Tyranny.' We have followed this controversy in its anxious stages, where these principles were constantly asserted and constantly denied, until it broke forth in battle; we have seen these principles adopted as the very frontlet of the republic, when it assumed its place in the family of nations, and then again when it ordained its Constitution; we have seen them avowed and illustrated in memorable words by the greatest authorities of the time; lastly, we have seen them embodied in public acts of the States collectively and individually; and now, out of this concurring, cumulative, and unimpeachable testimony, constituting a speaking aggregation absolutely without precedent, I offer you the American definition of a republican form of government. It is in vain that you cite philosophers or publicists, or the examples of former history. Against these I put the early and constant postulates of the fathers, the corporate declarations of the fathers, the avowed opinions of the fathers, and the public acts of the fathers, all with one voice proclaiming, first, that all men are equal in rights, and, secondly, that governments derive their just powers from the consent of the governed; and here is the American idea of a republic, which must be adopted in the interpretation of the National Constitution. You can not reject it. As well reject the Decalogue in determining moral duties, or as well reject the multiplication table in determining a question of arithmetic."

Maintaining that "the rebel States are not republican governments," Mr. Sumner said: "Begin with Tennessee, which disfranchises 283,079 citizens, being more than a quarter of its whole 'people.' Thus violating a distinctive principle of republican government, how can this State be recognized as republican? This question is easier asked than answered. But Tennessee is the least offensive on the list. There is Virginia, which disfranchises 549,019 citizens, being more than a third of its whole 'people.' There is Alabama, which disfranchises 436,030 citizens, being nearly one half of its whole 'people.' There is Louisiana, which disfranchises 350,546 citizens, being one half of its whole 'people.' There is Mississippi, which disfranchises 437,404 citizens, being much more than one half of its whole 'people.' And there is South Carolina, which disfranchises 412,408 citizens, being nearly two-thirds of its whole 'people.' A republic is a pyramid standing on the broad mass of the people as a base; but here is a pyramid balanced on its point. To call such a government 'republican' is a mockery of sense and decency. A monarch, 'surrounded by republican institutions,' which at one time was the boast of France, would be less offensive to correct principles, and give more security to human rights."

Of the Southern system of government he said: "It is essentially a monopoly, in a country which sets its face against all monopolies as unequal and immoral. If any monopoly deserves unhesitating judgment, it must be that which absorbs the rights of others and engrosses political power. How vain it is to condemn the petty monopolies of commerce, and then allow this vast, all-embracing monopoly of human rights."

Mr. Sumner maintained that the ballot was the great guarantee—"the only sufficient guarantee—being in itself peacemaker, reconciler, school-master, and protector." The result of conferring suffrage upon the negro will be, "The master will recognize the new citizen. The slave will stand with tranquil self-respect in the presence of the master. Brute force disappears. Distrust is at an end. The master is no longer a tyrant. The freedman is no longer a dependent. The ballot comes to him in his depression, and says, 'Use me and be elevated.' It comes to him in his passion, and says, 'Use me and do not fight.' It comes to him in his daily thoughts, filling him with the strength and glory of manhood."

Most beneficent results, it was thought, would flow from such legislation as that advocated by Mr. Sumner. "I see clearly," said he, "that there is nothing in the compass of mortal power so important to them in every respect, morally, politically, and economically—that there is nothing with such certain promise to them of beneficent results—that there is nothing so sure to make their land smile with industry and fertility as the decree of equal rights which I now invoke. Let the decree go forth to cover them with blessings, sure to descend upon their children in successive generations. They have given us war; we give them peace. They have raged against us in the name of slavery; we send them back the benediction of justice for all. They menace hate; we offer in return all the sacred charities of country together with oblivion of the past. This is our 'Measure for Measure.' This is our retaliation. This is our only revenge."

The following was the closing paragraph of Mr. Sumner's speech: "The Roman Cato, after declaring his belief in the immortality of the soul, added, that if this were an error, it was an error which he loved. And now, declaring my belief in liberty and equality as the God-given birthright of all men, let me say, in the same spirit, if this be an error, it is an error which I love; if this be a fault, it is a fault which I shall be slow to renounce; if this be an illusion, it is an illusion which I pray may wrap the world in its angelic arms."

On the seventh of February, the subject being again before the Senate, Mr. Henderson, of Missouri, moved to strike out the constitutional amendment proposed by the committee and insert the following:

"ARTICLE 14. No State, in prescribing the qualifications requisite for electors therein, shall discriminate against any person on account of color or race."

Mr. Fessenden made a speech in favor of the report of the committee, and in reply to Mr. Sumner. Referring to the subject of constitutional amendments, Mr. Fessenden said: "Something has been said, also, on different occasions, with reference to a disposition that is said to prevail now to amend the Constitution, and the forbearance of Congress has been invoked with regard to that venerable and great instrument. I believe that I have as much veneration for the Constitution as most men, and I believe that I have as high an opinion of its wisdom; but, sir, I probably have no better opinion of it than those who made it, and it did not seem to them, as we learn from its very provisions, that it was so perfect that no amendment whatever could be made that would be, in the language of the Senator from Massachusetts, an improvement. Why, sir, they provided themselves, as we all know, in the original instrument, for its amendment. They, in the very earliest days of our history, amended it themselves."

The result of retaining the "Constitution as it is" would be this: "The continuance of precisely the same rule, and the fostering of a feeling which the honorable Senator from Massachusetts has well proven to be contrary to the very foundation principles of a republican government. There can be no question that such would be the result; and we should have in a portion of the States all the people represented and all the people acting, and in another portion of the States all the people represented and but a portion of the people only exercising political rights and retaining them in their own hands. Such has been the case, and such, judging of human nature as it is, we have a right to suppose will continue to be the case."

The measure proposed by the committee was not entirely satisfactory to Mr. Fessenden. "I am free to confess," said he, "that could I legislate upon that subject, although I can see difficulties that would arise from it, yet trusting to time to soften them, and being desirous, if I can, to put into the Constitution a principle that commends itself to the consideration of every enlightened mind at once, I would prefer something of that sort, a distinct proposition that all provisions in the constitution or laws of any State making any distinction in civil or political rights, or privileges, or immunities whatever, should be held unconstitutional, inoperative, and void, or words to that effect. I would like that much better; and I take it there are not many Senators within the sound of my voice who would not very much prefer it; but, after all, the committee did not recommend a provision of that description, and I stand here as the organ of the committee, approving what they have done, and not disposed to urge my own peculiar views, if I have any, against theirs, or to rely exclusively on my own judgment so far as to denounce what honorable and true men, of better judgments than myself, have thought best to recommend, and in which I unite and agree with them."

After having given objections to limiting the basis of representation to voters, Mr. Fessenden remarked: "And if you extend it to citizens, or narrow it to citizens, you make it worse so far as many of the States are concerned; for my honorable friends from the Pacific coast, where there is a large number of foreigners, would hardly be willing to have them cut off; and they have no benefit of political power in the legislation of the country arising from the number of those foreigners who make a portion of their population. The difficulty is, that you meet with troubles of this kind every-where the moment you depart from the principle of basing representation upon population and population alone. You meet with inequalities, with difficulties, with troubles, either in one section of the country or the other, and you are inevitably thrown back upon the original principle of the Constitution.

"It will be noticed that the amendment which we have thus presented has one good quality: it preserves the original basis of representation; it leaves that matter precisely where the Constitution placed it in the first instance; it makes no changes in that respect; it violates no prejudice; it violates no feeling. Every State is represented according to its population with this distinction: that if a State says that it has a portion, a class, which is not fit to be represented—and it is for the State to decide—it shall not be represented; that is all. It has another good point: it is equal in its operation; all persons in every State are to be counted; nobody is to be rejected. With the very trifling exception fixed by the original Constitution, all races, colors, nations, languages, and denominations form the basis.

But, sir, the great excellence of it—and I think it is an excellence—is, that it accomplishes indirectly what we may not have the power to accomplish directly. If we can not put into the Constitution, owing to existing prejudices and existing institutions, an entire exclusion of all class distinctions, the next question is, can we accomplish that work in any other way?"

Concerning the "counter-proposition" of Mr. Sumner, the speaker said: "It is, in one sense, like a very small dipper with a very long handle; for the preamble is very much more diffuse than the proposed enactment itself. I looked to see what came next. I supposed that after that preamble we should have some adequate machinery provided for the enforcement and security of these rights; that we should have the matter put to the courts, and if the courts could not accomplish it, that we should have the aid of the military power, thus shocking the sensibilities of my honorable friend from Indiana [Mr. Hendricks] again. I do not know what good it does to merely provide by law that the provisions of the Constitution shall be enforced, without saying how, in what manner, by what machinery, in what way, to what extent, or how it is to be accomplished. Why reënact the Constitution of the United States and put it in a bill? What do you accomplish by it? How is that a remedy? It is simply as if it read in this way: Whereas, it is provided in the Constitution that the United States shall guarantee to every State in the Union a republican form of government, therefore we declare that there shall be a republican form of government and nothing else."

Mr. Sumner had said, in his speech in opposition to the proposed amendment, "Above all, do not copy the example of Pontius Pilate, who surrendered the Savior of the world, in whom he found no fault at all, to be scourged and crucified, while he set at large Barabbas, of whom the Gospel says, in simple words, 'Now, Barabbas was a robber.'"

To this Mr. Fessenden responded: "Is it a 'mean compromise'—for so it is denominated—that the Committee of Fifteen and the House of Representatives, when they passed it, placed themselves in the situation of Pontius Pilate, with the negro for the Savior of the world and the people of the United States for Barabbas, as designated by the honorable Senator. Why, sir, I expected to hear him in the next breath go further than that, and say that with the Constitution of the United States and the constitutions of the States the negro had been crucified, and that now, by the amendment of the Constitution, the stone had been rolled away from the door of the sepulcher, and he had ascended to sit on the throne of the Almighty and judge the world! One would have been, permit me to say with all respect, in as good taste as the other."

In conclusion, Mr. Fessenden said: "I wish to say, in closing, that I commend this joint resolution to the careful consideration of the Senate. It is all that we could desire; it is all that our constituents could wish. It does not accomplish, as it stands now, all, perhaps, that it might accomplish; but it is an important step in the right direction. It gives the sanction of Congress, in so many words, to an important, leading, effective idea. It opens a way by which the Southern mind—to speak of it as the Southern mind—may be led to that which is right and just. I have hopes, great hopes, of those who were recently Confederates; and I believe that now that they have been taught that they can not do evil, to all the extent that they might desire, with impunity, and when their attention is turned of necessity in the right direction, the road will seem so pleasant to their feet, or, at any rate, will seem so agreeable to their love of power, that they will be willing to walk in the direction that we have pointed. If they do, what is accomplished? In process of time, under this constitutional amendment, if it should be adopted, they are led to enlarge their franchise. That necessarily will lead them to consider how much further they can go, what is necessary in order to fit their people for its exercise, thus leading to education, thus leading to a greater degree of civilization, thus bringing up an oppressed and downtrodden race to an equality, if capable of an equality—and I hope it may be—with their white brethren, children of the same Father.

"And, sir, if this is done, some of us may hope to live—I probably may not, but the honorable Senator from Massachusetts may—to see the time when, by their own act, and under the effect of an enlightened study of their own interests, all men may be placed upon the same broad constitutional level, enjoying the same rights, and seeking happiness in the same way and under the same advantages; and that is all that we could ask."

On the following day, the discussion was continued by Mr. Lane, of Indiana, who addressed the Senate in a speech of two hours' duration. Mr. Lane seldom occupied the time of the Senate by speech-making, but when he felt it his duty to speak, none upon the floor attracted more marked attention, both from the importance of his matter and the impressiveness of his manner.

Much of Mr. Lane's speech, on this occasion, was devoted to the general subject of reconstruction, since he regarded the pending measure as one of a series looking to the ultimate restoration of the late rebel States. He was opposed to undue haste in this important work. He said: "The danger is of precipitate action. Delay is now what we need. The infant in its tiny fingers plays to-day with a handful of acorns, but two hundred years hence, by the efflux of time, those acorns are the mighty material out of which navies are built, the monarch of the forest, defying the shock of the storm and the whirlwind. Time is a mighty agent in all these affairs, and we should appeal to time. We are not ready yet for a restoration upon rebel votes; we are not ready yet for a restoration upon colored votes; but, thank God! we are willing and able to wait. We have the Government, we have the Constitution of the United States, we have the army and the navy, the vast moral and material power of the republic. We can enforce the laws in all the rebel States, and we can keep the peace until such time as they may be restored with safety to them and safety to us."

Of the measure proposed by the committee, Mr. Lane remarked: "This amendment, as I have already endeavored to show, will do away with much of the irregularity now existing, and which would exist under a different state of things, the blacks being all free. So far as the amendment goes, I approve of it, and I think I shall vote for it, but with a distinct understanding that it is not all that we are required to do, that it is not the only amendment to the Constitution that Congress is required to make."

Mr. Lane expressed his opinion of Mr. Sumner's "counter-proposition" in the following language: "It is a noble declaration, but a simple declaration, a paper bullet that kills no one, and fixes and maintains the rights of no one."

Of Mr. Henderson's proposition, he said: "It is a simple amendment to the Constitution of the United States, that no one shall be excluded from the exercise of the right of suffrage on account of race or color. That begins at the right point. The only objection to it is, that its operation can not be immediate, and in the mean time the rebels may be permitted to vote, and its adoption by the various State Legislatures is exceedingly doubtful. I should not doubt, however, that we might secure its adoption by three-fourths of the loyal States who have never seceded; and I believe that whenever that question is presented, the Supreme Court of the United States will determine that a ratification by that number of States is a constitutional approval of an amendment so as to make it the supreme law of the land. I have no doubt about it.

"If the rebel States are to be organized immediately, the only question is whether the right of suffrage shall be given to rebel white men or loyal black men. The amendment of the Senator from Missouri meets that issue squarely in the face. Whatsoever I desire to do I will not do by indirection. I trust I shall always be brave enough to do whatsoever I think my duty requires, directly and not by indirection."

Mr. Lane, with several other Western Senators, had been counted as opposed to negro suffrage, hence his advocacy of the principle gave much strength to those who desired to take a position in advance of the proposition of the committee.

In reply to an oft-reiterated argument that a war of races would result from allowing suffrage to the negro, Mr. Lane remarked: "If you wish to avoid a war of races, how can that be accomplished? By doing right; by fixing your plan of reconstruction upon the indestructible basis of truth and justice. What lesson is taught by history? The grand lesson is taught there that rebellions and insurrections have grown out of real or supposed wrong and oppression. A war of races! And you are told to look to the history of Ireland, and to the history of Hungary. Why is it that revolution and insurrection are always ready to break out in Hungary? Because, forsooth, the iron rule of Austria has stricken down the natural rights of the masses. It is a protest of humanity against tyranny, oppression, that produces rebellion and revolution. So in the bloody history of the Irish insurrections. Suppose the English Parliament had given equal rights to the Irish, had enfranchised the Catholics in Ireland in the reign of Henry VIII, long ere this peace and harmony would have prevailed between England and Ireland. But the very fact that a vast portion of a people are disfranchised sows the seeds of continual and ever-recurring revolution and insurrection. It can not be otherwise. These insurrections and revolutions, which are but the protest of our common humanity against wrong, are one of the scourges in the hands of Providence to compel men to do justice and to observe the right. It is the law of Providence, written upon every page of history, that God's vengeance follows man's wrong and oppression, and it will always be so. If you wish to avoid a war of races, if you wish to produce harmony and peace among these people, you must enfranchise them all."

On the following day, February 9th, Mr. Johnson, of Maryland, occupied the time devoted by the Senate to a consideration of this question with a speech against the proposed amendment of the Constitution. Mr. Johnson said that when the Constitution was framed there was no such objection to compromising as now existed in the minds of some Senators. "The framers of the Constitution came to the conclusion that the good of the country demanded that there should be a compromise, and they proposed, as a compromise, the provision as it now stands; and that is, that for the purposes of representation, a person held in slavery, or in involuntary servitude, shall be esteemed three-fifths of a man and two-fifths property; and they established the same rule in relation to taxation. They very wisely concluded that, as it was all-important that some general rule should be adopted, this was the best rule, because promising more than any other rule to arrive at a just result of ascertaining the number of Representatives and ascertaining the quota of taxation."

Mr. Johnson did not think that the North needed such a provision as this amendment to render her able to cope with Southern statesmanship in Congress: "Are not the North and the statesmen of the North equal to the South and the statesmen of the South on all subjects that may come before the councils of the nation? What is there, looking to the history of the two sections in the past, which would lead us to believe that the North is inferior to the South in any thing of intellectual improvement or of statesmanship? You have proved—and I thank God you have proved—that if listening to evil counsels, rendered effective, perhaps, by your own misjudged legislation, and by the ill-advised course of your own population, exhibited through the press and the pulpit, a portion of the South involved the country in a war, the magnitude of which no language can describe—you have proved yourselves adequate to the duty of defeating them in their mad and, as far as the letter of the Constitution is concerned, their traitorous purpose. And now, having proved your physical manhood, do you doubt your intellectual manhood? Mr. President, in the presence in which I speak, I am restrained from speaking comparatively of the Senate as it is and the Senate as it has been; but I can say this, with as much sincerity as man ever spoke, that there is nothing to be found in the free States calculated to disparage them properly in the estimation of the wise and the good. They are able to conduct the Government, and they will not be the less able because they have the advice and the counsels of their Southern brethren."

In answer to the position that the Southern States were not possessed of a republican form of government, Mr. Johnson remarked: "Did our fathers consider that any one of the thirteen States who finally came under the provisions of that Constitution, and have ever since constituted a part of the nation, were not living under republican forms of government? The honorable member will pardon me for saying that to suppose it is to disparage the memory of those great and good men. There was not a State in the Union when the Constitution was adopted that was republican, if the honorable member's definition of a republican government is the one now to be relied upon. A property qualification was required in all at that time. Negroes were not allowed to vote, although free, in most of the States. In the Southern States the mass of the negroes were slaves, and, of course, were not entitled to vote. If the absence of the universal right of suffrage proves that the Government is not republican, then there was not a republican government within the limits of the United States when the Constitution was adopted; and yet the very object of the clause to guarantee a republican government—and the honorable member's citations prove it—was to prevent the existing governments from being changed by revolution. It was to preserve the existing governments; and yet the honorable member would have the Senate and the country believe that, in the judgment of the men who framed the Constitution, there was not a republican form of government in existence.

"The definition of the honorable member places his charge of antirepublicanism as against the present forms of constitution upon the ground of the right to vote. I suppose the black man has no more natural right to vote than the white man. It is the exclusion from the right that affects the judgment of the honorable member from Massachusetts. Voting, according to him, is a right derived from God; it is in every man inalienable; and its denial, therefore, is inconsistent and incompatible with the true

25

object of a free government. If it be such a right, it is not less a right in the white man than in the black man; it is not less a right in the Indian than in the white man or the black man; it is not less a right in the female portion of our population than in the male portion. Then the honorable member from Massachusetts is living in an antirepublican government, and he ought not to stay there a moment if he can find any government which would be a government according to his theory. None has existed since the world commenced, and it is not at all likely that any will exist in all time to come; but if there is any such government to be found on the face of the earth, let him leave Massachusetts, let him hug that angelic delusion which he hopes will encircle the whole world, and go somewhere, where he can indulge it without seeing before him every day conclusive evidence that no such illusion exists at home. Leave Massachusetts, I beg the honorable member, just as soon as you can, or you will never be supremely happy."

In conclusion, Mr. Johnson remarked, referring to the recent rebels: "Let us take them to our bosom, trust them, and as I believe in my existence, you will never have occasion to regret it. You will, if the event occurs, look back to your participation in it in future time with unmingled delight, because you will be able to date from it a prosperity and a national fame of which the world furnishes no example; and you will be able to date from it the absence of all cause of differences which can hereafter exist, which will keep us together as one people, looking to one destiny, and anxious to achieve one renown."

On Tuesday, February 13th, the Senate resumed the consideration of the Basis of Representation. Mr. Sumner proposed to amend the proviso recommended by the committee—"all persons therein of such race or color shall be excluded from the basis of representation"—by adding the words "and. they shall be exempt from taxation of all kinds."

Mr. Henderson, of Missouri, occupied the attention of the Senate, during a considerable part of this and the following day, in a speech against the proposition of the Committee of Fifteen, which he considered a compromise, surrendering the rights of the negro out of the hands of the General Government into the hands of States not fit to be intrusted with them. In favor of his own amendment prohibiting the States from disfranchising citizens on the ground of color, Mr. Henderson said: "I propose to make the State governments republican in fact, as they are in theory. The States now have the power and do exclude the negroes for no other reason than that of color. If the negro is equally competent and equally devoted to the Government as the Celt, the Saxon, or the Englishman; why should he not vote? If he pays his taxes, works the roads, repels foreign invasion with his musket, assists in suppressing insurrections, fells the forest, tills the soil, builds cities, and erects churches, what more shall he do to give him the simple right of saying he must be only equal in these burdens, and not oppressed? My proposition is put in the least offensive form. It respects the traditionary right of the States to prescribe the qualifications of voters. It does not require that the ignorant and unlettered negro shall vote. Its words are simply that 'no State, in prescribing the qualifications requisite for electors therein, shall discriminate against any person on account of color or race.' The States may yet prescribe an educational or property test; but any such test shall apply to white and black alike. If the black man be excluded because he is uneducated, the uneducated white man must be excluded too. If a property test be adopted for the negro, as in New York, the same test must apply to the white man. It reaches all the States, and not a few only, in its operation. I confess that, so far as I am personally concerned, I would go still further and put other limitations on the power of the States in regard to suffrage; but Senators have expressed so much distrust that even this proposition can not succeed, I have concluded to present it in a form the least objectionable in which I could frame it. It will be observed that this amendment, if adopted, will not prevent the State Legislatures from fixing official qualifications. They may prevent a negro from holding any office whatever under the State organization. It is a singular fact, however, that to-day, under the Federal Constitution, a negro may be elected President, United States Senator, or a member of the lower branch of Congress. In that instrument no qualification for office is prescribed which rejects the negro. The white man, not native born, may not be President, but the native-born African may be. The States, however, may, in this respect, notwithstanding this amendment, do what the Federal Constitution never did."

Mr. Henderson closed his speech with the following words: "The reasons in favor of my proposition are inseparably connected with all I have said. I need not repeat them. Every consideration of peace demands it. It must be done to remove the relics of the rebellion; it must be done to pluck out political disease from the body politic, and restore the elementary principles of our Government; it must be done to preserve peace in the States and harmony in our Federal system; it must be done to assure the happiness and prosperity of the Southern people themselves; it must be done to establish in our institutions the principles of universal justice; it must be done to secure the strongest possible guarantees against future wars; it must be done in obedience to that golden rule which insists upon doing to others what we would that others should do unto us; it must be done if we would obey the moral law that teaches us to love our neighbors as ourselves; in fine, it must be done to purify, strengthen, and perpetuate a Government in which are now fondly centered the best hopes of mankind."

Mr. Clark, of New Hampshire, addressed the Senate on the pending measure. He made the following interesting historical statements: "As the traveler who has passed a difficult road, when he comes to some high hill looks back to see the difficulties which he has passed, I turn back, and I ask the Senator to turn back, to consider what occurred, as I say, about six years ago. In the session of 1859-60, in the old Senate-chamber, a bill was brought into the Senate of the United States by the then Senator from Mississippi [Mr. Brown], who was chairman of the Committee on the District of Columbia, a place which my friend from Maine [Mr. Morrill] now so worthily fills—a bill in aid of the education of the children of this District. The bill proposed to grant certain fines and forfeitures to the use of the schools, and also proposed to tax the people ten cents on every hundred dollars of the property in this District for the purpose of educating the children. That bill proposed to tax the white man and the black man alike; and fearing that the property of the black man would be taxed to educate the child of the white man, I proposed an amendment to the bill, that the tax collected from the black man should go to educate the black man's child.

"There was also a further provision of the bill, that if the District raised a certain amount of money for the education of the children, the Government of the United States would appropriate a like amount from the Treasury. If, for instance, you raised $20,000 by taxes on the people in the District, the Government should pay $20,000 more, to be added to it for the education of the children of the District. I moved the amendment that no child whose father paid any portion of that tax for the education of the children should be excluded from the benefit of it, be he white or black; but that there might be no inconvenience felt, I agreed to an amendment that the black child should not be put into the same school with the white child, but that they should be educated in different schools to be provided for them; but if the black man paid for educating the children of the District, his child should be educated. There was at once an outcry, 'Why, this is social equality of the two races; this is political equality;' and they would not consent that the black child should be educated, even with the money of the black father. That amendment was declared to be carried in the Senate of the United States, and after declaring it was carried, the Senate adjourned, and after the adjournment, the chairman of that committee, Mr. Brown, appealed to me personally if I would not withdraw it. I said to him, 'No, I would never withdraw it; if you tax the black man, the black man should have a part of the money that you raise from him to educate his child.'

"After some days, the bill came up again in the Senate of the United States, and the Senator from Mississippi, the chairman of the Committee on the District of Columbia, got up and in open Senate appealed to me, 'Will the Senator from New Hampshire withdraw that amendment?' 'Never, Mr. President.' 'Then,' said the Senator from Mississippi, 'I will lay the bill aside, and will not ask the Senate to pass it;' and so the whole scheme failed, because they would not consent that the money of the black man should educate his own child, and they could not vote it to educate a white child.

"Now I turn back to that time six years ago, and I mark the road that we have come along. I mark where we struck the chains from the black man in this same District, whose child you could not educate six years ago; I mark, in this Senate, at this very session, that we have passed a bill in aid of the Freedmen's Bureau to secure to him his rights in this District;

I mark that all through this nation we have stricken off the chains of the slave and secured to the slave his rights elsewhere in the Union; and we have now come to the height of the hill, and are considering whether we will not enfranchise those very black men through all the country."

In favor of granting political rights to the negro, Mr. Clark made the following remarks: "Mr. President, the question of the negro has troubled the nation long. His condition as a slave troubled you; and his condition as a freedman troubles you. Are you sick, heart-sick of this trouble? and do you inquire when will it end? I will tell you. When you have given him equal rights, equal privileges, and equal security with other citizens; when you have opened the way for him to be a man, then will you have rendered exact justice which can alone insure stability and content.

"Sir, if I ever did hold that this Government was made or belonged exclusively to the white man, I should now be ashamed to avow it, or to claim for it so narrow an application. The black man has made too many sacrifices to preserve it, and endangered his life too often in its defense to be excluded from it. The common sentiment of gratitude should open its doors to him, if not political justice and equality.

"Mr. President, my house once took fire in the night-time; my two little boys were asleep in it, when I and their mother were away. The neighbors rushed into it, saved the children, and extinguished the flames. When I reached it, breathless and exhausted, the first exclamation was, 'Your children are safe.' Can you tell me how mean a man I should have been, and what execration I should have deserved, if the next time those neighbors came to my house I had kicked them out of it? Tell me, then, I pray you, why two hundred thousand black men, most of whom volunteered to fight your battles, who rushed in to save the burning house of your Government, should not be permitted to participate in that Government which they helped to preserve? When you enlisted and mustered these men, when your adjutant-general went South, and gathered them to the recruiting-office, and persuaded them to join your ranks, did he, or any one, tell them this was the white man's Government? When they came to the rendezvous, did you point to the sign over the door, 'Black men wanted to defend the white man's Government?' When you put upon them the uniform of the United States, did you say, 'Don't disgrace it; this is the white man's Government?' When they toiled on the march, in the mud, the rain, and the snow, and when they fell out of the ranks from sheer weariness, did you cheer them on with the encouragement that 'this is the white man's Government?'

"When they stood on picket on the cold, stormy night to guard you against surprise, did you creep up and warm their congealing blood with an infusion of the white man's Government? When, with a wild hurrah, on the 'double-quick,' they rushed upon the enemy's guns, and bore your flag where men fell fastest and war made its wildest havoc, where explosion after explosion sent their mangled bodies and severed limbs flying through the air, and they fell on glacis, ditch, and scarp and counterscarp, did you caution them against such bravery, and remind them that 'this was the white man's Government?' And when the struggle was over, and many had fought 'their last battle,' and you gathered the dead for burial, did you exclaim, 'Poor fools! how cheated! this is the white man's Government?' No, no, sir; you beckoned them on by the guerdon of freedom, the blessings of an equal and just Government, and a 'good time coming.'

"'White man's Government,' do you say? Go to Fort Pillow; stand upon its ramparts and in its trenches, and recall the horrid butchery of the black man there because he had joined you against rebellion, and then say, if you will, 'This is the white man's Government.' Go to Wagner. Follow in the track of the Massachusetts Fifty-fourth, as they went to the terrible assault, with the guns flashing and roaring in the darkness. Mark how unflinchingly they received the pelting iron hail into their bosoms, and how they breasted the foe! See how nobly they supported, and how heroically they fell with their devoted leader; count the dead; pick up the severed limbs; number the wounds; measure the blood spilled; and remember why and wherefore and in whose cause the negro thus fought and suffered, and then say, if you can, 'This is the white man's Government.' Go to Port Hudson, go to Richmond, go to Petersburg, go anywhere and every-where—to every battle-field where the negro fought, where danger was greatest and death surest—and tell me, if you can, that 'this is the white man's Government.' And then go to Salisbury and Columbia and Andersonville, and as you shudder at the ineffable miseries of those dens, and think of those who ran the dead-line, and were not shot, but escaped to the woods and were concealed and fed and piloted by the black men, and never once betrayed, but often enabled to escape and return to their friends, and then tell me if 'this is a white man's Government.'

"In ancient Rome, when one not a citizen deserved well of the republic, he was rewarded by the rights of citizenship, but we deny them, and here in America—not in the Confederate States of America, where, attempting to found a government upon slavery and the subjection of one race to another, it would have been fitting, if anywhere, but in the United States of America, the cardinal principle of whose Government is the equality of all men. After these black men have so nobly fought to maintain the one and overthrow the other, when they ask us for the necessary right of suffrage to protect themselves against the rebels they have fought, and with whom they are compelled to live, we coolly reply, 'This is the white man's Government.' Nay, more, and worse, we have refused it to them, and allowed it to their and our worst enemies, the rebels. Sir, from the dim and shadowy aisles of the past, there comes a cry of 'Shame! shame!' and pagan Rome rebukes Christian America.

"But not chiefly, Mr. President, do I advocate this right of the black man to vote because he has fought the battles of the republic and helped to preserve the Union, but because he is a citizen and a man—one of the people, one of the governed—upon whose consent, if the Declaration of Independence is correct, the just powers of the Government rest; an intelligent being, of whom and for whom God will have an account of us, individually and as a nation; whose blood is one with ours, whose destinies are intermingled and run with ours, whose life takes hold on immortality with ours, and because this right is necessary to develop his manhood, elevate his race, and secure for it a better civilization and a more enlightened and purer Christianity."

On the 15th of February, Mr. Sumner presented a memorial from George T. Downing, Frederick Douglass, and other colored citizens of the United States, protesting against the pending constitutional amendment as introducing, for the first time, into the Constitution a grant to disfranchise men on the ground of race or color. In laying this memorial before the Senate, Mr. Sumner said: "I do not know that I have at any time presented a memorial which was entitled to more respectful consideration than this, from the character of its immediate signers and from the vast multitudes they represent. I hope I shall not depart from the proper province of presenting it if I express my entire adhesion to all that it says, and if I take this occasion to entreat the Senate, if they will not hearken to arguments against the pending proposition, that they will at least hearken to the voice of these memorialists, representing the colored race of our country."

Mr. Williams, of Oregon, argued in favor of the resolution reported by the committee as the best measure before the Senate. He was for proceeding slowly in the work of reconstruction. In his opinion, neither the negro nor his master was now fit to vote. Upon this point he said: "It seems to me there can be little doubt that at this particular time the negroes of the rebel States are unfit to exercise the elective franchise. I have recently conversed with two officers of the Federal army from Texas, who told me that there, in the interior and agricultural portions of the State, the negroes do not yet know that they are free; and one of the officers told me that he personally communicated to several negroes for the first time the fact of their freedom. Emancipation may be known in the towns and cities throughout the South, but the probabilities are that in the agricultural portions of that country the negroes have no knowledge that they are free, or only vague conceptions of their rights and duties as freemen. Sir, give these men a little time; give them a chance to learn that they are free; give them a chance to acquire some knowledge of their rights as freemen; give them a chance to learn that they are independent and can act for themselves; give them a chance to divest themselves of that feeling of entire dependence for subsistence and the sustenance of their families upon the landholders of the South, to which they have been so long accustomed; give them a little time to shake the manacles off of their minds that have just been stricken from their hands, and I will go with the honorable Senator from Massachusetts to give them the right of suffrage. And I will here express the hope that the day is not far distant when every man born upon American soil, within the pale of civilization, may defend his manhood and his rights as a freeman by that most effective ballot which

"'Executes the freeman's will
As lightning does the will of God.'

Concerning the amendment proposed by Mr. Henderson, Mr. Williams said: "All the impassioned declamation and all the vehement assertions of the honorable Senator do not change or affect the evidence before our eyes that the people of these United States are not prepared to surrender to Congress the absolute right to determine as to the qualifications of voters in the respective States, or to adopt the proposition that all persons, without distinction of race or color, shall enjoy political rights and privileges equal to those now possessed by the white people of the country. Sir, some of the States have lately spoken upon that subject. Wisconsin and Connecticut, Northern, loyal, and Republican States, have recently declared that they would not allow the negroes within their own borders political rights; and is it probable that of the thirty-six States, more than six, at the most, would at this time adopt the constitutional amendment proposed by the gentleman?"

Notwithstanding the temporary darkness of the political sky, Mr. Williams saw brilliant prospects before the country. "This nation," said he, "is to live and not die. God has written it among the shining decrees of destiny. Inspired by this hope and animated by this faith, we will take this country through all its present troubles and perils to the promised land of perfect unity and peace, where freedom, equality, and justice, the triune and tutelar deity of the American Republic, will rule with righteousness a nation 'whose walls shall be salvation and whose gates praise.'"

At the close of this speech, the Senate being about to proceed to a vote upon the pending amendment, it was proposed to defer action and adjourn the question over to the following day, for the purpose of affording an opportunity for speeches by Senators who were not prepared to proceed immediately. Mr. Fessenden, who had the measure in charge, protested against the delays of the Senate. "This subject," said he, "has dragged along now for nearly two weeks. If members desire to address the Senate, they must be prepared to go on and do so without a postponement from day to day for the purpose of allowing every gentleman to make his speech in the morning, and then adjourning early every evening. We shall never get through in that way. I give notice to gentlemen that I shall begin to be a little more quarrelsome—I do not know that it will do any good—after to-day."

On the day following, Mr. Hendricks delivered a speech of considerable length in opposition to the constitutional amendment. After having maintained that the proposition did not rest the right of representation upon population, nor upon property, nor upon voters, Mr. Hendricks inquired: "Upon what principle do Senators propose to adopt this amendment to the Constitution? I can understand it if you say that the States shall be represented in the House of Representatives upon their population; I can understand it if you say that they shall be represented upon their voters; but when you say that one State shall have the benefit of its non-voting population and another State shall not, I can not understand the principle of equity and justice which governs you in that measure. Sir, if it does not stand upon a principle, upon what does it rest? It rests upon a political policy. A committee that had its birth in a party caucus brings it before this body, and does not conceal the fact that it is for party purposes. This measure, if you ever allow the Southern States to be represented in the House of Representatives, will bring them back shorn of fifteen or twenty Representatives; it will bring them back so shorn in their representation that the Republican party can control this country forever; and if you cut off from fifteen to thirty votes for President of the United States in the States that will not vote for a Republican candidate, it may be that you can elect a Republican candidate in 1868."

Mr. Hendricks thought that "this proposition was designed to accomplish three objects: first, to perpetuate the rule and power of a political party; in the second place, it is a proposition the tendency of which is to place agriculture under the control and power of manufactures and commerce forever; and, in the third place, it is intended, I believe, as a punishment upon the Southern States."

In reference to changing the basis of representation as a punishment for the Southern States, Mr. Hendricks said: "Now that the war is over; now that the Southern people have laid down their arms; now that they have sought to come again fully and entirely into the Union; now that they have pledged their honors and their fortunes to be true to the Union and to the flag; now that they have done all that can be done by a conquered people, is it right, after a war has been fought out, for us to take from them their political equality in this Union for the purpose of punishment? The Senator from Maine, the chairman of the committee, says that the right to control the suffrage is with the States, but if the States do not choose to do right in respect to it, we propose to punish them. You do not punish New York for not letting the foreigner vote until he resides there a certain period. You do not punish Indiana because she will not allow a foreigner to vote until he has been in the country a year. These States are not to be punished because they regulate the elective franchise according to their sovereign pleasures; but if any other States see fit to deny the right of voting to a class that is peculiarly guarded and taken care of here, then they are to be punished."

Referring to the speech of the Senator from New Hampshire, Mr. Hendricks asked: "Had the white men of this country a right to establish a Government, and thereby a political community? If so, they had a right to say who should be members of that political community. They had a right to exclude the colored man if they saw fit. Sir, I say, in the language of the lamented Douglas, and in the language of President Johnson, this is the white man's Government, made by the white man for the white man. I am not ashamed to stand behind such distinguished men in maintaining a sentiment like that. Nor was my judgment on the subject changed the day before yesterday by the lamentations of the Senator from New Hampshire, [Mr. Clark,] sounding through this body like the wailing of the winds in the dark forest, 'that it is a horrible thing for a man to say that this is a white man's Government.'

"Mr. President, there is a great deal said about the part the colored soldiers have taken in putting down this rebellion—a great deal more than there is any occasion for, or there is any support for in fact or history. This rebellion was put down by the white soldiers of this country."

Criticising sentiments toward the South, expressed by Senators, Mr. Hendricks said: "We hear a good deal said about blood now. Yesterday the Senator from Oregon [Mr. Williams] criticised the President for his leniency toward the South. A few days ago, the Senator from Ohio [Mr. Wade] made a severe criticism on the President for his leniency, and my colleague asks for blood. Mr. President, this war commenced with blood; nay, blood was demanded before the war. When the good men and the patriotic, North and South, representing the yearning hearts of the people at home, came here, in the winter and spring of 1861, in a peace congress, if possible to avoid this dreadful war, right then the Senator from Michigan [Mr. Chandler] announced to his Governor and the country that this Union was scarcely worth preserving without some blood-letting. His cry before the war was for blood. Allow me to say that when the Senator's name is forgotten because of any thing he says or does in this body, in future time it will be borne down upon the pages of history as the author of the terrible sentiment that the Union of the people that our fathers had cemented by the blood of the Revolution and by the love of the people; that that Union, resting upon compromise and concession, resting upon the doctrine of equality to all sections of the country; that that Union which brought us so much greatness and power in the three-quarters of a century of our life; that that Union that had brought us so much prosperity and greatness, until we were the mightiest and proudest nation on God's footstool; that that grand Union was not worth preserving unless we had some blood-letting!"

Mr. Chandler, of Michigan, replied: "The Senator from Indiana has arraigned me upon an old indictment for having written a certain letter in 1861. It is not the first time that I have been arraigned on that indictment of 'blood-letting.' I was first arraigned for it upon this floor by the traitor John C. Breckinridge; and I answered the traitor John C. Breckinridge; and after I gave him his answer, he went out into the rebel ranks and fought against our flag. I was arraigned by another Senator from Kentucky and by other traitors upon this floor. I expect to be arraigned again. I wrote the letter, and I stand by the letter; and what was in it? What was the position of the country when that letter was written? The Democratic party, as an organization, had arrayed itself against this Government—a Democratic traitor in the presidential chair, and a Democratic traitor in every department of this Government; Democratic traitors preaching treason upon this floor, and preaching treason in the hall of the other house; Democratic traitors in your army and in your navy; Democratic traitors controlling every branch of this Government. Your flag was fired upon, and there was no response. The Democratic party had ordained that this Government should be overthrown; and I, a Senator from the State of Michigan, wrote to the Governor of that State, 'Unless you are prepared to shed blood for the preservation of this great Government, the Government is overthrown.' That is all there was to that letter. That I said, and that I say again; and I tell that Senator if he is prepared to go down in history with the Democratic traitors who then coöperated with him, I am prepared to go down on that 'blood-letting' letter, and I stand by the record as then made." [Applause in the galleries.]

On the 19th of February, Mr. Howard, of Michigan, offered an amendment providing that the right of suffrage should be enjoyed by all persons of African descent belonging to the following classes: those who have been in the military service of the United States, those who can read and write, and those who possess $250 worth of property.

Mr. Yates, of Illinois, addressed the Senate for three hours on the pending amendment of the Constitution. On the 29th of January preceding, Mr. Yates had proposed a bill providing that no State or Territory should make any distinction between citizens on account of race, or color, or condition; and that all citizens, without distinction of race, color, or condition, should be protected in the enjoyment and exercise of all their civil and political rights, including the right of suffrage.

This bill Mr. Yates made the basis of his argument. His reason for preferring a bill to a constitutional amendment was presented as follows: "There is only one way of salvation for the country. Your amendments to the Constitution of the United States can not be adopted. If we have not the power now under the Constitution of the United States to secure full freedom, then, sir, we shall not have it, and there is no salvation whatever for the country. Let not freedom die in the house, and by the hands of her friends."

Mr. Yates maintained that the constitutional amendment abolishing slavery gave to Congress power to legislate to the full extent of the measure proposed by him. "Let gentlemen come forward," said he, "and meet the issue like men. Let them come forward and do what they have by the Constitution the clear power to do, and that is a *sine qua non* in order to carry into effect the constitutional prohibition of slavery. As for me, I would rather face the music and meet the responsibility like a man, and send to the people of the State of Illinois the boon of universal suffrage, and of a full and complete emancipation, than

Eng^d by G.E. Perine & Co. N. York

Richd Yates

RICHARD YATES.

SENATOR FROM ILLINOIS.

meet the taunt of Northern demagogues that I would force suffrage upon North Carolina, and Tennessee, and Delaware, while I had not the courage to prescribe it for our own free States. Sir, it will be the crime of the century if now, having the power, as we clearly have, we lack the nerve to do the work that is given us to do.

"Let me say to my Republican friends, you are too late. You have gone too far to recede now. Four million people, one-seventh of your whole population, you have set free. Will you start back appalled at the enchantment your own wand has called up? The sequences of your own teachings are upon you. As for me, I start not back appalled when universal suffrage confronts me. When the bloody ghost of slavery rises, I say, 'Shake your gory locks at me; I did it.' I accept the situation. I fight not against the logic of events or the decrees of Providence. I expected it, sir, and I meet it half way. I am for universal suffrage. I bid it 'All hail!' 'All hail!'

"Four million people set free! What will protect them? The ballot. What alone will give us a peaceful and harmonious South? The ballot to all. What will quench the fires of discord, give us back all the States, a restored Union, and make us one people? The ballot, and that alone. Is there no other way? None other under the sun. There is no other salvation.

"The ballot will lead the freedman over the Red Sea of our troubles. It will be the brazen serpent, upon which he can look and live. It will be his pillar of cloud by day, and his pillar of fire by night. It will lead him to Pisgah's shining height, and across Jordan's stormy waves, to Canaan's fair and happy land. Sir, the ballot is the freedman's Moses. So far as man is concerned, I might say that Mr. Lincoln was the Moses of the freedmen; but whoever shall be the truest friend of human freedom, whoever shall write his name highest upon the horizon of public vision as the friend of human liberty, that man—and I hope it may be the present President of the United States—will be the Joshua to lead the people into the land of deliverance."

Mr. Yates maintained that for the exercise of the right of suffrage there should be no test of intelligence, wealth, rank or race. To bring the people up to the proper standard, the ballot itself was "the greatest educator." He said: "Let a man have an interest in the Government, a voice as to the men and measures by which his taxes, his property, his life, and his reputation shall be determined, and there will be a stimulus to education for that man.

"As the elective franchise has been extended in this country, we have seen education become more universal. Look throughout all our Northern States at our schools and colleges, our academies of learning, our associations, the pulpit, the press, and the numerous agencies for the promotion of intelligence, all the inevitable offspring of our free institutions. Here is the high training which inspires the eloquence of the Senate, the wisdom of the cabinet, the address of the diplomatist, and which has developed and brought to light that intelligent and energetic mind which has elevated the character and contributed to the prosperity of the country. It is the ballot which is the stimulus to improvement, which fires the heart of youthful ambition, which stimulates honorable aspiration, which penetrates the thick shades of the forest, and takes the poor rail-splitter by the hand and points him to the shining height of human achievement, or which goes into the log hut of the tailor boy and opens to him the avenue of the presidential mansion."

Mr. Yates then declared his confidence in the triumph of the principle of universal suffrage: "It is my conscientious conviction that if every Senator on this floor, and every Representative in the other House, and the President of the United States, should, with united voices, attempt to oppose this grand consummation of universal equality, they will fail. It is too late for that. You may go to the head-waters of the Mississippi and turn off the little rivulets, but you can not go to the mouth, after it has collected its waters from a thousand rivers, and with accumulated volume is pouring its foaming waters into the Gulf, and say, 'Thus far shalt thou go and no further.'

"It is too late to change the tide of human progress. The enlightened convictions of the masses, wrought by the thorough discussions of thirty years, and consecrated by the baptism of precious blood, can not now be changed. The hand of a higher power than man's is in this revolution, and it will not move backward. It is of no use to fight against destiny. God, not man, created men equal. Deep laid in the solid foundations of God's eternal throne, the principle of equality is established, indestructible and immortal.

"Senators, sixty centuries of the past are looking down upon you. All the centuries of the future are calling upon you. Liberty, struggling amid the rise and wrecks of empires in the past, and yet to struggle for life in all the nations of the world, conjures you to seize this great opportunity which the providence of Almighty God has placed in your hands to bless the world and make your names immortal, to carry to full and triumphant consummation the great work begun by your fathers, and thus lay permanently, solidly, and immovably, the cap-stone upon the pyramid of human liberty."

On the 21st of February, the proposed amendment being again before the Senate, Mr. Buckalew, of Pennsylvania, delivered an elaborate speech in opposition to the measure. He had previously refrained from speech-making, supposing that "while the passions of the country were inflamed by the war, reason could not be heard." He regretted that questions pertaining to the war still occupied the attention of Congress to the exclusion of those connected with economy, revenue, finance, ordinary legislation, and the administration of justice—questions which require intelligence, investigation, labor, and the habits of the student. As an argument against changing the basis of representation as it existed, Mr. Buckalew gave statistical details, showing the various ratios of representation in the Senate, as possessed respectively by the East, West and South. He maintained that New England had too great a preponderance of power in the Senate, both as to membership and the chairmanships of committees. "While," said he, "the population of the East is less than one-seventh of the population of the States represented in the Senate, she has the chairmanships of one-third of the committees. The chairmanship of a committee is a position of much influence and power. The several distinguished gentlemen holding that position have virtual control over the transaction of business, both in committee and in the Senate."

Mr. Buckalew thus presented the effect of restoration of representation to the Southern States upon the relative position of New England: "Twenty-two Senators from the Southern States and two from Colorado—being double the number of those from the East—would reduce the importance of the latter in the Senate and remit her back to the condition in which she stood in her relations to the Union before the war. True, she would even then possess much more than her proportion of weight in the Senate, regard being had to her population, but she would no longer dominate or control the Government of the United States."

Mr. Buckalew argued at some length that representation should continue to be based upon population. He thought that the two-fifths added to the representative population in the South by the abolition of slavery would be counterbalanced by the mortality of the slave population since the outbreak of the war. He then presented the following objections to "any propositions of amendments at this time by Congress:"

"1. Eleven States are unrepresented in the Senate and House. They are not heard in debate which may affect their interests and welfare in all future time.

"2. Any amendment made at this time will be a partisan amendment.

"3. The members of this Congress were not chosen with reference to the subject of constitutional amendment.

"4. Whatever amendments are now proposed by Congress are to be submitted to Legislatures, and not to popular conventions in the States; and most of those Legislatures are to be the ones now in session.

"5. In submitting amendments at this time, we invite a dispute upon the question of the degree of legislative assent necessary to their adoption. If ratified by the Legislatures of less than three-fourths of all the States, their validity will be denied, and their enforcement resisted."

Mr. Wilson, of Massachusetts, replied to Mr. Buckalew's imputations against New England. "The Senator gave us to understand that he had not wasted reason, thought, and culture upon the stormy passions engendered by the war, but now, when reason had resumed her empire, he had come forth to instruct his country.

"The Senators from New England, unlike the Senator from Pennsylvania, remained not silent during the great civil war through which the nation has passed. They have spoken; they have spoken for the unity of their country and the freedom of all men. They have spoken for their country, their whole country, and for the rights of all its people of every race. Their past is secure, and the imputations of the Senator from Pennsylvania will pass harmless by them.

"When the Constitution was formed, New England had eight of the twenty-six Senators—nearly one-third of the body; now she has twelve of the seventy-two Senators—one-sixth of the body. Her power is diminishing in this body and will continue to diminish. When the Constitution was adopted, quite as great inequalities existed among the States as now. The illustrious statesmen who framed the Constitution knew and recognized that fact; they based the Senate upon the States, and upon the equality of the States. They were so determined in that policy of equal State representation in the Senate that they provided that the Constitution should never be amended in that respect without the consent of every State.

"The Senator suggests that the Senators from New England are actuated by local interests and love of power in their action regarding the admission of the Representatives of the rebel States. Nothing can be more unjust to those Senators. It is without the shadow of fairness or justice, or the semblance of truth. I can say before God that I am actuated by no local interests, no love of power, in opposing the immediate and unconditional admission of the rebel States into these chambers; and I know my associates from New England too well to believe for a moment that they are actuated by interest or the love of power. Thousands of millions of money have been expended, and hundreds of thousands of brave men have bled for the unity and liberty of the republic. I desire—my associates from New England desire—to see these vacant chairs filled at an early day by the Representatives of the States that rebelled and rushed into civil war. We will welcome them here; but before they come it is of vital importance to the country, to the people of all sections, to the interests of all, that all disturbing questions should be forever adjusted, and so adjusted as never again to disturb the unity and peace of the country. It is now the time to settle forever all matters that can cause estrangement and sectional agitations and divisions in the future. Nothing should be left to bring dissensions, and, it may be, civil war again upon our country. The blood poured out to suppress the rebellion must not be shed in vain."

Prominent Republican Senators bringing earnest opposition to bear against the proposed constitutional amendment, and a sentiment evidently gaining ground that it did not meet the requirements of the case, caused its friends to urge it with less zeal than had at first characterized them. Meanwhile, other important propositions coming up from the Committee of Fifteen, which occupied the attention of the Senate, as detailed in a subsequent chapter, the subject of changing the basis of representation was allowed to lie over for nearly a fortnight.

On the 5th of March, the subject being resumed, Mr. Pomeroy addressed the Senate. He feared that the nation was not ready to adopt a constitutional amendment such as the necessities of the country required. "This nation," said he, "although severely disciplined, has not yet reached the point of giving to all men their rights by a suffrage amendment; three-fourths of the States are not ready. And any patchwork, any 'step toward it' (as said the chairman of the committee) which does not reach it, I fear to take, because but one opportunity will ever be afforded us to step at all; and lost opportunities are seldom repeated."

Mr. Pomeroy did not think the case was without remedy, however, since "the last constitutional amendment embraced all, gave the most ample powers, even if they did not exist before; for, after having secured the freedom of all men wherever the old flag floats, it provided that Congress might 'secure' the same by 'appropriate legislation.'

"What more could it have said? And who are better judges of appropriate legislation than the very men who first passed the amendment and provided for this very case?

"Sir, what is 'appropriate legislation' on the subject, namely, securing the freedom of all men? It can be nothing less than throwing about all men the essential safeguards of the Constitution. The 'right to bear arms' is not plainer taught or more efficient than the right to carry ballots. And if appropriate legislation will secure the one, so can it also the other. And if both are necessary, and provided for in the Constitution as now amended, why, then, let us close the question of congressional legislation.

"Let us not take counsel of our own fears, but of our hopes; not of our enemies, but of our friends. By all the memories which cluster about the pathway in which we have been led; by all the sacrifices, suffering, blood, and tears of the conflict; by all the hopes of a freed country and a disenthralled race; yea, as a legacy for mankind, let us now secure a free representative republic, based upon impartial suffrage and that human equality made clear in the Declaration of Independence. To this entertainment let us invite our countrymen and all nations, committing our work, when done, to the verdict of posterity and the blessing of Almighty God."

On the day following, Mr. Saulsbury took the floor. His speech, ostensibly against the pending measure, was a palliation of the conduct of the Southern States, and a plea for their right of being admitted to representation in Congress. All that the Senator said directly upon the subject under discussion was contained in the following paragraph:

"Now, suppose your constitutional amendment passes. If it passes, it ought to meet with the respect of some body. If this constitutional amendment shall be presented to the States who are now represented in Congress, and shall be adopted by simply three-fourths of those States, is there any body that will have the least respect for it? Then suppose you could go with the bayonet—which I think now, under the brighter dawn of a better day which we begin to realize, you are not going to have the liberty to do—suppose you were to go with the bayonet and present it to the other eleven States, and they, acting under duress, not as free agents and as free men, could get some people in their section so miserable and poor in spirit and craven in soul as to vote to adopt in their Legislatures such an amendment, would it command the respect of any body in this land? Not at all. Open your doors, sir; admit the Representatives of the Southern States to seats in this body; require no miserable degrading oath of them; administer to them the very oath that you first took when you entered this body, and the only oath that the Constitution of the United States requires, and the only oath which Congress has any right to exact, an oath to support the Constitution of the United States; and then, if you think your Constitution is defective, if you think it needs further amendment, or if you have not sufficiently exhausted your bowels of mercy and love and kindness toward your sable friends whose shadows darken this gallery every day, submit your amendments to the States represented in the Congress of the United States; and if they choose, acting freely as citizens of their States, to agree to your amendments, it will command the respect of themselves, but still it will not command mine. I should despise a people who would voluntarily assume so degrading a position."

On the 7th of March, Mr. Sumner occupied the attention of the Senate for three hours, with a second speech in opposition to the proposed constitutional amendment. He used very strong language to express his abhorrence of the proposition: "It reminds me of that leg of mutton served for dinner on the road from London to Oxford, which Dr. Johnson, with characteristic energy, described 'as bad as bad could be, ill-fed, ill-killed, ill-kept, and ill-dressed.' So this compromise—I adopt the saying of an eminent friend, who insists that it can not be called an 'amendment,' but rather a 'detriment' to the Constitution—is as bad as bad can be; and even for its avowed purpose it is uncertain, loose, cracked, and rickety. Regarding it as a proposition from Congress to meet the unparalleled exigencies of the present hour, it is no better than the 'muscipular abortion' sent into the world by the 'parturient mountain.' But it is only when we look at the chance of good from it that this proposition is 'muscipular.' Regarding it in every other aspect it is infinite, inasmuch as it makes the Constitution a well-spring of insupportable thralldom, and once more lifts the sluices of blood destined to run until it comes to the horse's bridle. Adopt it, and you will put millions of fellow-citizens under the ban of excommunication; you will hand them over to a new anathema maranatha; you will declare that they have no political rights 'which white men are bound to respect,' thus repeating in a new form that abomination which has blackened the name of Taney. Adopt it, and you will stimulate anew the war of race upon race. Slavery itself was a war of race upon race, and this is only a new form of this terrible war. The proposition is as hardy as it is gigantic; for it takes no account of the moral sense of mankind, which is the same as if in rearing a monument we took no account of the law of gravitation. It is the paragon and master-piece of ingratitude, showing more than any other act of history what is so often charged and we so fondly deny, that republics are ungrateful. The freedmen ask for bread, and you send them a stone. With piteous voice they ask for protection. You thrust them back unprotected into the cruel den of their former masters. Such an attempt, thus bad as bad can be, thus abortive for all good, thus perilous, thus pregnant with a war of race upon race, thus shocking to the moral sense, and thus treacherous to those whom we are bound to protect, can not be otherwise than shameful.

Adopt it, and you will cover the country with dishonor. Adopt it, and you will fix a stigma upon the very name of republic. As to the imagination, there are mountains of light, so are there mountains of darkness; and this is one of them. It is the very Koh-i-noor of blackness. Adopt this proposition, and you will be little better than the foul Harpies who defiled the feast that was spread. The Constitution is the feast spread for our country, and you are now hurrying to drop into its text a political obscenity, and to spread on its page a disgusting ordure,

"'Defiling all you find,
And parting leave a loathsome stench behind.'"

Having presented his objections to the pending proposition, at great length, he summed them up as follows: "You have seen, first, how this proposition carries into the Constitution itself the idea of Inequality of Rights, thus defiling that unspotted text; secondly, how it is an express sanction of the acknowledged tyranny of taxation without representation; thirdly, how it is a concession to State Rights at a moment when we are recovering from a terrible war waged against us in the name of State Rights; fourthly, how it is the constitutional recognition of an oligarchy, aristocracy, caste, and monopoly founded on color; fifthly, how it petrifies in the Constitution the wretched pretensions of a white man's government; sixthly, how it assumes what is false in constitutional law, that color can be a 'qualification' for an elector; seventhly, how it positively ties the hands of Congress in fixing the meaning of a republican government, so that, under the guarantee clause, it will be constrained to recognize an oligarchy, aristocracy, caste, and monopoly founded on color, together with the tyranny of taxation without representation, as not inconsistent with such a government; eighthly, how it positively ties the hands of Congress in completing and consummating the abolition of slavery according to the second clause of the constitutional amendment, so that it can not, for this purpose, interfere with the denial of the elective franchise on account of color; ninthly, how it installs recent rebels in permanent power over loyal citizens; and, tenthly, how it shows forth, in unmistakable character, as a compromise of human rights, the most immoral, indecent, and utterly shameful of any in our history. All this you have seen, with pain and sorrow, I trust. Who that is moved to sympathy for his fellow-man can listen to the story without indignation? Who that has not lost the power of reason can fail to see the cruel wrong?"

Mr. Doolittle mentioned some facts which he thought would prove the apprehension of an increase of the basis of representation in the South to be without foundation. "The destruction of the population," said he, "both white and black, during the civil war, has been most enormous. Of the white population, there were in those States in 1860, of white males over twenty years of age, about one million six hundred thousand. Nearly one-third of that white population over twenty years of age has perished. The actual destruction of the black population since 1860 has been at least twenty-five per cent. of the whole population. The population of the South has been so destroyed and wasted and enfeebled in consequence of this war, that I do not for one, I confess, feel those apprehensions which some entertain that, if they are admitted to representation under the Constitution just as it stands, they will have any increase of Representatives. My opinion is, that after the next census their representation will be diminished unless emigration from the North or from Europe shall fill up their population and increase it so as to entitle it to an increased representation."

Mr. Doolittle argued that the amendment was capable of being evaded by a State disposed to disfranchise colored men: "I do not see," said he, "that there is any thing in the resolution which would prevent South Carolina or any other State from passing a law that any person who was born free, or whose ancestors were free, should exercise the elective franchise, and none others. That would exclude the whole of the colored population, and yet would leave the State to have its full representation. There is nothing which would prevent the State of South Carolina or any other State from saying that only those persons who had served in the military service, and their descendants, should exercise the elective franchise. That would exclude the colored population, and the Union population, too, if they refused to serve in the army."

Mr. Doolittle closed his remarks by advocating an amendment basing representation upon actual voters under State laws.

Mr. Morrill, of Maine, addressed the Senate in support of the proposition to amend the Constitution. He said: "Some amendment is rendered absolutely necessary, unless the American

Constitution is to give to the nation the expression of utterly contradictory sentiments, saying involuntary servitude no longer exists, in one portion of it; in another, bearing on its front in marked contrast, that three-fifths only of the 'other persons' are to still constitute the basis of representation."

He recalled a time not far remote when amendments of the Constitution were adopted by those who now oppose any alteration of the fundamental law: "I do not forget," said he, "that within the last five years a class of statesmen and politicians, who now resist all propositions for an amendment of the Constitution, here and elsewhere urged and demanded amendments of the Constitution of the nation. What were the circumstances then? Several States threatened to dissolve this Union; several States had taken an attitude hostile to the Government of the country. They demanded the extension, the protection, and the perpetuation of slavery; and upon that question the country was divided. Then amendments to the Constitution were proposed without number here, elsewhere, and every-where. Amendments to the Constitution seemed to be the order of the day. To what end, and for what purpose? To increase the power in the hands of the few who wielded the political power in those States, and who were demanding it.

Referring to an argument presented by the Senator from Wisconsin, Mr. Morrill remarked: "But yesterday we had an additional reason given why this amendment should not be adopted; and that was that it was wholly unnecessary, because, it was said, by the events which were transpiring in the country in regard to the recent slave population, there need be no apprehension of excess of representation based on the whole 'numbers' instead of three-fifths, from the important fact that they were passing away. If I gather the force of that argument, it is this: we are to base no legislation and no action upon the idea that this race, recently slave, now free, is part and parcel of the American people, the object of our care, solicitude, and protection. They are passing away—dying; let them be represented as slaves now, and let them never enter into the basis hereafter of the representative system. Sir, that is the old argument—an argument worthy of another period than this. Our people have been an inexorable people, in some respects, in regard to the races that have been within their power. In the march of our civilization across the continent, the iron heel of that civilization has rested upon the Indian, and he is passing away. We seem to contemplate the probable extinction of the Indians from our limits with composure. He is a nomad; he is a savage; he is a barbarian; he is not within our morals or our code of law; he is not within the pale of the Constitution, but flits upon the verge of it, outside our protection, the subject of our caprices, and sometimes, I think, of our avarice. And, now, if any consequence is to be attached to the remark of the honorable Senator from Wisconsin [Mr. Doolittle] yesterday, this 'inferior race' is not to be the subject of our solicitude. They, too, are passing away; it is not worth while to change your Constitution in regard to them. Let them be represented as two-fifths slaves on the old basis until they shall have perished, and then your Constitution will need no amendment. The laws of a fearful antagonism of superior and inferior races are expected to accomplish what, if American statesmanship does not incite, it contemplates with apparent satisfaction."

Mr. Wilson, of Massachusetts, profoundly regretted to see indications that the amendment was doomed to defeat. He said: "My heart, my conscience, and my judgment approve of this amendment, and I support it without qualification or reservation. I approve of the purpose for which it is introduced. I approve it because I believe it would sweep the loyal States by an immense majority; that no public man could stand before the people of the loyal States in opposition to it, or oppose it with any force whatever. I approve it because I believe if it were put in the Constitution every black man in America, before five years could pass, would be enfranchised and weaponed with the ballot for the protection of life, liberty, and property."

Referring to the opposition brought to bear against the measure by his colleague, Mr. Wilson said: "We are also told that it is immoral and indecent, an offense to reason and to conscience. Sir, this measure came into Congress with the sanction of the Committee on Reconstruction, composed as it is of men of individual honor and personal character, and as true to the cause of the colored race as any other men here or elsewhere. It comes to the Senate by an overwhelming vote of the House of Representatives. It is sustained by ninety-nine out of every hundred of the public journals that brought the present Administration into power, and were it submitted to the American people, it would, I am quite sure, be sustained by men in the loyal States who believe that the soldier who fought the battles of the republic is the equal of the traitor who fought against the country. I see no compromise in it, no surrender in it, no defilement of the Constitution in it, no implication that can be drawn from it against the rights or interests of the colored race. On the contrary, I believe the black men, from the Potomac to the Rio Grande, would go for it and rejoice to see it adopted."

Mr. Wilson described the results that would follow the adoption of this amendment. "Being incorporated in the Constitution, the practical effect would be this, and only this: it would raise up a party in every one of these States immediately in favor of the enfranchisement of the colored race. That party might be animated and influenced by the love of power, by pride, and by ambition. These men might begin the contest, for they would not like to yield the power of their States in Congress; they might begin the battle animated by no high and lofty motives; but as soon as the discussion commenced, it would address itself to the reason, to the heart, and to the conscience of the people. The advocates of negro enfranchisement would themselves speedily grow up to believe in the justice, equity, and right of giving the ballot to the black men. There would be discussion on every square mile of the rebel States. Appeals would be made to their pride, to their ambition, to their justice, to their love of fair play, to their equity; all the interests and passions, and all the loftier motives that can sway, control, and influence men, would impel them to action. They would coöperate with the friends of freedom throughout the country; would seek their counsel and aid. They would be the left wing of the great army of freedom, of elevation, and improvement in the country. We would give them our influence, our voices, and our aid in fighting the battle of enfranchisement. They would have the support and the prayers of the poor black men of the South; and before five years had passed away, there would not be a rebel State that did not enfranchise the bondman."

Referring to the policy of "enlightened Christian States," in refusing the right of suffrage to the negro, Mr. Wilson said: "After all the fidelity and heroic conduct of these men, prejudice, party spirit, and conservatism, and all that is base and mean on earth, combine to deny the right of suffrage to the brave soldier of the republic. God alone can forgive such meanness; humanity can not. After what has taken place, is taking place, I can not hope that the constitutional amendment proposed by the Senator from Missouri will receive a majority of three-fourths of the votes of the States. I, therefore, can not risk the cause of an emancipated race upon it. In the present condition of the nation we must aim at practical results, not to establish political theories, however beautiful and alluring they may be."

It was the understanding of the Senate that the discussion would close and the vote would be taken on the 9th of March. On that day Mr. Fessenden took the floor in reply to objections urged by those who had previously spoken. In reply to the objection that the advocates of this measure were wrong in attempting to accomplish by indirection that which they could not accomplish directly, Mr. Fessenden said: "If negro suffrage can be secured by the indirect action of an amendment of the Constitution which appeals to the interest of those who have hitherto been and who are yet probably the ruling class among whom this large population is situated, and with whom they live, it will be far better than to run the risk of all the difficulties that might arise from a forcible imposition, which would create ill-feeling, generate discord, and produce, perhaps undying animosities."

To the objection urged by Mr. Hendricks, that it was intended for a party purpose, Mr. Fessenden replied: "Has he any right to attack the motives of those who support it? Must it necessarily be attended with benefit to a particular party? If so, it is necessarily attended with injury to another party, of which the honorable Senator is a prominent member; and it would as well become me to say that his opposition to it is for party purposes and for party objects as it became him to say that its introduction and its support were intended for party purposes. It is well known here and out of this Senate that the honorable Senator from Indiana is a gentleman who never, in any of his addresses here, says any thing that is in the slightest degree calculated to effect a party purpose, and has so little of that party feeling which presses itself upon other men as to be hardly suspected of being a party man at all." [Laughter.]

Mr. Fessenden thus replied to the objections of two opponents of the measure: "The Senator [Mr. Hendricks] objected to this measure upon another ground, and that was, that in one sense it was intended as a punishment, and that was wrong; and in another sense it was what he called a bribe, a reward, and that was wrong. If he considers it a punishment, he differs very much from his leading associate on this question, the honorable Senator from Massachusetts, [Mr. Sumner,] for he does not consider it a punishment at all. The Senator from Massachusetts says there is nothing punitive in it. On the contrary, it is a reward to these States; it is conferring power upon them; it is strengthening power in the hands of the whites of the South, and only oppressing the colored race. Behold how doctors disagree! They operate upon the same patient, and are operating at the same time, with different remedies and in different directions.

"Suppose it is a punishment, and suppose it is a bribe, a reward; it does not differ very much from the principle upon which all criminal legislation is founded, to say the least of it. We punish men when they do wrong. I never heard that it was an objection to legislation that it punished those who perpetrate a wrong. I never heard that it was an objection to legislation that it held out rewards to those who did right."

Referring to Mr. Buckalew's argument, Mr. Fessenden remarked: "Eight out of sixteen pages of his speech were devoted to abuse of New England, and to showing that New England had too much power, and that it ought to be abridged in some way.

"He closed those remarks by saying (for which I was very much obliged to him) that he did not despise New England. We are happy to know it. I will say to him that New England does not despise him that I am aware of. [Laughter.] I am not aware that it is really affected in any degree by the elaborate attack of eight pages which he delivered against New England on that occasion, and which he thought were views so important that he could not be justified if he failed to give them utterance."

Of Mr. Sumner's part in the debate, Mr. Fessenden said: "On this subject I think he has occupied about eight or nine hours of the time of the Senate, and on the last occasion, while saying that principles were to be considered, he has undertaken to designate the character of this proposed amendment. I have already stated who the men were who were in favor of it. What does the Senator call it? I have chosen a few, and but a few, flowers of rhetoric from the speech of the honorable Senator: 'Compromise of human rights,' 'violating the national faith,' 'dishonoring the name of there public,' 'bad mutton,' 'new muscipular abortion,' 'a new anathema maranatha,' 'abomination,' 'paragon and masterpiece of ingratitude,' 'abortive for all good,' 'shocking to the moral sense,' 'the very Koh-i-noor of blackness,' 'essential uncleanliness,' 'disgusting ordure,' 'loathsome stench;' and the men who support it, if they pass it, will be 'Harpies,' 'Pontius Pilate, with Judas Iscariot on his back.'

"The Senator from Massachusetts makes several points against this proposition, to which my answer is the same. His first point is, that it recognizes 'the idea of inequality of rights founded on race or color.' I deny *in toto* the correctness, or even the plausibility, to a man of sense, any point that he has raised on the subject. There is not one of them that is tenable; and more than that, there is not one of them but what is just as tenable against the proposition he is in favor of to found representation on voters as this. What lawyer in the world ever heard that a denial is an admission? What lawyer ever heard that a penalty is a permission? By this proposition, we say simply this: 'If, in the exercise of the power that you have under the Constitution, you make an inequality of rights, then you are to suffer such and such consequences.' What sane man could ever pretend that that was saying, 'Make an inequality of rights and we will sanction it?' We do not deny—nobody can deny—that the power may be thus exercised. What we say by this amendment is, 'If you attempt to exercise it in this wrongful way, you create an inequality of rights; and if you do create an inequality of rights' —not we, but you—'if you undertake to do it under the power which exists in the Constitution, then the consequence follows that you are punished by a loss of representation.' That is all that is in it."

Having replied to the most of Mr. Sumner's objections in order, Mr. Fessenden said: "The last point of the Senator is, that this proposition is 'a compromise of human rights, the most immoral, indecent, and utterly shameful in our history.'

"Mr. President, I stand rebuked, but I do not feel so bad as I might. The Committee of Fifteen, the friends and associates of the honorable Senator, stand rebuked. More than two-thirds of the House of Representatives and a large majority of this body, all the political friends and associates of the Senator, stand charged with proposing a compromise of human rights the most immoral, indecent, and shameful in our history! All I can say with regard to that is, that neither on its face, in its effect, nor in its intention is it any compromise. None such was dreamed of."

Mr. Fessenden thus described the remarkable combination of Senators opposing the amendment: "I can not close, however, without saying how amusing seems to me the character of the opposition to this joint resolution. That opposition is composed of men of all shades of opinion. The Democrats on the other side of the House oppose it because they say it is unjust to the Southern States; my honorable friends who have been some time with us are opposed to it because—I do not know why, except that the President is opposed to it, and I believe that is the ground; my honorable friend from Massachusetts objects because it is unjust to the negro. Why, sir, just imagine all the gentlemen opposed to this resolution met in caucus together, and looking around at each other, would there not be a smile on all their faces to see what company they had fallen into? I think Senators would be surprised to find themselves there, and, like the countryman looking at the reel in the bottle, they would consider how the devil they did get there. [Laughter.] It would be a very strange meeting; and yet they are all against this proposition."

After a running debate between several Senators, the vote was taken upon the substitute proposed by Mr. Henderson as a constitutional amendment, viz.: "No State, in prescribing the qualifications requisite for electors therein, shall discriminate against any person on account of color or race." The amendment was lost—yeas, 10; nays, 37. The question was then taken on Mr. Sumner's substitute, which was simply a joint resolution providing 'there shall be no oligarchy, aristocracy, caste, or monopoly invested with peculiar privileges, and no denial of rights, civil or political, on account of color or race, anywhere within the United States." This resolution was lost—yeas, 8; nays, 39. The vote was then taken on the amendment proposed by Mr. Yates, providing that no State shall make or enforce any distinction between citizens of the United States on account of race or color, and that all citizens shall hereafter be protected in the exercise of all civil and political rights, including the right of suffrage. This amendment was lost—yeas, 7; nays, 38. The vote was then taken upon the original amendment as reported by the joint Committee of Fifteen. The following was the result:

YEAS—Messrs. Anthony, Chandler, Clark, Conness, Cragin, Creswell, Fessenden, Foster, Grimes, Harris, Howe, Kirkwood, Lane of Indiana, McDougall, Morgan, Morrill, Nye, Poland, Ramsey, Sherman, Sprague, Trumbull, Wade, Williams, and Wilson—25.

NAYS—Messrs. Brown, Buckalew, Cowan, Davis, Dixon, Doolittle, Guthrie, Henderson, Hendricks, Johnson, Lane of Kansas, Nesmith, Norton, Pomeroy, Riddle, Saulsbury, Stewart, Stockton, Sumner, Van Winkle, Willey, and Yates—22.

ABSENT—Messrs. Foot, Howard, and Wright—3.

Two thirds of the Senators not having voted for the joint resolution, it was lost. The defeat of the proposed constitutional amendment was accomplished by the combination of five "Radical" Senators with six "Conservatives," elected as Republicans, whose vote, added to the regular Democratic strength, prevented its adoption by the required constitutional majority of two-thirds.

The advocates of constitutional reform, though foiled in this attempt, were not disheartened. Their defeat taught them the important lesson that pet measures and favorite theories must be abandoned or modified in order to secure the adoption of some constitutional amendment to obviate difficulties of which all felt and acknowledged the existence.

Meanwhile other measures, designed to lead to the great end of reconstruction, were demanding and receiving the consideration of Congress.

CHAPTER XVI.

REPRESENTATION OF THE SOUTHERN STATES.

Concurrent Resolution—A "Venomous Fight"—Passage in the House—The Resolution in the Senate—"A Political Wrangle" Deprecated—Importance of the Question—"A Straw in a Storm"—Policy of the President—Conversation between two Senators—Mr. Nye's Advice to Rebels—"A Dangerous Power"—"Was Mr. Wade once a Secessionist?"—Garrett Davis' Programme for the President—"Useless yet Mischievous"—The Great Question Settled.

IT was understood when the Committee of Fifteen introduced the joint resolution proposing a constitutional amendment relating to the basis of representation, that this was only one of a series of measures which they thought essential to the work of reconstruction, and which they designed to propose at a proper time.

In pursuance of this plan, on the 20th of February, the day after the veto of the Freedmen's Bureau Bill, and while the amendment of the basis of reconstruction was pending in the Senate, Mr. Stevens brought before the House, from the Committee of Fifteen, a "Concurrent Resolution concerning the Insurrectionary States," as follows:

"*Be it resolved by the House of Representatives*, (the Senate concurring,) That in order to close agitation upon a question which seems likely to disturb the action of the Government, as well as to quiet the uncertainty which is agitating the minds of the people of the eleven States which have been declared to be in insurrection, no Senator or Representative shall be admitted into either branch of Congress from any of said States until Congress shall have declared such State entitled to such representation."

After the reading of this resolution, Mr. Grider, of Kentucky, a member of the Committee of Fifteen, offered the following minority report:

"The minority of the Committee on Reconstruction, on the part of the House, beg leave to report that said committee have directed an inquiry to be made as to the condition and loyalty of the State of Tennessee. There has been a large amount of evidence taken, some part of it conducing to show that at some localities occasionally there have been some irregularities and temporary disaffection; yet the main direction and weight of the testimony are ample and conclusive to show that the great body of the people in said State are not only loyal and willing, but anxious, to have and maintain amicable, sincere, and patriotic relations with the General Government. Such being the state of the facts, and inasmuch as under the census of 1860 Congress passed a law which was approved in 1863, fixing the ratio and apportioning to Tennessee and all the other States representation; and inasmuch as Tennessee, disavowing insurrectionary purposes or disloyalty, has, under the laws and organic law of said State, regularly elected her members and Senators to the Congress of the United States, in conformity to the laws and Constitution of the United States, and said members are here asking admission; and inasmuch as the House by the Constitution is the 'judge of the election, returns, and qualification of its members,' considering these facts and principles, we offer the following resolution, to-wit:

"*Resolved*, That the State of Tennessee is entitled to representation in the Thirty-ninth Congress, and the Representatives elected from and by said State are hereby admitted to take their seats therein upon being qualified by oath according to law."

Mr. Stevens then said: "Having heard an ingenious speech upon that side of the question, and not intending to make any speech upon this side, as I hope our friends all understand a question which has agitated not this body only, but other portions of the community, I propose to ask for the question. I think I may say without impropriety, that until yesterday there was an earnest investigation into the condition of Tennessee, to see whether by act of Congress we could admit that State to a condition of representation here, and admit its members to seats here; but since yesterday there has arisen a state of things which the committee deem puts it out of their power to proceed further without surrendering a great principle; without the loss of all their dignity; without surrendering the rights of this body to the usurpation of another power. I call the previous question."

Strenuous efforts were made by the Democratic minority to defeat the proposed joint resolution by means of "dilatory motions." Repeated motions were made to adjourn, to excuse certain members from voting, and to call the House, on all of which the yeas and nays were called. This "parliamentary tactics" consumed many hours. The minority seemed resolved to make the passage of the resolution a question of physical endurance. In reply to a proposition of Mr. Eldridge, of the minority, that they would allow business to proceed if debate should be allowed, Mr. Stevens said: "It is simply the return of the rebels of 1861. I sat thirty-eight hours under this kind of a fight once, and I have no objections to a little of it now. I am ready to sit for forty hours."

Late in the evening, a member of the minority proposed that the House should take a recess for an hour, that the door-keeper might have the hall fitted up as a dormitory. From indications, he thought such accommodations would be necessary. At length, Mr. Eldridge said: "We know our weakness and the strength and power of the numbers of the majority. We have not had the assistance which we expected from the other side of the House in our effort to obtain the privilege of debating the resolution. We know perfectly well that it has become a question of physical endurance. We know perfectly well that we can not stand out against the overpowering majority of this House any great length of time. We know if the majority will it, the resolution will pass without debate. We have done all we could. We therefore yield to that power, and throw the responsibility of this most extraordinary, this most revolutionary measure, upor the majority of the House."

To this Mr. Stevens answered: "The gentlemen accept their situation just as Jeff. Davis did his—because they can not help it. [Laughter.] I confess, sir, for so small a number, they have made a most venomous fight."

The vote was then taken upon the concurrent resolution, which passed the House—yeas, 109; nays, 40.

The hopes which had arisen in the minds of the minority that a considerable number of Republicans would permanently separate themselves from the party that elected them, and adhere to the policy and fortunes of the President, were disappointed. The imprudence of the President himself, in making his unfortunate speech of the 22d of February, tended to unite the Republicans in Congress against his policy, and render fruitless the efforts of his new Democratic friends in his favor.

On the 23d of February, Mr. Fessenden proposed that the pending constitutional amendment should give way, to enable the Senate to consider the concurrent resolution passed by the House concerning the representation of the Southern States.

Mr. Sherman thought it would be better and wiser to allow this matter to lie over for a few days. He thought it best not to press this "declaration of political opinion" while the public mind and Senators themselves were more or less affected by surrounding circumstances. "I think," said he, "that we ought not to postpone all the important business now pending in Congress for the purpose of getting into a political wrangle with the President."

Mr. Fessenden replied: "The Senator from Ohio says we are getting up a political wrangle with the President of the United States. When the President of the United States tells Congress that it is transcending its proper limits of authority, that it has nothing to do in the way of judgment upon the great question of reconstructing the rebel States, and Congress assumes to express its own sense upon that question, I think it is hardly a proper term to apply to such a state of things. I am not aware that there has been any effort anywhere to get up a political wrangle or engage in a political wrangle with the President. Certainly I have not. No man has ever heard me speak of him except in terms of respect, in my place here and elsewhere.

"I am not sensible myself of any excitement that would prevent my speaking upon this question precisely in the style which I deem it deserves. I am not carried away by passion. I have reflected, and I am ready to express my opinion upon the great question at issue; and the Senator will allow me to say that, in my judgment, the sooner the judgment of Congress is expressed, the better.

"He talks about important business to be done by this Congress. Sir, is there any thing more important than to settle the question whether the Senate and the House of Representatives of the United States have or have not something to say in relation to the condition of the late Confederate States, and whether it is proper to admit Senators and Representatives from them? If the President is right in his assumption—for the assumption is a very clear one—that we have nothing to say, we ought to admit these men at once, if they come here with proper credentials, and not keep them waiting outside the door."

Mr. Sherman said: "In my judgment, the events that transpired yesterday are too fresh in the mind of every Senator not to have had some influence upon him, and I think it as well to allow the influence of those events to pass away. I do not wish now myself, nor do I wish any Senator here, to reply to what was said yesterday by the President of the United States. I would prefer that the Senate of the United States, the only legislative body which can deliberate fully and freely without any limitation on the right of debate, should deliberate, reflect, and act calmly after the excitement of the events of the last two or three days has passed off."

Mr. Howe, of Wisconsin, remarked: "If there be passion and excitement in the country at this present time, I do not hold myself as an individual responsible for any share of it; and I am here to say that if I know myself—and if I do not know myself nobody about me knows me—I am as competent to consider this particular question to-day as I was the day before yesterday or last week, and, so far as my judgment informs me, quite as competent to consider it as I expect to be next week or the week after. And when the Senator from Ohio asks me to vote against proceeding to the consideration of any measure, either because I distrust my own fitness to consider it, or distrust the fitness of my associates about me, I must respectfully decline, not because I care particularly whether we take up this measure to-day or another day, but because I ask the Senate to vindicate their own course as individual men, and to say that they are not to be swept from the seat of judgment by what is said, or can be said, by the first magistrate of the nation, or by the lowest and the last magistrate of the nation."

The Senate, by a vote of 26 to 19, agreed to proceed to consider the concurrent resolution proposed by the Committee of Fifteen, which had already passed the House of Representatives.

Mr. Fessenden advocated the resolution in a speech of considerable length. He presented extracts from the President's speech of the day before, in which he had arrayed himself against the right of Congress to decide whether a rebel State is in condition to be represented.

Mr. Fessenden considered the pending resolution as "transcending in importance the question of the amendment of the Constitution, which had been under discussion for several days." He deemed the resolution necessary now, "in order that Congress may assert distinctly its own rights and its own powers; in order that there may be no mistake anywhere, in the mind of the Executive or in the minds of the people of this country; that Congress, under the circumstances of this case, with this attempted limitation of its powers with regard to its own organization, is prepared to say to the Executive and to the country, respectfully but firmly, over this subject they have, and they mean to exercise, the most full and plenary jurisdiction. We will judge for ourselves, not only upon credentials and the character of men and the position of men, but upon the position of the States which sent those men here. In other words, to use the language of the President again, when the question is to be decided, whether they obey the Constitution, whether they have a fitting constitution of their own, whether they are loyal, whether they are prepared to obey the laws as a preliminary, as the President says it is, to their admission, we will say whether those preliminary requirements have been complied with, and not he, and nobody but ourselves."

Mr. Fessenden made an extended argument on the subject of reconstruction, affirming that while the people of the rebel States had not passed from under the jurisdiction of the United States Government, yet having no existence as States with rights in the Union and rights to representation in Congress. "My judgment is," said he, "that we hold the power over the whole subject in our hands, that it is our duty to hold it in our hands, and to regard it as a matter of the most intense interest to the whole people, involving the good of the whole people, calling for our most careful consideration, and to be adjudged without passion, without temper, without any of that feeling which may be supposed to have arisen out of the unexampled state of things through which we have passed."

On the 26th of February, Mr. Sherman addressed the Senate on the pending concurrent resolution. He approved the principle but doubted the expediency of now reäffirming it. "I regard it," said he, "as a mere straw in a storm, thrown in at an inopportune moment; the mere assertion of a naked right which has never yet been disputed, and never can be successfully; a mere assertion of a right that we have over and over again asserted. My idea is that the true way to assert this power is to exercise it, and that it was only necessary for Congress to exercise that power in order to meet all these complicated difficulties."

Mr. Sherman regarded the President's speech as humiliating

and unworthy of his high office. A part of the speech he characterized as "the product of resentment, hatched by anger and passion, and hurled, without reflection, at those he believed wished to badger and insult him."

Mr. Sherman favored the prompt restoration of Tennessee. "I think our first duty," said he, "is at once to prepare a mode and manner by which she may be admitted into the Union upon such terms and conditions as will make her way back the way of pleasantness and peace."

Of the general question of reconstruction he said: "If I had any power in arranging a plan, I would mark the line as broad and deep between the loyal people who stood at our side and the rebels who fought against us as between heaven and hell."

"How can you do it?" asked Mr. Howard.

"Whenever loyal men," replied Mr. Sherman, "present a State organization, complying with such terms and conditions and tests of loyalty as you may prescribe, and will send here loyal Representatives, I would admit them; and whenever rebels send or come here, I would reject them."

"I fear the storm," said Mr. Sherman, near the conclusion of his speech. "I fear struggles and contentions in these eleven States, unless there is some mode by which the local power of those States may be put in loyal hands, and by which their voices may be heard here in council and in command, in deliberation and debate, as of old. They will come back here shorn of their undue political power, humbled in their pride, with a consciousness that one man bred under free institutions is as good, at least, as a man bred under slave institutions. I want to see the loyal people in the South, if they are few, trusted; if they are many, give them power. Prescribe your conditions, but let them come back into the Union upon such terms as you may prescribe. Open the door for them. I hope we may see harmony restored in this great Union of ours; that all these States and all these Territories may be here in council for the common good, and that at as speedy a moment as is consistent with the public safety."

Mr. Dixon addressed the Senate in opposition to the concurrent resolution, and in favor of the policy of the President. "It is my belief," said he, "that what is known as the policy of the President for the restoration of the late seceded States in this Government is the correct policy. I believe it is the only safe policy." Having been requested to state that policy, Mr. Dixon said: "It contemplates a careful, cautious, discriminating admission of a loyal representation from loyal States and districts in the appropriate House of Congress, by the separate action of each, every case to be considered by itself and decided on its own merits. It recognizes the right of every loyal State and district to be represented by loyal men in Congress. It draws the true line of distinction between traitors and true men. It furnishes to the States lately in rebellion the strongest possible inducement to loyalty and fidelity to the Government. It 'makes treason odious,' by showing that while the traitor and the rebel are excluded from Congress, the loyal and the faithful are cordially received. It recognizes and rewards loyalty wherever it is found, and distinguishes, as it ought, between a Horace Maynard and a Jefferson Davis."

Of the purpose expressed in this resolution to "close agitation," Mr. Dixon said: "The vast business interests of this country are eagerly intent on this question. The people of this country are mutually attracted, the North and the South, and they must sooner or later act together. Whatever Congress may do, this question will not cease to be agitated. Adjourn, if you see fit, without settling this question; leave it as it is; admit no member from Tennessee; and when you go through the States next fall which hold their elections for Congress, see whether agitation has ceased. Sir, a word of caution may not be unfit on that subject."

Mr. Dixon maintained that the Senate would surrender its independence by resolving that Senators should not be admitted from rebel States until Congress should have declared them entitled to such representation. "Upon the question of credentials," said he, "this whole question is before the Senate; and it is for us to consider on that question whether the member presenting himself here for admission is a traitor or whether he is true to his country."

"Suppose," said Mr. Trumbull, "that in a time of peace the Legislature of Tennessee is disloyal, and swears allegiance to the Emperor Maximilian, does the Senator deny the authority of Congress to inquire into the character of that Legislature?"

"I do," replied Mr. Dixon. "It is for the Senate, and not for Congress, to make the inquiry if a Senator from Tennessee in the supposed case presents himself."

Mr. Trumbull said: "He denies the authority of Congress to decide whether the constituency is traitorous or loyal!"

"That is another point," said Mr. Dixon.

"That is the very one I put," said Mr. Trumbull. "If all the members of the Legislature of Tennessee swear allegiance to the Emperor Maximilian, and send a Senator here, I want to know if Congress has a right to inquire into the character of that Legislature?"

"I will answer that by asking another question," said Mr. Dixon. "Suppose that was the case, that the Emperor Maximilian had entire control of the State of Tennessee, and a person claiming a right so to do should come here and offer himself as a member of the Senate, and should be received here; that, in judging of the qualifications, returns, and elections of the member, the Senate decided that he was a Senator, has Congress any thing to do with the question? I ask him if the House of Representatives can interfere? Is there an appeal to Congress or any other tribunal? I ask him if that man is not a Senator in spite of the world?"

"If," replied Mr. Trumbull, "the Senator means to ask me if the Senate has not the physical power to admit any body, elected or not, I admit they have the same right to do it that twelve jurymen would have, against the sworn and uncontradicted testimony of a hundred witnesses, to bring in a verdict directly against the evidence and perjure themselves. I suppose we have the physical power to commit perjury here, when we have sworn to support the Constitution. We might admit a man here from Pennsylvania Avenue, elected by nobody, as a member of this Senate; but we would commit perjury in doing it, and have no right to do it."

Mr. Trumbull made an extended reply, which assumed somewhat the form of a conversation, in which Mr. Dixon and other Senators participated. Mr. Trumbull claimed that it required the concurrent action of both houses of Congress to recognize any government in States where rebellion had overthrown it.

On the 28th of February, the concurrent resolution still pending, Mr. Nye, of Nevada, advocated its passage. He opposed the present admission of any member from the seceding States. "We are told," said he, "by the apologists of these men who are being elected on their merits as rebels, to the exclusion of Union men, that 'we must not expect too much of them.' I fully accede to this idea. A class that during its whole political life has aimed at a monopoly of wealth, a monopoly of labor, and a monopoly of political power; that engaged in the attempt at revolution in order to establish more fully and to perpetuate such monopoly; that, failing in this, has become more bitter by disappointment, should have time; and, sir, I am decidedly in favor of giving them all the time necessary for the most substantial improvement. I would say to these men, 'Go home! Go back and labor as industriously to disabuse the minds of your constituencies as you labored to mislead and impose upon them. Tell them that the Union Government always was and never can be any thing else than a just Government. Tell them that the Constitution has become the acknowledged sovereign, and that it presides in both houses of Congress. Inform them, while you are about it, that the rebel sympathizers and apologists in the North can do them no good; that they are acting as much out of time and propriety now as they did in the time of the war, when their encouragement only prolonged the conflict and added to Southern disaster. You may say to your constituencies that the majority in Congress is very tenacious on the subject of the Union war debt; that it is determined to keep faith with the national creditors; that it is bent on adopting and throwing around it all the safeguards and precautions possible; and that your admission just now, and your alliance with Northern sympathizers, would not be propitious in raising the value of our public securities. While you are conferring with your constituents, you may as well repeat to them the common political axiom that Representatives are elected to represent their constituents, and that it is not believed at the seat of Government that a disloyal constituency would make such a mistake as to send loyal Representatives to Congress. In short, you may as well say to your people that, as Congress represents the loyalty of the nation, South as well as North, and has much important work on hand, some of it requiring a two-thirds majority, it is not deemed wholly prudent to part with that majority out of mere comity to men from whom no assistance could be expected. Finally, by way of closing the suggestive instructions, you may give your constituents to understand that, as you went out of Congress rebel end foremost, you will not probably get into those vacant seats over yonder except that you come back Union end foremost.'"

Mr. Stewart, of Nevada, held opinions of the pending question different from those maintained by his colleague. He thought "the power to suspend the right of a State to representation might imply a dangerous power, and might imply a right to suspend it for any reason that Congress might see fit. The power to suspend the right of a State to be represented might hereafter be a terrible precedent." "There is no provision in the Constitution," said Mr. Stewart, "conferring such a power upon Congress. No authority of the kind is expressed in that instrument, nor can I find any place where it is implied." In another portion of his speech, which was very long, and occupied part of the session of the succeeding day, Mr. Stewart remarked: "In the darkest time of the rebellion, I deny that the right to represent Tennessee in this hall by those who were loyal ever was for a moment suspended, but their power to obey the law, their power to represent it was prevented by treason. They were overpowered, and they were denied the right of representation, not by Congress, not by the Government. This war was to maintain for them that right which rebellion had sought to take away from them, and had for a time suspended the harmonious relations of the State to the General Government; and it will be too much to admit that this Government has ever been in such a fix that the people thereof were really not entitled to the protection of the Constitution, and because they were denied it this war was brought on, this war was prosecuted."

Mr. Johnson opposed the resolution in a protracted speech in which he reviewed the entire subject of reconstruction. Of the condition and rights of the Southern States he said: "They are as much States as they were when the insurrection was inaugurated, and their relation to their sister States, and their consequent relation to the Government of the United States, is the same relation in which they stood to both when the insurrection was inaugurated. That would seem to follow logically as a necessary result, and if that is a necessary result, does it not also follow that they are entitled to representation in this chamber? Whether they can present persons who can take their seats, because they have individually committed crimes against the United States is another question; but I speak now of the right itself."

Mr. Johnson argued that holding secession sentiments a few years ago was no evidence of present disloyalty, and cited in proof of this proposition a newspaper article purporting to give secession resolutions drawn up by Mr. Wade, and passed at a meeting held at Cleveland in 1859, which was presided over by Joshua R. Giddings.

This called forth an answer from Mr. Wade, who said: "The Senator from Maryland called me in question for having been present at a meeting which he affirmed was held in Cleveland some seven years ago by persons called 'Sons of Liberty,' and he alleged that I there consented to certain resolutions that were passed which favored the doctrine of secession, and that I was chairman of the committee which reported them. Sir, the charge is a total forgery so far as I am concerned. I never was at any such meeting of the Sons of Liberty or any other sons. I never uttered such a sentiment in my life; I am not one of those who have or have had much association with gentlemen holding to secession principles. My associations have all been the other way. During the war that secession made my counsels were against it. I was for war to the death against the principle of secession, while many other gentlemen in my eye were either participants in or apologists for that sentiment. I am perfectly aware that a war is made—and I am willing to meet it anywhere—upon what are called Radicals of the country, and I am one of them. In olden times I was here in the Senate called an Abolitionist, but they have changed the name since. They have all got to be Abolitionists now, and they have changed my name to 'Radical.'

"Mr. President, in the history of mankind, so far as I have read or know it, there never has been a time when parties were so organized on radical principles of justice and right. The party with whom I act appeal to no expediency, to none of your political policies; we dig down to the granite of eternal truth, and there we stand, and they who assail us have to assail the great principles of the Almighty, for our principles are chained to his throne, and are as indestructible as the Almighty himself. I want no warfare with any body; but if you will make war upon such principles as we have adopted, it is the worse for you. You can not prevail.

"I have been in these political warfares for a long time; I claim to be an old soldier in them. I stood in this Senate when there were not five men with me to support me, and then I rose here and told those who were inveighing like demons against the principles that they called abolitionism, that I was an Abolitionist. To-day you are all Abolitionists, not voluntarily, but by compulsion. I have wondered a great deal why men did not learn more about these things than they seem to do. Our principles are assailed now with just the same virulence that they used to be when we were in a small minority. I do not hold that they have triumphed thus far because of any superior capacity on our part. Certainly not. Why is it, then, that we, from the smallest of all beginnings, have conquered the prejudices of the people and conquered the predominant party of this country which had stood completely dominating the whole nation for more than forty years? Why is it that we have conquered you, and now are triumphant here in this Senate and almost by two-thirds in both branches, with the whole nation at our backs? What miracle has wrought this change? None other than the great consoling fact that justice, liberty, and right are destined among the American people to succeed, and the gates of hell can not prevail against them, although they are trying at this particular time very hard to do it." [Laughter.]

On the 2d of March, the last day of the debate, Mr. Cowan first claimed the attention of the Senate in a speech two hours in length. He argued "that for any guilty part taken by the people in the late war, that the sufferings and losses they endured in that war were the natural and sufficient punishment; that after it they remain purged, and ought to be reädmitted to all their constitutional rights at once. That it is due to the dignity of the United States as a great nation, if she punishes the actual traitors who incited the rebellion, that it be done solemnly and according to the strictest form of law, in open courts, where the prisoners may have counsel and witnesses, so that they may make their defense, if they have any. That according to the Constitution and laws all the States are still in the Union; that secession ordinances could not repeal the one, nor war set aside the other; that they are neither dead by forfeiture or *felo de se*, but are now in full and perfect existence, with all their municipal machinery in full play. That the proposition of the Committee of Fifteen to amend the Constitution is fundamental and revolutionary, and destructive of the freedom of the States and the liberties of the people; that it is a threat to deprive them of their rights by compelling them either to admit negroes to the right of suffrage or to give up a share of their representation, which is theirs by law and the last amendment to the Constitution. That the resolution now before us from the same committee is also revolutionary and destructive, being an attempt to suspend the Constitution and laws in regard to representation in Congress over eleven States of the Union until Congress shall see fit to restore them. It is a declaration on the part of the members of the present House and Senate, that having the means of keeping these States from being represented here, they are going to do so as long as they please; that no one of these measures can be justified as a punishment for the rebellion; that the Constitution forbids them as bills of pains and penalties, and as *ex post facto* in their character."

Mr. Garret Davis, in the course of a speech in opposition to the resolution, suggested a summary solution of the present difficulties: "There is," said he, "a provision in the Constitution which requires the President to communicate to the two houses of Congress information as to the state of the Union, and to recommend to them such measures as he shall deem proper and expedient. What does this necessarily impose upon him? He has to ascertain what men compose the two houses of Congress. It is his right, it is his constitutional function, to ascertain who constitute the two houses of Congress. The members of the Senate who are in favor of the admission of the Southern Senators could get into a conclave with those Southern Senators any day, and they would constitute a majority of the Senate. The President of the United States has the constitutional option—it is his function, it his power, it is his right—and I would advise him to exercise it, to ascertain, where there are two different bodies of men both claiming to be the Senate, which is the true Senate. If the Southern members and those who are for admitting them to their seats constitute a majority of the whole Senate, the President has a right—and, by the Eternal! he ought to exercise that right forthwith, to-morrow, or any day—to recognize the Opposition in this body and the Southern members, the majority of the whole body, as the true Senate. And then what would become of you gentlemen? Oh, if the lion of the Hermitage, and that great statesman, the sage of Ashland, were here in the seat of power, how soon would they settle this question! They would say to, and they would inspire those to whom they spoke, 'You Southern men are kept out of your seats by violence, by revolution, against the Constitution, against right; the Union is dissolved, the Government is brought to an end by keeping the Senators from eleven States out of their seats when the Constitution expressly states that every State shall have two Senators.'

"There is no plainer principle of constitutional law than that the President has the right to ascertain and decide what body of men is the Senate and what the House of Representatives when there are two bodies of men claiming to be each. It is his right to do so, and the people of America will sustain him in the noble and manly and patriotic performance of his duty in determining the identity of the true House. It ought to have been done at the beginning of this session. When a petty clerk took upon himself to read the list of the Representatives of the people of the United States, and to keep the Representatives of eleven States out of their seats, the Constitution guaranteeing to them those seats for the benefit of their constituents and country, that subordinate never ought to have been tolerated for one day in the perpetration of so great an outrage. Whenever Andrew Johnson chooses to exercise his high function, his constitutional right of saying to the Southern Senators, 'Get together with the Democrats and the Conservatives of the Senate, and if you constitute a majority, I will recognize you as the Senate of the United States,' what then will become of you gentlemen? You will quietly come in and form a part of that Senate."

Mr. Doolittle opposed the passage of the resolution. Referring to the plan proposed by Mr. Davis, he said: "If such a thing should happen—which God in his mercy, I hope, will always prevent—that the Senate should be divided, and one portion should go into one room, and another into another, each claiming to be the Senate, I suppose the House of Representatives could direct its clerk to go to one body and not go to the other, and I do not know but the President of the United States would have the power, in case of such a division, to send his private secretary with messages to one body and not send them to the other. Perhaps that might occur; but it is one of those cases that are not to be supposed or to be tolerated."

Mr. Wilson advocated the resolution: "The nation," said he, "is divided into two classes; that the one class imperiously demands the immediate and unconditional admission into these halls of legislation of the rebellious States, *rebel end foremost;* that the other class seeks their admission into Congress, at an early day, *loyal end foremost.* He would hear, too, the blended voices of unrepentant rebels and rebel sympathizers and apologists mingling in full chorus, not for the restoration of a broken Union, for the unity and indivisibility of the republic has been assured on bloody fields of victory, but for the restoration to these vacant chairs of the 'natural leaders' of the South."

Referring to Mr. Davis' programme for the President's interference with the Senate, Mr. Wilson said: "Sir, there was a time when a Senator who should have said what we have recently heard on this floor would have sunk into his seat under the withering rebuke of his associates. No Senator or Representative has a right to tell us what the Executive will do. The President acts upon his own responsibility. We are Senators, this is the Senate of the United States, and it becomes us to maintain the rights and the dignity of the Senate of the United States. The people demand that their Senators and Representatives shall enact the needed measures to restore, at the earliest possible day, the complete practical relations of the seceded States to the National Government, and protect the rights and liberties of all the people, without regard to color, race, or descent."

Mr. Fessenden, having the resolution in charge, made a second speech, in which he answered objections which had been urged, and defended the Committee of Fifteen against imputations of a disposition to delay the work of reconstruction.

Mr. McDougal took occasion to say a few words against the resolution. He said: "I would not dare to vote for this proposition, because I have some regard for the great Judge who lives above. The question pending now, as practically useless as it will be as a rule, is yet mischievous. It is in the way of teaching bad precedents, false law, unsound loyalty. These things are like the worms that eat into the majestic oaks which are used to build vessels to ride the sea, and decay their strength, so that they fall down and make wrecks of navies."

Mr. Hendricks had moved to amend the resolution by inserting the words "inhabitants of" after the word "States." This amendment was rejected. The Senate then proceeded to take the vote on the concurrent resolution, which was passed—yeas, 29; nays, 18.

Thus the opinion of Congress was established, by a large majority, that the two houses should act conjointly upon the whole question of the representation of States, and that this question was entirely independent of the Executive.

CHAPTER XVII.

THE RECONSTRUCTION AMENDMENT—IN THE HOUSE.

A Constitutional Amendment Proposed and Postponed—Proposition by Mr. Stewart—The Reconstruction Amendment—Death of its Predecessor Lamented—Opposition to the Disfranchisement of Rebels—"The Unrepentent Thirty-three"—Nine-tenths Reduced to One-twelfth—Advice to Congress—The Committee Denounced—Democratic and Republican Policy Compared—Authority without Power—A Variety of Opinions—An Earthquake Predicted—The Joint Resolution Passes the House.

WHILE the joint resolution proposing a modification of the basis of representation was the subject of consideration in the Senate, a constitutional amendment relating to the rights of citizens was made the topic of brief discussion in the House. It had been previously introduced and referred to the Committee of Fifteen. From this committee it was reported back by Mr. Bingham. It was proposed in the following form:

"Article —. That Congress shall have power to make all laws which shall be necessary and proper to secure to the citizens of each State all privileges and immunities of citizens in the several States, and to all persons in the several States equal protection in the rights of life, liberty, and property."

This proposition was introduced on the 26th of February, and was debated during the sessions of three successive days.

Many members of the legal profession saw in the final clause a dangerous centralization of power. It was considered objectionable as seeming to authorize the General Government to interfere with local laws on the subject of property, the legal rights of women, and other matters hitherto considered wholly within the domain of State legislation; hence the Republican majority unanimously voted to postpone the amendment until April.

After this postponement, and the failure of the amendment relating to the basis of representation to pass the Senate, the subject of reconstruction was in the hands of the Committee of Fifteen until the 30th of April.

Individuals had, from time to time, introduced propositions on the subject, which were referred to the appropriate committee. The one which attracted most attention and excited greatest interest was a proposition in the Senate, by Mr. Stewart, of Nevada. This was in favor of a joint resolution providing that each of the States lately in rebellion shall be recognized as having resumed its relations with the Government, and its Representatives shall be admitted to Congress whenever it shall have amended its Constitution so as to provide—

"1. There shall be no distinction in civil rights among its citizens by reason of race or color or previous condition of servitude; 2. That all debts incurred in aid of the rebellion shall be repudiated; 3. That all claim for compensation for liberated slaves shall be relinquished; and 4. That the elective franchise be extended to all persons on the same terms, irrespective of race, color, or previous condition, provided that none be disfranchised who were qualified voters in 1860; and that upon these conditions being ratified by a majority of the present voting population of each State, (including all qualified to vote in 1860,) a general amnesty shall be proclaimed as to all who engaged in the rebellion."

This proposition had peculiar significance, since it emanated from a gentleman who, though elected as a Republican, had ever since the veto of the Freedmen's Bureau acted with the Conservatives. Mr. Sumner, "with open arms," welcomed the Senator from Nevada as "a new convert to the necessity of negro suffrage." Mr. Wilson was thankful to the author of this proposition for placing the whole question "on the basis of universal liberty, universal justice, universal suffrage, and universal amnesty." The resolution was referred to the Committee of Fifteen, with whom Mr. Wilson had no doubt it would receive "serious consideration."

On the 30th of April, Mr. Stevens reported from the Committee of Fifteen a joint resolution providing for the passage of the following amendment to the Constitution:

"ARTICLE —.

"SEC. 1. No State shall make or enforce any law which shall abridge the privileges or immunities of citizens of the United States; nor shall any

State deprive any person of life, liberty, or property without due process of law; nor deny to any person within its jurisdiction the equal protection of the laws.

"SEC. 2. Representatives shall be apportioned among the several States which may be included within this Union according to their respective numbers, counting the whole number of persons in each State, excluding Indians not taxed. But whenever in any State the elective franchise shall be denied to any portion of its male citizens not less than twenty-one years of age, or in any way abridged, except for participation in rebellion or other crime, the basis of representation in such State shall be reduced in the proportion which the number of male citizens shall bear to the whole number of such male citizens not less than twenty-one years of age.

"SEC. 3. Until the 4th day of July, in the year 1870, all persons who voluntarily adhered to the late insurrection, giving it aid and comfort, shall be excluded from the right to vote for Representatives in Congress and for electors for President and Vice-President of the United States.

"SEC. 4. Neither the United States nor any State shall assume or pay any debt or obligation already incurred, or which may hereafter be incurred, in aid of insurrection or of war against the United States, or any claim for compensation for loss of involuntary service or labor.

"SEC. 5. The Congress shall have power to enforce, by appropriate legislation, the provisions of this article."

This proposed amendment to the Constitution was accompanied by two bills, one of which provided that when any State lately in insurrection should have ratified the amendment, its Senators and Representatives, if found duly elected and qualified, should be admitted as members of Congress. The other bill declared the high ex-officials of the late Confederacy ineligible to any office under the Government of the United States.

The proposed constitutional amendment was by a vote of the House made the special order for Tuesday, the 8th of May. On that day Mr. Stevens occupied the attention of the House with a brief argument in favor of the amendment. Referring to the death in the Senate of the amendment previously proposed, Mr. Stevens said: "But it is dead, and unless this (less efficient, I admit) shall pass, its death has postponed the protection of the colored race perhaps for ages. I confess my mortification at its defeat. I grieved especially because it almost closed the door of hope for the amelioration of the condition of the freedmen. But men in pursuit of justice must never despair. Let us again try and see whether we can not devise some way to overcome the united forces of self-righteous Republicans and unrighteous Copper-heads. It will not do for those who for thirty years have fought the beasts at Ephesus to be frightened by the fangs of modern catamounts."

Of the present proposition, Mr. Stevens said: "It is not all that the committee desired. It falls far short of my wishes, but it fulfills my hopes. I believe it is all that can be obtained in the present state of public opinion. Not only Congress, but the several States are to be consulted. Upon a careful survey of the whole ground, we did not believe that nineteen of the loyal States could be induced to ratify any proposition more stringent than this."

Referring to the section prohibiting rebels from voting until 1870, Mr. Stevens said: "My only objection to it is that it is too lenient. Here is the mildest of all punishments ever inflicted on traitors. I might not consent to the extreme severity denounced upon them by a provisional governor of Tennessee—I mean the late lamented Andrew Johnson of blessed memory—but I would have increased the severity of this section."

Mr. Blaine called attention to the fact that most of the persons whom the third section of the amendment was designed to disfranchise, had their political rights restored to them by the Amnesty Proclamation, or had been pardoned by the President.

Mr. Finck opposed the proposition in a speech of which the following are extracts: "Stripped of all disguises, this measure is a mere scheme to deny representation to eleven States; to prevent indefinitely a complete restoration of the Union, and perpetuate the power of a sectional and dangerous party.

"Sir, the whole scheme is revolutionary, and a most shallow pretext for an excuse to exclude the vote of eleven States in the next Presidential election. You can not exact conditions in this way from any State in the Union; no more from Georgia than from Massachusetts. They are each equal States in the Union, held together by the same Constitution, neither being the superior of the other in their relation to the Federal Government as States."

Commenting on the first section, designed to insert a recognition of civil rights in the Constitution, Mr. Finck said: "If it is necessary to adopt it in order to confer upon Congress power over the matters contained in it, then the Civil Rights Bill, which the President vetoed, was passed without authority, and is clearly unconstitutional."

To this inference, Mr. Garfield replied: "I am glad to see this first section here, which proposes to hold over every American citizen without regard to color, the protecting shield of law. The gentleman who has just taken his seat undertakes to show that because we propose to vote for this section, we therefore acknowledge that the Civil Rights Bill was unconstitutional. The Civil Rights Bill is now a part of the law of the land. But every gentleman knows it will cease to be a part of the law whenever the sad moment arrives when that gentleman's party comes into power. It is precisely for that reason that we propose to lift that great and good law above the reach of political strife, beyond the reach of the plots and machinations of any party, and fix it in the serene sky, in the eternal firmament of the Constitution, where no storm of passion can shake it, and no cloud can obscure it. For this reason, and not because I believe the Civil Rights Bill unconstitutional, I am glad to see that first section here."

Mr. Garfield opposed the section disfranchising rebels as "the only proposition in this resolution that is not bottomed clearly and plainly upon principle—principle that will stand the test of centuries, and be as true a thousand years hence as it is to-day."

Mr. Thayer, while favoring the proposed amendment in all other particulars, was opposed to the third section. "I think," said he, "that it imperils the whole measure under consideration. What will continue to be the condition of the country if you adopt this feature of the proposed plan? Continual distraction, continued agitation, continued bickerings, continued opposition to the law, and it will be well for the country if a new insurrection shall not spring from its bosom."

Mr. Boyer denounced the proposition as "an ingenious scheme to keep out the Southern States, and to prevent the restoration of the Union until after the next Presidential election."

Mr. Kelley, if he "could have controlled the report of the Committee of Fifteen, would have proposed to give the right of suffrage to every loyal man in the country." He advocated the amendment, however, in all its provisions. He especially defended the third section. "This measure," said he, "does not propose to punish them; on the contrary, it is an act of amnesty, and proposes, after four years, to reinvest them with all their rights, which they do not possess at this time because of their crime."

The passage of the resolution was next advocated by Mr. Schenck. Referring to the third section, he denied the principle advanced by Mr. Garfield that there was any thing inconsistent or wrong in making it an exclusion for a term of years instead of exclusion altogether. "If there be any thing in that argument," said he, "in case of crime, you must either not sentence a man to the penitentiary at all, or else incarcerate him for the term of his natural life. Or, to compare it to another thing, which perhaps better illustrates the principle involved, when a foreigner arrives upon our shores we should not say to him, 'At the end of five years, when you have familiarized yourself with our institutions, and become attached to them, we will allow you to become a citizen, and admit you to all the franchises we enjoy,' but we should require that he be naturalized the moment he touches our soil, or else excluded from the rights of citizenship forever."

Mr. Schenck thought the loyal and true people throughout the land were "full ready to declare that those who have proved traitors, and have raised their parricidal hands against the life of the country, who have attempted to strike down our Government and destroy its institutions, should be the very last to be trusted to take any share in preserving, conducting, and carrying on that Government and maintaining those institutions."

Mr. Smith opposed the resolution in a speech which, if it added nothing to the arguments, contributed, by its good humored personalities and its harmless extravagancies, to the amusement of the auditors.

On the following day, May 9th, the consideration of the subject was resumed, and Mr. Broomall addressed the House in favor of the resolution. He began by counting the votes that would probably be cast against the amendment. "It would meet the opposition," said he, "of the unrepentant thirty-three of this body. It was also to be expected that the six Johnsonian new converts to Democracy would oppose and vote against this measure, commencing with the gentleman from New York, [Mr. Raymond,] who, I believe, has the disease in the most virulent form, thence down to the gentleman from Kentucky, [Mr. Smith,] who preceded me on this question, and who has the mildest and most amiable type of the infection. Upon them, too, arguments are useless. There must, then, be thirty-nine votes against the measure, and I want there to be no more."

To the objection urged against the third section of the proposed amendment, that it would disfranchise nine-tenths of all the voters of the South, Mr. Broomall replied: "This is a grand mistake. There were in 1860 one million one hundred and twenty thousand voters in those eleven States. We may take seven hundred and fifty thousand as the number of individuals in the South who rendered aid and comfort to the enemy, not counting the comparatively few though powerful leaders who rendered aid and comfort outside of the army. But, sir, we do not propose to disfranchise even these seven hundred and fifty thousand. Supposing two hundred and fifty thousand of the rebel army were lost, we have five hundred thousand actual voters in the South to be disfranchised by this measure, if they come within the meaning of it. But do they come within the meaning of this provision? Why, sir, it does not embrace the unwilling conscripts; it does not embrace the men who were compelled to serve in the army. It would be fair to say three hundred thousand of these people belonged to the unwilling class, who were forced into the army by rigid conscription laws and the various contrivances of the leading rebels. This will leave two hundred thousand; and I say now it is utterly impossible, in my opinion, that the number of people in the South who can be operated upon by this provision should exceed two hundred thousand, if, indeed, it should reach the one half of that number. Is this nine-tenths of the voters of the South? Why, it is about one in every twelve."

Mr. Shanklin opposed the amendment as intended "to disfranchise the people of the Southern States who have gone into this rebellion, until the party in power could fasten and rivet the chains of oppression for all time to come, and hedge themselves in power, that they may rule and control those people at will."

Mr. Shanklin closed his speech with the following advice to Congress: "Discharge your joint Committee on Reconstruction; abolish your Freedmen's Bureau; repeal your Civil Rights Bill, and admit all the delegates from the seceded States to their seats in Congress, who have been elected according to the laws of the country and possess the constitutional qualification, and all will be well."

Mr. Raymond spoke in favor of the amendment, except the

disfranchisement clause. He had opposed the Civil Rights Bill on the ground of want of constitutional power in Congress to pass it. He favored the first section of this amendment, since it gave the previous acts of Congress a constitutional basis.

In answer to Mr. Broomall's "ingenious argument," Mr. Raymond said: "It seems to me idle to enter into such calculations, which depend on a series of estimates, each one of which can not be any thing more than a wild and random guess. I take it that we all know perfectly well that the great masses of the Southern people 'voluntarily adhered to the insurrection;' not at the outset, not as being originally in favor of it, but during its progress, sooner or later, they voluntarily gave in their adhesion to it, and gave it aid and comfort. They did not all join the army. They did not go into the field, but they did, at different times, from various motives and in various ways, give it aid and comfort. That would exclude the great body of the people of those States under this amendment from exercising the right of suffrage."

Mr. Raymond asserted that all that was offered to the rebel legislatures of the Southern States, in return for the concessions required of them, was "the right to be represented on this floor, provided they will also consent not to vote for the men who are to represent them! The very price by which we seek to induce their assent to these amendments we snatch away from their hands the moment that assent is secured. Is there any man here who can so far delude himself as to suppose for a moment that the people of the Southern States will accede to any such scheme as this? There is not one chance in ten thousand of their doing it."

Mr. McKee advocated the amendment. He thought that opposition to its third section was a rebuke to those States which had passed laws disfranchising rebels. To obviate all objections to this section, however, he proposed a substitute forever excluding "all persons who voluntarily adhered to the late insurrection" from holding "any office under the Government of the United States."

Mr. Eldridge did not intend "to make an argument on the merits of the joint resolution." His remarks were mostly in derogation of the committee by whom the measure was recommended. "The committee," said he, "report no facts whatever, and give us no conclusion. They simply report amendments to the Constitution. Was that the purpose for which the committee was organized? Was it to change the fundamental law of the land under which we of the loyal States assembled here? Was that the duty with which the committee was charged? Were they to inquire and report an entire change of the fundamental law of the nation which would destroy the States and create an empire? I say they were charged with no such duty. The resolution can not fairly be construed as giving to the committee any such power, any such jurisdiction. The committee stands resisting the restoration of this Union, and I hope that no further business will be referred to it. It has rendered itself unworthy of the high duty with which it was charged."

Mr. Eldridge asserted: "The whole scheme is in the interest of party alone, to preserve and perpetuate the party idea of this Republican disunion party."

The debate thus entering "the domain of partisan controversy," Mr. Boutwell, in a speech which followed, undertook to show how the proposition before the House "traverses the policy of the Democratic party with reference to the reconstruction of the Government." Mr. Boutwell described the policy of the Democratic party, "which," said he, "they laid down as early as 1856 in the platform made at Cincinnati, wherein they declared substantially that it was the right of a Territory to be admitted into this Union with such institutions as it chose to establish, not even by implication admitting that the representatives of the existing Government had any right to canvass those institutions, or to consider the right of the Territory to be recognized as a State.

"Now, sir, from that doctrine, which probably had its origin in the resolutions of 1798, the whole of their policy to this day has legitimately followed. First, we saw its results in the doctrine of Mr. Buchanan, announced in 1860, that, while the Constitution did not provide for or authorize the secession of a State from this Union, there was no power in the existing Government to compel a State to remain in the Union against its own judgment. Following that doctrine, they come legitimately to the conclusion of to-day, in which they are supported, as I understand, by the President of the United States upon the one side, and, as I know, by the testimony of Alexander H. Stephens, late Vice-President of the so-called Confederacy, upon the other. That doctrine, is that these eleven States have to-day, each for itself, an existing and unquestionable right of representation in the Government of this country, and that it is a continuous right which has not been interrupted by any of the events of the war."

On the other hand, Mr. Boutwell thus defined the position of "the Union party," which, he said, "stands unitedly upon two propositions. The first is equality of representation, about which there is no difference of opinion. The second is, that there shall be a loyal people in each applicant State before any Representative from that State is admitted in Congress. And there is a third: a vast majority of the Republican party, soon to be the controlling and entire force of that party, demand suffrage for our friends, for those who have stood by us in our days of tribulation. And for myself, with the right, of course, to change my opinion, I believe in the Constitutional power of the Government to-day to extend the elective franchise to every loyal male citizen of the republic."

Mr. Spalding favored the amendment, including the third section, to which exception had been taken by some of his friends. He asked, "Is it exceptionable? Is it objectionable? If it be so, it is, in my judgment, for the reason that the duration of the period of incapacity is not extended more widely. I take my stand here, that it is necessary to ingraft into that enduring instrument called the Constitution of the United States something which shall admonish this rebellious people, and all who shall come after them, that treason against the Government is odious; that it carries with it some penalty, some disqualification; and the only one which we seek to attach by this amendment is a disqualification in voting— not for their State and county and town officers, but for members of Congress, who are to be the law-makers, and for the Executive of the United States, this disqualification to operate for the short period of four years."

Mr. Miller advocated all the sections of the proposed amendment except the third. Of this he said: "Though it seems just on its face, I doubt the propriety of embodying it with the other amendments, as it may retard, if not endanger, the ratification of the amendment in regard to representation, and we can not afford to endanger in any manner a matter of such vital importance to the country."

Mr. Eliot had voted against the former amendment, which was passed by the House and rejected by the Senate. The present proposed amendment, while it was not all he could ask, was not open to the objections which then controlled his vote. In advocating the third section, he said: "It is clear, upon adjudged law, that the States lately in rebellion, and the inhabitants of those States, by force of the civil war, and of the Union triumph in that war, so far have lost their rights to take part in the Government of the Union that some action on the part of Congress is required to restore those rights. Pardon and amnesty given by the President can not restore them. Those men can not vote for President or for Representatives in Congress until, in some way, Congress has so acted as to restore their power. The question, then, is very simple: Shall national power be at once conferred on those who have striven, by all means open to them, to destroy the nation's life? Shall our enemies and the enemies of the Government, as soon as they have been defeated in war, help to direct and to control the public policy of the Government—and that, too, while those men, hostile themselves, keep from all exercise of political power the only true and loyal friends whom we have had, during these four years of war, within these Southern States?"

It had been argued against the third section that it could not be enforced, that it would be inoperative. To this objection Mr. Shellabarger replied: "It will not require standing armies. You can have registry laws. Upon this registry list you may place the names of men who are to be disqualified, and you may also have the names of all who are qualified to vote under the law. There they will stand, there they will be, to be referred to by your Government in the execution of its laws. And when it comes to this House or to the Senate to determine whether a man is duly elected, you can resort to the ordinary process applicable to a trial in a contested election case in either body, as to whether he has been elected by the men who were entitled to elect him."

Thursday, May 10th, was the last day of this discussion in the House. Mr. Randall first took the floor and spoke in opposition to the joint resolution. To the friends of the measure he said: "It is intended to secure what you most wish: an entire disagreement to the whole scheme by the eleven Southern States, and a continued omission of representation on this floor."

Mr. Strouse, in opposing the amendment, occupied most of his time in reading an editorial from the New York Times, which he characterized as "sound, patriotic, statesmanlike, and just."

Mr. Strouse expressed, as his own opinion, "that the States are, and never ceased to be, in law and in fact, constituent parts of our Union. If I am correct in this opinion, what necessity exists for these amendments of the Constitution? Let the States be represented in the Senate and House by men who can conscientiously qualify as members; and after that, when we have a full Congress, with the whole country represented, let any amendment that may be required be proposed, and let those most interested have an opportunity to participate in the debates and deliberations of matters of so much moment to every citizen."

Mr. Banks regarded the pending amendment as the most important question which could be presented to the House or to the country. "It is my belief," said he, "that reörganization of governments in the insurgent States can be secured only by measures which will work a change in the basis of political society. Any thing that leaves the basis of political society in the Southern States untouched, leaves the enemy in condition to renew the war at his pleasure, and gives him absolute power to destroy the Government whenever he chooses.

"There are two methods by which the change I propose can be made: one by extending the elective franchise to the negro, the other by restrictions upon the political power of those heretofore invested with the elective franchise—a part of whom are loyal and a part of whom are disloyal, a part of whom are friends and a part of whom are enemies.

"I have no doubt that the Government of the United States has authority to extend the elective franchise to the colored population of the insurgent States, but I do not think it has the power. The distinction I make between authority and power is this: We have, in the nature of our Government, the right to do it; but the public opinion of the country is such at this precise moment as to make it impossible we should do it. The situation of opinion in these States compels us to look to other means to protect the Government against the enemy.

"I approve of the proposition which disfranchises the enemies of the country. I think it right in principle. I think it necessary at this time. If I had any opinion to express, I should say to the gentlemen of the House that it is impossible to organize a government in the insurgent States, and have the enemies of the country in possession of political power, in whole or in part, in local governments or in representation here.

"An enemy to the Government, a man who avows himself an enemy of its policy and measures, who has made war against the Government, would not seem to have any absolute right to share political power equally with other men who have never been otherwise than friends of the Government.

"A pardon does not confer or restore political power. A general act of amnesty differs from an individual pardon only in the fact that it applies to a class of offenders who can not be individually described. It secures immunity from punishment or prosecution by obliterating all remembrance of the offense; but it confers or restores no one to political power.

"There is no justification for the opinion so strongly expressed, that this measure will fail because the rebel States will not consent to the disfranchisement of any portion of their own people. The proposition is for the loyal States to determine upon what terms they will restore to the Union the insurgent States. It is not necessary that they should participate in our deliberations upon this subject, and wholly without reason that they should have the power to defeat it. It is a matter of congratulation that they have not this power. We have the requisite number of States without them.

"I do not believe that there is a State in this Union where at least a clear majority of the people were not from the beginning opposed to the war; and could you remove from the control of public opinion one or two thousand in each of these States, so as to let up from the foundations of political society the mass of common people, you would have a population in all these States as loyal and true to the Government as the people of any portion of the East or West.

"The people knew that it was the rich man's war and the poor man's fight. The legislation of the insurgent States exempted, to a great degree, the rich men and their sons, on account of the possession of property, while it forced, at the point of the bayonet, and oftentimes at the cost of life, the masses of the people to maintain their cause. There is nothing in the whole war more atrocious than the cruel measures taken by the rebel leaders to force the people who had no interest in it, and were averse to sharing its dishonor and peril."

Mr. Banks remarked of the amendment: "It will produce the exact result which we desire: the immediate restoration of the governments of the States to the Union, the recognition of the loyal people, and the disfranchisement of the implacable and unchangeable public enemies of the Union, and the creation of State governments upon the sound and enduring basis of common interest and common affection."

Mr. Eckley advocated the joint resolution, citing a number of historical and political precedents in favor of its provisions. Of the disfranchising clause, he said: "The only objection I have to the proposition is, that it does not go far enough. I would disfranchise them forever. They have no right, founded in justice, to participate in the administration of the Government or exercise political power. If they receive protection in their persons and property, are permitted to share in the nation's bounties, and live in security under the broad ægis of the nation's flag, it is far more than the nation owes them."

Mr. Longyear favored the amendment, but disliked the third section, of which he said: "Let us then reject this dead weight, and not load down good provisions, absolutely essential provisions, by this, which, however good in and of itself, can not be enforced. I regard this provision, if adopted, both worthless and harmless, and, therefore, I shall vote for the proposed amendment as a whole, whether this be rejected or retained."

Mr. Beaman held a similar opinion. He said: "We very well know that such a provision would be entirely inoperative, because electors for President and Vice-President can be appointed by the Legislatures, according to a practice that has always obtained in South Carolina. The provision does not extend to the election of Senators, and, consequently, it can operate only to affect the election of members of this House, and that only for a period of four years."

Mr. Rogers denounced the proposed amendment in emphatic terms. He said: "The first section of this programme of disunion is the most dangerous to liberty. It saps the foundation of the Government; it destroys the elementary principles of the States; it consolidates every thing into one imperial despotism; it annihilates all the rights which lie at the foundation of the union of the States, and which have characterized this Government and made it prosperous and great during the long period of its existence. It will result in a revolution worse than that through which we have just passed; it will rock the earth like the throes of an earthquake, until its tragedy will summon the inhabitants of the world to witness its dreadful shock.

"In the third section, you undertake," said Mr. Rogers, "to enunciate a doctrine that will, if carried out, disfranchise seven or eight million people, and that will put them in a worse condition than the serfs of Russia or the downtrodden people of Poland and Hungary, until the year 1870."

Mr. Farnsworth advocated the amendment, but did not regard the third section as of any practical value. It did not provide punishment adequate to the guilt of the various offenders. "There is a large class of men," said he, "both in the North and South, equally—yea, and more—guilty than thousands of the misguided men who will be disfranchised by this provision, who will not be affected by it. I allude to those politicians and others at the South, who, keeping themselves out of danger, set on the ignorant and brave to fight for what they were told by these rascals were 'their rights;' and to other politicians, editors, 'copper-heads' in the North, some of whom were and are members of Congress, who encouraged them and discouraged our soldiers."

Mr. Bingham spoke in favor of the amendment. He preferred that the disfranchising clause should be embodied in an act of Congress. "I trust," said he, "that this amendment, with or without the third section, will pass this House, that the day may soon come when Tennessee—loyal Tennessee—loyal in the very heart of the rebellion, her mountains and plains blasted by the ravages of war and stained with the blood of her faithful children fallen in the great struggle for the maintenance of the Union, having already conformed her constitution and laws to every provision of this amendment, will at once, upon its submission by Congress, irrevocably ratify it, and be, without further delay, represented in Congress by her loyal Representatives and Senators.

"Let that great example be set by Tennessee, and it will be worth a hundred thousand votes to the loyal people in the free North. Let this be done, and it will be hailed as the harbinger of that day for which all good men pray, when the fallen pillars of the republic shall be restored without violence or the noise of words or the sound of the hammer, each to its original place in the sacred temple of our national liberties, thereby giving assurance to all the world that, for the defense of the republic, it was not in vain that a million and a half of men, the very elect of the earth, rushed to arms; that the republic still lives, and will live for evermore, the sanctuary of an inviolable justice, the refuge of liberty, and the imperishable monument of the nation's dead, from the humblest soldier who perished on the march, or went down amid the thunder and tempest of the dread conflict, up through all the shining roll of heroes and patriots and martyrs to the incorruptible and immortal Commander-in-chief, who fell by an assassin's hand in the capital, and thus died that his country might live."

The hour having arrived when, by understanding of the House, the discussion should close, Mr. Stevens closed the debate with a short speech. "I am glad," said he, "to see great unanimity among the Union friends in this House on all the provisions of this joint resolution except the third one. I am not very much gratified to see any division among our friends on that which I consider the vital proposition of them all. Without that, it amounts to nothing. I do not care the snap of my finger whether it be passed or not if that be stricken out. I should be sorry to find that that provision was stricken out, because, before any portion of this can be put into operation, there will be, if not a Herod, a worse than Herod elsewhere to obstruct our actions. That side of the house will be filled with yelling secessionists and hissing copper-heads. Give us the third section or give us nothing. Do not balk us with the pretense of an amendment which throws the Union into the hands of the enemy before it becomes consolidated. Do not, I pray you, admit those who have slaughtered half a million of our countrymen until their clothes are dried, and until they are reclad. I do not wish to sit side by side with men whose garments smell of the blood of my kindred. Gentlemen seem to forget the scenes that were enacted here years ago. Many of you were not here. But my friend from Ohio [Mr. Garfield] ought to have kept up his reading enough to have been familiar with the history of those days, when the men that you propose to admit occupied the other side of the House; when the mighty Toombs, with his shaggy locks, headed a gang who, with shouts of defiance on this floor, rendered this a hell of legislation.

"Ah, sir, it was but six years ago when they were here, just before they went out to join the armies of Catiline, just before they left this hall. Those of you who were here then will remember the scene in which every Southern member, encouraged by their allies, came forth in one yelling body because a speech for freedom was being made here; when weapons were drawn, and Barksdale's bowie-knife gleamed before our eyes. Would you have these men back again so soon to reënact those scenes? Wait until I am gone, I pray you. I want not to go through it again. It will be but a short time for my colleague to wait. I hope he will not put us to that test."

At the close of his remarks, Mr. Stevens moved the previous question.

Mr. Garfield hoped that it would be voted down, that he might have an opportunity to offer a substitute for the third section, forever excluding the persons therein specified "from holding any office of trust or profit under the Government of the United States."

Nevertheless, the previous question was sustained, and a vote was taken on the joint resolution proposing the constitutional amendment as it came from the committee. The following are the yeas and nays:

YEAS—Messrs. Alley, Allison, Ames, Anderson, Delos R. Ashley, James M. Ashley, Baker, Baldwin, Banks, Barker, Baxter, Beaman, Benjamin, Bidwell, Bingham, Blaine, Blow, Boutwell, Bromwell, Broomall, Buckland, Bundy, Reader W. Clarke, Sidney Clarke, Cobb, Conkling, Cook, Cullom, Darling, Davis, Dawes, Defrees, Delano, Deming, Dixon, Dodge, Donnelly, Driggs, Dumont, Eckley, Eggleston, Eliot, Farnsworth, Ferry, Garfield, Grinnell, Griswold, Abnber C. Harding, Hart, Hayes, Henderson, Higby, Holmes, Hooper, Hotchkiss, Asahel W. Hubbard, Chester D. Hubbard, Demas Hubbard, James R. Hubbell, Hulburd, James Humphrey, Ingersoll, Jenckes, Julian, Kasson, Kelley, Kelso, Ketcham, Kuykendall, Laflin, George V. Lawrence, William Lawrence, Loan, Longyear, Lynch, Marston, McClurg, McIndoe, McKee, McRuer, Mercur, Miller, Moorhead, Morrill, Morris, Moulton, Myers, Newell, O'Neill, Orth, Paine, Patterson, Perham, Pike, Plants, Price, William H. Randall, Raymond, Alexander H. Rice, John H. Rice, Rollins, Sawyer, Schenck, Scofield, Shellabarger, Spalding, Stevens, Stilwell, Thayer, Francis Thomas, John L. Thomas, Trowbridge, Upson, Van Aernam, Burt Van Horn, Robert T. Van Horn, Ward, Warner, Elihu B. Washburne, Henry D. Washburn, William B. Washburn, Welker, Williams, James F. Wilson, Stephen F. Wilson, Windom, Woodbridge, and the Speaker—128.

NAYS—Messrs. Ancona, Bergen, Boyer, Chanler, Coffroth, Dawson, Eldridge, Finck, Glossbrenner, Goodyear, Grider, Aaron Harding, Harris, Kerr, Latham, Le Blond, Marshall, McCullough, Niblack, Phelps, Radford, Samuel J. Randall, Ritter, Rogers, Ross, Rosseau, Shanklin, Sitgreaves,

Smith, Strouse, Taber, Taylor, Thornton, Trimble, Whaley, Winfield, and Wright—37.

Applause on the floor and in the galleries greeted the announcement that two-thirds of the House having voted in the affirmative the joint resolution was passed.

The heavy majority by which this measure passed the House indicated an effect of the President's steady opposition, the opposite of what was anticipated. The amendment secured two votes which were cast against the Civil Rights Bill, while it lost no vote which that measure received.

It is remarkable that the joint resolution should have been carried with such unanimity when so many Republicans had expressed dissatisfaction with the third section. This is accounted for, however, by the pressure of the previous question, in which fifteen Democrats joined forces with the radical Republicans to force the undivided issue upon the House. A large minority of the Republican members were thus prevented from voting against the clause disfranchising the late rebels until 1870.

In the Senate, as will be seen, the amendment assumed a shape more in accordance with their wishes.

CHAPTER XVIII.

THE RECONSTRUCTION AMENDMENT—IN THE SENATE.

DIFFERENCE BETWEEN DISCUSSIONS IN THE HOUSE AND IN THE SENATE—MR. SUMNER PROPOSES TO POSTPONE—MR. HOWARD TAKES CHARGE OF THE AMENDMENT—SUBSTITUTES PROPOSED—THE REPUBLICANS IN COUNCIL—THE DISFRANCHISING CLAUSE STRICKEN OUT—HUMOROUS ACCOUNT BY MR. HENDRICKS—THE PAIN AND PENALTIES OF NOT HOLDING OFFICE—A SENATOR'S PIETY APPEALED TO—HOWE VS. DOOLITTLE—MARKETABLE PRINCIPLES—PRAISE OF THE PRESIDENT—MR. MCDOUGALL'S CHARITY—VOTE OF THE SENATE—CONCURRENCE IN THE HOUSE.

THE joint resolution providing for amendments to the Constitution in relation to the rights of citizens, the basis of representation, the disfranchisement of rebels, and the rejection of the rebel debt, having passed the House of Representatives on the 10th of May, awaited only similar action of the Senate to prepare it to go before the several State Legislatures for final consideration. A fortnight had elapsed before it was taken up by the Senate. That body was much behind the House of Representatives in the business of the session. Notwithstanding the great size of the latter, it was accustomed to dispatch business with much greater rapidity than the Senate. The hour rule, limiting the length of speeches, and the previous question putting a boundary upon debate, being part of the machinery of the House, caused legislation to go on to final completion, which would otherwise have been swallowed up and lost in interminable talk.

The Senate, consisting of a smaller number, did not realize the need of such restrictions. Senators sometimes indulged themselves in speeches of such length as, if permitted in the House, would have proved an insurmountable obstacle to legislation.

The contrast between the discussions in the two houses of Congress was never more marked than in connection with the amend-

Eng'd by G.E. Perine & Co. N.Y.

E. D. Morgan

HON. E. D. MORGAN

SENATOR FROM NEW YORK.

ment relating to reconstruction. In this case the members of the House by special rule limited themselves to half an hour in the delivery of their speeches, which were consequently marked by great pertinency and condensation. In the Senate the speeches were in some instances limited only by the physical ability of the speakers to proceed. In one instance—the case of Garrett Davis —a speech was prolonged four hours, occupying all that part of the day devoted to the discussion. The limits of a volume would be inadequate for giving more than a mere outline of a discussion conducted upon such principles, and protracted through a period of more than two weeks.

The joint resolution was taken up by the Senate on the 23d of May. Mr. Sumner preferred that the consideration of the question should be deferred until the first of July. "We were able," said he, "to have a better proposition at the end of April than we had at the end of March, and I believe we shall be able to accept a better proposition just as the weeks proceed. It is one of the greatest questions that has ever been presented in the history of our country or of any country. It should be approached carefully and solemnly, and with the assurance we have before us all the testimony, all the facts, every thing that by any possibility can shed any light upon it."

The Senate proceeded, however, to the consideration of the joint resolution. Owing to the ill-health of Mr. Fessenden, who, as Chairman of the joint Committee on Reconstruction, would probably have taken charge of the measure, Mr. Howard opened the discussion and conducted the resolution in its passage through the Senate. He addressed the Senate in favor of all the sections of the proposed amendment except the third. "It is due to myself," said he, "to say that I did not favor this section of the amendment in the committee. I do not believe, if adopted, it will be of any practical benefit to the country."

Mr. Clark offered a substitute for the third section—the disfranchising clause—the following amendment, which, with slight modifications, was ultimately adopted:

"That no person shall be a Senator or Representative in Congress, or permitted to hold any office under the Government of the United States, who, having previously taken an oath to support the Constitution thereof, shall have voluntarily engaged in any insurrection or rebellion against the United States, or given aid or comfort thereto."

Mr. Wade offered a substitute for the whole bill, providing that no State shall abridge the rights of any person born within the United States, and that no class of persons, as to whose right to suffrage discrimination shall be made by any State except on the ground of intelligence, property, or rebellion, shall be included in the basis of representation. "I do not suppose," said Mr. Wade, "that if I had been on the committee I could have drawn up a proposition so good as this is that they have brought forward; and yet it seems to me, having the benefit of what they have done, that looking it over, reflecting upon it, seeing all its weak points, if it have any, I could, without having the ability of that committee, suggest amendments that would be beneficial."

Referring to the third section of the joint resolution, Mr. Wade remarked: "I am for excluding those who took any leading part in the rebellion from exercising any political power here or elsewhere now and forever; but as that clause does not seem to effect that purpose, and will probably effect nothing at all, I do not think it is of any consequence that it should have a place in the measure."

On the 24th of May, Mr. Stewart spoke three hours on the constitutional amendment. He advocated the extension to the States lately engaged in rebellion of all civil and political rights on condition of their extending impartial suffrage to all their people. He announced his policy as that of "protection for the Union and the friends of the Union, and mercy to a fallen foe. Mercy pleaded generous amnesty; justice demanded impartial suffrage. I proposed pardon for the rebels and the ballot for the blacks." Of the Committee on Reconstruction, Mr. Stewart said: "I realize the difficulties which they have been called upon to encounter. They have acted a noble part in their efforts to harmonize conflicting opinions. I rejoice in the manner in which the report is presented, and the liberal spirit manifested by the committee toward those who are anxious to aid in the perfection of their plan."

Mr. Johnson moved to strike out the third section, without offering a substitute.

Mr. Sherman offered a substitute for the second and third sections, apportioning representation according to the number of male citizens qualified to vote by State laws, and apportioning direct taxes according to the value of real and personal property.

The constitutional amendment was not again brought up for consideration in the Senate until Tuesday, May 29th. The several days during which the discussion was suspended in the Senate were not fruitless in their effect upon the pending measure. The amendment was carefully considered by the majority in special meetings, when such amendations and improvements were agreed upon as would harmonize the action of the Republicans in the Senate.

The first action of the Senate, when the subject was resumed, was to vote upon Mr. Johnson's motion to strike out the third section, which was passed unanimously—yeas, 43; nays, 0.

Mr. Howard, acting for the committee, then offered a series of amendments to the joint resolution under consideration. The first of these provided for the insertion as a part of section one, the following clause:

"All persons born in the United States, and subject to the jurisdiction thereof, are citizens of the United States and of the States wherein they reside."

Another modification moved by Mr. Howard was the insertion, in place of the third section already stricken out, a clause disabling certain classes of rebels from holding federal offices. This amendment was substantially the same as that previously proposed by Mr. Clark.

It was proposed to amend section four, which, as passed by the House, simply repudiated the rebel debt, by inserting the following clause:

"The obligations of the United States incurred in suppressing insurrection, or in defense of the Union, or for payment of bounties or pensions incident thereto, shall remain inviolate."

Such were the amendments to the pending measure which the majority saw proper to propose.

At a subsequent period of the debate, Mr. Hendricks, in a speech against the joint resolution, gave his view of the manner in which these amendments were devised. Being spoken, in good humor, by one whom a fellow-Senator once declared to be "the best-natured man in the Senate," and having, withal, a certain appropriateness to this point, his remarks are here presented:

"For three days the Senate-chamber was silent, but the discussions were transferred to another room of the Capitol, with closed doors and darkened windows, where party leaders might safely contend for a political and party policy. When Senators returned to their seats, I was curious to observe who had won and who lost in the party lottery. The dark brow of the Senator from New Hampshire [Mr. Clark] was lighted with a gleam of pleasure. His proposed substitute for the third section was the marked feature of the measure. But upon the lofty brow of the Senator from Nevada [Mr. Stewart] there rested a cloud of disappointment and grief. His bantling, which he had named universal amnesty and universal suffrage, which he had so often dressed and undressed in the presence of the Senate, the darling offspring of his brain, was dead; it had died in the caucus; and it was left to the sad Senator only to hope that it might not be his last. Upon the serene countenance of the Senator from Maine, the Chairman of the Fifteen, there rested the composure of the highest satisfaction; a plausible political platform had been devised, and there was yet hope for his party."

On the 30th of May, the Senate, as in Committee of the Whole, proceeded in the consideration of the constitutional amendment. The several clauses were taken up separately and in order.

Mr. Doolittle was desirous of amending the first section, relating to the rights of citizens, by inserting a clause excepting from its operation "Indians not taxed." His proposition was rejected.

"The Committee of Fifteen," said Mr. Doolittle, referring to the Civil Rights Bill, "fearing that this declaration by Congress was without validity unless a constitutional amendment should be brought forward to enforce it, have thought proper to report this amendment."

"I want to say to the honorable Senator," Mr. Fessenden replied, "that he is drawing entirely upon his imagination. There is not one word of correctness in all that he is saying; not a particle; not a scintilla; not the beginning of truth."

The first and second sections of the amendment were accepted in Committee of the Whole, with little further attempt at alteration.

The third section, cutting off late Confederate officials from eligibility to Federal offices, provoked repeated attempts to modify and emasculate it. Among them was a motion by Mr. Saulsbury to amend the final clause by adding that the President, by the exercise of the pardoning power, may remove the disability.

It augured the final success of the entire amendment in the Senate, that the numerous propositions to amend, made by those unfavorable to the measure, were voted down by majorities of more than three-fourths.

Mr. Doolittle, speaking in opposition to the third section, said that it was putting a new punishment upon all persons embraced within its provisions. "If," said he, "by a constitutional amendment, you impose a new punishment upon offenders who are guilty of crime already, you wipe out the old punishment as to them. Now, I do not propose to wipe out the penalties that these men have incurred by their treason against the Government. I would punish a sufficient number of them to make treason odious."

"How many would you like to hang?" asked Mr. Nye.

"You stated the other day that five or six would be enough to hang," replied Mr. Doolittle.

"Do you acquiesce in that?" asked Mr. Nye.

"I think I ought to be satisfied," replied Mr. Doolittle, "if you are satisfied with five or six.

"The insertion of this section," said Mr. Doolittle, continuing his remarks, "tends to prevent the adoption of the amendment by a sufficient number of States to ratify it. What States to be affected by this amendment will ratify it?"

"Four will accept that part of it," said Mr. James H. Lane.

"What four?" asked Mr. Doolittle.

"Virginia, Tennessee, Arkansas, and Louisiana," replied Mr. Lane. "I saw some gentlemen on Monday from Tennessee, who told me that this particular clause would be the most popular thing that could be tendered. And the very men that you want to hang ought to accept it joyfully in lieu of their hanging." [Laughter.]

"I do not know who those particular gentlemen were," said Mr. Doolittle. "Were they the gentlemen that deserved hanging or not?"

"They were Conservatives from Tennessee," replied Mr. Lane.

"I deem this section as the adoption of a new punishment as to the persons who are embraced within its provisions," said Mr. Doolittle.

"They seem to have peculiar notions in Wisconsin in regard to officers," said Mr. Trumbull; "and the Senator who has just taken his seat regards it as a punishment that a man can not hold an office. Why, sir, how many suffering people there must be in this land! He says this is a bill of pains and penalties because certain persons can not hold office; and he even seems to think it would be preferable, in some instances, to be hanged. He wants to know of the Senator from Ohio if such persons are to be excepted. This clause, I suppose, will not embrace those who are to be hanged. When hung, they will cease to suffer the pains and penalties of being kept out of office.

"Who ever heard of such a proposition as that laid down by the Senator from Wisconsin, that a bill excluding men from office is a bill of pains, and penalties, and punishment? The Constitution of the United States declares that no one but a native-born citizen of the United States shall be President of the United States. Does, then, every person living in this land who does not happen to have been born within its jurisdiction undergo pains, and penalties, and punishment all his life because by the Constitution he is ineligible to the Presidency? This is the Senator's position."

Mr. Willey spoke in favor of the pending clause of the joint resolution. "I hope," said he, "that we shall hear no more outcry about the injustice, the inhumanity, and the want of Christian spirit in thus incorporating into our Constitution precautionary measures that will forever prohibit these unfaithful men from again having any part in the Government."

"The honorable Senator," remarked Mr. Davis in reply, "is a professor of the Christian religion, a follower of the lowly and humble Redeemer; but it seems to me that he forgot all the spirit of his Christian charity and faith in the tenor of the remarks which he made."

"This cry for blood and vengeance," exclaimed Mr. Saulsbury, "can not last forever. The eternal God who sits above, whose essence is love, and whose chief attribute is mercy, says to all his creatures, whether in the open daylight or in the silent hours of the night, 'Be charitable; be merciful.'"

Mr. Doolittle proposed two amendments to section three: the first to limit its application to those who "*voluntarily* engaged in rebellion," and the second to except those "who have duly received amnesty and pardon."

These propositions were both rejected by large majorities, only ten Senators voting for them. The third section, as proposed by Mr. Howard, was then adopted by a vote of thirty against ten.

The death of General Scott having been the occasion of an adjournment of Congress, the consideration of the constitutional amendment was not resumed until the 4th of June. Mr. Hendricks moved to amend by including in the basis of representation in the Southern States three-fifths of the freedmen. Mr. Van Winkle offered an amendment providing that no person not excluded from office by the terms of the third section shall be liable to any disability or penalty for treason after a term of years. Both of these propositions were rejected by the Senate.

On the 5th of June, Mr. Poland, Mr. Stewart, and Mr. Howe addressed the Senate in favor of the constitutional amendment. Mr. Poland did not expect to be able to say any thing after six months' discussion of this subject. He took more hopeful views of the President's tractability than many others. "Although these propositions," said he, "may not, in all respects, correspond with the views of the President, I believe he will feel it to be his patriotic duty to acquiesce in the plan proposed, and give his powerful influence and support to procure their adoption."

"While it is not the plan that I would have adopted," said Mr. Stewart, "still it is the best that I can get, and contains many excellent provisions."

"I shall vote for the Constitutional amendment," said Mr. Howe, "regretfully, but not reluctantly. I shall vote for it regretfully, because it does not meet the emergency as I hoped the emergency would be met; but I shall not vote for it reluctantly, because it seems to me just now to be the only way in which the emergency can be met at all."

An issue of some personal interest arose between Mr. Howe and his colleague, Mr. Doolittle, which led them somewhat aside from the regular channel of discussion.

"He has been a most fortunate politician," said Mr. Howe, "always to happen to have just those convictions which bore the highest price in the market."

"That I ever intended in the slightest degree," replied Mr. Doolittle, "to swerve in my political action for the sake of offices or the price of offices in the market, is a statement wholly without foundation."

Mr. Howe had said in substance that in 1848 Mr. Doolittle

was acting with the Free Democratic party in New York, which was stronger than the Democratic party in that State. In 1852, when he left the Free Democratic party, and acted with the Democratic party in Wisconsin, the Democratic party was in the majority in that State. He did not leave the Democratic party and join the Republican party in 1854, but only in 1856, and then Wisconsin was no longer a Democratic State.

Mr. Doolittle, after having given a detailed account of his previous political career, remarked: "During the last six months, in the State of Wisconsin, no man has struggled harder than I have struggled to save the Union party, to save it to its platform, to save it to its principles, to save it to its supremacy. For six months, from one end of Wisconsin to the other—ay, from Boston to St. Paul—by every one of a certain class of newspapers I have been denounced as a traitor to the Union party because I saved it from defeat. Sir, it is not the first time in the history of the world that men have turned in to crucify their savior."

On the same day, June 6th, Messrs. Hendricks, Sherman, Cowan, and others having participated in the discussion, the Senate voted on another amendment offered by Mr. Doolittle, apportioning Representatives, after the census of 1870, according to the number of legal voters in each State by the laws thereof. This proposition was rejected—yeas, 7; nays, 31.

On the 7th of June, Mr. Garrett Davis occupied the entire time devoted to the constitutional amendment in opposing that measure, denouncing Congress, and praising the President. "There is a very great state of backwardness," said he, "in both houses of Congress in relation to the transaction of the legitimate, proper, and useful portion of the public business; but as to the business that is of an illegitimate and mischievous character, and that is calculated to produce results deleterious to the present and the future of the whole country, there has been a good deal, much too much, of progress made."

Of President Johnson Mr. Davis said: "He seems to be the man for the occasion; and his ability, resources, courage, and patriotism have developed to meet its great demands. If this ark which holds the rights and liberties of the American people is to be rescued and saved, he will be one of the chief instruments in the great work, and his glory and fame will be deathless."

On the 8th of June, the last day of the discussion, the constitutional amendment was opposed by Messrs. Johnson, McDougall, and Hendricks, and defended by Messrs. Henderson, Yates, and Howard.

"Let us bring back the South," said Mr. Johnson, in closing his remarks, "so as to enable her to remove the desolation which has gone through her borders, restore her industry, attend to her products, instead of keeping her in a state of subjection without the slightest necessity. Peace once existing throughout the land, the restoration of all rights brought about, the Union will be at once in more prosperous existence than it ever was; and throughout the tide of time, as I believe, nothing in the future will ever cause us to dream of dissolution, or of subjecting any part, through the powerful instrumentality of any other part, to any dishonoring humiliation."

"I went down once on the Mississippi," remarked Mr. McDougall, "at the opening of the war. I met a general of the Confederate army, and I took him by the hand and took him to my state-room, on board of my gun-boat. Said he, 'General,' throwing his arms around me, 'how hard it is that you and I have to fight.' That was the generosity of a combatant. I repeated to him, 'It is hard,' and he and I drank a bottle of wine or two—just as like as not. [Laughter.] This thing of bearing malice is one of the wickedest sins that men can bear under their clothes."

Speaking of the third section, which had encountered great opposition, as inflicting undue punishment upon prominent rebels, Mr. Henderson said: "If this provision be all, it will be an act of the most stupendous mercy that ever mantled the crimes of rebellion."

"Let us suppose a case," said Mr. Yates. "Here is a man—Winder, or Dick Turner, or some other notorious character. He has been the cause of the death of that boy of yours. He has shot at him from behind an ambuscade, or he has starved him to death in the Andersonville prison, or he has made him lie at Belle Isle, subject to disease and death from the miasma by which he was surrounded. When he is upon trial and the question is, 'Sir, are you guilty, or are you not guilty?' and he raises his blood-stained hands, deep-dyed in innocent and patriotic blood, the Senator from Pennsylvania rises and says, 'For God's sake! do not deprive him of the right to go to the legislature.' The idea is that if a man has forfeited his life, it is too great a punishment to deprive him of the privilege of holding office."

Speaking of radicalism, Mr. Yates remarked: "My fear is not that this Congress will be too radical; I am not afraid of this Congress being shipwrecked upon any proposition of radicalism; but I fear from timid and cowardly conservatism which will not risk a great people to take their destiny in their own hands, and to settle this great question upon the principles of equality, justice, and liberality. That is my fear."

Mr. Doolittle moved that the several sections of the amendment be submitted to the States as separate articles. This motion was rejected—yeas, 11; nays, 33.

The vote was finally taken upon the adoption of the constitutional amendment as a whole. It passed the Senate by a majority of more than two-thirds, as follows:

YEAS—Messrs. Anthony, Chandler, Clark, Conness, Cragin, Creswell, Edmunds, Fessenden, Foster, Grimes, Harris, Henderson, Howard, Howe, Kirkwood, Lane of Indiana, Lane of Kansas, Morgan, Morrill, Nye, Poland, Pomeroy, Ramsey, Sherman, Sprague, Stewart, Sumner, Trumbull, Wade, Willey, Williams, Wilson, and Yates—33.

NAYS—Messrs. Cowan, Davis, Doolittle, Guthrie, Hendricks, Johnson, McDougall, Norton, Riddle, Saulsbury, and Van Winkle—11.

On the 13th of June, the joint resolution, having been modified in the Senate, reäppeared in the House for the concurrence of that branch of Congress. There was a short discussion of the measure as amended in the Senate. Messrs. Rogers, Finck, and Harding spoke against the resolution, and Messrs. Spalding, Henderson, and Stevens in its favor.

"The first proposition," said Mr. Rogers, "was tame in iniquity, injustice, and violation of fundamental liberty to the one before us."

"I say," said Mr. Finck, "it is an outrage upon the people of those States who were compelled to give their aid and assistance in the rebellion. You propose to inflict upon these people a punishment not known to the law in existence at the time any offense may have been committed, but after the offense has been committed."

"Let me tell you," said Mr. Harding, "you are preparing for revolutions after revolutions. I warn you there will be no peace in this country until each State be allowed to control its own citizens. If you take that from them, what care I for the splendid machinery of a national government?"

Mr. Stevens briefly addressed the House before the final vote was taken. He had just risen from a sick-bed, and ridden to the Capitol at the peril of his life. During the quarter of an hour which he occupied in speaking, the solemnity was such as is seldom seen in that assembly. Members left their seats, and gathered closely around the venerable man to hear his brave and solemn words. From his youth he had hoped to see our institutions freed from every vestige of human oppression, of inequality of rights, of the recognized degradation of the poor and the superior caste of the rich. But that bright dream had vanished. "I find," said he, "that we shall be obliged to be content with patching up the worst portions of the ancient edifice, and leaving it in many of its parts to be swept through by the tempests, the frosts, and the storms of despotism."

It might be inquired why, with his opinions, he accepted so imperfect a proposition. "Because," said he, "I live among men, and not among angels; among men as intelligent, as determined, and as independent as myself, who, not agreeing with me, do not choose to yield their opinions to mine." With an enfeebled voice, yet with a courageous air, he charged the responsibility for that day's patchwork upon the Executive. "With his cordial assistance," said Mr. Stevens, "the rebel States might have been made model republics, and this nation an empire of universal freedom; but he preferred 'restoration' to 'reconstruction.'"

The question was taken, and the joint resolution passed the House by a vote of over three-fourths—120 yeas to 32 nays. From the necessary absence of many members, the vote was not full, yet the relative majority in favor of this measure was greater than in the former vote.

The following is the Constitutional Amendment as it passed both Houses of Congress:

"ARTICLE —.

"SEC. 1. All persons born or naturalized in the United States, and subject to the jurisdiction thereof, are citizens of the United States and of the State wherein they reside. No State shall make or enforce any law which shall abridge the privileges or immunities of citizens of the United States; nor shall any State deprive any person of life, liberty, or property without due process of law; nor deny to any person within its jurisdiction the equal protection of the laws.

"SEC. 2. Representatives shall be apportioned among the several States according to their respective numbers, counting the whole number of persons in each State, excluding Indians not taxed. But when the right to vote at any election for the choice of electors for President and Vice-President of the United States, Representatives in Congress, the executive and judicial officers of a State, or the members of the Legislature thereof, is denied to any of the male inhabitants of such State, being twenty-one years of age, and citizens of the United States, or in any way abridged, except for participation in rebellion or other crime, the basis of representation therein shall be reduced in the proportion which the number of such male citizens shall bear to the whole number of such male citizens twenty-one years of age in such State.

"SEC. 3. No person shall be a Senator or Representative in Congress, or elector of President and Vice-President, or hold any office, civil or military, under the United States or under any State, who, having previously taken an oath as a member of Congress, or as an officer of the United States, or as a member of any State Legislature, or as an executive or judicial officer of any State, to support the Constitution of the United States, shall have engaged in insurrection or rebellion against the same, or given aid or comfort to the enemies thereof. But Congress may, by a vote of two-thirds of each House, remove such disability.

"SEC. 4. The validity of the public debt of the United States, authorized by law, including debts incurred for payment of pensions and bounties for services in suppressing insurrection or rebellion, shall not be questioned. But neither the United States nor any State shall assume or pay any debt or obligation incurred in aid of insurrection or rebellion against the United States, or any claim for the loss or emancipation of any slave; but all such debts, obligations, and claims shall be held illegal and void.

"SEC. 5. The Congress shall have power to enforce, by appropriate legislation, the provisions of this article."

The President was requested to send the Amendment to the several States for ratification.

On the 22d of June, President Johnson sent a message to Congress informing them that the Secretary of State had transmitted to the Governors of the several States certified copies of the proposed amendment. "These steps," said the President, "are to be considered as purely ministerial, and in no sense whatever committing the Executive to an approval of the recommendation of the amendment." It seemed to the President a serious objection to the proposition "that the joint resolution was not submitted by the two houses for the approval of the President, and that of the thirty-six States which constitute the Union, eleven are excluded from representation."

The President having no power under the Constitution to veto a joint resolution submitting a constitutional amendment to the people, this voluntary expression of opinion could not have been designed to have an influence upon the action of Congress. The document could have been designed by its author only as an argument with the State Legislatures against the ratification of the Constitutional Amendment, and as a notice to the Southern people that they were badly treated.

The President's message was received by Congress without comment, and referred to the Committee on Reconstruction.

CHAPTER XIX.

REPORT OF THE COMMITTEE ON RECONSTRUCTION.

An important State Paper—Work of the Committee—Difficulty of obtaining information—Theory of the President—Taxation and Representation—Disposition and doings of the Southern People—Conclusion of the Committee—Practical Recommendations.

ON the 8th of June, the day on which the constitutional amendment passed the Senate, the report of the joint Committee on Reconstruction was presented to Congress. This important State paper had been looked for with great interest and no little anxiety by the people in all parts of the country. It was drawn up with marked ability, and was destined to have a most important bearing upon public opinion in reference to the great subject which, in all its bearings, it brought to the view of Congress and the country.

The committee having had unrivalled opportunities for obtaining information, their conclusions commanded the respect of those who differed from them, and obtained the almost unanimous approval of the party which carried the war to a successful close.

Referring to the nature of the work which was required of them, the committee said:

"Such an investigation, covering so large an extent of territory, and involving so many important considerations, must necessarily require no trifling labor, and consume a very considerable amount of time. It must embrace the condition in which those States were left at the close of the war; the measures which have been taken toward the reörganization of civil government, and the disposition of the people toward the United States—in a word, their fitness to take an active part in the administration of national affairs."

The first step to be taken by the committee, that of obtaining required information, and the difficulties attending it, were thus set forth:

"A call was made on the President for the information in his possession as to what had been done, in order that Congress might judge for itself as to the grounds of belief expressed by him in the fitness of States recently in rebellion to participate fully in the conduct of national affairs. This information was not immediately communicated. When the response was finally made, some six weeks after your committee had been in actual session, it was found that the evidence upon which the President seemed to have based his suggestions was incomplete and unsatisfactory. Authenticated copies of the constitutions and ordinances adopted by the conventions in three of the States had been submitted; extracts from newspapers furnished scanty information as to the action of one other State, and nothing appears to have been communicated as to the remainder. There was no evidence of the loyalty of those who participated in these conventions, and in one State alone was any proposition made to submit the action of the convention to the final judgment of the people.

"Failing to obtain the desired information, and left to grope for light wherever it might be found, your committee did not deem it either advisable or safe to adopt, without further examination, the suggestions of the President, more especially as he had not deemed it expedient to remove the military force, to suspend martial law, or to restore the writ of *habeas corpus*, but still thought it necessary to exercise over the people of the rebellious States his military power and jurisdiction. This conclusion derived greater force from the fact, undisputed, that in all those States, except Tennessee, and, perhaps, Arkansas, the elections which were held for State officers and members of Congress had resulted almost universally in the defeat of candidates who had been true to the Union, and in the election of notorious and unpardoned rebels—men who could not take the prescribed oath of office, and who made no secret of their hostility to the Government and the people of the United States.

"Under these circumstances, any thing like hasty action would have been as dangerous as it was obviously unwise. It appeared to your committee that but one course remained, viz.: to investigate carefully and thoroughly the state of feeling and opinion existing among the people of these States; to ascertain how far their pretended loyalty could be relied upon, and thence to infer whether it would be safe to admit them at once to a full participation in the Government they had fought for four years to destroy. It was an equally important inquiry whether their restoration to their former relations with the United States should only be granted upon certain conditions and guarantees, which would effectually secure the nation against a recurrence of evils so disastrous as those from which it had escaped at so enormous a sacrifice."

The theory of the President, and those who demanded the immediate admission of Southern Senators and Representatives, was stated in the report to amount to this:

"That, inasmuch as the lately insurgent States had no legal right to separate themselves from the Union, they still retain their positions as States, and, consequently, the people thereof have a right to immediate representation in Congress, without the imposition of any conditions whatever; and, further, that until such admission, Congress has no right to tax them for the support of the Government. It has even been contended that, until such admission, all legislation affecting their interests is, if not unconstitutional, at least unjustifiable and oppressive.

"It is moreover contended that, from the moment when rebellion lays down its arms, and actual hostilities cease, all political rights of rebellious communities are at once restored; that because the people of a State of the Union were once an organized community within the Union, they necessarily so remain, and their right to be represented in Congress at any and all times, and to participate in the government of the country under all circumstances, admits of neither question nor dispute. If this is indeed true, then is the Government of the United States powerless for its own protection, and flagrant rebellion, carried to the extreme of civil war, is a pastime which any State may play at, not only certain that it can lose nothing, in any event, but may be the gainer by defeat. If rebellion succeeds, it accomplishes its purpose and destroys the Government. If it fails, the war has been barren of results, and the battle may be fought out in the legislative halls of the country. Treason defeated in the field has only to take possession of Congress and the Cabinet."

The committee in this report asserted:

"It is more than idle, it is a mockery to contend that a people who have thrown off their allegiance, destroyed the local government which bound their States to the Union as members thereof, defied its authority, refused to execute its laws, and abrogated every provision which gave them political rights within the Union, still retain through all the perfect and entire right to resume at their own will and pleasure all their privileges within the Union, and especially to participate in its government and control the conduct of its affairs. To admit such a principle for one moment would be to declare that treason is always master and loyalty a blunder."

To a favorite argument of the advocates of immediate restoration of the rebel States, the report presented the following reply:

"That taxation should be only with the consent of the people, through their own representatives, is a cardinal principle of all free governments; but it is not true that taxation and representation must go together under all circumstances and at every moment of time. The people of the District of Columbia and of the Territories are taxed, although not represented in Congress. If it be true that the people of the so-called Confederate States have no right to throw off the authority of the United States, it is equally true that they are bound at all times to share the burdens of Government. They can not, either legally or equitably, refuse to bear their just proportion of these burdens by voluntarily abdicating their rights and privileges as States of the Union, and refusing to be represented in the councils of the nation, much less by rebellion against national authority and levying war. To hold that by so doing they could escape taxation, would be to offer a premium for insurrection—to reward instead of punishing treason."

Upon the important subject of representation, which had occupied much of the attention of the committee and much of the time of Congress, the report held the following words:

"The increase of representation, necessarily resulting from the abolition of slavery, was considered the most important element in the questions arising out of the changed condition of affairs, and the necessity for some fundamental action in this regard seemed imperative. It appeared to your committee that the rights of these persons, by whom the basis of representation had been thus increased, should be recognized by the General Government. While slaves they were not considered as having any rights, civil or political. It did not seem just or proper that all the political advantages derived from their becoming free should be confined to their former masters, who had fought against the Union, and withheld from themselves, who had always been loyal. Slavery, by building up a ruling and dominant class, had produced a spirit of oligarchy adverse to republican institutions, which finally inaugurated civil war. The tendency of continuing the domination of such a class, by leaving it in the exclusive possession of political power, would be to encourage the same spirit and lead to a similar result. Doubts were entertained whether Congress had power, even under the amended Constitution, to prescribe the qualifications of voters in a State, or could act directly on the subject. It was doubtful in the opinion of your committee whether the States would consent to surrender a power they had always exercised, and to which they were attached. As the best, not the only method of surmounting all difficulty, and as eminently just and proper in itself, your committee comes to the conclusion that political power should be possessed in all the States exactly in proportion as the right of suffrage should be granted without distinction of color or race. This, it was thought, would leave the whole question with the people of each State, holding out to all the advantages of increased political power as an inducement to allow all to participate in its exercise. Such a proposition would be in its nature gentle and persuasive, and would tend, it was hoped, at no distant day, to an equal participation of all, without distinction, in all the rights and privileges of citizenship, thus affording a full and adequate protection to all classes of citizens, since we would have, through the ballot-box, the power of self-protection.

"Holding these views, your committee prepared an amendment to the Constitution to carry out this idea, and submitted the same to Congress. Unfortunately, as we think, it did not receive the necessary constitutional support in the Senate, and, therefore, could not be proposed for adoption by the States. The principle involved in that amendment is, however, believed to be sound, and your committee have again proposed it in another form, hoping that it may receive the approbation of Congress."

The action of the people of the insurrectionary States, and their responses to the President's appeals, as showing their degree of preparation for immediate admission into Congress, was thus set forth in the report:

"So far as the disposition of the people of the insurrectionary States and the probability of their adopting measures conforming to the changed condition of affairs can be inferred, from the papers submitted by the President as the basis of his action, the prospects are far from encouraging. It appears quite clear that the antislavery amendments, both to the State and Federal Constitutions, were adopted with reluctance by the bodies which did adopt them; and in some States they have been either passed by in silence or rejected. The language of all the provisions and ordinances of the States on the subject amounts to nothing more than an unwilling admission of an unwelcome truth. As to the ordinance of secession, it is in some cases declared 'null and void,' and in others simply 'repealed,' and in no case is a refutation of this deadly heresy considered worthy of a place in the new constitutions.

"If, as the President assumes, these insurrectionary States were, at the close of the war, wholly without State governments, it would seem that before being admitted to participate in the direction of public affairs, such governments should be regularly organized. Long usage has established, and numerous statutes have pointed out, the mode in which this should be done. A convention to frame a form of government should be assembled under competent authority. Ordinarily this authority emanates from Congress; but under the peculiar circumstances, your committee is not disposed to criticise the President's action in assuming the power exercised by him in this regard.

"The convention, when assembled, should frame a constitution of government, which should be submitted to the people for adoption. If adopted, a Legislature should be convened to pass the laws necessary to carry it into effect. When a State thus organized claims representation in Congress, the election of Representatives should be provided for by law, in accordance with the laws of Congress regulating representation, and the proof, that the action taken has been in conformity to law, should be submitted to Congress.

"In no case have these essential preliminary steps been taken. The conventions assembled seem to have assumed that the Constitution which had been repudiated and overthrown, was still in existence, and operative to constitute the States members of the Union, and to have contented themselves with such amendments as they were informed were requisite in order to insure their return to an immediate participation in the Government of the United States. And without waiting to ascertain whether the people they represented would adopt even the proposed amendments, they at once called elections of Representatives to Congress in nearly all instances before an Executive had been chosen to issue certificates of election under the State laws, and such elections as were held were ordered by the conventions. In one instance, at least, the writs of election were signed by the provisional governor. Glaring irregularities and unwarranted assumptions of power are manifest in several cases, particularly in South Carolina, where the convention, although disbanded by the provisional governor on the ground that it was a revolutionary body, assumed to district the State."

The report thus sets forth the conduct naturally expected of the Southern people, as contrasted with their actual doings:

"They should exhibit in their acts something more than unwilling submission to an unavoidable necessity—a feeling, if not cheerful, certainly not offensive and defiant, and should evince an entire repudiation of all hostility to the General Government by an acceptance of such just and favorable conditions as that Government should think the public safety demands. Has this been done? Let us look at the facts shown by the evidence taken by the committee. Hardly had the war closed before the people of these insurrectionary States come forward and hastily claim as a right the privilege of participating at once in that Government which they had for four years been fighting to overthrow.

"Allowed and encouraged by the Executive to organize State governments, they at once place in power leading rebels, unrepentant and unpardoned, excluding with contempt those who had manifested an attachment to the Union, and preferring, in many instances, those who had rendered themselves the most obnoxious. In the face of the law requiring an oath which would necessarily exclude all such men from Federal office, they elect, with very few exeptions, as Senators and Representatives in Congress, men who had actively participated in the rebellion, insultingly denouncing the law as unconstitutional.

"It is only necessary to instance the election to the Senate of the late Vice President of the Confederacy—a man who, against his own declared convictions, had lent all the weight of his acknowledged ability and of his influence as a most prominent public man to the cause of the rebellion, and who, unpardoned rebel as he is, with that oath staring him in the face, had the assurance to lay his credentials on the table of the Senate. Other rebels of scarcely less note or notoriety were selected from other quarters. Professing no repentance, glorying apparently in the crime they had committed, avowing still, as the uncontradicted testimony of Mr. Stephens and many others proves, an adherence to the pernicious doctrines of secession, and declaring that they yielded only to necessity, they insist with unanimous voice upon their rights as States, and proclaim they will submit to no conditions whatever preliminary to their resumption of power under that Constitution which they still claim the right to repudiate."

Finally the report thus presented the "conclusion of the committee:"

"That the so-called Confederate States are not at present entitled to representation in the Congress of the United States; that before allowing such representation, adequate security for future peace and safety should be required; that this can only be found in such changes of the organic law as shall determine the civil rights and privileges of all citizens in all parts of the republic, shall place representation on an equitable basis, shall fix a stigma upon treason, and protect the loyal people against future claims for the expenses incurred in support of rebellion and for manumitted slaves, together with an express grant of power in Congress to enforce these provisions. To this end they have offered a joint resolution for amending the Constitution of the United States, and two several bills designed to carry the same into effect."

The passage of the Constitutional Amendment by more than the necessary majority has been related. One of the bills to which reference is made in the above report—declaring certain officials of the so-called Confederate States ineligble to any office under the Government of the United States—was placed in the amendment in lieu of the disfranchising clause. The other bill provided for "the restoration of the States lately in insurrection to their full rights" so soon as they should have ratified the proposed amendment. This bill was defeated in the House by a vote of 75 to 48. Congress thus refused to pledge itself in advance to make the amendment the sole test of the reädmission of rebel States. Congress, however, clearly indicated a disposition to restore those States "at the earliest day consistent with the future peace and safety of the Union." The report and doings of the Committee of Fifteen, although by many impatiently criticised as dilatory, resulted, before the end of the first session of the Thirty-ninth Congress, in the reconstruction of one of the States lately in rebellion.

CHAPTER XX.

RESTORATION OF TENNESSEE.

ASSEMBLING OF THE TENNESSEE LEGISLATURE—RATIFICATION OF THE CONSTITUTIONAL AMENDMENT—RESTORATION OF TENNESSEE PROPOSED IN CONGRESS—THE GOVERNMENT OF TENNESSEE NOT REPUBLICAN—PROTEST AGAINST THE PREAMBLE—PASSAGE IN THE HOUSE—NEW PREAMBLE PROPOSED—THE PRESIDENT'S OPINION DEPRECATED AND DISREGARDED—PASSAGE IN THE SENATE—THE PRESIDENT'S APPROVAL AND PROTEST—ADMISSION OF TENNESSEE MEMBERS—MR. PATTERSON'S CASE.

THE most important practical step in the work of reconstruction taken by the Thirty-ninth Congress was the restoration of Tennessee to her relations to the Union. Of all the recently rebellious States, Tennessee was the first to give a favorable response to the overtures of Congress by ratifying the Constitutional Amendment.

Immediately on the reception of the circular of the Secretary of State containing the proposed amendment, Governor Brownlow issued a proclamation summoning the Legislature of Tennessee to assemble at Nashville on the 4th of July.

There are eighty-four seats in the lower branch of the Legislature of Tennessee. By the State Constitution, two-thirds of the seats are required to be full to constitute a quorum. The presence of fifty-six members seemed essential for the legal transaction of business. Every effort was made to prevent the assembling of the required number. The powerful influence of the President himself was thrown in opposition to ratification.

On the day of the assembling of the Legislature but fifty-two members voluntarily appeared. Two additional members were secured by arrest, so that the number nominally in attendance was fifty-four, and thus it remained for several days. It was ascertained that deaths and resignations had reduced the number of actual members to seventy-two, and a Union caucus determined to declare that fifty-four members should constitute a quorum. Two more Union members opportunely arrived, swelling the number present in the Capitol to fifty-six. Neither persuasion nor compulsion availed to induce the two "Conservative members" to occupy their seats, and the house was driven to the expedient of considering the members who were under arrest and confined in a committee room, as present in their places. This having been decided, the constitutional amendment was immediately ratified. Governor Brownlow immediately sent the following telegraphic dispatch to Washington:

"NASHVILLE, TENNESSEE, *Thursday*, July 19—12 M.

"*To Hon. E. M. Stanton, Secretary of War, Washington, D. C.*

"My compliments to the President. We have carried the Constitutional Amendment in the House. Vote, 43 to 18; two of his tools refusing to vote.

"W. G. BROWNLOW."

On the 19th of July, the very day on which Tennessee voted to ratify the amendment, and immediately after the news was received in Washington, Mr. Bingham, in the House of Representatives, moved to reconsider a motion by which a joint resolution relating to the restoration of Tennessee had been referred to the Committee on Reconstruction.

This joint resolution having been drawn up in the early part of the session, was not adapted to the altered condition of affairs resulting from the passage of the constitutional amendment in Congress. The motion to reconsider having passed, Mr. Bingham proposed the following substitute:

"Joint resolution declaring Tennessee again entitled to Senators and Representatives in Congress.

"*Whereas*, The State of Tennessee has in good faith ratified the article of amendment to the Constitution of the United States, proposed by the Thirty-ninth Congress to the Legislatures of the several States, and has also shown, to the satisfaction of Congress, by a proper spirit of obedience in the body of her people, her return to her due allegiance to the Government, laws, and authority of the United States: Therefore,

"*Be it resolved by the Senate and House of Representatives of the United States of America in Congress assembled*, That the State of Tennessee is hereby restored to her former, proper, practical relation to the Union, and again entitled to be represented by Senators and Representatives in Congress, duly elected and qualified, upon their taking the oaths of office required by existing laws."

On the following day, this joint resolution was the regular order, and gave rise to a brief discussion.

Mr. Boutwell desired to offer an amendment providing that Tennessee should have representation in Congress whenever, in addition to having ratified the constitutional amendment, it should establish an "equal and just system of suffrage." Mr. Boutwell, although opposed to the joint resolution before the House, had no "technical" objections to the immediate restoration of Tennessee. "I am not troubled," said he, "by the informalities apparent in the proceedings of the Tennessee Legislature upon the question of ratifying the constitutional amendment. It received the votes of a majority of the members of a full house, and when the proper officers shall have made the customary certificate, and filed it in the Department of State, it is not easy to see how any legal objection can be raised, even if two-thirds of the members were not present, although that proportion is a quorum according to the constitution of the State."

Mr. Boutwell declared that his objections to the pending measure were vital and fundamental. The government of Tennessee was not republican in form, since under its constitution more than eighty thousand male citizens were deprived of the right of suffrage. The enfranchisement of the freedmen of Tennessee should be the beginning of the great work of reconstruction upon a republican basis. "We surrender the rights of four million people," said Mr. Boutwell in concluding his remarks; "we surrender the cause of justice; we imperil the peace and endanger the prosperity of the country; we degrade ourselves as a great party which has controlled the government in the most trying times in the history of the world."

Mr. Higby thought that Tennessee should not be admitted without a restriction that she should not be allowed any more representation than that to which she would be entitled were the constitutional amendment in full operation and effect.

Mr. Bingham advocated at considerable length the immediate restoration of Tennessee. "Inasmuch," said he, "as Tennessee has conformed to all our requirements; inasmuch as she has, by a majority of her whole legislature in each house, ratified the amendment in good faith; inasmuch as she has of her own voluntary will conformed her constitution and laws to the Constitution and laws of the United States; inasmuch as she has by her fundamental law forever prohibited the assumption or payment of the rebel debt, or the enslavement of men; inasmuch as she has by her own constitution declared that rebels shall not exerercise any of the political power of the State or vote at elections; and thereby given the American people assurance of her determination to stand by this great measure of security for the future of the Republic, Tennessee is as much entitled to be represented here as any State in the Union."

Mr. Finck, Mr. Eldridge, and other Democrats favored the resolution, while they protested against and "spit on" the preamble.

The question having been taken, the joint resolution passed the House, one hundred and twenty-five voting in the affirmative, and twelve in the negative. These last were the following: Messrs. Alley, Benjamin, Boutwell, Eliot, Higby, Jenckes, Julian, Kelley, Loan, McClurg, Paine, and Williams.

The announcement of the passage of the joint resolution was greeted with demonstrations of applause on the floor and in the galleries.

On the day succeeding this action in the House, the joint resolution came up for consideration in the Senate. After a considerable discussion, the resolution as it passed the House was adopted by the Senate.

In place of the preamble which was passed by the House, Mr. Trumbull proposed the following substitute:

> "*Whereas*, In the year 1861, the government of the State of Tennessee was seized upon and taken possession of by persons in hostility to the United States, and the inhabitants of said State, in pursuance of an act of Congress were declared to be in a state of insurrection against the United States; and whereas said State government can only be restored to its former political relations in the Union by the consent of the law-making power of the United States; and whereas the people of said State did on the 22d of February, 1865, by a large popular vote adopt and ratify a constitution of government whereby slavery was abolished, and all ordinances and laws of secession and debts contracted under the same were declared void; and whereas a State government has been organized under said constitution which has ratified the amendment to the Constitution of the United States abolishing slavery, also the amendment proposed by the Thirty-ninth Congress, and has done other acts proclaiming and denoting loyalty: Therefore."

Mr. Sherman opposed the substitution of this preamble. "These political dogmas," said he, "can not receive the sanction of the

President; and to insert them will only create delay, and postpone the admission of Tennessee."

"I pay no regard," said Mr. Wade, "to all that has been said here in relation to the President probably vetoing your bill, for any thing he may do, in my judgment, is entirely out of order on this floor. Sir, in olden times it was totally inadmissible in the British Parliament for any member to allude to any opinion that the king might entertain on any thing before the body; and much more, sir, ought an American Congress never to permit any member to allude to the opinion that the Executive may have upon any subject under consideration. He has his duty to perform, and we ours; and we have no right whatever under the Constitution to be biased by any opinion that he may entertain on any subject. Therefore, sir, I believe that it is, or ought to be, out of order to allude to any such thing here. Let the President do what he conceives to be his duty, and let us do ours, without being biased in any way whatever by what it may be supposed he will do."

Mr. Brown entered his disclaimer. "Republicanism," said he, "means nothing if it means not impartial, universal suffrage. Republicanism is a mockery and a lie if it can assume to administer this government in the name of freedom, and yet sanction, as this act will, the disfranchisement of a large, if not the largest, part of the loyal population of the rebel States on the pretext of color and race."

The question being taken on the passage of the preamble as substituted by the Senate, together with the resolution of the House, resulted in twenty-eight Senators voting in the affirmative, and four in the negative. The latter were Messrs. Brown, Buckalew, McDougal, and Sumner.

The House concurred in the amendment of the Senate, without discussion, and the joint resolution went to the President for his approval.

On the 24th of July, the President, not thinking it expedient to risk a veto, signed the joint resolution, and at the same time sent to the House his protest against the opinions presented in the preamble. After having given his objections to the preamble and resolution at considerable length, the President said: "I have, notwithstanding the anomalous character of this proceeding, affixed my signature to the resolution. [General applause and laughter.] My approval, however, is not to be construed as an acknowledgment of the right of Congress to pass laws preliminary to the admission of duly-qualified representatives from any of the States. [Great laughter.] Neither is it to be considered as committing me to all the statements made in the preamble, [renewed laughter,] some of which are, in my opinion, without foundation in fact, especially the assertion that the State of Tennnessee has ratified the amendment to the Constitution of the United States proposed by the Thirty-ninth Congress." [Laughter.]

After the reading of the Pesident's Message, Mr. Stevens said: "Inasmuch as the joint resolution has become a law by the entire and cordial approval of the President, [laughter,] I am joint committee on reconstruction to ask that that committee be discharged from the further consideration of the credentials of the members elect from the State of Tennessee, and to move that the same be referred to the Committee of Elections of this House."

This motion was passed. At a later hour of the same day's session, Mr. Dawes, of the Committee on Elections, having permission to report, said that the credentials of the eight Representatives elect from Tennessee had been examined, and were found in conformity with law. He moved, therefore, that the gentlemen be sworn in as members of the House from the State of Tennessee.

Horace Maynard and other gentlemen from Tennessee then went forward amid applause, and took the oath of office.

On the day following, Joseph S. Fowler was sworn in, and took his seat as a Senator from Tennessee.

The next day Mr. Fowler presented the credentials of David T. Patterson as a Senator elect from Tennessee. A motion was made that these credentials be referred to the Committee on the Judiciary, with instructions to inquire into the qualifications of Mr. Patterson.

The circumstances in this case were peculiar. Mr. Patterson had been elected circuit judge by the people of East Tennessee in 1854. His term of office expired in 1862, after Tennessee had passed the ordinance of secession and became a member of the Southern Confederacy. He was a firm, avowed, and influential Union man, and in the exercise of the duties of his office did much to protect the interests of loyal men. Persons who were opposed to secession, which with lawless violence was sweeping over the State, felt the importance of having the offices filled by Union men. Mr. Patterson was urged to again become a candidate for judge. He reluctantly consented, and was elected by a large majority over a rebel candidate. Governor Harris sent his commission, with peremptory orders that he should immediately take the oath to support the Southern Confederacy. Judge Patterson delayed and hesitated, and consulted other Union men as to the proper course to be pursued. They advised and urged him to take the oath. By so doing he could afford protection, to some extent, to Union men, against acts of lawless violence on the part of rebels. He was advised that, if he did not accept the office, it would be filled by a rebel, and the people would be oppressed by the civil as well as the military power of the rebels. He yielded to these arguments and this advice, and took the oath prescribed by the Legislature, which in substance was that he would support the Constitution of Tennessee and the Constitution of the Confederate States. He declared at the time that he owed no allegiance to the Confederate Government, and did not consider that part of the oath as binding him at all.

Judge Patterson held a few terms of court in counties when he could organize grand juries of Union men, and did something toward preserving peace and order in the community. He aided the Union people and the Union cause in every possible way, and thus became amenable to the hostility of the secessionists, who subjected him to great difficulty and danger. He was several times arrested, and held for some time in custody. At times he was obliged to conceal himself for safety. He spent many nights in out-buildings and in the woods to avoid the vengeance of the rebels.

In September, 1863, the United States forces under General Burnside having taken possession of Knoxville, Mr. Patterson succeeded, with his family, in making his escape to Knoxville, and did not return to his home until after the close of the rebellion.

The Committee on the Judiciary having taken into consideration the above and other palliating circumstances, proposed a resolution that Mr. Patterson "is duly qualified and entitled to hold a seat in the Senate." On motion of Mr. Clark this resolution was amended to read, "that, upon taking the oaths required by the Constitution and the laws, he be admitted to a seat in the Senate."

It was, however, thought better by the Senate to pass a joint resolution that in the case of Mr. Patterson there should be omitted from the test oath the following words: "That I have neither sought, nor accepted, nor attempted to exercise the functions of any office whatever under any authority, or pretended authority, in hostility to the United States." This joint resolution having passed the Senate, was immediately sent to the House of Representatives, then in session, and at once came up before that body for consideration. The resolution was eloquently advocated by Messrs. Maynard and Taylor, and opposed by Mr. Stokes, all of Tennessee.

"On the night of the 22d of February last," said Mr. Stokes, "I delivered a speech in Nashville, and there and then declared, if admitted as a member of this House, I would freeze to my seat before I would vote to repeal the test oath. [Long-continued applause on the floor and in the galleries.] I have made the same declaration in many speeches since then.

"Sir, I regard the test oath passed by the United States Congress as the salvation of the Union men of the South as well as of the North. I regard it as sacred as the flaming sword which the Creator placed in the tree of life to guard it, forbidding any one from partaking of the fruit thereof who was not pure in heart. Sir, this is no light question. Repeal the test oath and you permit men to come into Congress and take seats who have taken an oath to the Confederate Government, and who have aided and assisted in carrying out its administration and laws. That is what we are now asked to do. Look back to the 14th of August, 1861, the memorable day of the proclamation issued by Jefferson Davis, ordering every man within the lines of the confederacy who still held allegiance to the Federal Government to leave within forty-eight hours. That order compelled many to seek for hiding-places who could not take the oath of allegiance to the Confederate Government. When the rebel authorities said to our noble Governor of Tennessee, 'We will throw wide open the prison doors and let you out, if you will swear allegiance to our government,' what was his reply? 'You may sever my head from my body, but I will never take the oath to the Confederate Government.'"

Eng^d by G. E. Perine & Co. N. York.

W. B. Stokes.

W. B. STOKES

REPRESENTATIVE FROM TENNESSEE.

Mr. Conkling said: "I should be recreant to candor were I to attempt to conceal my amazement at the scene now passing before us. Only eight short days ago and eleven States were silent and absent here, because they had participated in guilty rebellion, and because they were not in fit condition to share in the government and control of this country. Seven short days ago we found one of these States with loyalty so far retrieved, one State so far void of present offenses, that the ban was withdrawn from her, and she again was placed on an equal footing with the most favored States in the Union. The doors were instantly thrown open to her Senators and Representatives, the whole case was disposed of, and the nation approved the act. Here the matter should have rested; here it should have been left forever undisturbed. But no; before one week has made its round, we are called upon to stultify ourselves, to wound the interests of the nation, to surrender the position held by the loyal people of the country almost unanimously, and the exigency is that a particular citizen of Tennessee seeks to effect his entrance to the Senate of the United States without being qualified like every other man who is permitted to enter there.

"We are asked to drive a ploughshare over the very foundation of our position; to break down and destroy the bulwark by which we may secure the results of a great war and a great history, by which we may preserve from defilement this place, where alone in our organism the people never lose their supremacy, except by the recreancy of their Representatives; a bulwark without which we may not save our Government from disintegration and disgrace. If we do this act, it will be a precedent which will carry fatality in its train. From Jefferson Davis to the meanest tool of despotism and treason, every rebel may come here, and we shall have no reason to assign against his admission, except the arbitrary reason of numbers."

Mr. Conkling closed by moving that the joint resolution be laid on the table, which was carried by a vote of eighty-eight to thirty-one.

During the same day's session — which was protracted until seven o'clock of Saturday morning, July 28th—the same subject came up again in the Senate, on the passage of the resolution to admit Mr. Patterson to a seat in the Senate upon his taking the oaths required by the Constitution and laws. After some discussion, the resolution passed, twenty-one voting in the affirmative and eleven in the negative.

Mr. Patterson went forward to the desk, and the prescribed oaths having been administered, he took his seat in the Senate. Thus, on the last day of the first session of the Thirty-ninth Congress, Tennessee was fully reconstructed in her representation.

CHAPTER XXI.

NEGRO SUFFRAGE.

Review of the Preceding Action—Efforts of Mr. Yates for Unrestricted Suffrage—Davis's Amendment to Cuvier—The "Propitious Hour"—The Mayor's Remonstrance—Mr. Willey's Amendment—Mr. Cowan's Amemdment for Female Suffrage—Attempt to Out-radical the Radicals—Opinions for and against Female Suffrage—Reading and Writing as a Qualification—Passage of the Bill—Objections of the President—Two Senators on the Opinions of the People—The Suffrage Bill becomes a Law.

ON the rëassembling of the Thirty-ninth Congress for the second session, December 3d, 1866, immediately after the preliminaries of opening had transpired, Mr. Sumner called up business which had been introduced on the first day of the preceding session—a year before—which still remained unfinished—the subject of suffrage in the District of Columbia. In so doing, the Senator from Massachusetts said: "It will be remembered that it was introduced on the first day of the last session; that it was the subject of repeated discussions in this chamber; that it was more than once referred to the Committee on the District of Columbia, by whose chairman it was reported back to the Senate. At several different stages of the discussion it was supposed that we were about to reach a final vote. The country expected that vote. It was not had. It ought to have been had. And now, sir, I think that the best way is for the Senate in this very first hour of its coming together to put that bill on its passage. It has been thoroughly debated. Every Senator here has made up his mind on the question. There is nothing more to be said on either side. So far as I am concerned, I am perfectly willing that the vote shall be taken without one further word of discussion; but I do think that the Senate ought not to allow the bill to be postponed. We ought to seize this first occasion to put the bill on its passage. The country expects it; the country will rejoice and be grateful if you will signalize this first day of your coming together by this beautiful and generous act."

Objection being raised to the immediate consideration of the subject, it was decided that it must be deferred under a rule of the Senate until after the expiration of six days from the commencement of the session.

It is proper here to present a brief record of the proceedings upon the subject during the preceding session. The passage of a bill in the House of Representatives, and the discussion upon the subject in that body are given in a preceding chapter. This bill, as Mr. Morrill subsequently said in the Senate, was not an election bill, and conferred no right of voting upon any person beyond what he had before. It was a mere declaration of a right to vote. As such, the bill was favorably received by the Senate Committee to whom it was referred, and was by them reported back with favor, but was never put upon its passage.

Meanwhile the Senate Committee had under consideration a bill of their own, which they reported on the 10th of January. This bill provided for restricted suffrage, requiring the qualification to read and write. Mr. Yates, an original and uncompromising advocate of universal suffrage was opposed to this restriction. He was a member of the Committee on the District of Columbia, but had been prevented from being present in its deliberations when it was resolved to report the bill as then before the Senate. Fearing that the bill might pass the Senate with the objectionable restrictions, Mr. Yates moved that it be recommitted, which was done.

At a meeting of the committee called to reconsider the bill, Mr. Yates argued at length and with earnestness against disfranchisement on the ground of inability to read and write. The committee reversed their former decision, and reported the bill substantially in the form in which it subsequently became a law. The bill being before the Senate on the 16th of January, 1866, Mr. Garrett Davis opposed it in a speech of great length. He made use of every argument and referred to every authority within his reach to prove the inferiority of the negro race. After giving Cuvier's definition of the "negro," the Senator remarked: "The great naturalist might have added as other distinctive characteristics of the negro; first, that his skin exhales perpetually a peculiar pungent and disagreeable odor; second, that 'the hollow of his foot makes a hole in the ground.'" The Senator drew a fearful picture of the schemes of Massachusetts to use the negro voters, whom it was her policy to create in the South.

This subject did not again come up in the Senate until after the lapse of several months. On the 27th of June it was "disentombed" from what many supposed was its final resting place. Mr. Morrill proposed as an amendment that the elective franchise should be restricted to persons who could read and write. This was rejected; fifteen voting in the affirmative, and nineteen in the negative.

Mr. Willey opposed the bill before the Senate in a speech of considerable length. He advocated the bestowal of a qualified and restricted suffrage upon the colored people of the District. His chief objection to the measure before the Senate was that it was untimely. "Any thing not essential in itself," said he, "or very material to the welfare of the nation, or a considerable part of the nation, if it is calculated to complicate our difficulties, or inflame party passions or sectional animosities, had better be left, it appears to me, to a more propitious hour."

The "propitious hour" hoped for by the Senator, did not come around until after the opening of the second session. The subject did not again seriously occupy the attention of the Senate, with the exception of Mr. Sumner's effort to have it taken up on the first day of the session, until the 10th day of December, 1866.

On that day, Mr. Morrill, who, as Chairman of the Committee on the District of Columbia, had the bill in charge, introduced the subject with a speech of considerable length. "This measure," said he, "not only regulates the elective franchise in this District, but it extends and enlarges it. The principal feature of the bill is that it embraces the colored citizens of the District of Columbia. In this particular it is novel, and in this particular it is important. In this particular it may be said to be inaugurating a policy not only strictly for the District of Columbia, but in some sense for the country at large. In this respect it is, I suppose, that this bill has received so large a share of the public attention during the last session and the recess of the Congress of the United States."

Mr. Morrill called attention to the remonstrance of the Mayor of Washington, who had informed the Senate that in an election held for the purpose of ascertaining the sentiments of the voters of the city upon the subject, some six thousand five hundred were opposed to the extension of the elective franchise, while only thirty or forty were in favor of it.

"These six or seven thousand voters," said Mr. Morrill, "are only one in thirty at most of the people of this District, and it is very difficult to understand how there could be more significance or probative force attached to these six or seven thousand votes than to an equal number of voices independent of the ballot, under the circumstances. This is a matter affecting the capital of the nation, one in which the American people have an interest, as indirectly, at least, touching the country at large. What the National Congress pronounce here as a matter of right or expediency, or both, touching a question of popular rights, may have an influence elsewhere for good or for evil. We can not well justify the denial of the right of suffrage to colored citizens on the protest of the voters of the corporation of Washington. We may not think fit to grant it simply on the prayer of the petitioners. Our action should rest on some recognized general principle, which, applied to the capital of the nation, would be equally just applied to any of the political communities of which the nation is composed."

In closing his speech, Mr. Morrill remarked: "In a nation of professed freemen, whose political axioms are those of universal liberty and human rights, no public tranquillity is possible while these rights are denied to portions of the American people. We have taken into the bosom of the Republic the diverse elements of the nationalities of Europe, and are attempting to mold them into national harmony and unity, and are still inviting other millions to come to us. Let us not despair that the same mighty energies and regenerating forces will be able to assign a docile and not untractable race its appropriate place in our system."

Mr. Willey's amendment, proposed when the subject was last considered in the previous session, six months before, being now the pending question, its author addressed the Senate in favor of some restrictions upon the exercise of the elective franchise. "There ought to be some obligation," said he, "either in our fundamental laws in the States, or somewhere, by some means requiring the peoole to educate themselves; and if this can be accomplished by disqualifying those who are not educated for the exercise of the right of suffrage, thus stimulating them to acquire a reasonable degree of education, that of itself, it seems to me, would be a public blessing."

"I am against this qualification of reading and writing," said Mr. Wilson; "I never did believe in it. I do not believe in it now. I voted against it in my own State, and I intend to vote against it here. There was a time when I would have taken it, because I did not know that we could get any thing more in this contest; but I think the great victory of manhood suffrage is about achieved in this country."

"Reading and writing, as a qualification for voting," said Mr. Pomeroy, "might be entertained in a State where all the people were allowed to go to school and learn to read and write; but it seems to me monstrous to apply it to a class of persons in this community who were legislated away from school, to whom every avenue of learning was shut up by law."

Some discussion was elicited by a proposition made by Mr. Anthony to attach to Mr. Willey's amendment a provision excluding from the right to vote all "who in any way voluntarily gave aid and comfort to the rebels during the late rebellion."

This was opposed by Mr. Wilson. "We better not meddle with that matter of disfranchisement," said he. "There are but few of these persons here, so the prohibition will practically not amount to any thing. As we are to accomplish a great object, to establish universal suffrage, we should let alone all propositions excluding a few men here. Disfranchisement will create more feeling and more bitterness than enfranchisement."

Mr. Willey's amendment was finally so much "amended" that he could not support it himself, and it received but one affirmative vote, that of Mr. Kirkwood.

Mr. Cowan proposed to amend the bill by striking out the word "male" before the word "person," that females might enjoy the elective franchise. "I propose to extend this privilege," said he, "not only to males, but to females as well; and I should like to hear even the most astute and learned Senator upon this floor give any better reason for the exclusion of females from the right of suffrage than there is for the exclusion of negroes.

"If you want to widen the franchise so as to purify your ballot-box, throw the virtue of the country into it; throw the temperance of the country into it; throw the purity of the country into it; throw the angel element—if I may so express myself—into it. [Laughter.] Let there be as little diabolism as possible, but as much of the divinity as you can get."

The discussion being resumed on the following day, Mr. Anthony advocated Mr. Cowan's amendment. "I suppose," said he, "that the Senator from Pennsylvania introduced this amendment rather as a satire upon the bill itself, or if he had any serious intention, it was only a mischievous one to injure the bill. But it will not probably have that effect, for I suppose nobody will vote for it except the Senator himself, who can hardly avoid it, and I, who shall vote for it because it accords with a conclusion to which I have been brought by considerable study upon the subject of suffrage."

After having answered objections against female suffrage, Mr. Anthony remarked in conclusion: "I should not have introduced this question; but as it has been introduced, and I intend to vote for the amendment, I desire to declare here that I shall vote for it in all seriousness, because I think it is right. The discussion of this subject is not confined to visionary enthusiasts. It is now attracting the attention of some of the best thinkers in the world, both in this country and in Europe; and one of the very best of them all, John Stuart Mill, in a most elaborate and able paper, has declared his conviction of the right and justice of female suffrage. The time has not come for it, but the time is coming. It is coming with the progress of civilization and the general amelioration of the race, and the triumph of truth, and justice, and equal rights."

Mr. Williams opposed the pending amendment. "To extend the right of suffrage to the negroes in this country," said he, "I think is necessary for their protection; but to extend the right of suffrage to women, in my judgment, is not necessary for their protection. Wide as the poles apart are the conditions of these two classes of persons. The sons defend and protect the reputation and rights of their mothers; husbands defend and protect the reputation and rights of their wives; brothers defend and protect the reputation and rights of their sisters; and to honor, cherish, and love the women of this country is the pride and the glory of its sons.

"When the women of this country come to be sailors and soldiers; when they come to navigate the ocean and to follow the plow; when they love to be jostled and crowded by all sorts of men in the thoroughfares of trade and business; when they love the treachery and the turmoil of politics; when they love the dissoluteness of the camp, and the smoke of the thunder, and the blood of battle better than they love the affections and enjoyments of home and family, then it will be time to talk about making the women voters; but until that time, the question is not fairly before the country."

Mr. Cowan defended his amendment and his position. "When the time comes," said he, "I am a Radical, too, along with my fellow Senators here. By what warrant do they suppose that I am not interested in the progress of the race? If the thing is to be bettered, I want to better it."

Mr. Morrill replied to the speech of Mr. Cowan. "Does any suppose," said Mr. Morrill, "that he is at all in earnest or sincere in a single sentiment he has uttered on this subject? I do not imagine he believes that any one here is idle enough for a moment to suppose so. If it is true, as he intimates, that he is desirous of becoming a Radical, I am not clear that I should not be willing to accept his service, although there is a good deal to be repented of before he can be taken into full confidence. [Laughter.]

"When a man has seen the error of his ways and confesses it, what more is there to be done except to receive him seventy and seven times? Now, if this is an indication that the honorable Senator means to out-radical the Radicals, 'Come on, Macduff,' nobody will object, provided you can show us you are sincere. That is the point. If it is mischief you are at, you will have a hard time to get ahead. While we are radical we mean to be rational. While we intend to give every male citizen of the United States the rights common to all, we do not intend to be forced by our enemies into a position so ridiculous and absurd as to be broken down utterly on that question, and who ever comes here in the guise of a Radical and undertakes to practice that probably will not make much by the motion. I am not surprised that those of our friends who went out from us and have been feeding on the husks desire to get in ahead; but I am surprised at the indiscretion and the want of common sense exercised in making so profound a plunge at once! If these gentlemen desire to be taken into companionship and restored to good standing, I am the first man to reach out the hand and say, 'Welcome back again, so that you are repentant and regenerated;' but, sir, I am the last man to allow that you shall indorse what you call Radicalism for the purpose of breaking down measures which we propose!"

"He alleges," replied Mr. Cowan, "that I am not serious in the amendment I have moved; that I am not in earnest about it. How does he know? By what warrant does he undertake to say that a brother Senator here is not serious, not in earnest? I should like to know by what warrant he undertakes to do that. He says I do not look serious.. I have not perhaps been trained in the same vinegar and persimmon school, [laughter;] I have not been doctrinated into the same solemn nasal twang which may characterize the gentleman, and which may be considered to be the evidence of seriousness and earnestness. I generally speak as a man, and as a good-natured man, I think. I hope I entertain no malice toward any body. But the honorable Senator thinks that I want to become a Radical. Why, sir, common charity ought to have taught the honorable Senator better than that. I think no such imputation, even on the part of the most virulent opponent that I have, can with any justice be laid to my door. I have never yielded to his radicalism; I have never truckled to it. Whether it be right or wrong, I have never bowed the knee to it. From the very word 'go' I have been a Conservative; I have endeavored to save all in our institutions that I thought worth saving."

Mr. Wade had introduced the original bill, and had put it upon the most liberal principle of franchise. "The question of female suffrage," said he, "had not then been much agitated, and I knew the community had not thought sufficiently upon it to be ready to introduce it as an element in our political system. While I am aware of that fact, I think it will puzzle any gentleman to draw a line of demarcation between the right of the male and the female on this subject. Both are liable to all the laws you pass; their property, their persons, and their lives are affected by the laws. Why, then, should not the females have a right to participate in their construction as well as the male part of the community? There is no argument that I can conceive or that I have yet heard that makes any discrimination between the two on the question of right.

"I shall give a vote on this amendment that will be deemed an unpopular vote, but I am not frightened by that. I have been accustomed to give such votes all my life almost, but I believe they have been given in the cause of human liberty and right and in the way of the advancing intelligence of our age; and whenever the landmark has been set up the community have marched up to it. I think I am advocating now the same kind of a principle, and I have no doubt that sooner or later it will become a fixed fact, and the community will think it just as absurd to exclude females from the ballot-box as males."

Mr. Yates opposed the pending amendment, deeming it a mere attempt on the part of the Senator from Pennsylvania to embarrass this question. "Logically," said he, "there are no reasons in my mind which would not permit women to vote as well as men, according to the theory of our government. But that question, as to whether ladies shall vote or not, is not at issue now. I confess that I am for universal suffrage, and when the time comes, I am for suffrage by females as well as males."

"While I will vote now," said Mr. Wilson, "or at any time, for woman suffrage as a distinct, separate measure, I am unalterably opposed to connecting that question with the pending question of negro suffrage. The question of negro suffrage is now an imperative necessity; a necessity that the negro should possess it for his own protection; a necessity that he should possess it that the nation may preserve its power, its strength, and its unity."

"Why was the consideration of this measure discontinued at the last session, and the bill not allowed to pass the Senate?" asked Mr. Hendricks.

"The bill passed the House of Representatives early in the session," replied Mr. Wilson. "It came to the Senate early in December. That Senator, I think, knows very well that we had not the power to pass it for the first five or six months of the session; that is, we had not the power to make it a law. We could not have carried it against the opposition of the President of the United States, and we had assurances of gentlemen who were in intimate relations with him that his signature would not be obtained. It would not have been wise for us to pass the bill if it was to encounter a veto, unless we were able to pass it over that veto. The wise course was to bide our time until we had that power, and that power came before the close of the session, but it came in the time of great pressure, when other questions were crowding upon us, and it was thought best by those who were advocating it, especially as the chairman of the committee, the Senator from Maine, [Mr. Morrill,] was out of the Senate for many days on account of illness, to let the bill go over until this December."

Mr. Johnson opposed the pending amendment. "I think if it was submitted to the ladies," said he—"I mean the ladies in the true acceptation of the term—of the United States, the privilege would not only not be asked for, but would be rejected. I do not think the ladies of the United States would agree to enter into a canvass and undergo what is often the degradation of seeking to vote, particularly in the cities, getting up to the polls, crowded out and crowded in. I rather think they would feel it, instead of a privilege, a dishonor."

Mr. Johnson was unwilling to vote for the amendment with a view to defeat the bill. "I have lived to be too old," said he, "and have become too well satisfied of what I think is my duty to the country to give any vote which I do not believe, if it should be supported by the votes of a sufficient number to carry the measure into operation, would redound to the interests and safety and honor of the country."

"The women of America," said Mr. Frelinghuysen, "vote by faithful and true representatives, their husbands, their brothers, their sons; and no true man will go to the polls and deposit his ballot without remembering the true and loving constituency that he has at home. More than that, sir, ninety-nine out of a hundred, I believe nine hundred and ninety-nine out of a thousand, of the women in America do not want the privilege of voting in any other manner than that which I have stated. In both these regards there is a vast difference between the situation of the colored citizens and the women of America.

"The learned and eloquent Senator from Pennsylvania said yesterday with great beauty that he wanted to cast the angel element into the suffrage system of America. Sir, it seems to me, that it would be ruthlessly tearing the angel element from the homes of America; and the homes of the people of America are infinitely more valuable than any suffrage system. It will be a sorry day for this country when those vestal fires of piety and love are put out."

On the next day, December 12th, the discussion being resumed, Mr. Brown advocated the amendment. "I stand," said he, "for universal suffrage, and as a matter of fundamental principle do not recognize the right of society to limit it on any ground of race, color, or sex. I will go further and say that I recognize the right of franchise as being intrinsically a natural right; and I do not believe that society is authorized to impose any limitation upon it that does not spring out of the necessities of the social state itself."

Believing "that the metaphysical always controls the practical in all the affairs of life," Mr. Brown gave the "abstract grounds" upon which he deemed the right of woman to the elective franchise rested. Coming finally to the more practical bearings of the subject, he answered the objection, that "if women are entitled to the rights of franchise, they would correspondingly come under the obligation to bear arms." "Are there not large classes," he asked, "even among men in this country, who are exempt from service in our armies for physical incapacity and for other reasons? And if exemptions which appertain to males may be recognized as valid, why not similar exemptions for like reasons when applied to females? Does it not prove that there is nothing in the argument so far as it involves the question of right? There are Quakers and other religious sects; there are ministers of the Gospel; persons having conscientious scruples; indeed, all men over a certain age who under the laws of many of the States are released from service of that character. Indeed, it is the boast of this republic that ours is a volunteer military establishment. Hence I say there is nothing in the position that because she may not be physically qualified for service in your army, therefore you have the right to deny her the franchise on the score of sex."

In closing an extended speech, Mr. Brown remarked: "Even though I recognize the impolicy of coupling these two measures in this manner and at this time, I shall yet record my vote in the affirmative as an earnest indication of my belief in the principle, and my faith in the future."

Mr. Davis made another protracted speech against both the amendment and the original bill. "The great God," said he, "who created all the races, and in every race gave to man woman, never intended that woman should take part in national government among any people, or that the negro, the lowest, should ever have coördinate and equal power with the highest, the white race, in any government, national or domestic."

In conclusion, Mr. Davis advised the late rebels to "resist this great, this most foul, cruel, and dishonoring enslavement. Men of the South, exhaust every peaceful means of redress, and when your oppressions become unendurable, and it is demonstrated that there is no other hope, then strike for your liberty, and strike as did your fathers in 1776, and as did the Hollanders and Zealanders, led by William the Silent, to break their chains, forged by the tyrants of Spain."

"When it is necessary," said Mr. Sprague, "that woman shall vote for the support of liberty and equality, I shall be ready to cast my vote in their favor. The black man's vote is necessary to this at this time. Do not prostrate all the industrial interests of the North by a policy of conciliation and of inaction. Delays are dangerous, criminal. When you shall have established, firmly and fearlessly, governments at the South friendly to the republic; when you shall have ceased from receiving terms and propositions from the leaders of the rebellion as to their reconstruction; when you shall have promptly acted in the interest of liberty, prosperity will light upon the industries of your people, and panics, commercial and mercantile revolutions, will be placed afar off; and never, sir, until that time shall have arrived. And as an humble advocate of all industrial interests of the free people of the North, white and black, and as an humble representative of these interests, I urge prompt action to-day, to-morrow, and every day until the work has been completed. Let no obstacle stand in the way now, no matter what it may be. You will save your people from poverty and free principles from a more desperate combat than they have yet witnessed. Ridicule may be used in this chamber, calumny may prevail through the country, and murder may be a common occurrence South to those who stand firmly thus and who advocate such measures. Let it be so; for greater will be the crowning glory of those who are not found wanting in the day of victory. Let us, then, press to the vote; one glorious step taken, then we may take others in the same direction."

"The objection," said Mr. Buckalew, "which I have to a large extension of suffrage in this country, whether by Federal or State power, is this: that thereby you will corrupt and degrade elections, and probably lead to their complete abrogation hereafter. By pouring into the ballot-boxes of the country a large mass of ignorant votes, and votes subjected to pecuniary or social influence, you will corrupt and degrade your elections and lay the foundation for their ultimate destruction."

"After giving some considerable reflection to the subject of suffrage," said Mr. Doolittle, "I have arrived at the conclusion that the true base or foundation upon which to rest suffrage in any republican community is upon the family, the head of the family; because in civilized society the family is the unit, not the individual."

Mr. Pomeroy was in favor of the bill without the proposed amendment. "I do not want to weigh it down," said he, "with any thing else. There are other measures that I would be glad to support in their proper place and time; but this is a great measure of itself. Since I have been a member of the Senate, there was a law in this District authorizing the selling of these people. To have traveled in six years from the auction-block to the ballot with these people is an immense stride, and if we can carry this measure alone, of itself, we should be contented for the present."

The vote being taken on Mr. Cowan's amendment conferring the elective franchise upon women, the result was yeas, nine; nays, thirty-seven. The following are the names of those who voted in the affirmative:

Messrs. Anthony, Brown, Buckalew, Cowan, Foster, Nesmith, Patterson, Riddle, and Wade.

Mr. Dixon then moved to amend the bill by adding a proviso:

"That no person who has not heretofore voted in this District shall be permitted to vote unless he shall be able, at the time of offering to vote, to read and also write his own name."

"I would deny to no man," said Mr. Dixon, "the right of voting solely on account of his color; but I doubt the propriety of permitting any man to vote, whatever his race or color, who has not at least that proof of intelligence which the ability to read and write furnishes."

"What is the test?" asked Mr. Saulsbury. "A person who can read and write. Is it his name, or only read and write?"

"His name," said one.

"Read and write his name!" continued Mr. Saulsbury. "A wonderful amount of education to qualify a man for the discharge of the high office and trust of voting! Great knowledge of the system of government under which we live does this impart to the voter!"

"If this were really an intelligence qualification," said Mr. Cowan, "I do not know what I might say; but of the fact that the ability of a man merely to write his own name and read it, is intelligence, I am not informed. To write a man's name is simply a mechanical operation. It may be taught to any body, even people of the most limited capacity, in twenty minutes; and to read it afterward certainly would not be very difficult."

"I understand the amendment to include," said Mr. Willey, "the qualification of reading generally, and also of writing his name; two tests, one the reading generally, and the other the writing his own name."

"Where is its precision?" asked Mr. Cowan; "where is it to end, and who shall determine its limits? I will put the case of a board belonging to the dominant party, and suppose they have the statute amended by my honorable friend from Connecticut before them, and a colored man comes forward and proposes to vote. They put to him the question, 'Can you write your name and read?' 'Oh, yes.' 'Well, let us see you try it.' He then writes his name and he reads it, and he is admitted if he is understood to belong to that party. But suppose, as has recently happened, that this dark man should come to the conclusion to vote on the other side, and it were known that he meant to vote on the other side, what kind of a chance would he have? Then the man of the dominant party, who desires to carry the election, says, 'You shall not only write your name and read it, but you must read generally. I have read the senatorial debates upon this question, and the honorable Senator from West Virginia, who originated this amendment, was of opinion that a man should read generally. Now, sir, read generally, if you please.' 'Well,' says he, 'what shall I read?' Read a section of the *Novum Organum*, or some other most difficult and abstruse thing, or a few sections from Okie's Physiology."

On the 13th of December, the last day of the discussion, Mr. Anthony occupied the chair during a portion of the session, and Mr. Foster took the floor in favor of the amendment proposed by his colleague. "The honorable Senator from Pennsylvania," said he, "from the manner in which he treats this subject, I should think, was now fresh from his reading of 'Much A-do about Nothing,' and was quoting Mr. Justice Dogberry, who said, 'To be a well-favored man is the gift of fortune, but to read and write comes by nature.' The Senator from Pennsylvania and others seem inclined to say, 'Away with writing and reading till there is need of such vanity.' I believe that the idea of admitting men to the elective franchise who can neither read nor write is going backward and downward.

"Who are the men who come forward to deposit their ballots in the ballot-boxes? They are the people of this country, to whom all questions must ultimately go for examination and correction. They correct the mistakes which we make, and which Congress makes, and which the Supreme Court makes. The electors at the ballot-boxes are the grand court of errors for the country. Now, sir, these Senators propose to allow men who can not read and write to correct our mistakes, to become members of this high court of errors.

"The honorable Senator from Massachusetts says he wants to put the ballot into the hands of the black man for his protection. If he can not read the ballot, what kind of protection is it to him? A written or printed slip of paper is put into the hands of a man, black or white, and if he can not read it, what is it to him? What does he know about it? What can he do with it? How can he protect himself by it? As well might the honorable Senator from Massachusetts put in the hands of a child who knew nothing of firearms a loaded pistol, with which to protect himself against his enemies. The child would be much more likely to endanger himself and his friends by the pistol than to protect himself. A perfectly ignorant man who can not read his ballot is much more likely to use it to his own detriment, and to the detriment of the country, than he is to use it for the benefit of either."

"The argument in favor of making the right to vote universal," said Mr. Frelinghuysen, in making a second speech upon the question, "is that the ballot itself is a great education; that by its

32

encouraging the citizen, by its inspiring him, it adds dignity to his character, and makes him strive to acquire learning. Secondly, that if the voting depended on learning, no inducement is extended to communities unfavorable to the right of voting in the colored man to give him the opportunity to learn; they would rather embarrass him, to prevent his making the acquisition, unless they were in favor of his voting; while if voting is universal, communities, for their own security, for their own protection, will be driven to establish common schools, so that the voter shall become intelligent."

Pursuing a similar line of thought, Mr. Wilson said: "Allow the black men to vote without this qualification and they will demand education, the school-houses will rise, school-teachers will be employed, these people will attend the schools, and the cause of education will be carried forward in this District with more rapidity than at any other period in its history. Give the negro the right of suffrage, and before a year passes round, you will see these men, who voted that they should not have the right to vote, running after them, and inquiring after the health of their wives and children. I do not think the Senator from Kentucky [Mr. Davis] will be examining their pelvis or shins, or making speeches about the formation of their lips, or the angle of their foreheads on the floor of the Senate. You will then see the Democracy, with the keen scent that always distinguishes that party, on the hunt after the votes of these black men, [laughter;] and if they treat them better than the Republicans do, they will probably get their votes, and I hope they will.

"And it will be just so down in these rebel States. Give the negroes of Virginia the right to vote, and you will find Wise and Letcher and the whole tribe of the secessionists undertaking to prove that from the landing at Jamestown in 1620 the first families of the Old Dominion have always been the champions and the special friends of the negroes of Old Virginia, and that there is a great deal of kindred between them, [laughter;] that they are relations, brethren; that the same red blood courses in the veins of many of them. They will establish all these things, perhaps by affidavits. [Laughter.] And I say to you, sir, they will have a good opportunity to get a good many of their votes, for in these respects they have the advantage of us poor Republicans."

Of the pending amendment, Mr. Hendricks said: "I propose

to vote for it, not because I am in favor, as a general proposition, of an intelligence qualification for the right to vote, but because in this particular instance, I think it to be proper to prescribe it."

"I shall vote," said Mr. Lane, "to enfranchise the colored residents of this District because I believe it is right, just, and proper; because I believe it is in accordance with those two grand central truths around which cluster every hope for redeemed humanity, the common fatherhood of God above us and the brotherhood of universal mankind."

"The bill for Impartial Suffrage in the District of Columbia," said Mr. Sumner, "concerns directly some twenty thousand colored persons, whom it will lift to the adamantine platform of equal rights. If it were regarded simply in its bearings on the District it would be difficult to exaggerate its value; but when it is regarded as an example to the whole country under the sanction of Congress, its value is infinite. It is in the latter character that it becomes a pillar of fire to illumine the footsteps of millions. What we do here will be done in the disorganized States. Therefore, we must be careful that what we do here is best for the disorganized States.

"When I am asked to open the suffrage to women, or when I am asked to establish an educational standard, I can not on the present bill simply because the controlling necessity under which we act will not allow it. By a singular Providence we are now constrained to this measure of enfranchisement for the sake of peace, security, and reconciliation, so that loyal persons, white or black, may be protected and that the Republic may live. Here in the District of Columbia we begin the real work of reconstruction by which the Union will be consolidated forever."

The question was taken upon Mr. Dixon's amendment, which was lost; eleven voting for, and thirty-four against the proposition. The vote was then taken upon the bill to regulate the elective franchise in the District of Columbia. It passed the Senate, thirty-two voting in the affirmative, and thirteen in the negative.

On the following day, December 14th, the bill came before the House of Representatives and passed without discussion; one hundred and eighteen voting in the affirmative, and forty-six in the negative.

On the 7th of January, the President returned the bill to the Senate with his objections. The Veto Message was immediately read by the Secretary of the Senate.

The President's first objection to the bill was that it was not in accordance with the wishes of the people to whom it was to apply, they having "solemnly and with such unanimity" protested against it.

It seemed to the President that Congress sustained a relation to the inhabitants of the District of Columbia analogous to that of a legislature to the people of a State, and "should have a like respect for the will and interests of its inhabitants."

Without actually bringing the charge of unconstitutionality against this measure, the President declared "that Congress is bound to observe the letter and spirit of the Constitution, as well in the enactment of local laws for the Seat of Government, as in legislation common to the entire Union."

The Civil Rights Bill having become a law, it was, in the opinion of the President, a sufficient protection for the negro. "It can not be urged," said he, "that the proposed extension of suffrage in the District of Columbia is necessary to enable persons of color to protect either their interests or their rights."

The President argued that the negroes were unfitted for the exercise of the elective franchise, and "can not be expected correctly to comprehend the duties and responsibilities which pertain to suffrage. It follows, therefore, that in admitting to the ballot-box a new class of voters not qualified for the exercise of the elective franchise, we weaken our system of government instead of adding to its strength and durability. It may be safely assumed that no political truth is better established than that such indiscriminate and all-embracing extension of popular suffrage must end at last in its destruction."

The President occupied a considerable portion of his Message with a warning to the people against the dangers of the abuse of legislative power. He quoted from Judge Story that the legislative branch may absorb all the powers of the government. He quoted also the language of Mr. Jefferson that one hundred and seventy tyrants are more dangerous than one tyrant.

The statements of the President in opposition to the bill were characterized by Mr. Sherman as "but a *resume* of the arguments already adduced in the Senate," hence but little effort was made by the friends of the measure to reply.

Mr. Sherman, in noticing the President's statements in regard to the danger of invasions by Congress of the just powers of the executive and judicial departments, said, "I do not think that there is any occasion for such a warning, because I am not aware that in this bill Congress has ever assumed any doubtful power. The power of Congress over this District is without limit, and, therefore, in prescribing who shall vote for mayor and city council of this city it can not be claimed that we usurp power or exercise a doubtful power.

"There can be but little danger from Congress; for our acts are but the reflection of the will of the people. The recent acts of Congress at the last session, those acts upon which the President and Congress separated, were submitted to the people, and they decided in favor of Congress. Unless, therefore, there is an inherent danger from a republican government, resting solely upon the will of the people, there is no occasion for the warning of the President. Unless the judgment of one man is better than the combined judgment of a great majority, he should have respected their decision, and not continue a controversy in which our common constituency have decided that he was wrong."

The last speech, before taking the vote, was made by Mr. Doolittle. "Men speak," said he, "of universal negro suffrage as having been spoken in favor of in the late election. There is not a State in this Union, outside of New England, which would vote in favor of universal negro suffrage. When gentlemen tell me that the people of the whole North, by any thing that transpired in the late election, have decided in favor of universal, unqualified negro suffrage, they assume that for which there is no foundation whatever."

The question being taken whether the bill should pass over the President's veto, the Senate decided in the affirmative by a vote of twenty-nine yeas to ten nays.

The next day, January 8th, the bill was passed over the veto by the House of Representatives, without debate, by a vote of one hundred and thirteen yeas to thirty-eight nays. The Speaker then declared that notwithstanding the objections of the President of the United States, the act to regulate the elective franchise in the District of Columbia had become a law.

CHAPTER XXII.

THE MILITARY RECONSTRUCTION ACT.

Proposition by Mr. Stevens—"Piratical Governments" not to be Recognized—The Military Feature Introduced—Mr. Schofield's Dog—The Only Hope of Mr. Hise—Conversation Concerning the Reconstruction Committee—Censure of a Member—A Military Bill Reported—War Predicted—The "Blaine Amendment"—Bill Passes the House—In the Senate—Proposition to Amend—Mr. McDougall Desires Liberty of Speech—Mr. Doolittle Pleads for the Life of the Republic—Mr. Sherman's Amendment—Passage in the Senate—Discussion and Nonconcurrence in the House—The Senate Unyielding—Qualified Concurrence of the House—The Veto—"The Funeral of the Nation"—The Act—Supplementary Legislation.

SOON after the passage of the bill extending the elective franchise in the District of Columbia, Congress was occupied in devising and discussing a practical and efficient measure for the reconstruction of the rebel States. The germ of the great "Act for the more efficient government of the rebel States" is to be found in the previous session of Congress in a proposition made by Mr. Stevens on the 28th of May "to enable the States lately in rebellion to regain their privileges in the Union."

The Constitutional Amendment had been eliminated in the Senate of features which Mr. Stevens regarded as of great importance. There was an indisposition on the part of the House to declaring by an act of Congress that the rebel States should be restored on the sole condition of their accepting and ratifying the Constitutional Amendment. The bill proposed by Mr. Stevens was designed by its author as a plan of restoration to take the place of the proposition which accompanied the Constitutional Amendment. This bill recognized the *de facto* State governments at the South as valid "for municipal purposes." It required the President to issue a proclamation within six months calling conventions to form legitimate State constitutions, which should be ratified by the people. All male citizens above twenty-one years of age should be voters, and should be eligible to membership in these constitutional conventions. All persons who held office under the "government called the Confederate States of America," or swore allegiance thereto, were declared to have forfeited their citizenship, and were required to be naturalized as foreigners before being allowed to vote. All citizens should be placed upon an equal footing in the reörganized States.

On the 28th of July, the last day of the session, Mr. Stevens brought this bill to the notice of the House, without demanding any action upon it. He made a solemn and affecting appeal to the House, and insisted upon it as the great duty of Congress to give all loyal men, white and black, the means of self-protection. "In this, perhaps my final action," said he, "on this great question, upon careful review, I can see nothing in my political course, especially in regard to human freedom, which I could wish to have expurged or changed."

On the 19th of December, 1866, a few days after the reässembling of Congress for the second session, Mr. Stevens called up his bill for the purpose of amending it and putting it in proper shape for the consideration of Congress after the hollidays.

On the 3d of January, 1867, Mr. Stevens addressed the House in favor of his plan of reconstruction. "This bill," said he, "is designed to enable loyal men, so far as I could discriminate them in these States, to form governments which shall be in loyal hands, and may protect them from outrages."

As an amendment to this bill, Mr. Ashley, chairman of the Committee on Territories, offered a substitute which was intended to establish provisional governments in the rebel States.

Mr. Pike brought in review before the House three modes of dealing with the rebel States which had been proposed for the consideration and decision of Congress. The first was the immediate admission of the States into a full participation in the Government, treating them as if they had never been in rebellion. The second was "the let-alone policy, which would merely refuse them representation until they had adopted the constitutional amendments." The third mode was "the immediate action by Congress in superseding the governments of those States set up by the President in 1865, and establishing in their place governments founded upon loyalty and universal suffrage. The policy last mentioned was advocated by Mr. Pike. "It has got to be time for action," said he, "if we are to fulfill the reasonable expectations of the country during the life of this Congress."

On the 7th of January Mr. Stevens proposed to amend his bill by inserting a provision that no person should be disfranchised as a punishment for any crime other than insurrection or treason. He gave as a reason for proposing this amendment that in North Carolina, and other States where punishment at the whipping-post deprives the person of the right to vote, they were every day whipping negroes for trivial offenses. He had heard of one county where the authorities had whipped every adult negro they knew of.

On the 8th of January a speech was made by Mr. Broomall advocating the passage of the bill before the House. "Can the negro in the South preserve his civil rights without political ones?" he asked. "Let the convention riot of New Orleans answer; let the terrible three days in Memphis answer. In the latter city three hundred negroes, who had periled their lives in the service of their country, and still wore its uniform, were compelled to look on while the officers of the law, elected by white men, set their dwellings in flames and fired upon their wives and children as they escaped from the doors and windows. Their churches and school-houses were burned because they were their churches and school-houses. Yet no arrest, no conviction, no punishment awaits the perpetrators of these deeds, who walk in open day and boast of their enormities, because, forsooth, this is a white man's Government."

On the 16th of January the discussion was resumed. Mr. Paine first addressed the House. He opposed the second section of the bill, which recognized the *de facto* governments of the rebel States as valid for municipal purposes. "I am surprised," said he, "that the gentleman from Pennsylvania should be ready, voluntarily, to assume this burden of responsibility for the anarchy of murder, robbery, and arson which reigns in these so-called *de facto* governments. He may be able to get this fearful burden upon his back; but if he does, I warn him of the danger that the sands of his life will all run out before he will be able to shake it off. He will have these piratical governments on his hands voluntarily recognized as valid for municipal purposes until duly altered. He will have gratuitously become a copartner in the guilt which hitherto has rested upon the souls of Andrew Johnson and his Northern and Southern satellites, but which thenceforth will rest on his soul also until he can contrive duly to alter these governments. And so it will happen that the great Union party to which he belongs, and to which I belong, will become implicated, for how long a time God only knows, in this unspeakable iniquity which daily and hourly cries to Heaven from every rood of rebel soil for vengeance on these monsters."

Mr. Bingham moved to refer the two bills—that of Mr. Stevens and that of Mr. Ashley—to the Committee on Reconstruction. He opposed these bills as "a substantial denial of the right of the great people who saved this republic by arms to save it by fundamental law." He advocated the propriety of making the proposed Constitutional Amendment the basis of reconstruction. It had already received the ratification of the Legislatures representing not less than twelve millions of the people of this nation. The fact that all the rebel States which had considered the amendment in their Legislatures had rejected it did not invalidate this mode of reconstruction. "Those insurrectionary States," said he, "have no power whatever as States of this Union, and can not lawfully restrain, for a single moment, that great body of freemen who cover this continent from ocean to ocean, now organized States of the Union and represented here, in their fixed purpose and undoubted legal right to incorporate the amendment into the Constitution of the United States."

Mr. Bingham maintained that Congress has the power, without restriction by the Executive or the Supreme Court, to "propose amendments to the Constitutions, and to decide finally the question of the ratification thereof, as well as to legislate for the nation." "I look upon both these bills," said Mr. Bingham, "as a manifest departure from the spirit and intent of our Constitutional Amendment. I look upon it as an attempt to take away from the people of the States lately in rebellion that protection which you have attempted to secure to them by your Constitutional Amendment."

Mr. Dawson, in a speech of an hour's duration, maintained

the doctrine, which he announced as that which had given shape to presidential policy, "that the attempt at secession having been suppressed by the physical power of the Government, the States, whose authority was usurped by the parties to the movement, have never, at any time, been out of the Union; and that having once expressed their acquiescence in the result of the contest and renewed their allegiance to the Union, they are, at the same time, restored to all the rights and duties of the adhering States."

On the other hand, the policy of Congress, in the opinion of Mr. Dawson, was "a shameless outrage upon justice and every conservative principle,"—a "usurpation of Federal powers and a violation of State rights."

Mr. Maynard gave expression to his opinions by asking the significant question, "Whether the men who went into the rebellion did not by connecting themselves with a foreign government, by every act of which they were capable, denude themselves of their citizenship—whether they are not to be held and taken by this Government now as men denuded of their citizenship, having no rights as citizens except such as the legislative power of this Government may choose to confer upon them? In other words, is not the question on our part one of enfranchisement, not of disfranchisement?"

On the 17th of January, Mr. Baker addressed the House in favor of referring the pending bill to the Committee on Reconstruction. He was opposed to the use of the term "Government," without qualification or restriction, as applied to the lately revolted States. He opposed the second section, as causing the *de facto* governments to become valid for municipal purposes long before the scheme of reconstruction contemplated by the bill is effectuated. "To recognize them in advance," said he, "would be to incur the danger of further embarrassing the whole subject by the illogical consequences of our own illogical procedure."

At this stage Mr. Stevens arose and modified his substitute by withdrawing the second section, which contained the provision objected to by Mr. Baker as well as by his "ardent friend" Mr. Paine. Mr. Baker objected to that feature of the bill which provided that none should be deprived of the right to vote as a punishment for any crime save insurrection or treason. "The penitentiaries of these States," said he, "might disgorge their inmates upon the polls under the operation of this bill."

Mr. Grinnell was opposed to sending the question to the Committee on Reconstruction. He did not think it the most modest proposition in the world for Mr. Bingham to urge the reference to his committee of a great question which the House generally desired to consider. "Let us have no delay," said he, "no recommitment, rather the earliest action upon this bill, as the requirement of the people who have saved the country, what the suffering implore, what justice demands, and what I believe God will approve."

"It is to my mind most clear," said Mr. Donnelly, in a speech upon the pending question, "that slavery having ceased to exist, the slaves became citizens; being citizens they are a part of the people, and being a part of the people no organization deserves a moment's consideration at our hands which attempts to ignore them."

Of the Southern States as under rebel rule, Mr. Donnelly remarked: "The whites are to make the laws, execute the laws, interpret the laws, and write the history of their own deeds; but below them, under them, there is to be a vast population—a majority of the whole people—seething and writhing in a condition of suffering, darkness, and wretchedness unparalleled in the world. And this is to be an American State! This is to be a component part of the great, humane, Christian republic of the world."

"It is hard," said Mr. Eldridge, in a speech against the bill, "sad to stand silently by and see the republic overthrown. It is indeed appalling to those accustomed from early childhood to revere and love the Constitution, to feel that it is in the keeping of those having the power and determination to destroy it. With the passage of this bill must die every hope and vestige of the government of the Constitution. It is indeed the final breaking up and dissolution of the union of the States by the usurpation and revolutionary act of Congress."

"Your work of restoration," said Mr. Warner, "will never commence until the Congress of the United States assumes to be one of the departments of the General Government. It will never commence until you have declared, in the language of the Supreme Court, that the Executive, as commander-in-chief of the army and navy, 'can not exercise a civil function.'"

"In less than two brief years of office," said Mr. Warner,

speaking of the President, "he has exercised more questionable powers, assumed more doubtful constitutional functions, obliterated more constitutional barriers, and interposed more corrupt schemes to the expression of the popular sentiment or will of the people than all other Executives since the existence of the Government."

Mr. Spalding feared that the bill, should it become a law, would be found defective in not affording any protection to that loyal class of the inhabitants of those communities upon whom the elective franchise was conferred. "These colored men," said he, "who are now recognized by the Government as possessing the rights of freemen, are to be in jeopardy of being shot down like so many dogs when they attempt to visit the polls." He then offered an amendment, which was accepted by Mr. Stevens, by which a section was added to the bill suspending the writ of *habeas corpus* in the ten rebel States, and placing them under martial law until they should be admitted to representation in Congress under the provisions of the bill. In this section thus introduced may be seen the origin of that feature which, in an enlarged and extended form, gave character to the important measure ultimately adopted by Congress, which is popularly known as the "Military Reconstruction Bill."

The discussion was continued by Mr. Koontz. "It is a solemn, imperative duty," said he, "that this nation owes to its colored people to protect them against their own and the nation's foes. It would be a burning, lasting disgrace to the nation were it to hand them over to their enemies. I know of no way in which this protection can be better given than by extending to them the elective franchise. Place the ballot in the hands of the black man and you give him that which insures him respect as well as protection."

Mr. Scofield maintained that the ratification of the Constitutional Amendment by three-fourths of the loyal States was all that was necessary. "Twenty-three of the twenty-six States elected Legislatures instructed to adopt it. Very soon these twenty-three States, having a population in 1860 of twenty-one million five hundred thousand, and not less than twenty-seven millions now, will send to a perfidious Secretary the official evidence of the people's will. Delaware, Maryland, and Kentucky alone give a negative answer. Who, then, stands in the way?

One old man who is charged by law with the duty of proclaiming the adoption of the amendment, but who has determined to incorporate into the Union the *debris* of the late Confederacy—he stands in the way."

"The Secretary is clever in work of this kind. An English nobleman was at one time exhibiting his kennel to an American friend, and passing by many of his showiest bloods, they came upon one that seemed nearly used up. 'This,' said the nobleman, 'is the most valuable animal in the pack, although he is old, lame, blind, and deaf.' 'How is that?' inquired the visitor. The nobleman explained: 'His education was good, to begin with, and his wonderful sense of smell is still unimpaired. We only take him out to catch the scent, and put the puppies on the track, and then return him to the kennel.' Do not suppose that I intend any comparison between the Secretary of State and that veteran hunter. Such a comparison would be neither dignified nor truthful, because the Englishman went on to say, 'I have owned that dog for thirteen years, and, hard as he looks, he never bit the hand that fed him nor barked on a false trail.'"

The laughter and applause which followed, were checked by the Speaker's gavel, which Mr. Schofield mistook for a notice to quit. "Has my time expired?" asked he. "It has not," replied the Speaker. "The Chair called you to order," said Mr. Stevens, in his seat, "for doing injustice to the dog."

Mr. Ward, who next addressed the House, presented a novel theory of the rebel war. "The people of the South," said he, "did not make war upon our republican form of government, nor seek to destroy it; they only sought to make two republics out of one. They are now, and have been all the time, as much attached to our system of free republican government as those who abuse them for disloyalty."

Mr. Ward presented his view of the state of things which would result from the passage of the pending bill. "These negro judges," said he, "will sit and hold this election backed by the United States army. That is rather an elevated position for the new-made freedman; the *habeas corpus* suspended, martial law proclaimed, the army at the back of the negro conducting an election to reconstruct States."

Mr. Plants addressed the House in favor of the pending bill. Of the reception given by the rebels to the proposed constitutional amendment, he said: "They have not only refused to accept the more than generous terms proposed, but have rejected them with contumely, and with the haughty and insulting bravado of assumed superiority demand that the nation shall submit to such terms as they shall dictate."

Mr. Miller, while advocating the pending measure, favored its reference to the Committee on Reconstruction. He gave a detailed account of the Constitutional Amendment, and its progress toward ratification among the Legislatures. He showed that the progress of reconstruction was delayed through fault of the rebels themselves. "It is not the desire of the great Republican party," said he, "to retard the restoration of those ten States to full political rights, but on the contrary they are anxious for a speedy adjustment, in order to secure adequate protection to all classes and conditions of men residing therein, and at the same time afford ample security to the United States Government against any future refractory course that might be pursued on the part of those States."

On the 21st of January the discussion was resumed by Mr. Kerr in a speech against the bill. He quoted extensively from judicial decisions and opinions to show that the rebel States were still entitled to their original rights in the Union. "The undisguised and most unrighteous purpose of all this kind of legislation," said he, "is to usurp powers over those States that can find no warrant except in the fierce will of the dominant party in this Congress. It is alike at war with every principle of good and free government, and with the highest dictates of humanity and national fraternity."

Mr. Higby was in favor of the pending bill, and opposed its reference to the Committee on Reconstruction. He preferred that it should be retained in the House, where it could be changed, matured, and finally passed. He contended that the rebel States should not come into the Union under any milder conditions than those imposed upon Territories recently passed upon in Congress. "Impartial suffrage," said he, "is required of each of those Territories as a condition precedent to their becoming States; and shall South Carolina, upon this basis of reconstruction, become a part of this Union upon different terms and principles entirely from those implied by the votes we have just given?"

Mr. Trimble denounced the pending legislation in violent terms. "By this act," said he, "you dissolve their connection with the Government of the United States, blot them out of existence as freemen, and degrade them to the condition of negro commonwealths. We have this monstrous proposition: to declare martial law in ten States of this Union; and in making this declaration, we, in my judgment, step upon the mangled ruins of the Constitution; for the Constitution plainly gives this power neither to the executive nor the legislative department of the Government."

Mr. Dodge, although a Republican, and in favor of "protecting the best interests of the colored man," could not vote for either of the propositions before the House. "The result of the passage of this bill," said he, "if it shall become operative, will be to disfranchise nearly the entire white population of the Southern States, and at the same time enfranchise the colored people and give them the virtual control in the proposed organization of the new State governments."

Mr. Dodge was particularly opposed to the military feature proposed by Mr. Spalding. "This is not likely," said he, "in the nature of things, to bring about an early reorganization of the South. The commercial, the manufacturing, and the agricultural interests of this country, as they look at this matter, will see in it a continuance of taxation necessary to support this military array sent to these ten States."

"This bill, if executed," said Mr. Hise, in the course of a speech against the measure, "will in effect establish corrupt and despotic local governments for all those States, and place in all the offices the most ignorant, degraded, and corrupt portion of their population, who would rule and ruin without honesty or skill the actual property-holders and native inhabitants, making insecure life, liberty, and property, and still holding those States in their Federal relations subject to the most rapacious, fierce, and unrelenting despotism that ever existed, that of a vindictive and hostile party majority of a Congress in which they have no voice or representation, and by which irresponsible majority they would be mercilessly oppressed for that very reason; and this will be continued, I fear, until the country shall again be precipitated into civil war."

Since the "beneficent conservative power" of the President was overcome by two-thirds of Congress, Mr. Hise could see safety for the nation in but one direction. "Our only hope," said he, "of the preservation of a free government is in the judicial department of the government, and in the decisions of the Supreme Court pronouncing your acts unconstitutional and void."

Mr. Raymond preferred the Constitutional Amendment as the basis of reconstruction, and blamed the party in power for abandoning that policy. "Last year," said he, "that man was untrue to his party obligations who did not stand by it; this year the man is declared to be faithless to his party who does."

Having spoken at considerable length against the pending measure, Mr. Raymond said: "For these reasons, sir, reasons of policy and of authority, I do not think we ought to pass this bill. I do not believe it would be at all effective in securing the objects at which we aim, or that it would conduce in the slightest degree to promote peace and secure equal rights among the people upon whom it is to take effect. And I can not help believing that it contains provisions directly at war with specific and peremptory prohibitions of the Constitution."

Mr. Raymond defended the Secretary of State against the accusations of Mr. Schofield. Mr. Seward was not "a perfidious old man," but one "venerable, not more for age than for the signal services to his country and the cause of freedom every-where, by which his long and laborious life, devoted wholly, from early manhood, to the public service, has been made illustrious." The Secretary of State acted under law. If Congress expected him to act under the theory that three-fourths of the loyal States were sufficient for the ratification of the Constitutional Amendment, they should pass a law to that effect.

"The man," said Mr. Shellabarger, "who is now the acting President of the United States, once said to me, in speaking of a bill like the one now before the House, that it was a measure to dissolve the Union. That proposition has been so often repeated by members upon the other side of this hall, that I have thought the House would probably pardon me if I should attempt to condense into a few sentences a suggestion or two in regard to that declaration, repeated so often and worn out so thoroughly as it is."

Mr. Shellabarger maintained the right of governments to withhold from those who discard all the obligations pertaining to their citizenship the powers and rights which come alone from performing these obligations. "This identical principle," said he, "was asserted at the origin of your Government in the legislation of every one of the States of the Confederation; was repeated and reënacted by three, at least, of the first Congresses under the Constitution, and has been virtually reënacted by being kept in force by every subsequent Congress which ever met under the Constitution."

"I see such diversity of opinion on this side of the House," said Mr. Stevens, "upon any question of reconstruction, that, if I do not change my mind, I shall to-morrow relieve the House from any question upon the merits of this bill by moving to lay it on the table."

On the 26th of January the discussion was renewed. Mr. Ross, considering the argument on the constitutionality of the measure exhausted, endeavored to show that the bill was "in clear conflict with the action of the party in power during the entire progress of the war, and in conflict with the clearly-expressed opinions of the Executive of the nation, the Supreme Court, and the Congress of the United States."

Mr. Ashley withdrew his amendment to Mr. Stevens' bill that the House might, in Committee of the Whole, have an opportunity to perfect the bill so as to send it to the Senate within two or three days.

"I ask the gentleman," said Mr. Conkling, "to state his objection to having a subject like this committed to a committee which has now no work upon its hands, and which has a right to report at any time."

"The Committee on Reconstruction," replied Mr. Ashley, "have held no meetings during this entire session up to this hour. Several bills proposed by gentlemen have been referred to that committee during this session, upon which they have taken no action. If the committee ever gets together again—which I doubt, as it is a large committee, composed of both branches of Congress—I have but little hope of their being able to agree. The chairman of the committee on the part of the Senate, as is well known, is absorbed in his efforts to perfect the financial measures of the country, and I fear that if this bill goes to that committee it will go to its grave, and that it will not, during the life of the Thirty-ninth Congress, see the light.

If I were opposed to these bills, I would vote to send them to that committee as sending them to their tomb."

"There is no difficulty," responded Mr. Conkling, "in having prompt consideration of any thing which may be sent to the committee. It was created originally solely to deal with this subject. It was, at first, broken into four sub-committees, that the work of gathering evidence might be more advantageously and speedily carried on. It became one committee, usually working together, only during a few weeks immediately preceding the bringing forward of its ultimate propositions. It would not be decorous for me to praise the committee or the work it did, but I may say with propriety that if it ever was a good committee, if it ever should have been created and composed as it was, it is a good committee now—better than it ever was before; better, because more familiar with this subject, because its members, having now become acquainted with each other's views, and having become accustomed to act with each other, and having studied the whole subject committed to them, can proceed with much more hope of good results than ever before. Having a right to report at any time, and being led, on the part of this House, by the distinguished gentleman from Pennsylvania [Mr. Stevens], I see no reason why it can not consider and digest wisely and promptly whatever may be referred to it and make report."

"We are now considering a report from that very committee," said Mr. Stevens. "That committee made a report, and I have offered a substitute for the bill which they reported. If the gentleman thinks the report of that committee is best, then let him vote against my substitute. But why send this subject back again to the committee? The gentleman knows as well as I do how many different opinions there are in that committee; some of us believe in one thing, and some of us in another; some of us are very critical, and some of us are not. The idea that we can consider any thing in that committee, constituted as it is, in less than a fortnight, it seems to me is wholly out of the question; and as we have only about some twenty working days in which to mature this bill in both branches of Congress, if we send this subject to that committee and let it take its time to consider it, and then have it reported here and considered again, I certainly need not say to gentlemen that that would be an end of the matter, at least for this session."

"The gentleman from Pennsylvania concurred in that report,' replied Mr. Conkling. "He had his full share in molding it and making it precisely what it was. He supported it then; now he offers a substitute for it. Why? Because the time which has elapsed since then, and the events which have transpired, have modified, he thinks, the exigencies of the case. Is not that as applicable to the judgment of the committee as to his own? Is it not proper that it should have the opportunity of acting for once in the light of all the facts and circumstances as they are to day?"

"Two or three bills on this subject," said Mr. Stevens, "have been referred during this session to that committee. Why has not the committee acted on them?"

"If I were the chairman of the committee on the part of this House," replied Mr. Conkling, I should be able to answer that question, because then I could tell why I had not called the committee together. But as I am only a subordinate member of the committee, whose business it is to come when I am called, and never to call others, I am entirely unable to give the information for which the gentleman inquires."

"If I could have any assurance," said Mr. Ashley, "that this committee would be able to report promptly a bill upon which this House could probably agree, I would not hesitate a single moment to vote for the reference of this measure to that committee; but, believing that they will be unable to agree, I shall vote against a recommitment."

In describing the character of the opposition arrayed against the Congressional plan of reconstruction, Mr. Ashley used the following emphatic language: "Why, sir, the assumption, the brazen-faced assumption of men who during the entire war were in open or secret alliance with the rebels, coming here now and joining hands with the apostate at the other end of the avenue, who is the leader, the recognized leader of a counter-revolution—a negative rebellion, as I said awhile ago—passes comprehension."

"If intended to apply to us," said Mr. Winfield, speaking for the Democratic members, "it is a base and unfounded slander."

"So far as I am concerned, it is a base lie," said Mr. Hunter. For using these words, "condemned by gentlemen every-where, as well as by parliamentary law," the House passed a vote of censure on Mr. Hunter, and he was required to go forward and receive a public reprimand from the Speaker.

On the 28th of January, the House having resumed the consideration of the bill to restore to the rebel States their full political rights, Mr. Julian expressed his belief that the time had come for action, and that having the great subject before them, they should proceed earnestly, and with little delay, to mature some measure which would meet the demand of the people. "Let us tolerate no further procrastination," said he; "and while we justly hold the President responsible for the trouble and mal-administration which now curse the South and disturb the peace of the country, let us remember that the national odium already perpetually linked with the name of Andrew Johnson will be shared by us if we fail in the great duty which is now brought to our doors."

Mr. Julian differed with many others in his opinion of the real wants of the rebel States. "What these regions need," said he, "above all things, is not an easy and quick return to their forfeited rights in the Union, but *government*, the strong arm of power, outstretched from the central authority here in Washington, making it safe for the freedmen of the South, safe for her loyal white men, safe for emigrants from the Old World and from the Northern States to go and dwell there; safe for Northern capital and labor, Northern energy and enterprise, and Northern ideas to set up their habitation in peace, and thus found a Christian civilization and a living democracy amid the ruins of the past."

"It would seem," said Mr. Cullom, "that the men who have been struggling so hard to destroy this country were and still are the instruments, however wicked, by which we are driven to give the black man justice, whether we will or no.

"By the unholy persistence of rebels slavery was at last overthrown. Their contempt of the Constitutional Amendment, now before the country, will place in the hands of every colored man of the South the ballot."

The bill before the House was referred to the Committee on Reconstruction by a vote of eighty-eight to sixty-five.

On the 4th of February, Mr. Williams, of Oregon, introduced into the Senate "A bill to provide for the more efficient government of the insurrectionary States," which was referred to the Committee on Reconstruction.

Eng^d by G.E. Perine & Co. N. York.

Geo H Williams

GEO. H. WILLIAMS.

SENATOR FROM OREGON.

This bill, having been considered by the Committee, was adopted by them, and was reported by their chairman to the House, on the 6th of February, in the following form:

"*Whereas*, the pretended State Governments of the late so-called Confederate States of Virginia, North Carolina, South Carolina, Georgia, Mississippi, Alabama, Louisiana, Florida, Texas, and Arkansas were set up without the authority of Congress and without the sanction of the people; and *whereas* said pretended governments afford no adequate protection for life or property, but countenance and encourage lawlessness and crime; and *whereas* it is necessary that peace and good order should be enforced in said so-called States until loyal and Republican State Governments can be legally established: Therefore,

"*Be it enacted by the Senate and House of Representatives of the United States of America in Congress assembled*, That said so-called States shall be divided into military districts and made subject to the military authority of the United States, as hereinafter prescribed; and for that purpose Virgina shall constitute the first district, North Carolina and South Carolina the second district, Georgia, Alabama, and Florida the third district, Mississippi and Arkansas the fourth district, and Louisiana and Texas the fifth district.

"SEC. 2. *And be it further enacted*, That it shall be the duty of the General of the army to assign to the command of each of said districts an officer of the regular army not below the rank of brigadier general, and to detail a sufficient force to enable such officer to perform his duties and enforce his authority within the district to which he is assigned.

"SEC. 3. *And be it further enacted*, That it shall be the duty of each officer assigned, as aforesaid, to protect all persons in their rights of person and property, to suppress insurrection, disorder, and violence, and to punish, or cause to be punished, all disturbers of the public peace and criminals; and to this end he may allow civil tribunals to take jurisdiction of and to try offenders, or when in his judgment it may be necessary for the trial of offenders he shall have power to organize military commissions or tribunals for that purpose, any thing in the constitution and laws of the so-called States to the contrary notwithstanding; and all legislative or judicial proceedings or processes to prevent the trial or proceedings of such tribunals, and all interference by said pretended State governments with the exercise of military authority under this act shall be void and of no effect.

"SEC. 4. *And be it further enacted*, That courts and judicial officers of the United States shall not issue writs of *habeas corpus* in behalf of persons in military custody unless some commissioned officer on duty in the district wherein the person is detained shall indorse upon said petition a statement certifying upon honor that he has knowledge or information as to the cause and circumstances of the alleged detention, and that he believes the same to be rightful; and further, that he believes that the indorsed petition is preferred in good faith and in furtherance of justice, and not to hinder or delay the punishment of crime. All persons put under military arrest, by virtue of this act, shall be tried without unnecessary delay, and no cruel or unusual punishment shall be inflicted.

"SEC. 5. *And be it further enacted*, That no sentence of any military commission or tribunal hereby authorized, affecting the life or liberty of any person, shall be executed until it is approved by the officer in command of the district; and the laws and regulations for the government of the army shall not be affected by this act, except in so far as they conflict with its provisions."

Mr. Stevens, having been remonstrated with by a Democratic member for expressing a wish to bring the question to vote without a prolonged debate, replied: "I am very willing that the debate which has been going on here for three weeks shall all be read over by the gentleman whenever he can take time to read it." "On behalf of the American people," said the same member, "I ask more time for debate." "I will see what the American people think of it in the morning. If they are generally for a prolongation of the debate, of course I will go with them. But I will wait until then, in order to ascertain what the people want."

On the following day, February 7th, Mr. Stevens introduced the discussion with a brief speech. "This bill provides," said he, that "the ten disorganized States shall be divided into five military districts, and that the commander of the army shall take charge of them through his lieutenants as governors, or you may call them commandants if you choose, not below the grade of brigadiers, who shall have the general supervision of the peace, quiet, and the protection of the people, loyal and disloyal, who reside within those precincts; and that to do so he may use, as the law of nations would authorize him to do, the legal tribunals wherever he may deem them competent; but they are to be considered of no validity *per se*, of no intrinsic force, no force in consequence of their origin, the question being wholly within the power of the conqueror, and to remain until that conqueror shall permanently supply their place with something else. I will say, in brief, that is the whole bill. It does not need much examination. One night's rest after its reading is enough to digest it."

"Of all the various plans," said Mr. Brandegee, "which have been discussed in this hall for the past two years, to my mind it seems the plainest, the most appropriate, the freest from constitutional objection, and the best calculated to accomplish the master aims of reconstruction.

"It begins the work of reconstruction at the right end, and employs the right tools for its accomplishment. It begins at the point where Grant left off the work, at Appomattox Court-house, and it holds those revolted communities in the grasp of war until the rebellion shall have laid down its spirit, as two years ago it formally laid down its arms."

Mr. LeBlond characterized the Committee on Reconstruction as "the maelstrom committee, which swallows up every thing that is good and gives out every thing that is evil."

"There is nothing left," said he, in the conclusion of his speech, "but quiet submission to your tyranny, or a resort to arms on the part of the American people to defend themselves.

"I do not desire war; but as one American citizen, I do prefer war to cowardly submission and total destruction of the fundamental principles of our Government. In my honest conviction, nothing but the strong arm of the American people, wielded upon the bloody battle-field, will ever restore civil liberty to the American people again."

"Is it possible," said Mr. Finck, "that in this Congress we can find men bold enough and bad enough to conspire against the right of trial by jury, the great privilege of *habeas corpus;* men who are willing to reverse the axiom that the military should be subordinate to the civil power, and to establish the abhorred doctrine resisted by the brave and free men of every age, that the military should be superior to the civil authority?"

"It does not seem to me," said Mr. Pike, "that the change proposed to be made by this bill in the management of the Southern States is so violent as gentlemen on the other side would have us suppose. They seem to believe that now the people of those States govern themselves; but the truth is, since the suppression of the rebellion, that is, since the surrender of the rebel armies in 1865, the government of those States have been virtually in the hands of the President of the United States.

"This bill does not transfer the government of those States from the people to the officers of the army, but only from the President to those officers."

Mr. Farnsworth, who next addressed the House, gave numerous authenticated instances of outrages and murders perpetrated by rebels upon Union soldiers and citizens. "It is no longer a question of doubt," said he, "it can not be denied that the loyal men, the Union soldiers and the freedmen in these disorganized and disloyal States are not proteeted. They are murdered with impunity; they are despoiled of their goods and their property; they are banished, scattered, driven from the country."

Mr. Rogers denounced the pending bill in most emphatic language. "You will carry this conflict on," said he, "until you bring about a war that will shake this country as with the throes of an earthquake; a war that will cause the whole civilized world to witness our dreadful shock and fill nature with agony in all her parts, with which the one we have passed through is not at all to be compared."

He eulogized President Johnson in the highest terms. "Free government," said he, "brought him from a poor boy to as great a man as ever lived, and he deserves as much credit as Washington and will yet receive it. He will not submit to have the citadel of liberty invaded and destroyed without using the civil and military powers to prevent it. He will maintain the Constitution, sir, even to the spilling of blood."

Mr. Bingham proposed to amend the bill to make it accord with his theory by substituting the phrase "the said States" for the words "so-called States." He also proposed some limitation of the extent to which the *habeas corpus* should be suspended. "When these men," said he, "shall have fulfilled their obligations, and when the great people themselves shall have put, by their own rightful authority, into the fundamental law the sublime decree, the nation's will, that no State shall deny to any mortal man the equal protection of the laws—not of the laws of South Carolina alone, but of the laws national and State, and above all, sir, of the great law, the Constitution of our own country, which is the supreme law of the land, from Georgia to Oregon, and from Maine to Florida—then, sir, by assenting thereto those States may be restored at once. To that end, sir, I labor and for that I strive."

"Unless the population of these States," said Mr. Lawrence, "is to be left to the merciless rule of the rebels, who employ the color of authority they exercise under illegal but *de facto* State governments to oppress all who are loyal without furnishing them any protection against murder and all the wrongs that rebels can inflict on loyal men, we can not, dare not refuse to pass this bill."

Since, however, the bill did not propose any "plan of reorganizing State governments in the late rebel States," Mr. Lawrence read amendments which he desired to introduce at the proper time, providing that the laws of the District of Columbia, "not locally inapplicable," should be in force in the rebel territory and that the United States courts should have jurisdiction.

Mr. Hise declared this a "stupid, cruel, unwise, and unconstitutional measure." "If I had not been prepared," said he, "by other measures hitherto adopted and others hitherto introduced into this House, I should not have been less startled at the introduction of this than if I had received the sudden intelligence that the ten States enumerated in this bill had been sunk by some great convulsion of nature and submerged under an oceanic deluge."

"This is not, strictly speaking, a measure of reconstruction," said Mr. Ingersoll, "but a measure looking simply to the enforcement of order. It seems to me clear, then, that, not only under the laws of war and under the laws of nations, but under the express authority of the Constitution itself, Congress possesses the rightful authority to establish military governments, as proposed by the bill under consideration."

Referring to Mr. LeBlond's anticipated war, Mr. Ingersoll said: "I desire to ask the gentleman where he is going to get his soldiers to make war upon the Government and the Congress of the United States? You will hardly find them in the rebel States. They have had enough of war; they have been thoroughly whipped, and do not desire to be whipped again. You will not get them from the loyal people of the Northern or Southern States. If you get any at all, you may drum up a few recruits from the Democratic ranks, but in the present weak and shattered condition of that party you would hardly be able to raise a very formidable army, and I tell the gentleman if the party decreases in the same ratio in the coming year as it has in the last, the whole party together would not form a respectable *corps d'armée.*"

"How about the bread and butter brigade?" interposed a member.

"I did not think of that heroic and patriotic band," replied Mr. Ingersoll, "but I do not apprehend much danger from that source; it would be a bloodless conflict; we would have no use either for the sword or musket; all that would be necessary to make a conquest over them would be found in the commissary department. Order out the bread and butter and peace would be restored."

Mr. Shanklin warned the House of the danger of establishing military governments in the South. "You may be in the plenitude of power to-day," he said, in conclusion, "and you may be ousted to-morrow. And I hope, if you do not cease these outrages upon the people of the country, such as you propose here, such as are attempting to be inflicted by your Freedmen's Bureau and your Civil Rights Bills, that the time will not be long before that army which the gentleman from Illinois [Mr. Ingersoll] seemed to think could not be raised—an army armed with ballots, and not with bayonet—will march to the polls and hurl the advocates of this and its kindred measures out of their places, and fill them with men who appreciate more highly and justly the rights of citizens and of freemen, with statesmen whose minds can grasp our whole country and its rights and its wants, and whose hearts are in sympathy with the noble, the brave, and the just, whether they live in the sunny South or the ice-bound regions of the North."

"I hail this measure," said Mr. Thayer, "as interrupting this baleful calm, which, if not disturbed by a proper exercise of legislative power upon this subject, may be succeeded by disaster and collision. It furnishes at least an initial point from which we can start in the consideration and adjustment of the great question of reconstruction. I regard this as a measure which lays the grasp of Congress upon this great question—a grasp which is to hold on to it until it shall be finally settled. I regard it as a measure which is to take that great question out of that sea of embarrassment and sluggish inactivity in which, through the course which the President has thought proper to pursue, it now rests."

"For our neglect," said Mr. Harding, of Illinois, "to exert the military power of the Government, we are responsible for the blood and suffering which disgrace this republic. Let us go back, then, or rather let us come up to where we were before, and exercise jurisdiction over the territory conquered from the rebels, which jurisdiction the President has given up to those rebels, to the great suffering and injury of the Government and of loyal people."

"Let it be remembered all the time," said Mr. Shellabarger, "that your country has a right to its life, and that the powers of your Government are given for its preservation. Let it be remembered that one portion of your republic has fallen into a state of rebellion, and is still in a state of war against your Government, and that the powers of the Government are to be exercised for the purposes of the protection and the defense of the loyal, and the disloyal too, in that part of the republic; and that, for the purpose of that defense, you are authorized to suspend the privilege of the writ of *habeas corpus,* and to exercise such extraordinary powers as are necessary to the preservation of the great life of the nation. Let these things be remembered; and then let it also be remembered that the law-making power of the Government not only controls the President, but controls the purposes and the ends and the objects of war, and, of course, the movements of the armies that are to be employed in war. Let these things be remembered, and it seems to me that all the difficulties with which it is sought to surround this measure will at once disappear."

"What carried our elections overwhelmingly?" asked Mr. Hotchkiss. "It was the story of the Southern refugees told to the people of the North and the West. They told us they demanded protection. They enlisted the sympathy of Northern soldiers by telling that the very guerrillas who hung upon the skirts of our army during the war were now murdering Southern soldiers who fought on the Union side, and murdering peaceful citizens, murdering black men who were our allies. We promised the people if we were indorsed we would come back here and protect them, and yet not a step has been taken."

Mr. Griswold regretted to vote against a measure proposed by those whom he believed to "have at heart the best interest of the whole country." "It seems to me," said he, "that the provisions of this bill will lead us into greater danger than is justified by the evils we seek to correct. It is, Mr. Speaker, a tremendous stride that we propose to make by this bill to subject to military control ten million people who have once been partners of this common country, and who are to be united with us in its future trials and fortunes. This bill proposes to place all the rights of life, liberty, and happiness exclusively in the control of a mere military captain. This bill contains no provisions for the establishment in the future of civil governments there; it simply provides that for an indefinite period in the future a purely military power shall have exclusive control and jurisdiction there. That is, therefore, to me, another and a very serious objection to this bill."

"There is a necessity," said Mr. Raymond, for some measure of protection to the people of the Southern States. I think it is clear that life, liberty, and property are not properly guarded by law, are not safe throughout those Southern States. They are not properly protected by the courts and judicial tribunals of those States; they are not properly protected by the civil authorities that are in possession of political power in those States."

Of the pending bill, he said: "It is a simple abnegation of all attempts for the time to protect the people in the Southern States by the ordinary exercise of civil authority. It hands over all authority in those States to officers of the army of the United States, and clothes them as officers of the army with complete, absolute, unrestricted power to administer the affairs of those States according to their sovereign will and pleasure. In my opinion there has not occurred an emergency which justifies a resort to this extreme remedy. The military force ought to follow the civil authority, and not lead it, not take its place, not supersede it."

"We must compel obedience to the Union," said Mr. Garfield, "and demand protection for its humblest citizen wherever the flag floats. We must so exert the power of the nation that it shall be deemed both safe and honorable to have been loyal in the midst of treason. We must see to it that the frightful carnival of blood now raging in the South shall continue no longer. The time has come when we must lay the heavy hand of military authority upon these rebel communities and hold them in its grasp till their madness is past."

Mr. Stevens having expressed a wish to have an immediate vote, Mr. Banks remarked: "I believe that a day or two devoted to a discussion of this subject of the reconstruction of the Government will bring us to a solution in which the two houses of Congress will agree, in which the people of this country will sustain us, and in which the President of the United States will give us his support."

"I have not the advantage," replied Mr. Stevens, "of the secret negotiations which the distinguished gentleman from Massachusetts [Mr. Banks] has, and from which he seems to expect such perfect harmony between the President and the Congress of the United States within a few days. If I had that advantage, I do not know what effect it might have upon me. Not having it, I can not, of course, act upon it."

"In the remarks which I made," said Mr. Banks, "I made no allusion to any negotiations with the President. I have had no negotiations with the President of the United States, nor do I know his opinions, and in the vote which I shall give upon this question, neither the gentleman from Pennsylvania [Mr. Stevens] nor any other man has the right to assume that I accept the policy of the Executive in the smallest particular. I hope for a change of his position; I think that it is not impossible. At all events, I think it is something which is worth our while to try for."

The previous question was moved by Mr. Stevens; but a majority refusing to second the motion, the discussion was continued.

Mr. Kasson denied the existence of a right in Congress "to establish a military government over people who have been in insurrection." He proposed as a substitute for the pending measure "A bill to establish an additional article of war for the more complete suppression of the insurrection against the United States." This provided for a division of the rebel territory into military districts, as did the original bill, and authorized commanders to declare martial law wherever it should be necessary for the "complete suppression of violence and disorder."

Mr. Ashley moved an amendment providing for the restoration to loyal owners of property confiscated by the rebel government, and providing that military government should cease so soon as the people of the rebel States should adopt State constitutions securing to all citizens equal protection of the laws, including the right of the elective franchise, and should ratify the proposed amendment to the Constitution.

Mr. Raymond thought that, on account of the great diversity of opinion, the whole subject should be referred to a select committee, who should be instructed to report within three or four days a bill which should "provide temporarily for the protection of rights and the preservation of the peace in the States lately in rebellion, and also for the speedy admission of those States to their relations in the Union upon the basis of the Constitutional

Amendment." Thus he hoped a result could be reached which "would command the support of Congress and of the country, and the approval, or at least the assent, of the Executive."

Mr. Boutwell remarked that previous propositions having been referred to the Committee on Reconstruction, they had agreed upon the bill before the House with a unanimity which no other report had ever obtained, nor had any bill submitted by that committee ever been so carefully considered as this. "To-day," said he, "there are eight millions and more of people, occupying six hundred and thirty thousand square miles of the territory of this country, who are writhing under cruelties nameless in their character—injustice such as has not been permitted to exist in any other country in modern times; and all this because in this capital there sits enthroned a man who, so far as the executive department is concerned, guides the destinies of the republic in the interest of rebels; and because, also, in those ten former States rebellion itself, inspired by the executive department of this Government, wields all authority, and is the embodiment of law and power every-where. Until in the South this obstacle to reconstruction is removed, there can be no effectual step taken toward the reorganization of the Government."

"A well man needs no remedies," said Mr. Niblack, in a speech against the bill; "it is only when he is sick that you can require him to submit to medicinal applications. A country at peace does not need and ought not to allow martial law and other summary remedies incident to a state of war. The highest and dearest interests of this country are made subordinate to party exigencies and to special and particular interests. No wonder, then, that trade languishes and commerce declines."

On the 12th of February, Mr. Bingham proposed an amendment making the restoration of the rebel States conditional upon their adoption of the Constitutional Amendment, and imposing upon them, meanwhile, the military government provided by the pending bill.

Mr. Kelley advocated the bill as reported from the committee. "This," said he, "is little more than a mere police bill. The necessity for it arises from the perfidy of the President of the United States. Had he been true to the duties of his high office and his public and repeated pledges, there would have been no necessity for considering such a bill."

"Throughout the region of the unreconstructed States," said Mr. Maynard, "the animating, life-giving principle of the rebellion is as thoroughly in possession of the country and of all the political power there to-day as it ever has been since the first gun was fired upon Fort Sumter. The rebellion is alive. It is strong—strong in the number of its votaries, strong in its social influences, strong in its political power, strong in the belief that the executive department of this Government is in sympathy and community of purpose with them, strong in the belief that the controlling majority of the supreme judiciary of the land is with them in legal opinion, strong in the belief that the controversy in this body between impracticable zeal and incorrigible timidity will prevent any thing of importance being accomplished or any legislation matured."

"It is," said Mr. Allison, "because of the interference of the President of the United States with the military law which exists in those States that this bill is rendered necessary. In my judgment, if we had to-day an Executive who was desirous of enforcing the laws of the United States to protect loyal men in those States, instead of defending the rebel element, this bill would not be needed."

Mr. Blaine submitted an amendment providing that any one of the "late so-called Confederate States" might be restored to representation and relieved of military rule when, in addition to having accepted the Constitutional Amendment, it should have conferred the elective franchise impartially upon all male citizens over twenty-one years of age.

Mr. Blaine maintained that the people in the elections of 1866 had declared in favor of "universal, or, at least, impartial suffrage as the basis of restoration."

On the 13th of February the discussion was continued. "That the spirit of rebellion still lives," said Mr. Van Horn, of New York, "and now thrives in the South no sane man can deny; that the determination exists to make their rebellion honorable and the loyalty of the South a lasting disgrace and a permanent badge of dishonor is equally true and can not be denied. The leaders of the rebellion, being in power in all the ten States unreconstructed, still defy the authority of the United States to a great extent, and deny the power of the loyal millions of the country, who have saved our nation's life against their treason and rebellion, to prescribe terms of settlement of this great controversy, and deny also that they have lost any rights they had before the war or committed any treason against the Government."

The measure before the House, as it came from the Committee on Reconstruction, "was not intended as a reconstruction bill," according to the interpretation of Mr. Stevens. "It was intended simply as a police bill to protect the loyal men from anarchy and murder, until this Congress, taking a little more time, can suit gentlemen in a bill for the admission of all those rebel States upon the basis of civil government."

The various amendments proposed were designed by their authors to add a plan of reconstruction to the pending bill. Of these Mr. Boutwell remarked: "Without examining into the details of the amendments, I have this to say, that any general proposition for the restoration of these States to the Union upon any basis not set forth in an act of Congress is fraught with the greatest danger to future peace and prosperity of the republic."

The amendments of Mr. Bingham and Mr. Blaine were finally combined by their authors. The combination made an amendment providing that the "States lately in insurrection" should be restored and relieved of military rule upon their ratification of the Constitutional Amendment and adoption of impartial suffrage. In order to "disentangle what seemed so much entangled," it was moved that the bill be recommitted to the Judiciary Committee, with instructions to report back immediately the amendment of Messrs. Blaine and Bingham.

Mr. Stevens then addressed the House, premising that in his state of health a few words must suffice. He felt a moral depression in viewing the condition of the party responsible for the doings of Congress. "For the last few months," said he, "Congress has been sitting here, and while the South has been bleeding at every pore, Congress has done nothing to protect the loyal people there, white or black, either in their persons, in their liberty, or in their property."

Of his previous bill, which had been consigned to its tomb in being referred to the Committee on Reconstruction, Mr. Stevens said: "I thought it was a good bill; I had labored upon it in conjunction with several committees of loyal men from the South for four months; I had altered and realtered it, written and rewritten it four several times, and found that it met the approbation of numerous societies and meetings in all the Southern States. It was, therefore, not altogether my fault if it was not so good a bill as might be found; but I did think that, after all, it was uncivil, unjust, indecent not to attempt to amend it and make it better, to see whether we could do something to enable our friends in the Southern States to establish institutions according to the principles of republican government."

Mr. Stevens deprecated a disposition among his friends to be hypercritical in relation to mere verbal details. "If I might presume upon my age," said he, "without claiming any of the wisdom of Nestor, I would suggest to the young gentlemen around me that the deeds of this burning crisis, of this solemn day, of this thrilling moment, will cast their shadows far into the future and will make their impress upon the annals of our history, and that we shall appear upon the bright pages of that history just in so far as we cordially, without guile, without bickering, without small criticisms, lend our aid to promote the great cause of humanity and universal liberty."

The question being taken on the motion to refer to the Committee on the Judiciary, it was decided in the negative—yeas, 69; nays, 94. The question was then taken on the passage of the bill. It passed the House—one hundred and nine voting in the affirmative, and fifty-five in the negative.

"I wish to inquire, Mr. Speaker," said Mr. Stevens, "if it is in order for me now to say that we indorse the language of good old Laertes, that Heaven rules as yet, and there are gods above."

At the evening session of the Senate on the same day, the bill "to provide for the more efficient government of the insurrectionary States" was announced as having passed the House, and at once received its first reading. Mr. Williams gave notice of his intention to propose an amendment, but on the following day, when the Senate proceeded to consider the subject, he said that being impressed with the necessity of the passage of the bill, and fearing that any amendment might endanger if not defeat it, he had concluded not to present his amendment.

Mr. Johnson said that the adoption of the amendment would make the bill much less objectionable to him, although he could not vote for it even if amended. He then offered the amend-

34

ment, which was substantially the same as that proposed by Messrs. Bingham and Blaine in the House of Representatives.

Mr. Stewart regretted that the Senator from Oregon had changed his mind in regard to this amendment. "The military bill without that," said he, "is an acknowledgment that, after two years of discussion and earnest thought, we are unable to reconstruct, and are compelled to turn the matter over to the military. It seems to me that the people of the United States want and demand something more than a military government for the South."

Several Senators thought Mr. Stewart was unnecessarily troubled about military governments in the South. "Are we," asked Mr. Morrill, "who have stood here for five long, bloody years, and witnessed the exercise of military power over these rebel States, to be frightened now by a declaration of that sort? That is not the temper in which I find myself to-day. I have got so accustomed, if you please, to the exercise of this authority——"

"That is the trouble," said Mr. Stewart.

"That has not been our trouble that we have exercised power," said Mr. Morrill; "that has been the salvation of the nation. The trouble has been from the hesitation to exercise authority when authority was required."

Mr. Wilson thought that the wisest course would be to pass the bill just as it came from the House. If it was to be amended at all, he would propose an amendment that all citizens should "equally possess the right to pursue all lawful avocations and receive the equal benefits of the public schools."

"I think the amendments," said Mr. Howard, "entirely incompatible with the scheme and provisions of the bill itself, and that gentlemen will discover that incompatibility on looking into it."

Mr. Henderson thought that the remedy proposed by him long before would be found the only cure for the ills of the nation. "I offered," said he, "twelve months ago, a proposition, as a constitutional amendment, that was to give political rights to the negroes. Some Senators said it was a humbug, that it was Jacob Townsend's Sarsaparilla, or some thing to that effect, that it would amount to nothing. Now, I will ask what other protection can you give to a Union man in the Southern States than the ballot?"

Since the bill must be passed both Houses and go to the President by the following Tuesday, in order to give Congress time to pass it over his veto, Mr. Williams, who had the bill in charge, was desirous of having it passed upon in the Senate on the evening of the day of this discussion, February 15th. Several Senators protested against this as unreasonable haste. "It is extraordinary," said Mr. Doolittle, "that a bill of this kind, that proposes to establish a military despotism over eight million people and a country larger than England, France, and Spain combined, is to be pressed to a vote in this Senate the first day it is taken up for consideration."

"If the measure will not bear argument," said Mr. Hendricks, "then let it be passed in the dark hours of the night. I think it is becoming, when despotism is established in this free land, that the best blood that ever ran in mortal veins was shed to make free, that that despotism shall be established when the sun does not shed its bright light upon the earth. It is a work for darkness and not for light."

"He talks about establishing a despotism," said Mr. Henderson, "and gets into a perfect fret about it. Why, sir, the Southern States have presented nothing but a despotism for the last six years. During the rebel rule it was a despotism, the veriest despotism ever established upon earth; and since the rebel rule ceased, the President of the United States certainly has governed the Southern States without ever consulting Congress on the subject."

The Senate held an evening session for the consideration of this bill. Mr. Hendricks proposed to modify the pending amendment so as to provide for impartial rather than universal suffrage. He thought that States should be allowed to limit suffrage. Mr. Saulsbury would not vote for this amendment because he was unwilling to "touch, taste, or handle the unclean thing." On the other hand, Mr. Davis could vote for it because he preferred a "little unclean thing" to "a big one." Mr. Hendricks finally withdrew his amendment.

Mr. Doolittle hoped that the majority would seriously weigh this question because on it might depend whether the people of the South would accept the Constitutional Amendment, and accept the proposition necessary to get rid of military despotism.

"Make them," said Mr. Wilson.

"I ask," said Mr. Doolittle, "if that is the true language of a statesman, to say to a people who have been educated in the largest liberty, a people in whose veins the Anglo-Saxon blood is flowing, which for a thousand years has been fighting against despotism of every form, 'You must accept this position at the point of the bayonet, or forever live with the bayonet at your throats?' Is that the way to make peace?"

"I think it is statesmanship," replied Mr. Wilson, "to settle this question of reconstruction upon the solid basis of the perfect equality of rights and privileges among citizens of the United States. Colored men are citizens, and they have just as much right as this race whose blood has been fighting against oppression for a thousand years, as he says, and any settlement of this civil war upon any other basis than perfect equality of rights and privileges among citizens of the United States is not statesmanship; it is mere trifling; only keeping open questions for future controversy. Nothing is settled unless it is settled upon the basis of justice."

"I shall vote for this amendment," said Mr. Lane, "believing that it is necessary to make a perfect system for the restoration of the lately rebellious States."

"The amendment," said Mr. Johnson, "is objectionable to me only upon the ground that it denies to those States the right of coming into the Union entitled to representation until they extend the suffrage, because I believe the right of suffrage is a matter with which the Congress of the United States has no concern."

"I know perfectly well," said Mr. Buckalew, "that a vote for this amendment, although given under circumstances which do not commit me to the proposition as a final one, will be misunderstood and perverted. It will be said throughout the country of each of those who stand in the position in which I stand, that we have departed, to some extent at least, from that position which we have hitherto maintained, and maintained against all the influences of the time, against the pressure of circumstances which have swept many from our side and carried them into the large and swollen camp of the majority. Sir, I for one am ambitious of being known as one among that number of men who have kept their faith, who have followed their convictions, who have obeyed the dictation of duty in the worst of times, who did not bend when the storm beat hardest and strongest against them, but kept their honor unsullied, their faith intact, their self-respect unbroken and entire."

"My object is," said Mr. Henderson, when proposing to modify the pending amendment, "to secure the franchise, and after that is secured, to go forward and establish civil governments in the Southern States."

Extended arguments against the measure were made by Mr. Johnson and Mr. Hendricks. At twelve o'clock the minority desired to adjourn, and the friends of the measure would have been willing to do so could an understanding have been had as to an hour on the following day when the vote would be taken.

Mr. McDougall would submit to no such limitation upon free speech. "I do not expect myself," said he, "to speak at any great length, but yet if upon careful consideration I should choose to do so, or if possessing the recollections of past times and memories and reasons and considerations that yet lay in my hidden memories I shall choose to talk for a longer period, I shall claim the right to do so."

"I am anxious to give my views on this subject," said Mr. Davis. "I do not feel able to give them at this late hour of the night; still, I believe I could hang on for three or four hours if I was disposed to do so, [laughter,] but I believe that to-morrow I should not occupy more than at the farthest two hours of the time of the Senate."

Numerous amendments were proposed, much discursive talk was indulged in, and many motions to adjourn were voted down. At length, three o'clock of Saturday morning, February 16th, having arrived, an adjournment was brought about by means of a very long amendment proposed by Mr. Henderson as a substitute for the entire bill. This opening up a new discussion, the friends of the pending bill saw the impossibility of coming to a speedy vote, and consented to an adjournment.

On the reässembling of the Senate on Saturday, February 16th, Mr. Doolittle delivered a very long speech in opposition to the bill, and in vindication of his political course which had been called in question by the "Radicals of Wisconsin." "I rise," said he, "to plead for what I believe to be the life of the republic, and for that spirit which gives it life. I stand here, also, to answer for myself; because, foreseeing and resisting from the beginning what I knew must follow as the logical consequences of the adoption of certain fundamental heresies originating in Massachusetts, and of which the honorable Senator upon my right [Mr. Sumner] is the advocate and champion, I have been for more than eighteen months denounced in my State by many of my former political associates and friends."

At the evening session of the Senate, Mr. Saulsbury and Mr. Davis delivered extended speeches against the measure. "I appeal to you, sir," said Mr. Saulsbury; "I appeal to those who exercise political power in this country now, by all the memories that cluster around the glorious past; by the recollection of the noble deeds and heroic sufferings of our ancestors, for you and for me, for your posterity and for my posterity; by all the bright realizations which might be ours in this present hour; by all the bright future and all the glories which are in that immediate future, stop your aggressions upon the Constitution of your country."

The vote having been taken on the amendment proposed by Mr. Johnson and the substitute of Mr. Henderson, they were both rejected.

Mr. Sherman then offered an amendment in the nature of a substitute, the preamble of which declared that "No legal State governments or adequate protection for life or property now exist in the rebel States." It retained the military feature of the original bill, with the modification that the President, instead of the General of the army, should appoint district commanders. The most important part of the amendment was a plan of reconstruction, which added a new section to the bill in the following form:

"Sec. 5. *And be it further enacted*, That when the people of any one of said rebel States shall have formed a Constitution of government in conformity with the Constitution of the United States in all respects, framed by a convention of delegates elected by the male citizens of said State twenty-one years old and upward, of whatever race, color, or previous condition of servitude, who have been resident in said State for one year previous to the day of such election, except such as may be disfranchised for participation in the rebellion, or for felony at common law, and when such Constitution shall provide that the elective franchise shall be enjoyed by all such persons as have the qualifications herein stated for electors of delegates, and when such Constitution shall be ratified by a majority of the persons voting on the question of ratification who are qualified as electors of delegates, and when such Constitution shall have been submitted to Congress for examination and approval, and Congress shall have appointed the same, and when said State, by a vote of its Legislature elected under said Constitution, shall have adopted the amendment to the Constitution of the United States proposed by the Thirty-ninth Congress, and known as article fourteen, and when said article shall have become a part of the Constitution of the United States, said State shall be declared entitled to representation in Congress, and Senators and Representatives shall be admitted therefrom on their taking the oath prescribed by law, and then and thereafter the preceding sections of this act shall be inoperative in said State."

Mr. Sherman made a brief speech in explanation of the bill. "All there is material in the bill," said he, "is in the first two lines of the preamble and the fifth section, in my judgment. The first two lines may lay the foundation, by adopting the proclamation issued first to North Carolina, that the rebellion had swept away all the civil governments in the Southern States; and the fifth section points out the mode by which the people of those States, in their own manner, without any limitations or restrictions by Congress, may get back to full representation in Congress."

After numerous propositions to amend, and speeches against the bill by Messrs. Hendricks, Cowan, Buckalew and McDougall, the Senate reached a vote upon the bill at six o'clock on Sunday morning. Twenty-nine voted in the affirmative, namely:

Messrs. Anthony, Brown, Cattell, Chandler, Conness, Cragin, Creswell, Fogg, Frelinghuysen, Grimes, Howard, Howe, Kirkwood, Lane, Morgan, Morrill, Poland, Pomeroy, Ramsey, Ross, Sherman, Stewart, Trumbull, Van Winkle, Wade, Willey, Williams, Wilson, and Yates.

Ten voted in the negative, to-wit:

Messrs. Buckalew, Cowan, Davis, Doolittle, Hendricks, McDougall, Nesmith, Norton, Patterson, and Saulsbury.

The Senate amended the title of the bill by substituting the word "rebel" for "insurrectionary." Thus passed in the Senate the great measure entitled "A bill to provide for the more efficient government of the rebel States."

On Monday, February 18th, the bill, as amended, came before the House. Mr. Stevens moved that the amendments of the Senate be non-concurred in, and that the House ask a Committee of Conference.

Mr. Boutwell opposed the amendment. "If I did not believe," said he, "that this bill, in the form in which it now comes to us from the Senate, was fraught with great and permanent danger to the country, I would not attempt to resist further its passage."

He objected to the bill on the ground that it proposed to reconstruct the rebel State governments at once, through the agency of disloyal men, and that it gave additional power to the President when he had failed to use the vast power which he already possessed in behalf of loyalty and justice.

Mr. Stokes saw in the bill the principle of universal amnesty and universal suffrage. "I would rather have nothing," said he, "if these governments are reconstructed in a way that will place the rebels over Union men."

"Now, what has the Senate done?" Mr. Stevens asked. "Sent back to us an amendment which contains every thing else but protection. It has sent us back a bill which raises the whole question in dispute as to the best mode of reconstructing these States by distant and future pledges which this Congress has no authority to make and no power to execute. What power has this Congress to say to a future Congress, When the Southern States have done certain things, you shall admit them, and receive their members into this House?"

"Our friends," said he, in another part of his remarks, "who love this bill, love it now because the President is to execute it, as he has executed every law for the last two years, by the murder of Union men, and by despising Congress and flinging into our teeth all that we seek to have done."

Mr. Stevens thought that in two hours a Committee of Conference could frame a bill and report it to the House free from all these difficulties—free from all this extraneous matter—which would protect every loyal man in the Southern States, and do no injustice to the disloyal.

Mr. Blaine supported the bill as it came from the Senate. "Congress," said he, "no more guarantees, under this bill, the right of any rebel in any State to vote than did Congress guarantee to the rebels in Tennessee the right to vote."

"Although this bill," said Mr. Wilson of Iowa, "does not attain all I desire to accomplish, it does embrace much upon which I have insisted. It reaches far beyond any thing which the most sanguine of us hoped for a year ago. It secures equal suffrage to all loyal men; it sets aside the pretended governments which now abuse power in the rebel States; it insists on the ratification of the Constitutional Amendment, under the operation of which all the rebels who now occupy official position in the States affected by this bill will be rendered ineligible to office, State or national; it presents an affirmative policy, on the part of Congress, hostile to that of the President; it demonstrates the ability of Congress to agree upon a given line of future action; and, finally, it reserves to Congress jurisdiction over the whole case when the people of any Southern disorganized State may present a Constitution and ask for admission to this body as a part of the governing power of the nation. There is too much of good in this to be rejected. I will vote to concur in the amendment of the Senate."

Mr. Bingham maintained that in the bill, as it passed the House, they had voted as extensive powers to the President as were conferred upon him by the bill as amended by the Senate. The former bill provided that the General in command of the army should detail army officers; but all officers of the army are under command of the Commander-in-chief as constituted by the supreme law of the land. "For myself," said he, "I had rather that my right hand should forget its cunning, and that my tongue should cleave to the roof of my mouth, than to find myself here so false to my own convictions, and so false to the high trust committed to me by that people who sent me here as to vote against this bill."

"This bill," said Mr. Farnsworth, "provides a platform ten steps in advance of the platform upon which we went to the people last fall. We then only expected the ratification of the amendment to the Constitution proposed by Congress at its last session, and the formation of Constitutions, republican in form, which should give the people there the right to send loyal men here as Senators and Representatives. But by this bill we extend impartial suffrage to the black man—universal suffrage."

"I am one of those who believe we ought to do something," said Mr. Schenck. "I believe we ought to declare to these rebel States, as we do by this bill, that they shall be put under martial law, and held by the strong hand to keep the peace until they have complied with whatever conditions are imposed upon them. But while we do this, I think it equally important to announce to them, to announce to the country, to announce to our constituents as the completion of the whole platform upon which we go before the nation, the terms which we require of them."

Mr. Garfield favored the Senate amendment. "There are some gentlemen," said he, "who live among the eagles on the high mountain peaks, beyond the limit of perpetual frost, and they see the lineaments in the face of freedom so much clearer than I do, whenever any measure comes here that seems almost to grasp our purpose, they rise and tell us it is all poor and mean and a surrender of liberty."

"These terms embrace, in my judgment," said Mr. Thayer, "every guarantee, every safeguard, and every check which it is proper for us to demand or apply. Upon these foundations we can safely build, for by them we retain the final control of the question in our own hands."

Mr. Hotchkiss opposed the bill as amended. "If you allow this bill to go into operation as it now stands," said he, "without making any amendment of its provisions, and permit these elections to be held, as they must necessarily be held under this bill, under the authority, control, and regulation of the rebel governments in those States, there will be no security whatever, and you will have the elections in New Orleans held under the control of Mayor Monroe and the mob which he used to such fell purpose last summer. That is the entertainment to which this bill invites us.

"I regard this as a flank movement," said Mr. Bromwell, "by which is to be brought about that darling scheme of certain politicians—universal amnesty and universal suffrage. Whether it end in universal suffrage or not, one thing is certain, it is universal amnesty."

"It would be emphatically," said Mr. Donnelly, "a government of rebels. I say a government of rebels, because although the amendment which has reached us from the Senate contains the words, 'Except such as may be disfranchised for participation in the rebellion,' that disfranchisement has to come from the rebels themselves, and surely there is no man upon this floor weak enough to suppose that they will so disfranchise themselves."

Mr. LeBlond opposed both bills. Of the one before the House, he said: "This bill is quite as infamous, quite as absurd, as the bill that the distinguished gentleman from Pennsylvania, [Mr. Stevens,] who is Chairman of the Committee on Reconstruction, contends for and hangs so tenaciously to. It confers all the powers that that bill gives; it confers all the powers that the most radical could claim consistently."

"I shall content myself," said Mr. Eldridge, "with denouncing this measure as most wicked and abominable. It contains all that is vicious, all that is mischievous in any and all of the propositions which have come either from the Committee on Reconstruction or from any gentleman upon the other side of the House."

"If you do not take this bill," said Mr. Delano, "although in all its parts it does not suit you, what are you likely to give the American people? Nothing. I will not return to my constituents admitting that I have failed to try to do something in this great trial of the nation. It is not for rebels that I legislate; it is not for the right of those who have sought to destroy this Government that I extend mercy; but it is for the liberties, rights, and welfare of my country, for all parts of it."

"If this bill be passed, said Mr. Banks, "in my belief there will be no loyal party known and no loyal voice heard in any of these States, from Virginia to Texas."

Many members subsequently presented arguments and opinions for and against the bill, in speeches limited to fifteen minutes in length. This occupied a session protracted until near midnight.

On the following morning, February 19th, a vote was taken, and the House refused to concur in the amendments of the Senate, and asked a Committee of Conference.

The action of the House having been announced in the Senate, that body immediately proceeded to consider a motion made by Mr. Williams, that they insist on their amendment and agree to the conference. The proposition to give the subject into the hands of a Committee of Conference was opposed by many Senators, who thought a question of so much importance should be deliberated upon in a full Senate. If such a committee were appointed, their report could only be adopted or rejected without modification or amendment. They would only have the power which they possess over a nomination by the President—power to reject a nominee without naming another.

"The result arrived at by the Senate in reference to this bill," said Mr. Conness, "was after the most mature consideration that was ever given to any proposition that came before this body, resulting in an unanimity, at least on this side of the chamber, unparalleled in legislative proceedings—a result hailed by the country at large, demanded by the most intelligent and powerful of the American press, alike acceptable to the industrial and commercial interests of the country, which suffer from a continual disorganization of the country affecting its vital industries."

"The fact that it is a very important bill," said Mr. Williams, only makes it the more necessary, as it seems to me, to adopt the usual practice in such cases"—that of appointing a Committee of Conference.

Mr. Sumner favored the appointment of such a committee. The Senate had made its best endeavor, the House had refused to concur, and now to ask that body to vote upon the question again without a Committee of Conference would kill the bill. In such a case there could be no hope during the session for any just and beneficent measure either of protection or reconstruction.

Mr. Fessenden had taken no part in the debate upon the bill when it was on its passage. A majority of his political friends having determined that the measure which passed the Senate was the best that could be accomplished, he had deemed it his duty not to present his individual objections to the bill. "I would have very much preferred," said he, "the Military Bill, as it was called, pure and simple, without having any thing else upon it, and leaving to other legislation, if it was judged expedient, what else might be done."

Mr. Trumbull had not before said a word in reference to this bill. He never regarded the Military Bill as it came from the House of Representatives as of the slightest importance. Section fourteenth of the Freedmen's Bureau Bill conferred all the powers given in the Military Bill. If these had not been used for the protection of the loyal people of the South, would the reiteration of the statute be to any purpose? Yet Mr. Trumbull thought the amendment put upon the bill by the Senate contained every guarantee that had ever been asked for by any one. He was unwilling that a great question like this, open in all its parts, should be submitted to a Committee of Conference.

The vote was finally taken, after a prolonged discussion. The

Engd by Geo E Perine & Co N.Y.

John Conness

HON. JOHN CONNESS.

SENATOR FROM CALIFORNIA.

Senate insisted on its amendment, and refused to appoint a Committee of Conference.

The bill having gone back to the House of Representatives, they resolved by a vote of one hundred and twenty-six to forty-six to recede from their disagreement to the amendment of the Senate, and to concur in the same with amendments, providing that no person excluded from holding office by the recently proposed Constitutional Amendment should be eligible for membership in the convention to frame a constitution for any of the rebel States, nor should any such person be allowed to vote for members of such convention. Another amendment proposed by the House was the addition of a section (sixth) to the bill providing that until the rebel States should be admitted to representation in Congress, any civil governments existing therein should be deemed provisional only, and subject to the paramount authority of the United States, who may at any time abolish, modify, control, or supersede them.

This qualified concurrence on the part of the House having been announced in the Senate, that body proceeded immediately to consider the question of acquiescence.

Mr. Sherman said that his only objection to the amendment of the House was, that it disfranchised ten or fifteen thousand leading rebels from voting at the elections, yet he was willing to agree to the amendment.

Mr. Sumner congratulated Mr. Sherman on the advanced step he had taken. "To-morrow," said Mr. Sumner, "I hope to welcome the Senator to some other height."

Mr. Sherman was unwilling to admit that he had come to Mr. Sumner's stand-point. He was willing to accept the bill, although it excluded a few thousand rebels from voting, yet "I would rather have them all vote," said he, "white and black, under the stringent restrictions of this bill, and let the governments of the Southern States that are about now to rise upon the permanent foundation of universal liberty and universal equality, stand upon the consent of the governed, white and black, former slaves and former masters."

Then followed an extended discussion of the question as to whether the Senate should agree to the amendments proposed by the House. Mr. Doolittle proposed and advocated an amendment providing that nothing in the bill should be construed to disfranchise persons who have received pardon and amnesty. This amendment was rejected—yeas, 8; nays, 33.

The vote was then taken upon the final passage of the bill as amended by the House; it passed the Senate—yeas, 35; nays, 7.

The Bill "to provide for the more efficient government of the rebel States," having thus passed both houses of Congress on the 20th of February, it was immediately submitted to the President for his approval.

On the second of March the President returned the bill to the House, in which it originated, with his objections, which were so grave that he hoped a statement of them might "have some influence on the minds of the patriotic and enlightened men with whom the decision must ultimately rest."

The Veto Message was immediately read by the clerk of the House of Representatives. The following extracts present the President's principal objections to the measure:

"The bill places all the people of the ten States therein named under the absolute domination of military rulers. * * * *

"It is not denied that the States in question have each of them an actual government, with all the powers, executive, judicial, and legislative which properly belong to a free State. They are organized like the other States of the Union, and like them they make, administer, and execute the laws which concern their domestic affairs. An existing *de facto* government, exercising such functions as these, is itself the law of the State upon all matters within its jurisdiction. To pronounce the supreme law-making power of an established State illegal is to say that law itself is unlawful. * * *

"The military rule which it establishes is plainly to be used, not for any purpose of order or for the prevention of crime, but solely as a means of coercing the people into the adoption of principles and measures to which it is known that they are opposed, and upon which they have an undeniable right to exercise their own judgment.

"I submit to Congress whether this measure is not, in its whole character, scope, and object, without precedent and without authority, in palpable conflict with the plainest provisions of the Constitution, and utterly destructive to those great principles of liberty and humanity for which our ancestors on both sides of the Atlantic have shed so much blood and expended so much treasure.

* * * * + * * *

"The power thus given to the commanding officer over all the people of each district is that of an absolute monarch. His mere will is to take the place of all law. The law of the States is now the only rule applicable to the subjects placed under his control, and that is completely displaced by the clause which declares all interference of State authority to be null and void. He alone is permitted to determine what are rights of person or property, and he may protect them in such way as in his discretion may seem proper. It places at his free disposal all the lands and goods in his district, and he may distribute them without let or hinderance to whom he pleases. Being bound by no State law, and there being no other law to regulate the subject, he may make a criminal code of his own; and he can make it as bloody as any recorded in history, or he can reserve the privilege of acting upon the impulse of his private passions in each case that arises. He is bound by no rules of evidence; there is indeed no provision by which he is authorized or required to take any evidence at all. Every thing is a crime which he chooses to call so, and all persons are condemned whom he pronounces to be guilty. He is not bound to keep any record or make any report of his proceedings. He may arrest his victims wherever he finds them, without warrant, accusation, or proof of probable cause. If he gives them a trial before he inflicts the punishment, he gives it of his grace and mercy, not because he is commanded so to do.

* * * * * * * *

"Cruel or unusual punishment is not to be inflicted, but who is to decide what is cruel and what is unusual? * * * * * Each officer may define cruelty according to his own temper, and if it is not usual, he will make it usual. Corporal punishment, imprisonment, the gag, the ball and chain, and the almost insupportable forms of torture invented for military punishment lie within the range of choice. The sentence of a commission is not to be executed without being approved by the commander, if it affects life or liberty, and a sentence of death must be approved by the President. This applies to cases in which there has been a trial and sentence. I take it to be clear, under this bill, that the military commander may condemn to death without even the form of a trial by a military commission, so that the life of the condemned may depend upon the will of two men instead of one.

"It is plain that the authority here given to the military officer amounts to absolute despotism.

* * * * * * * *

"I come now to a question which is, if possible, still more important. Have we the power to establish and carry into execution a measure like this? I answer certainly not, if we derive our authority from the Constitution, and if we are bound by the limitations which it imposes. This proposition is perfectly clear; that no branch of the Federal Government, executive, legislative, or judicial, can have any just powers except those which it derives through and exercises under the organic law of the Union. Outside of the Constitution we have no legal authority more than private citizens, and within it we have only so much as that instrument gives us. This broad principle limits all our function and applies to all subjects. It protects not only the citizens of States which are within the Union, but it shields every human being who comes or is brought under our jurisdiction. We have no right to do in one place more than in another that which the Constitution says we shall not do at all. If, therefore, the Southern States were in truth out of the Union, we could not treat their people in a way which the fundamental law forbids. * * * * *

"If an insurrection should take place in one of our States against the authority of the State government, and end in the overthrowing of those who planned it, would they take away the rights of all the people of the counties where it was favored by a part or a majority of the population? Could they for such a reason be wholly outlawed and deprived of their representation in the Legislature? I have always contended that the Government of the United States was sovereign within its constitutional sphere; that it executed its laws like the States themselves, by applying its coercive power directly to individuals; and that it could put down insurrection with the same effect as a State and no other. The opposite doctrine is the worst heresy of those who advocated secession, and can not be agreed to without admitting that heresy to be right.

* * * * * * * *

"This is a bill passed by Congress in time of peace. There is not in any one of the States brought under its operation either war or insurrection. The laws of the States and of the Federal Government are all in undisturbed and harmonious operation. The courts, State and Federal, are open and in the full exercise of their proper authority. Over every State comprised in these five military districts life, liberty, and property are secured by State laws and Federal laws, and the national Constitution is every-where enforced and every-were obeyed.

* * * * * * * *

"Actual war, foreign invasion, domestic insurrection—none of these appear, and none of these in fact exist. It is not even recited that any sort of war or insurrection is threatened."

"Upon this question of constitutional law and the power of Congress," the President gave quotations from "a recent decision of the Supreme Court *ex parte* Milligan." Having commented upon this opinion, the President proceeded with his objections:

"I need not say to the Representatives of the American people that their Constitution forbids the exercise of judicial power in any way but one; that is, by the ordained and established courts. It is equally well known that, in all criminal cases, a trial by jury is made indispensable by the express words of that instrument. I will not enlarge on the inestimable value of the right thus secured to every freeman, or speak of the danger to public liberty, in all parts of the country, which must ensue from a denial of it anywhere, or upon any pretense. * * * * * * *

"The United States are bound to guaranty to each State a republican form of government. Can it be pretended that this obligation is not palpably broken if we carry out a measure like this, which wipes away every vestige of republican government in ten States, and put the life, property, liberty and honor of all the people in each of them under the domination of a single person clothed with unlimited authority.

* * * * * * * * *

"The purpose and object of the bill—the general intent which pervades it from beginning to end—is to change the entire structure and character of the State governments, and to compel them by force to the adoption of organic laws and regulations which they are unwilling to accept if left to themselves. The negroes have not asked for the privilege of voting; the vast majority of them have no idea what it means. This bill not only thrusts it into their hands, but compels them, as well as the whites, to use it in a particular way. If they do not form a Constitution with prescribed articles in it, and afterward elect a Legislature which will act upon certain measures in a prescribed way, neither blacks nor whites can be relieved from the slavery which the bill imposes upon them. Without pausing here to consider the policy or impolicy of Africanizing the Southern part of our territory, I would simply ask the attention of Congress to that manifest, well-known, and universally-acknowledged rule of constitutional law which declares that the Federal Government has no jurisdiction, authority, or power to regulate such subjects for any State. To force the right of suffrage out of the hands of the white people and into the hands of the negroes is an arbitrary violation of this principle.

"This bill imposes martial law at once, and its operations will begin so soon as the General and his troops can be put in place. The dread alternative between its harsh rule and compliance with the terms of this measure is not suspended, nor are the people afforded any time for free deliberation. The bill says to them, Take martial law first, then deliberate.

* * * * * * * * * *

"The bill also denies the legality of the governments of ten of the States which participated in the ratification of the amendment to the Federal Constitution abolishing slavery forever within the jurisdiction of the United States, and practically excludes them from the Union. * * *

"That the measure proposed by this bill does violate the Constitution in the particulars mentioned, and in many other ways which I forbear to enumerate is too clear to admit of the least doubt.

* * * * * * * * * *

"I am thoroughly convinced that any settlement, or compromise, or plan of action which is inconsistent with the principles of the Constitution, will not only be unavailing, but mischievous; that it will but multiply the present evils instead of removing them. The Constitution, in its whole integrity and vigor, throughout the length and breadth of the land, is the best of all compromises. Besides, our duty does not, in my judgment, leave us a choice between that and any other. I believe that it contains the remedy that is so much needed, and that if the coördinate branches of the Government would unite upon its provisions, they would be found broad enough and strong enough to sustain, in time of peace, the nation which they bore safely through the ordeal of a protracted civil war. Among the most sacred guarantees of that instrument are those which declare that 'each State shall have at least one Representative,' and that 'no State, without its consent, shall be deprived of its equal suffrage in the Senate.' Each house is made the 'judge of the elections, returns, and qualifications of its own members,' and may, 'with the concurrence of two-thirds, expel a member.'"

* * * * * * * * * *

"And is it not far better that the work of restoration should be accomplished by simple compliance with the plain requirements of the Constitution, than by a recourse to measures which, in effect, destroy the States, and threaten the subversion of the General Government? All that is necessary to settle this simple but important question, without further agitation or delay, is a willingness, on the part of all, to sustain the Constitution, and carry its provisions into practical operation. If to-morrow either branch of Congress would declare that, upon the presentation of their credentials, members constitutionally elected, and loyal to the General Government, would be admitted to seats in Congress, while all others would be excluded, and their places remain vacant until the selection by the people of loyal and qualified persons; and if, at the same time, assurance were given that this policy would be continued until all the States were represented in Congress, it would send a thrill of joy throughout the entire land, as indicating the inauguration of a system which must speedily bring tranquillity to the public mind.

"While we are legislating upon subjects which are of great importance to the whole people, and which must affect all parts of the country, not only during the life of the present generation, but for ages to come, we should remember that all men are entitled at least to a hearing in the councils which decide upon the destiny of themselves and their children. At present ten States are denied representation, and when the Fortieth Congress assembles, on the fourth day of the present month, sixteen States will be without a voice in the House of Representatives. This grave fact, with the important questions before us, should induce us to pause in a course of legislation, which, looking solely to the attainment of political ends, fails to consider the rights it transgresses, the law which it violates, or the institutions which it imperils.

"ANDREW JOHNSON."

After the reading of the message, the question came up, "Shall the bill pass, the objections of the President to the contrary notwithstanding?"

Mr. Eldridge declared that it would be the duty of the minority, if it were within their physical power, to defeat the bill. "But we are conscious," said he, "that no effort of ours can prevent its passage, and the consequent accomplishment of a dissolution of the Union, and the overthrow and abandonment of our constitution of government. We can only, in the name of the Constitution, in the name of the republic, in the name of all we hold dear on earth, earnestly, solemnly protest against this action of this Congress."

Mr. LeBlond said that "the passage of this bill would be the death-knell of republican liberty upon this continent." He declared his willingness, if a sufficient number on his side of the House would stand by him, to resist to the utmost extremity of physical exhaustion the passage of this bill, which would "strike a death-blow to this Government."

Mr. Stevens would not be discourteous to those who were opposed to this bill: "I am aware," said he, "of the melancholy feelings with which they are approaching this funeral of the nation." He was unwilling, however, to lose the opportunity to pass the bill at once, and send it to the Senate, that the House might proceed to other matters.

The vote was taken, and the House passed the bill over the President's veto—yeas, 135; nays, 48. The announcement of this result was followed by great applause on the floor and in the galleries.

The immense numbers that had assembled in the galleries of the House to witness these proceedings went immediately to the other end of the Capitol to see the reception which the Veto Message would receive in the Senate. The consideration of the subject, however, was deferred until the evening session.

The Veto Message having been read in the Senate by the Secretary, the pending question at once became whether the bill should pass notwithstanding the objections of the President?

Mr. Johnson advocated the passage of the bill over the veto. "It contains," said he, speaking of the President's message, "some legal propositions which are unsound, and many errors of reasoning. I lament the course he has thought it his duty to pursue, because I see that it may result in continued turmoil and peril, not only to the South, but to the entire country. I see before me a distressed, a desolated country, and in the measure before you I think I see the means through which it may be rescued and restored erelong to prosperity and a healthful condition, and the free institutions of our country preserved."

In reply to a charge of inconsistency brought against him by Mr. Buckalew, Mr. Johnson said: "Consistency in a public man can never properly be esteemed a virtue when he becomes satisfied that it will operate to the prejudice of his country. The pride of opinion, which more or less belongs to us all, becomes, in my judgment, in a public man, a crime when it is indulged at the sacrifice or hazard of the public safety." He urged upon the people of the South their acceptance of the terms proposed by Congress. In view of the probability these overtures should be rejected, harsher measures would be resorted to.

Mr. Saulsbury expressed his admiration for the wisdom of the President in "vetoing the most iniquitous bill that ever was presented to the Federal Congress." "I hope," said he, "that there may be no man within the limits of these ten States who will participate in his own disgrace, degradation, and ruin: let them maintain their honor. If there be wrath in the vials of the Almighty, if there be arrows of vengeance in his quiver, such iniquity and injustice can not finally prove successful."

Mr. Hendricks disagreed with the Senator from Delaware that the people of the South, at once and without consideration, must turn their backs upon the proposition now made them in order to maintain their honor. He hoped they would bring to the consideration of the subject the coolest judgment and the highest patriotism. He was still opposed to the bill; he approved of the President's veto. His judgment against the measure had been "fortified and strengthened by that able document."

The discussion of the question was continued by Messrs. Buckalew, Dixon, and Davis, who spoke against the bill. The friends of the measure were content to let the subject go without a further word from them, save the solemn and final declaration of their votes.

The question being taken, the bill was passed over the veto by a vote of almost four-fifths. Thirty-eight Senators voted for the bill in its final passage, and but ten were found willing to stand by the President and his veto.

The bill whose progress through Congress has thus been traced became a law of the land in the following form:

"An Act to provide for the more efficient government of the rebel States

"*Whereas*, no legal State governments or adequate protection for life or property now exists in the rebel States of Virginia, North Carolina, South Carolina, Georgia, Mississippi, Alabama, Louisiana, Florida, Texas, and Arkansas; and *whereas* it is necessary that peace and good order should be enforced in said States until loyal and republican State governments can be legally established: therefore,

"*Be it enacted by the Senate and House of Representatives of the United States of America in Congress assembled*, That said rebel States shall be divided into military districts and made subject to the military authority of the United States, as hereinafter prescribed; and for that purpose Virgina shall constitute the first district, North Carolina and South Carolina the second district, Georgia, Alabama, and Florida the third district, Mississippi and Arkansas the fourth district, and Louisiana and Texas the fifth district.

"SEC. 2. *And be it further enacted*, That it shall be the duty of the President to assign to the command of each of said districts an officer of the army not below the rank of brigadier general, and to detail a sufficient military force to enable such officer to perform his duties and enforce his authority within the district to which he is assigned.

"SEC. 3. *And be it further enacted*, That it shall be the duty of each officer assigned, as aforesaid, to protect all persons in their rights of person and property, to suppress insurrection, disorder, and violence, and to punish, or cause to be punished, all disturbers of the public peace and criminals; and to this end he may allow local civil tribunals to take jurisdiction of and to try offenders, or when in his judgment it may be necessary for the trial of offenders he shall have power to organize military commissions or tribunals for that purpose, and all interference, under color of State authority, with the exercise of military authority under this act shall be null and void.

"SEC. 4. *And be it further enacted*, That all persons put under military arrest by virtue of this act shall be tried without unnecessary delay, and no cruel or unusual punishment shall be inflicted, and no sentence of any military commission or tribunal hereby authorized, affecting the life or liberty of any person, shall be executed until it is approved by the officer in command of the district; and the laws and regulations for the government of the army shall not be affected by this act, except in so far as they conflict with its provisions: *Provided*, That no sentence of death under the provisions of this act shall be carried into effect without the approval of the President.

"SEC. 5. *And be it further enacted*, That when the people of any one of said rebel States shall have formed a constitution of government in conformity with the Constitution of the United States in all respects, framed by a convention of delegates elected by the male citizens of said State twenty-one years old and upward, of whatever race, color, or previous condition, who have been resident in said State for one year previous to the day of such election, except such as may be disfranchised for participation in the rebellion or for felony at common law, and when such constitution shall provide that the elective franchise shall be enjoyed by all such persons as have the qualifications herein stated for electors of delegates, and when such Constitution shall be ratified by a majority of the persons voting on the question of ratification who are qualified as electors for delegates, and when such constitution shall have been submitted to Congress for examination and approval, and Congress shall have approved the same, and when said State, by a vote of its Legislature elected under said constitution, shall have adopted the amendment to the Constitution of the United States, proposed by the Thirty-ninth Congress, and known as article fourteen, and when said article shall have become a part of the Constitution of the United States, said State shall be declared entitled to representation in Congress, and Senators and Representatives shall be admitted therefrom on their taking the oath prescribed by law, and then and thereafter the preceding sections of this act shall be inoperative in said State: *Provided*, That no person excluded from the privilege of holding office by said proposed amendment to the Constitution of the United States, shall be eligible to election as a member of the convention to frame a constitution for any of said rebel States, nor shall any such person vote for members of such convention.

"SEC. 6. *And be it further enacted*, That, until the people of said rebel States shall be by law admitted to representation in the Congress of the United States, any civil government which may exist therein shall be deemed provisional only, and in all respects subject to the paramount authority of the United States at any time to abolish, modify, control, or supersede the same; and in all elections to any office under such provisional governments all persons shall be entitled to vote, and none others, who are entitled to vote under the provisions of the fifth section of this act; and no person shall be eligible to any office under such provisional governments who would be disqualified from holding office under the provisions of the third article of said Constitutional Amendment."

The friends of this measure were dissatisfied with it on the ground of its incompleteness in not containing provisions for carrying it into effect in accordance with the purpose of its framers. This record would be incomplete without a statement of what was done to perfect the measure in the succeeding Congress. The Fortieth Congress, meeting on the 4th of March, immediately upon the close of its predecessor, proceeded without delay to perfect and pass over the President's veto a bill supplementary to the act to provide for the more efficient government of the rebel States. By this act it was provided that the commanding general of each district should cause a registration to be made of the male citizens twenty-one years of age in his district, qualified to vote under the former act. In order to be registered as a voter under this act, a person is required to swear that he has not been disfranchised for participation in any rebellion or civil war against the United States, nor for felony; that he has never been a member of any State Legislature, nor held any executive or judicial office in any State and afterward engaged in insurrection or rebellion against the United States, or given aid or comfort to the enemies thereof; that he has never taken an oath as a member of Congress of the United States, or as a member of any State Legislature, or as an executive or judicial officer of any State, to support the Constitution of the United States, and afterward engaged in insurrection or rebellion against the United States, or given aid or comfort to the enemies thereof, and that he will faithfully support the Constitution and obey the laws of the United States, and encourage others to do so.

Persons thus qualified shall vote at elections held for the purpose of selecting delegates to the conventions for framing constitutions for the States.

A majority of voters so qualified shall determine whether constitutional conventions shall be held in the several States, and shall vote for delegates who shall be as numerous as the members of the most numerous branch of the Legislature of such State in the year 1860. This convention having framed a constitution, it shall be submitted to the people, and if ratified by a majority of the qualified voters, it shall be forthwith transmitted to Congress. If this constitution is satisfactory to Congress, and found to be in accordance with the provisions of the act of which this is supplementary, the State shall be declared entitled to representation. All elections are required to be by ballot, and all officers acting under the provisions of this act are required to take the test oath.

CHAPTER XXIII.

OTHER IMPORTANT ACTS.

EQUALIZING BOUNTIES—THE ARMY—THE DEPARTMENT OF EDUCATION—SOUTHERN HOMESTEADS—THE BANKRUPT LAW—THE TARIFF—REDUCTION OF TAXES—CONTRACTING THE CURRENCY—ISSUE OF THREE PER CENTS.—NEBRASKA AND COLORADO—TENURE OF OFFICE.

THE great national measures, whose progress through Congress has been given in detail, occupied the attention of that body continuously, from the first days of its existence to the closing hours of its last session. No day passed which was not rendered important by something said or done upon questions which concern not only the nation, but humanity, and which are of interest not only for the present, but for all time to come. While these great measures were passing through Congress, making it memorable, and absorbing the public attention, there was a constant undercurrent of patient, laborious legislation upon subjects of less interest to the public, but of real importance to the country.

One of the first duties devolving upon the Thirty-ninth Congress was the great work of disbanding the vast volunteer army which had suppressed the rebellion, saved the country, and earned the undying gratitude of the nation. The soldiers of the republic were to be paid for their distinguished services, their reasonable demands for equalization of bounty were to be met, and a suitable number retained in the service for the necessities of the nation on a "peace footing." Near the close of the first session, a bill to equalize soldiers' bounties, introduced by Mr. Schenck of Ohio, passed the House by a nearly unanimous vote, but was lost in the Senate. Subsequently, the Senate attached to the Civil Appropriation Bill a provision for paying additional bounty, differing materially from the bill which passed the House. This being in such shape that it could not be easily detached, became a law.

During the first session, Congress passed the "Act to increase and fix the military peace establishment of the United States." By this law the regular army consists of five regiments of artillery, ten regiments of cavalry, and forty-five regiments of infantry. It acknowledged the services and claims of the volunteer officers and men who served in the recent war by providing that a large proportion of the commissions in the new service should be conferred upon them. At the same time the standard of attainment and talent was not lowered, since the law provided for such an examination as must exclude the unqualified and relieve the army from some who unworthily held commissions.

The important fact that general intelligence is one of the greatest safeguards of the nation was fully recognized by the Thirty-ninth Congress. Of this they gave permanent proof in establishing a Bureau of Education. Early in the first session, Mr. Donnelly, of Minnesota, introduced a resolution instructing the joint Committee on Reconstruction to inquire into the expediency of establishing a National Bureau of Education "to enforce education, without regard to color." The necessity for such a measure was set forth in the preamble to arise from the fact that "republican institutions can find permanent safety only upon the basis of the universal intelligence of the people," and that "the great disasters which have afflicted the nation and desolated one-half its territory are traceable in a great degree to the absence of common schools and general education among the people of lately rebellious States." This resolution passed the House by a large majority.

This subject was subsequently referred to an able select committee, of which Mr. Garfield was chairman. On the 5th of June he reported a bill to establish a Department of Education. The measure was supported by Messrs. Donnelly, Garfield, Banks, and Boutwell, and opposed by Messrs. Pike, Rogers, and Randall. The bill passed the House on the 19th of June and went to the Senate, where it was referred to the Committee on the Judiciary. The bill went over, in the press of business, to the second session, and passed the Senate on the 28th of February, 1867.

A measure indirectly connected with the subject of reconstruction, destined to have an important influence upon the future of Southern society, was introduced by Mr. Julian on the 7th of

February, 1866. This was a bill for the disposal of the public lands for homesteads to actual settlers, without distinction of color, in the States of Alabama, Mississippi, Louisiana, Arkansas, and Florida, providing that the quantity of land selected by any one person should be eighty acres, and not one hundred and sixty acres, as provided in the Homestead Bill of 1862. The necessity of this measure, as shown by Mr. Julian, arose from the abolition of slavery and the demands of free labor. It was designed to cut off land speculation in the Southern country. "Without some provision of this kind." said Mr. Julian, "rebel speculators now hovering over the whole of that region, and hunting up the best portion of it, and the holders of Agricultural College scrip can come down upon it at one fell swoop and cheat the actual settler, whether white or black, out of his rights, or even the possibility of a home in that region, driving the whole of them to some of our Western Territories or to starvation itself."

The bill was finally passed in the House on the 28th of February, 1867, with an amendment excluding from the benefit of the act persons who have borne arms against the United States, or given aid and comfort to its enemies.

A work of legislation of much importance, destined to have beneficent effect upon the business interests of the country, was the passage of the Bankrupt Law, which was finally enacted near the close of the Thirty-ninth Congress. The Bankrupt Bill passed the House of Representatives as early as May, 1866, but the Senate objecting to the entire principle of the bill, it was postponed till December. On the reässembling of Congress for the second session, the consideration of the Bankrupt Bill was resumed, and after much opposition in the Senate, it finally received the support of a decisive majority in that body of all shades of politics. The perfection and final passage of this measure were among the last acts of the Thirty-ninth Congress.

The Bankrupt Law of 1800 was enacted in the interest of creditors, and that of 1841 for the benefit of debtors. The law of 1867 was framed with a view to protect the interests of both parties. The passage of this important law is due mainly to the energy and perseverance of Thomas A. Jenckes, of Rhode Island.

The subject of the tariff occupied, first and last, a considerable share of the time and attention of the Thirty-ninth Congress. In the early part of the first session numerous petitions poured in upon Congress in favor of a protective tariff. In June and July the subject was discussed, and a Tariff Bill passed the House by a vote of ninety-four to fifty-three. The friends of protection said of this bill that though not perfect, it was "a decided improvement on the tariff in existence." The bill, on its introduction to the Senate was postponed till December.

There was soon after introduced into the House a revised Tariff Bill, entitled a bill "to protect the revenue." Gradually many of the features which the advocates of protection regarded as most important, were eliminated from the bill. This was passed in the Senate on the 24th of July, with amendments in which the House was unwilling to concur. A Committee of Conference was appointed, who made a report which was accepted by both Houses of Congress. The bill greatly modified and "enfeebled" as its original friends regarded it, finally passed on the day before the close of the first session.

The subject of diminishing taxation, as far as consistent with the obligations of the nation to its creditors, early enlisted and occupied the attention of the Thirty-ninth Congress. The principle upon which Congress acted was announced by the distinguished chairman of the Committee of Ways and Means, Mr. Morrill, to be "*The abolition or speedy reduction of all taxes which tend to check development, and the retention of all those which like the income tax fall chiefly on realized wealth.*"

In the midst of many conflicting interests, and in the face of remonstrances, protests, and prayers from every trade and profession, Congress proceeded to work out the difficult question. As a result of most patient and careful investigation, Congress found itself able to reduce to the extent of one hundred millions of dollars per annum, the taxation resting upon the shoulders of the American people.

On the subject of finance and the national currency great diversity of opinion existed among leading members of the Thirty-ninth Congress. Unanimity prevailed upon the opinion that the currency should sooner or later be subjected to suitable contraction, but there was diversity of sentiment as to the ways and means by which this result should be achieved without involving the country in commercial and financial disaster.

"I am for specie payments," remarked Mr. Stevens, on one occasion, "when we can arrive at them without crushing the community to death. I am for arriving at specie payments, and still allowing the business of the country to go on and thrive, and the people engaged in business to pay the taxes which you impose on them. I say that there is not a man in the community who would not as soon have one dollar in greenbacks as one dollar in gold. No one expects to be paid in gold until a general resumption by the banks of specie payment; nobody now knows any other currency than greenbacks, and, therefore, I am in favor of keeping that currency. In my judgment, we have not more circulation now than the expanded business of the country requires.

"This war has given an immense impulse to every thing. Whence this precipitation? We have barely got out of the war against the rebels before we have a war made upon the business community, upon the manufacturing interests, and upon all others."

"When this great Republican party was made up," said Mr. Wentworth, "we, who were originally Democrats, took up a cross, and it was a great cross. [Laughter.] We were told that if we went into that thing, we should have to lay down at the feet of the irresponsible paper-money men. Now, I want to know of the gentleman distinctly, whether, if he could, he would resume specie payments to-morrow?"

"If," replied Mr. Stevens, "I could have specie payment to-morrow, without deranging the business of the country, I would. If it would derange the business of the country to return to specie payment at once, I would postpone it a little. I voted for the Legal-tender Bill; and I am glad I did so, for the country would not have survived without it."

"Would you compromise on a year?" asked Mr. Wentworth.

"No, sir; nor on two years," replied Mr. Stevens. "England did not resume specie payment the year after the wars with France. The Bank of England issued paper money, but the Government had £14,000,000 in the stock of that bank to give it security, and the Government prevented it from resuming specie payment until it thought it best. Now, when that great war of twenty-five years was over, did England attempt, in 1814 and 1815, to return to specie payment? They had afloat but £20,000,000, or $100,000,000, and they began with their one-pound notes. In a few years they took their two-pound notes;

afterward they took their five-pound notes. But they never resumed full specie payment until the latter part of the year 1822. Does my friend from Illinois expect me to be wiser than the great men of England?"

"Does my friend from Pennsylvania deny," asked Mr. Garfield, "that in 1819 the law for resuming specie payment was passed, to go into effect gradually at first, and completely in 1823, and that the full resumption of specie payment actually took place early in the Spring of 1821—only about a year and three-quarters from the passage of the law?"

"Yes," answered Mr. Stevens, "except in very large sums. The law authorized them to go on until the first of January, 1823."

"But they resumed in 1821, about a year and three-quarters earlier," said Mr. Garfield.

"About a year earlier," said Mr. Stevens. "But the law did not pass until four years after the war. Do gentlemen here expect, when England, with almost all the commerce of the world at her command, was unable to resume specie payments for eight years after the conclusion of her wars, and then did it by such gradual legislation that there should be no shock to the business of the country—do gentlemen expect that we are to put it into the power of one man to compel the resumption of specie payments in a single year?"

"I want to know," said Mr. Wentworth, "if the power, and the patronage, and the influence of the great Republican party, so called, is to be used to deprive us of our natural standard of value. Now, I wish, while we go together, to be perfectly honest. Nobody respects the talents of my friend from Pennsylvania [Mr. Stevens] more than I do. He knows more than all of us put together. [Laughter.] I want him to state to the House, fairly and candidly, whether, if we follow him, he will lead us to specie payment; or whether, if he could, he would."

"I will say to my friend," replied Mr. Stevens, "that in this case I do not act as a member of the Republican party."

"I have followed the gentlemen," said Mr. Wentworth, "because I supposed him to be a Republican leader."

"If I believed," said Mr. Stevens, "that we could resume specie payments in a month without crushing the interests of the country, without injuring the laborer, without breaking down the manufacturer, without oppressing the people, without decreasing the revenues of the Government; if I had the power, I would order every bank in the country, State and national, and the Government also, to resume specie payment."

"Suppose McCulloch could do that," said Mr. Wentworth, "and give all our boys their money at par."

"If he could do it, I would give him great credit," said Mr. Stevens.

"I believe he can," said Mr. Wentworth.

"My friend is large," said Mr. Stevens, "and has faith like two grains of mustard-seed."

Plans were devised, and ultimately carried through Congress, by which the great volume of paper currency should be gradually reduced at a certain fixed rate, so that the people might know how to calculate the future, and be enabled to provide against a commercial crash.

The first measure designed to accomplish this result was popularly called the Loan Bill, which was amendatory of an act "to provide ways and means to support the Government." When first considered, in March, 1866, it was defeated in the House. It was soon after brought up again in a modified form, and passed both the House and Senate by large majorities. The act provided that the Secretary of the Treasury might receive treasury notes, or "other obligations issued under any act of Congress," in exchange for bonds. The contraction of the currency was restricted and limited by the provision that not more than ten millions of dollars might be retired and canceled within six months from the passage of the act, and thereafter not more than four millions of dollars in any one month.

A financial problem of great importance presented itself for solution in the second session of the Thirty-ninth Congress. A large amount of compound-interest notes, weighed down with accrued interest, had ceased to float as currency, and lay in the vaults of the banks and the coffers of capitalists, awaiting redemption. The question arose as to how they should be redeemed, and the nation saved the payment of the immense amounts of interest which must accumulate in course of time. The House of Representatives proposed to pass an act authorizing and directing the Secretary of the Treasury to issue legal-tender notes, without interest, not exceeding $100,000,000, in place of the compound-interest bearing notes.

To this proposition the Senate would not accede, and passed a substitute which the House would not accept. A Committee of Conference reported a modification of the Senate's substitute, which finally became a law, providing that, for the purpose of redeeming and retiring compound-interest notes, the Secretary of the Treasury should issue temporary loan certificates, to the amount of $50,000,000, at a rate of interest not exceeding three per cent. per annum.

While the greater share of the attention of the Thirty-ninth Congress was occupied with efforts to reconstruct the eleven States which had forfeited their rights by rebellion, the Territories of Colorado and Nebraska applied for admission to the Union. Congress voted to admit both, but the President obstructed their entrance with his vetoes. Congress, on reconsideration, admitted Nebraska, the objections of the President to the contrary notwithstanding. Colorado was not so fortunate, since her people had been so unwise as to prejudice their cause by restricting the enjoyment of political rights by ingrafting the word "white" into their fundamental law. By this mistake they forfeited the favor of the "Radicals," who refused to champion their cause against the President. Incidental to this, Congress ordained that political rights should not be restricted in the Territories on account of race or color.

The manifest evils of unrestricted Executive patronage—the bane of American politics—early enlisted the efforts of the Thirty-ninth Congress to provide a remedy. A bill to regulate appointments to and removals from office was introduced by Mr. Henderson into the Senate near the close of the first session, and referred to the Committee on the Judiciary, but never saw the light as an act of Congress.

The President's power of removal and appointment having been unsparingly used during the recess of Congress, the country became convinced that a remedy should be applied which would be effectual for time to come. On the first day of the second session, Mr. Williams brought before the Senate a bill to "regulate the tenure of offices," which was subsequently referred to the joint Committee on Retrenchment. On the 10th of December Mr. Edmunds, chairman of this committee, reported the bill to the Senate, with amendments. In bringing forward the measure, Mr. Edmunds asserted that they were acting in no spirit of hostility to any party or administration whatever, but for "the true republican interest of the country under all administrations, and under the domination of all parties in the growth before the nation in the future." After grave consideration and protracted discussion in both houses of Congress, the bill was passed near the close of the session. On the 2d of March the bill encountered the veto of the President, who saw in the measure serious interference with the ability of the Executive to keep his oath to preserve, protect, and defend the Constitution of the United States. The bill was immediately passed over the veto without debate.

The act thus passed provides that officers appointed by and with the advice and consent of the Senate shall hold their offices until their successors are in like manner appointed and qualified. Members of the Cabinet hold their offices during the term of the President by whom they are appointed, and for one month thereafter, subject to removal by consent of the Senate.

CHAPTER XXIV.

THE PRESIDENT AND CONGRESS.

THE PRESIDENT'S TREATMENT OF THE SOUTH—FIRST ANNUAL MESSAGE—MR. SUMNER'S CRITICISM—THE PRESIDENT TRIUMPHANT—HE DAMAGES HIS CAUSE—HUMOR OF MR. STEVENS—VETOES OVERRIDDEN—THE QUESTION SUBMITTED TO THE PEOPLE—THEIR VERDICT—SUMMARY OF VETOES—IMPEACHMENT—CHARGES BY MR. ASHLEY—REPORT OF THE COMMITTEE.

THE Thirty-ninth Congress is remarkable for having run its entire career with the constant opposition of the Executive obstructing its progress. In all representative governments, a contest between the executive and the legislative branches of the government has sooner or later arisen, which has invariably ended in the defeat of the former. The hopelessness of the contest on the part of the executive, and the pertinacity with which it has been waged, have given it a mock-heroic character.

During the months which intervened between the death of Abraham Lincoln and the assembling of Congress, Andrew Johnson had ample time to preöccupy the field and intrench himself against what he termed a coördinate branch "hanging on the verge of the Government."

In June, 1865, delegates from the South were first admitted to private interviews with the President. On the 17th of June he issued his proclamation providing for the restoration of civil government in Georgia and Alabama, in which he excludes negroes from the category of loyal citizens entitled to vote. The President soon after proceeded to appoint provisional governors for the Southern States—a step which was viewed with joy by the late rebels, and sorrow by the Union men of the North. The character of these appointments may be seen in a sentiment uttered by Governor Perry soon after his elevation to office: "There is not now in the Southern States," said he, "any one who feels more bitterly the humiliation and degradation of going back into the Union than I do." Governor Perry saved himself from dismissal by assuring the people that the death of Mr. Lincoln was no loss to the South, while he had every hope that Mr. Johnson, an old slaveholding Democrat, would be an advantage.

In Alabama, under the provisional government established by Mr. Johnson, the convention prohibited negroes from testifying in the courts. Rebels throughout the South at once began to make their arrangements for taking part in the government. In November, Governor Perry made a public demand that when Congress met the Clerk of the House should place on the roll the names of Representatives from the rebel States.

When South Carolina hesitated to adopt the Constitutional Amendment abolishing slavery, President Johnson assured the Governor that the clause giving Congress the power to enforce it by appropriate legislation really limited congressional control over the negro question. After this assurance, South Carolina accepted the Constitutional Amendment.

In August and September, 1865, Democratic conventions indorsed the President's policy, and Democratic papers began to praise him. Republicans were unwilling to believe that they had been deserted, and hoped that after the assembling of Congress all differences would disappear.

The message of the President, read at the opening of the Thirty-ninth Congress, placed him in direct opposition to the leaders of the Republican party, and at variance with his own policy. "A concession of the elective franchise," said he, "to the freedmen, by act of the President of the United States, must have been extended to all colored men, wherever found, and must have established a change of suffrage in the Northern, Middle, and Western States, not less than in the Southern and Southwestern."

Every one could see that the President possessed as much power to admit the black man to the right of suffrage in the rebel States as to appoint provisional governors over them.

While Congress was in session, and actually employed in legislating for the restoration of the rebel States, Mr. Johnson substantially declared that Congress had no control over the subject, by removing the provisional governor of Alabama, and handing the State Government over to the officers elected by the people.

The Senate having requested information from the President as to the condition of the rebel States, the President, on the 20th of December, sent in a message which Mr. Sumner characterized as an attempt to "whitewash" the unhappy condition of the rebel States. The message of the President was accompanied by reports from General Grant and General Schurz, in which Congress found evidence that the late rebels had little sense of national obligation, and were chiefly anxious to regain political power, and compensate themselves for the loss of slavery by keeping the negroes in abject servitude.

The passage of the Freedmen's Bureau Bill, by a large majority in Congress, and its veto by the President, presents the next phase in the contest. To Republicans the most alarming feature in the Veto Message was the evidence it gave that the President was ready at once to give to traitors who had fought fiercely for four years to destroy the Union an equal voice with loyal men in determining the terms of its reconstruction.

In this instance the President prevailed. The bill failed to pass over the veto, from the fact that six Senators—Dixon, Doolittle, Morgan, Norton, Stewart, and Van Winkle—who had voted for the bill, now sided with the President. This was the first and last triumph of the President.

Two days after, on the 22d of February, the President greatly damaged his cause by denouncing a Senator and a Representative, and using the slang of the stump against the Secretary of the Senate in the midst of an uproarious Washington mob. The people were mortified that the Executive of the nation should have committed so serious an indiscretion.

The incident received notice in Congress in a humorous speech of Thaddeus Stevens, who declared that the alleged speech could never have been delivered; that it was "a part of the cunning contrivanee of the copperhead party, who have been persecuting our President;" that it was "one of the grandest hoaxes ever perpetrated."

Congress, now aware that it must achieve its greatest works of legislation over the obstructing veto of the President, moved forward with caution and deliberation. Every measure was well weighed and carefully matured, since, in order to win its way to the favor of a triumphant majority in Congress and the country, it must be as free as possible from all objectionable features.

Impartial suffrage, as provided in the District of Columbia Suffrage Bill, being a subject upon which the people had not yet spoken, the Senate determined that it would be better not to risk the uncertainty of passing the measure over the inevitable veto until the people should have an opportunity of speaking at the ballot-box.

The President applied his veto to the Civil Rights Bill and the second Freedmen's Bureau Bill, but a majority of more than the requisite two-thirds placed these measures among the laws of the land. In the House of Representatives, Mr. Raymond was the only Republican member who voted to sustain the veto of the Civil Rights Bill. The temptation to be friends of the President, in order to aid him in the distribution of patronage, was very great with members of Congress, and the wonder is that so many were able to reject it all, and adhere to principles against which the Executive brought to bear all his power of opposition.

On the adjournment of Congress in July, at the close of the first session, the contest was still continued, though in another arena. Members of Congress went to their several districts, submitted their doings to their constituents, and took counsel of the people. The President also traversed the States from the Atlantic to the Mississippi. He made numerous speeches, and endeavored to popularize his policy.

The people gave their verdict at the ballot-box in favor of Congress. The reëlection of Congress was the rejection of the President. The ruin of the President's fortunes was shared by his followers. No gentleman ever entered the House of Representatives with more *eclat* than that with which Mr. Raymond took his seat as a member of the Thirty-ninth Congress, but his constituents did not see proper to elect him for a second term. Delano and Stillwell, of the West, were left at home. Cowan, in the Senate, elected six years before as a Republican, was superseded, and Doolittle was instructed by his Legislature to resign.

The message of the President at the opening of the second session displayed no disposition to yield to the people or to Congress. He declared to a State delegation that waited on him that he was too old to learn.

One of the first acts of Congress after reässembling was to accept the sanction of the people for impartial suffrage, and pass the District Suffrage Bill over the President's veto. The President deemed it due to his consistency to return bills, with his "objections thereto in writing," to the very last. Among the last doings of the Thirty-ninth Congress was the passage of the Tenure-of-office Bill and the Military Reconstruction Bill over vetoes. In humiliating contrast with the circumstances one year before, when the veto of the Freedmen's Bureau Bill prevailed, the veto of the Military Reconstruction Bill had but ten supporters in the Senate.

The following is a complete list of the bills vetoed by the President during the Thirty-ninth Congress, and of the bills which were passed over the veto, and those which became laws without the President's signature:

First Session.—To enlarge the powers of the Freedmen's Bureau; vetoed February 19, 1866.

To protect all persons in the United States in their civil rights, and furnish the means of their vindication; vetoed; and passed, April 9, 1866, over veto.

For the admission of the State of Colorado into the Union; vetoed May, 1866.

To enable the Montana and New York Iron Mining and Manufacturing Company to purchase a certain amount of the public lands not now in market; vetoed June, 1866.

To continue in force and to amend an act entitled "an act to establish a bureau for the relief of freedmen and refugees, and for other purposes;" vetoed; passed, July 16, 1866, over veto.

For the admission of the State of Nebraska into the Union; not signed; failed through the adjournment of Congress.

Second Session.—To regulate the elective franchise in the District of Columbia; vetoed; passed, January 8, 1867, over veto.

To admit the State of Colorado into the Union; vetoed January 18, 1867.

For the admission of the State of Nebraska into the Union; vetoed; passed, February 9, 1867, over veto.

To provide for the more efficient government of the insurrectionary States; vetoed; passed, March 2, 1867, over veto.

To regulate the tenure of office; vetoed; passed, March 2, 1867, over veto.

Bills which became laws without the President's signature, the constitutional limit of ten days having expired without their return:

To repeal section 13 of "an act to suppress insurrection, to punish treason and rebellion, to seize and confiscate the property of rebels, and for other purposes," approved July 17, 1862; became a law January 22, 1867.

To regulate the franchise in the Territories of the United States; became a law January 31, 1867.

To regulate the duties of the Clerk of the House of Representatives, in preparing for the organization of the House, and for other purposes; became a law February 20, 1867.

To declare the sense of an act entitled "an act to restrict the jurisdiction of the Court of Claims, and to provide for the payment of certain demands for quartermasters' stores and subsistence supplies furnished to the army of the United States;" became a law February 22, 1867.

RECAPITULATION.—Vetoes, 10; pocket vetoes, 1; laws passed over vetoes, 6; vetoes sustained, 4; became laws without signature, 4.

As President Johnson proceeded in his career of opposition to the legislative branch of the Government, the conviction fastened upon the minds of some that he was guilty of crimes rendering him liable to impeachment. On the 7th of January, 1867, Hon. James M. Ashley, of Ohio, brought before the House of Representatives articles of impeachment, as follows:

"I do impeach Andrew Johnson, Vice-President and acting President of the United States, of high crimes and misdemeanors.

"I charge him with a usurpation of power and violation of law:

"In that he has corruptly used the appointing power;

"In that he has corruptly used the pardoning power;

"In that he has corruptly used the veto power;

"In that he has corruptly disposed of public property of the United States;

"In that he has corruptly interfered in elections, and committed acts which, in contemplation of the Constitution, are high crimes and misdemeanors; Therefore,

"*Be it resolved*, That the Committee on the Judiciary be, and they are hereby, authorized to inquire into the official conduct of Andrew Johnson, Vice-President of the United States, discharging the powers and duties of the office of President of the United States, and to report to this House whether, in their opinion, the said Andrew Johnson, while in said office, has been guilty of acts which are designed or calculated to overthrow, subvert, or corrupt the Government of the United States, or any department or office thereof; and whether the said Andrew Johnson has been guilty of any act, or has conspired with others to do acts, which, in contemplation of the Constitution, are high crimes and misdemeanors, requiring the interposition of the constitutional power of this House; and that said committee have power to send for persons and papers, and to administer the customary oath to witnesses."

This resolution was adopted by a vote of one hundred and eight to thirty-eight.

Near the close of the session, the Committee on the Judiciary, having in charge the question of impeachment, made a report.

Truly Your friend
J. M. Ashley

The condition in which the subject was left by the Thirty-ninth Congress will be seen from the following extract:

"The duty imposed upon the committee by this action of the House was of the highest and gravest character. No committee, during the entire history of the Government, has ever been charged with a more important trust. The responsibility which it imposed was of oppressive weight and of most unpleasant nature. Gladly would the committee have escaped from the arduous labor imposed upon it by the resolution of the House; but once imposed, prompt, deliberate, and faithful action, with a view to correct results, became its duty, and to this end it has directed its efforts.

"Soon after the adoption of the resolution by the House, the Hon. James M. Ashley communicated to the committee, in support of his charges against the President of the United States, such facts as were in his possession, and the investigation was proceeded with, and has been continued almost without a day's interruption. A large number of witnesses have been examined, many documents collected, and every thing done which could be done to reach a conclusion of the case. But the investigation covers a broad field, embraces many novel, interesting, and important questions, and involves a multitude of facts, while most of the witnesses are distant from the capital, owing to which, the committee, in view of the magnitude of the interests involved in its action, has not been able to conclude its labors, and is not, therefore, prepared to submit a definite and final report. If the investigation had even approached completeness, the committee would not feel authorized to present the result to the House at this late period of the session, unless the charge had been so entirely negatived as to admit of no discussion, which, in the opinion of the committee, is not the case. Certainly, no affirmative report could be properly considered in the expiring hours of this Congress.

"The committee, not having fully investigated all the charges preferred against the President of the United States, it is deemed inexpedient to submit any conclusion beyond the statement that sufficient testimony has been brought to its notice to justify and demand a further prosecution of the investigation.

"The testimony which the committee has taken will pass into the custody of the Clerk of the House, and can go into the hands of such committee as may be charged with the duty of bringing this investigation to a close, so that the labor expended upon it may not have been in vain.

"The committee regrets its inability definitely to dispose of the important subject committed to its charge, and presents this report for its own justification, and for the additional purpose of notifying the succeeding Congress of the incompleteness of its labors, and that they should be completed."

With the acceptance of this report, the impeachment was at an end so far as the action of the Thirty-ninth Congress was concerned. The subject was handed over to the consideration of the Fortieth Congress.

CHAPTER XXV.

PERSONAL.

CONTESTED SEATS—MR. STOCKTON VOTES FOR HIMSELF—NEW JERSEY'S LOSS OF TWO SENATORS—LOSSES OF VERMONT—SUICIDE OF JAMES H. LANE—DEATH IN THE HOUSE—GENERAL SCOTT—LINCOLN'S EULOGY AND STATUE—MR. SUMNER ON FINE ARTS IN THE CAPITOL—CENSURE OF MR. CHANLER—PETITION FOR THE EXPULSION OF GARRET DAVIS—GRINNELL ASSAULTED BY ROUSSEAU—THE ACTION OF THE HOUSE—LEADER OF THE HOUSE.

MATTERS of interest relating to the members of the Thirty-ninth Congress remain to be noticed. Some names of members appear in the opening scenes of Congress which were substituted by others before the close. This was occasioned partly through successful contests for seats by persons who, after an investigation of their claims, were declared to have been legally elected, but failed, through fraud or mistake, to receive their credentials. The right of Mr. Voorhees, of Indiana, to a seat in the Thirty-ninth Congress was contested by Henry D. Washburn. The testimony in this case was laid before the Committee on Elections early in the session, and after patient hearing of the parties and careful consideration of the subject, the committee reported in favor of Mr. Washburn and unseated Mr. Voorhees.

The seat in Congress taken at the opening of the session by James Brooks, of New York, was decided by the committee, after consideration of the claims of the contestant, to belong to William E. Dodge, a merchant of New York city.

The right of John P. Stockton, of New Jersey, to a seat in the Senate having been disputed on account of irregularity in his election, the Senate came to a vote on the question, after considerable discussion, on the 23d of March, 1866. Mr. Stockton was declared entitled to his place by the close vote of 22 to 21, he giving the decisive vote in favor of himself. There arose a very exciting debate as to the right of a Senator to vote for himself under such circumstances. Mr. Stockton finally yielded to the arguments against his right to sit in judgment on his own case, and he was unseated March 27th by a vote of 22 to 21. For a time the seat thus vacated, to which New Jersey was entitled in the Senate, remained unoccupied on account of the refusal of the Republican Speaker of the New Jersey Senate to give his vote in favor of the nominee of the Union caucus, Mr. Cattell. On account of the nearly equal balance of the parties, the choice was long deferred, but eventually made in favor of Mr. Cattell. The other seat held by New Jersey in the Senate was practically vacant for a considerable time on account of the illness of its incumbent, Mr. William Wright, who consequently resigned and eventually died before the expiration of the Thirty-ninth Congress.

Other seats in Congress were vacated by death. Of all the States, Vermont suffered most severely in this respect. A part of the proceedings of the Thirty-ninth Congress consists of funeral addresses and eulogies upon Judge Collamer, a distinguished Senator from Vermont, whose term of service, had he lived, would have expired with the close of this Congress. He died, lamented by the nation, on the 8th of November, 1865. One who took a prominent part in the funeral obsequies of Mr. Collamer was Solomon Foot, the surviving Senator from Vermont. A man termed, from his length of service, "the father of the Senate," long its presiding officer, of purest morals, incorruptible integrity, and faithful industry, he died universally lamented on the 28th of March, 1866. Mr. Foot's death created a profound impression, since it exhibited, in a most remarkable manner, the effect of Christianity in affording its possessor a happy close of life.

The death of another Senator stands forth in striking contrast with that of Mr. Foot. On the first of July, 1866, Senator James H. Lane shot himself at Leavenworth, Kansas. While on his way home from Washington, when at St. Louis, he had intimated a determination to commit suicide. His friends watched him closely, and obtained possession of his pocket-knife lest he might use it for the fatal purpose. Mr. Lane having reached Leavenworth, two of his friends invited him to ride with them on Sabbath afternoon. After getting into the carriage, he expressed a desire to return to his room for his cane, refusing to allow any one to go for him. Mr. Lane having returned with his cane, they drove to the heights overlooking the city. He entered cheerfully into the conversation, remarking upon the beauty of the city and landscape. On returning, they had to pass through a gate that separated two fields. One of the gentlemen alighted to open the gate. At the same time Mr. Lane stepped down from the carriage, and, passing around behind it, said, "Good-by, gentlemen," and instantly discharged a pistol with its muzzle in his mouth. The ball passed out at the top of his head, near the center of the skull, producing a fatal wound. The unhappy man lingered for a few days in a state of unconsciousness and died. Thus ended the stirring, troubled life of one who as a politician had occupied no inconsiderable space in the public eye.

A number of seats in the House of Representatives were vacated by death. James Humphrey, an able and honored member from New York, died in Brooklyn on the 16th of June, 1866. During the second session of the Thirty-ninth Congress, two members of the House of Representatives were removed by death—Philip Johnson, of Pennsylvania, in his third term of Congressional service, and Henry Grider, of Kentucky, a veteran member, who, having served in Congress from 1843 to 1847, was more recently a member of the Thirty-seventh, Thirty-eighth, and Thirty-ninth Congresses.

Congress was called upon to pay funeral honors to others than its members. The death of General Scott, so long the illustrious chief of the military establishment of the nation, was regarded with due solemnity and honor by Congress, who deputized a large committee to attend the funeral obsequies at West Point. An equestrian statue of the distinguished General was voted by Congress to adorn the public grounds of the national capital.

The name of Abraham Lincoln, the nation's martyred President, was always pronounced with profoundest respect and sincerest gratitude in the halls of Congress. His birthday, February 12th, was celebrated by the adjournment of Congress, and such an assembly as the hall of Representatives has rarely witnessed, to hear a eulogy pronounced by Mr. Bancroft, the American historian. An appropriation of ten thousand dollars was made to pay a young artist, Miss Minnie Ream, to model a statue of Abraham Lincoln. This proposition elicited an animated discussion, and was the occasion of a most interesting address by Mr. Sumner on Art in the Capitol. "Surely this edifice," said he, "so beautiful and interesting, should not be opened to the experiments of untried talent. Only the finished artists should be invited to its ornamentation.

"Sir, I doubt if you consider enough the character of this edifice in which we are now assembled. Possessing the advantage of an incomparable situation, it is one of the first-class structures in the world. Surrounded by an amphitheater of hills, with the Potomac at its feet, it resembles the capitol in Rome, surrounded by the Alban hills, with the Tiber at its feet. But the situation is grander than that of the Roman capitol. The edifice itself is worthy of the situation. It has beauty of form and sublimity in proportions, even if it lacks originality in conception. In itself it is a work of art. It ought not to receive in the way of ornamentation any thing which is not a work of art. Unhappily this rule has not always prevailed, or there would not be so few pictures and marbles about us worthy of the place they occupy. But bad pictures and ordinary marbles should warn us against adding to their number."

Perhaps no Congress in the history of the country presents fewer disagreeable incidents of a personal nature than this. The Democrats in Congress being in such a small minority as to be unable to *do* any thing effectual either to impede or advance legislation, could only present their vain protests in words. Chafing under the difficulties they encountered, it is not surprising that at times they used language so ill-timed and unparliamentary as to call forth the censure of the House.

On one occasion, Mr. Chanler, of New York, submitted a resolution "that the independent, patriotic, and constitutional course of the President of the United States, in seeking to protect, by the veto power, the rights of the people of this Union against the wicked and revolutionary acts of a few malignant and mischievous men meets with the approval of this House, and deserves the cordial support of all loyal citizens of the United States."

For introducing this resolution, the House voted to censure Mr. Chanler as having "attempted a gross insult to the House."

Before the vote was taken, Mr. Chanler said: "If by my defiance I could drive your party from this hall, I would do so; if by my vote I could crush you, I would do so, and put the whole party, with your leader, the gentleman from Pennsylvania [Mr. Stevens], into that political hell surrounded by bayonets referred to by him in his argument on Thursday last."

In the Senate a petition was presented from citizens of New York praying that Garret Davis be expelled from the Senate, and, "with other traitors, held to answer to the law for his crime, since he stood in the attitude of an avowed enemy of the Government"—since he had made the declaration in reference to the Civil Rights Bill "that if the bill should become a law, he should feel compelled to regard himself as an enemy of the Government, and to work for its overthrow."

"It is true," replied Mr. Davis, "that I used in substance the words that are imputed to me in that petition; but, as a part of their context, I used a great many more. As an example of garbling, the petition reminds me of a specimen that I heard when I was a young man. It was to this effect: 'The Bible teaches "that there is no God."' When those words were read in connection with the context, the passage read in about these terms: 'The fool hath said in his heart that there is no God.' That specimen of the Bible was about as fair as this garbled statement is of what I said upon the matter to which it refers."

The most serious subject coming up for the censure of the House was an assault made by Mr. Rousseau, of Kentucky, upon Mr. Grinnell, of Iowa. In many of its features this incident resembles the "affairs" of a personal character which were of frequent occurrence when Southern members were in Congress before the war. In February, 1866, Mr. Rousseau, in the course of a speech on the Freedmen's Bureau Bill, made the remark, "If you intend to arrest white people on the *ex parte* statement of negroes, and hold them to suit your convenience for trial, and fine and imprison them, then I say that I oppose you; and if you should so arrest and punish me, I would kill you when you set me at liberty."

To this Mr. Grinnell replied, "I care not whether the gentleman was four years in the war on the Union side or four years on the other side, but I say that he degraded his State and uttered a sentiment I thought unworthy of an American officer when he said that he would do such an act on the complaint of a negro against him."

To this Mr. Rousseau, on the following day, replied: "I pronounce the assertion that I have degraded my State and uttered a sentiment unworthy an American officer to be false, a vile slander, and unworthy to be uttered by any gentleman upon this floor."

Some months after this, Mr. Rousseau, in a public speech delivered in New York city, denounced Mr. Grinnell as a "pitiable politician from Iowa." In a speech made in the House on the 11th of June, Mr. Rousseau said of Mr. Grinnell: "I do not suppose that any member of this House believed a word he said. When a member can so far depart from what every body believes he ought to know and does know is the truth, it is a degradation, not to his State, but to himself."

"When any man," replied Mr. Grinnell—"I care not whether he stands six feet high, whether he wears buff and carries the air of a certain bird that has a more than usual extremity of tail, wanting in the other extremity—says that he would not believe what I utter, I will say that I was never born to stand under an imputation of that sort.

"The gentleman begins courting sympathy by sustaining the President of the United States preparatory to his assault upon me. Now, sir, if he is a defender of the President of the United States, all I have to say is, God save the President from such an incoherent, brainless defender, equal in valor in civil and in military life. His military record—who has read it? In what volume of history is it found?"

Mr. Rousseau determined to resent the insult which he conceived to be offered him in this speech by inflicting a bodily chastisement upon Mr. Grinnell. On the morning of June 14th, Mr. Rousseau informed a military friend of his purpose of flogging Mr. Grinnell. The person so informed procured a pistol and waited in the capitol until the close of the day's session, in order to be present at the flogging and see "fair play." Two other friends of Mr. Rousseau, also armed with pistols, happened to be present when the scene transpired. While Mr. Grinnell was passing from the House through the east portico of the capitol, he was met by Mr. Rousseau, who, in an excited manner, said, "I have waited four days for an apology for words spoken here upon this floor."

"What of that?" asked Mr. Grinnell.

"I will teach you what of that," said Mr. Rousseau, who then proceeded to strike Mr. Grinnell about the head and shoulders with a rattan, stopping occasionally to lecture him, and saying, "Now, you d—d puppy and poltroon, look at yourself."

After receiving half a dozen blows, Mr. Grinnell exclaimed, "I do n't want to hurt you."

"I do n't expect you to hurt me, you d—d scoundrel," said Mr. Rousseau, "but you tried to injure me upon the floor of the House. And now look at yourself; whipped here; whipped like a dog, disgraced and degraded! Where are your one hundred and twenty-seven thousand constituents now?"

A committee was appointed to investigate this disgraceful affair. In just one month after the transaction, a report was presented, signed by Messrs. Spalding, Banks, and Thayer, stating the facts in the case, and recommending the expulsion of Mr. Rousseau. They also proposed a resolution to express disapproval of the reflections made by Mr. Grinnell upon the character of Mr. Rousseau. The "views of the minority" were also presented by Messrs. Raymond and Hogan. They recommended that the punishment of Mr. Rousseau should be a public reprimand by the Speaker. After protracted discussion, the House came to a final decision. The motion to expel, requiring two-thirds, failed by a few votes. The motion by which the Speaker was directed to publicly reprimand Mr. Rousseau was carried by a vote of 89 to 30. There were not enough in favor of the motion to disapprove of Mr. Grinnell's remarks to call the ayes and noes. Mr. Rousseau endeavored to evade the execution of the sentence by sending his resignation to the Governor of Kentucky. The House declared that a member could not dissolve his connection with the body under such circumstances, without its consent. On the 21st of July, the execution of the order was of the House having been demanded, Mr. Rousseau appeared at the bar, when the Speaker said, "General Rousseau, the House of Representatives have declared you guilty of a violation of its rights and privileges in a premeditated personal assault upon a member for words spoken in debate. This condemnation they have placed on their journal, and have ordered that you shall be publicly reprimanded by the Speaker at the bar of the House. No words of mine can add to the force of this order, in obedience to which I now pronounce upon you its reprimand."

Early in the second session of the Thirty-ninth Congress, an interesting case came up relating to the privileges and immunities of a member of Congress. Charles V. Culver, Representative of the Twentieth District of Pennsylvania, having been engaged very extensively in banking, made a failure in business. In June, 1866, during the session of Congress, one of his creditors caused his arrest upon a contract for the return of certain bonds and notes alleged to have been lent to him, charging that the debt incurred thereby was fraudulently contracted by Culver. In default of required security, Mr. Culver was committed to jail, where he remained until the 18th of December. Mr. Culver claimed his immunity as a member of Congress, under the clause of the Constitution which provides that Senators and Representatives "shall in all cases, except treason, felony, and breach of the peace, be privileged from arrest during their attendance at the sessions of their respective houses, and in going to and returning from the same." The judge decided that the offense fell under the constitutional exception, and was to be regarded as a "breach of the peace." From this remarkable decision an appeal was made to the House of Representatives itself, as "the highest court of the nation, and depository of its supreme authority." The case was referred to the Judiciary Committee, who reported a resolution, unanimously adopted by the House, directing the Speaker to issue his warrant to the Sergeant-at-Arms, commanding him to deliver forthwith Charles V. Culver from the custody of the sheriff and jailor of Venango County, and make return to the House of the warrant, and the manner in which he may have executed the same. The Sergeant-at-Arms proceeded immediately to execute the order of the House, and in a short time the Speaker announced that Mr. Culver was unrestrained in his seat as a member of the Thirty-ninth Congress.

Among the numerous distinguished men who constituted the Thirty-ninth Congress, no one towered so conspicuously above the rest as to be universally recognized and followed as the "leader." This title has been frequently applied to Thaddeus Stevens. He was in many respects the most prominent figure in the Thirty-ninth Congress. His age, his long fidelity to the principles of the Republican party, his uncompromising spirit, and his force of character made him a conspicuous and influential member of the House, but did not cause him to be generally recognized or implicitly followed as a leader.

In so large a legislative body, composed of so many men of independent thought and action, acknowledging no parliamentary leader, it is remarkable that the wheels of legislation should run so smoothly, and that after all the disagreement in discussion, great results should be at last so harmoniously wrought out. This is partly due to the patriotic spirit which pervaded the minds of its members, inducing them to lay aside minor differences of opinion for the good of that common country for which their constituents had lately made such tremendous sacrifice. The result is also owing to the parliamentary ability and tact of him who sat patiently and faithfully as Speaker of the House. Deprived by his position of opportunity of taking part in the discussions, which his genius and experience fitted him to illustrate, he nevertheless did much to direct the current of legislation which flowed smoothly or turbidly before him. The resolution of thanks to the Speaker, moved by a member of the minority, and passed unanimously by the House, was no unmeaning compliment, but was an honor fairly earned and justly paid.

The labor of presiding over the Senate—a much lighter task, owing to the smaller number which composed the body—was faithfully performed by Mr. Foster. His remarks to the Senate on retiring from the chair as President *pro tempore*, and closing a career of twelve years as a member of the body, were most beautiful and impressive.

Benjamin F. Wade, "a Senator from Ohio," having been duly elected President *pro tempore* of the Senate, took the "iron-clad oath" and assumed his seat as acting Vice-President of the United States without ostentation or remark.

At twelve o'clock noon of March 4, 1867, the Thirty-ninth Congress closed its existence, handing over its great enactments to the country, and its unfinished business to its successor, which immediately came into life.

BIOGRAPHICAL INDEX

OF THE

THIRTY-NINTH CONGRESS.

(The numbers appended to the following sketches refer to preceding pages of the book.)

[The names of Republicans are printed in ROMAN ; of Democrats in *ITALICS*.]

JOHN B. ALLEY was born in Lynn, Massachusetts, January 7, 1817. Having learned the art of shoemaking, he devoted himself to the shoe and leather trade. After having served several years in the City Council of Lynn, he was chosen a member of the Governor's Council in 1851. He was a member of the Massachusetts Senate in 1852, and of the State Constitutional Convention held in the following year. In 1858 he was elected a Representative in Congress from Massachusetts. He entered upon his fourth Congressional term in 1865 as a member of the Thirty-Ninth Congress ; and was succeeded in the Fortieth Congress by General Butler.

WILLIAM B. ALLISON was born in Wayne County, Ohio, March 2, 1829. He was educated at Alleghany College, Pennsylvania, and at Western Reserve College, Ohio. From 1851 to 1857 he practiced law in Ohio, and subsequently settled in Dubuque, Iowa. He was a member of the Chicago Convention of 1860. As a member of the Governor's staff, in 1861, he rendered efficient service in raising troops for the war. In 1862 he was elected a Representative in the Thirty-Eighth Congress, from Ohio. He was re-elected in 1864, and again in 1866. —527.

OAKES AMES was born in Easton, Massachusetts, January 10, 1804. He has devoted most of his life to the business of manufacturing, taking but little public part in politics. Having served for two years as a member of the Executive Council of his State, he was, in 1862, 1864, and 1866, elected a Representative in Congress, from Massachusetts.—31.

SYDENHAM E. ANCONA was born in Warwick, Pennsylvania, November 20, 1824. Removing to Berks County, he was, for a number of years, connected with the Reading Railroad Company. In 1860 he was elected a Representative to the Thirty-Seventh Congress from Pennsylvania, and was subsequently returned to the Thirty-Eighth and Thirty-Ninth Congresses. He was succeeded in the Fortieth Congress by *J. Lawrence Getz.*

GEORGE W. ANDERSON was born in Tennessee, May 22, 1832. Having received a liberal education, he adopted the profession of law. In 1853 he settled in Missouri, where he soon after became editor of the "North-East Missourian." In 1858 he was elected to the State Legislature. In 1862 he was chosen a State Senator, and served as such until he was elected a Representative from Missouri to the Thirty-Ninth Congress. He was re-elected to the Fortieth Congress.

HENRY B. ANTHONY was born of Quaker ancestry, at Coventry, Rhode Island, April 1, 1815. He graduated at Brown University in 1833. He became editor of the "Providence Journal" in 1838. He was chosen Governor of Rhode Island in 1849, and served two terms. In 1859 he was elected a Senator in Congress from Rhode Island, and was subsequently re-elected for a second term, which ends in 1871.—36, 37, 487, 488, 497.

SAMUEL M. ARNELL was born in Maury County, Tennessee, May 3, 1834. He studied at Amherst College, Massachusetts, and adopted the profession of law, which he practiced in Columbia, Tennessee. In April, 1865, he was elected a member of the Legislature of Tennessee, and in the following August was elected a Representative in Congress. The Tennessee delegation not being admitted at the opening of the Thirty-Ninth Congress, he continued to hold his seat in the Legislature. He was the author of the Franchise Law, which became a part of the Constitution of Tennessee, and of the Civil Rights Bill of Tennessee. He took his seat as a member of the Thirty-Ninth Congress at the opening of its second session, and was re-elected to the Fortieth Congress.

DELOS R. ASHLEY studied and practiced the profession of law in Monroe, Michigan. In 1849 he removed to California, where he was elected District Attorney in 1851. He was elected to the Assembly in 1854, and to the State Senate in 1856. He subsquently held the office of Treasurer of State. Having removed to Nevada in 1864, he was elected the Representative from that State to the Thirty-Ninth Congress, and was re-elected to the Fortieth Congress.

JAMES M. ASHLEY was born in Pennsylvania, November 14, 1824. He spent several years of his early life in a printing-office, and was some time a clerk on Ohio and Mississippi steamboats. He studied law, and was admitted to the bar in 1849, but immediately engaged in the business of boat-building. He subsequently went into the wholesale drug business in Toledo. In 1858 he was elected a Representative from Ohio to the Thirty-Sixth Congress, and has been a member of every succeeding Congress, including the Fortieth.—306, 503, 513, 515, 525, 566.

JEHU BAKER was born in Fayette County, Kentucky, November 4, 1822. He received a good education, and entered the profession of law. Having settled in Illinois, he was, in 1864, elected a Representative from that State to the Thirty-Ninth Congress, and was re-elected in 1866.—340, 560.

JOHN D. BALDWIN was born in North Stonington, Connecticut, September 28, 1810. He graduated at Yale College. Having studied law, and gone through a course of theological studies, he published a volume of poems, and became connected with the press, first in Hartford, and then in Boston, where he was editor of the "Daily Commonwealth." He subsequently became proprietor of the "Worcester Spy." In 1860 he was a delegate to the Chicago Convention. In 1862 he was elected a Representative in Congress from Massachusetts, and was re-elected in 1864 and 1866.

NATHANIEL P. BANKS was born in Waltham, Massachusetts, January 30, 1816. His parents, being poor, could afford him no advantages of education save those of the common school. He was editor of a newspaper first in Waltham and then in Lowell. He studied law, but did not practice. In 1848 he was elected to the Legislature. He served in both Houses, and officiated part of the time as Speaker. He was President of the Convention, held in 1853, for revising the Constitution of Massachusetts. From 1853 to 1857 he was a Representative in Congress. During his second term in Congress he held the office of Speaker of the House, with unsurpassed acceptability and success. In 1857 he was elected Governor of Massachusetts, and held the office for three successive terms. During the late rebellion he served as a Major-General of Volunteers. In 1865 he was elected a member of the Thirty-Ninth Congress, and was re-elected in 1866.—25, 31, 445, 524, 525, 539, 553.

ABRAHAM A. BARKER was born in Lovell, Maine, March 30, 1816. He received a common-school education, and engaged in agricultural pursuits. He was an early and earnest advocate of temperance and anti-slavery. In 1854 he removed to Pennsylvania, and entered upon the lumber business and mercantile pursuits. In 1860 he was a delegate to the Chicago Convention. In 1864 he was elected to represent the Seventeenth District of Pennsylvania in the Thirty-Ninth Congress. He was succeeded in the Fortieth Congress by Daniel J. Morrell.

PORTUS BAXTER was born in Brownington, Vermont. He received a liberal education, and engaged in mercantile and agricultural pursuits. In 1852 and 1856 he was a Presidential Elector. In 1860 he was elected a Representative from Vermont to the Thirty-Seventh Congress, and was re-elected to the Thirty-Eighth and Thirty-Ninth Congresses. He was succeeded in the Fortieth Congress by Worthington C. Smith.

FERNANDO C. BEAMAN was born in Chester, Vermont, June 28, 1814, and was removed in boyhood to New York. He received an English education at the Franklin County Academy, and studied law in Rochester. In 1838 he removed to Michigan, and engaged in the practice of his profession. He served six years as Prosecuting Attorney for the county of Lenawee, and four years as Judge of Probate. In 1856 he was a Presidential Elector. In 1860 he was elected a Representative from Michigan to the Thirty-Seventh Congress, and was successively re-elected to the Thirty-Eighth, Thirty-Ninth, and Fortieth Congresses.—447.

JOHN F. BENJAMIN was born in Cicero, New York, January 23, 1817. After having spent three years in Texas, he settled in Missouri, in 1848, and engaged in the practice of law. He was a member of the Missouri Legislature in 1851 and 1852, and was a Presidential Elector in 1856. He entered the Missouri Cavalry as a private, in 1861, and by a series of promotions reached the rank of Lieutenant-Colonel. He resigned to accept the appointment of Provost-Marshal for the Eighth District of Missouri. He was a delegate to the Baltimore Convention of 1864, and was the same year elected a Representative from Missouri to the Thirty-Ninth Congress, and in 1866 was re-elected.—366.

TEUNIS G. BERGEN was born in Brooklyn, New York, October 6, 1806, He received an academical education at Flatbush, and engaged in surveying and horticulture. He served the town of New Utrecht as supervisor for twenty-three years. He was a member of the State Constitutional Convention of 1846. In 1860 he was a member of the Democratic Conventions of Charleston and Baltimore. In 1864 he was elected a Representative from New York to the Thirty-Ninth Congress. At the close of his Congressional term he was elected a member of the New York Constitutional Convention of 1867. He was succeeded in the Fortieth Congress by *Demas Barnes*.

JOHN BIDWELL was born in Chautauqua county, N. Y., August 5, 1819. In 1829 he removed with his father to Erie, Pennsylvania, and two years after to Ashtabula county, Ohio, where, through his own exertions he obtained an academical education. In 1838 he taught school in Darke County, Ohio, and subsequently taught two years in Missouri. In 1841 he emigrated to California, one of the first adventurers on the wild overland route. At the breaking out of the war with Mexico, he entered the service of the United States as a private, and reached the rank of Major. He was among the first who discovered gold on Feather River in 1848. In 1849 he was elected to the State Constitutional Convention, and to the Senate of the first Legislature of California. In 1860 he was a delegate to the Charleston Convention, and refused to sanction the secession movement there made. In 1863 he was appointed Brigadier General of California militia, when it was necessary to organize in order to preserve the peace of the State. In 1864 he was a member of the Baltimore Convention, which renominated Lincoln. The same year he was elected a Representative from California to the Thirty-Ninth Congress. He was not a candidate for re-election to Congress, since nearly all the papers in the State had hoisted his name as candidate for Governor. He failed, however, to receive the nomination for that office by the Republican Convention. He was succeeded in the Fortieth Congress by *James A. Johnson*.—31.

JOHN A. BINGHAM was born in Pennsylvania in 1815. Having received an academical education, and spending two years in a printing-office, he entered Franklin College, in Ohio, but owing to ill-health, did not prosecute his studies to graduation. He was admitted to the bar in 1840, and from 1845 to 1849 he was Prosecuting Attorney for the county of Tuscarawas. In 1854 he was elected a Representative from Ohio to the Thirty-Fourth Congress, and was re-elected to the Thirty-Fifth, Thirty-Sixth, and Thirty-Seventh Congresses. In 1864 he was appointed a Judge-Advocate in the Army, and Solicitor of the Court of Claims. He was Assistant Judge-Advocate in the trial of the Assassination Conspirators, in May, 1865. In 1865 he took his seat for his fifth term of service in Congress and was re-elected to the Fortieth Congress.—25, 67, 237, 285, 319, 357, 434, 448, 474, 475, 505, 520, 526, 537.

JAMES G. BLAINE was born in Washington County, Pennsylvania, in 1830. After graduating at Washington College, 1847, he removed to Maine and became editor of the "Kennebec Journal," and "Portland Advertiser. He was four years a member of the Maine Legislature, and served two years as Speaker of the House. In 1862 he was elected a Representative from Maine to the Thirty-Eighth Congress, and was successively re-elected to the Thirty-Ninth and Fortieth Congresses.—333, 437, 527, 528, 536.

HENRY T. BLOW was born in Southampton county, Virginia, July 15, 1817. In 1830 he removed to Missouri, and soon after graduated at the St. Louis University. He engaged extensively in the drug and lead business. He served four years in the Senate of Missouri. In 1861 he was appointed by President Lincoln Minister to Venezuela, but resigned the position before the expiration of a year. In 1862 he was elected a Representative from Missouri to the Thirty-Eighth Congress, and was re-elected to the Thirty-Ninth. He was succeeded in the Fortieth Congress by Carman A. Newcomb.

GEORGE S. BOUTWELL was born in Brookline, Massachusetts, January 28, 1818, and removed to Groton in 1835. He was engaged in mercantile business as clerk and proprietor for several years, and subsequently entered the profession of the law. From 1842 to 1850 he was a member of the Massachusetts House of Representatives. In 1849 and 1850 he was Bank Commissioner. In 1851 he was elected Governor of Massachusetts, and served two terms. He was a member of the Massachusetts Constitutional Convention of 1853. He was eleven years a member and Secretary of the Massachusetts Board of Education, and ten years a member of the Board of Overseers of Harvard College. He was appointed Commissioner of the Internal Revenue, in July, 1862, and organized the Revenue system. In 1863 he took his seat as a Representative in Congress from Massachusetts, and was re-elected to the Thirty-Ninth and Fortieth Congresses. He is the author of a "Manual of the School System, and School Laws of Massachusetts," "Educational Topics and Institutions," "A Manual of the Revenue System," and a volume just published, entitled "Speeches on Reconstruction."—31, 91, 442, 475, 526, 528, 536, 553.

BENJAMIN M. BOYER was born in Montgomery county, Pennsylvania, January 22, 1823. He graduated at the University of Pennsylvania, and adopted the profession of law. In 1848 he was elected District Attorney for the county of Montgomery. In 1864 he was elected a Representative from Pennsylvania to the Thirty-Ninth Congress, and was re-elected to the Fortieth Congress.—54, 438.

ALLEN A. BRADFORD was born in Friendship, Maine, July 23, 1815. In 1841 he emigrated to Missouri, where he was admitted to the bar in 1843. He held the office of Clerk of the Circuit Court of Atchinson County, and subsequently removed to Iowa, where he was appointed Judge of the Sixth Judicial Circuit. Resigning this office in 1855, he went to Nebraska, and became a member of the Legislative Council. Having, in 1860, settled in Colorado, he was appointed Judge of the Supreme Court for that territory, and held this office until he was elected a delegate to the Thirty-Ninth Congress from Colorado. He was succeeded in the Fortieth Congress by George M. Chilcott.

AUGUSTUS BRANDAGEE was born in New London, Conn., July 15, 1828. He graduated at Yale College in 1849, and at the Yale Law School in 1851. From 1854 to 1861 he served in the Connecticut Legislature, of which he was Speaker in the latter year. He was a Presidential Elector in 1861, and was elected a Representative to the Thirty-Eighth Congress from Connecticut in 1863, and was re-elected in 1865. He was succeeded in the Fortieth Congress by Henry H. Starkweather.

HENRY H. P. BROMWELL was born in Baltimore, Maryland, August 26, 1823. Having spent seven years of his boyhood in Ohio, he went to Illinois in 1836, and came to the bar in 1853. He was subsequently an editor, Judge of a County Court, and Presidential Elector. In 1864 he was elected a Representative from Illinois to the Thirty-Ninth Congress, and in 1866 was re-elected to the Fortieth Congress.—349, 538.

JAMES BROOKS was born in Portland, Maine, November 10, 1810. When eleven years old he became a clerk in a store. At sixteen he was a school-teacher, and at twenty-one graduated at Waterville College. After several years spent in traveling and writing letters for the press, he was, in 1835, elected to the Legislature of Maine. In 1836 he established the "New York Daily Express," of which he has since been chief editor. In 1847 he was elected to the General Assembly of New York. In 1849 and again in 1851 he was elected a Representative in Congress. In 1863 he was returned to Congress. In December, 1865, he took his place as a member of the Thirty-Ninth Congress, but held it only until the 6th of April following, his seat having been successfully contested by William E. Dodge. In 1866 he was elected a Representative from New York to the Fortieth Congress. —17, 20, 25, 335, 336, 568.

JOHN M. BROOMALL was born in Upper Chichester, Pennsylvania, in 1816. Having received a common-school education, he devoted himself to legal studies and pursuits. In 1861 he was a Presidential Elector. In 1862 he was elected to represent the Seventh Pennsylvania District in Congress. Two years later was re-elected to the Thirty-Ninth Congress, and was re-elected to the Fortieth Congress.—223, 360. 439, 504.

B. GRATZ BROWN is grandson of John Brown, who was United States Senator from Kentucky in 1805. He was born in Lexington, Kentucky, May 28, 1826. Having graduated at Yale College and studied law, he settled at St. Louis, Mo., where he edited the "Missouri Democrat," from 1854 to 1859, and was a member of the State Legislature. He raised a regiment at the breaking out of the war, which he commanded during its term of service. He was among the foremost champions of freedom in Missouri, and was elected a Senator in Congress from that State for the term commencing in 1863 and ending in 1867. He was succeeded by Charles D. Drake.—285, 477, 493.

CHARLES R. BUCKALEW was born in Columbia County, Pennsylvania, December 28, 1821. He was admitted to practice law in 1843, and was elected Prosecuting Attorney for his native county in 1845. In 1850 he was elected a Senator in the State Legislature, which office he held for a series of years. In 1854 he was a Commissioner to exchange the ratifications of a treaty with Paraguay. He was a Presidential Elector in 1856, and Chairman of the State Democratic Committee in 1857. He was appointed by President Buchanan Minister to Ecquador in 1858, and held the position until 1861. He was, in 1863, elected United States Senator from Pennsylvania for the term ending 1869.—296, 401, 413, 494, 532, 535, 547, 548.

RALPH P. BUCKLAND was born in Leyden, Massachusetts, January 20, 1812, and was removed by his parents to Ohio in the same year. From 1831 to 1834 he was clerk in a large cotton commission house in New Orleans. Returning to Ohio, he took an academical course of study at Kenyon College. Having studied law, he was admitted to the bar in 1837. He was a member of the Philadelphia Whig Convention of 1848. In 1855 and 1857 was elected to the Senate of Ohio. In 1861 he was appointed Colonel of the Seventy-Second Ohio Infantry, and commanded a brigade in the battle of Shiloh. He was promoted to the rank of Brigadier General, and participated in the siege of Vicksburg. He was subsequently assigned to the command of the District of Memphis, and defeated Forrest in his attack on that city. At the close of the war he was brevetted a Major General of Volunteers. In 1864, while absent in the field, he was elected a Representative from Ohio to the Thirty-Ninth Congress, and was re-elected in 1866.

HEZEKIAH S. BUNDY was born in Marietta County, Ohio, August 15, 1817. Having been left an orphan when a mere boy, and the support of the family devolving upon him, his opportunities for attaining an education were limited. From 1835 to 1846 he was engaged in mercantile pursuits, and subsequently turned his attention to farming and the furnace business. Meanwhile he studied law, and was admitted to the bar in 1850. He served two terms in the House of Representatives of Ohio, and was, in 1855, elected State Senator. In 1860 he was a Presidential Elector, and in 1864 he was elected a Representative from Ohio to the Thirty-Ninth Congress. He was succeeded in the Fortieth Congress by John T. Wilson.

WALTER A. BURLEIGH was the Delegate from Dakota Territory in the Thirty-Ninth Congress. He received a common-school education, studied medicine, and practiced his profession for a number of years. He was subsequently appointed an Indian Agent, and removed to the West. Soon after the organization of the Territory of Dakota he was elected to represent its interests in Congress, and was re-elected to the Fortieth Congress.

WILLIAM B. CAMPBELL was born in Tennessee, and served as Captain of mounted Volunteers in the Florida War. He served for some time in the State Legislature, and was a Representative in Congress from 1837 to 1843. He commanded the first regiment of Tennessee Volunteers in the Mexican War, and at its close he was elected a Circuit Judge. From 1851 to 1853 he was Governor of Tennessee. In 1865 he was elected a Representative from Tennessee to the Thirty-Ninth Congress, but was not admitted until July, 1866. He died of disease of the heart at his residence in Lebanon, Tennessee, August 19, 1867.

ALEXANDER G. CATTELL was born in Salem, New Jersey, in 1816. He received a commercial education, and began his business-life, as a clerk, at the age of thirteen. Before reaching his majority he had advanced to the head of a large and flourishing business. In 1840 he was elected to the General Assembly of New Jersey, and in 1844 he was a member of the Convention called to frame a new Constitution for that State. He subsequently became the head of the extensive mercantile house of A. G. Cattell & Co., of Philadelphia. During a residence of nine years in that city he was several times elected to the City Council, and was President of the Corn Exchange Association, which, largely through his exertions, recruited and equipped two and a half regiments for service in the late war. Having resumed his residence in New Jersey, he was, in 1866, elected a Senator in Congress from that State.—569.

ZACHARIAH CHANDLER was born in Bedford, New Hampshire, December 10, 1813. He received an academical education, and removed to Michigan, where he engaged extensively in mercantile pursuits and in banking. In 1851 he held the office of Mayor of Detroit. In 1852 he was an unsuccessful candidate for Governor of Michigan. He entered the United States Senate, during the Thirty-Fifth Congress, as the successor of General Cass. In 1863 he was re-elected to the Senate for the term ending in 1869.—27, 397.

JOHN W. CHANLER was born in the City of New York in 1826. In 1859 and 1860 he was a memberof the General Assembly of New York. In 1862 he was elected a Representative from New York to the Thirty-Eighth Congress, and was re-elected to the Thirty-Ninth and Fortieth Congresses.—64, 156, 337, 338, 571.

J. FRANCISCO CHAVES was born in New Mexico in 1833. He studied medicine in New York, and subsequently devoted several years to mercantile pursuits and cattle-raising. In 1861 he entered the military service as Major of the First New Mexico Infantry, and after seeing much active service was mustered out as Lieutenant-Colonel. In 1865 he was elected a Delegate from New Mexico to the Thirty-Ninth Congress.

DANIEL CLARK was born in Stratham, New Hampshire, October 24, 1809. He graduated at Dartmouth College in 1834, and was admitted to the bar in 1837. From 1842 to 1857 he was repeatedly a member of the New Hampshire Legislature. In 1857 he was elected a Senator in Congress from New Hampshire, and in 1861 he was re-elected for the term ending in 1867. At the close of the first session of the Thirty-Ninth Congress he resigned his seat in the Senate, having been appointed U. S. District Judge for New Hampshire.—28, 201, 202, 388, 453, 455, 456, 479.

READER W. CLARKE was born in Bethel, Clermont County, Ohio, May 18, 1812. He learned the art of printing, but subsequently studied law, and was admitted to the bar in 1836. In 1840 and 1841 he was a member of the Ohio Legislature. He was a delegate to the Baltimore Convention of 1844, and was a Presidential Elector in the same year. For six years succeeding 1846 he held the office of Clerk of the Courts of Clermont County. He was a delegate to the Chicago Convention of 1860. In 1864 he was elected a Representative from Ohio to the Thirty-Ninth Congress, and was re-elected to the Fortieth Congress.

SIDNEY CLARKE was born in Southbridge, Massachusetts, October 16, 1831. He adopted the profession of an editor, and published the "Southbridge Press." He emigrated to Kansas in 1858, and settled in Lawrence. In 1862 he was a member of the Kansas Legislature. He served during the rebellion as Captain of Volunteers, and Assistant Provost Marshal General for Kansas, Nebraska, Colorado, and Dakota. In 1864 he was elected the Representative from Kansas to the Thirty-Ninth Congress, and was re-elected to the Fortieth.—88.

AMASA COBB was born in Crawford County, Illinois, September 27, 1823. He emigrated to Wisconsin Territory in 1842, and engaged in the lead-mining business. He served as a private in the Mexican War, and at the close of this service he commenced the practice of law. He served as District Attorney, State Senator, and Adjutant-General of Wisconsin. He was subsequently a member of the State Legislature, and was chosen Speaker. He was Colonel of the Fifth Wisconsin Regiment in the war, and was elected a Representative from Wisconsin to the Thirty-Eighth, Thirty-Ninth, and Fortieth Congresses.

ALEXANDER H. COFFROTH was born in Somerset, Pennsylvania, May 18, 1828. He commenced the practice of law in 1851. He was a delegate to the Charleston Convention in 1860, and was elected a Representative to the Thirty-Eighth Congress. He appeared as a member of the Thirty-Ninth Congress, but his seat was successfully contested by William H. Koontz.

SCHUYLER COLFAX was born in New York City, March 23, 1823. He became a printer, and settled in Indiana, 1836. He was for many years editor and publisher of the "South Bend Register." In 1850 he was a member of the Indiana Constitutional Convention. He was a delegate and secretary of the Whig National Conventions of 1848 and 1852. He was elected a Representative from Indiana to the Thirty-Fourth Congress, and has been a member by re-election of each succeeding Congress. He was elected Speaker of the Thirty-Eighth Congress, and was re-elected to the same office in the Thirty-Ninth and Fortieth Congresses.—12, 20, 289, 306, 363, 501, 574, 576.

ROSCOE CONKLING, son of Alfred Conkling, a member of the Seventeenth Congress, was born at Albany, in 1828. Having entered the profession of law, he successively held the offices of of District Attorney for Oneida County and Mayor of Utica. In 1859 he took his seat as a member of the Thirty-Sixth Congress from New York, and remained a Representative in Congress by successive re-elections until the 4th of March, 1867, when he entered the United States Senate as the successor of Ira Harris.—628, 330, 348, 363, 481, 513, 514.

JOHN CONNESS was born in Ireland in 1822, and came to America when thirteen years of age. He was an early emigrant to California, where he engaged in mercantile and mining pursuits. In 1852 he was elected to the State Legislature, and served in that capacity for a series of years. In 1863 he was elected United States Senator from California for the term ending in 1869.—540.

BURTON C. COOK was born in Monroe County, New York, May 11, 1819. He received a collegiate education, and entered upon the profession of law in Illinois. After serving as State Attorney for six years, he was elected to the State Senate in 1852, and was a member of that body until 1860. In 1864 he was elected a Representative from Illinois to the Thirty-Ninth Congress, and was re-elected to the Fortieth Congress.—223, 350, 351.

EDMUND COOPER was born in Maury County, Tennessee. He graduated at the Harvard Law School, and entered upon the practice of law at Columbia, and afterwards at Shelbyville, Tennessee. He has served in the Tennessee Legislature, and was a member of the Constitutional Convention of 1865. In August, 1865, he was elected a Representative from Tennessee to the Thirty-Ninth Congress, but was not admitted until near the close of the first session. While waiting at Washington to be admitted to Congress, he acted as Private Secretary to President Johnson. In November, 1867, he was appointed by the President to act as Assistant Secretary of the Treasury.

EDGAR COWAN was born in Westmoreland County, Pennsylvania, September 19, 1815. He graduated at Franklin College, Ohio, in 1839. Having been at different times clerk, boat-builder, schoolmaster, and student of medicine, he studied law and practiced the profession until 1861, when he was elected United States Senator from Pennsylvania for the term ending 1867. He was succeeded by Simon Cameron.—96, 100, 133, 135, 195, 216, 273, 429, 460, 487, 489, 496, 535, 564.

AARON H. CRAGIN was born in Weston, Vermont, February 3, 1821. He studied law in Albany, New York, and in 1847 removed to Lebanon, New Hampshire, where he practiced his profession. From 1852 to 1855 he was a member of the New Hampshire Legislature. He was a Representative from New Hampshire in the Thirty-Fifth and Thirty-Sixth Congresses. In 1865 he entered the Senate of the United States for the term ending in 1871.

JOHN A. J. CRESWELL was born in Port Deposit, Maryland, November 18, 1828. He graduated at Dickinson College in 1848, and was admitted to the bar in 1850. He was successively a member of the Maryland House of Delegates, Assistant Adjutant-General for the State and a Representative in the Thirty-Eighth Congress. In 1865 he was chosen a United States Senator for the unexpired term of T. H. Hicks, deceased.—134, 136.

SHELBY M. CULLOM was born in Wayne County, Kentucky, November 27, 1829, and was removed to Illinois, when scarcely a year old, by his parents, who settled in Tazewell County. He spent two years as a student at the Mount Morris Seminary. Having studied law, he entered upon the practice of his profession in Springfield, and was immediately elected City Attorney. In 1856 he was elected to the State Legislature, and was re-elected in 1860, and chosen Speaker of the House. In 1856 was a Fillmore Elector for the State at large. In 1864 he was elected a Representative from Illinois to the Thirty-Ninth Congress. In 1866 he was re-elected by more than double his former majority.—516.

CHARLES V. CULVER was born in Logan, Ohio, September 6, 1830. Having settled in Western Pennsylvania, he engaged in business pursuits, and especially in banking. He was largely concerned in railroads and other public enterprises. In 1864 he was elected a Representative from the Twentieth District of Pennsylvania to the Thirty-Ninth Congress. He was succeeded in the Fortieth Congress by Darwin A. Finney.—575.

WILLIAM A. DARLING was born in Newark, New Jersey, December 17, 1817. He shortly after settled in New York City, where he received a commercial education, and devoted himself to the wholesale business. He became a Director of the Mercantile Library Association, and served eleven years as officer and private of the Seventh Regiment, National Guard. From 1847 to 1854 he was Deputy Receiver of Taxes for New York City. In 1860 he was a Presidential Elector, and in 1863 and 1864 was President of the Union and Republican Organization of New York City. In 1864 he was elected a Representative from New York to the Thirty-Ninth Congress. He was nominated for the Fortieth Congress, and was defeated by *Fernando Wood* by 1600 majority, in a District giving Hoffman (Dem.) for Governor nearly 6000 majority.—81.

GARRETT DAVIS was born at Mt. Sterling, Kentucky, September 10, 1801. Having received an English and classical education, he studied law, and was admitted to the bar in 1823. With his professional labors he joined a considerable attention to agricultural pursuits. In 1833 he was elected to the Legislature, and was twice re-elected. He was a member of the State Constitutional Convention in 1839. From the latter year to 1847 he was in Congress, representing the District in which Henry Clay resided, of whom he was a warm personal and political friend. In 1861 he was elected a Senator in Congress from Kentucky, and was re-elected in 1867.—24, 136, 171, 199, 208, 243, 287, 296, 430, 458, 460, 484, 493, 498, 531, 533, 534, 548, 572.

THOMAS T. DAVIS was born in Middlebury, Vermont, August 22, 1810.

Having removed to the State of New York, he graduated at Hamilton College in 1831, and was admitted to the bar in Syracuse in 1833. He has devoted much attention to business relating to railroads, manufactures, and mining. In 1862 he was elected a Representative from New York to the Thirty-Eighth Congress, and was re-elected to the Thirty-Ninth. He was succeeded in the Fortieth Congress by Dennis McCarthy.—63, 361.

HENRY L. DAWES was born in Cummington, Massachusetts, October 30, 1816. Having graduated at Yale College in 1839, he engaged successively in school-teaching, editing a newspaper, and practicing law. From 1848 to 1853 he was a member of the Legislature of Massachusetts. In 1853 he was chosen District Attorney for the Western District of the State, and held the office until 1856, when he was elected a Representative from Massachusetts to the Thirty-Fifth Congress. He has been a member of every subsequent Congress, including the Fortieth.—30, 478.

JOHN L. DAWSON was born in Uniontown, Pennsylvania, February 7, 1813. He was educated at Washington College, adopted the profession of law, and was, in 1845, appointed by President Polk United States Attorney for the Western District of Pennsylvania. Since 1844 he has been a member of most of the Democratic National Conventions. In 1850 he was elected a Representative to the Thirty-Second Congress, and was re-elected to the Thirty-Third, in which he served as Chairman of the Committee on Agriculture, and was the author of the Homestead Bill which passed in 1854. In 1855 he was appointed by President Pierce Governor of Kansas, but declined the office. In 1862 he was elected a Representative from Pennsylvania to the Thirty-Eighth Congress, and was re-elected to the Thirty-Ninth. He was succeeded in the Fortieth Congress by John Covode.—144, 505.

JOSEPH H. DEFREES was born in White County, Tennessee, May 13, 1812. When eight years old he removed to Piqua, Ohio, and a few years after, he entered a printing-office, in which he obtained the most of his early education. In 1831 he established a newspaper in South Bend, Indiana, and two years after removed to Goshen, where he engaged in mercantile pursuits. In 1836 he was elected Sheriff of Elkhart County. In 1849 he was elected to the House of Representatives of Indiana, and in 1850 to the State Senate. In 1864 he was elected a Representative from Indiana to the Thirty-Ninth Congress. His successor in the Fortieth Congress is William Williams.

COLUMBUS DELANO was born in Shoreham, Vermont, in 1809. When eight years old he removed to Mount Vernon, Ohio, where he studied law and was admitted to the bar in 1831. In 1844 he was elected a Representative from Ohio to the Twenty-Ninth Congress. In 1860 he was a delegate to the Chicago Convention. In 1861 he was appointed Commissary General of Ohio. Two years after he was a member of the Ohio Legislature. In 1864 he was a delegate to the Baltimore Republican Convention, and was in the same year elected a Representative from Ohio to the Thirty-Ninth Congress. His successor in the Fortieth Congress is *George W. Morgan.*—236, 285 539, 564.

HENRY C. DEMING was born in Connecticut. He graduated at Yale College in 1836, and at the Harvard Law School in 1838. He had been a member of the Lower House and Senate of Connecticut, and for six years Mayor of Hartford, when in 1861 he went into the war as Colonel of the Twelfth Connecticut Regiment. He participated in the capture of New Orleans, and was Mayor of that city until 1863, when he returned to his native State, and was soon after elected a Representative in the Thirty-Eighth Congress, and was re-elected in 1865. He was succeeded in the Fortieth Congress by *Richard D. Hubbard.*—31.

CHARLES DENISON was born in Wyoming Valley, Pennsylvania, January 23, 1818. He graduated at Dickinson College in 1839, and entered the profession of law. In 1862 he was elected a Representative from Pennsylvania to the Thirty-Eighth Congress, and was re-elected in 1864. He was succeeded in the Fortieth Congress by *George W. Woodward.*

ARTHUR A. DENNY was born in Indiana, in 1822, and removed in boyhood to Illinois. In 1851 he removed to Washington Territory, and was a member of the Territorial Legislature from 1853 to 1861. He was four years Register of the Land Office at Olympia, and was subsequently elected a Delegate from Washington Territory to the Thirty-Ninth Congress. He was succeeded by Alvan Flanders in the Fortieth Congress.

JAMES DIXON was born in Enfield, Connecticut, in 1814. He graduated at Williams' College in 1834, and soon after entered upon the practice of law. In 1837 he was elected to the Legislature of Connecticut, and was twice re-elected. He was a Representative in Congress from Connecticut from 1845 to 1849. In the latter year he was elected to the State Senate. He was elected United States Senator from Connecticut in 1857, and was re-elected in 1863.—423, 425, 495, 548.

NATHAN F. DIXON, son of a Senator of the same name, was born in Westerly, Rhode Island, May 1, 1812, and graduated at Brown University in 1833. After attending the Law Schools at New Haven and Cambridge, he was admitted to the bar in 1837. From 1840 to 1849 he was a member of the General Assembly of Rhode Island, and after having served in the Thirty-First Congress, was again elected to the Legislature. In 1863 he was elected a Representative from Rhode Island to the Thirty-Eighth Congress, and entered upon his second Congressional term in 1865. He was in 1866 re-elected to the Fortieth Congress.

WILLIAM E. DODGE was born in Hartford, Connecticut, September 4, 1805. Early in life he went to New York City, where he engaged actively in business. He has been forty years at the head of one of the most extensive manufacturing and importing establishments in the country. He was many years President of the National Temperance Society, and has long been a prominent promoter of benevolent enterprises in New York City. Having established his right to the seat held by *James Brooks*, he was admitted a member of the Thirty-Ninth Congress in the spring of 1866. He was succeeded by *James Brooks* in the Fortieth Congress.—511, 568.

IGNATIUS DONNELLY was born in Philadelphia, November 3, 1831, and was educated at the Central High School of his native city. He studied law and was admitted to the bar in 1853. He emigrated to Minnesota in 1857, and two years after was elected Lieutenant Governor of that State, and held the office two terms. In 1862 he was elected a Representative from Minnesota to the Thirty-Eighth Congress, and was re-elected to the Thirty-Ninth and Fortieth Congresses.—145, 156, 333, 507, 238, 553.

JAMES R. DOOLITTLE was born in Hampton, New York, January 3, 1815. He graduated at Geneva College in 1834, became a lawyer, and for several years held the office of District Attorney for Wyoming County. In 1851 he removed to Wisconsin, and two years after was elected Judge of the First Judicial Circuit of that State. In 1857 he was elected a United States Senator from Wisconsin, and in 1863 was re-elected for the term ending in 1869.—28, 38, 285, 408, 431, 456, 457, 458, 459, 460, 462, 495, 501, 531, 532, 533, 541, 564.

JOHN F. DRIGGS was born in Kinderhook, New York, March 8, 1813. He served an apprenticeship in the sash and door-making business, and soon after set up as a master mechanic in New York City. He took no part in politics until 1844, when he assisted in the reform movement by which James Harper was elected Mayor of New York. He was soon after appointed Superintendent of Blackwell's Island Penitentiary. In 1856 he removed to East Saginaw, Michigan, and was two years after elected President of that town. In 1859 he was elected to the Michigan Legislature. Two years after he was appointed Register at the Land Office for the Saginaw District, and held the office until his election as a Representative from Michigan to the Thirty-Eighth Congress in 1862. He was returned by increased majorities to the Thirty-Ninth and Fortieth Congresses.

EBENEZER DUMONT was born in Vevay, Indiana, November 23, 1814. He was educated at the Indiana University, and adopted the profession of law. In 1838 he was elected a member of the Indiana Legislature, and from 1839 to 1845 held the office of County Treasurer. He served in the Mexican War as a Lieutenant Colonel, and was subsequently a member of the State Legislature, a Presidential Elector, and President of the State Bank. At the breaking out of the rebellicn, he was appointed Colonel of the Seventh Regiment of Indiana Volunteers, and fought in the battle of Philippi, in West Virginia. Having been promoted to the rank of Brigadier General, he commanded a brigade at the battle of Murfreesboro. He was subsequently assigned to the military command of Nashville, and from that place led an expedition against John Morgan, capturing nearly all of his command. In 1862, while yet in the army, he was elected a Representative from Indiana to the Thirty-Eighth Congress, and was re-elected in 1864. His successor in the Fortieth Congress is John Coburn.

EPHRAIM R. ECKLEY was born in Jefferson County, Ohio, December 9, 1812, and was admitted to the bar in 1837. From 1843 to 1853 he served in the House of Representatives and in the Senate of Ohio. In the Civil War he was Colonel of the Twenty-Sixth and Eightieth Regiments of Ohio Volunteers. He fought in several battles, and at Corinth commanded a brigade. In 1862 he was elected a Representative from Ohio to the Thirty-Eighth Congress, and was re-elected to the Thirty-Ninth and Fortieth.—447.

GEORGE F. EDMUNDS was born in Richmond, Vermont, February 1, 1828, and was admitted to the bar in 1849. In 1854 he entered the Vermont Legislature, and served three years as Speaker. In 1861 and 1862 he served in the State Senate, and was the Presiding Officer of that body. He was appointed to the vacancy in the United States Senate occasioned by the death of Solomon Foot, and entered upon the duties of that position in April, 1866.—559, 560.

BENJAMIN EGGLESTON was born in Corinth, New York, January 3, 1816. He removed to Ohio in 1831, and gave his attention to commercial pursuits. He has been identified with many important public enterprises. He was for many years Chairman of the Board of Public Works of Cincinnati, and President of the City Council. He was for some years a member of the State Legislature. In 1860 he was a delegate to the Chicago Convention, and was a Presidential Elector in the election of that year. In 1864 he was elected a Representative from Ohio to the Thirty-Ninth Congress, and was re-elected in 1866.

CHARLES A. ELDRIDGE was born at Bridport, Vermont, February 27, 1821. He removed to the State of New York, where he was admitted to the bar in 1846. In 1848 he removed to Fond du Lac, Wisconsin, and served in the Senate of that State in 1854 and 1855. In 1862 he was elected a Representative from Wisconsin to the Thirty-Eighth Congress, and was returned to the Thirty-Ninth and Fortieth Congresses.—226, 242, 355, 419, 441, 476, 507, 539, 546.

THOMAS D. ELIOT was born in Boston, March 20, 1808. Having graduated at Columbia College, Washington, in 1825, he settled as a lawyer in New Bedford. Having served in both branches of the Massachusetts Legislature, he first entered Congress in 1855 for an unexpired term. In 1858 he was elected a Representative from Massachusetts to the Thirty-Sixth Congress, and has been returned to every succeeding Congress, including the Fortieth.—31, 95, 138, 157 295, 296, 306, 347, 443.

JOHN F. FARNSWORTH was born of New England parentage, in Eaton, Lower Canada, March 27, 1820, but was early removed to the Territory of Michigan. In 1843 he settled in St. Charles, Illinois, and entered upon the practice of law. In 1846 he left the Democratic Party with which he had acted, and joined the "Liberty Party." In 1856 and again in 1858 he was elected to Congress, from what was then known as the Chicago District. In 1861 he raised the Eighth Illinois Cavalry Regiment, of which he was Colonel until his promotion to the rank of Brigadier General. The severe service in which he was engaged in the Peninsular Campaign brought on a disability which necessitated his resignation. In the fall of 1862 he was elected a Representative from Illinois to the Thirty-Eighth Congress, and was re-elected in 1864 and 1866, on both occasions receiving the largest majorities given by any district in the United States.—61, 333, 339, 448, 519, 537.

JOHN H. FARQUHAR was born in Frederick County, Maryland, December 20, 1818. With his widowed mother he removed to Indiana in 1833, and was employed as civil engineer upon some of the earliest public improvements of the State. In 1841 he was elected Secretary of the Indiana Senate. In 1843 he was Chief Clerk of the Indiana House of Representatives, and was the same year admitted to the bar in Brookfield. In 1844 he was a delegate to the National Convention which nominated Henry Clay. In 1852 he was candidate for Presidential Elector on the Scott ticket, and in 1860 on the Lincoln ticket. In 1861 he was commissioned a Captain in the Nineteenth United States Infantry, and was detailed as mustering and disbursing officer for Indiana. In 1864 he was elected a Representative from Indiana to the Thirty-Ninth Congress, and was succeeded by *William S. Holman* in the Fortieth Congress.

THOMAS W. FERRY was born in Mackinac, Michigan, June 1, 1827. He has been occupied extensively in the lumber trade and in banking. In 1850 he was elected to the House of Representatives of Michigan, and in 1856 to the State Senate. For eight years he was an efficient member of the Republican State Committee, and was a delegate and a Vice-President of the Chicago Convention of 1860. In 1864 he was elected a Representative from Michigan to the Thirty-Ninth Congress, and was re-elected in 1866.

WILLIAM PITT FESSENDEN was born at Boscawen, New Hampshire, October 16, 1860. He graduated at Bowdoin College in 1823, and in 1827 entered upon the practice of law in Portland, Maine. In 1832 he was a delegate to the Convention which nominated Henry Clay. In the same year he was elected to the Maine Legislature, and again in 1840. In 1841 he was elected a Representative in Congress, and declined a re-election. In 1845, 1846, and 1853 he served his fellow citizens in the State Legislature. In 1853 he was elected a United States Senator from Maine, and was re-elected in 1859. Upon the resignation of Mr. Chase as Secretary of the Treasury, in July, 1864, he was appointed to that office. On the 4th of March following he resigned his seat in the Cabinet, and re-entered the United States Senate, to which he had been elected for the term ending in 1871. In the Senate he has held the important positions of Chairman of the Finance Committee and of the Joint Committee on Reconstruction. He has received the degree of LL.D. from Bowdoin College and Harvard University.—27, 42, 136, 271, 224, 373, 377, 380, 394, 412, 419, 421, 432, 453, 456, 540.

WILLIAM E. FINCH was born in Ohio in 1822, and at the age of twenty-one was admitted to the bar. In 1851 he was elected to the State Senate. In the following year he was a delegate to the Convention which nominated General Scott for President. In 1861 he was again elected a State Senator. In 1862 he was elected a Representative from Ohio to the Thirty-Eighth Congress, and was re-elected to the Thirty-Ninth. He was succeeded by *Philadelph Van Trump* in the Fortieth Congress.—437, 462, 476, 519.

GEORGE G. FOGG was a newspaper editor, of New Hampshire, until his appointment by President Lincoln as United States Minister Resident for Switzerland. He made a considerable fortune while there by investing his salary in United States Securities when they were very low in Europe. At the opening of the second session of the Thirty-Ninth Congress he took his seat in the Senate, having been appointed to fill the unexpired term of Daniel Clark, which closed on the 4th of March, 1867. He was succeeded by James W. Patterson.

SOLOMON FOOT was born in Cornwall, Vermont, November 19, 1802, and graduated at Middlebury College in 1826. Having occupied some years in teaching, he studied law, and was admitted to the bar in 1831. He was for many years a member of the State Legislature of Vermont, and State Attorney. From 1843 to 1847 he was a Representative in Congress. In 1851 he was elected a Senator in Congress from Vermont, was re-elected in 1857, and again in 1863. For several years he held the office of President *pro tem.* of the Senate. He died in Washington, March 28, 1866.—253, 269.

LAFAYETTE S. FOSTER, a lineal descendant of Miles Standish, was born in Franklin, Connecticut, November 22, 1806. In 1828 he graduated at Brown

University, which honored him with the degree of LL.D. in 1850. He was admitted to the bar in 1831. He was six times a member of the Connecticut Legislature, and two years Mayor of the city of Norwich. In 1855 he was elected a United States Senator for Connecticut, and was re-elected in 1862. He was chosen President *pro tem.* of the Senate at the extra session in 1865, and by the elevation of Andrew Johnson to the Presidency became Acting Vice-President of the United States. His service of twelve years in the Senate closed March 4, 1867, when he was succeeded by Orris S. Ferry.—23, 137, 187, 288, 306, 497, 576.

JOSEPH S. FOWLER was born near Steubenvile, Ohio. He was left dependent on his own resources when very young, but by energy and perseverance succeeded in attaining a thorough collegiate education. Having adopted the profession of teaching, he was elected to a college Professorship of Mathematics in Tennessee. He was subsequently for some years at the head of a flourishing seminary of learning near Nashville. He was conspicuous for his staunch loyalty, and when the State Government passed out of the hands of the rebels he was elected to the important office of Comptroller of Tennessee. In 1865 he was elected a Senator in Congress from Tennessee, but with his colleagues was not admitted to a seat until near the close of the first session of the Thirty-Ninth Congress.—478.

FREDERICK T. FRELINGHUYSEN was born at Millstone, New Jersey, August 4, 1817. His grandfather, of the same name, was a member of the Continental Congress, and was a United States Senator from 1793 to 1796. Young Frederick having been left an orphan at an early age was adopted and reared by his uncle, Hon. Theodore Frelinghuysen. He graduated at Rutgers College, and studied law. He was appointed Attorney General of New Jersey in 1861, and was re-appointed in 1866. On the 24th of January, 1867, he took his seat as a United States Senator from New Jersey having been elected for the unexpired term of *William Wright*, deceased, which will end March 4, 1869.—492, 497.

JAMES A. GARFIELD was born in Orange, Cuyahoga County, Ohio, November 19, 1831. He graduated at Williams College, Massachusetts, in 1856, and was for some years principal of a flourishing Seminary of learning at Hiram, Ohio. In 1859 and 1860 he was a member of the Ohio Senate. In 1861 he entered the army as Colonel of the Forty-Second Regiment of Ohio Volunteers, and in the following year was commissioned a Brigadier General. He served as Chief of Staff to General Rosecrans. He fought at the battles of Shiloh, Corinth, and Chicamauga. For gallant service in the last-named battle he was promoted to the rank of Major General. In 1862 he was elected a Representative from Ohio to the Thirty-Eighth Congress, and was re-elected to the Thirty-Ninth and Fortieth Congresses.—144, 438, 450, 524, 540, 538, 553, 557.

ADAM J. GLOSSBRENNER was born in Hagerstown, Maryland, August 31, 1810. He was apprenticed at an early age to the printing-business. When seventeen years of age he journeyed westward, and became foreman in the office of the "Ohio Monitor," and afterwards of the "Western Telegraph." In 1829 he returned to Pennsylvania and settled in York, and there published the "York Gazette." In 1849 he was elected Sergeant-at-arms of the House of Representatives for the Thirty-First Congress, and held the same office through the four following Congressional terms. In 1861 he was private secretary to President

Buchanan. In 1864 he was elected a Representative from Pennsylvania to the Thirty-Ninth Congress.

CHARLES GOODYEAR was born in Schoharie County, New York, April 26, 1805. He graduated at Union College in 1824, and entered upon the practice of law in 1827. In 1839 he was elected to the New York Legislature, and in 1841 was appointed First Judge of Schoharie County. In 1845 he was elected a Representative to the Twenty-Ninth Congress, and twenty years after was elected to the Thirty-Ninth Congress. During the interval he devoted his attention to the business of banking. His successor in the Fortieth Congress is *John V. L. Pruyn.*

HENRY GRIDER was born in Kentucky, July 16, 1796. He was a private in the last war with England. He subsequently divided his attention between agriculture and law. In 1827 and 1831 he was elected to the Legislature of Kentucky, and in 1833 to the State Senate. As early as 1843 he was elected a Representative to Congress from Kentucky and held the position until 1847. He was re-elected to the Thirty-Seventh, Thirty-Eighth, and Thirty-Ninth Congresses. He died before the expiration of the last term for which he was elected.—417, 570.

JAMES W. GRIMES was born in Deering, New Hampshire, October 16, 1816. He graduated at Dartmouth College in 1836, and soon after removed to Iowa, where he was, in 1838, elected to the first Territorial Legislature. From 1854 to 1858 he was Governor of Iowa. In 1859 he was elected a Senator in Congress, and was in 1865 elected for a second term, which will end in 1871. In 1865 he received the degree of LL.D. from Iowa College. He was a delegate to the Peace Congress of 1861. For a number of years he has been Chairman of the Committee on Naval Affairs.

JOSIAH B. GRINNELL was born in New Haven, Vermont, December 22, 1821. He received a collegiate and theological education. In 1855, he went to Iowa, where he turned his attention to farming, and became the most extensive wool-grower in the State. He was four years a member of the Iowa Senate, and two years a special agent for the General Post Office. In 1862 he was elected a Representative from Iowa to the Thirty-Eighth Congress, and was re-elected to the Thirty-Ninth. He was succeeded by William Loughridge in the Fortieth Congress.—70, 153, 507, 572, 573, 574.

JOHN A. GRISWOLD was born in Rensselaer County, New York, in 1822. He has been engaged in the iron trade and business of banking. He was once Mayor of the City of Troy. In 1862 he was elected a Representative from New York to the Thirty-Eighth Congress, was re-elected in 1864, and again in 1866.—523.

JAMES GUTHRIE was born near Bardstown, Kentucky, in 1795. Having spent some years in trading with New Orleans as the owner of flatboats, he settled in Louisville as a lawyer, at the age of twenty-five. He was at one time shot by a political opponent, and was in consequence laid up for three years. He served nine years in the State Legislature and six years in the Kentucky Senate. He subsequently took an active part in the banking business, and was President of the Nashville and Louisville Railroad. He was President of the Kentucky Constitutional Convention of 1851. In 1853 he became Secretary of the Treasury under President Pierce. He was a delegate to the Chicago Convention of 1864. In 1865 he was elected United States Senator from Kentucky for the term ending in 1871.—46, 134, 160, 210, 214.

ROBERT S. HALE was born in Chelsea, Vermont, September 24, 1822, and graduated at the University of Vermont in 1842. He settled for the practice of law at Elizabethtown, New York. He subsequently held the position of Judge of Essex County, Regent of the University of New York, and Presidential Elector. In 1864 he was elected a Representative from New York to the Thirty-Ninth Congress, and was succeeded in the Fortieth Congress by Orange Ferris.—82, 372.

AARON HARDING was born in Greene County, Kentucky. He was admitted to the bar in 1833. He was elected to the Kentucky Legislature in 1840. In 1861 he was elected a Representative from Kentucky to the Thirty-Seventh Congress and was re-elected to the Thirty-Eighth and Thirty-Ninth Congresses. His successor in the Fortieth Congress is *J. Proctor Knott.*—361, 462.

ABNER C. HARDING was born in East Hampton, Connecticut, February 10, 1807. He practiced law in the State of New York, and subsequently in Illinois. He was for many years engaged extensively in farming and railroad management. In 1848 he was a member of the Illinois Constitutional Convention, and subsequently of the Legislature. In 1862 he enlisted as a private in the Eighty-Third Illinois Infantry, and became its Colonel. He was promoted to the rank of Brigadier General. In 1864 he was elected a Representative from Illinois to the Thirty-Ninth Congress, and was re-elected in 1866.—522.

BENJAMIN G. HARRIS was born in Maryland, December 13, 1806. He was for a time a student of Yale College, and afterwards studied at the Cambridge Law School. He returned to his native State and engaged in the practice of law and agriculture. He served for several years in the Maryland House of Delegates. In 1863, and again in 1865, he was elected a Representative to Congress from Maryland. In May, 1865, he was arrested and tried by court-martial for violating the Fifty-Sixth Article of War, and was declared guilty; but the President ordered the sentence of the court to be remitted in full. He was succeeded in the Fortieth Congress by *Frederick Stone.*

IRA HARRIS was born in Charleston, New York, May 31, 1802. He graduated at Union College in 1824, and soon after entered upon the practice of law in Albany, and for many years devoted attention exclusively to his profession. In 1844 he was elected to the New York Legislature, and served two terms. In 1846 he was a delegate to the State Constitutional Convention, and was the same year elected to the State Senate. In 1847 he was elected Judge of the Supreme Court, and held the office twelve years. In 1861 he was elected a Senator in Congress from New York for the term ending in 1867, when he was succeeded by Roscoe Conkling.

ROSWELL HART was born in Rochester, New York, in 1821. He graduated at Yale College in 1843, and was admitted to the bar in 1847, but entered immediately upon mercantile pursuits. In 1864 he was elected a Representative from New York to the Thirty-Ninth Congress. His successor in the Fortieth Congress is Lewis Selye.

ISAAC R. HAWKINS was born in Maury County, Tennessee, May 16, 1818. He was engaged in agricultural pursuits until twenty-two years of age, when he commenced the study of law. In 1843 he settled, for the practice of law, in Huntington, Tennessee, where he now resides. He served as a Lieutenant in the Mexican War. In 1860 he was elected to the Legislature of Tennessee. He was a delegate to the Peace Congress of 1861, and in the spring and summer of that year was actively engaged in making speeches throughout his State against secession. In September, 1862, he entered the army as Lieutenant-Colonel of the Seventh Tennessee Cavalry. In 1864 he was captured by the enemy at Union City, Tennessee, and was imprisoned at Mobile and Macon. He was one of the fifty officers placed by the rebels under fire of the Federal force off Charleston. Having been exchanged, he commanded the cavalry force in Western Kentucky until the close of the war. In August, 1865, he was elected a Representative from Tennessee to the Thirty-Ninth Congress, and was re-elected to the Fortieth Congress.

RUTHERFORD B. HAYES was born in Delaware, Ohio, October 4, 1822. He graduated at Kenyon College, and subsequently at the Cambridge Law School. He was City Solicitor for Cincinnati from 1858 to 1861. He went into the army at the opening of the war as Major of the Twenty-Third Ohio Volunteers, and reached the rank of Brigadier General. In 1864 he was elected a Representative from Ohio to the Thirty-Ninth Congress. He was, in 1866, re-elected to the Fortieth Congress, but having been elected Governor of Ohio in 1867, he resigned his seat in Congress, and was succeeded by Samuel F. Carey.

JAMES H. D. HENDERSON was born in Livingston County, Kentucky, July 23, 1810. In 1817 he removed with his parents to Missouri, and learned the printing business in Jefferson City. He subsequently published a weekly newspaper at Bowling Green, Missouri. At the age of twenty-five he entered the ministry of the Cumberland Presbyterian Church, and after preaching for a time in Missouri, he accepted the pastoral charge of a congregation in Pennsylvania. Having held this position eight years, he resigned in 1851, and soon after emigrated to Oregon. There he engaged in agricultural pursuits, but was active in preaching and lecturing against slavery, intemperance, gambling, and other popular vices. He was elected to the office of Superintendent of Common Schools for Oregon. In 1864 he was elected the Representative from Oregon to the Thitry-Ninth Congress. He was succeeded by Rufus Mallory.

JOHN B. HENDERSON was born in Virginia, November 16, 1826, and at ten years of age removed with his parents to Missouri. He taught school as a means of support while attaining an academical education. He studied law, and was admitted to the bar in 1848. He was subsequently twice elected to the Missouri Legislature. In 1856 he was a Democratic Presidential Elector, and was a delegate to the Charleston Convention of 1860. On the expulsion of Trusten Polk from the United States Senate, he was appointed to fill the vacancy. In 1863 he was elected for the full term, ending in 1869.—161, 377, 382, 386, 388, 461, 530, 531, 533, 534, 559.

THOMAS A. HENDRICKS was born in Muskingum County, Ohio, September 7, 1819. He was educated at South Hanover College. He studied law at Chambersburg, Pennsylvania, and settled in Indiana for the practice of his profession. In 1848 he served in the State Legislature, and was a prominent member of the Indiana Constitutional Convention of 1850. In 1851 he was elected a Representative in Congress from Indiana, and served two terms. In

1855 he was appointed Commissioner of the General Land Office, and held that office until his resignation in 1859. In 1860 he was the Democratic candidate for Governor of Indiana, and was defeated by Henry S. Lane. In 1863 he was elected United States Senator from Indiana, for the term ending in 1869.—28, 108, 136, 211, 218, 296, 306, 395, 432, 455, 459, 460, 491, 498, 531, 532, 533, 535, 548.

WILLIAM HIGBY was born in Essex County, New York, August 18, 1813. He graduated at the University of Vermont in 1840, and practiced law in New York until 1850, when he removed to California. Three years after he was elected District Attorney of Cavaleras County, and held the office until 1859. He was subsequently a member of the State Senate. In 1863 he was elected a Representative from California to the Thirty-Eighth Congress, and was successively re-elected to the Thirty-Ninth and Fortieth Congresses.—356, 357, 358, 575, 510.

RALPH HILL was born in Trumbull County, Ohio, October 12, 1827, and was left in early life entirely dependent upon his own exertions. After taking an academical course of study, he attended the New York State and National Law School at Ballston Spa, where he graduated to the degree of LL.B., in 1851. In the following year he settled in the practice of his profession at Columbus, Indiana. In 1864 he was elected a Representative from Indiana to the Thirty-Ninth Congress. His successor in the Fortieth Congress is Morton C. Hunter.—356.

ELIJAH HISE was born in Pennsylvania, and removed in early life to Lexington, Kentucky. Having studied law, he established himself in Russellville, Kentucky, for the practice of his profession. He served as member of the State Legislature and a Judge of the Superior Court of Kentucky. He was long regarded as one of the most eloquent and effective political speakers of Kentucky. In 1865 he was elected a Representative from Kentucky to the Thirty-Ninth Congress. In May, 1867, he was re-elected to the Fortieth Congress, and a few days after committed suicide, alleging the gloomy political prospects of the country as a reason for the act. His successor in the Fortieth Congress is Jacob S. Galladay.—511, 521.

PHINEAS W. HITCHCOCK was born in New Lebanon, New York, November 30, 1831. Having graduated at Williams College, Massachusetts, in 1855, he studied law, and emigrated to Nebraska Territory in 1857. In 1861 he was appointed by President Lincoln Marshal of the Territory, and held this office until his election as a Delegate from Nebraska to the Thirty-Ninth Congress.

JOHN HOGAN was born in Ireland, January 2, 1805, and came with his father to Baltimore, Maryland, in 1817. He was apprenticed to a shoemaker, and obtained the rudiments of education in the Asbury Sunday School. In 1826 he removed to Illinois, where he engaged in mercantile pursuits. In 1836 he was a member of the State Legislature, in 1838 Commissioner of the Board of Public Works, and in 1841 Register of the Land Office by appointment of President Harrison. He removed to St. Louis, and engaged in mercantile pursuits and banking. In 1857 he was appointed by President Buchanan Postmaster at St. Louis. In 1864 he was elected a Representative to Congress from Missouri, and was succeeded in the Fortieth Congress by William A. Pile.

E. D. HOLBROOK was born in Elyria, Ohio, in 1836. Having received a common-school education, he studied law, and emigrated to Idaho. In 1864 he was elected the Delegate from that Territory to the Thirty-Ninth Congress, and was re-elected in 1866.

SIDNEY T. HOLMES was born in Schaghticoke, Rensselaer County, New York, in 1815. He received an academical education, and after having spent five years in civil engineering, studied law, and entered upon the practice of his profession in 1841. In 1851 he was elected Judge and Surrogate for Madison County, and held the office until 1864, when he was elected a Representative from New York to the Thirty-Ninth Congress. His successor in the Fortieth Congress is John C. Churchill.

SAMUEL HOOPER was born in Marblehead, Massachusetts, February 3, 1808. Having received a commercial education, he established himself as merchant in Boston. He has long been a partner in the commercial house of William Appleton & Co. In 1851 he was elected to the Massachusetts House of Representatives, and in 1857 to the State Senate. In 1861 he was elected a Representative from Massachusetts to the Thirty-Seventh Congress, to fill the vacancy occasioned by the resignation of William Appleton. He has been re-elected to the Thirty-Eighth, Thirty-Ninth, and Fortieth Congresses.—30.

GILES W. HOTCHKISS is a member of the bar in Binghamton, New York. In 1862 he was elected a Representative from New York to the Thirty-Eighth Congress, and was re-elected in 1864. He was succeeded in the Fortieth Congress by William S. Lincoln.—523, 538.

JACOB M. HOWARD was born in Shaftsbury, Vermont, July 10, 1805, and graduated at Williams College in 1830. Having taught in an academy and studied law in Massachusetts, he removed to Michigan in 1832. In 1838 he was a member of the State Legislature, and in 1841 was elected a Representative in Congress from Michigan. He subsequently served for six years as Attorney General of the State. In 1862 he was elected to a vacancy in the United States Senate, and in 1865 he was re-elected for the term ending in 1871.—36, 196, 398, 423, 453, 455, 530.

TIMOTHY O. HOWE was born in Livermore, Maine, February 7, 1816 Having received an academical education at the Readfield Seminary, he studied law, and was admitted to the bar in 1839. He was elected to the Legislature of Maine in 1845, and in the same year removed to Green Bay, Wisconsin. Five years after he was elected a Circuit Judge, and held the office until his resignation in 1855. In 1861 he was elected a Senator in Congress from Wisconsin, and was re-elected in 1867.—421, 459.

ASAHEL W. HUBBARD was born in Haddam, Connecticut, January 18, 1819. In 1838 he removed to Indiana, and engaged in school-teaching. He entered upon the profession of law in 1841, and was in 1847 elected to the Indiana Legislature, in which he served three terms. He removed to Iowa in 1857, and was soon after elected Judge of the Fourth Judicial District of that State. In 1862 he was elected a Representative from Iowa to the Thirty-Eighth Congress, and was re-elected to the Thirty-Ninth and Fortieth Congresses.

CHESTER D. HUBBARD was born in Hamden, Connecticut, November 25, 1814. In the following year he was removed to Pennsylvania, and thence to

Wheeling, Virginia, in 1819. Having graduated at Wesleyan University, Connecticut, in 1840, he returned to Wheeling, and engaged actively in business pursuits. In 1852 he was elected to the lower House of the Virginia Legislature. He was a delegate to the Richmond Convention which passed the ordinance of secession, and opposed that movement with so much ardor that he was expelled from the Convention. He was a member of the Wheeling Convention which organized the restored government of Virginia, and after the formation of the new State of West Virginia, was elected to the State Senate. He was elected a Representative from West Virginia to the Thirty-Ninth Congress, and was re-elected to the Fortieth Congress.

DEMAS HUBBARD was born in Winfield, New York, January 17, 1806. Having received an academic education he gave his attention to farming and the practice of law. He was for many years a member and Chairman of the Board of Supervisors of Chenango County, and from 1838 to 1840 was a member of the New York Legislature. In 1864 he was elected a Representative from New York to the Thirty-Ninth Congress. His successor in the Fortieth Congress is William C. Fields.

JOHN H. HUBBARD was born in Salisbury, Connecticut, in 1805. He was brought up a farmer and received a common-school education. He was admitted to the bar in 1826. He was five years Prosecuting Attorney for Litchfield County, and two terms a member of the State Senate. In the spring of 1863 he was elected a Representative from Connecticut to the Thirty-Eighth Congress, and was re-elected in 1865. He was succeeded in the Fortieth Congress by *William H. Barnum*.—148.

EDWIN N. HUBBELL was born in Coxsackie, New York, August 13, 1813. Having received an academical education, he gave his attention to manufacturing and farming, and held for some time the office of County Supervisor. In 1864 he was elected a Representative from New York to the Thirty-Ninth Congress. He was succeeded in the Fortieth Congress by Thomas Cornell.

JAMES R. HUBBELL was born in Delaware County, Ohio, in 1824. Having received a common-school education, he studied and practiced the profession of law. He served four terms in the House of Representatives of Ohio, of which he was twice the Speaker. In 1856 he was a Presidential Elector. In 1864 he was elected a Representative from Ohio to the Thirty-Ninth Congress. He was succeeded in the Fortieth Congress by Cornelius S. Hamilton, deceased.

CALVIN T. HULBURD was born in Stockholm, New York, June 5, 1809. After having graduated at Middlebury College, Vermont, and studied law at Yale College, he engaged in agricultural pursuits. In 1842 he was elected to the Legislature of New York, and was twice re-elected. In 1862 he was elected a Representative from New York to the Thirty-Eighth Congress, and was re-elected to the Thirty-Ninth and Fortieth Congresses.

JAMES HUMPHREY was born in Fairfield, Connecticut, October 9, 1811, and in 1831 graduated at Amherst College, of which his father, Rev. Heman Humphrey, was President. After having been principal of an academy in Connecticut, he studied law, and commenced the practice of his profession in Louisville, Kentucky, where he remained only one year. In 1838 he removed to the

City of New York for the practice of the law. In 1859 he was elected a member of Congress, and served one term. After remaining in private life a few years, he was elected a member of the Thirty-Ninth Congress, but died before its close, on the 16th June, 1866.—570.

JAMES M. HUMPHREY was born in Erie County, New York, September 21, 1819. He received a common-school education and studied law. From 1857 to 1859 he was District Attorney at Buffalo. He was a member of the State Senate from 1862 to 1865, when he was elected a Representative from New York to the Thirty-Ninth Congress. He was re-elected to the Fortieth.

JOHN W. HUNTER, a banker of Brooklyn, New York, was elected a Representative from New York to the Thirty-Ninth Congress to fill the vacancy occasioned by the death of James Humphrey. He took his seat December 4, 1866. His successor in the Fortieth Congress is *William E. Robinson.*—515.

EBEN C. INGERSOLL was born in Oneida County, New York, December 12, 1831. He removed with his father to Illinois in 1843. Having received an academical education at Paducah, Kentucky, he studied law, and located in Peoria, Illinois, for the practice of his profession. In 1856 he was elected to the Illinois Legislature. He served as Colonel of Illinois Volunteers in the Civil War. On the death of Owen Lovejoy, March 25, 1864, he was elected a Representative from Illinois for the remainder of the Thirty-Eighth Congress, and was re-elected to the Thirty-Ninth and Fortieth Congresses.—521.

THOMAS A. JENCKES was born in Providence, Rhode Island, in 1818. Having graduated at Brown University in 1838, he entered upon the profession of law. In 1863 he was elected a Representative from Rhode Island to the Thirty-Eighth Congress, and was re-elected to the Thirty-Ninth and Fortieth Congresses.—31, 320, 332, 340, 554.

PHILIP JOHNSON was born in Warren County, New Jersey January 17, 1818, and removed to Pennsylvania in 1839. He was educated at Lafayette College, and having studied law, he was admitted to the bar in 1848. He was two years a member of the State Legislature, and was Chairman of the Democratic State Convention in 1857. In 1860 he was elected a Representative from Pennsylvania to the Thirty-Seventh Congress, and was subsequently twice re-elected. He died before the expiration of the term for which he was elected as a member of the Thirty-Ninth Congress.—90, 570.

REVERDY JOHNSON was born in Annapolis, Maryland, May 21, 1796. He was educated at St. John's College, in his native town, and studied law with his father. The first office which he held was that of State Attorney. In 1817 he removed to Baltimore for the practice of his profession, and was three years after appointed Chief Commissioner of Insolvent Debtors. In 1821 he was elected to the Senate of Maryland, and was re-elected for a second term. In 1845 he was elected a Senator in Congress from Maryland, but resigned in 1849 to accept the position of Attorney General, to which he had been appointed by President Taylor. Subsequently he devoted many years to the uninterrupted practice of his profession. He was a delegate to the Peace Congress of 1861, and was in in the following year elected a United States Senator from Maryland for the term ending in 1869.—24, 36, 96, 136, 163, 198, 203, 264, 270, 271, 384, 427, 454, 455, 461, 492, 528, 532, 533, 534, 547.

MORGAN JONES was born in New York City, February 26, 1832, and was educated at the school of St. James' Church. He adopted the business of a plumber, which he conducted in the City of New York. He served as a City Councilman for several years, and was subsequently elected a member of the Board of Aldermen, of which he was made President. In 1864 he was elected a member of the Thirty-Ninth Congress, and was succeeded in the Fortieth Congress by *John Fox*.

GEORGE W. JULIAN was born in Wayne County, Indiana, May 5, 1817. After spending three years as school-teacher, he studied law, and commenced the practice of the profession in 1840. In 1845 he was a member of the State Legislature. Having become an earnest advocate of anti-slavery principles, he attended the Buffalo Convention of 1848, which nominated Van Buren and Adams, and subsequently, as a candidate for Presidential Elector on their ticket made a laborious canvass of his district. In 1849 he was Representative in Congress from Indiana. In 1852 he was a candidate for Vice-President of the United States on the ticket with John P. Hale. In 1860 he was re-elected Representative in Congress, and has since been a member of the Thirty-Eighth, Thirty-Ninth, and Fortieth Congresses.—31, 74, 364, 516, 553, 554.

JOHN A. KASSON was born near Burlington, Vermont, January 11, 1822. Having graduated at the University of Vermont, he studied law in Massachusetts, and practiced the profession for a time in St. Louis, Missouri. In 1857 he removed to Iowa, and was appointed a Commissioner to report upon the condition of the Executive Departments of Iowa. In 1861 he was appointed Assistant Postmaster-General, but resigned the position in the following year, when he was elected a Representative to Congress from Iowa. He was re-elected in 1864 to the Thirty-Ninth Congress. His successor in the Fortieth Congress is Grenville M. Dodge.—72, 363, 525.

WILLIAM D. KELLEY was born in Philadelphia in the spring of 1814. He was left an orphan when very young, dependent for support and education wholly upon his own resources. Having been errand-boy in a book-store, and copy-reader in a printing-office, in his fourteenth year he apprenticed himself in a jewelry establishment. Having learned his trade, he removed to Boston, where he remained four years working at his trade, and giving, meanwhile, considerable time to reading and study. Returning to Philadelphia, he studied law, and was admitted to the bar in 1841. From 1846 for a period of ten years he held the office of Judge of the Court of Common Pleas of Philadelphia. In 1856, on the repeal of the Missouri Compromise, he left the Democratic party, and became the Republican candidate for Congress, but was defeated. In 1860 he was a delegate to the Chicago Republican Convention, and was, in the fall of the same year, elected a Representative from Pennsylvania to the Thirty-Seventh Congress, and was re-elected to the Thirty-Eighth, Thirty-Ninth, and Fortieth Congresses.—51, 58, 79, 348, 349, 438, 526.

JOHN R. KELSO was born in Franklin County, Ohio, March 23, 1831. At the age of nine years he removed with his parents to North-western Missouri, then a wilderness. After surmounting great obstacles he succeeded in obtaining an education, and graduated at Pleasant Ridge College in 1858. He soon after became principal of an academy at Buffalo, Missouri. On the breaking out of the rebellion he was the first in his county to volunteer in defense of the Union, and immediately took the field as captain of a company of daring and enterprising men. With his company he was detailed to hunt the bushwhackers, who, from their hiding-places, were committing the most atrocious outrages upon the loyal people. His name became a terror to the rebels and guerillas of the Southwest. He took part in over sixty fierce conflicts, and in personal encounter killed twenty-six armed rebels with his own hand. At the close of his service in the war he was elected a Representative from Missouri to the Thirty-Ninth Congress. He declined re-nomination. and resumed his profession of teaching in Springfield, Missouri. His successor in the Fortieth Congress is Joseph J. Gravelly.

MICHAEL C. KERR was born in Titusville, Pennsylvania, March 15, 1827. He was left an orphan at the age of twelve years, and through his own exertions obtained an academical education. He taught school for a time, and, in 1851, graduated in the Law Department of the University of Louisville, and soon after located in New Albany, Indiana. In 1856 he was elected to the Legislature of Indiana, and served two terms. In 1862 he was elected reporter of the decisions of the Supreme Court, and held the office two years, publishing five volumes of reports. In 1864 he was elected a Representative from Indiana to the Thirty-Ninth Congress, and was re-elected to the Fortieth Congress.—147, 236, 362, 510.

JOHN H. KETCHAM was born in Dover, New York, December 21, 1831. Having received an academical education, he devoted his attention to agricultural pursuits. In 1856 and 1857 he was a member of the New York House of Representatives, and of the State Senate in 1860 and 1861. He entered the military service in 1862 as Colonel of the One Hundred and Fiftieth New York Regiment, and became a Brigadier General by brevet. He resigned his position in the army in March, 1865, having been elected a Representative from New York to the Thirty-Ninth Congress. He was re-elected to the Fortieth Congress.—31.

SAMUEL J. KIRKWOOD was born in Hartford County, Maryland, December 20, 1813, and received an academical education in Washington. Having removed to Ohio he studied law, and was admitted to the bar in 1843. He was four years Prosecuting Attorney for Richland County, and was a member of the Ohio Constitutional Convention in 1850. Having removed to Iowa, he was elected to the State Senate in 1856. He was Governor of Iowa from 1860 to 1864, and, in January, 1866, he was elected a United States Senator from Iowa for the unexpired term of James Harlan, ending in 1867, at which date he was succeeded by his predecessor, who was re-elected.—487.

WILLIAM H. KOONTZ, a lawyer by profession, was elected a Representative from Pennsylvania to the Thirty-Ninth Congress. He successfully contested the seat taken by Alexander H. Coffroth, and was admitted near the close of the first session. He was, in 1866, re-elected to the Fortieth Congress.—508.

ANDREW J. KUYKENDALL was born in Gallatin County, Illinois, March 3, 1815, and became a lawyer. From 1842 to 1846 he was a member of the Illinois House of Representatives, and was, from 1850 to 1852, a member of the State Senate. He was Major of the Thirty-First Illinois Infantry, but resigned on account of ill health in the early part of the war. In 1864 he was elected a Representative to Congress from Illinois, and was succeeded in the Fortieth Congress by Green B. Raum.

ADDISON H. LAFLIN was born in Lee, Massachusetts, October 24, 1823. He graduated at Williams College in 1843. He afterward settled in Herkimer County, New York, and became engaged extensively in the manufacture of paper. In 1857 he was elected State Senator. In 1864 he was elected a Representative to the Thirty-Ninth Congress, and was re-elected in 1866.

HENRY S. LANE was born in Montgomery County, Kentucky, February 24, 1811. After having obtained an academical education, he studied law, and removed to Indiana, where he engaged in the practice of his profession. In 1837 he was elected to the Indiana Legislature. In 1840 he was elected a Representative in Congress from Indiana. He served under General Taylor in the Mexican War as Lieutenant-Colonel of Volunteers. He was President of the first Republican National Convention which met in Philadelphia, July 4, 1856. In 1861 he was elected Governor of Indiana, but resigned the office two days after his inauguration to accept the position of Senator in Congress, to which he was elected for the term ending in 1867. He was succeeded by Oliver P. Morton.—213, 381, 383, 499, 532.

JAMES H. LANE was born in Lawrenceburg, Indiana, June 22, 1814. He served as a soldier through the Mexican War, and soon after his return in 1849 was elected Lieutenant-Governor of Indiana. He was an active Democratic politician, and as such was elected a Representative in Congress from Indiana in 1853. Soon after the close of his Congressional term, he went to Kansas, where he actively aided in the work of erecting a Free-State Government. He was President of the Topeka and the Leavenworth Constitutional Conventions, and was elected by the people Major General of the Free-State Troops. On the admission of Kansas into the Union, he was elected a Senator in Congress from that State. Soon after the breaking out of the Rebellion, he was appointed by President Lincoln a Brigadier General of Volunteers. He was a member of the Baltimore Convention of 1864. In 1865 he was re-elected by the Legislature of Kansas a Senator in Congress. On the 1st of July, 1866, while at Fort Leavenworth on leave of absence from the Senate on account of ill-health, he committed suicide.—171, 201, 279, 284, 285, 457, 569.

GEORGE R. LATHAM was born in Prince William County, Virginia, March 9, 1832. He engaged in teaching school, and while in that employment studied law, and was admitted to the bar in 1859. During the Presidential Campaign of 1860, he edited a paper in Grafton, Virginia. At the breaking out of the Rebellion, he entered the army as Captain, and became Colonel of the Second Virginia Volunteers. In 1864 he was elected a Representative from West Virginia to the Thirty-Ninth Congress, and was succeeded in the Fortieth Congress by Bethuel M. Kitchen.

GEORGE V. LAWRENCE, whose father, Joseph Lawrence, was a member of Congress, was born in Washington County, Pennsylvania, in 1818. He received a liberal education at Washington College, and engaged in agricultural pursuits. He was in 1844 elected a member of the Pennsylvania House of Representatives, and was three times re-elected. He served five terms in the State Senate, of which, during his last term of service, he was the Presiding Officer,

In 1864 he was elected a Representative from Pennsylvania to the Thirty-Ninth Congress, and was re-elected in 1866.

WILLIAM LAWRENCE was born in Mount Pleasant, Ohio, June 26, 1819. He graduated at Franklin College, Ohio, in 1838, and subsequently taught school in McConnellsville. In 1840 he graduated in the Law Department of Cincinnati College. In 1841 he located in Bellefontaine, Ohio, for the practice of law. In 1842 he was appointed Commissioner of Bankrupts for Logan County. In 1845 he was elected Prosecuting Attorney, and in the same year became proprietor of the "Logan Gazette," of which he was two years the editor. In 1846 he was elected a Representative in the Legislature, and was re-elected in the following year. In 1849 and 1850 he was a member of the Ohio Senate, and again in 1854, having in the interval held the office of Reporter for the Supreme Court. He was the originator of many legislative acts of great importance to the State, among the rest one relating to land titles, known as "Lawrence's Law," and the *Ohio Free Banking Law*, similar in some respects to the existing National Banking Law. In 1854 he was one of the signers to a call for a State Convention in opposition to the "Kansas-Nebraska Bill." In 1856 he was elected a Judge of the Court of Common Pleas, and in 1861 was re-elected for a term of five years. In 1862 he had command as Colonel of the Eighty-Fourth Regiment of Ohio Volunteers for three months. In September, 1863, President Lincoln gave him the commission of Judge of the U. S. District Court of Florida, which he declined. In 1864 he was elected a Representative from Ohio to the Thirty-Ninth Congress, and in 1866 he was re-elected.—343, 345, 520.

FRANCIS C. LEBLOND was born in Ohio, and became a lawyer. In 1851 and in 1853 he was elected to the State Legislature and served as Speaker. In 1862 he was elected a Representative from Ohio to the Thirty-Eighth Congress, and was re-elected in 1864. His successor in the Fortieth Congress is *William Mungen.*—243, 306, 519, 538, 547.

JOHN W. LEFTWICH was born in Bedford County, Virginia, September 7, 1826. He removed with his parents to Tennessee in 1834, and was occupied in farm work in summer, and attending school in winter, until twenty years of age. He served as a private in the Mexican War, and on his return attended the Jefferson Medical College of Philadelphia, where he graduated in 1850. He practiced medicine in Middle Tennessee two years, and then removed to Memphis, where he was occupied with mercantile pursuits until the breaking out of the war. Being loyal to the Union, he found it necessary after the battle of Fort Donaldson to cross the Federal lines. After the occupation of Memphis by the Federal forces in June, 1862, he returned to find that his personal property had been confiscated by the rebels. He resumed business, however, and was elected President of the Memphis Chamber of Commerce on its reorganization. He was elected a Representative from Tennessee to the Thirty-Ninth Congress, to which, with his colleagues, he was admitted in July, 1866. He was nominated for re-election by the "Conservative Party," and was defeated by David A. Nunn.

BENJAMIN F. LOAN was born in Hardinsburg, Kentucky, in 1819. In 1838 he removed to Missouri and engaged in the practice of law. At the breaking out of the rebellion he entered the army, and was appointed Brigadier General. In 1862 he was elected a Representative from Missouri to the Thirty-Eighth Congress, and was re-elected to the Thirty-Ninth and Fortieth Congresses.

JOHN W. LONGYEAR was born in Shandaken, Ulster County, New York, October 22, 1820. Having acquired an academical education, he removed to Michigan in 1844. He studied law, and was admitted to the bar in 1846. In 1862 he was elected a Representative from Michigan to the Thirty-Eighth Congress, and was re-elected in 1864. His successor in the Fortieth Congress is Austin Blair.—447.

JOHN LYNCH was born in Portland, Maine, February 15, 1825. After receiving an academical education he entered upon mercantile pursuits in his native city. After serving two years in the State Legislature he was, in 1864, elected a Representative from Maine to the Thirty-Ninth Congress, and was re-elected in 1866.

SAMUEL S. MARSHALL was born in Illinois, and was educated at Cumberland College, Kentucky. He devoted himself to the practice of law in Illinois, and was elected to the State Legislature in 1846. He served two years as State Attorney, and, in 1851, was elected a Judge of the Circuit Court, and held the office until 1854, when he was elected a Representative from Illinois to the Thirty-Fourth Congress and was re-elected in 1856. He was a delegate to the Chicago Democratic Convention of 1864, and was the same year elected a Representative to the Thirty-Ninth Congress. He was re-elected in 1866.—148, 352.

GILMAN MARSTON was born in Orford, New Hampshire. In 1837 he graduated at Dartmouth College, and in 1840 at the Dane Law School. He commenced the practice of law in the following year. In 1845 he was elected to the New Hampshire Legislature, and served four years. In 1859 he was elected a Representative from New Hampshire to the Thirty-Sixth Congress, and was re-elected in 1861. In June, 1861, he was appointed Colonel of the Second Regiment of New Hampshire Volunteers, and in 1863 was promoted to the rank of Brigadier General. He participated in many battles, and on the fall of Richmond retired from the army. Early in 1865 he was re-elected a Representative in Congress from New Hampshire. His successor in the Fortieth Congress is Jacob H. Ela.—31.

JAMES M. MARVIN was born in Ballston, New York, February 27, 1809. He spent his boyhood on a farm, and received an academical education. When not in public life he has been occupied in managing a large estate. In 1846 he was elected to the Legislature of New York, and subsequently held, for three terms, the office of County Supervisor. In 1862 he was elected a Representative from New York to the Thirty-Eighth Congress, and was re-elected to the Thirty-Ninth and Fortieth Congresses.

HORACE MAYNARD was born in Westborough, Massachusetts, August 30, 1814. He graduated at Amherst College in 1838. Soon after, he removed to Tennessee, and was appointed Professor of Mathematics in the University of East Tennessee. While holding this position he studied law, and was admitted to the bar in 1844. He was a Presidential Elector in 1852, and in 1856 was elected a Representative from Tennessee to the Thirty-Fifth Congress, and was twice re-elected. He was in Washington as a member of the Thirty-Seventh Congress when the rebels took possession of Tennessee. His property was confiscated, and his family was driven from their home in East Tennessee. He was a delegate to the Baltimore Republican Convention of 1864, and was the same year re-elected a Representative from Tennessee to the Thirty-Ninth Congress, and was admitted to his seat in July, 1866. He was re-elected to the Fortieth Congress.—17, 424, 478, 480, 506, 527.

JOSEPH W. McCLURG was born in St. Louis County, Missouri, February 22, 1818, and was educated at Miami University, Ohio. He subsequently spent two years as a teacher in Louisiana and Mississippi. In 1841 he went to Texas, where he was admitted to the bar, and became Clerk of a Circuit Court. In 1844 he settled in Missouri as a merchant. At the outbreak of the civil war he suffered severe losses at the hands of rebels, and abandoning his business he served for a time as Colonel of Cavalry. He was a member of the Missouri State Convention of 1862, and was in that year elected a Representative from Missouri to the Thirty-Eighth Congress, and was re-elected in 1864 and 1866.

HIRAM McCULLOUGH was born in Cecil County, Maryland, September 20, 1813. He was educated at the Elkton Academy, studied law, and was admitted to the bar in 1838. From 1845 to 1851 he was a member of the Maryland Senate. In 1852 he was appointed by the Legislature one of the codifiers of the laws of Maryland, and aided in making the present code of that State. In 1864 he was elected a Representative from Maryland to the Thirty-Ninth Congress, and was re-elected in 1866.

JAMES A. McDOUGALL was born at Bethlehem, New York, November 19, 1817, and was educated at the Albany Grammar School. He assisted in the survey of the first railroad ever built in this country. In 1837 he removed to Illinois and engaged in the practice of law. In 1842 he was chosen Attorney General of Illinois, and two years after was re-elected. In 1849 he originated and accompanied an exploring expedition to the far West. He soon after emigrated to California, and in 1850 was elected Attorney General of that State. From 1853 to 1855 he served as a Representative in Congress from California. In 1861 he was elected United States Senator for California for the term ending with the expiration of the Thirty-Ninth Congress. He died in Albany, New York, in the summer of 1867.—136, 137, 163, 277, 287, 432, 461, 533, 535.

WALTER D. McINDOE was born in Scotland, March 30, 1819. He emigrated to New York City in his fifteenth year, and was a clerk in that city, and afterwards in Charleston and St. Louis. He subsequently settled in Wisconsin, and engaged in the lumber trade. In 1850 he was a member of the Wisconsin Legislature, and was twice re-elected. In 1856, and in 1860, he was a Presidential Elector. In 1862 he was elected a Representative from Wisconsin to fill a vacancy in the Thirty-Seventh Congress, and was re-elected to the Thirty-Eighth and Thirty-Ninth Congresses. His successor in the Fortieth Congress is Cadwalader C. Washburn.

SAMUEL McKEE was born in Montgomery County, Kentucky, November 4, 1833. In 1858 he graduated at the Miami University, Ohio, and afterwards at the Cincinnati Law School in 1858. He subsequently practiced law until 1862, when he entered the Union army as Captain of the Fourteenth Kentucky Cavalry. He was thirteen months a prisoner in Libby Prison. In 1865 he was elected a Representative from Kentucky to the Thirty-Ninth Congress.—152, 361, 441.

DONALD McRUER was born in Maine in 1826. He received an academical education, and engaged in mercantile pursuits. Removing to California, he settled in San Francisco. He held for some time the office of Harbor Commissioner for that State. In 1864 he was elected a Representative from California to the Thirty-Ninth Congress. He was succeeded by *Samuel B. Axtell* in the Fortieth Congress.

ULYSSES MERCUR was born in Towanda, Pennsylvania, August 12, 1818. He graduated at Jefferson College, in 1842, and was admitted to the bar in the following year. In 1861 he was elected President Judge of the Thirteenth Judicial District of Pennsylvania, for a term of ten years, but resigned in 1864 when he was elected a Representative from Pennsylvania to the Thirty-Ninth Congress. In 1866 he was re-elected to the Fortieth Congress.

GEORGE F. MILLER was born in Chilisquaque, Northumberland County, Pennsylvania, September 5, 1809. Having obtained an academical education, he studied law, and was admitted to the bar in 1833. He was for several years Secretary of the Lewisburg University. He took an active interest in local politics, but frequently declined nominations for County and State offices. In 1864 he was elected a Representative from Pennsylvania to the Thirty-Ninth Congress, and was re-elected in 1866.—443, 510.

JAMES K. MOORHEAD was born in Pennsylvania, in 1806. He spent his youth on a farm and as an apprentice to a tanner. He was a contractor for building the Susquehanna branch of the Pennsylvania Canal, on which he originated a passenger packet line. In 1836 he removed to Pittsburg, where he became President of a company for the improvement of the navigation of the Monongahela, and subsequently was President of several telegraph companies. In 1859 he was re-elected a Representative to the Thirty-Sixth Congress from Pennsylvania, and has been re-elected to every succeeding Congress, including the Fortieth.—31.

EDWIN D. MORGAN was born in Washington, Massachusetts, February 8, 1811. At the age of seventeen he became a clerk, and three years later a partner in a wholesale grocery house in Hartford, Connecticut. In 1836 he settled in New York City, and embarked extensively in mercantile pursuits. In 1849 he was chosen an Alderman of the city, and soon after was elected a member of the State Senate, in which he served two terms. Since 1856 he has been Chairman of the National Republican Committee. In 1858 he was elected Governor of New York, and re-elected in 1860. During his administration, 223,000 troops were sent into the field from New York. Governor Morgan was appointed by President Lincoln a Major General of Volunteers. In 1863 he was elected United States Senator from New York for the term ending in 1869.

JUSTIN S MORRILL was born in Strafford, Vermont, April 14, 1810. He received an academical education, and subsequently gave his attention to mercantile and agricultural pursuits. In 1854 he was elected a Representative from Vermont to the Thirty-Fourth Congress, and was re-elected to the Thiry-Fifth, Thirty-Sixth, Thirty-Seventh, Thirty-Eighth and Thirty-Ninth Congresses. In 1867 he became a United States Senator from Vermont for the term ending in 1873, succeeding Luke P. Poland, who became the successor of Mr. Morrill as a Representative in the Fortieth Congress.—17, 19, 29, 555.

LOT M. MORRILL was born at Belgrade, Maine, in 1815. He studied at Waterville College, and was admitted to the bar in 1839. In 1854 he was a member of the Maine Legislature, and in 1856 he was President of the State Senate. In 1858 he was elected Governor of Maine, and was twice re-elected. In 1861 he was elected United States Senator from Maine for the unexpired term of Vice-President Hamlin. In 1863 he was re-elected to the Senate for the term ending in 1869.—28, 204, 205, 207, 408, 484, 485, 489, 530.

DANIEL MORRIS was born in Seneca County, New York, January 4, 1812. He was bred a farmer, taught school for a time, and finally became a lawyer. Having been District Attorney for Yates County, and member of the State Legislature, he was in 1862 elected a Representative from New York to the Thirty-Eighth Congress, and in 1864 was re-elected. His successor in the Fortieth Congress is William H. Kelsey.

SAMUEL W. MOULTON was born in Wareham, Massachusetts, January 20, 1822. Having acquired a common-school education, at the age of twenty he emigrated to the West, and spent a year at Covington, Kentucky, where he commenced the study of law. He subsequently went to Mississippi, where he taught school, and continued the study of law. In 1845 he settled in Illinois, and soon after commenced the practice of law. In 1852 he was elected to the Legislature of Illinois, and was continuously re-elected until 1859. He was the author of the Free-School System of Illinois. He held the position of Chairman of the Board of Education for a number of years. He was a candidate for Presidential Elector on the Democratic ticket in 1856. On the breaking out of the Rebellion he joined the Republican party, and was in 1863 elected President of the Union League of Illinois. In 1864 he was elected Representative from the State at large to the Thirty-Ninth Congress, and was succeeded by John A. Logan in the Fortieth Congress.—149.

LEONARD MYERS was born in Attleborough, Pennsylvania, November 13, 1827. Having entered the profession of law, and settled in Philadelphia, he became Solicitor for two municipal districts in that city. He digested the ordinances for the consolidation of the city, and has translated several works from the French. In 1862 he was elected a member of the Thirty-Eighth Congress, and was re-elected to the Thirty-Ninth and Fortieth Congresses.

JAMES W. NESMITH was born in Washington County, Maine, July 23, 1820. When quite young, he removed to New Hampshire, emigrated to Ohio in 1838, subsequently spent some time in Missouri, and finally settled in Oregon in 1843. In 1853 he was appointed United States Marshal for Oregon. In 1857 he was appointed Superintendent of Indian Affairs for Oregon and Washington Territories. In 1861 he became United States Senator from Oregon for the term ending in 1867, when he was succeeded by Henry W. Corbett.

WILLIAM A. NEWELL is a native of Ohio, and a graduate of Rutger's College. He studied medicine, and took up his residence in Allentown, New Jersey. He was a member of Congress from that State from 1847 to 1851. In 1856 he was elected Governor of New Jersey, and held the office till 1860. He was again elected a Representative to Congress in 1864, and was succeeded in the Fortieth Congress by *Charles Haight.*

WILLIAM E. NIBLACK was born in Dubois County, Indiana, May 19,

1822, and spent his early life on a farm. He attended the Indiana University at intervals during three years, and afterwards devoted some time to surveying and civil engineering. In 1845 he commenced the practice of law, and in 1849 he was elected a Representative in the State Legislature. In the following year he was elected to the State Senate. In January, 1854, he was appointed Judge of the Third Judicial Circuit, to fill a vacancy, and was, in the following fall, elected to the office for the term of six years. In 1857 he was elected a Representative from Indiana to the Thirty-Fifth Congress, and was re-elected in 1859. After the close of the Thirty-Sixth Congress he served one term in the State Legislature. In 1864 he was again elected a Representative in Congress from Indiana, and was re-elected to the Fortieth Congress.—526.

JOHN A. NICHOLSON was born in Laurel, Delaware, November 17, 1827. Having graduated at Dickinson College, Pennsylvania, he studied law, and settled in Dover, Delaware, where he was admitted to the bar in 1850. In 1865 he entered Congress as a Representative from Delaware, and was re-elected to the Fortieth Congress.—361.

THOMAS E. NOELL was born in Perryville, Missouri, April 3, 1839. He was admitted to the bar at nineteen years of age, and practiced until 1861, when he was appointed a Military Commissioner for the arrest of disloyal persons. He subsequently went into the ranks of the State militia, and reached the rank of Major. In 1862 he was appointed a Captain in the Nineteenth Regiment of Regular United States Infantry. In 1864 he was elected a Representative from Missouri to the Thirty-Ninth Congress, and was re-elected in 1866.

DANIEL S. NORTON was born in Mount Vernon, Ohio, April 12, 1829. After being educated at Kenyon College, he served in the Mexican War. He subsequently went to California, and thence to Nicaragua, where he spent a year. Returning to Ohio, he studied law, and was admitted to the bar in 1852. He emigrated to Minnesota in 1855, and was, two years after, elected to the State Senate, to which he was three times re-elected. In 1865 he was elected a Senator in Congress from Minnesota for the term ending in 1871.

JAMES W. NYE was born in Madison County, New York, June 10, 1815, and entered the profession of law. In 1861 he was appointed by President Lincoln Governor of Nevada Territory. He held this office until the admission of Nevada into the Union, when he was elected a Senator from the new State for the term ending in 1871.—425, 457.

CHARLES O'NEILL was born in Philadelphia, March 21, 1821. Having graduated at Dickinson College, and studied law, he was admitted to the bar in 1843. He served five years in the House of Representatives and Senate of Pennsylvania. In 1862 he was elected a Representative to the Thirty-Eighth Congress. In 1865 he entered upon his second term in Congress, and was re-elected to the Fortieth Congress.

GODLOVE S. ORTH was born near Lebanon, Pennsylvania, April 22, 1817. He was educated at the Pennsylvania College, Gettysburg. In 1839 he was admitted to the bar, and removed to Indiana, locating in Lafayette. In 1843 he was elected to the Indiana Senate, and served six years. A part of the time he was President of that body. In 1848 he was a Whig candidate for Presidential Elector. In 1861 he was a member of the "Peace Congress." In 1862, Indiana being threatened with a sudden invasion, the Governor made a call for volunteers to meet the emergency. Mr. Orth immediately responded with two hundred men, who elected him their Captain. He was placed in command of the U. S. Ram "Horner," which cruised the Ohio river, and did much to restore and maintain quiet along its shores. In 1862 he was elected a Representative from Indiana to the Thirty-Eighth Congress, and was re-elected to the Thirty-Ninth and Fortieth Congresses.—336.

HALBERT E. PAINE was born at Chardon, Ohio, February 4, 1826. Having graduated at the Western Reserve College in 1845, he studied law, and located in Cleveland. In 1857 he removed to Milwaukee, Wisconsin. He entered the army in 1861 as Colonel of the Fourth Wisconsin Regiment, and soon rose to the rank of Brigadier General. He lost a leg in June, 1863, at the last assault on Port Hudson. Resigning his commission in 1865, he was elected a Representative to the Thirty-Ninth Congress from Wisconsin, and was re-elected to the Fortieth Congress.—504, 506.

DAVID T. PATTERSON was born at Cedar Creek, Green County, Tennessee, February 28, 1819. He was educated at Meadow Creek Academy and Greenville College. He followed for some time the business of a paper-maker, but gave attention to the study of law, and was admitted to the bar in 1841, and practiced in Greenville. Here he married a daughter of Andrew Johnson. In 1854 he was elected Judge of the First Judicial Circuit of Tennessee. In May, 1865, he was elected a United States Senator from Tennessee for the term ending in 1869. After a protracted consideration and discussion of his case, he was sworn in near the close of the first session of the Thirty-Ninth Congress.—478, 482.

JAMES W. PATTERSON was born in Hanniker, New Hampshire, July 2, 1823. He graduated at Dartmouth College in 1848. He was Professor of Mathematics in Dartmouth College from 1854 to 1859, and was then transferred to the chair of Astronomy and Meteorology. He was four years Secretary of the Board of Education of New Hampshire, and in 1862 he was a member of the State Legislature. He was elected a Representative from New Hampshire to the Thirty-Eighth and Thirty-Ninth Congresses. At the expiration of the latter Congress he became United States Senator from Vermont for the term ending in 1873.

SIDNEY PERHAM was born in Woodstock, Maine, March 27, 1819. Until his thirty-fourth year he was a farmer and a teacher. In 1852 he was elected a member of the State Board of Agriculture, and served two years. In 1855 he was a member of the Maine Legislature, and officiated as Speaker. In 1856 he was a Presidential Elector. In 1858 he was elected Clerk of a County Court, which position he held until 1862, when he was elected a Representative from Maine to the Thirty-Eighth Congress. He was re-elected to the Thirty-Ninth and Fortieth Congresses.

CHARLES E. PHELPS was born in Guilford, Vermont, May 1, 1833. Having graduated at Princeton College in 1853, he came to the Maryland bar in 1855. In 1862 he was made Lieutenant-Colonel of the Seventh Maryland Volunteers, and was discharged, on account of wounds, in 1864. He was elected a Representative from Maryland to the Thirty-Ninth Congress, and was re-elected in 1866.—156.

FREDERICK A. PIKE was born in Calais, Maine, where he now resides. He adopted the profession of law, and served some time as Attorney for the County. He was several years a member, and during one term Speaker, of the Maine House of Representatives. In 1862 he was elected a Representative from Maine to the Thirty-Seventh Congress, and was re-elected to the Thirty-Eighth, Thirty-Ninth, and Fortieth Congresses.—348, 503, 504, 519, 553.

TOBIAS A. PLANTS was born in Beaver County, Pennsylvania, March 17, 1811. After teaching school for several years, he studied law, and was admitted to the bar in 1841. Having settled in Ohio, he served in the State Legislature from 1858 to 1861. In 1864 he was elected a Representative from Ohio to the Thirty-Ninth Congress, and was re-elected in 1866.—509.

LUKE P. POLAND was born in Westford, Vermont, November 1, 1815. Having received an academical education, he studied law, and was admitted to the bar in 1836. In 1839 and 1840 he was Register of Probate for Lamoille County. In 1843 he was a member of the State Constitutional Convention, and in the following year was elected Prosecuting Attorney for his County. In 1848 he was elected by the Legislature one of the Judges of the Supreme Court of Vermont. This position he continued to hold by annual elections until November, 1865, when he was appointed to fill the vacancy in the United States Senate occasioned by the death of Judge Collamer. His term of service in the Senate closing March 4, 1867, he took his seat as a Representative from Vermont in the Fortieth Congress.—28, 459.

SAMUEL C. POMEROY was born in Southampton, Massachusetts, January 3, 1816. He entered Amherst College in 1836, and in 1838 went to Monroe County, New York, where he resided four years. He returned to his native town in 1842, and having espoused the Anti-Slavery cause, he labored zealously to advance its principles. Annually for eight years he ran on the Anti-Slavery ticket for the Massachusetts Legislature, without success, until 1852, when he was elected over both Whigs and Democrats. In 1854 he aided in organizing the New England Emigrant Aid Society, and was its financial agent, and the same year he conducted a colony to Kansas. He was a member of the Territorial Defense Committee, and was active in his efforts to protect the settlers from the border ruffians. During the famine in Kansas, he was Chairman of the Relief Committee. He was a delegate to the Republican National Conventions of 1856 and 1860. In 1861 he was elected a Senator in Congress from Kansas, and was re-elected in 1867 for the term ending in 1873.—404, 487, 495.

THEODORE M. POMEROY was born in Cayuga, New York, December 31, 1824. He graduated at Hamilton College, and adopted the profession of law. From 1850 to 1856 he was District Attorney for his native county, and in 1857 was a member of the New York Legislature. In 1860 he was elected a Representative from New York to the Thirty-Seventh Congress, and has been re-electd to the Thirty-Eighth, Thirty-Ninth, and Fortieth Congresses.—30.

HIRAM PRICE was born in Washington County, Pennsylvania, January 10, 1814. Removing to Iowa, he settled in the City of Davenport, and was made

President of the State Bank of Iowa. In 1862 he was elected a Representative from Iowa to the Thirty-Eighth Congress, and was re-elected to the Thirty-Ninth and Fortieth Congresses.—30.

WILLIAM RADFORD was born in Poughkeepsie, New York, June 24, 1814. He settled in New York City in 1829, and engaged in mercantile pursuits. In 1862 he was elected a Representative from New York to the Thirty-Eighth Congress, and was re-elected in 1864. He was succeeded in the Fortieth Congress by William H. Robertson.

ALEXANDER RAMSAY was born near Harrisburg, Pennsylvania, September 8, 1815. In 1841 he was elected Clerk of the Pennsylvania House of Representatives. From 1843 to 1847 he was a Representative in Congress from Pennsylvania. In 1849 he was appointed, by President Taylor, the first Territorial Governor of Minnesota, and held the office until 1853. During his term of office, he negotiated some important Indian treaties. From 1858 to 1862 he held the office of Governor of the State of Minnesota. In 1863 he was elected a United States Senator from Minnesota for the term ending in 1869.

SAMUEL J. RANDALL was born in Philadelphia, in 1828. He was for many years engaged in mercantile pursuits. He served four years in the Philadelphia City Council and one term in the State Senate. In 1862 he was elected a Representative to the Thirty-Eighth Congress, and was re-elected to the Thirty-Ninth and Fortieth Congresses.—79, 444.

WILLIAM H. RANDALL was born in Kentucky. He studied law, and was admitted to the bar in 1835. Having held the office of Clerk of the Circuit Court for a number of years, he was, in 1862, elected a Representative to Congress from Kentucky, and was re-elected in 1864. His successor in the Fortieth Congress is *George M. Adams.*

HENRY J. RAYMOND was born in Lima, New York, January 24, 1820. He was brought up on a farm, and became teacher in a district school when sixteen years of age. In 1840 he graduated at the University of Vermont, and soon after went to New York City, where, in 1841, he became managing editor of the "New York Tribune." He subsequently became the leading editor of the "New York Courier and Enquirer." In 1849 he was elected to the New York Legislature, and having been re-elected, was made Speaker of the House. In 1851 he established the "New York Times." He was subsequently elected Lieutenant-Governor of New York, and was again a member of the General Assembly. In 1864 he was elected a Representative from New York to the Thirty-Ninth Congress, and was succeeded in the Fortieth Congress by Thomas E. Stewart.—31, 155, 234, 314, 317, 328, 364, 370, 372, 439, 440, 512, 524, 525, 564.

ALEXANDER H. RICE was born in Newton, Massachusetts, in August, 1818. He graduated at Union College in 1844, and subsequently engaged in the manufacture of paper. In 1853 he was elected a member and President of the City Council of Boston. In 1856 and 1857 he was Mayor of Boston. In 1858 he was elected a Representative from Massachusetts to the Thirty-Sixth Congress, and was re-elected to the Thirty-Seventh, Thirty-Eighth, and Thirty-Ninth Congresses. He was succeeded in the Fortieth Congress by Ginery Twitchell.

JOHN H. RICE was born in Mount Vernon, Maine, February 5, 1816. Having been successively sheriff, lumberman, and lawyer, he was, in 1852, elected State Attorney of Maine. He held this office until 1860, when he was elected a Representative from Maine to the Thirty-Seventh Congress. He was re-elected to the Thirty-Eighth and Thirty-Ninth Congresses. He was succeeded in the Fortieth Congress by John A. Peters.

GEORGE REED RIDDLE was born in New Castle, Delaware, in 1817. He was educated at Delaware College. Devoting himself to civil engineering, he was occupied for some years in locating and constructing canals and railroads. He afterwards studied law, and was admitted to the Delaware bar in 1848. In 1850 he was chosen a Representative in Congress from Delaware, and was re-elected in 1852. In 1864 he was elected a United States Senator for the term ending in 1869, and died in Washington, March, 1867.

BURWELL C. RITTER was born in Kentucky, January 10, 1810. He has devoted his life to agricultural pursuits. In 1843, and again in 1850, he was a member of the State Legislature. In 1865 he was elected a Representative from Kentucky to the Thirty-Ninth Congress. *John Young Brown* was elected as his successor in the Fortieth Congress.—149.

ANDREW J. ROGERS was born in Hamburg, New Jersey, July 1, 1828. He spent his youth as an assistant in a hotel and in a country store. He studied law while engaged in school-teaching, and was admitted to the bar in 1852. In 1862 he was elected a Representative from New Jersey to the Thirty-Eighth Congress, and in 1864 was re-elected. He was succeeded in the Fortieth Congress by John Hill.—59, 222, 306, 325, 447, 462, 520, 553.

EDWARD H. ROLLINS was born in Rollingford, New Hampshire, October 3, 1824. Having received an academical education, he taught school for some time, and subsequently engaged in mercantile pursuits. From 1855 to 1857 he was a member of the New Hampshire Legislature, and during two years was Speaker of the House. In 1856 he was Chairman of the State Republican Committee. In 1860 he was elected a Representative from New Hampshire to the Thirty-Seventh Congress, and was re-elected to the Thirty-Eighth and Thirty-Ninth Congresses. His successor in the Fortieth Congress is Aaron F. Stevens.

EDMUND G. ROSS was born in Wisconsin. He learned the art of printing, and became an editor. In 1856 he removed to Kansas, and took an active part in the affairs of the territory. He was a member of the Kansas Constitutional Convention of 1858. From that time until 1861 he was a member of the State Legislature. He served in a Kansas regiment during the rebellion, and reached the rank of Major. He subsequently became editor of the "Lawrence Tribune." In July, 1866, he was appointed a Senator in Congress from Kansas for the unexpired term of James H. Lane, deceased.

LEWIS W. ROSS was born in Seneca County, New York, December 8, 1812. He was removed in boyhood to Illinois. He was educated at Illinois College, and adopted the profession of law. He was elected to the State Legislature in 1840 and 1844. He was a Democratic Presidential Elector in 1848, and a delegate to the Charleston and Baltimore Conventions of 1860. In 1861 he was a member of the State Constitutional Convention, and in the following year was elected a Representative from Illinois to the Thirty-Eighth Congress. He was re-elected to the Thirty-Ninth and Fortieth Congresses.—513.

LOVELL H. ROUSSEAU was born in Stanford, Kentucky, August 4, 1818. He studied law, and removed to Indiana in 1841. He was three years a member of the Indiana House of Representatives, and three years a member of the State Senate. He served as a Captain in the Mexican War, and on his return settled in Louisville, Kentucky. In 1860 he was elected to the Senate of Kentucky, and after serving through the stormy session of 1861 he resigned, to raise a regiment for the war. In June, 1861, he was commissioned a Colonel, and in October of the same year was made a Brigadier General. In October of the following year he was promoted to the rank of Major General for his gallantry in the battles of Shiloh and Stone River. In 1865 he was elected a Representative from Kentucky to the Thirty-Ninth Congress. At the close of his Congressional term he was commmissioned a Brigadier General in the Regular Army, and assigned to the command of the newly acquired possessions of the United States in the North-west.—31, 151, 572, 573, 574.

WILLARD SAULSBURY was born in Kent County, Delaware, June 2, 1820. He was educated at Delaware College and Dickinson College. Having studied law, he was admitted to the bar in 1845. In 1850 he was appointed Attorney General of Delaware, and held the office five years. In 1859 he was elected a United States Senator from Delaware, and was re-elected in 1865 for the term ending in 1871.—24, 44, 124, 127, 136, 192, 219, 287, 306, 405, 456, 458, 496, 531, 534, 548.

PHILETUS SAWYER was born in Whiting, Addison County, Vermont. After receiving a common-school and business education, he removed to Wisconsin and engaged in the lumber trade. In 1857 and 1861 he was elected to the Wisconsin Legislature. He served as Mayor of Oshkosh in 1863 and 1864. In the latter year he was elected a Representative from Wisconsin to the Thirty-Ninth Congress, and was re-elected in 1866.

ROBERT C. SCHENCK was born in Franklin, Ohio, October 4, 1809. He graduated at Miami University in 1827. He studied law under Thomas Corwin, and was admitted to the bar in 1831. He was elected to the Ohio Legislature in 1841, and served two terms. In 1842 he was elected a Representative from Ohio to the Twenty-Eighth Congress, and served four successive terms. At the close of Thirty-First Congress, in 1851, he was appointed by President Fillmore Minister to Brazil, and negotiated several important treaties with South American Governments. After his return in 1853, he became largely interested in railroad enterprises, and was President of a line from Fort Wayne, Indiana, to the Mississippi. At the breaking out of the rebellion he offered his services to the Government, and was commissioned a Brigadier General, May 17, 1861. He was in numerous engagements, including both the Bull Run battles, where he displayed much skill and bravery. He was promoted to the rank of Major General in August, 1862, and was assigned to the command of the Middle Department, including Baltimore, Maryland, in which he rendered efficient service to the country. Having been re-elected to Congress, he resigned his commission in December, 1863, and took his seat in the Thirty-Eighth Congress. He was re-elected to the Thirty-Ninth and Fortieth Congresses.—31, 352, 353, 354, 366, 439, 537, 552.

GLENNI W. SCOFIELD was born in Chautauque County, March 11, 1817. He graduated at Hamilton College in 1840, and removed to Warren, Pennsylvania, where he was admitted to the bar in 1843. In 1850 and 1851 he was a Representative in the Pennsylvania Legislature, and from 1857 to 1859 was a State Senator. In 1861 he was appointed President Judge of the Eighteenth Judicial District of the State. In 1865 he was elected a Representative from Pennsylvania to the Thirty-Eighth Congress, and was re-elected to the Thirty-Ninth and Fortieth Congresses.—56, 508.

GEORGE S. SHANKLIN was born in Jessamine County, Kentucky. He engaged in the practice of law, and in agricultural affairs. He was several years a member of the Kentucky Legislature, and was Commonwealth's Attorney of a Judicial District. He was a member of the Philadelphia Convention of 1856 which nominated Fillmore. In 1865 he was elected a Representative from Kentucky to the Thirty-Ninth Congress. He was succeeded in the Fortieth Congress by *James B. Beck*.—151, 440, 552.

SAMUEL SHELLABARGER was born in Clark County, Ohio, December 10, 1817. He graduated at the Miami University in 1841. He studied law, and having been admitted to the bar practiced in the city of Springfield, Ohio. In 1852 and 1853 he was a member of the Ohio Legislature. In 1860 he was elected a Representative from Ohio to the Thirty-Seventh Congress. He was re-elected to the Thirty-Ninth and Fortieth Congresses.—156, 231, 238, 345, 444, 512, 522.

JOHN SHERMAN was born in Lancaster, Ohio, May 10, 1823. He studied law, and was admitted to the bar in 1844. He was a delegate to the Whig Conventions of 1848 and 1852. In 1854 he was elected a Representative from Ohio to the Thirty-Fourth Congress, and was re-elected to the Thirty-Fifth, Thirty-Sixth, and Thirty-Seventh Congresses. In the memorable contest for the Speakership of the House which occurred in 1859 he was the Republican candidate, and through a long series of ballotings lacked but one or two votes of an election. On the resignation of Senator Chase in 1861, he was elected a Senator in Congress from Ohio, and in 1866 he was re-elected for the term ending in 1873.—27, 98, 161, 420, 422, 454, 460, 476, 500, 501, 534, 535, 541.

CHARLES SITGREAVES was born in Easton, Pennsylvania, April 22, 1803. He adopted the profession of law and settled in New Jersey. In 1831 and 1833 he was a member of the New Jersey Assembly. In 1834 and 1835 he was member and President of the Legislative Council. From 1852 to 1854 he served in the State Senate. He subsequently held the positions of Mayor of Phillipsburg, President of the Belvidere and Delaware Railroad Company, and Trustee of the State Normal School. In 1864 he was elected a Representative from New Jersey to the Thirty-Ninth Congress, and was re-elected in 1866.

ITHAMAR C. SLOAN was born in Madison County, New York. He adopted the profession of law, and removed to Wisconsin in 1854. In 1858 and 1860 he was elected District Attorney of Rock County. In 1862 he was elected a Representative from Wisconsin to the Thirty-Eighth Congress, and was re-elected to the Thirty-Ninth Congress. He was succeeded in the Fortieth Congress by Benjamin F. Hopkins.—334, 335.

GREEN CLAY SMITH was born in Richmond, Kentucky, July 2, 1830. He graduated at Transylvania College in 1849, and in the Law Department of the same institution in 1852. He served in the Mexican War as Second Lieutenant, and at the breaking out of the rebellion was commissioned to command the Fourth Kentucky Cavalry. In 1862 he was appointed a Brigadier General, and subsequently reached the rank of Major General. After participating in numerous battles, he resigned his military commission in December, 1863, to take his seat as a Representative from Kentucky in the Thirty-Eighth Congress. He was re-elected a member of the Thirty-Ninth Congress, but before the expiration of his term he was appointed by the President Governor of the Territory of Montana.—439.

RUFUS P. SPALDING was born at West Tisbury, Martha's Vineyard, Massachusetts, May 3, 1798. He entered Yale College in 1813, and graduated in 1817. After studying law he emigrated to Cincinnati, Ohio, where he remained one year, and then went to Arkansas. Having spent a year and a half in that State he returned to Ohio, and practiced his profession successively in Warren, Ravenna, and Akron, and finally at Cleveland, where he now resides. In 1839 he was elected to the Ohio Legislature. He was re-elected in 1841, and made Speaker of the House. In 1849 he was elected Judge of the Supreme Court of Ohio. In 1862 he was elected a Representative from Ohio to the Thirty-Eighth Congress, and was re-elected to the Thirty-Ninth and Fortieth Congresses.—319, 443, 508.

WILLIAM SPRAGUE was born in Cranston, Rhode Island, September 11, 1830. He was educated chiefly at the Irving Institute, Tarrytown, New York. He subsequently spent several years in the counting-room of his uncle, upon whose death he came into possession of one of the largest manufacturing interests in the country. In 1861 he was elected Governor of Rhode Island. He entered with zeal into the national cause at the breaking out of the rebellion, and was with the Rhode Island Volunteers at the first battle of Bull Run. In 1862 he was elected a Senator in Congress from Rhode Island for the term ending in 1869.—27, 494.

JOHN F. STARR was born in Philadelphia in 1818. He removed to New Jersey in 1844, and engaged in business pursuits. In 1863 he was elected a Representative from New Jersey to the Thirty-Ninth Congress. He was succeeded in the Fortieth Congress by William Moore.

THADDEUS STEVENS was born in Caledonia County, Vermont, April 4, 1793. He graduated at Dartmouth College in 1814, and in the same year removed to Pennsylvania. While teaching in an academy he studied law, and in 1816 was admitted to the bar in the County of Adams. In 1833 he was elected to the Legislature of Pennsylvania, and served four terms, rendering signal service to the State by originating the school-system of Pennsylvania. He early espoused the cause of anti-slavery, and became an earnest advocate of equal rights. In 1836 he was elected a member of the Convention to revise the State Constitution, and refused to append his name to the amended instrument, because it restricted suffrage on account of color. In 1838 he was appointed a Canal Commissioner. In 1842 he removed to Lancaster, where he now resides. In 1848 he was elected a Representative from Pennsylvania to the Thirty-First Congress. He was re-elected to the Thirty-Second, Thirty-Sixth, Thirty-Seventh,

Thirty-Eighth, Thirty-Ninth, and Fortieth Congresses.—18, 24, 29, 34, 48, 156, 308, 325, 333, 336, 357, 366, 417, 418, 435, 436, 449, 463, 478, 502, 503, 504, 513, 514, 518, 524, 528, 535, 536, 547, 555, 557, 563, 575.

WILLIAM M. STEWART was born in Wayne County, New York, August 9, 1827, and removed with his father to Ohio in 1835. He entered Yale College in 1848, where he remained eighteen months. He then went to California and spent two years in the mining business. In 1852 he commenced studying law, and was soon after elected District Attorney for the County of Nevada. In 1854 he was appointed to perform the duties of Attorney General of California, and subsequently practiced law in Nevada City and Downieville. In 1860 he removed to that part of Utah territory which is now Nevada, and served in the Territorial Legislature of the following year. He was a member of the Constitutional Convention of 1863. He was soon after elected a United States Senator from the new State of Nevada for the term ending in 1869.—28, 100, 107, 202, 275, 427, 435, 454, 456, 459, 530.

THOMAS N. STILWELL was born in Butler County, Ohio, August 29, 1830. He was educated at Miami University and Farmer's College. He studied law, and, removing to Indiana in 1852, he was admitted to the bar, and practiced until 1855, when he engaged in banking. In 1856 he was a Representative in the Indiana Legislature. He raised a regiment of volunteers for the war, and served some time as Quartermaster. In 1864 he was elected a Representative from Indiana to the Thirty-Ninth Congress, and was succeeded in the Fortieth Congress by John P. C. Shanks. He was appointed by President Johnson United States Minister to Venezuela.—564.

JOHN P. STOCKTON was born in Princeton, New Jersey, August 2, 1825. His father and grandfather were United States Senators, and his great-grandfather was one of the signers of the Declaration of Independence. He graduated at Princeton College in 1843, and, having studied law, was admitted to the bar in 1849. He was appointed by the Legislature of New Jersey to revise the laws of the State. As reporter in chancery, he published three volumes of Reports, which bear his name. In 1858 he was appointed by President Buchanan Minister Resident to Rome. In 1865 he appeared in Congress as a Senator from New Jersey. The question of his right to the seat underwent long discussion, and at length was decided against him on the 27th of March, 1866.—568.

WILLIAM B. STOKES was born in Chatham County, North Carolina, September 9, 1814. His father was killed by an accident while emigrating to Tennessee in 1818. He enjoyed but few advantages of early education, and devoted himself to agricultural pursuits. In 1849 he was elected a Representative in the Tennessee Legislature, and was re-elected in 1851. He was elected to the State Senate in 1855. In 1859 he was elected a Representative from Tennessee to the Thirty-Sixth Congress. At the close of his Congressional term he took a bold stand and made numerous speeches against secession in Tennessee. In 1862 he recruited and commanded a regiment of cavalry, which saw much hard fighting and did valuable service. At the close of the war he was brevetted Brigadier General. In 1865 he was elected a Representative from Tennessee to the Thirty-Ninth Congress, and was admitted in July, 1866. He was re-elected to the Fortieth Congress.—480, 536.

MYER STROUSE was born in Germany, December 16, 1825. He came with his father to America in 1832, and settled in Pottsville, Pennsylvania. Having received an academical education, he studied law. From 1848 to 1852 he edited the "North American Farmer," in Philadelphia, and subsequently devoted himself to the practice of law. In 1862 he was elected a Representative to the Thirty-Eighth Congress, and was re-elected in 1864. His successor in the Fortieth Congress is Henry L. Cake.—444.

CHARLES SUMNER was born in Boston, January 6, 1811. He graduated at Harvard College in 1830, spent three years in the Cambridge Law School, and was admitted to the bar in 1834. For three years he edited the "American Jurist," and was subsequently Reporter of the United States Circuit Court. He published several volumes of Reports, and has devoted much attention to literary pursuits. He published in 1850 two volumes of "Orations;" in 1853 a work on "White Slavery in the Barbary States;" and in 1856 a volume of "Speeches and Addresses." In 1851 he was elected a United States Senator from Massachusetts. In 1856 he was assaulted in the Senate Chamber by Preston S. Brooks, of South Carolina, and so seriously injured that he sought restoration by a temporary absence in Europe. Just before his departure he was elected to the Senate for a second term, and in 1863 was re-elected for a third term ending in 1869.—15, 26, 28, 99, 108, 373, 374, 380, 386, 392, 406, 413, 435, 453, 483, 499, 540, 541, 563, 571.

STEPHEN TABER, whose father, Thomas Taber, was a Member of Congress, was born in Dover, Dutchess County, New York. Having received an academical education, he devoted himself to agriculture in Queens County, on Long Island. In 1860 and 1861 he was elected to the State Legislature. In 1863 he was elected a Representative to the Thirty-Ninth Congress and was re-elected to the Fortieth Congress.

NATHANIEL G. TAYLOR was born in Carter County, Tennessee, December 29, 1819, and graduated at Princeton College in 1840. He studied law and was admitted to the bar in 1843, but subsequently became a minister in the Methodist Episcopal Church South. In 1852 he was a Presidential Elector, and in 1854 was elected a Representative in Congress from Tennessee. In 1865 he was re-elected a Representative in the Thirty-Ninth Congress, and was admitted to his seat in July, 1866. R. R. Butler was elected as his successor in the Fortieth Congress.—480.

NELSON TAYLOR was born in South Norwalk, Connecticut, June 8, 1821. He served through the Mexican War as Captain in the First Regiment of New York Volunteers. He subsequently went to California, and was elected a member of the State Senate in 1849. In 1853 he was elected Sheriff of San Joaquin County, California. In 1861 he entered the military service as Colonel of the Seventy-Second Regiment of New York Volunteers, and became a Brigadier General. In 1864 he was elected a Representative from New York to the Thirty-Ninth Congress. His successor in the Fortieth Congress is *John Morrissey.*

M. RUSSELL THAYER was born in Petersburg, Virginia, January 27, 1819, and graduated at the University of Pennsylvania in 1840. He studied law, and having been admitted to the bar in 1842, he located in Philadelphia. In 1862 he was elected a Representative in the Thirty-Eighth Congress, and was re-elected to the Thirty-Ninth. His successor in the Fortieth Congress is Caleb N. Taylor.—83, 325, 438, 522, 538.

FRANCIS THOMAS was born in Frederick County, Maryland, February 3, 1799. He was educated at St. John's College, Annapolis. He studied law, and was admitted to practice at Frederick in 1820. He was elected to the Maryland Legislature in 1822, 1827, and 1829, when he was chosen Speaker. In 1831 he was elected a Representative in Congress, and served for ten consecutive years. In 1841 he declined a renomination for Congress. In the fall of that year he was elected Governor of Maryland, and served until January, 1845. In 1848 he supported Van Buren and Adams on the Buffalo Anti-Slavery platform. In 1850 he was a member of the Maryland Constitutional Convention. At the breaking out of the Rebellion he raised a brigade of 3,000 volunteers for the military service. In March, 1863, he originated and assisted in securing popular approval of a measure which resulted in the emancipation of all the slaves of Maryland. He was re-elected a Representative from Maryland to the Thirty-Sixth, Thirty-Seventh, Thirty-Eighth, Thirty-Ninth, and Fortieth Congresses.

JOHN L. THOMAS, Jr., was born in Baltimore, May 20, 1835, and was educated at the Alleghany County Academy. He studied law, and was admitted to the bar in 1856. He was appointed Solicitor for the City of Baltimore in 1861, and held the office two years. In 1863 he was elected State Attorney for Maryland, and in 1864 he served as a delegate to the State Constitutional Convention. In 1865 he was elected a Representative to the Thirty-Ninth Congress to fill a vacancy occasioned by the resignation of E. H. Webster. He was succeeded in the Fortieth Congress by *Stephenson Archer.*

ANTHONY THORNTON was born in Bourbon County, Kentucky, November 19, 1814. He graduated at the Miami University, and having studied law, he settled in Illinois. He was a member of the Illinois Constitutional Conventions of 1847 and 1862. In 1850 he was a member of the State Legislature. In 1864 he was elected a Representative from Illinois to the Thirty-Ninth Congress. His successor in the Fortieth Congress is *Albert G. Burr.*—228.

LAWRENCE S. TRIMBLE was born in Fleming, Kentucky, August 26, 1825. He received an academical education, and entered the profession of law. In 1851 and 1852 he was a member of the Kentucky Legislature. From 1856 to 1860 he was Judge of the Equity and Criminal Court of the First Judicial District of the State. He was subsequently for five years President of the New Orleans and Ohio Railroad Company. In 1865 he was elected a Representative from Kentucky to the Thirty-Ninth Congress, and was re-elected to the Fortieth Congress.—152, 342, 511.

ROWLAND E. TROWBRIDGE was born in Elmira, New York, June 18, 1821, and when a child removed to Michigan with his parents, who were among the first settlers that penetrated the wilderness back of the old French settlements. He graduated at Kenyon College, and engaged in the business of farming. In 1856 and 1858 he was elected a member of the Michigan Senate. In 1860 he was elected a Representative from Michigan to the Thirty-Seventh Congress. He was re-elected to the Thirty-Ninth and Fortieth Congresses.

LYMAN TRUMBULL was born in Colchester, Connecticut, in 1813. He entered the profession of law, and removed to Illinois. He was a member of the State Legislature in 1840, and was Secretary of State in 1841 and 1842. He was a Justice of the Supreme Court of Illinois from 1848 to 1853. In 1854 he was elected a Representative for Illinois to the Thirty-Fourth Congress, and was soon after elected a Senator in Congress for the term commencing in 1855. He was re-elected in 1861, and again in 1867.—22, 28, 45, 98, 104, 105, 108, 120, 136, 158, 162, 171, 188, 190, 199, 209, 216, 253, 269, 424, 457, 476, 540.

CHARLES UPSON was born in Southington, Hartford County, Connecticut, March 19, 1821. He received an academical education, and at the age of sixteen he commenced teaching school, in which he was employed during the winters of seven years. He attended the law school of Yale College for some time, and in 1845 removed to Michigan. In 1848 he was elected County Clerk, and in 1852 Prosecuting Attorney for St. Joseph County. In 1854 he was elected to the State Senate. In 1860 he was elected Attorney General of Michigan, and declined a renomination. In 1862 he was elected a Representative from Michigan to the Thirty-Eighth Congress, and was re-elected to the Thirty-Ninth and Fortieth Congresses.

HENRY VAN AERNAM was born in Marcellus, New York, March 11, 1819. After receiving an academical education and graduating at a medical college, he settled as a physician and surgeon in Franklinville, New York. In 1858 he was a member of the State Legislature. In 1862 he entered the army as surgeon of the One Hundred and Fifty-Fourth New York Regiment. He resigned this position in 1864, and was elected a Representative from New York to the Thirty-Ninth Congress, and was re-elected to the Fortieth Congress.

BURT VAN HORN was born in Newfane, Niagara County, New York, October 28, 1823, and was educated at the Madison University. He was elected to the New York Legislature in 1858, and served three terms. In 1860 he was elected a Representative from New York to the Thirty-Seventh Congress. He was re-elected to the Thirty-Ninth and Fortieth Congresses.—87, 527.

ROBERT T. VAN HORN was born in Indiana County, Pennsylvania, May 19, 1824. After serving an apprenticeship in a printing-office, he studied law, and was admitted to the bar in 1849. He subsequently published a newspaper two years in Pomeroy, Ohio. In 1855 he emigrated to Kansas City, Missouri, where he established a newspaper which is now the "Daily Journal of Commerce." In 1861 he was elected Mayor of Kansas City. He was in the military service as Major and Lieutenant-Colonel from 1861 to 1864. He was wounded and taken prisoner at Lexington, Missouri, and after his exchange saw much active service in Tennessee. While still in the army, he was elected a member of the Missouri Senate, and in 1864 he was elected a Representative from Missouri to the Thirty-Ninth Congress, and was re-elected in 1866.

PETER G. VAN WINKLE was born in the City of New York, September 7, 1808, and removed to Parkersburg, West Virginia, in 1835. He was a member of the Virginia Constitutional Convention of 1850, and of the Wheeling Convention of 1861. He aided in forming the Constitution of West Virginia in 1862. He became a member of the Legislature of that State at its organization, and in November, 1863, he was elected a United States Senator from West Virginia for the term ending in 1869.—194, 459.

DANIEL W. VOORHEES was born in Fountain County, Indiane, September 26, 1828. He graduated at the Indiana Asbury University in 1849, and commenced the practice of law in 1851. He held the office of United States District Attorney for three years, by appointment of President Buchanan. In 1860 he was elected a Representative to Congress from Indiana, and re-elected in 1862. He appeared in December, 1865, as a member of the Thirty-Ninth Congress, but remained only a short time, his seat having been successfully contested by Henry D. Washburn.—568.

BENJAMIN F. WADE was born in Feeding Hills Parish, Massachusetts, October 27, 1800. He received a common-school education, and was employed for some time in teaching. At the age of twenty-one he removed to Ohio and engaged in agriculture. He subsequently studied law, and was admitted to the bar in 1828. Thereafter he successively held the offices of Justice of the Peace, Prosecuting Attorney for Ashtabula County, State Senator, and Judge of the Circuit Court. In 1851 he was elected a United States Senator from Ohio, and has been twice re-elected, his third term ending in 1869. In March, 1867, he was elected President, *pro tempore*, of the Senate, and thus became acting Vice-President of the United States.—15, 28, 50, 276, 279, 283, 428, 454, 477, 490, 576.

ANDREW H. WARD is a lawyer by profession, and a resident of Cynthiana, Kentucky. He was a Representative from the Sixth District of Kentucky to the Thirty-Ninth Congress. His successor in the Fortieth Congress is *Thomas L. Jones*.—509.

HAMILTON WARD was born in Salisbury, New York, July 3, 1829. He worked on a farm until nineteen years of age, and was favored with but few facilities for acquiring education. In 1848 he began the study of law, and was admitted to the bar in 1851. In 1856 he was elected District Attorney for Alleghany County, and was re-elected in 1862. At an early period of the war he was appointed by the Governor a member of the Senatorial Military Committee, and in that capacity aided in raising several regiments of volunteers for the army. In 1864 he was elected a Representative from New York to the Thirty-Ninth Congress, and was re-elected in 1866.—306, 361.

SAMUEL L. WARNER was born in Wethersfield, Connecticut, in 1829. He received an academical education, and having studied law at the Yale and Harvard Law Schools, was admitted to the bar in 1853. He was soon after appointed Executive Secretary of State. In 1857 he was a member of the Connecticut Legislature. In 1860 he was a delegate and a Secretary of the Baltimore Convention. In 1861 he was elected Mayor of Middletown, and served two terms. In 1865 he was elected a Representative from Connecticut to the Thirty-Ninth Congress. His successor in the Fortieth Congress is *Julius Hotchkiss*.—507.

ELLIHU B. WASHBURN was born in Livermore, Maine, September 23 1816. After serving an apprenticeship in the printing-office of the "Kennebec Journal," he studied law at Harvard University. He subsequently removed to Illinois, and settled in Galena. In 1852 he was elected a Representative from Illinois to the Thirty-Third Congress. He has been elected to every succeeding Congress including the Fortieth, and has been longer in continuous service than any other member of the House.—30.

HENRY D. WASHBURN was born in Windsor, Vermont, March 28, 1832 In his youth he served one year as an apprentice to the tanner's trade, and subsequently was employed as a school-teacher. In 1853 he graduated at the New York State and National Law School, and settled in Newport, Indiana. In 1854 he was appointed Auditor of Vermillion County, and in 1856 was elected to the same position. In 1861 he raised a company of volunteers, of which he was elected Captain. He was soon after made Lieutenant-Colonel of the Eighteenth Indiana Infantry, and was commissioned Colonel June, 1862. He saw much active service, and was breveted a Major General July 26, 1865. He contested the seat held by D. W. Voorhees as a Representative from Indiana, and was declared by the Committee on Elections to be entitled to the place. He was re-elected to the Fortieth Congress.—568.

WILLIAM B. WASHBURN was born in Winchendon, Massachusetts, January 31, 1820. He graduated at Yale College in 1844, and subsequently engaged in the business of manufacturing. In 1850 he was a Senator, and in 1854 a Representative, in the Legislature of Massachusetts. He was subsequently President of Greenfield Bank. In 1862 he was elected a Representative to the Thirty-Eighth Congress, and was re-elected to the Thirty-Ninth and Fortieth Congresses.

MARTIN WELKER was born in Knox County, Ohio, April 25, 1819. When a farmer's boy and a clerk in a store, he applied himself diligently to study, and without the aid of schools obtained a liberal education. At the age of eighteen he commenced the study of law, and was admitted to the bar in 1840. In 1851 he was elected Judge of the Court of Common Pleas for the Sixth District of Ohio, and served five years. In 1857 he was elected Lieutenant Governor of Ohio, and served one term, declining a renomination. At the beginning of the war he served three months as a staff officer with the rank of Major, and was then appointed Judge Advocate General of the State. In 1862 he was Assistant Adjutant General of Ohio, and Superintendent of the draft. In 1864 he was elected a Representative from Ohio to the Thirty-Ninth Congress and was re-elected to the Fortieth Congress.

JOHN WENTWORTH, grandson of a member of the Continental Congress of 1778, was born in Sandwich, New Hampshire, March 5, 1815. He graduated at Dartmouth College, and completed a course of legal study in Harvard University. In 1836 he removed to Illinois, and settled in Chicago. He conducted the "Chicago Democrat," as editor and proprietor, for twenty-five years. In 1837 he became a member of the Board of Education, and occupied that position many years. In 1842 he was elected a Representative from Illinois to the Twenty-Eighth Congress, and subsequently served in the Twenty-Ninth, Thirtieth, Thirty-First, and Thirty-Second Congresses. In 1857 and 1860 he was Mayor of Chicago, and was a member of the State Constitutional Convention of 1861. In 1864 a Representative in Congress for his sixth term. His successor in the Fortieth Congress is Norman B. Judd. In 1867 the degree of LL.D. was conferred upon him by Dartmouth College.—18, 556, 557.

KELLIAN V. WHALEY was born in Onondaga County, New York, May 6, 1821. When quite young he removed with his father to Ohio, where he was favored with few educational advantages. At the age of twenty-one he settled in Western Virginia, and engaged in the lumber and mercantile business. He was an active opponent of secession in 1860, and as such was elected a Representative in the Thirty-Seventh Congress. He acted as an Aid to Governor Pierpont in organizing regiments, and was in command in the battle of Guandotte, when he was taken prisoner, in November, 1861. He made his escape from his captors, however, and was soon able to take his seat in Congress. He was re-elected to the Thirty-Eighth and Thirty-Ninth Congresses. His successor in the Fortieth Congress is Daniel Polsley.

WAITMAN T. WILLEY was born on Buffalo Creek, Monongalia County, Virginia, October 18, 1811. He graduated at Madison College in 1831, and was admitted to the bar. From 1841 to 1855 he was Clerk of the Courts of Monongalia County and the Judicial Circuit. He was a member of the Virginia Constitutional Convention of 1850. He was a delegate to the Richmond Convention held in the winter of 1860-61. In 1861 he was a member of the Wheeling Constitutional Convention. In 1863 he was elected a Senator in Congress from West Virginia, and has since been re-elected for the term commencing in 1865 and ending in 1871. In 1863 he received the degree of LL.D. from Alleghany College of Pennsylvania.—458, 485, 486, 496.

GEORGE H. WILLIAMS was born in Columbia County, New York, March 23, 1823. He received an academical education, and studied law. Immediately after being admitted to the bar in 1844 he removed to Iowa. In 1847 he was elected Judge of the First Judicial District of Iowa. In 1852 he was a Presidential Elector. In 1853 he was appointed by President Pierce Chief Justice of the Territory of Oregon, and was re-appointed by President Buchanan in 1857. He was a member of the Convention which framed the Constitution of Oregon. In 1864 he was elected a United States Senator from Oregon for the term ending in 1871.—393, 488, 516, 517, 529, 531, 539, 540, 559.

THOMAS WILLIAMS was born in Greensburg, Westmoreland County, Pennsylvania, August 28, 1806. He graduated at Dickinson College in 1825, and studied law. He was admitted to the bar in 1828, and settled in Pittsburg. From 1838 to 1841 he was member of the State Senate. In 1860 he was a Representative in the State Legislature. In 1862 he was elected a Representative from Pennsylvania to the Thirty-Eighth Congress. He was re-elected to the Thirty-Ninth and Fortieth Congresses.

HENRY WILSON was born in Farmington, New Hampshire, February 16, 1812. His parents were in very humble circumstances, and at ten years of age he was apprenticed to a farmer till he was twenty-one. On attaining his majority, he went to Natick, Massachusetts, where he learned the trade of shoemaking, and worked at the business nearly three years. He then secured an academical education, and, after teaching school a short time, engaged in shoe-manufacturing, which he continued for several years. In 1841 and 1842 he was a Senator, and in 1844, 1845, 1856, and 1850, a Representative, in the Legislature of Massachusetts. In 1851 and 1852 he was re-elected a member of the State Senate, of which he was President. In 1855 he was elected a United States Senator from Massachusetts to succeed Edward Everett, and in 1859 was re-elected for the full term. In the recess of Congress in the summer of 1861, he raised the Twenty-Second Regiment of Massachusetts Volunteers, of which he was commissioned Colonel. He subsequently served on General McClellan's staff, until the meeting of Congress in December. During the war he occupied the arduous and responsible position in the Senate of Chairman of the Committee of Military Affairs. At the opening of the Thirty-Ninth Congress he entered upon his third Senatorial term, which will end in 1871.—15, 95, 97, 101, 135, 214, 402, 410, 431, 435, 437, 487, 491, 498, 530, 531, 532.

JAMES F. WILSON was born in Newark, Ohio, October 19, 1828. He entered upon the profession of law, and removed to Iowa in 1853. In 1856 he was elected a member of the Iowa Constitutional Convention. In 1857 he was elected a Representative, and in 1859 a Senator, in the State Legislature. In 1861 he was President of the Iowa Senate. In that year he was elected a Representative from Iowa to fill a vacancy in the Thirty-Seventh Congress. He was re-elected to the Thirty-Eighth, Thirty-Ninth, and Fortieth Congresses.—31, 51, 220, 237, 239, 288, 294, 325, 536.

STEPHEN F. WILSON was born at Columbia, Pennsylvania, September 4, 1821. He received his education at Wellsboro' Academy, where he subsequently engaged for a short time in teaching. He finally became a lawyer, and was, in 1863, elected a State Senator. In 1864 he was chosen a Representative from Pennsylvania to the Thirty-Ninth Congress, and was re-elected to the Fortieth Congress.

WILLIAM WINDOM was born in Belmont County, Ohio, May 10, 1827. He received an academical education, and studied law. He was admitted to the bar in 1850, and was soon after elected Prosecuting Attorney for Knox County, Ohio. In 1853 he removed to Minnesota, and settled in Winona. In 1858 he was elected a Representative from Minnesota to the Thirty-Sixth Congress, and was re-elected to the Thirty-Seventh, Thirty-Eighth, Thirty-Ninth, and Fortieth Congresses.—229.

CHARLES H. WINFIELD was born in Orange County, New York, April 22, 1822. He studied law, and was admitted to the bar in 1846. From 1850 to 1856 he was District Attorney for Orange County. He was elected a Representative to the Thirty-Eighth Congress from New York, and was in 1864 re-elected for a second term. He was succeeded in the Fortieth Congress by Charles H. Van Wyck.—20, 515.

FREDERICK E. WOODBRIDGE was born in Vergennes, Vermont, August 29, 1818. He graduated at the University of Vermont in 1840, and was admitted to the bar in 1842. He served three years as a Representative, and two years as a Senator, in the Vermont Legislature. He subsequently served three years as Auditor of State. In 1863 he was elected a Representative from Vermont to the Thirty-Eighth Congress, and was re-elected to the Thirty-Ninth and Fortieth Congresses.

EDWIN R. V. WRIGHT was born in Hoboken, New Jersey, January 2, 1812. He learned the trade of a printer, and in 1835 edited and published the "Jersey Blue." He studied law, and was admitted to the bar in 1839. He was elected to the State Senate in 1843. He subsequently held for five years the office of District Attorney for Hudson County. In 1859 he was the Democratic Candidate for Governor of New Jersey, and was defeated by a small majority. He was elected a Representative from New Jersey to the Thirty-Ninth Congress, and was succeeded in the Fortieth Congress by George A. Halsey.—363.

WILLIAM WRIGHT was born in Clarkstown, Rockland County, New York, in 1791. In 1823 he removed to Newark, New Jersey, and held the office of Mayor of that city for a number of years. He was a Representative in Congress four years, commencing in 1843. In 1853 he was elected United States Senator for the term ending in 1859. In 1863 he was again elected to the Senate for the term ending in 1869. He died before the expiration of the term for which he was elected.—276, 569.

RICHARD YATES was born in Warsaw, Kentucky, in 1818. Having studied one year at the Miami University, Ohio, he removed to Illinois, and graduated at Illinois College in 1838. He studied at the Law School of Lexington, Kentucky, and having been admitted to the bar, he settled in Jacksonville, Illinois. In 1842 he was elected to the State Legislature, and served until 1850. In 1851 he was elected a Representative in Congress from Illinois, and served two terms. He was subsequently President of a railroad for several years. In 1861 he was elected Governor of Illinois for the term of four years. During his administration, 258,000 troops were raised in Illinois and sent to the field. He was not only active in his State in promoting the success of the national cause, but he frequently encouraged the regiments of Illinois by his presence with them in the camp and on the field. In 1865 he was elected a Senator in Congress from Illinois for the term ending in 1871.—28, 272, 398, 400, 461, 462, 484, 491.

ANALYTICAL INDEX.

THE END.

www.ingramcontent.com/pod-product-compliance
Lightning Source LLC
LaVergne TN
LVHW021049110826
845150LV00001B/26

* 9 7 8 1 4 2 5 5 6 8 2 7 6 *